200
The

"Judges as persons, or courts as institutions, are entitled to
no greater immunity from criticism than other persons
or institutions . . . [J]udges must be kept mindful of their limitations and
of their ultimate public responsibility by a vigorous
stream of criticism expressed with candor however blunt."
—*Felix Frankfurter*

". . . while it is proper that people should find fault when
their judges fail, it is only reasonable that they should recognize the
difficulties. . . . Let them be severely brought to book,
when they go wrong, but by those who will take the trouble
to understand them."
—*Learned Hand*

THE LAW SCHOOL

THE UNIVERSITY OF CHICAGO

upreme Court Review

EDITED BY

DENNIS J. HUTCHINSON

DAVID A. STRAUSS

AND GEOFFREY R. STONE

 THE UNIVERSITY OF CHICAGO PRESS

CHICAGO AND LONDON

INTERNATIONAL STANDARD BOOK NUMBER: 978-0-226-36325-7

LIBRARY OF CONGRESS CATALOG CARD NUMBER: 60-14353

THE UNIVERSITY OF CHICAGO PRESS, CHICAGO 60637

THE UNIVERSITY OF CHICAGO PRESS, LTD., LONDON

© 2007 BY THE UNIVERSITY OF CHICAGO, ALL RIGHTS RESERVED, PUBLISHED 2007

PRINTED IN THE UNITED STATES OF AMERICA

The paper used in this publication meets the minimum requirements of American National Standard for Information Sciences–Permanence of Paper for Printed Library Materials, ANSI Z39.48-1984. ⊚

TO RALPH LERNER

For a half-century, teacher and scholar
Of the texts
That make liberty both a promise
and an imperative

CONTENTS

CASS R. SUNSTEIN

CLEAR STATEMENT PRINCIPLES AND NATIONAL SECURITY: HAMDAN AND BEYOND

The Supreme Court has often declined to answer the most fundamental questions about the relationship between individual rights and national security. Instead it has said that if the executive seeks to enter into constitutionally sensitive domains, or to depart from standard adjudicative forms, clear congressional permission is required. This approach reflects a form of what I shall call *liberty-promoting minimalism*. It is liberty-promoting insofar as it gives liberty the benefit of interpretive doubt. It is minimalist insofar as it avoids the most fundamental issues of constitutional law and to that extent reflects a form of judicial self-restraint. Those who embrace liberty-promoting minimalism ask the national legislature to give unambiguous authorization for serious intrusions on freedom; but they are reluctant to rule that when so authorized, the President may not act as he wishes to protect the nation's security.

Liberty-promoting minimalism can be found at diverse stages of American history. During the Civil War period, President Lincoln suspended the writ of habeas corpus, but Chief Justice Roger Taney

Cass R. Sunstein is Karl N. Llewellyn Distinguished Service Professor, Law School and Department of Political Science, University of Chicago.

AUTHOR'S NOTE: I am grateful to Eric Posner, John Schmidt, Geoffrey Stone, and David Strauss for valuable comments on a previous draft and to Matthew Johnson and Matthew Tokson for excellent research assistance.

ruled that the President could not suspend the writ on his own.[1] During World War I, Justices Brandeis and Holmes argued not only for use of the First Amendment to invalidate legislation, but also for narrow construction of congressional authorizations to the executive.[2] Justice Holmes insisted that "it would take very strong language to convince me that Congress ever intended to give such a practically despotic power to any one man."[3] In fact a clear statement principle, rather than the Constitution by itself, underlies one of the most celebrated free speech decisions in American history: Judge Learned Hand's in the *Masses* case.[4] During World War II, the Court struck down the detention of concededly loyal Japanese Americans on the West Coast,[5] relying in large part on the absence of unambiguous statutory authorization for the detention.[6] The Court said, somewhat remarkably, that "[i]n interpreting a wartime measure we must assume that their purpose was to allow for the greatest possible accommodation between those liberties and the exigencies of war."[7]

During the Korean War, the Court refused to allow President Truman to seize the nation's steel mills, notwithstanding his claim that steel was an indispensable component in nearly all weapons and war materials. In the Steel Seizure Case,[8] the Court emphasized that there "is no statute that expressly authorizes the President to take possession of the property as he did here. Nor is there any act of Congress to which our attention has been directed from which such a power can fairly be implied."[9] A similar approach prevailed

---

[1] See *Ex parte Merryman*, 17 F Cases 144 (Cir Ct Md 1861); William H. Rehnquist, *All the Laws But One* 36–38 (1999); Geoffrey R. Stone, *Perilous Times: Free Speech in Wartime from the Sedition Act of 1798 to the War on Terrorism* 84–87 (2004). Notably, however, Lincoln ignored Taney. See id.

[2] *U.S. v Bureleson*, 255 US 407, 417 (1921) (Brandeis, J, dissenting); id at 436 (Holmes, J, dissenting).

[3] Id at 437.

[4] See *Masses Publishing Co. v Patten*, 244 F 535 (SDNY 1917); see generally Stone, *Perilous Times* at 164–70 (cited in note 1), for a detailed discussion.

[5] 320 US 81 (1943).

[6] Id at 297.

[7] Id at 300.

[8] *Youngstown Sheet & Tube Co. v Sawyer*, 343 US 579 (1952).

[9] Id at 585. It would be possible to understand the majority opinion not as demanding clear congressional authorization, but simply as saying that the relevant statutes are not fairly interpreted to grant the relevant authority to the President. Unlike the other cases I am discussing, the Steel Seizure Case need not be seen as reflecting a clear statement principle.

at the height of the Cold War, when the Court protected speech through an aggressive clear statement approach in *Yates v United States*.[10]

The requirement of fair adjudicative procedure, backed by a clear statement principle, was crucial in *Duncan v Kahanamoku*,[11] involving the imposition of martial law in Hawaii during World War II. Civilians in Hawaii had been imprisoned after a trial in military tribunals; the central question was whether those tribunals had the legal authority to try civilians. In its narrow ruling, the Court held that they did not. The Court acknowledged that the statutory language and history were unclear and stressed, as relevant to the interpretive question, "the birth, development, and growth of our political institutions."[12] Because "courts and their procedural safeguards are indispensable to our system of government," the Court would not construe an ambiguous statute to authorize the displacement, by the executive, of ordinary courts with military tribunals.[13]

In its initial encounter with the war on terror, the Court did not invoke a clear statement principle, but a plurality of the Supreme Court squarely emphasized fair procedure.[14] In the key part of the prevailing opinion in the *Hamdi* case, the plurality said that an enemy combatant must be supplied with "notice of the factual basis for his classification, and a fair opportunity to rebut the Government's factual assertions before a neutral decisionmaker."[15] What is most noteworthy about the plurality's reasoning is its insistence on the right to a fair hearing, one of the "essential liberties that remain vibrant even in times of security concerns."[16]

Since the attacks of 9/11, clear statement principles, demanding explicit authorization to the executive, have been under exceedingly severe pressure, above all from those who insist on the broad constitutional prerogatives of the President. The pressure has taken two different forms. On one view, the document, as originally un-

---

[10] 354 US 298 (1957).

[11] 327 US 304 (1946).

[12] Id at 319.

[13] Id at 323.

[14] *Hamdi v Rumsfeld*, 542 US 507 (2004). Note that Justices Souter and Ginsburg did invoke a clear statement principle, calling for unambiguous congressional authorization for a detention of an American citizen. See id at 544–45 (Souter, J, dissenting in part).

[15] Id at 2651 ("There remains the possibility that the standards we have articulated could be met by an appropriately authorized and properly constituted military tribunal").

[16] Id at 2652.

derstood, gave "the war power" to the President and essentially authorized him to do whatever must be done to protect the nation.[17] On a more functional view, the particular circumstances of the war on terror justify an especially strong role for the executive and a weak one for the judiciary—and also make it hazardous to require specific congressional authorization for presidential action.[18] For those who emphasize these points, legislative enactments should be construed generously to the President, so as to fit with contemporary needs or to avoid the constitutional problems that might be produced by intrusions on his authority. At its most extreme, the resulting view calls for a kind of presidential unilateralism, authorizing the Commander-in-Chief to act entirely on his own.[19]

The Supreme Court's various opinions in *Hamdan v Rumsfeld* are highly technical; they focus on numerous legal provisions, including the Detainee Treatment Act,[20] the Authorization for the Use of Military Force (AUMF),[21] the Uniform Code of Military Justice (UCMJ),[22] and the Geneva Conventions.[23] The Court was closely divided on the interpretation of these provisions—with disagreements manifesting themselves on no fewer than seven major points. Indeed, it is not easy to find an opinion, in the Court's entire history, in which the Justices divided on so many points; I hereby nominate *Hamdan* as the all-time champion on this count. But as the sheer number of specific disagreements suggests, the underlying split within the Court was far more general, and had nothing to do with any particular provision.

In essence, the prevailing view in *Hamdan* can be captured in a single idea: *If the President seeks to depart from standard adjudicative forms through the use of military tribunals, the departure must be authorized by an explicit and focused decision from the national legislature.*[24]

---

[17] A version of this view can be found in John Yoo, *The Powers of War and Peace* (2005).

[18] A version of this view is defended in Eric Posner and Adrian Vermeule, *Terror in the Balance* (2007).

[19] See Richard Pildes and Samuel Issacharoff, *Between Civil Libertarianism and Executive Unilateralism: An Institutional Process Approach to Right during Wartime*, 5 Theoretical Inquiries in Law (online edition), No 1, Art 1 (2004) (http://www.bepress.com/til/default/vol5/iss1/art1); Cass R. Sunstein, *Minimalism at War*, 2004 Supreme Court Review 47.

[20] Pub L No 109-148, 119 Stat 2739.

[21] 115 Stat 224, note following 50 USC 1541 (2000 ed, Supp III).

[22] 10 USC 101–1805.

[23] Full text available at http://www.genevaconventions.org.

[24] A narrower reading would say that Congress had expressly limited the President's

This idea has considerable importance. If it is generalized, the analysis in *Hamdan* can be taken as a wholesale repudiation of the view of those who claim, on originalist or functionalist grounds, that something like the "war power" is concentrated in the President. And if that view is repudiated, the requirement of clear congressional authorization might well apply in many other domains, at least where the executive seeks to intrude into the realm of liberty or departs from practices that are historically entrenched. After *Hamdan*, presidential unilateralism stands on very shaky ground.

By contrast, the view of at least two dissenters, and possibly three, is this: *If the Commander-in-Chief seeks to interpret ambiguous provisions in a way that he deems necessary to protect national security, he is entitled to do so, at least if his judgment is not plainly foreclosed by historical understandings.* This view embodies a clear statement principle of its own—a principle that requires an explicit statement from the national legislature if it seeks to cabin the President's power to protect national security in a time of war. A distinctive feature of this view is that it builds on standard principles of administrative law so as to permit the executive to interpret ambiguous provisions as he sees fit, so long as his interpretation is reasonable.

The difference between the two views points out a serious gap in the canonical opinion of Justice Robert Jackson in the Steel Seizure Case[25]—an opinion on which both the prevailing opinion and the dissenters rely.[26] Jackson famously distinguished among three kinds of cases: those in which the President has acted with express or implied congressional authorization, those in which the President has acted amid congressional silence, and those in which the President has acted in defiance of congressional limits on his authority.[27] Here is the question that Justice Jackson did not explicitly ask (and whose importance he appears not to have noticed):

authority, as the Court indeed suggested it had. But as we shall see, I do not believe that there are such express limitations; what the majority requires is clear authorization. Of course, it is a nice question whether the *Hamdi* majority would have allowed the President to do as he did here if Congress had said nothing at all; complete congressional silence would have made it harder to rule against the President.

[25] 343 US at 593 (Jackson, J, concurring).

[26] *Hamdan v Rumsfeld*, 126 S Ct 2749, 2774 n 23; id at 2800 (Kennedy, J, concurring); id at 2824 (Thomas, J, dissenting) (2006).

[27] 343 US at 609.

When legislative enactments are susceptible to more than one interpretation, what is the appropriate background rule? Should the President's interpretations of ambiguous terms prevail? Or should a clear statement be required from Congress, at least in certain domains? In which domains?

My principal goal here is to demonstrate that the underlying disagreement in *Hamdan* has everything to do with the appropriate clear statement principle. As we shall see, the Court's opinion necessarily if opaquely answered certain questions about the constitutional power of the President, in a way that went well beyond anything the Court has done in the past. For this reason, too, the Court's reasoning has immense importance. If it continues to be followed, it is likely to have implications for many other questions, including the legality of warrantless wiretapping by the National Security Agency.

I attempt to offer a sympathetic understanding of the Court's requirement of clear congressional authorization, not to evaluate it. But I shall raise two questions about the Court's approach. First, the best course might well have been to abstain. The underlying provisions presented quite difficult questions; much could be said on behalf of a refusal to resolve those questions until a trial had been completed. Second, the Court's decision would have been greatly strengthened if it had been able to invoke the Avoidance Canon. The Court did not contend that it was interpreting the relevant provisions so as to ensure that the President did not intrude on constitutionally sensitive interests on his own; if it had been able to do so, its ruling would have been much more secure. The Court's conclusion would have been better supported if it had invoked due process concerns in order to rule, very narrowly, that the President was obliged to provide Hamdan with a right to see the contrary evidence unless (*a*) compelling reasons required otherwise and (*b*) a fair trial was possible without conferring that right. Without the Avoidance Canon, the dissenters probably had the better view on the merits, because the President is entitled to deference in the face of ambiguity in the relevant legal provisions.

Notwithstanding my objections to the Court's analysis, the general requirement of clear congressional authorization has considerable appeal. It deserves judicial endorsement in other domains in which liberty is seriously threatened, at least where the threat raises serious constitutional questions.

I. Multiple Paths

Salim Ahmed Hamdan was captured by militia forces in Afghanistan in November 2001, amid hostilities between the United States and the Taliban. Turned over to the United States military shortly after his capture, Hamdan was taken to Guantanamo Bay in June 2002. In 2003, the President concluded that he was eligible for trial by military commission. In 2004, Hamdan was charged with only one count, involving a conspiracy to commit offenses triable by military commission, including violations of the law of war. He filed petitions for writs of mandamus and habeas corpus, raising multiple objections to the proposed trial. Hamdan acknowledges that he was bodyguard and driver for Osama Bin Laden, but he denies a role in the attacks of September 11, 2001.

A. OPTIONS

As we shall see, the Court had many options, and it will provide a helpful orientation to outline them at the outset. To hold in the President's favor, the Court had six principal routes:

1. It could have refused to reach the merits, on the ground that the Detainee Treatment Act of 2005 (DTA) deprived the Supreme Court of jurisdiction (and provided a special procedure that Hamdan was required to follow to challenge his detention and trial).

2. It could have refused to reach the merits, on the ground that principles of abstention required federal courts to allow the case to proceed to trial.

3. It could have held that military commissions were authorized by some act of Congress; candidates include the Authorization for the Use of Military Force and the Uniform Code of Military Justice.

4. It could have held that in light of the President's constitutional authority as Commander-in-Chief, the relevant acts of Congress and the Geneva Conventions should be construed to permit the President to create military commissions. Under this approach, the constitutional backdrop permits the President to construe ambiguous provisions as the President sees fit.

5. It could have invoked principles of administrative law to conclude that in light of the President's expertise and ac-

countability, he should be allowed to interpret ambiguous provisions in the relevant statutes, so long as his interpretations are reasonable.[28]

6. It could have held that even if Congress has said otherwise, the President has the constitutional authority to create military commissions—authority that Congress cannot eliminate or even significantly restrict.

To hold against the President, the Court had two principal options:

1. It could have held that fairly interpreted, the relevant statutes or the Geneva Conventions (or both) prohibit the President from creating and using military commissions of this kind.

2. It could have held that Congress must give unambiguous authorization to enable the President to convene military commissions, and that the relevant sources of law failed to provide such authorization. The requirement of unambiguous authorization might have been based on background principles calling for adherence to the ordinary standards of criminal justice. Alternatively, the requirement might have been based on a desire to avoid a possible constitutional problem (though Hamdan did not raise an objection under the Due Process Clause or the Confrontation Clause).

The government argued for options (3) and (4). It contended that the relevant sources of law "recognized" the President's authority to create military commissions—and hence that the President's authority was not a creation of Congress at all. Indeed, the government argued that as Commander-in-Chief, the President could try Al Qaeda combatants in military commissions even in the face of legislative silence. The "President's war power under Article II, Section 2 of the Constitution includes the inherent authority to create military commissions even in the absence of any statutory authorization, because that authority is a necessary and longstanding component of his war powers."[29]

The most obvious precedent, apparently offering a great deal

---

[28] See Eric A. Posner and Cass R. Sunstein, 116 *Chevronizing Foreign Relations Law*, Yale L J (forthcoming 2007).

[29] 2005 US Briefs 184, at p 21.

of help to the government, was the Court's unanimous decision in *Ex Parte Quirin*.[30] In that case, the Court authorized President Roosevelt to try Nazi saboteurs in military commissions. It did so with reference to Article 15 of the Laws of War, which, in its view, was best read to authorize such commissions. Article 15, the precursor of Article 36 of the Uniform Code of Military Justice, says that "the provisions of these articles conferring jurisdiction upon courts martial shall not be construed as depriving military commissions . . . or other military tribunals of concurrent jurisdiction in respect of offenders or offenses that by statute or by the law of war may be triable by such military commissions . . . or other military tribunals." Pointedly declining "to determine to what extent the President as Commander in Chief has constitutional power to create military commissions without the support of Congressional legislation," the Court said that with this provision, "Congress has authorized trial of offenses against the law of war before such commissions."[31]

The reading of Article 15 in *Ex Parte Quirin* was highly vulnerable on the text; Article 15 need not be read as specifically authorizing trial before military commissions. The Court's reading was evidently inspired by a belief that, at least in some circumstances, the President may well have the power to create military commissions on his own. Thus the Court said that an "important incident to the conduct of war is the adoption of measures by the military command . . . to seize and subject to disciplinary measures those enemies who in their attempt to thwart or impede our military effort have violated the law of war."[32] After *Ex Parte Quirin*, it would be reasonable to think that Article 36 of the Uniform Code of Military Justice essentially authorizes the President to create military commissions to try suspected terrorists, at least when there has been a declaration of war or an authorization for the use of military force.[33] But in *Hamdan*, the Court rejected this view.

---

[30] 317 US 1 (1942).

[31] Id at 29.

[32] Id at 28–29.

[33] Perhaps there is a difference between the two; perhaps a declaration of war permits more in the way of presidential discretion than an authorization for the use of military force. But declarations of war have been exceedingly rare in the nation's history, and authorization for the use of military force appears to have become the functional equivalent.

The *Hamdan* decision was issued in the midst of a broad and far-reaching debate about presidential power to protect the nation's security, and the dispute within the Court cannot be appreciated without reference to that debate, of which the Justices were surely aware. On the one hand, Justice Jackson's concurring opinion in the Steel Seizure Case has had a dominant role in public discussion and indeed set its basic terms, having played a key role in the confirmation hearings for Chief Justice Roberts and Justice Alito.[34] On the other hand, the Bush administration has made some aggressive claims about the President's power to act unilaterally. In a much-discussed memorandum in 2002, the Office of Legal Counsel of the Department of Justice contended that as Commander-in-Chief, the President has inherent authority to torture suspected terrorists—authority that Congress might well not be permitted to override.[35] In other contexts, the executive offered exceedingly broad arguments about the President's power to act on his own to protect the nation, and some lower courts explicitly suggested that something like "the war power" had been vested in the President.[36]

At the same time, a range of disputes involved the appropriate presumption, or clear statement principle, to apply in the face of ambiguous legislation.[37] What was unsettled was the direction in which any clear statement principle should run. Should the President, as Commander-in-Chief, be presumed to have the authority to act to protect national security, at least when Congress has not

---

[34] Note, for example, the large place of Justice Jackson's concurrence in the confirmation hearings of Chief Justice Roberts and Justice Alito. See Confirmation Hearing on the Nomination of John G. Roberts, Jr., To Be Chief Justice of the Supreme Court, Committee on the Judiciary, 109th Cong, 1st Sess (Sept 12–15, 2005), Serial No J-109-37, available online at http://www.gpoaccess.gov, at pp 153–54, 253, 279; Confirmation Hearing on the Nomination of Samuel J. Alito, Jr., To Be an Associate Justice of the Supreme Court, Committee on the Judiciary, 109th Cong, 2d Sess (Jan 9–13, 2006), Serial No J-109-56, available online at http://www.gpoaccess.gov, at 323–27. (Roberts hearings available online at http://www.asksam.com/ebooks/releases.asp?file=JGRHearing.ask&dn=Contents; Alito hearings available at http://www.asksam.com/ebooks/releases.asp?file=Alito_Hearing.ask).

[35] See Office of Legal Counsel, Memorandum for Alberto Gonzales, Counsel to the President, Re: Standards of Conduct for Interrogation under 18 USC 2340–2340A (Aug 1, 2002) (copy on file with author).

[36] *Al Odah v United States*, 321 F3d 1134 (DC Cir 2003); *Center for National Security Studies v U.S. Department of Justice*, 331 F3d 918 (DC Cir 2003); *U.S. v Moussaoui*, 382 F3d 453 (4th Cir 2004).

[37] See, e.g., Posner and Vermeule, *Terror in the Balance* (cited in note 18); Pildes and Issacharoff, 5 Theoretical Inquiries in Law (cited in note 19).

said otherwise? Or should principles of constitutional liberty, or liberty in general, forbid the President from acting unless he can claim clear congressional permission? Justice Jackson's concurrence does not answer these questions, which will be decisive in many actual and imaginable controversies.

B. JUSTICE STEVENS: CLEAR STATEMENTS AND FAIR TRIALS

The prevailing opinion, and in most respects the majority opinion, was written by Justice Stevens. For the most part, the Court did not explicitly embrace clear statement principles at all. It purported to adhere closely to the text, context, and history of the relevant provisions. Nonetheless, we shall see that the Court's approach is best understood as rooted, at all crucial points, in a clear statement principle of an identifiable kind—one that requires congressional authorization to be explicit rather than implicit, and that rejects claims of unilateral or exclusive presidential authority.

1. *The Detainee Treatment Act.* The first issue was whether the writ of certiorari should be dismissed under the authority of the Detainee Treatment Act (DTA), which provided a special procedure for judicial review of detention of enemy combatants. Under the DTA, the United States Court of Appeals for the District of Columbia Circuit has exclusive jurisdiction "to determine the validity of any final decision" of a military commission.[38] Review is limited to specified grounds, including compliance with federal law, statutory and constitutional.

While the relevant section is said to "take effect on the date of enactment," it does not specify whether it applies to pending claims.[39] The government contended that the text of the statute applies to all claims, including pending ones, and that under established doctrine, the failure of Congress to exempt pending cases creates a presumption against the Court's exercise of jurisdiction.[40] The Court rejected the argument. It emphasized that other provisions of the DTA expressly proclaim their applicability to pending cases, and there was no such express proclamation in the disputed section here. In the Court's view, Congress's failure to

---

[38] *Hamdan*, 126 S Ct at 2763 (2006) (quoting Detainee Treatment Act, Pub L No 109-148, § 1005(e)(2), 119 Stat 2739, 2740 (2005)).

[39] Id at 2763 (quoting Pub L No 109-148, § 1005(h)(1), 119 Stat 2739, 2743 (2005)).

[40] See id at 2763.

include such a provision in that section suggested that it did not mean to apply that section to pending cases.[41]

2. *Abstention.* The government argued that even if the Court had jurisdiction, it should abstain and thus refuse to address the merits until Hamdan's trial was complete. In the government's view, abstention was mandatory under principles of comity, ensuring against a premature attack on an ongoing military proceeding.[42] The Court responded that comity principles did not apply. It emphasized two points. First, Hamdan is not a member of the armed forces of the United States, and hence military discipline was not at issue.[43] Second, the military commission was not part of an integrated system of military courts, and hence Hamdan could not use a system of appeal to civilian courts.[44] The Court found it relevant that the pertinent "review bodies clearly lack the structural insulation from military influence" that would make abstention principles applicable.[45]

It is worth pausing over this point. In refusing to abstain, the Court suggested that comity principles would call for abstention only when appellate review ensured a degree of protection against "military influence." This suggestion, reflecting an unmistakable concern for procedural fairness, animates other parts of the Court's opinion as well.

3. *Conspiracy and the law of war.* Did the President have the authority to convene a military commission here? On this question, the Court said a great deal, offering far more analysis and detail than it had in *Ex Parte Quirin*. The Court began with the important conclusion that the AUMF did not affect the President's authority under preexisting statutes. Implied repeals are disfavored, and the general and abstract language of the AUMF, giving the President the power to use force, should not be taken to overcome specific limitations in existing law, including the limitations in the UCMJ.[46] As we shall see, this conclusion has general implications.

The Court acknowledged that military commissions have a long

---

[41] Id at 2769.

[42] Id.

[43] Id at 2771.

[44] Id.

[45] Id.

[46] Id at 2775.

history. In its view, that history was a product of "military necessity," and limited to that context.[47] Nor was the authority to create such tribunals purely a presidential prerogative; hence any form of presidential unilateralism, intimated by Justice Thomas's dissent, misdescribed the law. In the Court's view, the relevant authority "can derive only from the powers granted jointly to the President and Congress in time of war."[48] In a pointed paragraph, the Court noted that while the President is Commander-in-Chief of the Armed Forces, the Constitution explicitly grants a number of war-related powers of Congress, including the authority to declare war, to make rules concerning captures on land and water, to raise and support armies, and to define and punish offenses against the law of nations.[49] This paragraph seemed to be a clear rejection of general claims of a distinctly presidential "war power," or broad executive authority to protect the nation's security.

The Court declined to resolve the question whether the President could, under circumstances of "military necessity," create military commissions "without the sanction of Congress."[50] And the Court went out of its way to suggest that it had "no occasion to revisit" the *Quirin* Court's conclusion that Article 15 authorized military commissions—a conclusion that it described as "controversial."[51] In its view, however, *Ex Parte Quirin* gave no "sweeping mandate" to the President to create commissions whenever he wished.[52] At most, *Quirin* allowed the President to convene such commissions "where justified under the 'Constitution and laws,'" including the law of war.[53]

All this led to the central question: Did the law of war justify trying Hamdan in a military commission? On this point, Justice Kennedy refused to speak, and hence Justice Stevens wrote for a 4–3 plurality. He began the analysis by pointing to the common law, which allowed for military commissions in only three circumstances. The first involved places in which martial law had been declared; the second involved temporary military government over

---

[47] Id at 2773.

[48] Id.

[49] Id at 2773–74.

[50] Id at 2774.

[51] Id.

[52] Id.

[53] Id at 2775.

occupied territories. The third, and the relevant context here, involved commissions "convened as an 'incident of the conduct of war' when there is a need 'to seize and subject to disciplinary measures those enemies who in their attempt to thwart or impede our military effort have violated the law of war.'"[54] For the executive, the problem was that Hamdan was charged not with a violation of the law of war itself, but with "conspiracy" to violate the law of war, over a period from 1996 to November 2001. Most of this period preceded the attacks of 9/11 and the enactment of the AUMF. In the plurality's view, the offense of "conspiracy" to violate the law of war is not itself triable by military commission.

In reaching this conclusion, the plurality did not deny that Congress has the power to characterize conspiracy as a war crime; the difficulty was that it had not done so. By itself, this objection was not fatal, for the common law of war could suffice to justify trial in a military commission even if Congress had not spoken. But to support prosecution in such a commission, the plurality said that the historical precedent on that point "must be plain and unambiguous,"[55] so to avoid the concentration of adjudicative and punitive power in military hands. In *Ex Parte Quirin*, the violation of the law or war was plain. With respect to conspiracy, however, history provided no such plain support.

This point was "indicative of a broader" problem, which was the executive's failure to "satisfy the most basic precondition" for military tribunals, which is "military necessity."[56] Hence the plurality emphasized that the record showed that there was no urgent need for imposition or execution of judgment; recall that Hamdan had been arrested in 2001 and charged only in 2004. These are not the circumstances that call for use of a military commission. In the plurality's view, Hamdan could not be tried for conspiracy.

4. *The UCMJ and fair procedures.* Now speaking for the Court, Justice Stevens went on to conclude that even if Hamdan had been legitimately charged with an offense against the law of war, the commission could not proceed, because the specified procedures violated the UCMJ. A key point here is that under the regulations governing the commission, both Hamdan and his lawyer could be

---

[54] Id at 2776.
[55] Id at 2780.
[56] Id at 2785.

excluded from part of the proceeding if either the appointing authority or the presiding officer so decided—for reasons of national security or other reasons specified in the regulations. And if the proceedings were closed, Hamdan and his lawyer could be prevented from learning the evidence against him. In addition, hearsay and other evidence could be included whenever it "would have probative value to a reasonable person," and various kinds of information could be deemed "protected," and hence withheld from the defense, if it concerned "national security interests."[57] Hence some of the standard rules, calling for fairness to the defense, might not be followed in the military tribunal.

The Court concluded that to this extent, the rules governing the tribunal were inconsistent with the UCMJ. Under that statute, military tribunals are supposed, "so far as practicable," to "apply the principles of law and rules of evidence generally recognized in the trial of criminal cases in the United States district courts."[58] In addition, rules and regulation "shall be uniform insofar as practicable."[59] Any procedural rules must therefore be consistent with the UCMJ; and the rules in military commissions must be the same as those in court-martial proceedings unless such uniformity is shown to be impracticable. The Court acknowledged that a sufficient determination of "impracticability" could justify a departure from the usual rules.[60] But here the President's determination was inadequate. There was, in fact, no official determination that it would be impracticable to follow the rules for courts-martial. In any event, nothing in the record explained why those rules would not be practicable. The Court said that the general danger of international terrorism, by itself, would not require a variance from the ordinary rules.[61]

Here again the Court emphasized that a military commission must be a "tribunal of true exigency" rather than "a more convenient adjudicatory tool"; and it read the UCMJ in this light.[62] One implication is that Congress could expressly authorize military commissions even in the circumstances in which the Presi-

---

[57] Id at 2786–87.

[58] Id at 2790 (quoting Unif Code Mil Justice, Art 36, 10 USCS § 836(a)).

[59] 126 S Ct at 2790 (quoting Unif Code Mil Justice Art 36, 10 USCS § 836(b)).

[60] 126 S Ct at 2791.

[61] Id at 2792.

[62] Id at 2793.

dent sought to try Hamdan. Another implication is that the analysis would be very different in a genuine emergency. But without explicit authorization or an emergency, a military tribunal, not following the standard procedures, would be unacceptable.

5. *The Geneva Conventions.* The Court's final conclusion was that the procedures violated the Geneva Conventions and in particular Common Article 3. The Court began by concluding that the Conventions are subject to judicial enforcement. The reason is that the UCMJ conditions the authority to create military commissions on compliance with the law of war; to that extent, the Geneva Conventions are a part of the law of war and enforceable as such. The Court added that the key provision of the Geneva Conventions—Common Article 3—does in fact apply to the conflict with Al Qaeda. Common Article 3 applies in a "conflict not of an international character occurring in the territory of one of the High Contracting Parties."[63] The executive construed Common Article 3 not to apply because the conflict with Al Qaeda is indeed international in character and scope. The Court responded that the words "not of an international character" refer to conflicts that are not between or among nations—and hence that the war with Al Qaeda, reflecting a conflict between a nation and a terrorist organization, does fall within the literal language.[64]

Finally, the Court reached the merits. The key provision of Common Article 3 requires that Hamdan be tried before a "regularly constituted court affording all the judicial guarantees which are recognized as indispensable by civilized peoples."[65] The Court concluded that this provision was violated, because the military commission was not "regularly constituted."[66] The regular military courts are the courts-martial, not military commissions. This point does not mean that Common Article 3 always bans military commissions as such. But in order for them to be legitimate, the executive must show that a practical need justifies departure from the use of court-martial proceedings. Hence the Court's analysis of Common Article 3 tracked its analysis of the UCMJ: The ex-

---

[63] Id at 2795.

[64] Id.

[65] Id at 2796 (quoting 6 UST at 3320 (Art 3, 1(d))).

[66] 126 S Ct at 2796.

ecutive may use the procedures of military commissions only if it demonstrated some kind of necessity.[67]

A plurality also concluded that "the judicial guarantees recognized as indispensable by civilized peoples" require the procedural safeguards afforded by customary international law, and that those safeguards include the right to be tried in one's presence and to be privy to the evidence.[68] Here again, no practical need had been shown to justify a departure from the requisite guarantees. The plurality said that at least in the absence of "express statutory provision to the contrary, information used to convict a person of a crime must be disclosed to him."[69] Thus Common Article 3 required both "regular" courts and a right to see the evidence on which a conviction might be based.

C. JUSTICE BREYER AND ACTIVE LIBERTY

Justice Breyer, joined by Justices Kennedy, Souter, and Ginsburg, offered a revealing one-page concurrence, designed to specify the theme of the Court's holding. In his view, that holding "rests upon a single ground: Congress has not issued the Executive a 'blank check.'"[70] Because there was no emergency, judicial insistence on consultation with Congress was entirely proper. The task was to decide how to deal with the current danger through democratic means.

Justice Breyer's separate opinion is worth noting for three reasons. First, he underlines a general point that might be lost in the details of Justice Stevens's opinion, which is that the President must ask Congress, in express terms, for "the authority he believes necessary."[71] I shall have more to say about this point below, which seems to organize the central message of the Court. Second, there

---

[67] There is an evident puzzle here. If a military commission is not "regularly constituted," and hence violates Common Article 3, why would it be legitimate under circumstances of necessity? Why would it become "regularly constituted" simply because necessity required it?

[68] Id at 2797 (quoting 6 UST at 3320 (Art 3, 1(d))).

[69] 126 S Ct at 2798.

[70] Id at 2799.

[71] Id. Note that Justice Breyer does not say whether this principle would be followed if Congress had said nothing at all. It is not clear how the problem in *Hamdi* would be analyzed if Congress had said nothing about military tribunals, rather than enacting relevant statutes with several ambiguities. Of course, an aggressive form of liberty-protecting minimalism would say that silence is not enough.

is an evident connection between Justice Breyer's plea for congressional specification and his recent argument that hard cases
should be assessed with close reference to the ideal of "active
liberty," which calls for democratic self-government.[72] Justice
Breyer appears to believe that this ideal requires a degree of democratic engagement, involving the national legislature, on the appropriate response to danger of terrorism, at least when there is
no emergency. The *Hamdan* decision is difficult to understand
without an emphasis on this point, which is central to the Court's
liberty-promoting minimalism. Third, there is no question that
five members of the Court are in agreement with Justice Breyer's
brief opinion. Recall that it was signed by four members of the
Court, and perhaps Justice Stevens would have signed it if not for
the fact that by doing so, he would have ensured the existence of
not one but two majority opinions.[73]

D. JUSTICE KENNEDY AS (RELATIVE) MINIMALIST

Justice Kennedy wrote separately—essentially to agree with the
prevailing opinion, but to offer a greater degree of caution. His
principal claim was that under both the UCMJ and the Geneva
Conventions, the President must use the ordinary procedures for
courts-martial unless there is some demonstrated need to do otherwise. Here no such need had been shown. On his view, Common
Article 3 requires an inquiry very much like that required by the
UCMJ, with "at the least, a uniformity principle similar to that
codified in" domestic law.[74] More particularly, a military commission would be "regularly constituted" only if "some practical
need explains deviations from court-martial practice."[75] The military commission was significantly different from courts-martial
in terms of its composition and structure, and the relevant differences could not be justified by reference to practicability.

Justice Kennedy declined to offer his view on several questions,
most prominently whether a conspiracy charge could be tried be-

---

[72] See Stephen Breyer, *Active Liberty* (2005).

[73] It is true that Justice Stevens might have incorporated Justice Breyer's arguments in
his own opinion, but it seems clear that Justice Breyer, and perhaps the public more
generally, had an interest in this very simple separate statement of the grounds of the
holding.

[74] 126 S Ct at 2803.

[75] Id at 2804.

fore a military commission and whether Common Article 3 requires the presence of the accused at all stages of a criminal trial.

E. JUSTICE SCALIA: THE PASSIVE VIRTUES?

Justice Scalia's opinion, joined by Justices Thomas and Alito,
was restricted to the two justiciability issues. First, Justice Scalia
contended that the DTA eliminated the Court's jurisdiction. He
emphasized that by its plain terms, it said that "no court, justice,
or judge" shall have jurisdiction to consider habeas applications
from Guantanamo Bay detainees except through the specified
routes.[76] Hence the Supreme Court had been deprived of jurisdiction—particularly in view of the established principle requiring
clear exemptions for pending cases. Having found a denial of jurisdiction, he concluded that there was no constitutional problem
with the DTA under the Suspension Clause. The first reason was
that Hamdan, as an enemy alien detained abroad, lacked rights
under that clause. The second reason was that Congress had not
eliminated judicial review entirely, but merely created a substitute
remedy, and an adequate one, through the postdecision review
process in the D.C. Circuit.

Second, Justice Scalia contended that whatever the meaning of
the DTA, the Court should exercise its equitable discretion and
decline to hear the merits. Considerations of comity required this
course, especially because of the need for "*interbranch* comity at
the federal level."[77] The order of the district court, enjoining proceedings deemed necessary, by the President, for the protection
of American citizens against terrorist attacks, "brings the Judicial
Branch into direct conflict with the Executive in an area where
the Executive's competence is maximal and ours is virtually non-
existent."[78] While the obligation is to "avoid such conflict[,] the
Court rushes headlong to meet it."

Justice Scalia's opinion is not implausibly understood as a tribute
to the passive virtues[79]—the idea that the Court should decline,
when it can, to resolve especially contentious and difficult issues.

---

[76] Id at 2810 (quoting § 1005(e)(1), 119 Stat at 2742).

[77] 126 S Ct at 2822.

[78] Id.

[79] See Alexander Bickel, *The Least Dangerous Branch* (1965). Note, however, that Justice
Scalia's pronouncements about the Suspension Clause reach into constitutionally sensitive
territory.

It would have been interesting, and in a way elegant, if Justice Scalia had simply stopped there. Ironically, however, Justice Scalia did not rest content with his own argument. Instead he joined, in full, Justice Thomas's dissenting opinion, which expressed a view on the merits of every issue in the case.

F. JUSTICE THOMAS: THE PRESIDENT'S "BROAD CONSTITUTIONAL AUTHORITY"

Justice Thomas's dissenting opinion began with a distinctive understanding of the President's constitutional authority. In his view, the "primary responsibility" to protect national security rests with the President.[80] Indeed, the Constitution "confer[s] on the President broad constitutional authority to protect the Nation's security as he sees fit."[81] Shifting from the Constitution to governing statutes, he emphasized the AUMF, which, in his view, independently authorizes the use of military commissions, because that authority is included within the power to use force.

After this ambitious start, Justice Thomas proceeded to explain his particular disagreements with the Court. The common law of war, far from being frozen in time, "is flexible and evolutionary in nature," and it "affords a measure of respect for the judgment of military commanders."[82] In his view, membership in Al Qaeda— a group of war criminals—is itself legitimately punishable under the Laws of War, and the same is certainly true of conspiracy to commit war crimes. As a matter of history, Justice Thomas rejected Justice Stevens's claim that conspiracy was not so punishable. In addition, he emphasized the need to respect "what is quintessentially a policy and military judgment, namely, the appropriate military measures to take against those" involved in the 9/11 attacks.[83] The punishment of conspiracy was fully supported by the nature of the conflict against international terrorism, for we "are not engaged in a traditional battle with a nation-state, but with a worldwide, hydra-headed enemy, who lurks in the shadows conspiring to reproduce the atrocities of September 11, 2001."[84] Thus

---

[80] 126 S Ct at 2823.

[81] Id.

[82] Id at 2829.

[83] Id at 2838.

[84] Id.

the plurality's view—forbidding use of military commissions against conspiracies—"would sorely hamper the President's ability to confront and defeat a new and deadly enemy."[85]

Justice Thomas also concluded that the UCMJ does not limit the President's inherent power to convene military commissions. On the contrary, it expressly recognizes that power. What the Court reads as a restriction is, in Justice Thomas's view, a grant of discretion. Thus Article 36 of the UCMJ tells the President to use ordinary principles and rules, but only "so far as he considers practicable."[86] Hence Article 36 is best taken to allow the President "to depart from the procedures applicable in criminal cases whenever he alone does not deem such procedures 'practicable.'"[87] Far from limiting the President's options, Article 3 gives him "unfettered authority to prescribe military commission procedure."[88] And even if Article 36 could be construed to require procedural uniformity in the absence of some relevant finding of impracticability, that finding could be discerned in public statements of the Secretary of Defense, explaining why military commissions were needed.

Finally, Justice Thomas contended that the Geneva Conventions were unhelpful to Hamdan, and for multiple reasons. First, they did not provide the basis for justiciable claims at all; "diplomatic measures by political and military authorities were the exclusive mechanisms for" their enforcement.[89] In addition, Common Article 3 applies only to "armed conflict not of an international character occurring in the territory of one of the High Contracting Parties."[90] The executive reasonably concluded that this article does not apply to Al Qaeda detainees, because the relevant conflicts are international in nature. In Justice Thomas's view, that reasonable conclusion deserved deference from the Court.

In any case, Hamdan's commission was in full compliance with Common Article 3. The commission was "regularly constituted" in light of the fact that military commissions had been used at many stages in the nation's history. Moreover, the anticipated pro-

---

[85] Id.

[86] Id at 2840 (quoting 10 USC § 836(a)).

[87] 126 S Ct at 2840.

[88] Id.

[89] Id at 2844.

[90] Id at 2846 (quoting 6 UST at 3318).

cedures provided "the judicial guarantees which are recognized as indispensable by civilized peoples."[91] It is true that Hamdan might be barred from the proceedings and denied access to certain evidence; but the exclusion or denial would occur only for specific reasons, including a desire to protect classified intelligence. In any case, no such bar or denial would be acceptable, under the existing regulations, if it would make the trial unfair. Hence there was no denial here of what "civilized peoples" would accept. In Justice Thomas's view, "the President's understanding of the requirements of Common Article 3 is entitled to 'great weight.'"[92] Most generally, the President's "findings about the nature of the present conflict . . . represent a core exercise of his commander-in-chief authority that this Curt is bound to respect."[93]

G. JUSTICE ALITO'S (RELATIVE) MINIMALISM

Justice Alito's separate opinion had essentially the same relationship to that of Justice Thomas as Justice Kennedy's had to that of Justice Stevens—broad agreement, but a plea for greater caution. Justice Alito contended that it was unnecessary to reach several of the questions explored by Justice Thomas—including the constitutional power of the President, whether membership in Al Qaeda was a violation of the law of war, and whether Common Article 3 was enforceable. Most of his opinion patiently explained his conclusion that whether or not it was enforceable, Common Article 3 had not been violated. He contended that the words "regularly constituted" mean not "usually in place" but properly constituted under domestic law—and the military commissions here were so constituted.[94] With respect to the guarantees "recognized as indispensable by civilized peoples," he suggested that it was speculative, and therefore premature, to conclude that Hamdan might be prejudiced by the exclusion of certain evidence. Any such possibility should be assessed in the review proceeding for Hamdan's case in particular.

---

[91] 126 S Ct at 2847.
[92] Id at 2849.
[93] Id.
[94] See id at 2851.

II.   Clear Statements and Clear Principles

My goals in this section are twofold. First and foremost, I attempt to explain the real division in the Court—a division that involved the appropriate presumption, or clear statement principle, with which to approach the technical issues. Second, I shall attempt a sympathetic reconstruction of the Court's approach. Despite the sympathetic character of the reconstruction, I am not at all sure that the Court was correct. Because of the complexity and delicacy of the underlying issues, it might well have been best if the Court had simply abstained. There would be real advantages in waiting for Hamdan's trial and seeing, rather than speculating about, the relevant procedure before resolving the merits. Of course, there are countervailing considerations; a number of people, and not merely Hamdan, might have been subjected to arguably unlawful proceedings, which, once terminated and invalidated, might have had to be replicated. I am here not to press the argument for abstention, but to understand the broader ideas that lie beneath the surface of the Court's opinion. As we shall see, those broader ideas have considerable appeal.

A.   technicalities

One of the most remarkable features of the *Hamdan* decision is the sheer number of issues on which the Court divided—by margins of 5–3, 4–3, or 4–2. The Justices divided over (1) the Court's jurisdiction (5–3); (2) abstention (5–3); (3) the legality of using military commissions to try a conspiracy charge (4–3); (4) the legality of using a military commission lacking the rules and procedures of courts-martial (5–3); (5) the enforceability of the Geneva Conventions (5–2); (6) the applicability of Common Article 3 to the war with Al Qaeda (5–2); and (7) the meaning of Common Article 3 (5–3). Each of these questions is highly technical and complex. In many of them, and plausibly in all of them, the legal materials were ambiguous. For at least some of the seven issues, the legal materials would surely leave an objective reader unsure, concluding that the standard interpretive sources made both positions plausible. For other issues, one of the two positions was stronger, but it would be hard to argue that the alternative view was utterly implausible and not susceptible to a good-faith defense.

I shall not attempt to demonstrate these points by parsing all the technical questions in detail, but I shall shortly turn to the most important of them. By way of background, let us pause over the differences between the military commissions proposed by the President and courts-martial approved by the UCMJ—differences that obviously concerned both the President and the Court. As noted, the President's procedures allow a military commission to be closed, and evidence to be withheld from the defendant and his lawyer, if the appointing authority or the presiding officer decides to do so in order to protect classified or classifiable information, the physical safety of participants, intelligence and law enforcement activities, or other national security interests.[95] In addition, evidence is admissible in the President's proposed military commissions so long as it "would have probative value to a reasonable person."[96] Hearsay evidence, evidence obtained through coercion, and unsworn testimony may therefore be admitted. The defendant and his counsel may also be deprived of access to "protected information," including classified information, if it is "probative" and if its admission would not deny the defendant "a full and fair trial."[97]

In the President's version of military commissions, decisions are to be made by a panel consisting of at least three and possibly seven or more members, all of them officers in the United States Armed Forces (and not necessarily with judicial experience). A verdict of guilty need not be supported by a unanimous panel; a two-thirds vote would suffice for guilt and for any sentence except for the death penalty.[98] An appeal can be taken to a three-member panel consisting of military officers and chosen by the Secretary of Defense; only one member is required to have judicial experience.[99] The panel is asked to make a recommendation to the Secretary of Defense, who can remand for further proceedings or forward the record to the President with a recommendation for final disposition. The President makes the "final decision" unless he has delegated that task to the Secretary.[100] In all these ways,

[95] Id at 2786.
[96] Id.
[97] Id at 2787.
[98] Id.
[99] Id.
[100] Id.

the commission's proceedings depart from the generally recognized principles and rules for courts-martial.

Article 36 of the UCMJ, emphasized by the Court, directs the President to apply the principles and rules set forth in the UCMJ in military tribunals "so far as he considers practicable," and it adds that uniform regulations must be used "insofar as practicable."[101] The Court was evidently concerned about the disparities between procedures in military commissions and procedures in courts-martial. But it would be possible to read the "practicability" provisions to say that the President is allowed to depart from the usual principles essentially as he pleases, subject to something akin to arbitrariness review. On this view, the President may establish distinctive rules and principles if he wishes, so long as he is making a good-faith (and not unreasonable) judgment about practicability. And on this view, the unique circumstances of the war on terror—and of trials of those allegedly associated with Al Qaeda—could support a judgment that the standard rules are simply not practicable. The fact that the word "practicable" is preceded by "so far as he considers" lends strength to this interpretation. After all, the President, and no one else, is entitled to make judgments about what is, in fact, "practicable."

The competing position is also possible to sketch. On that view, the word "practicable" does not merely mean as the President reasonably sees fit. On the contrary, it imposes a serious constraint. In ordinary language, the suggestion that one must follow a certain course of action insofar as it is "practicable" operates as a restriction, not a license. Perhaps the President is obliged to make and to support a finding of genuine impracticability—and perhaps he failed to do so here. At first glance, this position seems somewhat weaker than the alternative view, defended by Justice Thomas; a potentially closed trial of Osama Bin Laden's driver and bodyguard—closed only to the extent that national security so requires—appears to satisfy whatever restriction is imposed by the words "so far *as he considers* practicable." But reasonable people can differ on this point.

Or consider the question whether Common Article 3 applies to the war with Al Qaeda. At first glance, that war is certainly a conflict "of international character"—and hence Common Article

---

[101] 10 USC § 836(a).

3 does not apply. On the other hand, perhaps a conflict has an international character only if it is a conflict among or between nations. This conclusion might be supported on the ground that the President has interpreted this ambiguous phrase not to apply to the conflict with Al Qaeda; it is standard to defer to presidential interpretations of ambiguous provisions in treaties. But if the words "of international character" are read in their context, perhaps the President's interpretation is inconsistent with them. At least if we consider the principle of deference to executive interpretations, the dissenters seem to have the stronger argument here as well. But the standard legal tools do not foreclose the conclusion, on this question, of either the Court or the dissent.

While I cannot demonstrate the point here, I believe that something of this kind can be said about all of the issues that divide the Justices in *Hamdan*. Is "conspiracy" to violate the law of war itself a violation of the law of war? The plurality is right to say that the historical materials do not unambiguously justify an affirmative answer; but Justice Thomas is right to say both that the common law of war need not be fixed and rigid and that the President's position is not without historical support. Would the proposed procedure violate guarantees recognized as indispensable by civilized peoples? Hamdan would be subjected to a genuine trial, not to a summary proceeding, and he was entitled to counsel. Justice Alito had a fair point in suggesting that it "makes no sense to strike down the entire commission structure based on speculation that some evidence might be improperly admitted in some future case." On the other hand, the right to see the evidence is among the most fundamental guarantees of a fair system of criminal justice, and perhaps the divergences between ordinary procedures, and those laid out for military commission, raise serious problems of unfairness.

B. THE REAL DIVISION

We should now be able to see that the real division in the Court involved not the technicalities, but two intimately related and much more general issues: the appropriate clear statement principles and the constitutional background. This claim is easiest to establish for Justice Thomas's dissenting opinion, which comes close to acknowledging its general motivation. But a clear statement principle is even more central to Justice Stevens's opinion, which cannot possibly be understood without it.

Recall that Justice Thomas begins with a sustained treatment of the constitutional allocation of power, emphasizing that the founding document "confer[s] upon the President broad constitutional authority to protect the Nation's security in the manner he deems fit."[102] Thus his analysis is undergirded by a distinctive understanding of the Commander-in-Chief authority, one that recognizes presidential authority, at least when it has not been clearly limited by Congress. Consider too the fact that at several key moments, Justice Thomas emphasizes that courts should defer to the interpretive judgments of the President. In suggesting that the President is entitled to depart from the standard procedural rules, Justice Thomas offers the language of deference, suggesting the need to accept the informed judgments of the Chief Executive. And in calling for deference to the President's interpretation of Common Article 3, Justice Thomas invokes the conventional view that the executive receives deference with respect to ambiguous treaty provisions. He adds that the Court's "duty to defer . . . is only heightened by the fact that he is acting pursuant to his constitutional authority as Commander in Chief and by the fact that the subject matter of Common Article 3 calls for a judgment about the nature and character of an armed conflict."[103]

We might therefore understand his opinion in the following way: *In light of the President's position as Commander-in-Chief, and his distinctive expertise in the domain of national security, he is entitled to interpret ambiguous statutes as he sees fit. If Congress wants to cabin his power, it must do so explicitly.* We might even say that Justice Thomas is suggesting a kind of *Chevron* principle for the war on terror—one that accords the President the same power, with respect to ambiguous statutory provisions, that regulatory agencies have with respect to the statutes that they administer.[104] If the Environmental Protection Agency is permitted to interpret ambiguous provisions of the Clean Air Act (so long as its interpretations are reasonable), perhaps the President has the same power with respect to the AUMF, the UCMJ, and Common Article 3,

---

[102] 126 S Ct at 2823.

[103] Id at 2825.

[104] For general discussion, see Posner and Sunstein, Yale L J (cited in note 28).

at least insofar as the question is how to handle the war with Al Qaeda.

Justice Stevens's opinion, emphasizing the legal details, is less transparent in its treatment of the constitutional backdrop and relevant clear statement principles. But it is evidently motivated by a particular view about that backdrop and those principles. Recall that at a key moment, Justice Stevens acknowledges the President's authority as Commander-in-Chief, but goes on to specify, in pointed terms, a wide range of war-related powers that the founding document gives to Congress, not the President. Recall too that in exploring whether the charge of conspiracy can be tried in military commissions, Justice Stevens requires that the precedent "be plain and unambiguous"—so as to avoid concentrating both adjudicative and punitive power "in military hands."[105] And in emphasizing the absence of an adequate showing that ordinary procedures are not "practicable," Justice Stevens seems to be calling for clear congressional permission for any departure from those principles. Justice Breyer's brief opinion—asking the President to go to Congress "to seek the authority he believes necessary"—signals the underlying idea.[106]

On this view, *Hamdan* reflects a kind of narrow nondelegation principle, one that will not lightly take ambiguous statutes to grant the President broad authority to create military commissions as he sees fit (at least when there is no emergency). More particularly, the basic claim is that Congress must speak clearly if it seeks to allow the executive to depart from the usual methods for conducting criminal trials. Unless Congress has unambiguously said otherwise, and if history or circumstances of emergency do not clearly warrant, the government is forbidden to deprive people (including enemy combatants) of their liberty except through the ordinary channels and procedures, with their important guarantees against error and unfairness. The outcome in *Hamdan*—the diverse conclusions on seven difficult questions of law—cannot plausibly be explained without resort to a principle of this kind. It is in this respect that the ruling reflects a form of liberty-promoting minimalism, closely connected with an identifiable strand of decisions in the Court's past.

---

[105] 126 S Ct at 2780.

[106] Id at 2799.

Two clarifications are important here. First, the Court's ruling was far from minimalist; the Court did not issue a narrow, incompletely theorized opinion. On the contrary, the Court resolved questions to which it did not need to speak, and it showed a degree of theoretical ambition. When I say that the decision reflects liberty-promoting minimalism, I mean only to suggest that it fits easily with other decisions in which the Court protected individual rights, in the face of national security concerns, by requiring clear legislative authorization.

Second, the clear statement principle in *Hamdan* could be understood narrowly or broadly. Most narrowly, the principle merely requires congressional authorization for a departure from standard adjudicative forms, at least where there is no emergency and where tradition does not clearly support the departure. Most broadly, the principle requires clear congressional authorization whenever the executive intrudes into the domain of individual liberty.[107] By contrast, the breadth of the dissenting view is plain; it suggests that when a legal provision is ambiguous, the executive is permitted to offer a reasonable interpretation of his choice.

C. WHICH CLEAR STATEMENT?

The two sides in *Hamdan* thus disagreed on the question that Justice Jackson did not answer—and that turns out to be crucial to the application of his tripartite framework. While Justice Jackson concluded that the President lacked authority to seize the steel industry, he did not specify the appropriate background principle in the face of statutory ambiguity. In the face of real ambiguity in the governing provisions, we cannot say whether Congress should be taken to have authorized presidential action, or forbidden it, without specifying the appropriate background principles. Much of the time, legislative enactments will be relevantly ambiguous, because Congress will not have anticipated the particular questions. (Both *Hamdi* and *Hamdan* attest to the pervasiveness of ambiguity; as we shall see, the debate over wiretapping by the National Security Agency falls in the same category, because of ambiguity in the AUMF, and because of the need to sort out the relationship between the AUMF and the Foreign Intelligence Sur-

---

[107] This reading creates some tension with *Hamdi*, as discussed below; a possible reconciliation is that the authorization was clear in that case.

veillance Act.[108]) Which side is right? What, if any, is the appropriate clear statement principle?

1. *Constitutional avoidance.* We can approach these questions by observing that the Court's approach would be easiest to defend if it were undergirded by a constitutional provision that protects individual rights, such as the Due Process Clause or the Confrontation Clause. We have seen that in dealing with conflicts between national security and rights, the Court has often used a principle of constitutional avoidance, insisting that unless Congress has been clear, the executive may not enter into constitutionally sensitive domains.[109] The Avoidance Canon is fundamental to the whole area, and we should be able to agree that this canon is properly used to prevent the President from raising serious due process or confrontation problems without clear congressional authorization. The least controversial form of liberty-promoting minimalism is a simple use of the idea of constitutional avoidance.

But the Court did not explicitly point to Due Process or Confrontation Clause concerns in *Hamdan*. It did not fortify its argument by pointing to the potential problems in convicting people of a criminal offense without allowing them to attend the hearing and to see the evidence on which conviction rests. And, in fact, Hamdan did not even argue that the proposed trial would raise serious constitutional questions—or that relevant statutes should be construed so as to make it unnecessary to resolve those questions.

An argument to this effect would hardly have been unimaginable. Hamdan might have been able to contend that he had a right to attend the trial under the Confrontation Clause. And if tried by a U.S. court on territory controlled by the United States, Hamdan would be entitled to claim that he has not been provided with the process that is "due." Under *Hamdi*, the requisite amount of process might well be influenced, at least in part, by the familiar balancing test of *Mathews v Eldridge*.[110] Of course, defendants in criminal trials are entitled to the constitutionally specified rights, such as the right to counsel and to confront witnesses, and it is not entirely clear to what extent the rights of a criminal defendant

---

[108] See infra at 37–41.

[109] Pildes and Issacharoff, 5 Theoretical Inquiries in Law (cited in note 19).

[110] 424 US 319 (1976).

will or should be elaborated by reference to the *Mathews* balancing test. But beyond the constitutional specifications, the extent of the appropriate procedure may well reflect explicit or implicit attention to the three factors identified in *Mathews*: the defendant's interest; the likelihood of error and the probable value of additional safeguards; and the government's interest in avoiding more extensive procedures. Under this test, it is not at all clear that Hamdan could be tried without access to the evidence against him. At the very least, the government would have to muster an extremely good reason for denying him such access—and even if it could do so, it would probably have to show that the trial was otherwise fair.

The Court did not discuss these possibilities—perhaps because Hamdan did not raise them, or contend in any way that the proposed procedure would violate his constitutional rights. But the Court's emphasis on Hamdan's right to see the evidence against him, and to attend the trial, suggests that a concern about due process, if only Due Process Writ Small, played a large role in its decision. Because the Avoidance Canon was not in play, the Court's ruling must be understood as resting on the implicit assumption that a departure from the standard adjudicative forms is impermissible unless clearly authorized by Congress (or justified by tradition or necessity). That idea lacks the support of a constitutional concern; but it certainly does not lack appeal.

2. *Avoidances*. Whatever the nature of the clear statement principle, it runs into a competing argument, grounded in the President's own claims of constitutional authority. Suppose that the President has a legitimate argument that a limitation on his discretion would violate the Commander-in-Chief Clause. If so, then there are two applicable clear statement principles, not merely one. Perhaps ambiguous statutes should be construed favorably to the President, so as to avoid the constitutional issue that would otherwise arise; perhaps Congress should be asked to speak clearly if it seeks to intrude on what might well be the constitutional prerogatives of the Commander-in-Chief. And, indeed, *Ex Parte Quirin* seems to be animated by a clear statement principle in the President's favor—with the apparent thought that the commission procedure there at issue raised no serious question of individual rights. We can certainly imagine cases in which the individual rights claim has no constitutional backing, whereas the President's

claim is plausible; this was apparently the view of Justice Thomas in *Hamdan*.

If competing clear statements are in play, there are two possibilities. Perhaps the competing principles are offsetting; if so, neither is helpful, and the decision must be resolved on some other ground. Much more plausibly, the individual rights claim deserves a kind of interpretive priority and thus defeats the President's claim so long as the statutory provision is ambiguous. In support of this view, consider the fact that the Due Process Clause has priority over the exercise of executive power under the Commander-in-Chief Clause, or for that matter the exercise of congressional power under the Commerce Clause. Under the founding document, individual rights operate as a trump on government authority; a similar idea justifies the interpretive primacy of clear statement principles on behalf of such rights.

3. *Hamdan without avoidance.* But if constitutional avoidance was not involved in *Hamdan* (and recall that the Court did not contend that it was), the Court's approach is far more vulnerable, and there is much to be said for Justice Thomas's approach. This is not because of his (extravagant and implausible[111]) claims about the constitutional allocation of authority to the President, but because it makes sense to allow the President to interpret ambiguous statutory terms, so long as his interpretations are reasonable. At the very least, ambiguous treaty provisions are subject, under the most conventional of principles, to executive interpretation—a point that greatly undermines the Court's treatment of the Geneva Conventions.

Perhaps the UCMJ is not analogous. Perhaps the UCMJ is analogous to the Administrative Procedure Act (APA) or the Freedom of Information Act (FOIA); for the latter statutes, executive interpretations do not receive deference.[112] The reason is that neither the APA nor FOIA is plausibly taken as a delegation of law-interpreting power to the executive. Both statutes limit the authority of the executive in general terms; they are not analogous to organic statutes, such as the Clean Air Act and the Occupational Safety and Health Act, whose rulemaking provisions are reasonably taken as a grant of law-interpreting power as well. Perhaps

---

[111] See Sunstein, *Minimalism at War* (cited in note 19).

[112] See Posner and Sunstein, *Chevronizing Foreign Relations Law* (cited in note 28).

the UCMJ imposes general limits on what the executive may do, so that executive interpretations are neither here nor there. On this view, Congress is not probably read, in the UCMJ, to have given the executive the power to interpret its ambiguities. But even if this is so, recall that the key provision authorizes the President to follow ordinary principles "so far as he considers practicable." Very plausibly, that provision should, above all in the circumstances of the war on terror, be taken to permit him to convene military commissions of the kind contemplated here. At least this is so if constitutional avoidance does not argue otherwise.

The best response would take the following form. Perhaps the Court was not motivated by constitutional concerns, to which it did not refer, but instead by a more general unwillingness to allow a departure from traditional adjudicative institutions and procedures unless Congress explicitly authorizes the departure. On this view, the clear statement principle is defended by reference to a commitment to the standard judicial forms—no matter the identity or the nationality of the defendant. Because of the centrality of those standard forms to Anglo-American law, and to the most basic principles of individual liberty, the President must adhere to them unless they are explicitly displaced by the national legislature. On this view, the Court's approach is essentially Burkean;[113] it requires respect for traditional institutions, designed to protect liberty, unless traditions themselves justify a departure from them (and do so unambiguously).

This idea is not without appeal.[114] But it should be clear that thus understood, *Hamdan* is in a different conceptual universe from *Ex Parte Quirin*, which required no such clear statement— and which, on the contrary, seemed to construe the relevant statute aggressively in a way that would fit with the President's claim of constitutional authority. Under emergency conditions, or when individual liberty is not at stake, the approach in *Ex Parte Quirin* is most plausible. In *Hamdan*, the Court was evidently motivated by a belief that there was no emergency and that an invalidation of the procedure could not possibly compromise national secu-

---

[113] See Cass R. Sunstein, *Burkean Minimalism*, 105 Mich L Rev 353 (2006).

[114] Note, however, Justice Thomas's twofold response: In fact, traditions support use of military commissions to try conspiracy to violate the law of war; and the war with Al Qaeda is unprecedented, and the common law of war must adapt to fit with that unprecedented war.

rity—perhaps because it believed that if a military commission were truly indispensable, Congress would authorize it. What is clear is that at least in a particular domain, *Hamdan* resolves the unanswered question in Justice Jackson's tripartite framework by requiring an explicit statement from Congress.

4. *Legal process?* There is an alternative interpretation of the prevailing opinion in *Hamdan*. The idea of clear statement principles played a role in Justice Thomas's dissenting opinion, but perhaps the majority was not thinking in terms of those principles at all. Perhaps the plurality, or the majority, was operating in terms of the "legal process" approach to interpretation—taking Congress to consist of reasonable people with reasonable purposes, and understanding the legal materials accordingly.[115] On this view, the question is how to see the statutes as sensible or coherent, or how to cast them in the best constructive light. Perhaps this approach— less axiomatic or formalized than one that speaks in terms of clear statement—is what is actually animating the result, or the results, in *Hamdan*.

There is no reason to doubt that some of those who signed the Court's opinion were thinking at least roughly in these terms. The problem with this view is that it is necessary to explain why the prevailing understanding is, in fact, the most reasonable one to attribute to Congress. If so, the idea must be that the standard adjudicative forms should be assumed to apply—unless an emergency is involved. And if that is the idea, it must be because clear congressional authorization should be required if the executive is to be permitted to depart from those forms. Justice Breyer's separate opinion came close to endorsing this point. Hence the legal process approach must ultimately depend on a kind of clear statement principle, even if it is not articulated.[116]

5. *Abstention.* In view of the novelty and delicacy of the underlying questions, a great deal can be said on behalf of a genuinely minimalist course: abstention. That course would have made it unnecessary to resolve disputed questions about the AUMF, the UCMJ, and the Geneva Conventions. To the extent that the Supreme Court should demonstrate the passive virtues, there are

---

[115] See Henry Hart and Albert Sacks, *The Legal Process* 1374, 1378 (William Eskridge and Philip Frickey, eds, 1994)

[116] Note that Hart and Sacks themselves emphasize the importance of clear statement principles. See id.

advantages to leaving those questions undecided. There is a further point, emphasized by Justice Alito and with considerable importance. If the Court had abstained, it would have had an opportunity to resolve the central questions after a trial, and thus after learning about the actual (rather than hypothesized) nature of the particular procedures. Recall that the Court was concerned that Hamdan might have been tried without an opportunity to be present or to hear some of the evidence against him. But the Court did not know if, in fact, Hamdan would have been denied these rights. Perhaps the Court's concerns would turn out to be irrelevant to Hamdan's actual trial, in a way that would bear on both the UCMJ and the Geneva Conventions. A trial may or may not have offered the safeguards deemed indispensable by civilized peoples. If the Court had abstained, it would have known a great deal more.

Abstention might also have had the additional advantage of making it unnecessary to resolve complex questions about the DTA. To be sure, the question of jurisdiction would ordinarily have to be resolved first, and it would have been awkward to abstain without resolving the jurisdictional question. But the Court would have been within its legitimate bounds in saying that a decision to abstain, and hence not to exercise jurisdiction, would make it unnecessary to rule on whether the DTA applied to pending claims.[117] Certainly comity does have its claims; by refusing to abstain, the Court intervened in ongoing military procedures at an exceedingly early stage.

But there are reasonable counterarguments. In this unconventional setting, not involving standard military practices, perhaps the Court was right to assess Hamdan's claim that he would be subject to a procedure that was potentially unlawful and unfair. A decision to abstain would have subjected Hamdan to a long delay— one year? two years?—before obtaining an authoritative ruling on the legality of the trial. And Hamdan would not be the only victim of such a long delay; others, and possibly significant numbers of others, would face the same problem. If the illegality of the commission procedure were clear, the argument for abstention would be weak. In addition, it might be desirable for the Court to tell the executive in advance what procedures it should use, rather

---

[117] A possible objection is that a failure to rule on this point would create excessive uncertainty; surely it is useful to know whether the DTA applies to pending claims. But because the number of pending claims is so small, the concern here is minor.

than making the executive guess. No one denies that it is awkward for the Court to abstain and then to overturn the conviction and require a new proceeding, after Hamdan had been convicted by the commission (on the basis of a trial involving national security issues, informants, and so forth). But in view of the difficulty and novelty of those issues, and the difficulty of resolving them without seeing the actual procedure in action, the course of abstention would have had many virtues.

D. OF HAMDI AND HAMDAN

I have understood *Hamdan* to be rooted most narrowly in a clear statement principle that requires express congressional authorization for a departure from standard adjudicative forms. This understanding has the advantage of reducing the evident tension between the outcome there and the outcome in *Hamdi*.[118]

Recall that in *Hamdi*, Justice Souter, in an opinion joined by Justice Ginsburg, contended that the AUMF should not be construed to overcome the Nondetention Act—and hence that explicit congressional authorization was required for the detention of Hamdi. This approach embodied a kind of clear statement principle, asking Congress to amend the Nondetention Act if it saw fit. The plurality plainly rejected this position, ruling that the AUMF is best read (implicitly) to include the power of detention. In *Hamdan*, by contrast, the Court took a position evidently akin to that of Justice Souter in *Hamdi*, refusing to read the AUMF broadly and finding that explicit authorization was required for the use of military commissions. Here are the obvious questions: Why was a repeal by implication found in *Hamdi* but rejected in *Hamdan*? If *Hamdi* is correct, mustn't *Hamdan* be wrong, and vice-versa?

If the two outcomes are to be reconciled, there are several possibilities.

1. Perhaps it is clear that by tradition and necessity, detention is incidental to the authority to use force—whereas neither tradition nor necessity clearly supports the use of military commissions, at least not in the distinctive circumstances of *Hamdan*. This view is not implausible in the abstract.

---

[118] I am grateful to Eric Posner for discussions of this point.

But is it clearly right? This is a question about historical understanding, and the answer is not obvious.

2. Perhaps the key point is that the President did not make an adequate finding about practicability, and that the UCMJ requires such a finding—and the AUMF does not alter the UCMJ insofar as it so requires. No such problem can be found in *Hamdi*. But is it so clear that the President's finding was inadequate? It would be easy to say that the departures from standard procedures are well suited to the war with Al Qaeda, and that, to this extent, adherence to those procedures would hardly be practicable.

3. Perhaps the best reconciliation is that *Hamdan* rests on a distinctive and quite narrow clear statement principle, governing the use of nontraditional institutions for adjudicating guilt or innocence. Perhaps this principle does not apply to detentions. An approach of this sort might particularly appeal to Justices who are reluctant to second-guess military decisions, such as those involving detention, but who are more willing to insist on the traditional adjudicative forms. But this idea has problems of its own. After all, detention is a deprivation of liberty too. Why should a clear statement be required for military commissions but not for detentions?

To this last question, the best answer must incorporate my first attempt at reconciliation. It emphasizes that as a matter of history and logic, an authorization to use force includes the power to detain enemy combatants. The creation of military commissions is different. At the very least, this argument certainly seems reasonable.

III. BEYOND HAMDAN: THE WIRETAPPING CONTROVERSY

Hamdan has implications for a wide range of questions involving the President's authority in connection with the war on terror. In many circumstances, Congress has not spoken clearly, and if an unambiguous statement is required, the President will not be authorized to act.

As an obvious example, consider the intense controversy over the warrantless wiretapping by the National Security Agency (NSA). During the period from 2001 to the present, the NSA has engaged in foreign surveillance, without a warrant, of commu-

nications involving Al Qaeda. Many people contend that this surveillance is unlawful, on the ground that it violates either the
Foreign Intelligence Surveillance Act (FISA) or the Fourth
Amendment.[119] The executive branch argues otherwise.[120] The
simple question is this: Is the President permitted to engage in
foreign surveillance without a warrant?

At first glance, the question would seem to be negative, because
the FISA regulates the area, and it generally requires the President
to obtain a warrant from the special court created by FISA.[121] But
two arguments are available to the executive branch. First, the
AUMF might be taken to permit the President to engage in warrantless surveillance of communications involving Al Qaeda. On
this view, surveillance is permitted by any statute that authorizes
the use of force; if the President is permitted to use force against
Al Qaeda, surely he is permitted to monitor their communications.

To see the point, suppose that the President authorized surveillance of Al Qaeda on the battlefields of Afghanistan. Under
the AUMF, such authorization would plainly be lawful. Is it so
clear that the President is not authorized, by the AUMF, to monitor a conversation from Osama Bin Laden to (say) Los Angeles?
If he is so authorized, is he not permitted to monitor conversations
from any member of Al Qaeda to the United States? This argument might well be supported by reference to *Hamdi*, which (as
we have seen) understood the power to detain to be an aspect of
the authority to use force, notwithstanding the claim that the
Nondetention Act provided the governing law. Perhaps the AUMF
has the same relationship to FISA that it has to the Nondetention Act. Perhaps it displaces both of them, so long as the President
is operating within its terms.

Second, it might be urged that as Commander-in-Chief, the
President has the inherent power to engage in foreign surveillance
under the Constitution. On the most extreme version of this view,
Congress cannot limit that power even if it chooses to do so.
Foreign surveillance is a presidential prerogative, akin to dictation
of the movement of troops, and perhaps Congress cannot limit

---

[119] See, e.g., Beth Nolan et al, *NSA Spying: A Letter to Congress*, available at http://
www.nybooks.com/articles/18650 (Feb 9, 2006).

[120] See Department of Justice, Legal Authorities Supporting the Activities of the National
Security Agency Described by the President (Jan 19, 2006).

[121] 50 USC 1803–04.

that prerogative—at the very least, after a declaration of war or an authorization for the use of force. On a less extreme version of this argument, legislative enactments such as FISA should be interpreted, if fairly possible, to conform with, rather than to intrude on, the President's constitutional authority. On this view, the AUMF should be taken to authorize the President to engage in foreign surveillance, and FISA should not be understood to dictate otherwise, at least insofar as the conversations involve Al Qaeda or others connected with the attacks of 9/11. This view offers a clear statement principle: Ambiguous congressional enactments must be construed to fit with a plausible claim of constitutional authority.

Before *Hamdan*, these arguments were vulnerable but hardly frivolous. To be sure, the AUMF does not, in terms, give the President the authority to engage in foreign surveillance; it is not specific on this point. But as we have seen, the *Hamdi* plurality ruled that as a matter of history and necessity, detention is incidental to the power to use force; and it is plausible to see foreign surveillance in the same terms. It is true that the Commander-in-Chief Clause does not specifically empower the president to engage in foreign surveillance. But several lower courts have held that the President does, in fact, have that power.[122] As a matter of text, it is not at all clear that foreign surveillance is included within the President's constitutional authority. But the law seems to be in his favor.

The best argument to the contrary would point to FISA. As noted, that statute specifically governs foreign surveillance; perhaps the specific statute should prevail over the more general one, which is the AUMF. In any case, implied repeals are disfavored, and AUMF should not lightly be taken to repeal FISA. Indeed, FISA's text specifically anticipates circumstances of war and makes provision for how the executive branch must proceed under those circumstances[123]—an apparently serious obstacle to the NSA program. The executive's strongest response is that the AUMF may be the more specific statute insofar as it deals with Al Qaeda and

---

[122] See, e.g., *In re Sealed Case*, 310 F3d 717, 742 (Foreign Intel Surv Ct of Rev 2002); *United States v Truong Dinh Hung*, 629 F2d 908 (4th Cir 1980); *U.S. v Brown*, 484 F2d 418 (5th Cir 1973); *U.S. v Butenko*, 484 F2d 418 (5th Cir 1973). For a contrary view, see *Zweibon v Mitchell*, 516 F2d 594 (DC Cir 1975).

[123] 50 USC 1811.

that the AUMF and FISA should be read, if fairly possible, to fit with the President's plausible claim of constitutional authority. But perhaps this reading is not fairly possible; and perhaps FISA, even if applicable, does not intrude on any constitutional power that the President might have. If the Fourth Amendment raises serious doubts about warrantless foreign surveillance, the Avoidance Canon would offer an additional argument in favor of a narrow construction of the President's power. But perhaps there is no serious Fourth Amendment objection; the underlying doctrine is quite technical and one or another exception to the warrant requirement might apply.

Even before *Hamdan*, there were powerful objections to the warrantless wiretapping by NSA. After *Hamdan*, the President's claims have been seriously weakened. The *Hamdan* Court said that even though Commander-in-Chief, the President lacks the authority to countermand the judgments of Congress with respect to the uses of military commissions. The Court did not reject the possibility that the President could create such commissions on his own, without any statute at all; but the Court made it clear that the President must follow any relevant congressional enactment. Indeed, the Court specifically referred to the presumption against implied repeals in refusing to hold that the UCMJ had been altered by the AUMF. As with military commissions, so too, plausibly, with foreign surveillance: just as the AUMF does not affect the UCMJ, so does it leave FISA unaltered.

After *Hamdan*, then, it would be easy to write an opinion suggesting, very simply, that whatever the constitutional authority of the President, he cannot override the procedures specified in FISA, and that the AUMF is too general to displace those procedures. Even if the President has inherent authority to engage in foreign surveillance, that authority is not exclusive and hence is subject to congressional restrictions as embodied in FISA—restrictions that grant the executive considerable flexibility to procure a warrant, so long as it has probable cause.[124] Such an opinion would simply track the Court's analysis in *Hamdan*.

To be sure, we could imagine other possibilities. Justice Thomas might well be tempted to adapt some version of his *Hamdan* dissent to this context. Such an analysis might begin with the constitu-

---

[124] See 50 USC 1842.

tional understandings on which Justice Thomas relies, seeing national security as the President's distinctive domain. Plausibly, the President's constitutional claims are stronger in the context of foreign surveillance than in the context of *Hamdi*. There is an argument that history vindicates the power of surveillance more convincingly than the power to create military tribunals; the President might contend that Congress has long been involved in the latter question, while also allowing unilateral surveillance power for most of our history. At least in the context of an emergency, the President might be able to distinguish *Hamdi*; outside of the context of an emergency, the need for secrecy might support his position. The President might also rely on the AUMF, informed by the emphasis in *Hamdi* on what normally accompanies the power to use force; foreign surveillance might be seen as a normal accompaniment of that power, no less than the power to detain.

The difficulty is to preserve *Hamdan* while also ruling in the President's favor in connection with wiretapping. There are two options here. Perhaps foreign surveillance fits more easily within the President's constitutional authority than does the convening of military commissions, at least in nonemergency circumstances and of the kind created in *Hamdan*. Or perhaps the AUMF is a better source for a power to wiretap than for convening such commissions; perhaps the power to engage in surveillance of those against whom force has been authorized, such as Al Qaeda members, is more akin to the detention upheld in *Hamdi* than the commissions struck down in *Hamdan*. Or perhaps *Hamdan* really had everything to do with the need to ensure the standard forms of adjudication, allowing a departure only when Congress, or some kind of emergency, clearly required it.

In its analysis of these questions in the immediate aftermath of *Hamdan*, the Department of Justice attempted to argue along these general lines, contending that its previous analysis was unaffected by the Court's ruling.[125] The Department emphasized that under section 109 of FISA, electronic surveillance is banned "except as authorized by statute"[126]—a recognition that statutory provisions might permit such surveillance. The relevant provisions of the UCMJ have no analogous exception. In this respect, FISA might

---

[125] See Letter to The Honorable Charles Schumer, July 10, 2006 (on file with the author).

[126] 50 USC 1809(a)(1).

seem to be more closely akin to the Nondetention Act, which expressly allows detention "pursuant to an Act of Congress."[127] Moreover, the UCMJ is specifically focused on armed conflict and wars, while FISA makes separate provision for wartime.[128] The Department contends that it is more natural to read the AUMF to provide authority to engage in electronic surveillance than to override the UCMJ, designed as the latter is for wartime. Finally, Congress is specifically authorized, by the Constitution, to define and punish offenses against the law of nations, at issue in *Hamdan*, and to make rules for the regulation of the armed forces; with respect to foreign surveillance, the Constitution gives no similar power to Congress. In the Department's view, the power to collect foreign surveillance is "a direct corollary" of the President's power to conduct military campaigns. In the context of surveillance, the President might even be able to show that congressional limitations could prevent him from performing his constitutional duty.

Arguments of these sorts are not entirely implausible. After all, the Court was badly divided in *Hamdan*, and it would not be a stunning surprise to see a future decision cabining the reach of the Court's analysis. But at least it can be said that after *Hamdan*, the President's claims on behalf of warrantless wiretapping are significantly weakened, and any defense of those claims faces a serious uphill battle. To be sure, FISA contains an exception, from its criminal prohibitions, for other laws that authorize surveillance, but after *Hamdan*, the AUMF is probably too abstract and general to provide that authorization. FISA does not generally exempt war from its orbit; on the contrary, it makes express provision for war, allowing a fifteen-day period of warrantless surveillance.[129] In addition, and importantly, FISA was explicitly amended after the attacks of 9/11, and in a way that pointedly refuses to give the President the authority to engage in surveillance as he sees fit.[130]

Even if the power to engage in foreign surveillance is a legitimate inference from the power to conduct military campaigns, it

---

[127] 18 USC 4001(a).

[128] 50 USC 111.

[129] 50 USC 1811.

[130] See, e.g., 50 USC 1805(c) (2)(B), 18 USC 1805(e)(1), 18 USC 1805(e)(2). For a good summary of the changes made in FISA by Pub L 107-56, see the compilation by the Congressional Research Service, available at http://www.fas.org/sgp/crs/intel/m071906 .pdf.

is hard to show that the restrictions in FISA would impermissibly interfere with that power. Perhaps the President can argue that in order to conduct such campaigns, he needs to be able to engage in foreign surveillance even when he cannot show probable cause. But to the extent that FISA requires a warrant for wiretapping communications that involve the United States, it is hard to see how this argument can be made into a persuasive constitutional challenge to FISA.

In the first judicial encounter with the NSA program, a federal district court went well beyond liberty-promoting minimalism.[131] The court held that the program violated the Fourth and First Amendments, and was unlawful, because unconstitutional, whatever Congress said. Indeed, the court said that even if the AUMF gave the executive the relevant authority, the program must be invalidated on constitutional grounds.[132] To say the least, the court's approach was puzzling. The First Amendment ruling was adventurous on the precedents, for it is hardly clear that any "chilling effect" on speech, from warrantless surveillance, amounts to a constitutional infirmity. The Supreme Court has never said whether foreign surveillance of this kind violates the Fourth Amendment.[133] In these circumstances, it would be far better to construe the relevant statutes in a way that would avoid the constitutional questions,[134] rather than to rule that Congress and the President, even if acting in concert, could not authorize a program of the sort at issue. This kind of liberty-promoting minimalism would have the additional advantage of fitting with a large number of decisions in the nation's past.

The broadest point is that in *Hamdan*, the Court declined to give deference to the President's interpretation of ambiguous provisions. It rejected presidential unilateralism. It refused to embrace clear statement principles favoring executive discretion. It declined to defer to what the President claimed to be his greater expertise. For these reasons, any presidential action, not vindicated by history or required by emergency, is likely to need clear congressional

---

[131] *ACLU v NSA*, 2006 US Dist LEXIS 57338 (ED Mich 2006).

[132] Id at 57370–72.

[133] The issue is left open in *U.S. v U.S. Dist. Ct*, 407 US 297 (1972).

[134] Of course the constitutional questions must be serious in order to merit avoiding, and an exploration of the First and Fourth Amendment problems is beyond the scope of my discussion here.

authorization, at least if it intrudes into the domain of liberty. Under the approach in *Hamdan*, the warrantless wiretapping is in serious trouble, and the same point could be made about many other presidential efforts to construe ambiguous statutes in a way that jeopardizes interests that have a plausible claim to protection by reference to constitutional principles or long-standing traditions.

IV. Conclusion

In *Hamdan*, the Court had several options. Exercising the passive virtues, it might have refused to reach the merits at all. A committed minimalist would be especially drawn to abstention— on the ground that such an approach would leave all of the central issues undecided, including the meaning and the validity of the DTA. Reaching the merits, the Court might have followed *Quirin* to rule that military commissions were authorized by Congress and that no provision of law precluded the President's action here. Speaking more ambitiously, the Court might have relied on the President's power as Commander-in-Chief, most plausibly to suggest that all of the (ambiguous) provisions, in federal statutes and the Geneva Conventions, should be construed as he (reasonably) saw fit. On this approach, a clear statement principle might have operated in the President's favor.

Instead the Court ruled that key provisions of domestic and international law banned the President from convening the proposed commission. Those provisions were certainly ambiguous. I have suggested that the Court's opinion is best understood as undergirded by a simple clear statement principle: If the President is going to try people in military commissions, and thus depart from the standard procedures governing adjudication, it must be pursuant to unambiguous authorization from Congress.[135] This suggestion, supported by Justice Breyer's concurring opinion, borrows from, and extends, a number of past decisions in which the Court demanded a clear statement from Congress to permit intrusions on constitutionally sensitive interests.

But *Hamdan* was nonetheless distinctive. The prevailing opinion reached far and wide; it is not plausibly characterized as minimalist.

---

[135] Note, however, that it is unclear whether the Court would have so insisted if it had been faced with real congressional silence, as opposed to ambiguous enactments.

No constitutionally sensitive interest was involved, or at least the Court did not say that it was; and the operative clear statement principle was (mostly) implicit, not on the surface of the opinion. At the same time, the Court necessarily offered a limited reading of the President's powers as Commander-in-Chief; and it did so without anything like a sustained discussion. Both the majority and the principal dissent invoked Justice Jackson's tripartite framework from the Steel Seizure Case. But they resolved, if only implicitly, a question that Justice Jackson did not pose: What is the appropriate presumption in the face of congressional ambiguity? The Court's answer, at least in the context of a criminal trial, was that the presumption would operate against presidential authority. The dissenting view was that in light of the distinctive constitutional position of the Commander-in-Chief, the President may construe ambiguities as he reasonably sees fit.

Hamdan was concerned, of course, with the President's power to convene military commissions, and for this reason it need not resolve other issues, such as the President's power to engage in warrantless wiretapping. But it is reasonable to read the decision to embrace a narrow reading of the AUMF and to indicate that outside of the context of military necessity, inherent presidential powers will generally be subject to legislative limitations. Even more significantly, *Hamdan* might be taken to suggest that when military necessity and genuine emergencies are not involved, the Court will not invoke a clear statement principle so as to read legislation sympathetically to presidential prerogatives. In this way, *Hamdan* is written in an altogether different spirit from *Ex Parte Quirin*, and may well mark a large-scale difference between the Court's posture in World War II and its posture in the war on terror.

To evaluate the Court's decision, it would be necessary to parse the relevant provisions in some detail; that has not been my goal here. But if the governing provisions are generally taken as ambiguous, we can say that the views of the dissenters would certainly be convincing *if* the President has a plausible claim of constitutional authority to create military commissions *or* if the distinctive competence of the executive justified deference to its interpretations. And, indeed, Justice Thomas offered reasonable arguments to this effect. It would be easiest to respond to those arguments if the result would be to raise serious constitutional questions—a genuine problem in previous cases involving national security and individual rights. If the President's interpretation of an ambiguous provision raised a serious constitutional problem, it should be rejected. And we could imagine a trial that would indeed raise due process questions—by, for example, convicting Hamdan on the basis of evidence not disclosed to him or his counsel. But no constitutional objection was offered in *Hamdan*.

I have suggested that a great deal could be said on behalf of abstention and a refusal to assess the merits at all. But it is hard to deplore a decision insisting that if there is no emergency, and if American institutions seek to try a suspected terrorist in a military commission lacking the standard guarantees of procedural fairness, it must be a result of a clear and focused decision by the national legislature.

RICHARD A. POSNER

A NOTE ON RUMSFELD v FAIR AND THE LEGAL ACADEMY

The Supreme Court's 8–0 decision (Justice Alito not participating) in *Rumsfeld v Forum for Academic & Institutional Rights, Inc. (FAIR)*[1] was neither momentous nor unexpected (a decision the other way would have been both). Its chief interest lies in the participation of the legal professoriat in the litigation. The suit was in effect an academic project, from which we can learn some things about the faculties of today's law schools, especially elite law schools like Harvard and Yale.

The background to the suit was the policy of the armed forces of not permitting homosexuals to serve. The policy is firm,[2] but leeway in its administration is created by uncertainty as to what precisely is meant by saying that someone is a "homosexual"—is it a matter of preference or orientation, on the one hand, or behavior on the other? It is that ambiguity that enabled the Defense Department in 1993, in a compromise with President Clinton, who had attempted to end the ban outright, to adopt its "don't ask, don't tell" directive. The directive provides that homosexual orientation is not a bar to service unless manifested by homosexual "conduct,"

Richard A. Posner is Judge, U.S. Court of Appeals for the Seventh Circuit; Senior Lecturer, University of Chicago Law School.

AUTHOR'S NOTE: I thank William Eskridge, Steven Shavell, and Geoffrey Stone for helpful comments on a previous draft.

[1] 126 S Ct 1297 (2006).

[2] 10 USC § 654.

broadly and somewhat oddly defined as a homosexual act, a *statement* that the person is homosexual, or a marriage or attempted marriage to someone of the same sex.[3] So military recruiters no longer ask applicants for military service what their sexual orientation is, but members of the armed forces who disclose their homosexual orientation are to be discharged.

So there is discrimination against homosexuals in the military (though not outright exclusion), and the response of most law schools, beginning in the 1970s, has been to deny the Judge Advocate General's Corps (plural—each service has its own JAG corps) the same assistance in recruiting law students that the schools' career-placement offices provide to law firms and other potential employers who promise, as the JAG corps cannot, not to discriminate against applicants for employment on the basis of their sexual orientation. Not that the law schools single out JAG or other military recruiters. The denial of assistance applies to all employers who refuse to hire homosexuals. Nor are JAG recruiters (or other discriminators) banned from the law school campus. But they are denied the extensive assistance that the law schools offer recruiters who, so to speak, take the pledge. That assistance includes, as explained in the amicus curiae brief of the National Association for Law Placement, "notifying employers of the days or weeks set aside for interviewing 'seasons,' inviting and accepting employers' requests to be included in the process, taking students' requests for interviews with particular employers, and scheduling the interviews at times that fit within students' and employers' needs. . . . Some schools provide teleconferencing or videoconferencing services to facilitate long-distance interviewing. . . . Other schools may even go so far as to provide lodging at the school's own expense for recruiters who travel from other cities."[4] There is much more: for example, "many schools have recurring 'meet the employer nights,' or gatherings on campus at which students and employers' representatives can meet in a cordial, low-pressure, event that is more like a cocktail reception than an interview or meeting."[5]

---

[3] Policy on Homosexual Conduct in the Armed Forces, Memorandum from Secretary of Defense Les Aspin to the Secretaries of the Army, Navy, and Air Force, and to the Chairman of the Joint Chiefs of Staff (July 19, 1993).

[4] *Rumsfeld v Forum for Academic & Institutional Rights, Inc.*, Brief of NALP et al, Lexsee 2004 US Briefs 1152; 2005 US S Ct Briefs LEXIS 622, at *10 (Sept 20, 2005) (footnotes omitted).

[5] Id at *10 (footnotes omitted).

All this largesse is denied to military recruiters and other employers who do not promise not to discriminate against homosexuals. The law schools are discriminating against such recruiters.

Congress's response to this discrimination is a law known as the Solomon Amendment, which in its present form[6] provides that if any part of an institution of higher education (thus including a university's law school) prevents military recruiters "from gaining access to campuses, or access to students . . . on campuses, for purposes of military recruiting in a manner that is at least equal in quality and scope to the access to campuses and to students that is provided to any other employer," the entire institution is denied federal funding.[7]

The law schools reluctantly complied, lest their universities lose federal funding. But a liberal lawyer named Joshua Rosenkranz, formerly head of the Brennan Center for Justice at New York University, organized the Forum for Academic and Institutional Rights, a coalition of law schools and law professors, to challenge the constitutionality of the Solomon Amendment. FAIR sought an injunction against its enforcement, lost in the district court, won in the court of appeals,[8] and lost again in the Supreme Court. FAIR's argument was that the Solomon Amendment imposes an unconstitutional condition on the receipt of federal funds: to obtain such funding a law school must in effect mute its opposition to discrimination against homosexuals by providing the same hospitality to military recruiters that it extends to employers who pledge not to discriminate.

A number of amicus curiae briefs were submitted. One of these, filed on behalf of a large number of Harvard Law School professors, opposed the government on a different ground from FAIR's: namely, that there is no violation of the Solomon Amendment as long as the law school, rather than singling out military recruiters, denies placement assistance to all employers who refuse to promise not to discriminate against homosexuals. The brief actually argues *against* holding the Solomon Amendment unconstitutional, because the professors' "concern, first and foremost, is in furthering the eradication of invidious discrimination. Accordingly, we are deeply

---

[6] 10 USC § 983 (Supp 2005).

[7] Id. There are a few exceptions, but they are not germane to my analysis.

[8] *Forum for Academic & Institutional Rights, Inc. v Rumsfeld*, 340 F3d 219 (3d Cir 2004).

concerned about an opinion that would accept the assertion that the Solomon Amendment requires nothing more than equal access—but then conclude that the statute is nonetheless unconstitutional because it infringes upon associational rights, compels unwilling speech, or restricts expressive conduct." For "such an approach could encourage attempts by discriminatory employers, educational institutions or other groups to evade compliance with various pieces of federal civil rights legislation . . . by asserting that granting equal treatment without regard to race or sex would send a 'message' with which they disagree."[9]

The Supreme Court rejected the suggested interpretation, which bordered on the absurd. As the Court pointed out (and remember that eight Justices, including the four liberal Justices, agreed), the interpretation would defeat the purpose of the Solomon Amendment because it would allow the law schools to continue their policy of excluding military recruiters without any change at all. Congress would have achieved nothing by its law. Nullification is not an accepted method of statutory interpretation.

Turning to the constitutional issue—the issue pressed by FAIR and decided in its favor by the court of appeals—the Supreme Court said that "the Solomon Amendment neither limits what law schools may say nor requires them to say anything. Law schools remain free under the statute to express whatever views they may have on the military's congressionally mandated employment, all the while retaining eligibility for federal funds."[10] To the argument that the assistance that the law school placement services offer to compliant employers includes (compelled) speech in the form of "send[ing] e-mails or post[ing] notices on bulletin boards on an employer's behalf," the Court responded that Congress "can prohibit employers from discriminating in hiring on the basis of race. The fact that this will require an employer to take down a sign reading 'White Applicants Only' hardly means that the law should be analyzed as one regulating the employer's speech rather than conduct."[11]

Just as no one would suppose that that employer had had a change of heart, so no one reading the notices sent to students or employers

---

[9] *Rumsfeld v Forum for Academic & Institutional Rights, Inc.*, Brief of Professors William Alford et al, Lexsee 2004 US Briefs 1152; 2005 US S Ct Briefs LEXIS 630, at *21–22 (Sept 21, 2005) (footnote omitted).

[10] 126 S Ct at 1307.

[11] Id at 1308.

by law school placement offices would think that the law school
was expressing its agreement with the policies of prospective employers. Law firms that represent cigarette companies or pornog-
raphers, the law departments of giant corporations that pollute the
atmosphere or sell munitions to Third World dictators, the offices
of the general counsel of the CIA and the Defense Department,
right-wing and left-wing public interest firms—all are welcome to
"meet the employer" nights. No one, least of all the law schools
themselves, thinks that by extending this welcome the law schools
or their faculties endorse the policies of their employer guests. All
that the law school is "expressing" by its hospitality gestures to
prospective employers of its students is its desire to help the students, for the law school's sake as well as the students' own, get
good jobs. (Successful graduates tend to be loyal alumni.) A law
school can if it wants make emphatically clear that it is hosting JAG
recruiters only because it must do so or cost its university huge
amounts of federal money. "We have held that high school students
can appreciate the difference between speech a school sponsors and
speech the school permits because legally required to do so, pursuant to an equal access policy. Surely students have not lost that
ability by the time they get to law school."[12]

There is more to the opinion (Chief Justice Roberts's graceful
maiden effort), but I have quoted enough to convey its thrust and
tone, except that it is interesting that all the other seven Justices
who participated in the decision joined in the Chief Justice's polite
but unmistakable rebuke of the legal professoriat for overreaching:
"In this case, FAIR has attempted to stretch a number of First
Amendment doctrines well beyond the sort of activities these doctrines protect."[13] FAIR "plainly overstates the expressive nature of
[the law schools'] activity and the impact of the Solomon Amendment on it, while exaggerating the reach of our First Amendment
precedents."[14]

The Harvard professors (who did their stretching on the principles of statutory interpretation) were right that invalidating the
Solomon Amendment would foster discrimination by educational
institutions by curtailing the government's authority to use its

---

[12] Id at 1310.
[13] Id at 1313.
[14] Id.

spending power to prevent discrimination. It would even empower conservative law schools—and there are some (Ave Maria, for example)—to refuse to assist employers who will not promise *not* to hire homosexuals. But the Harvard professors' solution—an untenable interpretation of the amendment—raises a question of academic integrity. FAIR's constitutional arguments were weak, but the Harvard professors' statutory argument bordered on the frivolous. A lawyer whom you hire to represent you can in perfect good faith make any argument on your behalf that is not downright frivolous. But the professors were not parties to *Rumsfeld v FAIR* and so a reader of their amicus curiae brief might expect the views expressed in it to represent their best professional judgment on the meaning of the Solomon Amendment. The brief identifies them as full-time faculty members of the Harvard Law School rather than as concerned citizens, and one expects law professors when speaking *ex cathedra* as it were to be expressing their true belief rather than making any old argument that they think might have a 5 percent chance of persuading a court. They could have said "we happen to be law professors but we're also citizens and it is in the latter capacity that we have decided to participate as amici curiae." But they did not. I cannot imagine that all the professors who subscribed to the Harvard brief thought that interpreting the Solomon Amendment as a nullity was the best interpretation. I doubt also that they are interpretive nihilists, who believe that the meaning of a text is entirely in the eye of the beholder.

I do not make the same criticism of the law schools themselves, or of their association (the Association of American Law Schools, another amicus curiae), or of FAIR itself insofar as it is composed of law schools (but it also has law professors as members). Of course a law school (and its university) would prefer to have federal money given to it without strings attached, especially strings that will get it in trouble with students and faculty members who are strongly hostile to the military's policy on homosexuals. The law school merely wants to have its cake and eat it—and who doesn't? It is not an edifying desire—it is embarrassing for a law school to have to tell its irate homosexual students that it loves them but loves federal money even more—but the reality is that universities nowadays are giant corporations and behave accordingly, whatever their pretensions. It is hyperbole for the AALS to argue that the price of a law school's retaining its federal funding is to "abandon its commitment to fight discrimination"[15] or that the issue in the case is the right of a university to decide what may be taught,[16] but one understands that this is merely lawyer rhetoric in the service of a conventional client interest.

But one cannot say the same for the Harvard professors' amicus brief, or for the brief filed on behalf of a large majority of the faculty of the Yale Law School. That brief states flatly that the Defense Department's enforcement of the Solomon Amendment "trample[s] upon the [Yale Law School] Faculty Members' academic freedom" by forcing them "to assist the military in telling some Yale Law students that they are not fit to serve in our country's armed forces because of their sexual orientation."[17] To bolster this extravagant claim, the brief cites a case in which the Supreme Court held that the First Amendment entitled the NAACP to organize a boycott of merchants who discriminated against blacks:[18] "The Court's decision in *Claiborne* makes it clear that the First Amendment fully protects the Faculty Members' refusal to cooperate with or assist, to disassociate from, and thereby to protest against, the military's discrimination against their gay, lesbian, and bisexual students."[19] Ignored is an elementary distinction: the NAACP was not trying to bite the hand that fed it. The logic of the Yale professors' interpretation of *Claiborne* is that if the Yale Law School refused to allow the federal government to audit its use of federal funds on the ground that money saved by the auditors might be diverted to the war in Iraq, the First Amendment would entitle Yale to bar the auditors but keep the money.

No student could think that by virtue of Yale's bowing to the Solomon Amendment, the law school faculty was complicit with the military policy on homosexuals. If the Yale hospital treats a homophobe who has cancer, is the Yale medical faculty complicit in homophobia? That is the logic of the Yale professors' brief. One

---

[15] *Rumsfeld v Forum for Academic & Institutional Rights, Inc.*, Brief for the Association of American Law Schools, Lexsee 2004 US Briefs 1152; 2005 US S Ct Briefs LEXIS 637, at *16 (Sept 21, 2005).

[16] Id at *29–30.

[17] *Rumsfeld v Forum for Academic & Institutional Rights, Inc.*, Brief Amici Curiae of Robert A. Burt et al, Lexsee 2004 US Briefs 1152; 2005 US S Ct Briefs LEXIS 637, at *2–3 (Sept 21, 2005).

[18] Id at 13–14, discussing *National Association for the Advancement of Colored People v Claiborne*, 458 US 898, 911 (1982).

[19] Brief Amici Curiae of Robert A. Burt et al (note 17 above), at 14.

is not surprised that the brief fails to note a countervailing First Amendment interest. In discriminating against military recruiters (or recruiters for other institutions that discriminate against homosexuals), the law schools limit their students' exposure to views concerning military policy that are contrary to the orthodoxy that dominates the law school community. If the Solomon Amendment is censorship, so is the law schools' discrimination against military recruiters.

It is no answer to the audit hypothetical that the government has a legitimate interest in auditing government grants but not in discriminating against homosexuals. The military's discrimination against homosexuals is legal, and the Yale professors' brief makes no effort to evaluate the reasons for the discrimination, which may not be entirely the product of ignorance and malice, as the professors believe.

What is especially curious about the law professor amicus curiae briefs is how conventional they are. In all but one instance[20] the professors did not write the briefs themselves but instead hired a practicing lawyer to do so. No doubt they approved what he wrote, and I am told that at least in the case of the Yale professors' brief the intellectual input by the professors was substantial. I would be more comfortable had it been insubstantial. For there is nothing in any of these briefs that distinguishes them from the ordinary product of practicing lawyers.

The way in which a law professor could be a true friend of the court would be by offering an academic perspective on a case. Long gone are the days when elite law schools were dominated by law professors who identified with the practicing legal profession rather than with a distinctive legal academic culture. That culture might have a contribution to make to the judicial consideration of a case like *Rumsfeld v FAIR*. Yet absent from the briefs is any discussion of why our armed forces want to continue a ban on homosexuals that has been abandoned by most of the countries that we consider

---

[20] *Rumsfeld v Forum for Academic & Institutional Rights, Inc.*, Brief for Amicus Curiae of the American Association of University Professors, Lexsee 2004 US Briefs 1152; 2005 US S Ct Briefs LEXIS 641, at *2–3 (Sept 21, 2005). The brief makes the remarkable assertion that "a faculty is entitled to make the academic judgment that assisting recruitment by an employer that refuses to hire openly gay students is akin to failing a student in class merely for being gay." Id at 12. That is like saying that teaching evolution to a class that contains believers in biblical inerrancy is akin to flunking a student because he's a fundamentalist Christian.

to be our peers and what effect invalidating the Solomon Amendment would have. Maybe the military has reason to believe that
lifting the ban would undermine military morale, complicate recruitment, and further strain our already overstretched military. If
so, this belief would have to be weighed against the harm to homosexuals (indeed, the harm to the military itself) from the ban.
For what it is worth, I have long considered that harm significant.[21]
But the military perforce recruits heavily from a segment of the
American male population that might be deeply upset if it thought
that homosexuals were entitled to serve with them; and that anxiety—that prejudice—is something that a conscientious administration would have to weigh, especially when the nation is at war. (And
I am referring not to the "war on terrorism," a locution imprecise
and misleading, but rather to our military combat in Iraq and Afghanistan.)

As for the consequences of invalidating the Solomon Amendment—another topic on which law professors might be expected
to have an opinion—one would be that fewer students from elite
law schools would be hired by the military because JAG recruiters
wouldn't have the same access to those students as other recruiters
would. Some of the discouraged students would be homosexual.
Homosexuals as I have said are not excluded by the armed forces;
they are forced to stay in the closet. (The situation was practically
though not legally identical before "don't ask, don't tell.") Many
homosexuals today are unwilling to remain closeted, but some are
willing, even some who attend schools like Harvard and Yale. If
they are recruited into a JAG corps, this may hasten the end of the
formal ban on homosexuals. But what is more important, as Peter
Berkowitz has pointed out, is that most students at such law schools,
whatever their sexual orientation, are liberal.[22] The more of them
who are recruited for JAG service, the sooner the ban will collapse.

The practical causes and real-world consequences of the ban on
homosexuals in the military, of the "don't ask, don't tell" policy,
and of the Solomon Amendment are the kind of sociopolitical facts
that academics are in a better position to investigate than practicing

---

[21] "It is terrible to tell people they are unfit to serve their country, unless they really
are unfit, which is not the case here." Richard A. Posner, *Sex and Reason* 321 (1992).

[22] Peter Berkowitz, *U.S. Military: 8, Elite Law Schools: 0, How Did So Many Professors
Misunderstand the Law?* Weekly Standard (March 20, 2006), http://www.weeklystandard
.com/Content/Public/Articles/000/000/011/959tzkai.asp?pg=2.

lawyers are. Inquiring into those facts and presenting the results to
the courts would be a more useful employment of law professors'
time than hiring practitioners to flog precedents. There is a sheep-
like character to all these professors signing on to a practitioner's
brief (the sheep being led by the goat). One might have thought
that some of these professors would speak in their own voice—
express an individual view. Can't a law professor at Harvard or Yale
write a brief? Well, maybe not any more; but he or she could do
the research that only academics can do well, and let the practitioner
convey the results in the brief. Do these professors perhaps not
care about the issue strongly enough to actually work on it? Do
they want more than to show that their heart is in the right place,
or at least in the same place as their students' hearts?

But Rosenkranz is on to something, though not to what he thinks
he's on to, when he says that "law schools are more than just vo-
cational schools that teach students to draft briefs and close deals.
Law schools are, and define themselves as, normative institutions.
They aspire to shape future lawyers who 'can profoundly change
our society, its mores and values,' and who will urge their visions
of justice on society at large. Law schools admonish their students
that 'issues of justice are at the core of [their] missions,' and urge
students 'to accept the challenge of more clearly defining a just
system.'"[23] Soaring rhetoric, but inaccurate. American law schools
are professional schools, not secular *madrasahs*, and they spend a
lot more time teaching their students how to defend society's "mores and values" than how to challenge them. The vast majority of
the students at the elite law schools become corporate lawyers and
defend the mores and values of giant corporations. Revolutionaries
they are not. Rosenkranz's brief invokes a selected subset of American mores and values in defense of his constitutional claim.

What is particularly revealing about the passage I've just quoted
is the uncritical assumption that legal education has a liberal agenda,
specifically a liberal agenda in which homosexual rights occupy a
high place. The Solomon Amendment must go *because* law schools
are normative institutions. Rosenkranz invokes "visions of justice"
(plural) but does not acknowledge the possibility that there is a
military vision of justice that challenges justice as homosexual rights.

---

[23] *Rumsfeld v Forum for Academic & Institutional Rights, Inc.*, Brief for the Petitioner,
Lexsee 2004 US Briefs 1152; 2005 US S Ct Briefs LEXIS 634, at *2 (Sept 21, 2005)
(record references omitted).

So comfortable are Rosenkranz and the legal professoriat with that agenda that it does not occur to him or to it to inquire into the practical dimensions of JAG recruiting at elite law schools, including the possibility that by discouraging military recruiters the schools are helping to perpetuate a conservative military culture; JAG recruiters are surely welcome at Ave Maria.

The left-liberal domination of elite law school faculties[24] has had the debilitating effect on the intellect that John Stuart Mill in *On Liberty* assigned to the groupthink of his day.[25] When you inhabit a cozy burrow of like thinkers, your ideas are not challenged and they grow flabby. They become unexamined habits of mind—articles of faith that when finally challenged provoke anger rather than reasoned response because the ability to reason about them has atrophied. Missing from the professors' briefs is an awareness that there are two sides to the issue of the right of homosexuals to full equality in the armed forces and that law professors could contribute more to a sound resolution by dispassionate study than by signing their names to conventional briefs written by practicing lawyers.[26] Even a sense of irony withers in an atmosphere of intellectual conformity. Law professors should be "reluctant to promiscuously hurl accusations of discrimination at the military, especially since many of the law professors had only a few years ago argued for, and won from the Supreme Court in *Grutter v Bollinger* (2003), a special exemption to classify at their law schools on the basis of race because of their presumed special expertise concerning the need in legal education for diverse student bodies."[27] The military has its needs as well, and perhaps even some expertise.

Judges sense a growing chasm between the professoriat and the judiciary. In *Rumsfeld v FAIR* we glimpse its breadth.

---

[24] Indeed of higher education in general. See, for example, Christopher F. Cardiff and Daniel B. Klein, *Faculty Partisan Affiliations in All Disciplines: A Voter-Registration Study*, 17 Critical Review 237 (2005).

[25] John Stuart Mill, *On Liberty* 36 (David Spitz ed, 1975 [1859]).

[26] A total of 82 Harvard and Yale law professors signed amicus curiae briefs in the *FAIR* case. Berkowitz, note 22 above.

[27] Id.

CURTIS A. BRADLEY

THE FEDERAL JUDICIAL POWER AND
THE INTERNATIONAL LEGAL ORDER

Richard Falk famously argued that domestic courts should operate
as "agents of the international order."[1] Recent academic debates
over the role of international law in the U.S. legal system, and over
the relevance of foreign and international materials in U.S. constitutional interpretation, are at least in part debates about this
proposition. Modern variants of Falk's claim can be found in the
works of scholars such as Harold Koh, Jennifer Martinez, and Anne-
Marie Slaughter.[2] These and other "internationalist" scholars consider the U.S. judiciary as part of a "global community of courts,"
emphasize the values of international cross-fertilization and har-
monization, and view international law as directly permeating, and
often having primacy within, the U.S. legal system. "Constitutionalist" or "revisionist" scholars, by contrast, distinguish between the
international and domestic legal systems, emphasize constitutional
structure as a limitation on the domestic effect of international law,
and generally advocate political branch rather than judicial control
over the domestic implementation of international legal obliga-

Curtis A. Bradley is the Richard and Marcy Horvitz Professor of Law at Duke Law School.

AUTHOR'S NOTE: Thanks to Kathy Bradley, Jack Goldsmith, Joost Pauwelyn, Eric Posner,
Paul Stephan, Carlos Vazquez, Mark Weisburd, and Ernest Young for helpful comments.

[1] Richard A. Falk, *The Role of Domestic Courts in the International Legal Order* 72 (1964).

[2] See, e.g., Harold Hongju Koh, *Transnational Legal Process*, 75 Neb L Rev 181 (1996);
Jennifer Martinez, *Towards an International Judicial System*, 56 Stan L Rev 429 (2003);
Anne-Marie Slaughter, *Judicial Globalization*, 40 Va J Intl L 1103 (2000).

tions.[3] The leading judicial proponent of the internationalist perspective is currently Justice Breyer; the leading judicial proponent of the constitutionalist perspective is currently Justice Scalia.

Debates between internationalists and constitutionalists encompass a wide variety of legal issues. These issues include the status in the U.S. legal system of customary international law, the circumstances under which treaties are domestically enforceable, the extent to which the federal government can delegate regulatory functions to international actors, and the relevance of federalism to U.S. foreign relations. The practical significance of these debates continues to grow, as the United States, despite its isolationist reputation, becomes increasingly enmeshed in international regimes. As the need and opportunities for international cooperation have increased, multilateral regulatory treaties have proliferated, as have international institutions established to administer them. These institutions include a growing number of dispute resolution bodies that consider issues that overlap and intersect with the issues considered by U.S. courts.

Sanchez-Llamas v Oregon[4] was an important test case for the internationalist perspective. The petitioners there, with the support of internationalist scholars, were seeking to have the Supreme Court create domestic remedies to help effectuate compliance with a multilateral treaty, and to set aside traditional state law procedures in order to implement an interpretation of the treaty that had been adopted by an international tribunal. In rejecting this effort in *Sanchez-Llamas*, the Court made clear that the Article III federal judicial power plays an important mediating role between the United States and the international legal system. Under the Court's approach, international law neither gives U.S. courts special powers nor limits their authority to decide cases, and U.S. courts are to consider the application of international law against the backdrop of traditional domestic remedial and procedural restrictions, even if the result is disuniformity in treaty interpretation.

While one should be cautious about reading too much into a single decision, the Court's approach to the federal judicial power in *Sanchez-Llamas* has potential relevance to a number of foreign

---

[3] Although hardly uniform in their approach to particular issues, scholars commonly associated with the constitutionalist approach include myself, Jack Goldsmith, Julian Ku, Eric Posner, Paul Stephan, Mark Weisburd, John Yoo, and Ernest Young.

[4] 126 S Ct 2669 (2006).

relations law issues. In this regard, *Sanchez-Llamas* may have broader significance than the more widely discussed decision issued by the Court a day later, *Hamdan v Rumsfeld*,[5] in which the Court held that the military commission system established by President Bush to try terrorist detainees was invalid. *Hamdan* may seem like a monumental decision, in that it repudiated one of the components of the Bush administration's legal strategy in the war on terrorism and seemed to give little deference to the administration's views about the scope of international law. The Court's decision there, however, ultimately rests on a particular construction of statutory provisions in the Uniform Code of Military Justice (provisions that Congress has since amended), and the Court's lack of deference may stem from facts specific to the war on terrorism, including the fact that the administration had never actually tried anyone in the military commission system that the Court was invalidating. Moreover, whereas Chief Justice Roberts wrote the majority opinion in *Sanchez-Llamas*, he did not even participate in *Hamdan*, so, to the extent that those decisions overlap, *Sanchez-Llamas* would seem to be a better indicator of the likely approach of the Roberts Court.

Part I of this essay briefly describes the *Sanchez-Llamas* decision and explains how the federal judicial power played a central role in the Court's analysis. As explained in this part, the majority viewed the federal judicial power as imposing both a *restraint* on the federal courts' ability to advance the international order, and a *protection* against the delegation of the federal courts' adjudicative functions to that order. Part II considers potential implications of these two functions of restraint and protection for various foreign relations law issues. Part III outlines several benefits of these two functions of the judicial power in light of the current conditions of the international adjudicative system.

I. Sanchez-Llamas and the Federal Judicial Power

This part briefly summarizes the *Sanchez-Llamas* decision and explains the central relevance of the federal judicial power to the decision. Next, it compares the decision with the Court's widely discussed decision a day later in *Hamdan v Rumsfeld*. Finally, it considers whether the treaty provision at issue in *Sanchez-Llamas*

---

[5] 126 S Ct 2749 (2006).

confers judicially enforceable individual rights, an issue expressly left open by the majority.

A. BACKGROUND[6]

The Vienna Convention on Consular Relations is a multilateral treaty that addresses a variety of issues concerning the exercise of consular functions and the privileges and immunities of consular officials.[7] *Sanchez-Llamas* concerned Article 36 of this Convention, which provides that when foreign nationals from other party countries are arrested, they are to be informed without delay that they have the right to have their consulate notified of the arrest and to communicate with the consulate.[8] Article 36 also states that these rights "shall be exercised in conformity with the laws and regulations of the receiving State, subject to the proviso, however, that the said laws and regulations must enable full effect to be given to the purposes for which the rights accorded under this Article are intended."[9] The United States ratified the Vienna Convention in 1969. At the same time, it also ratified an "optional protocol" to the treaty providing that disputes between nations arising under the treaty could be heard in the International Court of Justice (ICJ) that sits in The Hague, in the Netherlands.[10]

State police in the United States have often failed to inform foreign nationals of their rights under Article 36 when arresting them. Before the mid-1990s, however, these violations were rarely the subject of U.S. court litigation. This changed with the *Breard* case. There, a Paraguayan citizen on death row in Virginia filed a federal habeas corpus action alleging that he should receive either a new trial or sentencing proceeding because he had never been advised of his right to have his consulate notified of his arrest. As the lower courts began to deny him relief, and as his execution date approached, the nation of Paraguay filed an action against the United States in the ICJ, seeking to have the Court order a

---

[6] My description here draws on Curtis A. Bradley, *International Decisions: Sanchez-Llamas v Oregon*, 100 Am J Intl L 882 (2006).

[7] See Vienna Convention on Consular Relations, Apr 24, 1963, 21 UST 77, 596 UNTS 261.

[8] Id, Art 36(1)(b).

[9] Id, Art 36(2).

[10] See Optional Protocol Concerning the Compulsory Settlement of Disputes, Apr 24, 1963, 21 UST 77, 169, 596 UNTS 487, 488.

new trial for Breard. About five days before the scheduled execution, the ICJ issued a provisional order stating that the United States should "take all measures at its disposal" to ensure that Breard was not executed while the Court considered the case.[11]

At this point, the case had also reached the U.S. Supreme Court, which declined to grant a stay of execution, concluding that Breard's Vienna Convention claim had been procedurally defaulted because he had failed to raise it in a timely manner in the state courts.[12] While recognizing that it should give "respectful consideration to the interpretation of an international treaty rendered by an international court with jurisdiction to interpret such," the Court reasoned that absent "a clear and express statement to the contrary, the procedural rules of the forum State govern the implementation of the treaty in that State."[13] One such procedural rule in the United States, explained the Court, is that "assertions of error in criminal proceedings must first be raised in state court in order to form the basis for relief in habeas."[14] Although the U.S. government took the position that the ICJ's provisional order was not binding, the Secretary of State at that time, Madeline Albright, wrote a letter to Virginia's governor, asking him voluntarily to stay the execution. The governor declined, however, and Breard was executed. Paraguay subsequently withdrew its case from the ICJ.[15]

A similar case, *LaGrand*,[16] was initiated in the ICJ by Germany in 1999. *LaGrand* concerned two brothers of German citizenship on death row in Arizona, one of whom was executed shortly before Germany brought its case. The Court issued a provisional order directing the United States to take all measures at its disposal to stay the execution of the other brother. Once again, however, the

---

[11] See *Vienna Convention on Consular Relations (Paraguay v United States)*, Provisional Measures, 1998 ICJ Rep 248, para 41 (Apr 9).

[12] See *Breard v Greene*, 523 US 371, 375 (1998). A group of international law professors filed a statement with the Court unsuccessfully urging a stay of execution. See Statement Amicus Curiae of International Law Professors, *Republic of Paraguay v Gilmore*, No 97-1390 (US Supreme Court).

[13] 523 US at 375.

[14] Id.

[15] For additional discussion of the *Breard* litigation, see Curtis A. Bradley, *Breard, Our Dualist Constitution, and the Internationalist Conception*, 51 Stan L Rev 529 (1999); Agora: *Breard*, 92 Am J Intl L 666 (1998).

[16] *LaGrand (Federal Republic of Germany v United States)*, 2001 ICJ Rep 466, paras 67, 73, 77, 91 (June 27).

execution was carried out on schedule. Unlike Paraguay in the *Breard* case, however, Germany did not abandon its case at this point, but rather pressed on for a judgment. Subsequently, in June 2001, the ICJ issued a final decision, concluding that Article 36 of the Vienna Convention confers not only state-to-state rights but also individual rights, that the United States had violated these individual rights with respect to the German brothers, and that U.S. court application of procedural default rules had prevented "full effect" from being given to the rights under Article 36.[17] The ICJ also concluded that, in the future, when German nationals are sentenced to severe penalties in the United States without their Article 36 rights being respected, the United States would be obligated to provide for "review and reconsideration" of their convictions and sentences in light of the violation.[18] The ICJ noted, however, that this "obligation can be carried out in various ways" and that the "choice of means must be left to the United States."[19]

LaGrand set the stage for the *Avena* case.[20] In early 2003, Mexico filed an action against the United States in the ICJ on behalf of fifty-four Mexican nationals on death row throughout the United States, alleging that they had not been notified of their rights under Article 36 of the Vienna Convention. This was a particularly significant case, since it resembled a class action rather than just a challenge to a particular execution. In February 2003, the Court issued a provisional order directing the United States not to execute three of the individuals who appeared to be at greatest risk of execution in the coming months.[21] This time, none of the individuals was executed while the Court considered the case.

In March 2004, the ICJ issued its judgment on the merits. The Court held that the United States had violated the Vienna Convention rights of fifty-one Mexican nationals, and that it was required to provide these Mexican nationals with review and reconsideration of their convictions and sentences as a result of having failed to notify them of their consular rights. In its opinion,

---

[17] Id, paras 67, 73, 77, 91.

[18] Id, para 125.

[19] Id.

[20] *Case Concerning Avena and Other Mexican Nationals (Mexico v United States)*, 2004 ICJ No 128 (Judgment Mar 31).

[21] See *Case Concerning Avena and Other Mexican Nationals (Mexico v United States)*, Provisional Measures, 2003 ICJ 128 (Feb 5).

the Court reasoned that Article 36 confers individual rights, and that the proper remedy for a violation of these rights is "review and reconsideration of these nationals' cases by the United States courts . . . with a view to ascertaining whether in each case the violation of Article 36 . . . caused actual prejudice to the defendant in the process of administration of criminal justice."[22] The ICJ further suggested that procedural default rules should not be applied to bar this review and reconsideration because the application of such rules would prevent full effect from being given to the rights.[23]

After the *Avena* decision, the Executive Branch took the position that the ICJ had erred in its construction of the Convention. In a case involving one of the Mexican nationals covered by *Avena*—in which the Supreme Court granted a writ of certiorari but subsequently dismissed the writ as improvidently granted[24]—the Executive Branch filed a brief arguing, among other things, that Article 36 did not confer any private, judicially enforceable rights, that the article did not preclude application of procedural default rules, and that the *Avena* decision was not directly enforceable in U.S. courts.[25] The brief informed the Supreme Court, however, that President Bush had written a memorandum to the U.S. Attorney General stating that the United States, "in accordance with general principles of comity," would discharge its obligations under *Avena* by having its state courts provide review and reconsideration in the fifty-one cases covered by *Avena*, and that this memorandum would, it was argued, override state procedural default rules.[26] About a week later, the U.S. Secretary of State sent a letter to the UN Secretary-General stating that the United States was withdrawing from the optional protocol that gives the ICJ jurisdiction over Vienna Convention disputes.[27]

---

[22] See 2004 ICJ No 128, at para 121.

[23] Id, para 113.

[24] See *Medellin v Dretke*, 544 US 660 (2005).

[25] See Brief for the United States as Amicus Curiae Supporting Respondent, at 9, *Medellin v Dretke*, No 04-5928 (US Supreme Court, Feb 2005).

[26] See id at 38–48; Charles Lane, *U.S. Quits Pact Used in Capital Cases*, Wash Post, Mar 10, 2005, at A01.

[27] See Memorandum for the Attorney General, "Compliance with the Decision of the International Court of Justice in *Avena*" (Feb 28, 2005), at http://brownwelsh.com/Archive/2005-03-10_Avena_compliance.pdf.

B. SANCHEZ-LLAMAS AND THE FEDERAL JUDICIAL POWER

Sanchez-Llamas involved two consolidated state cases, one from Oregon and one from Virginia.[28] In each case, state police had failed to advise a foreign citizen of his rights under Article 36 of the Vienna Convention. In the Oregon case, a Mexican citizen was seeking suppression of incriminating statements as a remedy for the treaty violation, and in the Virginia case a Honduran citizen was seeking to overcome state rules of procedural default that would otherwise prevent him from raising the treaty violation for the first time in state postconviction proceedings. The Supreme Court granted certiorari on three questions: "(1) whether Article 36 of the Vienna Convention grants rights that may be invoked by individuals in a judicial proceeding; (2) whether suppression of evidence is a proper remedy for a violation of Article 36; and (3) whether an Article 36 claim may be deemed forfeited under state procedural rules because a defendant failed to raise the claim at trial."[29]

In an opinion authored by Chief Justice Roberts, a majority of the Court rejected the claims of both petitioners. The Court did not take a position on whether Article 36 confers judicially enforceable individual rights. The Court reasoned that, even if Article 36 does confer such rights, suppression of evidence is not an appropriate remedy for violations of that article, and that the article does not override state rules of procedural default.

The Court emphasized the federal judicial power in both its analysis of the suppression issue and its analysis of the procedural default issue. In concluding that there was no suppression of evidence remedy for violations of Article 36, the Court rejected the argument that it could use its remedial authority to promote state court compliance with Article 36. The Court explained that "our authority to create a judicial remedy applicable in state court must lie, if anywhere, in the treaty itself."[30] Imposing a remedy not provided for by the Convention, the Court noted, would be "enlarging the obligations of the United States under the Vienna Convention," which would be "entirely inconsistent with the ju-

---

[28] See 126 S Ct 2669 (2006).

[29] Id at 2677.

[30] Id at 2679.

dicial function."[31] The Court concluded that, "where a treaty does not provide a particular remedy, either expressly or implicitly, it is not for the federal courts to impose one on the States through lawmaking of their own."[32] In other words, regardless of whether fashioning a suppression remedy would promote U.S. compliance with Article 36, limitations on the judicial power meant that this was not an appropriate task for the federal courts.

In concluding that Article 36 did not override state rules of procedural default, despite the ICJ's view that it did, the Court similarly focused on the judicial power—this time as something to be protected rather than kept in check. The Court rejected the argument, advanced by a group of international law professors in an amicus curiae brief,[33] that the Court was obligated to accept as "authoritative" the ICJ's interpretation of the Vienna Convention. The Court explained that, although the ICJ's interpretation deserves "respectful consideration," when treaties are being applied as federal law, the ultimate authority to interpret them must rest with the domestic U.S. court system, not an international tribunal. Citing *Marbury v Madison*, the Court stated that "[i]f treaties are to be given effect as federal law under our legal system, determining their meaning as a matter of federal law 'is emphatically the province and duty of the judicial department,' headed by 'one Supreme Court' established by the Constitution."[34] Invoking *stare decisis*, the Court also reasoned that its "respectful consideration" of the ICJ's views "does not compel us to reconsider our understanding of the Convention in *Breard*."[35]

In sum, the Court's conception of the federal judicial power is that it operates both as a limitation on the federal courts' ability to participate in the international order, and also as a protection of the federal courts from that order. In particular, the Court appeared to deny itself a foreign affairs lawmaking power, even for the purpose of promoting treaty compliance, while at the same time suggesting that there are limitations on the extent to which

---

[31] Id.

[32] Id at 2680.

[33] See Brief of International Court of Justice Experts as Amici Curiae in Support of Petitioners, at 2–3, 20, 25 and n 41, *Sanchez-Llamas v Oregon*, Nos 04-10566, 05-51 (US Supreme Court).

[34] 126 S Ct at 2684.

[35] Id at 2683.

the federal judicial power may be diluted through U.S. participation in international adjudication.

Justice Breyer issued a dissent, joined by Justices Stevens and Souter, and joined in part by Justice Ginsburg.[36] These four Justices reasoned that Article 36 provides an individual right that can be invoked by criminal defendants in domestic proceedings. They also argued that sometimes suppression is an appropriate remedy for violations of Article 36, and that sometimes state procedural default rules must be set aside. Three of these Justices (but not Justice Ginsburg) thought it appropriate to remand for a determination of whether those remedies should be applied to these particular cases. Although these Justices stated that they would assume that the ICJ's interpretation was not binding on the Court, they suggested that it should be given more weight than it was given by the majority, in the interest of promoting uniformity of treaty interpretation.[37]

C. COMPARISON WITH HAMDAN

In public discussions, the *Sanchez-Llamas* decision was overshadowed by the Court's decision a day later in *Hamdan v Rumsfeld*.[38] In *Hamdan*, the Court invalidated the military commission system that President Bush had established after the September 11 attacks to try terrorist "enemy combatants." The Court based its decision, in part, on purported inconsistencies between the military commission system and a treaty provision—Common Article 3 of the 1949 Geneva Conventions.[39]

The Court's reliance on a treaty provision to invalidate Executive action in *Hamdan* might appear to be in tension with the limited judicial role for enforcing treaties suggested in *Sanchez-Llamas*. However, the Court in *Hamdan*, and Justice Kennedy in his concurrence, emphasized that the treaty provision there was

---

[36] See id at 2690–2709 (Breyer, J, dissenting).

[37] See id at 2700 (Breyer, J, dissenting). In what can only be described as a creative reading of the *Avena* decision, these Justices also suggested that a hearing in which procedural default rules were applied might itself satisfy the ICJ's requirement of "review and reconsideration," and that it would be consistent with *Avena* for states to apply procedural default rules as long as the defendant could pursue an ineffective assistance of counsel claim based on the failure of his lawyer to raise the Article 36 claim in time. See id at 2698, 2702–03 (Breyer, J, dissenting).

[38] See 126 S Ct 2749 (2006).

[39] See id at 2793–97.

being applied because Congress had implicitly directed its domestic application. The Court explained, for example, that "regardless of the nature of the rights conferred [by Common Article
3] . . . they are, as the Government does not dispute, part of the
law of war," and "compliance with the law of war is the condition
upon which the authority [for military commissions] set forth in
[the Uniform Code of Military Justice] is granted."[40] The Court
did not conceive of *Hamdan*, therefore, as a case in which courts
were being asked to act, independently of the political branches,
in providing remedies for breaches of international law. Nor, unlike in *Sanchez-Llamas*, was the Court being asked to defer to an
international body's construction of the treaty. Furthermore, both
decisions considered international law against the backdrop of traditional U.S. procedures. Whereas in *Sanchez-Llamas* these procedures included procedural default and *stare decisis*, in *Hamdan*
they concerned the procedures that had traditionally been used
for military courts-martial.[41] Even at the more general level of
respect for international law, *Sanchez-Llamas* and *Hamdan* are not
inconsistent. Whatever one may think of the Court's ultimate
conclusions in *Sanchez-Llamas*, it is difficult to dispute that the
Court took the international law arguments seriously. The Court
carefully parsed the language of Article 36, examined its drafting
history, and considered how other nations had been enforcing it.
Moreover, in considering the proper remedy and the effect of state
procedural rules, the Court treated the Article 36 violation in
much the same way that it would treat violations of other federal
law. The fact that it perceived structural and procedural restraints
on its ability to grant the relief requested does not show disrespect
for international law. As the Court explained, "[i]t is no slight to
the Convention to deny petitioners' claims under the same principles we would apply to an Act of Congress, or to the Constitution
itself."[42]

There is one way, however, in which the two decisions do seem
inconsistent. Traditionally, the Supreme Court has given substantial deference to the Executive Branch's interpretations of treaties,
stating, for example, that these interpretations are entitled to

---

[40] Id at 2794; see also id at 2774, 2786; id at 2802 (Kennedy, J, concurring).

[41] See, e.g., id at 2788 ("[T]he procedures governing trials by military commission historically have been the same as those governing courts-martial.").

[42] Id at 2688.

"great weight."[43] The majority in *Sanchez-Llamas* cited and quoted with approval from this line of authority and ultimately agreed with the Executive Branch's views regarding the implications of Article 36 for suppression of evidence and procedural default. In *Hamdan*, however, the Court interpreted Common Article 3 of the Geneva Conventions to apply to a conflict between the United States and a nonstate terrorist organization, and it did not appear to give much deference to a contrary interpretation by the Executive Branch.[44] It should be noted, however, that Chief Justice Roberts did not participate in *Hamdan*, so *Sanchez-Llamas* is probably a better indicator than *Hamdan* of how the Roberts Court is likely to approach treaty cases.[45] Moreover, the Court's lack of deference to the Executive Branch in *Hamdan* might have stemmed from factors specific to U.S. policy at Guantánamo Bay—such as the international public relations difficulties engendered by the U.S. detention facility and the long delay in initiating any military commission trials there—and may not be indicative of more general views relating to treaty deference.

D. PRIVATE ENFORCEMENT OF ARTICLE 36

As noted above, four Justices in *Sanchez-Llamas*—the three dissenting Justices, and Justice Ginsburg—made clear that they believed that Article 36 confers judicially enforceable private rights. The majority did not take a position on this issue, stating that it would "assume, without deciding, that Article 36 does grant [the petitioners] such rights."[46] This issue presumably will arise in other litigation—for example, on direct review where there is no procedural default bar, and where remedies other than suppression of evidence are sought (such as a new sentencing hearing). Prior to *Sanchez-Llamas*, the lower courts were divided on the issue.[47]

---

[43] See, e.g., *United States v Stuart*, 489 US 353, 369 (1989); *Sumitomo Shoji America, Inc. v Avagliano*, 457 US 176, 184–85 (1982); *Kolovrat v Oregon*, 366 US 187, 194 (1961).

[44] See 126 S Ct at 2795–96.

[45] Roberts recused himself in *Hamdan* because he had participated in the decision under review. In that decision, Roberts had joined in an opinion holding, among other things, that the Geneva Conventions do not confer judicially enforceable private rights. See *Hamdan v Rumsfeld*, 415 F3d 33, 38–40 (DC Cir 2005).

[46] 126 S Ct at 2677–78.

[47] Compare *Jogi v Voges*, 425 F3d 367 (7th Cir 2005) (concluding that Article 36 confers judicially enforceable private rights), with *United States v Jimenez-Nava*, 243 F3d 192, 195–98 (5th Cir 2001) (concluding that Article 36 does not confer judicially enforceable

Textually, this issue appears to be a closer one than the suppression and procedural default issues decided in *Sanchez-Llamas*. Article 36 imposes mandatory obligations on arresting authorities and specifically refers to "rights."[48] Moreover, some of the functional and constitutional concerns associated with implying a suppression remedy or an override of procedural default rules do not apply to this issue, since it is not uncommon for federal statutes to confer individual rights, including rights enforceable in state courts. On the other hand, there is no mention of judicial enforcement in the Vienna Convention, and the preamble to the Convention states that the purpose of the privileges and immunities set forth in the Convention "is not to benefit individuals but to ensure the efficient performance of functions by consular posts on behalf of their respective States." Although the ICJ has concluded that Article 36 does confer individual rights, its reasoning on this issue, like the procedural default issue, is presumably entitled only to "respectful consideration." Moreover, it is not entirely clear that this is a question of treaty interpretation, as opposed to a question of U.S. law governing the circumstances under which a law should be viewed as allowing for private enforcement.

This issue of private treaty enforcement implicates broader debates in the literature over the extent to which treaties should be viewed like federal statutes. On the one hand, the Supremacy Clause of the Constitution refers to treaties, along with federal statutes and the Constitution, as the "supreme Law of the Land."[49] On the other hand, treaties, unlike statutes, are international contracts, and by definition concern U.S. foreign relations. As a result, it is arguable that they should be less amenable than statutes to direct judicial enforcement. This may partially explain the special doctrine of "non-self-execution" that has existed since the early 1800s, pursuant to which some treaties are viewed as judicially unenforceable until they are implemented by Congress.[50] As treaties have grown in number and breadth, this concept of non-self-

---

private rights). Many courts prior to *Sanchez-Llamas* had avoided deciding this question, instead holding simply that Article 36 did not confer the particular remedies being sought in those cases (such as suppression of evidence).

[48] See Vienna Convention, Art 36(1)(b) ("The said authorities shall inform the person concerned without delay of his rights under this sub-paragraph.").

[49] US Const, Art VI.

[50] See *Foster v Neilson*, 27 US (2 Pet) 253, 314 (1829).

execution has also grown, to the dismay of internationalist commentators who view the doctrine as in tension with the Supremacy Clause and as undermining U.S. compliance with international law. Constitutionalist scholars, by contrast, tend to see the doctrine as a means of fostering democratic deliberation in the implementation of modern treaties.[51]

The term "self execution" has in turn become a highly confusing concept, in part because it is often used to mean different propositions.[52] It is sometimes used simply to suggest the lack of a need for implementing legislation. At other times, it is used to suggest judicial enforceability. In still other instances, it may denote the existence of a private cause of action. Litigants, not surprisingly, seek to use this ambiguity to their advantage. In *Sanchez-Llamas*, for example, the petitioners and their amicus supporters pointed out that when the Vienna Convention was originally submitted to the Senate, the State Department had testified that the Convention was "entirely self-executive and does not require any implementing or complementing legislation."[53] This statement, however, was probably intended simply to signify that the treaty did not need implementing legislation to become operative, not necessarily to suggest that the treaty would be privately enforceable in domestic courts.

The position of the current administration is that treaties are presumptively not enforceable by private parties. In its amicus brief in *Sanchez-Llamas*, the Executive Branch maintained that "[i]t is a long-established presumption that treaties and other international agreements do not create judicially enforceable individual rights."[54] It is far from clear, however, that there is any such general presumption, although it may be true that of the vast number of treaties today, most do not confer judicially enforceable individual rights. The Executive relies heavily on the *Head Money Cases* for

---

[51] See, e.g., Curtis A. Bradley and Jack L. Goldsmith, *Treaties, Human Rights, and Conditional Consent*, 149 U Pa L Rev 399, 457–59 (2000).

[52] See Carlos Manuel Vazquez, *The Four Doctrines of Self-Executing Treaties*, 89 Am J Intl L 695 (1995).

[53] See Brief for Petitioner Mario A. Bustillo, at 20, *Bustillo v Johnson*, No 05-51 (US Supreme Court, Dec 2005); Brief for Petitioner Moises Sanchez-Llamas, at 13, *Sanchez-Llamas v Oregon*, No 04-10566 (US Supreme Court, Dec 22, 2005); Brief of International Court of Justice Experts, at 20 (cited in note 33).

[54] Brief for the United States as Amicus Curiae Supporting Respondents, at 11, *Bustillo v Johnson*, Nos 05-51, 04-10566 (US Supreme Court, Jan 2006).

the purported presumption, but that decision (which stands for the different proposition that Congress has the authority to override treaties for purposes of U.S. law) contains language that cuts both ways. While noting that "[a] treaty is primarily a compact between independent nations" that "depends for the enforcement of its provisions on the interest and honor of the governments which are parties to it," the Court also observed that "a treaty may also contain provisions which confer certain rights upon the citizens or subjects of one of the nations residing in the territorial limits of the other, which partake of the nature of municipal law, and which are capable of enforcement as between private parties in the courts of the country."[55] Moreover, in some contexts, such as extradition and alien property rights, treaties (particularly bilateral treaties) have long been treated as conferring judicially enforceable private rights.[56]

The debate over whether treaties should be viewed like statutes is complicated even more by disagreements over the proper baseline. Whereas the Executive Branch resists the analogy to statutes out of concern that it would expand judicial enforcement of treaties, that may depend on the type of statute covered by the analogy. If modern treaties are like regulatory statutes, it is arguable that the presumption would still be against private enforcement.[57] Many important regulatory statutes, after all, have been found not to confer judicially enforceable individual rights.[58] Viewed this way, it is easier to see why the mere fact that treaties are listed in the Supremacy Clause is not dispositive of the issue of private judicial enforcement.

There are suggestions in *Sanchez-Llamas* that the majority might not be receptive to allowing private judicial enforcement of Article 36. The majority noted that "diplomatic avenues" are "the primary means of enforcing the Convention," and it stated that there "is reason to doubt" that Article 36 requires a judicial remedy.[59] The

---

[55] *Edye v Robertson (Head Money Cases)*, 112 US 580, 598 (1884).

[56] See, e.g., *Clark v Allen*, 331 US 503 (1947); *Asakura v Seattle*, 265 US 332 (1924); *United States v Rauscher*, 119 US 407 (1886).

[57] See Paul B. Stephan, *Private Remedies for Treaty Violations after Sanchez-Llamas*, 11 Lewis and Clark L Rev 65 (2007).

[58] See, e.g., *Gonzaga University v Doe*, 536 US 273 (2002) (Family Educational Rights and Privacy Act of 1974); *Alexander v Sandoval*, 532 US 275 (2001) (Section 602 of Civil Rights Act of 1964).

[59] 126 S Ct at 2680, 2682.

majority also made clear that it would give some deference to the Executive Branch's construction of Article 36, and the Executive Branch has for a number of years taken the position that this article does not confer judicially enforceable private rights.[60] As with many issues that the Roberts Court will address, Justice Kennedy's views are likely to be critical here. His vote and concurrence in *Hamdan* might suggest that he is receptive to private judicial enforcement of treaties. As noted above, however, Justice Kennedy made clear that the Court was enforcing the treaty provision in *Hamdan* because of an underlying statutory incorporation,[61] whereas there has been no statutory incorporation of Article 36 of the Vienna Convention.

II. POTENTIAL IMPLICATIONS FOR U.S. FOREIGN RELATIONS LAW

This part considers potential implications for U.S. foreign relations law of both the restrictive and protective roles for the judicial power envisioned in *Sanchez-Llamas*. The part concludes by assessing the implications of these functions for the enforceability of President Bush's 2005 memorandum, in which he stated that the United States would comply with the ICJ's decision in *Avena* by having state courts give effect to the decision in the fifty-one cases covered by the decision.

A. THE JUDICIAL POWER AS LIMITATION

The limiting function of the judicial power envisioned in *Sanchez-Llamas* is potentially relevant to at least four issues in U.S. foreign relations law: judicial federalism, the viability of dormant foreign relations preemption, the domestic application of customary international law, and the scope of the *Charming Betsy* canon of construction. The organizing theme for these issues concerns the default role of the courts. Under the internationalist approach, U.S. courts are to act independently from the political branches in promoting U.S. internationalism, subject to post hoc political branch correction. Under the constitutionalist approach as reflected in *Sanchez-Llamas*, by contrast, decisions about U.S. internationalism are to be made in the first instance by the political

---

[60] See *United States v Li*, 206 F3d 56, 63 (1st Cir 2000) (quoting view of State Department that the Vienna Convention is not a treaty "establishing rights of individuals").

[61] See note 40.

branches, through processes designed to protect structural constitutional values.

1. *Judicial federalism.* The conventional wisdom among internationalist scholars is that federalism is irrelevant to U.S. foreign relations law. Professor Louis Henkin reflects this view in stating that, "as regards U.S. foreign relations, the states 'do not exist.'"[62] There is Supreme Court dicta supporting this view, particularly in cases from the 1930s and 1940s.[63]

This conventional wisdom has never mapped well onto reality. States and localities routinely engage in a host of actions that can affect foreign relations, and almost none of it is subject to federal preemption.[64] They arrest and try foreign nationals, decide whether to apply foreign law and enforce foreign judgments, and form a variety of commercial and other relationships with other countries. Moreover, the federal political branches have long considered federalism in deciding which treaties to ratify, in attaching various reservations to U.S. ratification of treaties, and in crafting legislation to implement treaties.[65] And, whether it is claimed opportunistically or with genuine conviction, the political branches have often suggested that federalism places constitutional restrictions on their activities in foreign relations.[66] This has been true even in the Vienna Convention litigation: In the *Breard* litigation before the Supreme Court, the Executive Branch maintained that "our federal system imposes limits on the federal government's ability to interfere with the criminal justice system of the States."[67] In arguing the *LaGrand* case before the ICJ, the Executive Branch stated that "[f]ederal Government officials do not have legal power to stop peremptorily the enforce-

---

[62] Louis Henkin, *Foreign Affairs and the United States Constitution* 150 (2d ed 1996).

[63] See, e.g., *United States v Pink*, 315 US 203, 233 (1942) ("[P]ower over external affairs is not shared by the States; it is vested in the national government exclusively."); *United States v Belmont*, 301 US 324, 331 (1937) ("[I]n respect of our foreign relations generally, state lines disappear. As to such purpose . . . the State does not exist."). Both of these decisions involved the preemption of state law through a "sole executive agreement"—that is, an international agreement concluded with another country solely by the President.

[64] See generally Dennis J. Palumbo, *The States and American Foreign Relations* (1960); Jack L. Goldsmith, *Federal Courts, Foreign Affairs, and Federalism*, 83 Va L Rev 1617 (1997).

[65] See Curtis A. Bradley and Jack L. Goldsmith, *The Abiding Relevance of Federalism to U.S. Foreign Relations*, 92 Am J Intl L 675 (1998); Duncan B. Hollis, *Executive Federalism: Forging New Federalist Constraints on the Treaty Power*, 79 S Cal L Rev 1327 (2006).

[66] See Curtis A. Bradley, *The Treaty Power and American Federalism, Part II*, 99 Mich L Rev 98, 131–32 (2000) (providing examples).

[67] Brief for the United States as Amicus Curiae at 51, *Breard v Greene*, Nos 97-8214, 97-1390 (US Supreme Court).

ment of a criminal sentence by the state of Arizona."[68]

Recent academic debates on this topic have primarily concerned the extent to which federalism restricts the authority of the federal political branches. One issue that has generated particular controversy is whether the treaty power is subject to federalism restrictions. The Supreme Court's 1920 decision in *Missouri v Holland* holds that the treaty power is not subject to the federalism limitations applicable to legislation.[69] Academic debates have focused on the continued vitality of *Holland* in light of the Supreme Court's renewed commitment to federalism in the domestic arena, and the expansion of treatymaking to encompass a variety of matters that were traditionally of state and local concern.[70] A number of intermediate positions have arisen in the debate, including the proposition that "anti-commandeering" and state sovereign immunity limitations apply to the treaty power even if that power is not subject to the Article I limitations applicable to legislation,[71] and the proposition that federalism restricts executive agreements but not Article II treaties.[72]

Sanchez-Llamas reminds us that federalism can be relevant in a different way to foreign relations law—not as a limitation on the political branches, but rather as a limitation on the role of the courts. Federalism values were directly implicated in *Sanchez-Llamas*. The two consolidated cases arose from state courts, and they concerned issues of criminal law and procedure, core areas of state interest.[73] The Supreme Court did not question the authority of the political

---

[68] Counter-Memorial Submitted by the United States of America, *LaGrand Case*, para 124 (Mar 27, 2000), at http://www.icj-cij.org/icjwww/idocket/igus/igusframe.htm.

[69] See *Missouri v Holland*, 252 US 416 (1920).

[70] See Curtis A. Bradley, *The Treaty Power and American Federalism*, 97 Mich L Rev 390 (1998); David M. Golove, *Treaty-Making and the Nation: The Historical Foundations of the Nationalist Conception of the Treaty Power*, 98 Mich L Rev 1075 (2000); Bradley, 99 Mich L Rev (cited in note 66); Nicholas Quinn Rosenkranz, *Executing the Treaty Power*, 118 Harv L Rev 1867 (2005).

[71] See, e.g., Carlos Manuel Vazquez, *Treaties and the Eleventh Amendment*, 42 Va J Intl L 713 (2002); Carlos Manuel Vazquez, *Breard, Printz, and the Treaty Power*, 70 U Colo L Rev 1317 (1999).

[72] See, e.g., David Sloss, *International Agreements and the Political Safeguards of Federalism*, 55 Stan L Rev 1693 (2003).

[73] Cf. *United States v Morrison*, 529 US 598, 617 (2000) ("The regulation and punishment of intrastate violence that is not directed at the instrumentalities, channels, or goods involved in interstate commerce has always been the province of the States."); *United States v Lopez*, 514 US 549, 561 n 3 (1995) ("Under our federal system, the 'States possess primary authority for defining and enforcing the criminal law.'") (citations omitted).

branches to displace state law through the treaty power, noting that "where a treaty provides for a particular judicial remedy, there is no issue of intruding on the constitutional prerogatives of the States."[74] In rejecting the petitioners' arguments, however, the Court emphasized the relevance of federalism to the scope of the judicial power. The Court disclaimed any supervisory authority over state court proceedings, even for the purpose of effectuating compliance with international law.[75] The Court also stated that, "where a treaty does not provide a particular remedy . . . it is not for the federal courts to impose one on the States through lawmaking of their own."[76] Justice Ginsburg similarly emphasized judicial federalism in her concurrence. Noting that federal courts are allowed to apply procedural default rules to bar treaty claims, including claims under the Vienna Convention, Justice Ginsburg expressed the view that:

> it would be unseemly, to say the least, for this Court to command state courts to relax their identical, or even less stringent procedural default rules, while federal courts operate without constraint in this regard. That state of affairs, surely productive of friction in our federal system, should be resisted if there is a plausible choice, *i.e.*, if a reasonable interpretation of the federal statute and international accord would avoid the conflict.[77]

There is an often overlooked connection between this sort of judicial federalism and arguments for not enforcing federalism limits against the political branches. The most frequently cited argument for why the courts should not enforce federalism restraints is that state interests are adequately addressed in the political process.[78] To the extent that this argument has merit (and its empirical validity is contested), it may be particularly strong with respect to Article II treaties, which require the advice and consent of two-thirds of

---

[74] 126 S Ct at 2680.

[75] See id at 2679.

[76] Id at 2680.

[77] Id at 2689 (Ginsburg, J, concurring).

[78] See generally Jesse H. Choper, *Judicial Review and the National Political Process* (1980); Herbert Wechsler, *The Political Safeguards of Federalism: The Role of the States in the Composition and Selection of the National Government*, 54 Colum L Rev 543 (1954). See also *Garcia v San Antonio Metropolitan Transit Authority*, 469 US 528, 550–53 (1985).

the Senate.[79] These process protections, however, do not apply to actions by the federal judiciary. By subjecting the judicial power to federalism limitations, courts help ensure that the political process protections for federalism actually operate.[80]

2. *Viability of dormant foreign relations preemption.* Judicial federalism is in turn relevant to a separate foreign relations law issue, which is whether courts should subject state and local laws to "dormant" foreign relations preemption. The Constitution prohibits the states from engaging in certain foreign relations activities, such as treaty-making, and it grants the federal government broad authority to preempt other state foreign affairs activities. This constitutional structure might naturally be read to suggest that when states are not engaging in activities expressly prohibited by the Constitution, they are subject to preemption only when the political branches actually exercise their preemptive authority.[81] Some commentators contend, however, that the federal courts should enforce a "dormant" preemption to ensure that states do not unduly intrude on the ability of the United States to speak with "one voice."[82]

The Supreme Court has applied dormant foreign relations preemption only once, in the Cold War decision, *Zschernig v Miller.*[83] The issue there was the validity of an Oregon inheritance statute that effectively disallowed residents of communist countries from inheriting personal property from Oregonian decedents. Despite concluding that no treaty or federal statute preempted the state law, the Court held that the law was invalid because of its "direct impact upon foreign relations."[84] The Court reached this conclusion even though the Executive Branch had informed the Court that the

---

[79] But cf. Bradley, 97 Mich L Rev at 442–43 (cited in note 70) (questioning the extent to which state interests are protected in light of the Seventeenth Amendment, the rise of executive agreements, the opaque nature of the treaty-making process, and the vagueness of many of the treaty provisions that pose federalism issues).

[80] See Bradford R. Clark, *Separation of Powers as a Safeguard of Federalism,* 80 Tex L Rev 327 (2001).

[81] For an argument along these lines, see Goldsmith, 83 Va L Rev (cited in note 64).

[82] See, e.g., Henkin, *Foreign Affairs and the United States Constitution* at 139 (cited in note 62); Brannon P. Denning and Jack H. McCall, Jr., *The Constitutionality of State and Local "Sanctions" Against Foreign Countries: Affairs of State, States' Affairs, or a Sorry State of Affairs?* 26 Hastings Const L Q 307, 349–50 (1999); John Norton Moore, *Federalism and Foreign Relations,* 1965 Duke L J 248, 275–76.

[83] 389 US 429 (1968).

[84] Id at 441.

Oregon statute did *not* unduly interfere with foreign relations.[85] The Court in *Zschernig* thus envisioned itself as having an independent role in policing, and invalidating, state foreign affairs activities.

Some commentators thought that a 1994 decision, *Barclays Bank v Franchise Tax Board*,[86] might have spelled the end for dormant foreign relations preemption. There, the Court held that a California system for taxing multinational corporations, which had generated substantial foreign protest and Executive Branch complaint, did not unconstitutionally interfere with the ability of the national government to speak with "one voice." The Court explained that "[t]he Constitution does 'not make the judiciary the overseer of our government,'" and that, as a result, the Court would "leave it to Congress—whose voice, in this area, is the Nation's—to evaluate whether the national interest is best served by tax uniformity, or state autonomy."[87]

In subsequent decisions, the Supreme Court has latched onto a different doctrine—"obstacle" preemption—to displace state foreign relations activities.[88] In doing so, it has shown less tolerance for such activities than one might have predicted after *Barclays Bank*. Nevertheless, the Court has at the same time gone out of its way not to endorse *Zschernig*. In *American Insurance Association v Garamendi*, for example, the majority referred to *Zschernig* only in the passive voice, noting that "reliance [by the petitioners] is placed on our decision in *Zschernig v. Miller*," and it declined to rest its finding of preemption on the decision.[89] Justice Ginsburg's dissent, which was joined by three other Justices, treated *Zschernig* with even less enthusiasm, noting that, "[w]e have not relied on *Zschernig* since it was decided, and I would not resurrect that decision here."[90]

The limiting function of the judicial power reflected in *Sanchez-*

---

[85] See id at 460 (Harlan, J, concurring).

[86] 512 US 298 (1994).

[87] Id at 330–31 (citations omitted).

[88] See *American Insurance Association v Garamendi*, 539 US 396 (2003); *Crosby v National Foreign Trade Council*, 530 US 363 (2000).

[89] 539 US 396, 417 (2003). In a cryptic footnote, the majority suggested that dormant preemption might be appropriate only when a state "take[s] a position on a matter of foreign policy with no serious claim to be addressing a traditional state responsibility." Id at 420 n 11. Under that approach, *Zschernig* was wrongly decided, since Oregon in that case was legislating in the area of inheritance, a traditional state responsibility.

[90] 539 US at 439 (Ginsburg, J, dissenting).

Llamas suggests that the Roberts Court may be even less enthusiastic than the Rehnquist Court about dormant foreign relations preemption. Contrary to the approach in *Zschernig*, the Court in *Sanchez-Llamas* insisted that the "judicial function" did not give it a supervisory role over state courts, even in cases affecting foreign relations, and the Court at least suggested that federal preemption of state law must be grounded in law that has been approved by the federal political branches.

3. *Domestic application of customary international law.* One of the most controversial debates in foreign relations law in the last decade has concerned the domestic status of customary international law. Referred to historically as part of the "law of nations," customary international law is the law of the international community that "results from a general and consistent practice of states followed by them from a sense of legal obligation."[91] Despite occasional claims to the contrary, there now appears to be widespread agreement that, prior to *Erie v Tompkins*, customary international law had the status in the United States of general common law. That is, state and federal courts felt free to apply it in appropriate cases, but they did not view it as supreme federal law that would either preempt state law or provide a basis for federal question jurisdiction. This approach fits well with the text of the Supremacy Clause, which lists treaties, but not the law of nations, as preemptive federal law.

The post-*Erie* status of customary international law has generated significant disagreement among academic commentators. Internationalist commentators claim that customary international law automatically has the status today of federal common law and thereby preempts state law, serves as a source of federal question jurisdiction, and potentially even overrides Executive Branch authority.[92] Constitutionalist commentators, by contrast, have argued that customary international law has the status of federal common law only when the political branches have authorized courts to incorporate it as such.[93] As with many foreign relations law debates, intermediate positions have also arisen, with some commentators claiming that

[91] *Restatement (Third) of the Foreign Relations Law of the United States* § 102(1) (1987).

[92] See, e.g., Lea Brilmayer, *Federalism, State Authority, and the Preemptive Power of International Law*, 1994 Supreme Court Review 295; Louis Henkin, *International Law as Law in the United States*, 82 Mich L Rev 1555 (1984); Harold Hongju Koh, *Is International Law Really State Law?* 110 Harv L Rev 1824 (1997).

[93] See, e.g., Curtis A. Bradley and Jack L. Goldsmith, *Customary International Law as Federal Common Law: A Critique of the Modern Position*, 110 Harv L Rev 815 (1997).

customary international law might be federal law only for jurisdictional purposes,[94] or that customary international law might still operate as general common law despite the holding in *Erie* that "there is no more federal general common law."[95]

Customary international law comes up frequently in human rights litigation brought under the Alien Tort Statute. This statute, first enacted in 1789 as part of the Judiciary Act, provides simply that the federal district courts "shall have original jurisdiction of any civil action by an alien for a tort only, committed in violation of the law of nations or a treaty of the United States."[96] Ever since the Second Circuit's 1980 decision in *Filartiga v Pena-Irala*,[97] the statute has become a fount of international human rights litigation—that is, suits by aliens against other aliens for human rights abuses committed in other countries. Essentially all of these cases have involved alleged violations of the "law of nations," or customary international law, rather than treaties, because the United States has either not ratified the relevant human rights treaties or has ratified them subject to non-self-execution declarations that render them unenforceable in U.S. courts.

In allowing this litigation, the *Filartiga* decision and its progeny embraced an internationalist conception of the role of the federal courts. In explaining how Article III jurisdictional requirements were satisfied in *Filartiga* despite the lack of a treaty or statutory cause of action and the lack of diversity jurisdiction, the court there invoked the judiciary's federal common law powers and cited to "[t]he Framers' overarching concern that control over international affairs be vested in the new national government to safeguard the standing of the United States among the nations of the world."[98] The court concluded by describing its approach as "a small but important step in the fulfillment of the ageless dream to free all

---

[94] See, e.g., Michael D. Ramsey, *International Law as Part of Our Law: A Constitutional Perspective*, 29 Pepperdine L Rev 187 (2001).

[95] See, e.g., Alexander Aleinikoff, *International Law, Sovereignty, and American Constitutionalism: Reflections on the Customary International Law Debate*, 98 Am J Intl L 91 (2003); Ernest A. Young, *Sorting Out the Debate Over Customary International Law*, 42 Va J Intl L 365 (2002).

[96] 28 USC § 1350.

[97] 630 F2d 876 (2d Cir 1980).

[98] Id at 887. The court also incorrectly asserted that the law of nations "has always been part of the federal common law." Id at 885.

people from brutal violence."[99] The author of the opinion, Judge Irving Kaufman, extended this theme in a subsequent magazine article commenting on the decision, writing that "the articulation of evolved norms of international law by the courts" helps "form the ethical foundations for a more enlightened social order."[100] In other words, the court viewed its federal common law authority as a means of effectuating the needs of the international system and the court's views about the proper place of the United States in that system.

The Supreme Court's 2004 decision in *Sosa v Alvarez-Machain* was at least an initial step toward rejection of an internationalist approach to the application of customary international law.[101] In that case, the Court finally considered the propriety of using the Alien Tort Statute as a vehicle for international human rights litigation. While the Court held that a "modest" number of such claims could be pursued under the statute, the Court made clear that this conclusion stemmed from congressional authorization, not some independent judicial authority to effectuate international law. Thus, while the Court concluded that the Alien Tort Statute "was meant to underwrite litigation of a narrow set of common law actions derived from the law of nations," it also made clear that there was "no congressional mandate to seek out and define new and debatable violations of the law of nations."[102] The Court further emphasized that "the general practice has been to look for legislative guidance before exercising innovative authority over substantive law," and that courts should be "wary of impinging on the discretion of the Legislative and Executive Branches in managing foreign affairs."[103]

The limiting function of the judicial power embraced in *Sanchez-Llamas* suggests that the Roberts Court may move even further toward the constitutionalist perspective on this issue. The Court made clear in *Sanchez-Llamas* that to the extent that international law (in that case, a treaty right) comes into the U.S. legal system, it comes in subject to the usual remedial and procedural doctrines governing the application of domestic law. In *Sanchez-Llamas*, those

---

[99] Id at 890.

[100] Irving R. Kaufman, *A Legal Remedy for International Torture?* NY Times Mag 44 (Nov 9, 1980).

[101] 542 US 692 (2004).

[102] Id at 721, 728.

[103] Id at 726, 727.

doctrines included *stare decisis*, procedural default, and limits on criminal law remedies. In the context of the customary international law debate, the relevant limits are those applicable to post-*Erie* federal common law, including most notably the requirement that this law be derived from, and be consistent with, extant federal law.[104] The judicial federalism aspects of *Sanchez-Llamas*, discussed above, are also part of the limitations on post-*Erie* federal common law that are potentially relevant to the domestic judicial incorporation of customary international law.[105]

4. *Scope of the "Charming Betsy" canon.* There is a long-standing canon of construction pursuant to which U.S. courts will attempt to construe statutes, where reasonably possible, to avoid violations of international law.[106] A likely justification for the canon is that it helps the United States avoid unintended violations of international law by forcing the political branches to be clear when they intend to violate it.[107] Internationalist commentators have attempted to reshape the canon, however, so that it would become a vehicle for expanding U.S. law to be aligned more closely to the contours of international law, and for limiting the discretion of the political branches.

An early example of this effort was an attempt to have courts construe the Foreign Sovereign Immunities Act to disallow immunity for serious human rights violations, on the theory that there was no right to such immunity under international law. The Act specifically lists the grounds under which foreign sovereigns may be denied immunity and does not have a provision for human rights

---

[104] For an extended argument to this effect, see Curtis A. Bradley, Jack L. Goldsmith, and David H. Moore, *Sosa, Customary International Law, and the Continuing Relevance of Erie*, 120 Harv L Rev 869 (2007).

[105] Cf. Thomas W. Merrill, *The Common Law Powers of Federal Courts*, 52 U Chi L Rev 1, 15 (1985) ("[T]he federalism principle identified by *Erie* still exists but has been silently transformed from a general constraint on the powers of the federal government into an attenuated constraint that applies principally to one branch of that government—the federal judiciary.").

[106] See *Restatement (Third)*, § 114 ("Where fairly possible, a United States statute is to be construed so as not to conflict with international law or with an international agreement of the United States.") (cited in note 91); *Murray v Schooner Charming Betsy*, 2 Cranch 64, 118 (1804) ("[A]n act of Congress ought never to be construed to violate the law of nations if any other possible construction remains.").

[107] See Curtis A. Bradley, *The Charming Betsy Canon and Separation of Powers: Rethinking the Interpretive Role of International Law*, 86 Georgetown L J 479 (1998). See also Einer Elhauge, *Preference-Eliciting Statutory Default Rules*, 102 Colum L Rev 2162, 2238–41 (2002).

violations.[108] Nevertheless, some judges and commentators argued that the Act's provision for implied waiver of immunity should be construed as extending to situations in which foreign states effectively "waived" their immunity internationally by engaging in egregious conduct.[109] To date, all the circuit courts to consider this argument have rejected it, reasoning that their obligation is to apply the statute that Congress enacted, not mold it to the contours of international law.[110] This is also arguably the subtext of the Supreme Court's 1989 decision in *Argentine Republic v Amerada Hess Shipping Corp.*, in which the Court rejected an Alien Tort Statute–based exception to sovereign immunity.[111]

A more recent effort has concerned the Authorization for the Use of Military Force (AUMF) that Congress enacted in the wake of the September 11 attacks. The AUMF broadly authorizes the Executive to use "all necessary and appropriate force" against those responsible for the attacks. Some commentators have argued, citing to the *Charming Betsy* canon, that this authorization statute should be read "consistently" with international law, such that it would disallow interrogation and detention practices inconsistent with the Geneva Conventions.[112] Used this way, the canon would become a vehicle for judicial supervision of Executive Branch compliance with international law, rather than a doctrine designed to promote political branch deliberation.[113] Courts have not yet shown an inclination to read the AUMF in this fashion. In *Hamdi v Rumsfeld*,[114] the Supreme Court construed the AUMF as authorizing the "incidents of war" and conditioned the exercise of that authority only on compliance with constitutional requirements, not international law. In *Hamdan v Rumsfeld*,[115] the Court rejected the argument that

---

[108] See 28 USC §§ 1602–11.

[109] See, e.g., *Princz v Federal Republic of Germany*, 26 F3d 1166, 1183–84 (DC Cir 1994) (Wald, J, dissenting); Adam C. Belsky et al, Comment, *Implied Waiver Under the FSIA: A Proposed Exception to Immunity for Violations of Peremptory Norms of International Law*, 77 Cal L Rev 365 (1989).

[110] See, e.g., *Sampson v Federal Republic of Germany*, 250 F3d 1145 (7th Cir 2001).

[111] See 488 US 428 (1989).

[112] See, e.g., Harold Hongju Koh, *The Case Against Military Commissions*, 96 Am J Intl L 337, 341 n 24 (2002); Ingrid Brunk Wuerth, *Authorizations for the Use of Force, International Law, and the Charming Betsy Canon*, 46 BC L Rev 93 (2005).

[113] See Curtis A. Bradley and Jack L. Goldsmith, *Congressional Authorization and the War on Terrorism*, 118 Harv L Rev 2047, 2098–99 (2005) (criticizing this use of the canon).

[114] 542 US 507 (2004).

[115] 126 S Ct 2749 (2006).

the AUMF expanded President Bush's preexisting statutory authority to create military commissions, and it found that Congress in the Uniform Code of Military Justice had imposed international law restrictions on the use of military commissions, but the Court did not rely on the *Charming Betsy* canon.

Perhaps the most dramatic effort to extend *Charming Betsy* is with respect to constitutional interpretation. A number of commentators have argued that, just as with statutes, courts should construe the Constitution to avoid violations of international law.[116] It has been argued, for example, that the Eighth Amendment's "cruel and unusual punishments" clause should be interpreted to prohibit punishments disallowed under international law.[117] This would involve a substantial extension of the canon, since a narrower construction of the Constitution in these instances would not actually place the United States in violation of international law.[118] The Constitution does not mandate particular punishments, for example, regardless of how narrowly the Eighth Amendment is construed. Rather, such punishments are mandated by federal and state law, and if those laws are unambiguous there is no role for the *Charming Betsy* canon of construction.[119] Indeed, the United States would not be in violation of international law even if it lacked an Eighth Amendment, and even if it lacked a Constitution. It would violate international law only if it imposed punishments that violated international standards.

More importantly, this extension of the *Charming Betsy* canon calls upon the courts to use their interpretive power not to avoid an unintended violation of international law, but rather to ensure that the political branches do not violate international law or ac-

---

[116] See, e.g., Daniel Bodansky, *The Use of International Sources in Constitutional Opinion*, 32 Ga J Intl & Comp L 421, 427 (2004); Gordon A. Christenson, *Using Human Rights Law to Inform Due Process and Equal Protection Analyses*, 52 U Cin L Rev 3, 36 (1983); Joan Fitzpatrick, *The Relevance of Customary International Law Norms to the Death Penalty in the United States*, 25 Ga J Intl & Comp L 165, 179 (1995–96).

[117] See, e.g., Fitzpatrick, 25 Ga J Intl & Comp L at 179 (cited in note 116).

[118] See Curtis A. Bradley, *The Juvenile Death Penalty and International Law*, 52 Duke L J 485, 555–56 (2002) (explaining this point). See also Roger P. Alford, *Four Mistakes in the Debate on "Outsourcing Authority,"* 69 Alb L Rev 653, 673–74 (2006) (criticizing efforts to apply the *Charming Betsy* canon to the Constitution); John O. McGinnis, *Contemporary Foreign and International Law in Constitutional Construction*, 69 Alb L Rev 801, 803 n 4 (2006) (same).

[119] Cf. *Fund for Animals, Inc. v Kempthorne*, 472 F3d 872 (DC Cir 2006) (emphasizing that the canon about avoiding international law violations applies only when a statute is ambiguous).

quiesce in a violation of international law by the states. Instead of reserving the issue of international law compliance to the political branches, this approach attempts to take the issue away from the political process by constitutionalizing it.[120]

These efforts to expand the *Charming Betsy* canon to give courts a more affirmative role in aligning U.S. law with international law, and overseeing political branch compliance with international law, are at odds with the limited judicial role envisioned in *Sanchez-Llamas*. The Court there carefully restricted itself to the bounds of the particular treaty provision in question, and disclaimed independent remedial authority to help effectuate enforcement of the provision, even when such authority would align the United States more closely to the position of an international tribunal. As the Court explained, "our authority to create a judicial remedy applicable in state court must lie, if anywhere, in the treaty itself."[121]

B. THE JUDICIAL POWER AS PROTECTION

The protective function of the judicial power envisioned in *Sanchez-Llamas* also has potential implications for U.S. foreign relations law. Most notably, it suggests that regardless of whether the nondelegation doctrine has vitality in the international arena, there are limits on the extent to which the federal judicial power may be delegated to international institutions. These limits, as I will explain, are likely to be enforced most commonly through a presumption that the decisions and orders of international institutions are "non-self-executing" in the U.S. legal system. I also consider here the potential relevance of these limitations for the Supreme Court's citation of foreign and international materials in its constitutional interpretation decisions.

1. *Limits on adjudicative delegations.* There is a growing debate over whether the Constitution limits the extent to which the United States can delegate authority to international institutions.[122] A central issue in this debate is the proper analogy. If

---

[120] As explained in subsection B, the Supreme Court's controversial citation of foreign and international materials in recent constitutional interpretation decisions is distinguishable.

[121] 126 S Ct at 2679.

[122] Compare, for example, Julian G. Ku, *The Delegation of Federal Power to International Organizations: New Problems with Old Solutions*, 85 Minn L Rev 71 (2000), with David Golove, *The New Confederalism: Treaty Delegations of Legislative, Executive, and Judicial*

delegations of authority to international institutions are properly analogized to delegations of authority from Congress to U.S. administrative agencies, they may seem unproblematic, given the weakness of the nondelegation doctrine in the administrative agency context. The nondelegation doctrine has been applied to invalidate legislative delegations in only two cases, both decided in 1935, and the doctrine has often been described as having little if any modern vitality. Moreover, Supreme Court precedent suggests that, if anything, there are even fewer restraints on congressional delegations to the Executive in the area of foreign affairs.[123]

On the other hand, it is not clear that this is the proper analogy, since, unlike the Executive, international institutions have no direct electoral connection to U.S. voters. Moreover, international institutions are not subject to the public notice and comment, and congressional oversight, applicable to U.S. administrative agencies. An alternative analogy would be to delegations of governmental authority to private actors, which, although often allowed, are probably subject to greater constitutional restraints than delegations to the Executive.[124]

Most of the focus in this debate has been on legislative and regulatory delegations. Whatever the outcome of that debate, *Sanchez-Llamas* suggests that, at the very least, nondelegation concerns will have force in the context of international *adjudicative* delegations. In considering the weight to be given to the ICJ's interpretation of Article 36 of the Vienna Convention, the Court in *Sanchez-Llamas* noted that Article III of the Constitution vests the judicial power in the federal courts, and that this power extends to the interpretation of treaties. As a result, the Court reasoned, "If treaties are to be given effect as federal law under our legal system, determining their meaning as a matter of federal law 'is emphatically the province and duty of the judicial department,' headed by the 'one supreme Court' established by the Constitu-

Authority, 55 Stan L Rev 1697 (2003). See also Edward Swaine, *The Constitutionality of International Delegations*, 104 Colum L Rev 1492 (2004).

[123] See, e.g., *United States v Curtiss-Wright Export Corp.*, 299 US 304, 315 (1936). But cf. *NRDC v EPA*, 464 F3d 1, 9 (DC Cir 2006) (concluding that, if certain regulatory decisions made by the parties to the Montreal Protocol constituted binding law, it "would raise serious constitutional questions in light of the nondelegation doctrine, numerous constitutional procedural requirements for making law, and the separation of powers").

[124] I develop this analogy further in a forthcoming article, *Constitutional Process, Treaty Amendments, and Accountability*, which will be published in Law & Contemporary Problems.

tion."[125] The Court therefore resisted the conclusion that the President and Senate had delegated to the ICJ the authority to bind federal courts to its treaty interpretations.

There are a number of reasons why nondelegation concerns are likely to be given weight in the adjudicative context even if courts do not scrutinize other types of international delegations. First, whereas delegations of legislative or regulatory authority involve voluntary transfers of authority from the branches of government that would normally exercise that authority, with adjudicative delegations the political branches are delegating another branch's (i.e., the judiciary's) authority. Arguments about institutional consent and accountability for the initial delegation are therefore less applicable here.[126]

Second, the case law concerning limits on delegations to non-Article III tribunals, while hardly determinate, is more substantial than the case law for the nondelegation doctrine. Article III nondelegation concerns led the Supreme Court to invalidate the bankruptcy court system established by Congress in the early 1980s,[127] and, in upholding adjudicative delegations in other modern cases, the Court has repeatedly reaffirmed the existence of limits on the extent to which adjudicative authority can be vested in non-Article III tribunals.[128] Moreover, in other decisions that do not involve delegations per se, the Court has shown a willingness to guard the Article III judicial power from erosion.[129] There is also longstanding precedent to draw upon, including *Hayburn's Case* (which

---

[125] 126 S Ct at 2684.

[126] Cf. Eric A. Posner and Adrian Vermeule, *Interring the Nondelegation Doctrine*, 69 U Chi L Rev 1721 (2002) (relying on such arguments in questioning the nondelegation doctrine); see also id at 1755 ("Congress couldn't, for example, transfer to executive agents a power that the Constitution vests in some other institution, such as the Supreme Court."). For a similar reason, one could question the ability of the Senate and President to delegate, through a treaty, the full Congress's authority to determine whether the United States should go to war (assuming it has such authority). See Curtis A. Bradley, *International Delegations, the Structural Constitution, and Non-Self-Execution*, 55 Stan L Rev 1557, 1569–70 (2003).

[127] See *Northern Pipeline Construction Co. v Marathon Pipe Line Co.*, 458 US 50 (1982).

[128] See, e.g., *Peretz v United States*, 501 US 923, 936–39 (1991); *Commodity Futures Trading Commission v Schor*, 478 US 833, 847–56 (1986); *Thomas v Union Carbide Agricultural Products Co.*, 473 US 568, 582–89 (1985).

[129] See, e.g., *Plaut v Spendthrift Farm, Inc.*, 514 US 211, 218–19 (1995) (holding that it was unconstitutional for Congress to retroactively reopen final judgments by Article III courts because doing so interfered with the power of the federal judiciary "'to render dispositive judgments.'") (quoting Frank Easterbrook, *Presidential Review*, 40 Case W L Rev 905, 926 (1990)).

has come to stand for the proposition that Congress generally cannot vest the review of decisions of Article III courts in the Executive Branch),[130] and *United States v Klein* (which, although its holding is not very clear, may limit the ability of Congress to determine how federal courts adjudicate a case).[131] *Ex parte Milligan*, the famous Civil War–era decision disallowing the trial of a U.S. citizen by military commission (and much discussed in connection with the current war on terrorism), was also premised in part on Article III nondelegation concerns.[132] Scholarly commentary on the issue, while divided with respect to the proper organizing principle, does not evidence the same wholesale retreat as is the case with respect to the administrative nondelegation doctrine.[133]

Finally, as a predictive matter, one can expect that the federal courts will be more solicitous in preventing the loss of their own authority than that of the other branches.[134] In other modern contexts, the Supreme Court has resisted what it has perceived as political branch challenges to its judicial authority.[135] The latest indication of this is of course *Sanchez-Llamas* itself. The Court's approach in *Sanchez-Llamas* was foreshadowed in the earlier *Breard* decision, in which the Court emphasized that, notwithstanding a

---

[130] See 2 Dall 409 (1792). See also *Miller v French*, 530 US 327, 343 (2000) (describing *Hayburn's Case*).

[131] See 13 Wall 128, 146 (1872) (suggesting that Congress may not "prescribe rules of decision to the Judicial Department of the government in cases pending before it"). But cf. *Plaut*, 514 US at 218 ("Whatever the precise scope of *Klein* . . . later decisions have made clear that its prohibition does not take hold when Congress 'amend[s] applicable law.'") (citation omitted).

[132] See 4 Wall 2, 121 (1866) ("Every trial involves the exercise of judicial power; and from what source did the military commission that tried him derive their authority? Certainly no part of the judicial power of the country was conferred on them; because the Constitution expressly vests it 'in one supreme court and such inferior courts as the Congress may from time to time ordain and establish,' and it is not pretended that the commission was a court ordained and established by Congress.").

[133] See, e.g., James E. Pfander, *Article I Tribunals, Article III Courts, and the Judicial Power of the United States*, 118 Harv L Rev 643, 647–48 (2004) (describing academic theories).

[134] As lifetime appointees generally removed from party politics, Supreme Court Justices are more likely to be protective of institutional interests than members of Congress. Cf. Daryl J. Levinson and Richard H. Pildes, *Separation of Parties, Not Powers*, 119 Harv L Rev 2311 (2006) (arguing that members of Congress are unlikely to be institutionally protective, especially when Congress is controlled by the President's party).

[135] See, e.g., *Boerne v Flores*, 521 US 507, 536 (1997) ("When the political branches of the Government act against the background of a judicial interpretation of the Constitution already issued, it must be understood that in later cases and controversies the Court will treat its precedents with the respect due them under settled principles, including *stare decisis*, and contrary expectations must be disappointed.").

provisional order from the ICJ calling for a stay of execution, "this Court must decide questions presented to it on the basis of law."[136] The *Hamdan* decision, decided a day after *Sanchez-Llamas*, also fits this pattern, since the Court there emphasized the ultimate authority of the federal courts to interpret the relevant law.[137]

2. *Presuming non-self-execution*. None of this is to suggest that delegations of adjudicative authority to international institutions are inherently problematic, or that the Supreme Court will impose significant constitutional restraints on the ability of the United States to agree to such delegations. The United States has agreed to have international arbitral tribunals resolve treaty disputes since the early days of the nation, so some assignment of adjudicative authority to international actors is certainly allowed. Moreover, the Court's current standard for determining whether delegations to non-Article III tribunals are permissible is highly contextual and indeterminate,[138] and, especially in the international context, may require judgments for which the courts lack sufficient expertise. In addition, a central factor considered by the Court— whether the dispute in question concerns "public rights" (e.g., civil disputes between the government and private parties that historically could have been determined exclusively by the government)—may often weigh in favor of the permissibility of international delegations.[139]

---

[136] 523 US at 378. See also Sandra Day O'Connor, *Federalism of Free Nations*, 28 NYU J Intl L & Pol 35, 36–42 (1995–96) (raising the possibility that the vesting of decision-making authority in international tribunals would violate Article III).

[137] See 126 S Ct at 2775 ("Together, [federal statutes] at most acknowledge a general Presidential authority to convene military commissions in circumstances where justified under the 'Constitution and laws,' including the law of war. Absent a more specific congressional authorization, the task of this Court is . . . to decide whether Hamdan's military commission is so justified.").

[138] In evaluating whether such a delegation is permissible, the Supreme Court considers, among other things, "the extent to which the non-Article III forum exercises the range of jurisdiction and powers normally vested only in Article III courts, the origins and importance of the right to be adjudicated, and the concerns that drove Congress to depart from the requirements of Article III." *Schor*, 478 US at 851. The Court's ultimate functional inquiry is whether the delegation "impermissibly threatens the institutional integrity of the Judicial Branch." Id.

[139] This may be what saves the NAFTA Chapter 19 arbitral panels, which review whether a U.S. administrative agency has correctly applied *U.S. law* in making certain import decisions. See Ethan Boyer, *Article III, The Foreign Relations Power, and the Binational Panel System of NAFTA*, 13 Intl Tax and Bus Lawyer 101 (1996). Cf. Matthew Burton, Note, *Assigning the Judicial Power to International Tribunals: NAFTA Binational Panels and Foreign Affairs Flexibility*, 88 Va L Rev 1529 (2002) (defending the constitutionality of the tribunals based on the special need for flexibility in foreign affairs).

Because of the doctrinal uncertainties and difficulties of judicial line-drawing in this context, it is likely that Article III nondelegation concerns will be addressed most commonly through interpretive canons. Indeed, in domestic cases, the Court already uses the constitutional avoidance canon as a means of giving effect to Article III nondelegation concerns. In *Gomez v United States*,[140] for example, the Court construed the Federal Magistrates Act as not authorizing felony jury trial selection by magistrates, noting, "It is our settled policy to avoid an interpretation of a federal statute that engenders constitutional issues if a reasonable alternative interpretation poses no constitutional question."[141]

Importantly, the Court in *Sanchez-Llamas* did not suggest that the United States' delegation of judicial authority to the ICJ to resolve disputes under the Vienna Convention (through the Optional Protocol) was constitutionally problematic. The Court's Article III concern, rather, related to the *domestic effect* of the ICJ decision—the determination of the meaning of treaties "as a matter of federal law."[142] As I have argued elsewhere, courts can generally address this concern by presuming that the decisions of international adjudicative institutions are "non-self-executing" in the U.S. legal system—that is, that they do not by themselves create a rule of decision for U.S. courts.[143] By requiring political branch implementation, this presumption subjects international decisions to the filter of the U.S. democratic process, while preserving the traditional role of the federal courts to interpret and apply existing domestic law.

The D.C. Circuit has applied this non-self-execution approach in a number of cases involving the orders and decisions of international institutions. In *Diggs v Richardson*, the court concluded that a Security Council resolution prohibiting certain contacts with apartheid South Africa did not "confer on individual citizens rights that are judicially enforceable in American domestic

---

[140] 490 US 858 (1989).

[141] Id at 864. More controversially, the Court also uses this interpretive approach to address constitutional concerns associated with delegations from Congress to administrative agencies. See John F. Manning, *The Nondelegation Doctrine as a Canon of Avoidance*, 2000 Supreme Court Review 223; Cass R. Sunstein, *Nondelegation Canons*, 67 U Chi L Rev 315 (2000).

[142] 126 S Ct at 2684.

[143] See generally Bradley, 55 Stan L Rev at 1587–95 (cited in note 126).

courts."[144] Similarly, in *Committee of United States Citizens Living in Nicaragua v Reagan*,[145] the court reasoned that an ICJ decision prohibiting the United States from assisting rebel forces in Nicaragua was non-self-executing because the relevant treaty provisions evidenced "no intent to vest citizens who reside in a U.N. member nation with authority to enforce an ICJ decision against their own government."[146] Most recently, in *NRDC v EPA*,[147] the court held that decisions of the parties under the Montreal Protocol did not have the status of "judicially enforceable domestic law," reasoning that such status would raise "significant constitutional problems."[148]

3. *Citation of foreign and international materials.* The Court's resistance in *Sanchez-Llamas* to giving substantial weight to the ICJ's reasoning might be contrasted with recent decisions in which the Court has cited foreign and international materials in resolving issues of constitutional interpretation.[149] This practice has generated significant controversy, both in the academy and among policymakers.[150] Internationalist commentators point to the practice as evidence that the Supreme Court is moving to a more global conception of its role.[151]

This practice has been vigorously opposed by some Supreme Court Justices,[152] and it is possible that the practice will diminish with the new appointments to the Court.[153] In any event, this practice is distinguishable from efforts to give direct effect to in-

[144] See 555 F2d 848, 851 (DC Cir 1976).

[145] 859 F2d 929 (DC Cir 1988).

[146] Id at 938.

[147] 464 F3d 1 (DC Cir 2006).

[148] Id at 9. The court also suggested more broadly that the decisions were mere political commitments rather than binding international obligations.

[149] See, e.g., *Roper v Simmons*, 543 US 551 (2005); *Lawrence v Texas*, 539 US 558, 572–73 (2003); *Atkins v Virginia*, 536 US 304, 316 n 21 (2002).

[150] Compare, for example, Harold Hongju Koh, *International Law as Part of Our Law*, 98 Am J Intl L 43 (2004), with John O. McGinnis, *Foreign to Our Constitution*, 100 Nw U L Rev (2006).

[151] See, e.g., Melissa Waters, *Mediating Norms and Identity: The Role of Transnational Judicial Dialogue in Creating and Enforcing International Law*, 93 Georgetown L J 487 (2005).

[152] See, e.g., *Roper*, 543 US at 622–28 (Scalia, J, dissenting, along with Rehnquist and Thomas).

[153] In their confirmation hearings, both Chief Justice Roberts and Justice Alito suggested skepticism about reliance on foreign and international materials in constitutional interpretation. There may still be five Justices, however, that support such reliance.

ternational adjudicatory decisions. The Court has treated foreign and international materials as evidence that may be relevant to the interpretation of vague or uncertain constitutional provisions, not as sources of law that have direct and binding application in the U.S. legal system. Nor has it purported to use these materials in a *Charming Betsy* sort of way—that is, the Court has not claimed that the Constitution must be interpreted to avoid being inconsistent with these materials. Even in the Court's broadest endorsement of the practice—in the juvenile death penalty decision, *Roper v Simmons*—the Court made clear that, although the opinion of the world community may provide "respected and significant confirmation" for the Court's conclusions, it is "not controlling."[154] This phrasing-is similar to the "respectful consideration" that the Court in *Sanchez-Llamas* gave to the ICJ's reasoning.

Thus, as currently applied by the Court, the citation of foreign and international materials is not a threat to the Article III judicial power. The foreign and international materials are subject to discretionary selection by the Court, and are treated as nonbinding. This practice is in fact best viewed as potentially *enhancing* judicial discretion by giving the Court a broader array of materials to draw from in rationalizing its constitutional interpretations. Regardless of whether this practice is a proper method of constitutional interpretation, it is not likely to erode the authority of the federal courts.

C. IMPLICATIONS FOR ENFORCING THE PRESIDENT'S MEMORANDUM

Because the petitioners in *Sanchez-Llamas* were not part of the group of fifty-one Mexican nationals directly covered by the ICJ's judgment in *Avena*, the Court did not need to consider the legal status or effect of President Bush's February 2005 memorandum, in which he stated that the United States would give effect to the ICJ's judgment in its state courts. The Court simply noted in passing that "the United States has agreed to 'discharge its international obligations' in having state courts give effect to the decision in *Avena*."[155]

During the prior Term, the Court had before it a case that did

---

[154] 543 US at 578.

[155] 126 S Ct at 2685.

involve one of the fifty-one Mexican nationals, *Medellin v Dretke*.[156] The Court initially granted a writ of certiorari in that case, but subsequently dismissed the writ as improvidently granted. A principal reason for the dismissal was the possibility that Medellin might obtain the relief he was seeking in a Texas state court, as a result of the President's memorandum.[157]

After *Sanchez-Llamas*, however, the Texas Court of Criminal Appeals denied relief to Medellin, holding that the President's memorandum did not override Texas's law of procedural default.[158] In reaching this conclusion, the Texas court noted that the Supreme Court in *Sanchez-Llamas* had concluded that Article 36 of the Vienna Convention does not override state rules of procedural default, and that the ICJ's reasoning in *Avena* is not binding on U.S. courts. As a result, the Texas court concluded that neither Article 36 nor the *Avena* judgment created a legal basis for overriding Texas's law. With respect to the President's memorandum, the court, invoking the *Youngstown* steel seizure decision, reasoned that the President lacked the power to create preemptive federal law, and that the memorandum improperly "intrud[ed] into the independent powers of the judiciary."[159]

The implications of *Sanchez-Llamas* for the enforceability of the President's memorandum are less clear than this analysis suggests. As an initial matter, *Sanchez-Llamas* did not consider the effect of the ICJ's judgment, as opposed to its reasoning. It would not be illogical for the Court to both disagree with the ICJ's reasoning, as it did in *Sanchez-Llamas*, and nevertheless enforce the ICJ's judgment, just as U.S. courts often enforce foreign court judgments and commercial arbitral awards without endorsing their underlying reasoning. To be sure, ICJ judgments may be distinguishable in this regard given the interstate nature of ICJ dispute resolution and the subject matter of the disputes addressed by the ICJ,[160] but the Court in *Sanchez-Llamas* did not address that issue.

More fundamentally, *Sanchez-Llamas* is ultimately a decision

---

[156] See 544 US 660 (2005).

[157] Id at 666–67; see also id at 669 (Ginsburg, J, concurring).

[158] See *Ex parte Medellin*, 2006 Tex Crim App LEXIS 2236 (Tex Ct Crim App, Nov 15, 2006).

[159] Id at *45.

[160] See Curtis A. Bradley, *Enforcing the Avena Decision in U.S. Courts*, 30 Harv J L & Pub Pol 119 (2006); Mark L. Movsesian, *Understanding Sanchez-Llamas* (draft on file with author).

about judicial power, not Executive power. The Court made clear in *Sanchez-Llamas* that the *judiciary* lacks the authority to create remedies or legal rules that go beyond the terms of a treaty, even for the sake of facilitating enforcement of the treaty. While the Court also suggested that the judiciary should be protected from outside control, its focus was on control by non-U.S. actors, not the Executive. Indeed, the Court noted that U.S. courts should give deference to Executive Branch treaty constructions.[161]

The decision in *Sanchez-Llamas* therefore does not preclude the possibility that the Executive has some remedial lawmaking authority in this context not possessed by the judiciary, perhaps stemming from the President's obligation to "take Care that the Laws be faithfully executed."[162] Even though Article 36 of the Vienna Convention may not override state procedural default rules (as both the Executive and the Supreme Court have now concluded), the United States still has a treaty obligation to comply with the ICJ's judgment, pursuant to Article 94 of the United Nations Charter.[163] While Article 94 is almost certainly non-self-executing—that is, it does not of its own force give domestic effect to ICJ judgments[164]—the President's Take Care authority may include some ability to give legal effect to a non-self-executing treaty obligation. Or, to put it slightly differently, Article 94 could be read as implicitly delegating to the Executive Branch some authority to implement ICJ decisions, in the same way that foreign affairs statutes are often construed as implicitly delegating authority to the Executive.[165]

Certainly there must be limits on the authority of the President to create preemptive federal law, even in the area of foreign relations. Dicta in *American Insurance Association v Garamendi* sug-

[161] See 126 S Ct at 2685.

[162] US Const, Art II, § 3.

[163] See UN Charter, Art 94(1) ("Each member of the United Nations undertakes to comply with the decision of the International Court of Justice in any case to which it is a party.").

[164] See *Committee of United States Citizens Living in Nicaragua v Reagan*, 859 F2d 929, 937–38 (DC Cir 1988); A. Mark Weisburd, *International Judicial Decisions, Domestic Courts, and the Foreign Affairs Power*, 2004–05 Cato Sup Ct Rev 287, 299–304. The only enforcement mechanism mentioned in Article 94 is through the UN Security Council. See UN Charter, Art 94(2).

[165] Cf. Curtis A. Bradley, *Chevron Deference and Foreign Affairs*, 86 Va L Rev 649, 670–71 (2000); Carlos Manuel Vazquez, *Breard and the Federal Power to Require Compliance with ICJ Orders of Provisional Measures*, 92 Am J Intl L 683, 689 (1998).

gesting that state law can be preempted by the "foreign policy of the Executive Branch"[166] has been appropriately criticized.[167] The Supreme Court would not need to go as far as that dicta, however, to enforce the President's memorandum, since the underlying treaty commitment to comply with the ICJ's judgment makes compliance more than simply the foreign policy of the Executive Branch. Indeed, the Texas court acknowledged that the President might be able to accomplish this by entering into an executive agreement with Mexico.[168] If this is the case (and there may be federalism and other grounds for disputing it), it is not clear why the lack of this formality is dispositive.[169] While requiring an executive agreement would impose a process restraint on the Executive's ability to preempt state law, such a restraint is not (unlike the Article II treaty process, which involves the Senate) one that has any particular relationship to the protection of state interests.

III. Benefits of the Judicial Power's Two Functions in International Cases

The constitutionalist approach, as reflected in *Sanchez-Llamas*, envisions federal judges as agents of the domestic legal system, not the international order. This part outlines several benefits associated with this approach in light of the current nature of the international adjudicative system. In particular, it argues that the constitutionalist approach has the virtues of enhancing democratic input, compensating for the lack of horizontal checks and balances at the international level, allowing international law and decisions to be tailored to local conditions, and facilitating local acceptance of international decision making. It also argues that countervailing arguments about the need for the uniformity and the desirability of enhancing international law compliance are weak in this context.

---

[166] 539 US at 413.

[167] See Brannon P. Denning and Michael D. Ramsey, *American Insurance Association v. Garamendi and Executive Preemption in Foreign Affairs*, 46 Wm & Mary L Rev 825 (2004); Michael P. Van Alstine, *Executive Aggrandizement in Foreign Affairs Lawmaking*, 54 UCLA L Rev 309 (2006).

[168] See 2006 Tex Crim App LEXIS at *66–*67.

[169] But see Weisburd, 2004–05 Cato Sup Ct Rev at 313 (cited in note 164) ("Since the president's power to supersede state law in foreign affairs matters derives from his authority to bargain with foreign governments, the absence of a bargain eliminates any basis for presidential authority.").

A. THE INTERNATIONAL ADJUDICATIVE "SYSTEM"

Since World War II and the establishment of the United Nations, there has been a vast growth in the number and types of international institutions. As part of this growth, scores of adjudicative institutions have arisen, sometimes as stand-alone bodies, but often as constituent parts of broader organizations.[170] There are general tribunals like the ICJ; specialized tribunals in areas such as trade, human rights, and the law of the sea; ad hoc arbitral bodies such as the Iran-U.S. Claims Tribunal; regional tribunals such as in Europe and in the Inter-American system; and criminal tribunals, including the relatively new International Criminal Court (ICC).[171] Increasingly, in terms of the subject matters that they address and the ways in which they are structured, international adjudicatory institutions are resembling traditional domestic courts rather than simply interstate arbitral mechanisms. Although not a party to all of these institutions (such as the ICC), the United States has connections to many of them.

This description actually understates the extent of, and variations within, the international adjudicative "system." In part because separation of powers is less distinct in the international system than in some domestic systems, many international institutions that are not courts or tribunals nevertheless perform judicial or quasi-judicial functions. The Security Council, for example, routinely decides whether nations have acted in ways that threaten international peace and security.[172] Monitoring and inspection committees for human rights and arms control regimes regularly issue reports or decisions concerning compliance.[173] The

---

[170] See generally Julian G. Ku, *International Delegations and the New World Court Order*, 81 Wash L Rev 1, 25–31 (2006); Martinez, 56 Stan L Rev at 436–41 (cited in note 2); Cesare P. R. Romano, *The Proliferation of International Judicial Bodies: The Pieces of the Puzzle*, 31 Intl L and Pol 709 (1999).

[171] For a chart showing 125 international judicial and quasi-judicial bodies and mechanisms, see *The Project on International Courts and Tribunals—Synoptic Chart*, version 3.0 (Nov 2004), at http://www.pict-pcti.org/publications/synoptic_chart/Synop_C4.pdf.

[172] See, e.g., UN Security Council, Res 1718 (Oct 14, 2006) (concluding that nuclear test by North Korea created a threat to international peace and security and therefore imposing a variety of sanctions).

[173] See, e.g., Concluding Observations of the Human Rights Committee, United States of America, UN Doc A/50/40, para 279 (expressing the view that U.S. reservations to the International Covenant on Civil and Political Rights, including a reservation concerning the use of the death penalty for individuals who committed crimes while under the age of eighteen, were invalid because they were incompatible with the object and purpose of the Covenant); Human Rights Committee, General Comment 24(52), General Comment

same is true of various international law "commissions," such as the Inter-American Commission on Human Rights, which, although not constituted as a court, has issued a variety of adjudicatory rulings, including some relating to U.S. practices such as the death penalty.[174] "Conferences of parties" established under treaty regimes also frequently issue quasi-judicial "decisions" about how the treaty should be interpreted or applied.[175]

There are wide variations in the jurisdiction of these various institutions. Some, like the ICJ, can hear disputes only between nation-states. Others, like the Inter-American Court on Human Rights, are open to disputes between states and private parties. Moreover, different states often have differing jurisdictional relationships with the same institution. For example, some states may accept a tribunal's general or compulsory jurisdiction, whereas others may not. For the ICJ, sixty-six states currently accept its compulsory jurisdiction, which is only about one-third of all the members of the United Nations, and many of those sixty-six states have qualified their acceptance of this jurisdiction with reservations.[176] Similarly, some parties to a treaty may consent to adjudication with respect to disputes that arise under the treaty, while other parties to the treaty may not. For the Vienna Convention on Consular Relations, for example, there are 171 parties to the treaty, but only forty-five of them currently accept ICJ jurisdiction to resolve disputes under the treaty.[177] In addition, some states

on Issues Relating to Reservations Made Upon Ratification or Accession to the Covenant or the Optional Protocols Thereto, or in Relation to Declarations Under Article 41 of the Covenant, UN Doc CCPR C/21/Rev 1/Add 6 (1994) (expressing views about the circumstances under which reservations to the Covenant are disallowed, and stating that "[i]t necessarily falls to the Committee to determine whether a specific reservation is compatible with the object and purpose of the Covenant").

[174] See, e.g., Inter-American Commission on Human Rights, Report No 62/02, Case 12.285, Michael Domingues, United States (Oct 22, 2002) (concluding that customary international law prohibits the execution of individuals who commit their crimes prior to the age of eighteen).

[175] For example, decisions by the conference of parties under the Montreal Protocol were at issue in the *NRDC* case described in note 123.

[176] See Declarations Recognizing as Compulsory the Jurisdiction of the Court, at http://www.icj-cij.org/icjwww/ibasicdocuments/ibasictext/ibasicdeclarations.htm. The United States was originally a party to the ICJ's compulsory jurisdiction, but withdrew from that jurisdiction after the ICJ assumed jurisdiction over a case in the 1980s concerning U.S. military activities in Nicaragua. Only one of the five permanent members of the UN Security Council—Great Britain—is currently a party to the ICJ's compulsory jurisdiction, and its consent to that jurisdiction is subject to the proviso that it can "at any time . . . and with effect as from the moment of such notification, either add to, amend or withdraw" any of its reservations to the jurisdiction.

[177] See United Nations Treaty Collection, at http://untreaty.un.org.

may allow their citizens to file individual complaints with an institution, whereas others may not. This is optional, for example, with the Human Rights Committee that administers the International Covenant on Civil and Political Rights.[178]

Sometimes, even when the relevant parties to a controversy have not agreed to an institution's jurisdiction, the institution will nevertheless address the controversy through the issuance of an advisory opinion. The ICJ has done this on a number of occasions, perhaps most controversially when it opined in 2004 about the legality of Israel's construction of a security barrier in occupied Palestine.[179] Although the United States is not a party to the Inter-American Court on Human Rights, that Court has issued a number of advisory opinions relating to practices in the United States, including U.S. compliance with the Vienna Convention.[180] These advisory opinions are technically not "binding" under international law, although the line between binding and nonbinding international decisions is often unclear in light of the limited enforcement options associated with even binding decisions, as well as the possibility that nonbinding decisions will either be given substantial deference or treated as evidence of binding customary international law.

The jurisdiction of these various institutions frequently overlaps, such that different institutions may address the same questions and potentially reach different conclusions, and there is no established hierarchy among these institutions.[181] For example, as noted above, both the Inter-American Court on Human Rights and the ICJ have addressed issues of compliance with the Vienna

---

[178] See Optional Protocol to the International Covenant on Civil and Political Rights, UN Doc A/6316 (1966), 999 UNTS 302, *entered into force* March 23, 1976.

[179] See Advisory Opinion, Legal Consequences of the Construction of a Wall in the Occupied Palestinian Territory (July 9, 2004), at http://www.icj-cij.org/icjwww/idocket/ imwp/imwpframe.htm. For criticism of the ICJ's exercise of advisory jurisdiction in this case, see Michla Pomerance, *The ICJ's Advisory Jurisdiction and the Crumbling Wall Between the Political and the Judicial*, 99 Am J Intl L 26 (2005).

[180] See, e.g., Inter-American Court of Human Rights, "The Right to Information on Consular Assistance in the Framework of the Guaranties of the Due Process of Law," Adv Op OC-16/99, Inter-Am Ct HR (Ser A) No 16 (Oct 1, 1999).

[181] See generally Yuval Shany, *The Competing Jurisdictions of International Courts and Tribunals* (2003); see also Martinez, 56 Stan L Rev at 431 ("In many situations . . . it is as yet unclear what should happen when more than one court potentially has jurisdiction over the same case; unclear how one court should treat the decisions of another court; and unclear what should happen when courts reach inconsistent decisions.") (cited in note 2).

Convention, and they have expressed differing views about what the treaty requires.[182] Similarly, the International Criminal Tribunal for Former Yugoslavia has expressed views contrary to the ICJ concerning state responsibility for the actions of non-actors.[183]

The jurisdiction of international adjudicatory institutions also increasingly overlaps with the jurisdiction of domestic courts.[184] As its Vienna Convention decisions demonstrate, the ICJ is now addressing issues of domestic criminal law and procedure. International criminal tribunals address crimes that may also be addressed in domestic criminal law. A particularly direct intersection between international adjudication and domestic courts was evident in two NAFTA arbitral cases, *Loewen* and *Mondev*, in which NAFTA panels considered whether state court decision making in the United States had violated U.S. treaty obligations.[185]

The appointment process for the members of these institutions varies widely, with none of them appointed with the tenure and salary protections applicable to federal judges. Nor are these appointments typically subject to nearly as much transparency or public deliberation as with domestic judicial appointments.[186] Consider, for example, the ICJ. It consists of fifteen judges, from fifteen different nations. These judges are, according to the ICJ Statute,

---

[182] Whereas the Inter-American Court expressed the view that consular notice must be provided "at the time the accused is deprived of his freedom, or at least before he makes his first statement before the authorities," see Inter-American Court, The Right to Information on Consular Assistance, at para 106 (cited in note 180), the ICJ in *Avena* expressed the view that the notice should be given "as soon as it is realized that the person is a foreign national, or once there are grounds to think that the person is probably a foreign national" and that the notice need not necessarily be given at the time of the arrest or before questioning, see *Case Concerning Avena*, at paras 87–88 (cited in note 20).

[183] Compare *Case Concerning the Military and Paramilitary Activities in and Against Nicaragua (Nicaragua v United States of America)*, 1986 ICJ 14, para 115 (1986) (Judgment of 27 June 1986) (adopting narrow "effective control" standard for attribution of private conduct to states), with *The Prosecutor v Dusko Tadic*, IT-94-1-A, ICTY Appeals Chamber, para 145 (1999) (Judgment of 15 July 1999) (Merits) (adopting broader "overall control" standard).

[184] See Ernest A. Young, *Institutional Settlement in a Globalizing Judicial System*, 54 Duke L J 1143 (2005).

[185] See *The Loewen Group, Inc. v United States of America*, Case No ARB(AF)/98/3 (Award) (June 26, 2003), at http://www.state.gov/documents/organization/22094.pdf; *Mondev Int'l Ltd v United States of America*, Case No ARB(AF)/99/2 (Award) (Oct 11, 2002), at http://www.state.gov/documents/organization/14442.pdf.

[186] See Ruth Mackenzie and Philippe Sands, *International Courts and Tribunals and the Independence of the International Judge*, 44 Harv Intl L J 271, 277–78 (2003) ("In practice, the nomination and election of judges to international courts and tribunals are politicized processes, subject to little transparency, and to widely varying nomination mechanisms at the national level.").

supposed to be representative of the "main forms of civilization" and "the principal legal systems of the world."[187] The ICJ's membership has in fact been quite varied, although the five veto members of the Security Council have almost always had a judge on the court. (The current judges on the court are from the United States, the United Kingdom, Jordan, Madagascar, China, Sierra Leone, Venezuela, Japan, Germany, Slovakia, France, New Zealand, Mexico, Morocco, and Russia.) The judges are nominated by "national groups" in the Permanent Court of Arbitration (which are appointed by each nation), and then elected by the UN General Assembly and UN Security Council. These judges serve for nine-year terms and can be reelected. When a judge is elected or reelected to the ICJ, even when it is a U.S. judge, there is almost no public attention or debate in the United States.[188]

In many instances, the judges on international adjudicative bodies are likely to be "biased" in the sense that they will vote according to the preferences of their nation. One study of the ICJ, for example, found that ICJ judges vote for their home state about 90 percent of the time, and when their home state is not a party, they tend to vote for states that are similar to their home state in terms of wealth, culture, and political regime.[189] This is unsurprising, given that these judges are as a practical matter dependent on their nations for reappointment, and also potentially for other government positions.[190] As further noted by Eric Posner and Miguel Figueiredo, "These considerations are likely to weigh even more heavily in the calculations of judges from authoritarian states, as these judges do not necessarily have the option to take refuge in the private sector if they displease their government."[191] Even without such incentives, however, it is not surprising that judges

---

[187] ICJ Statute, Art 9.

[188] Based on a LexisNexis search of major newspapers, I could find no mention in U.S. newspapers of the reelection to the ICJ in 2005 of the current American judge, Thomas Buergenthal. Contrast that with the news coverage of the recent appointments of John Roberts and Samuel Alito to the U.S. Supreme Court.

[189] See Eric A. Posner and Miguel de Figueiredo, *Is the International Court of Justice Biased?* 34 J Legal Stud 539 (2005).

[190] For debate over whether judicial independence is desirable in international tribunals, compare Eric A. Posner and John C. Yoo, *Judicial Independence in International Tribunals*, 93 Cal L Rev 1 (2005) (arguing that it is not), with Laurence R. Helfer and Anne-Marie Slaughter, *Why States Create International Tribunals: A Response to Professors Posner and Yoo*, 93 Cal L Rev 899 (2005) (arguing that it is).

[191] Posner and Figueiredo, 34 J Legal Stud at 608 (cited in note 189).

would reflect the particular perspectives of their nations, which might be very different from the perspective of the party countries before them.

In sum, the international adjudicative system is highly varied and fragmented. It has scores of institutions of varying levels of specialization and types of jurisdiction, with often varying relationships to different states. It produces overlapping and sometimes conflicting decisions, some of which are formally binding and some of which are not, and some of which will reflect national biases.

Contrast this with the U.S. Supreme Court and its relationship to U.S. states. There is one centralized Supreme Court, and it has a hierarchical relationship to both the lower federal courts and, for issues of federal law, to the state courts. It applies law that is expressly stated in the Constitution to be part of the supreme law of the land and binding on state judges. Its judges are appointed from the U.S. bar in a process that involves substantial public attention and requires nomination by a nationally elected president and approval by a substantial number of senators, two of whom represent each state. The judges then enjoy lifetime tenure and salary protection. The judges may well be "political" in the sense that their votes are affected by their political preferences, but they are largely removed from direct political influences. In practice, the constitutional decisions of the Court nevertheless hew pretty closely to democratic preferences of the polity. As for its non-constitutional decisions, they are subject to override by a simple majority of the legislative branch. The Court decides only cases and controversies and will not issue advisory opinions. It now has well over 200 years of history and jurisprudence from which to draw. Perhaps most importantly, it is understood to be the national court for a single country of which the states are constituent parts. Even with all of this, its decisions and authority have sometimes been vigorously questioned, both by the states and by the federal political branches.

The only international adjudicatory institutions that bear some resemblance to the U.S. Supreme Court are two supranational courts in Europe—the European Court of Justice, and the European Court of Human Rights. These institutions are centralized tribunals, embedded in a connected geographic community that

shares a common drive for integration.[192] They have broad compulsory jurisdiction that is similar for all the member states, and
they have now developed an extensive jurisprudence. Not coin-
cidentally, national court relations with those institutions come
closest to the internationalist approach, with national courts generally treating the decisions of those institutions as authoritative.[193]
The United States is of course not a party to these institutions,
and they are not representative of the rest of the international
adjudicative system.

B. BENEFITS OF THE CONSTITUTIONALIST APPROACH

In light of the current state of the international adjudicative
system, there are a number of benefits to the constitutionalist
approach followed in *Sanchez-Llamas*: enhancing democratic input,
helping to compensate for the lack of horizontal checks and balances at the international level, ensuring that international decision making is tailored to local conditions, and facilitating domestic acceptance of such decision making.

First, by limiting judicial remedial creativity and denying international decisions direct domestic effect, the constitutionalist
approach enhances democratic input in the domestic application
and enforcement of international law. Under this approach, decisions about whether and how to comply with international law
are made in the first instance by the democratically accountable
political branches, rather than the courts. Such a democratic "filter" is particularly important for international law because the
processes of international lawmaking—both treaty-based and customary—are less transparent and involve less accountability than
domestic democratic lawmaking.[194]

---

[192] The European Court of Justice is the adjudicatory body of the European Union,
which now has twenty-seven member states. The European Court of Human Rights is
part of the Council of Europe, which has forty-six member states. All members of the
European Union are also members of the Council of Europe.

[193] Even for those courts, there are mediating doctrines that can limit the intrusiveness
of the courts on national decision making, such as the "margin of appreciation" and
"subsidiarity." See, e.g., Howard Charles Yourow, *The Margin of Appreciation Doctrine in
the Dynamics of European Human Rights Jurisprudence* (1996); George A. Bermann, *Taking
Subsidiarity Seriously: Federalism in the European Union and the United States*, 94 Colum L
Rev 331 (1994).

[194] See generally John O. McGinnis and Ilya Somin, *Should International Law Be Part of
Our Law?* 59 Stan L Rev (forthcoming 2007); Eric Stein, *International Integration and
Democracy: No Love at First Sight*, 95 Am J Intl L 489 (2001); Paul B. Stephan, *Accountability*

Customary international law implicates particular democratic legitimacy concerns.[195] Unlike a statute or treaty, customary international law does not involve any agreed-upon text voted upon by U.S. representatives. Moreover, the most populist branch of the government, the Congress, has at most a very indirect role in the formation of customary international law. Rather, U.S. involvement in customary international law formation comes primarily from the Executive Branch. Nor, even with this involvement, is there any guarantee that the U.S. position will prevail or that customary international law will reflect U.S. legal traditions and culture. The United States simply has one important voice in a community of over 190 diverse nations, many of whom may themselves be undemocratic. Finally, unlike with many treaties, the United States has no unilateral authority to withdraw from customary international law rules once those rules are established.

International adjudicatory institutions, despite offering potential benefits of expertise and enhancement of coordination, add yet another layer of democratic deficit. As noted above, the judges in these institutions are often appointed with little public attention or legislative oversight, and many of them may come from nondemocratic regimes. And, unlike domestic courts, these institutions are not embedded in, or closely monitored by, a domestic society. If U.S. judges were to act as agents of the international order and bypass the political branches with respect to the implementation of international law and decisions, they would only compound the democratic deficit.

A good model for enhancing democratic input is the way in which the United States processes dispute settlement decisions by the World Trade Organization (WTO). The international trade regime, despite its many benefits, is controversial because of its perceived tensions with other values, such as labor and environmental protection, and this controversy is exacerbated by concerns over perceptions about its lack of democratic legitimacy. Congress took account of these concerns in its implementing legislation for the WTO agreements, making clear that WTO dispute settlement decisions must be accepted and implemented by the political

and International Lawmaking: Rules, Rents, and Legitimacy, 17 Nw J Intl L & Bus 681 (1996–97).

[195] See Curtis A. Bradley, _The Costs of International Human Rights Litigation_, 2 Chi J Intl L 457, 465 (2001); McGinnis and Somin, 59 Stan L Rev (cited in note 194).

branches before they are applied by U.S. courts.[196] This requirement has ensured that there is democratic deliberation before WTO decisions result in changes to U.S. law, but at the same time it has not prevented the United States from complying with even the most controversial WTO decisions.

A second benefit of the constitutionalist perspective is that it helps compensate for the lack of horizontal checks and balances at the international level. Because there is no general legislative or executive body on the international plane, international adjudicative institutions (and other international institutions) typically operate without any significant horizontal supervision or feedback (again, the European institutions are a notable exception). While in theory the parties to the treaty establishing the institution could amend the treaty if the institution makes poor decisions, or exceeds its mandate, such amendments may require a supermajority vote or even unanimity among a highly diverse group of states, so this option is likely to provide only a very limited check.

The constitutionalist approach reflected in *Sanchez-Llamas* helps compensate for this problem by allowing for a subvertical check on international decision making. Under this approach, international decisions are still binding on the international plane, and nations will have reputational and other incentives to comply with the decisions. International institutions will not, however, be able to enlist domestic courts directly as their enforcement organs. The implementation of these decisions, rather, will turn in part on their persuasiveness on the relevant legal issues.

The usefulness of this subvertical check is illustrated by the ICJ's decision in *Avena*. The U.S. political branches have repeatedly resisted efforts over the years to have the U.S. death penalty regulated by international law.[197] Nevertheless, through the Vienna Convention cases, the ICJ moved into the sensitive realm of the death penalty, an issue made even more sensitive in the United States by considerations of federalism. Instead of simply determining whether there were breaches of the Convention (something that was not even contested), the ICJ ultimately opined about the ability of foreign nationals to raise claims under the Vienna Convention in U.S. domestic courts, and the relationship of the

---

[196] See Bradley, 55 Stan L Rev at 1594–95 (cited in note 126).
[197] See Bradley, 52 Duke L J at 516–35 (cited in note 118).

Vienna Convention to U.S. domestic procedures. It is unlikely that the United States could have expected these sorts of decisions when it ratified the Vienna Convention's optional protocol in 1969, but, as noted, there is no meaningful horizontal check on the ICJ's compliance with its jurisdictional mandates.[198]

A subvertical check was also useful in *Avena* simply because of the unclear and possibly confused nature of some of the ICJ's reasoning. With respect to the issue of procedural default, there are places in both *LaGrand* and *Avena* in which the ICJ suggests that the application of procedural default rules is problematic only where the failure of authorities to provide the consular notice is itself responsible for the failure of a defendant's lawyer to raise the violation until after conviction.[199] It is not clear how this would occur, however, since lawyers in the U.S. system are on constructive notice of their clients' legal rights, including presumably their Vienna Convention rights. By analogy, if a defendant fails to receive a *Miranda* warning, he is not allowed to raise the *Miranda* violation for the first time in postconviction proceedings on the theory that he and his lawyer were unaware of *Miranda* rights because they were not informed of them by the police. It is possible that the ICJ thought that criminal defendants should not bear the consequences of their lawyers' ignorance or mistakes, but, as the majority noted in *Sanchez-Llamas*, that view would be substantially inconsistent with well-settled features of the U.S. legal system.[200]

In any event, the ICJ never follows up on the idea that a Vienna Convention violation might itself be responsible for a lawyer's failure to raise the violation until after conviction. Rather, it simply concludes without further analysis that the application of procedural default rules in the cases before it violates the treaty, even though in none of those cases was there a showing that the lawyers' failure to raise the claim was caused by the lack of consular notification itself.[201] If the ICJ believed that the application of procedural default rules to bar Vienna Convention claims *inherently* violates the treaty, as its holding (although not its reasoning) sug-

---

[198] For other examples of jurisdictional expansion by international institutions over time, see Bradley, 55 Stan L Rev at 1577 (cited in note 126).

[199] See *LaGrand*, at paras 90–91 (cited in note 16); *Case Concerning Avena*, at para 112 (cited in note 20).

[200] See 126 S Ct at 2686 n 6.

[201] See *Case Concerning Avena*, at paras 113, 134 (cited in note 20).

gests, this would mean that even if a defendant's lawyer purposely avoided raising a Vienna Convention claim at trial, the defendant could raise the claim years later, something not allowed even for constitutional claims, even during the days of the Supreme Court's most expansive approach to habeas corpus.[202]

In his dissent in *Sanchez-Llamas*, Justice Breyer creatively attempted to clarify the ICJ's holding on this issue, suggesting both that a hearing at which the procedural default issue was considered would constitute "review and reconsideration" that would satisfy the ICJ's required remedy, and that procedural default rules could be applied to bar Vienna Convention claims if states allowed defendants to bring an ineffective assistance of counsel claim based on their counsel's failure to raise the Vienna Convention issue in a timely manner.[203] There is no hint of these glosses in *Avena*, however, and they would completely negate the ICJ's procedural default holding. If the procedural default hearing would itself satisfy the ICJ's requirements, then it makes no sense for the ICJ to have ruled that U.S. application of procedural default rules violated the treaty. As for the possibility of raising an ineffective assistance of counsel claim, the ICJ was made aware of that possibility in *LaGrand*, but it did not appear to affect the ICJ's analysis of procedural default.[204] Moreover, if defendants can in fact bring ineffective assistance of counsel claims based on Vienna Convention violations (as might be the case, subject to the usual stringent requirements of the ineffective assistance of counsel doctrine), then, once again under Justice Breyer's logic, the ICJ's finding of a conflict between the Vienna Convention and procedural default rules was erroneous.

It is possible, of course, that the ICJ, which has only one U.S. judge, was simply confused about how procedural default rules worked in the United States, which has both an adversarial system and a federal system of government. This would be entirely understandable given the complex body of domestic law implicated

---

[202] See *Fay v Noia*, 372 US 391 (1963) (allowing denial of habeas corpus relief where there has been "deliberate bypass").

[203] See 126 S Ct at 2699–2700 (Breyer, J, dissenting).

[204] See *LaGrand*, at para 71 (noting Germany's argument that "due to the doctrine of procedural default and the high postconviction threshold for proving ineffective counsel under United States law, Germany's intervention at a stage later than the trial phase could not 'remedy the extreme prejudice created by the counsel appointed to represent the LaGrands'") (cited in note 16).

by that issue. If so, however, this simply confirms the desirability of the domestic filter entailed by the constitutionalist approach.

A third advantage of the constitutionalist approach to international adjudicatory decisions is that it helps ensure that, when international decisions are implemented domestically, they are tailored to take into account local laws and conditions. Domestic legal systems vary substantially, and international adjudicative institutions will not have significant expertise with respect to any one particular system. As noted, this problem is evident in the ICJ's analysis of U.S. procedural default law in *Avena*. This is also an issue for international regulatory decisions, such as those issued by the WTO, which often intersect with complex bodies of federal statutory and administrative law, and sometimes state law as well. Even the ICJ seemed to recognize the value of this function in its pre-*Avena* Vienna Convention decisions, noting in *LaGrand*, for example, that the "choice of means [for implementing the Article 36 obligations] must be left to the United States."

Finally, this local filtering and tailoring will likely make the decisions more acceptable to those who disagree with them. Domestic actors will have a better sense of how international laws and decisions fit within the broader framework of the domestic legal system, and about what is acceptable in their polity. In a federal system like the United States, this includes considerations of what is acceptable at the state and local levels.[205] These considerations are particularly significant for international decisions, because, unlike a domestic court, international adjudicators are not typically able to draw upon a shared experience or culture to enhance acceptance of their decisions.[206] The U.S. Supreme Court, by contrast, does this regularly. To take just one example, consider *Missouri v Holland*, in which the Supreme Court (through Justice Holmes, a veteran of the Civil War) reminds readers that the development of the Constitution initiated by the Founders "has taken a century and has cost their successors much sweat and blood to prove that they created a nation," and then observes that "[t]he

---

[205] See, e.g., Karen Alter, *Resolving or Exacerbating Disputes? The WTO's New Dispute Resolution System*, 79 Intl Affairs 783, 793 (2003) ("Being products of their national political environment, and working within the same cultural and political context in which they adjudicate, national judges are far more likely to be in harmony with political sentiment.").

[206] See Movsesian, *Understanding Sanchez-Llamas* (cited in note 160) (making this point); see also Mark L. Movsesian, *Sovereignty, Compliance, and the World Trade Organization: Lessons from the History of Supreme Court Review*, 20 Mich J Intl L 775 (1999).

case before us must be considered in the light of our whole experience and not merely in that of what was said a hundred years
ago."[207]

C. COUNTERVAILING VALUES

There are two potential countervailing values in this context:
the need for uniformity in the interpretation and application of
international law, and the desirability of enhancing compliance
with international obligations. The dissenters in *Sanchez-Llamas*
emphasized the first value, noting that uniformity was "an important goal of treaty interpretation," and arguing that "the ICJ's
position as an international court specifically charged with the duty
to interpret numerous international treaties (including the Convention) provides a natural point of reference for national courts
seeking that uniformity."[208] This value was also emphasized by the
U.S. Supreme Court in its early decisions in explaining why states
owed more than "respectful consideration" to its decisions. In
Martin v Hunter's Lessee, for example, the Court emphasized the
need for uniformity in explaining why it had appellate jurisdiction
over state court interpretations of federal law:

> Judges of equal learning and integrity, in different states, might
> differently interpret a statute, or a treaty of the United States,
> or even the constitution itself: If there were no revising au-
> thority to control these jarring and discordant judgments, and
> harmonize them into uniformity, the laws, the treaties, and the
> constitution of the United States would be different in different
> states, and might, perhaps, never have precisely the same con-
> struction, obligation, or efficacy, in any two states. The public
> mischiefs that would attend such a state of things would be
> truly deplorable; and it cannot be believed that they could have
> escaped the enlightened convention which formed the consti-
> tution.[209]

This value of uniformity, however, is much weaker in the context
of international adjudication (outside of the European system) than
with respect to a national constitutional court like the Supreme
Court. The fragmented nature of the international adjudicatory

---

[207] 252 US at 433.
[208] 126 S Ct at 2700 (Breyer, J, dissenting).
[209] 14 US (1 Wheat) 304, 348 (1816).

system, and the highly varied nature of the jurisdictional relationships within that system, makes uniformity unlikely under any circumstances. As discussed, the various tribunals can and do differ among themselves, and much of their jurisprudence is formally binding only with respect to particular parties, or is merely advisory. The ICJ's Statute, for example, provides that ICJ decisions have "binding force" only "between the parties and in respect of that particular case."[210]

Although the United States participated in the international adjudicatory decisions at issue in *Sanchez-Llamas*, it is not a party to and does not participate in most of the international adjudicatory decisions that are issued, including most ICJ decisions. If it were bound only by the reasoning in cases in which it participated, this would do little to promote uniformity. On the other hand, it is difficult to see why the United States should be bound by the reasoning in cases litigated between other countries, with different jurisdictional relationships to the institution in question, in which the United States does not even have an opportunity to express its views.[211] Of course, that sort of precedential effect is common with national courts like the U.S. Supreme Court, but, as discussed, there are fundamental differences between most international adjudicatory institutions and the Supreme Court.

In addition to uniformity, it might be argued that the internationalist approach will enhance compliance with international legal obligations. Compliance is a particular concern with international law, given the absence of strong centralized enforcement machinery. If U.S. courts played a more active role in incorporating the output of international institutions, the argument goes, it would enhance the level of compliance with international legal obligations.

One problem with this argument is that it assumes that the output of international institutions will accurately reflect international legal obligations, whereas this is not necessarily the case. It is not obvious, for example, that the ICJ did a better job than the U.S. Supreme Court of interpreting the Vienna Convention.

---

[210] ICJ Statute, Art 59.

[211] The arguments for uniformity may be stronger with respect to the WTO, a centralized and specialized institution with wide membership, compulsory jurisdiction over the members, and repeat players. Even for the WTO, however, Congress has required that adjudicatory decisions be filtered through the U.S. democratic process (see text accompanying note 196).

Nor is it clear that the U.S. judiciary is institutionally better suited than the political branches to evaluate the content of international norms, whether treaty-based or customary. Moreover, often the goal of the internationalist conception is to advance purported goals of the international legal system where compliance is not at stake. This is the case, for example, with arguments in support of broad human rights litigation under the Alien Tort Statute—the United States is not required to provide for that litigation, and, indeed, it is almost unique in the world in doing so.[212]

In addition, since international law almost never requires a particular role for domestic courts,[213] there is no contradiction between the constitutionalist approach and compliance. Under that approach, the political branches simply play the lead role in making compliance decisions. As noted above, this approach has not generally resulted in U.S. noncompliance with WTO obligations. Even with respect to *Avena*, the Executive Branch has attempted to comply with the judgment despite disagreeing with the ICJ's reasoning. Whether the United States complies with Article 36 more generally will depend on a variety of factors beyond whether this article is determined to create judicially enforceable rights (the issue left open in *Sanchez-Llamas*). Those factors include most notably the degree to which the federal government educates and pressures state and local governments to comply—something it has already been doing in recent years, as the ICJ itself has acknowledged.[214]

Of course, one might question whether the political branches will make wise decisions about international law compliance. It is possible, for example, that the political branches will focus too much on short-term or parochial concerns, perhaps because of pressure from special interest groups. This objection, however, sweeps too broadly; taken to it logical extreme, it would suggest that U.S. courts should operate as the ultimate policymakers, a proposition at odds with the basic separation-of-powers structure

---

[212] See Beth Stephens, *Translating Filartiga: A Comparative and International Law Analysis of Domestic Remedies for International Human Rights Violations*, 27 Yale J Intl L 1, 17–18 (2002).

[213] See, e.g., Lori F. Damrosch et al, *International Law: Cases and Materials* 160–61 (4th ed 2001) ("International law requires a state to carry out its international obligations but, in general, how a state accomplishes that result is not of concern to international law or to the state system.").

[214] See *LaGrand*, at paras 121, 123–24 (cited in note 16).

of the Constitution. It is also at odds with various deference doctrines, including the *Chevron* doctrine in administrative law, whereby courts accept Executive Branch legal interpretations on the theory that the Executive is in a better position than the courts to make the relevant policy assessments relating to the interpretations.[215]

In any event, there are significant reasons to question whether the courts are functionally better suited than the political branches to make international compliance decisions. Courts will typically lack much of the relevant information to assess, for example, the likely consequences of noncompliance or undercompliance, or of different forms of compliance, including effects on reciprocity and on international cooperation more generally. Moreover, there is an inherent inconsistency in this call for a greater judicial role in promoting U.S. compliance, since it implicitly assumes that the political branches will make wise decisions concerning international commitments, including commitments giving authority to international institutions, while at the same time questioning their wisdom when it comes to compliance.

Conclusion

International tribunals can often play a useful role in facilitating international cooperation. As these tribunals continue to expand in number and authority, however, it will become increasingly important to understand their proper relationship with domestic courts. Despite the Supreme Court's controversial citation of foreign and international materials in some of its constitutional law decisions, and despite recent academic calls for greater "transnational judicial dialogue," the Court indicated in *Sanchez-Llamas* that it will insist on a certain degree of autonomy from the international legal system. Although the Court took international law seriously, it made clear that international law and decisions will be applied in the United States against the backdrop of the usual constitutional, procedural, and remedial doctrines that govern the domestic legal system. International dialogue has a role under this approach, but it is one whereby national courts act as independent interpreters and filters of international law, rather

---

[215] See Eric A. Posner and Cass Sunstein, *Chevronizing Foreign Relations Law*, 116 Yale L J (forthcoming 2007).

than as agents of the international order. This mediating role for domestic courts is normatively desirable in light of the highly fragmented and diverse nature of the international adjudicative system.

CYNTHIA ESTLUND

HARMONIZING WORK AND CITIZENSHIP: A DUE PROCESS SOLUTION TO A FIRST AMENDMENT PROBLEM

Until recently, public employee free speech cases had settled into a well-worn groove: If the employee suffered adverse action based on speech about a matter of public concern, then the employer had to show that the speech threatened legitimate managerial interests that outweighed the employee's interest in speaking out. Questions remained around the edges: What counts as "speech on matters of public concern"? What sort of employer showing does it take to outweigh the employee's interest in speaking out? How does the employee show that adverse action was motivated or caused by her speech? But the basic formula had become familiar.

   It turns out, however, that the familiar formula had been worked out within only a middling segment of the spectrum of possible First Amendment disputes between public employers and their employees. The Supreme Court's own pronouncements in the area concerned speech that, on the one hand, was related to the job—

Cynthia Estlund is the Catherine A. Rein Professor at the New York University School of Law.

Author's note: I wish to thank Samuel Estreicher, Samuel Issacharoff, Jason Solomon, Geoffrey Stone, and the participants in a faculty workshop at Rutgers School of Law–Newark for their helpful comments, and Jennifer Wagner and Keren Wheeler for excellent research assistance..

it either took place on the job, or was about the job, or both—but, on the other hand, was not actually *part* of the employee's job. In the last two Terms, however, the Supreme Court decided two cases that did not fit that mold, and that may serve as bookends on the Court's public employee free speech jurisprudence. *City of San Diego v Roe*,[1] decided per curiam in late 2004, involved off-duty speech that was not about the job or the employer: A police officer was fired for making and selling on-line pornographic videos starring himself in (and partially out of) a generic police uniform. The second and more important case, *Garcetti v Ceballos*,[2] decided by a bare majority last Term, involved speech uttered as part of the employee's actual job performance: A deputy district attorney claimed that he had suffered reprisals for opining in a memo that an arresting officer had made false statements in a search warrant affidavit. In both decisions the Court reversed pro-employee rulings by the Ninth Circuit.

City of San Diego and *Garcetti* offer an opportunity to reexamine what is at stake in the protection of public employee speech by looking at the problem from both ends of a wide spectrum: What is the appropriate relationship between the spheres of citizenship and of employment? Where does each begin and end? Both *City of San Diego* and *Garcetti* turn on the Court's answers to those questions: Roe lost because the Court deemed his role as employee, and the limited speech protections that go with it, to extend well beyond the job itself. And Ceballos lost because he was deemed to cease acting and speaking "as a citizen" while performing his job.

This article has two aims. The first is to critically assess the conception of the relationship between work and citizenship that is expressed in *City of San Diego* and especially *Garcetti*. Both decisions reflect an overly crimped conception of the public employee's role and liberties "as citizen," both outside the employment relationship and deep within it. In particular, *Garcetti*'s notion that public employees cease acting and speaking as citizens when they are carrying out their job duties reflects an underappreciation of the meaning of work to citizens and the meaning of citizenship to public sector workers.

A richer and more realistic appreciation of the civic significance

---

[1] 543 US 77 (2004) (per curiam).

[2] 126 S Ct 1951 (2006).

of public employment may suffice to show that *Garcetti* reaches the wrong result. But it does not necessarily identify the right result. That brings me to the second aim of this article. For while the *Garcetti* decision is troubling, there is no denying that the *Garcetti* problem is genuinely difficult. None of the alternatives presented to the Court under the First Amendment offered an especially palatable solution to that problem. On the one hand, the Court's resolution denies constitutional protection to employees who bring matters of public concern to light precisely when they are most likely to be well informed and are acting most conscientiously and consistently with their responsibilities. On the other hand, the Ninth Circuit's ruling would have subjected many routine personnel decisions, including many that are based on a straightforward evaluation of job performance, to First Amendment litigation and to potentially costly second-guessing under the *Pickering* balancing test.[3]

I argue here that the best solution to the *Garcetti* dilemma lies not squarely within the First Amendment but within due process jurisprudence. A public employee whose job may require her to speak on matters of public concern should be deemed—as a First Amendment gloss on the employment contract—to have a reasonable expectation that she will not be fired for conscientiously speaking out in the performance of her job. That reasonable expectation would function like a very narrow-gauged form of job security; it should give rise to a hybrid liberty-property interest that should trigger the right to due process of law. So the employee who claims that she was fired for speaking on matters of public concern in the course of doing her job should have the right to a fair hearing—though not necessarily a federal lawsuit—on whether that speech was in fact the basis for her discharge and whether the discharge was nonetheless justified.

The citizen's role as employee should not swallow up as much of her civic and private life as *City of San Diego* would have it. Neither should the employee's role as citizen drop out while she is performing her job as *Garcetti* would have it. But at least when the roles of citizen and employee are intertwined in the particularly nettlesome way that they are in the *Garcetti* scenario, none of the stark alternatives readily available under the First Amendment offers

---

[3] See *Pickering v Board of Education*, 391 US 563 (1968).

a sensible reconciliation of the two roles. The solution may lie instead in the cooler and less contentious environs of procedural due process.

Indeed, once we survey those environs, we may find that due process affords a better solution not only to the *Garcetti* problem but to the larger problem of reconciling the demands of employment and citizenship under the First Amendment. The overlapping roles and the competing demands of citizenship and employment have proved problematic for the Court at least since *Pickering*. When employees claim that they have suffered adverse treatment at work because of their protected speech, the right to bring a federal lawsuit is not obviously the best or most effective way—much less the most efficient and expeditious way—either to vindicate their liberty interests or to protect the public interest in hearing what public employees have to say.

I. SETTING THE STAGE: PUBLIC EMPLOYEE SPEECH RIGHTS BEFORE CITY OF SAN DIEGO AND GARCETTI

For much of the twentieth century, the "rights-privileges" distinction shielded public employers—and employment-at-will in the public sector—from the intrusion of constitutional norms.[4] But that doctrine came under pressure in the 1950s when government began to flex its muscles in its anti-Communist crusade. By the time of *Pickering v Board of Education* in 1968, "'the theory that public employment which may be denied altogether may be subjected to any conditions, regardless of how unreasonable, ha[d] been uniformly rejected.'"[5] *Pickering* brought the First Amendment into the public employment relationship, but it was a scaled-down First Amendment. The Court explained:

> the State has interests as an employer in regulating the speech of its employees that differ significantly from those it possesses in connection with regulation of the speech of the citizenry in general. The problem in any case is to arrive at a balance between the interests of the teacher, as a citizen, in commenting upon matters of public concern and the interest of the State, as an

---

[4] See *McAuliffe v City of New Bedford*, 155 Mass 216, 220 (1892) (Holmes) ("The petitioner may have a constitutional right to talk politics, but he has no constitutional right to be a policeman.").

[5] *Pickering v Board of Education*, 391 US 563, 568 (1968), quoting *Keyishian v Board of Regents*, 385 US 589, 605–06 (1967).

employer, in promoting the efficiency of the public services it performs through its employees.[6]

In ranking public employee speech rights somewhere between the oblivion of the old "rights-privileges" doctrine and the expansive speech protections accorded to "the citizenry in general," *Pickering* guaranteed a steady flow of doctrinal disputes for decades to come. The resolution of those disputes would require an understanding of what was at stake on both sides of the ledger—both in protecting employees' freedom of expression and in preserving public employers' residual managerial freedom. Two questions thus loomed large: Why constrain the government's regulation of its own employees' speech at all? And why allow the government more latitude in regulating its employees' speech than in regulating the speech of citizens generally?

On the latter question, *Pickering* was rather cursory. The government's greater power vis-à-vis its employees was based on "the interest of the State, as an employer, in promoting the efficiency of the public services it performs through its employees." Not much more was said on this matter for several decades. On the former question—why constrain the government's regulation of its own employees' speech at all?—*Pickering* was more forthcoming. The Court suggested two distinct rationales for its foray into the government workplace, one grounded in the intrinsic liberty interests of citizen employees, and one grounded in the instrumental value of public employee speech to public debate. The experience of McCarthy-era repression had taught the dangers of allowing government to leverage its power as employer into control of citizens' speech. Citizens who happen to be employed by the government should be no less free to express themselves than other citizens. But *Pickering* also reflected an appreciation of the *special* contribution that public employees can make to informed public debate.

Both rationales, as well as the nascent tension between them, were on display in *Pickering* itself. Pickering, a teacher, had been fired for writing a letter to the editor criticizing the school board for its allocation of funds between academics and athletics. His letter expressed "a difference of opinion between Pickering and the Board as to the preferable manner of operating the school system, a difference of opinion that clearly concern[ed] an issue of general public

---

[6] Id.

interest."[7] Indeed, the public had a particular interest in hearing Pickering's views as a teacher about the public schools:

> *Teachers are, as a class, the members of a community most likely to have informed and definite opinions as to how funds allotted to the operations of the schools should be spent.* Accordingly, it is essential that they be able to speak out freely on such questions without fear of retaliatory dismissal.[8]

But a few lines later the Court took the opposite tack, portraying Pickering as a citizen who was vulnerable to additional tools of government repression because of the incidental fact of his public employment: "[I]t is . . . perfectly clear that, were appellant a member of the general public," the First Amendment would sharply constrain the state's imposition of civil or criminal sanctions for such speech.[9] Like those sanctions,

> the threat of dismissal from public employment is . . . a potent means of inhibiting speech. . . . [I]n a case such as the present one, in which *the fact of employment is only tangentially and insubstantially involved in the subject matter of the public communication* made by a teacher, we conclude that it is necessary to regard the teacher as the member of the general public he seeks to be.[10]

So was Pickering protected because he was speaking as a teacher with special knowledge of his subject or because he was speaking as a "member of the general public" on matters that were only "tangentially and insubstantially" related to his employment? Was the problem that the government had deprived the public of the valuable voice of a public servant about the government agency he served? or that it had leveraged its power as employer into control of the individual's civic life? Both, it seems, in *Pickering* itself. But in future cases the two lenses deployed in *Pickering* would not always converge clearly on the same result.

Whether we read *Pickering* as ambiguous or contradictory or simply overdetermined, it left many unanswered questions about what kind of employee speech was protected. The next two cases—

---

[7] Id at 571.

[8] Id at 572 (emphasis added).

[9] Id at 573.

[10] Id at 574 (emphasis added).

Perry v Sindermann[11] and *Mt. Healthy Board of Education v Doyle*[12]—paralleled *Pickering*: Public educators had allegedly been punished for speaking to a public audience about the policies of their own educational institutions.[13] But the next major case, *Givhan v Western Line Consolidated School District*,[14] varied the formula: Yet another teacher had complained about school district policies, in this case alleged racial discrimination. And in this case the teacher had spoken not to the public at large but in private meetings with her own principal. That fact, though, was "largely coincidental" and not determinative, according to the Court: "This Court's decisions in *Pickering, Perry*, and *Mt. Healthy* do not support the conclusion that a public employee forfeits his protection against governmental abridgment of freedom of speech if he decides to express his views privately rather than publicly."[15]

Put that way, it is hard to disagree. It would have seemed paradoxical to deny free speech rights to "the public employee who arranges to communicate privately with his employer rather than to spread his views before the public."[16] Yet *Givhan* was actually a hard case under either of the two rationales articulated in *Pickering*. The employee who complains privately to her boss about public concerns cannot claim that she was *merely* exercising her rights as citizen, and that the government was *merely* leveraging its power as employer into control over her civic freedoms. Nor does she make a direct contribution to public debate—unless public debate is understood to go on within as well as outside of government agencies. *Givhan* thus suggests a new rationale for the protection of public employee speech—or a new dimension of the instrumental rationale: The public benefits from dissent and critical discussion within the government's own ranks, for greater accountability and

---

[11] 408 US 593 (1972).

[12] 429 US 274 (1977).

[13] Compare *Madison Joint School District No. 8 v Wisconsin Employment Relations Commission*, 429 US 167 (1976). The state court below had ruled that it was an unfair labor practice for a school board to allow public statements by nonunion teachers on matters subject to collective bargaining; that was a form of bargaining prohibited by the labor statute. The Supreme Court reversed on First Amendment grounds: the school board could not be required or even permitted to bar such statements at a public meeting. For present purposes, the case followed a familiar pattern: Public teachers opining about school-related issues in a public forum enjoy First Amendment protection.

[14] 439 US 410 (1979).

[15] Id at 414.

[16] Id.

reform can come from *within*, and not only by way of public debate and electoral pressure from without.

The Court took the occasion to review and revise its evolving doctrine in *Connick v Myers*,[17] in which a deputy district attorney was fired after circulating among her co-workers a questionnaire about office morale, confidence in supervisors, the office "rumor mill," and other issues affecting the office. In rejecting the claim, *Connick* formalized a new threshold test that the Court found implicit in *Pickering* and its progeny: A public employee enjoyed First Amendment protections, and the government was required to justify its actions, only when the employee spoke "as a citizen . . . on matters of public concern."[18] Moreover, that new protected category of speech on "matters of public concern" did not include speech about "internal office matters."[19]

Beyond the exclusion of most internal workplace grievances, the contours of the new category were sketched by the Court's review of *Pickering* and its progeny, all of which the Court maintained had involved matters of public concern (and all of which involved the policies of the employing agency itself): allocation of school district funds (*Pickering*); elevation of a two-year college to four-year status (*Perry*); a teacher dress code that was linked to public support for bond issues (*Mt. Healthy*); and alleged racial discrimination in the school district (*Givhan*). *Connick* added to the catalog of protected topics one item from Myers's questionnaire about perceived pressure on employees to work on political campaigns. Having previously held that such pressure raised constitutional concerns of its own, the Court would have been hard pressed to hold that it was not a matter of public concern.[20]

Even while cutting back on the scope of public employees' speech protections, *Connick* reinforced all of the extant rationales for those protections. The Court returned to the theme of protecting the basic liberties of citizens from the government's leveraging of its power as employer: "Our responsibility is to ensure that citizens are not deprived of fundamental rights by virtue of working for the government."[21] In justifying the "public concern" threshold, the

---

[17] 461 US 138 (1983).

[18] Id at 142, quoting *Pickering*, 392 US at 568.

[19] 461 US at 149.

[20] See *Branti v Finkle*, 445 US 507, 515–16 (1980); *Elrod v Burns*, 427 US 347 (1976).

[21] *Connick*, 461 US at 147.

Court leaned heavily on the instrumental rationale of enriching and informing public discourse. And in holding that part of Myers's internal office questionnaire was on "matters of public concern," the Court reinforced *Givhan*'s message that public discourse included at least some discourse within the government. While the Court cautioned that "the First Amendment does not require a public office to be run as a roundtable for employee complaints over internal office affairs,"[22] the First Amendment does apparently require employers to tolerate some internal criticism of its own policies when they bear on public concerns. Not much room, to be sure; the "limited First Amendment interest" at stake in the one question about pressure to work on political campaigns did "not require that Connick tolerate action which he reasonably believed would disrupt the office, undermine his authority, and destroy close working relationships."[23]

The next case, *Rankin v McPherson*,[24] added an important new data point: The question was "whether a clerical employee in a county constable's office was properly discharged for remarking, after hearing of an attempt on the life of the President, 'If they go for him again, I hope they get him.'"[25] The answer was no. McPherson's comment, triggered by a sensational news item and coupled with commentary on President Reagan's policies, was inescapably on a "matter of public concern," however crudely expressed. The fact that the comment was made in a private conversation with a co-worker, far from disqualifying the speech from protection, weighed in McPherson's favor at the balancing stage, for it undermined the employer's claim of disruption.[26] In overturning the discharge, the Court explained: "Vigilance is necessary to ensure that public employers do not use authority over employees to silence discourse, not because it hampers public functions but simply because superiors disagree with the content of employees' speech."[27]

Rankin was the first post-*Pickering* case in which the content of

[22] Id.

[23] Id at 154.

[24] 483 US 378 (1987).

[25] Id at 379.

[26] Id at 389. The fact that the employee was designated a "deputy constable" within a law enforcement agency was brushed aside given the actual nature of the employee's job: routine clerical work. Id at 380–81.

[27] Id at 384.

the employee's speech had nothing to do with the employer or its policies (putting aside the constable's feeble effort to link the speech to his agency's law enforcement mission). The speech contributed neither to informed public debate about the government agency nor to debate and accountability within the agency. But neither was the government merely leveraging its power as employer into the control of McPherson's civic life; for the fact of employment was not quite "incidental" to this speech within the workplace. The Court's reference to "silenc[ing] discourse" in this context implies something new and important: a recognition of the value of political discussion within the workplace—informal conversations among co-workers on public issues having nothing to do with their work or their employer—as an aspect of public discourse. The workplace is, after all, where discussion of political and social issues is most likely to take place outside home and family.[28] In the real life of most citizens, most public discourse is workplace discourse.[29]

The issue in the next case, *Waters v Churchill*, was a rather convoluted one involving motive and mistake of fact on which the Court split three ways.[30] But along the way the decision made two important moves. First, the entire Court seemed to agree that a nurse's criticism of a new staff rotation policy that she believed would harm patients—criticism uttered only to co-workers within the hospital—would be speech on a matter of public concern.[31] That apparent consensus fortifies the protected status of internal debate about the agency's own policies; for the employee who is fired for speaking at work about the employer's own policies has neither directly contributed to informed debate among the public at large nor been deprived of her background liberties as a citizen by virtue of the incidental fact of public employment. But she has contributed to

---

[28] See Robert Huckfeldt et al, *Political Environments, Cohesive Social Groups, and the Communication of Public Opinion*, 39 Am J Pol Sci 1025, 1031–32 (1995); Bruce C. Straits, *Bringing Strong Ties Back In: Interpersonal Gateways to Political Information and Influence*, 55 Pub Op Q 432, 446–47 (1991). The importance of these workplace conversations is magnified by the comparative heterogeneity of workplaces; the workplace is where most adults are most likely to have genuine interaction across racial and ethnic lines. See Cynthia Estlund, *Working Together: How Workplace Bonds Strengthen a Diverse Democracy* 7–12 (Oxford, 2003).

[29] Estlund, *Working Together* at 118–24 (cited in note 28).

[30] 511 US 661 (1994). We will return below to *Waters* and the Court's resort to process to resolve a First Amendment problem. See text accompanying notes 145–47.

[31] The plurality is initially tentative, but this conclusion is necessary to the disposition of the case, which is to remand on the question of whether the hospital was actually motivated by protected speech. See *Waters*, 511 US at 681–82.

critical engagement on public issues within the government.

So the Supreme Court's decisions through *Waters* recognize several reasons for injecting the First Amendment into the government workplace: to protect the basic liberties of citizens from the government's leveraging of its additional power as employer; to create space for informal "public discourse" within the workplace on politics and public issues in general; to enrich and inform public discourse about the government's operations and policies; and to foster critical engagement within government agencies about their own public mission. An employee's internal criticism might be a preliminary step toward public criticism; or it might seep out of the office and gain publicity even without the employee's going public. Even if it does not, the citizens who work within government are an especially important subset of the public whose informed views contribute to democratic self-governance. Whether internal dissent and disclosure on matters of public concern is protected because of its potential value to public debate outside the government or because of its value to internal debate and accountability, at least some of it is clearly protected under the Court's precedents.

It was first in *Waters* that the Court gave equal time to the other side of the ledger: Given the multiple interests served by public employees' freedom of speech, why afford them only a diluted version of the First Amendment? We learned in *Pickering* that "the State has interests as an employer in regulating the speech of its employees that differ significantly from those it possesses in connection with regulation of the speech of the citizenry in general,"[32] and that those interests were managerial in nature. But why were mere managerial needs adequate to outweigh fundamental First Amendment rights? Or, as the plurality put it in *Waters*, "[w]hat is it about the government's role as employer that gives it a freer hand in regulating the speech of its employees than it has in regulating the speech of the public at large?"[33]

The answer given in *Waters* is worth quoting at some length:

> [T]he extra power the government has in this area comes from the nature of the government's mission as employer. Government agencies are charged by law with doing particular tasks. Agencies hire employees to help do those tasks as effectively

[32] *Pickering*, 391 US at 568.
[33] *Waters*, 511 US at 671.

and efficiently as possible. When someone who is paid a salary
so that she will contribute to an agency's effective operation
begins to do or say things that detract from the agency's effective operation, the government employer must have some
power to restrain her. . . .

The key to First Amendment analysis of government employment decisions, then, is this: The government's interest in
achieving its goals as effectively and efficiently as possible is elevated from a relatively subordinate interest when it acts as sovereign to a significant one when it acts as employer. The government cannot restrict the speech of the public at large just in
the name of efficiency. But where the government is employing
someone for the very purpose of effectively achieving its goals,
such restrictions may well be appropriate.[34]

A government agency has the power to condition public employment on the sacrifice of freedom of expression that detracts from
"an agency's effective operation" because employees are hired precisely to contribute to the "agency's effective operation"; those
speech limitations are built into the contract of employment. *Waters*
is the Court's most coherent account of why the First Amendment
takes a smaller bite out of the government's power as employer
than it takes out of the government's power as sovereign. In explaining *why* the government has greater power to restrict its employees' speech, *Waters* provides further guidance as to the scope
of that power—guidance to which we will shortly return.[35]

But first we must fold in two more decisions, neither of which
fits the standard *Pickering-Connick* mold of individual disciplinary
decisions allegedly motivated by the employee's speech. *United
States Civil Service Commission v National Association of Letter Carriers
(Letter Carriers)*[36] and *United States v National Treasury Employees
Union (NTEU)*[37] both involved broad federal statutory restrictions
on employees' off-duty speech that had nothing to do with the
employees' job or agency. It was unclear whether *Pickering-Connick*
even applied in that context. As the Court observed in *NTEU*, and
could have said in *Letter Carriers* as well,

[u]nlike *Pickering* and its progeny, this case does not involve a

---

[34] Id at 674–75.

[35] See text between notes 54–55.

[36] 413 US 548 (1973).

[37] 513 US 454 (1995).

post hoc analysis of one employee's speech and its impact on that employee's public responsibilities. Rather the Government asks us to apply *Pickering* to Congress' wholesale deterrent to a broad category of expression by a massive number of potential speakers.[38]

This might lead one to surmise that both restrictions would be struck down. But that surmise would be only half right.

Letter Carriers upheld the Hatch Act's ban on partisan political activity by federal civil service employees. Congress's assumption in 1939 was that if employees were *allowed* to engage in partisan political activity, they could be *coerced* to do so and could be selected on that basis. In the heyday of rights-privileges, there was no doubt either that officials could lawfully discriminate against employees on the basis of partisan activity (absent legislation), or that Congress could lawfully address the problem by restricting employees' political activities. By 1973, however, one might have thought that the constitutionally appropriate way to prevent employers' political coercion and discrimination against public employees was to prohibit employers' coercion and discrimination rather than to prohibit employees' political activity.[39] But *Letter Carriers* deferred to Congress's judgment of 1939, depriving thousands of federal employees of the right to participate in political advocacy at the core of self-government.[40] *Letter Carriers* is a bit of a throwback—perhaps too early in the post-*Pickering* era to take full cognizance of the First Amendment interests of public employees. It also reflects the unusual deference accorded Congress and its elaborate civil service regime for federal employees. But that deference has its limits, as we saw in *NTEU*.

The Court in *NTEU* struck down a broad congressional ban on federal employees' acceptance of honoraria for making speeches or

---

[38] Id at 466–67.

[39] Indeed, one might have thought that the First Amendment itself prohibited discrimination against public employees on the basis of their political affiliation. And so held the Court a few years later in *Elrod v Burns*, 427 US 347 (1976), which effectively banned patronage-based personnel decisions in state and local government. The civil service laws had already done that in the federal government, and would seem to have largely obviated—in a speech-friendly way—the problem that the Hatch Act was meant to solve.

[40] Fortunately for them, Congress itself had a change of heart, and sharply cut back on the Hatch Act restrictions in 1993. The law now restricts only political activity that uses government property (offices, vehicles) or uniforms or otherwise risks being associated with the government. 5 USC § 7324 (2000). Those remaining restrictions seem uncontroversially valid under the principles of *Pickering-Connick*.

writing articles, regardless of the topic. The ban implicated the most basic and venerable rationale for imposing First Amendment constraints on government employers: The government had leveraged its power as employer, reached beyond the workplace nexus into the employees' lives as citizens, and restricted speech that was related to the employment only incidentally, if at all. In striking down the ban, the Court deployed the familiar *Pickering-Connick* terminology but seemed to unsettle its meaning. The ambiguity in the *NTEU* decision is encapsulated in two sentences:

> Respondents' expressive activities in this case fall within the protected category of citizen comment on matters of public concern rather than employee comment on matters related to personal status in the workplace. The speeches and articles for which they received compensation in the past were addressed to a public audience, were made outside the workplace, and involved content largely unrelated to their government employment.[41]

On one reading, *NTEU* simply applied *Pickering-Connick* to the broad-gauged ban on honoraria: Having found that all of the speech at issue was on matters of public concern, the Court cast a burden of justification on the government that it could not meet, given that, with few exceptions, the employees' speeches did not "even arguably have any adverse impact on the efficiency of the offices in which they work."[42] That reading is hard to credit, however, for the honorarium ban reached utterances on an almost infinite array of topics united only by the fact they were "largely unrelated to [the speakers'] government employment."[43] *NTEU* is thus hard to read as simply finding that all of the speech covered by the honorarium ban happened to "fall within the protected category of citizen comment on matters of public concern."

NTEU may instead have recast the *Pickering-Connick* mold by redefining the category of speech on "matters of public concern." Focusing on the first sentence quoted above, *NTEU* might define speech on "matters of public concern" to include all speech other than "employee comment on matters related to personal status in the workplace." Or, focusing on the second sentence, *NTEU* might define the category to include all speech "addressed to a public

---

[41] *NTEU*, 513 US at 466.

[42] Id at 464.

[43] Id at 466.

audience, . . . made outside the workplace, and involv[ing] content largely unrelated to their government employment." Either interpretation would afford broader protection for public employee speech that is outside the workplace nexus.

The difficulty of reconciling *NTEU* with *Pickering-Connick* highlights the fact that the Court's ordinary public employee speech cases—those reviewing individual adverse personnel actions—occupy only part of the spectrum of possible cases. All involved speech that was work related in one way or another: The employing agency was either the subject of the speech (*Pickering, Perry, Mt. Healthy*), the site of the speech (*Rankin*), or both (*Givhan, Connick,* and *Waters*). It was perhaps self-evident that speech that is either at work or about the employing agency would have *some* effect either within the workforce or on public perceptions of the agency. Those are the cases for which *Connick* prescribed a threshold public concern test that employees must meet in order to trigger a balancing of interests between the employer and employee. But *NTEU* put in doubt whether that same test applies to off-duty speech that is not about the work or the employer—where there is no nexus to the employment; in particular, are public employees' First Amendment rights in that context still confined to speech on matters of public concern? And what about speech at the other end of the spectrum of work-relatedness—speech that not only is uttered on the job and is *about* the employee's job but is *part* of his job?

That brings us to the two recent cases, *City of San Diego v Roe*,[44] decided per curiam early in the 2004 Term, and *Garcetti v Ceballos*,[45] decided by a split Court late in the 2005 Term. Among the Court's public employee speech cases, *City of San Diego* represents the furthest a government employer has reached *outside* of the workplace to discipline an employee for expressive activity, while *Garcetti* represents the furthest the Court has been asked to reach *inside* the employment relationship to protect an employee from sanctions based upon speech.

---

[44] 543 US 77 (2004) (per curiam).

[45] 126 S Ct 1951 (2006).

II. City of San Diego and Off-Duty Speech That Is "Unrelated to the Employment"

Roe was a San Diego police officer. His troubles began, as the Supreme Court tells the tale, when he

> made a video showing himself stripping off a police uniform and masturbating. He sold the video on the adults-only section of eBay, the popular online auction site. His user name was Codestud3@aol.com, a word play on a high priority police radio call. The uniform apparently was not the specific uniform worn by the San Diego police, but it was clearly identifiable as a police uniform.[46]

Roe's supervisor discovered the video while on eBay, and reported it to higher-ups. The department set up a sting operation in which Roe agreed to produce a custom video for an undercover police officer that "showed Roe, again in police uniform, issuing a traffic citation but revoking it after undoing the uniform and masturbating."[47] Roe's supervisors confronted him and ordered him to "cease displaying, manufacturing, distributing or selling any sexually explicit materials or engaging in any similar behaviors," online or otherwise.[48] He failed to comply fully and was fired. He sued, claiming the discharge violated his First Amendment rights.

The district court dismissed the suit, holding that none of his activities constituted expression on matters of public concern. The Ninth Circuit reversed. The court noted that

> [a]ll aspects of the production and sale of the videotapes were conducted while Roe was off-duty and away from his employer's premises and did not involve the use of any City or Department resources. . . . He never listed himself by name in any listing, and he never identified himself as a San Diego Police officer. . . . There is no evidence that Code3stud's real identity was ever discovered by anyone other than [his supervisor] and the other police officers involved in the investigation.[49]

The court recognized that it was faced with a novel twist on the

---

[46] 543 US at 78. Roe also sold custom videos and police equipment online. Id.

[47] Id at 79.

[48] Id, quoting *Roe v City of San Diego*, 356 F3d 1108, 1111 (9th Cir 2004).

[49] *Roe v City of San Diego*, 356 F3d 1108, 1110–11 (9th Cir 2004).

Pickering-Connick scenario, one involving "off-duty, non-work-re-lated speech."[50]

For guidance the court of appeals turned to *NTEU*, the ambiguities of which it resolved neatly if not uncontroversially:

> The Court concluded that the plaintiffs' "expressive activities . . . fall within the protected category of citizen comment on matters of public concern rather than employee comment on matters related to personal status in the workplace," *because* "[t]he speeches and articles for which [the plaintiffs] received compensation in the past were addressed to a public audience, were made outside the workplace, and involved content largely unrelated to their government employment."[51]

The court's addition of "because" between two declarative sentences is crucial; it reads *NTEU* as categorically *defining* all off-duty, non-work-related speech to a public audience as "speech on matters of public concern" rather than as independently *determining* (and requiring courts in future cases to determine) that the speech at issue was on matters of public concern. Having thus designated Roe's expression as speech on matters of public concern, the panel majority remanded the case for further proceedings under the balancing test. The Supreme Court's grant of certiorari preempted those further proceedings.

The Court's per curiam opinion began by recasting the meaning of *NTEU*:

> The Court has recognized the *right of employees to speak on matters of public concern*, typically matters concerning government policies that are of interest to the public at large, a subject on which public employees are uniquely qualified to comment. [citing *Connick* and *Pickering*] *Outside of this category*, the Court has held that when government employees speak or write on their own time on topics unrelated to their employment, the speech can have First Amendment protection, absent some governmental justification "far stronger than mere speculation" in regulating it [citing *NTEU*].[52]

Having thus separated its prior cases into two distinct categories,

---

[50] Id at 1112.

[51] Id at 1118 (emphasis added) (citing *NTEU*, 513 US at 466).

[52] *City of San Diego*, 543 US at 80 (emphasis added).

the Court proceeded to analyze Roe's speech under each line of cases.

So *City of San Diego* tells us that *NTEU* neither follows nor reconstructs *Pickering-Connick*; rather, it creates an alternative avenue of protection for public employees.[53] Employees who "speak or write on their own time on topics unrelated to their own employment" are not subject to the *Pickering-Connick* test at all. They enjoy both broader and stronger speech rights than those who speak at or about work. This may not be the full-fledged First Amendment that protects the citizens at large—the Court in *NTEU* reaffirmed *Letter Carriers* while distinguishing it[54]—but it is close.

In effect, *City of San Diego* and *NTEU* require the public *employer* to meet a threshold test in order to get the benefit of *Pickering-Connick*: Only if the speech had some nexus to the employment must the employee show that her speech is on a matter of public concern. This is important good news for public employees. *NTEU*, as read in *City of San Diego*, stakes out a large zone of liberty for citizens employed by the government: The government employer rarely has any business regulating off-duty, non-work-related speech, period. One assumes, of course, that public employers don't often make it their business to uncover and punish off-duty speech that has no effect on their operations. But it is now clearer than it was that the First Amendment stands guard against their doing so.

The super-protections of *NTEU* are in keeping with the Court's explanation in *Waters* of the government's greater power to regulate its employees' speech, which stems from the employer's need to pursue its mission through its employees. Where employee speech has no nexus to the job and no impact on the employer's operations, the justification for the government's broader power to suppress employees' speech simply runs out. This conclusion also resonates with the most basic goal of public employee speech protections: Absent some nexus between speech and employment, the government is simply using its power as employer to suppress the speech of citizens who happen to be its employees. At that point, something like the full force of the First Amendment, and not the narrower

---

[53] See id (describing NTEU's protections as stemming from a separate "line of cases" from *Pickering-Connick*); id at 82 (accord). The structure of *City of San Diego* confirms this. Only after determining that Roe's speech was not "unrelated to the employment" within the meaning of NTEU does the Court pose the standard threshold question under *Connick* whether the speech was on matters of public concern.

[54] *NTEU*, 513 US at 467.

and weaker protections of *Pickering-Connick*, govern. That much seems clear after *City of San Diego*.

But these few sentences of good news for employees are followed by several pages of bad news. First, the Court took an expansive view of the speech that is "related to the employment" and therefore subject to the middling protections of *Pickering-Connick*: "Far from confining his activities to speech unrelated to his employment, Roe took deliberate steps to link his videos and other wares to his police work, all in a way injurious to his employer."[55] How so, given that there was no discernible link to his employer, the San Diego Police Department? According to the Court, the generic law enforcement uniform and "the debased parody of an officer performing indecent acts while in the course of official duties brought the mission of the employer and the professionalism of its officers into serious disrepute."[56] The extension of the employer's legitimate interests to the general "mission" that it shares with thousands of law enforcement agencies across the country is troubling.[57] It allows public employers to punish some off-duty speech that is ideologically obnoxious to them even without any impact on or link to its particular operations. It remains to be seen, however, whether the requisite impact on employment will be as readily found in the case of off-duty speech less repugnant to judges than Roe's videos, or in the case of employment less exalted in its mission than law enforcement. But it now appears that employees fall outside the super-protections of *NTEU* not only if they speak at work or about the employer or its policies, but also if their speech is otherwise deemed to be detrimental to the employer or its mission.

Since Roe's speech was "related to the employment," *Pickering-Connick* applied. The first (and last) question was whether Roe's

---

[55] *City of San Diego*, 543 US at 81.

[56] Id.

[57] It is arguably in tension with *Rankin*, in which the Court brushed aside Constable Rankin's claim that his deputy's rash wish for the assassination of the President undermined the agency's law enforcement mission. There is no direct conflict between the cases, however. First, Roe was an actual police officer, not a clerical employee; that might have changed the result in *Rankin*. More importantly, the employers' claims of harm to the mission of law enforcement were put to different uses in the two cases. In *Rankin* that claimed harm failed to outweigh the employee's interest in speaking on a matter of public concern. The San Diego Police Department's similar claim of harm sufficed only to take the case out of *NTEU* and into the more employer-friendly analysis of *Pickering-Connick*; had Roe's speech been deemed to be of public concern, the tenuous harm to the employer's "law enforcement mission" might still have been insufficient justification for punishing Roe.

off-duty pornographic videos qualified as speech on matters of public concern. The Ninth Circuit had held that they did, reasoning that the category included "almost *any* matter other than speech that relates to internal power struggles within the workplace."[58] Recall from *Connick*: "We hold only that when a public employee speaks not as a citizen upon matters of public concern, but instead as an employee upon matters only of personal interest," no further review was called for.[59] The Ninth Circuit had drawn the inference that the former included all but the latter, and therefore included Roe's speech. The Supreme Court disagreed, and held that Roe's speech "does not qualify as a matter of public concern under any view of the public concern test."[60] So *City of San Diego* became the first of the Court's public employee speech cases to exclude from the category of matters of public concern speech that had no link to internal workplace grievances.

The Court went on to redescribe the public concern test in potentially restrictive terms: "[P]ublic concern is something that is a subject of legitimate news interest; that is, a subject of general interest and of value and concern to the public at the time of publication."[61] If this means that courts are to inquire into the *actual* interest of the general public "at the time of publication," it is in tension with earlier formulations of the public concern requirement, which seemed to ask whether members of the general public *would* or *should* be interested in the employee's speech if they knew of it.[62] The narrower reading would make for very bad First Amendment policy; for surely if public employees have something special to contribute to public debate—and the Court has repeatedly recognized that they do—it lies partly in their perception of problems

---

[58] *Roe v City of San Diego*, 356 F3d 1108, 1117 (9th Cir 2004), quoting *Tucker v California Department of Education*, 97 F3d 1204 (9th Cir 1996). In its view, the point of *Connick*'s threshold test was simply to avoid entangling courts in the innumerable employment disputes that arise out of mundane personnel disputes and grievances. The court had sought to mitigate the genuine perils of the public concern test by converting it from a protected category that the employee has to get her speech into, to a residual category that the employee has to avoid falling out of. See Cynthia Estlund, *Speech on Matters of Public Concern: The Perils of an Emerging First Amendment Category*, 59 Geo Wash L Rev 1 (1990).

[59] *Connick*, 461 US at 147.

[60] *City of San Diego*, 543 US at 84.

[61] Id at 83–84; the Court added, almost as an afterthought, "certain private remarks, such as negative comments about the President of the United States." Id at 84.

[62] See *NTEU*, 513 US at 466; *Waters v Churchill*, 511 US at 681–82; *Connick*, 461 US at 149; *Givhan*, 439 US 410, 414 (1979); *Pickering*, 391 US 563, 572 (1968).

within the government *before* the public becomes aware of them. But unless we are to conclude that the Court reversed one or more of its prior decisions silently and per curiam, we must read this formulation from *City of San Diego* broadly enough to include the entire catalog of matters of public concern identified in those decisions, not all of which were featured in the press or in actual public debate "at the time of publication."

In sum, *City of San Diego* proves to be an important case along several dimensions—too important, one might add, to be packed into a terse per curiam decision without full briefing and oral argument. Behind the doctrinal twists and turns, there lies a conception of the relationship between the public employee's job—which limits her speech rights—and her freedom as an individual and a citizen. That conception has both encouraging and troubling aspects, and I will return to it in Part IV below.

III. Garcetti and Speech-That-Is-the-Job

Whereas *City of San Diego* concerned speech at the outer reach of the employment nexus, *Garcetti* was about speech at its very center: speech that is part of the job itself.[63] *Garcetti* is much more important in practice than *City of San Diego*, if only because employers are far more likely to punish employees for speech that is part of their job than for speech that is off duty and unrelated to the job. The *Garcetti* issue hits home especially for those who pay attention to the Court: Nearly everyone who read the decision (and nearly everyone who reads this article) performs his or her job largely through verbal expression—in legal briefs, memos, or articles, in courtrooms or in classrooms.[64] Perhaps partly for that reason, the case attracted more attention than the usual public employee speech case.

While supervising a prosecution, Richard Ceballos, a deputy district attorney in Los Angeles County, California, was told by a defense attorney that there were inaccuracies in a search warrant affidavit. Ceballos investigated, and concluded that the affidavit "contained serious misrepresentations."[65] He consulted with his su-

---

[63] 126 S Ct 1951 (2006).

[64] Of course most of us are employed in the private sector (where the First Amendment does not reach); and some of us have tenure (which is the best kind of speech protection there is).

[65] Id at 1955.

pervisors, and then wrote a memo on his findings and recommended dismissal of the case. Following a meeting with members of the sheriff's department, Ceballos's supervisors decided to proceed with the case pending disposition of a defense motion challenging the search warrant. After a hearing on the motion, at which Ceballos testified under a defense subpoena, the motion was denied and the prosecution proceeded. Ceballos alleged that he then suffered various reprisals, including a demotion and the denial of a promotion. Ceballos sued, claiming that his First Amendment rights had been violated.

The bone of contention in the case was whether the First Amendment applies at all to speech that is uttered "pursuant to the employee's official duties."[66] Under Ninth Circuit precedent, that fact did not deprive Ceballos of First Amendment protection. In such cases the court must discern "the point of the speech in question: was it . . . to bring wrongdoing to light? Or to raise other issues of public concern, because they are of public concern? Or was the point to further some purely private interest?"[67] Because Ceballos, in disclosing police misconduct and possible perjury, was clearly acting to bring alleged wrongdoing to light, Judge Reinhardt for the panel majority applied *Pickering-Connick*: Ceballos's speech was "inherently a matter of public concern";[68] and the defendants could not meet their burden under the balancing test because "they offer[ed] no explanation as to how Ceballos' [speech] resulted in inefficiency or office disruption."[69] Ceballos was simply doing his job. Indeed, "[i]t is difficult to imagine how the performance of one's duties in this manner could be disruptive or inefficient—much less how any such 'disruption' or 'inefficiency' could outweigh the public's interest in the exposure of corrupt or unlawful practices in the Sheriff's Department."[70] So Ceballos's speech was protected, and the retaliation unlawful.

Judge O'Scannlain, in a special concurrence, deferred to circuit precedent but took the opportunity to lambast that precedent, which

---

[66] Id.

[67] *Ceballos v Garcetti*, 361 F3d 1168, 1174 (9th Cir 2004) (internal quotation marks omitted), quoting *Roth v Veteran's Administration of United States*, 856 F2d 1401, 1406 (9th Cir 1988).

[68] Id at 1174.

[69] Id at 1179.

[70] Id at 1180.

he believed "entirely ignored . . . *Connick*'s distinction between speech offered by a public employee acting *as an employee* in carrying out his or her ordinary employment duties and speech spoken by an employee acting *as a citizen* expressing his or her personal views on disputed matters of public import."[71] Indeed, "when public employees speak in the course of carrying out their routine, required employment obligations, they have no personal interest in the content of that speech that gives rise to a First Amendment right. Instead, their speech is, in actuality, the State's."[72] That was highlighted in this case by Ceballos's belief that he was *obligated* as a prosecuting attorney to reveal to the defense his doubts about the affidavit.

The Supreme Court took up the case, and heard arguments in the first week of the 2005 Term, and then again several months later—apparently to allow the newly confirmed Justice Alito to break a tie. At that point, the writing seemed to be on the wall. And, indeed, the Court eventually split 5–4 in favor of the employer, with Justice Alito in the majority.

Justice Kennedy, for the majority, began by reviewing the Court's precedents, which "have sought both to promote the individual and societal interests that are served when employees speak as citizens on matters of public concern and to respect the needs of government employers attempting to perform their important public functions."[73] Under those precedents, Ceballos did not lose protection because his memo "concerned the subject matter of [his] employment," for that was true in several cases, starting with *Pickering*, in which the Court had emphasized the instrumental value of public employee speech to public debate.[74] Nor did Ceballos lose protection because he spoke "inside his office"; *Givhan* had established that.[75] Moreover, "[m]any citizens do much of their talking inside their respective workplaces, and it would not serve the goal of treating public employees like 'any member of the general public,' to hold that all speech within the office is automatically exposed to restriction."[76] With this last sentence the Court both affirmed the

---

[71] Id at 1186–87 (O'Scannlain specially concurring) (emphasis in original).

[72] Id at 1189.

[73] *Garcetti v Ceballos*, 126 S Ct 1951, 1959 (2006).

[74] Id at 1959–60.

[75] Id at 1959.

[76] Id, quoting *Pickering*, 391 US at 573.

importance of workplace speech for citizens and planted the seeds of its suppression. The phrase, "any member of the general public," is from *Pickering*, in which the Court had observed that the school district's interest in limiting "teachers' opportunities to contribute to public debate [was] not significantly greater than its interest in limiting a similar contribution by any member of the general public."[77] In *Garcetti* that became "the goal of treating public employees like 'any member of the general public.'" A theme was in the making.

Ceballos lost neither because he spoke at work nor because he spoke about work, but because he spoke as part of his work: "his expressions were made pursuant to his duties as a calendar deputy"; he "spoke as a prosecutor fulfilling a responsibility to advise his supervisor about how best to proceed with a pending case."[78] The bottom line: "We hold that when public employees make statements pursuant to their official duties, the employees are not speaking as citizens for First Amendment purposes, and the Constitution does not insulate their communications from employer discipline."[79]

To be sure, the language on which the majority relied to delimit First Amendment protections—"the interests of the [employee], as a citizen, in commenting upon matters of public concern"—had been there all along. This clause from *Pickering* was repeated in every one of the Court's public employee speech decisions. But this was the first time that the phrase "as a citizen" was given independent significance. In *Connick*, in which this language was elaborated, the focus was on the content and purpose of the speech. Before *Garcetti*, it was fair to assume that an employee spoke "as a citizen" whenever she spoke on matters of public concern. But *Garcetti* held otherwise: "Ceballos did not act as a citizen when he went about conducting his daily professional activities, such as supervising attorneys, investigating charges, and preparing filings. . . . When he went to work and performed the tasks he was paid to perform, Ceballos acted as a government employee."[80] In explaining why Ceballos did not speak "as a citizen" when he expressed doubts about the police affidavit, the majority recurred to the theme of treating the employee like "any member of the general public":

---

[77] *Pickering*, 391 US at 573.

[78] Id at 1960.

[79] Id.

[80] *Garcetti*, 126 S Ct at 1960.

"Restricting speech that owes its existence to a public employee's professional responsibilities does not infringe *any liberties the employee might have enjoyed as a private citizen*. It simply reflects the exercise of employer control over what the employer itself has commissioned or created."[81]

Having thus downgraded the free speech interests at stake in the case, the majority turned to the other side of the ledger. In the ordinary *Pickering-Connick* case, the interests of the government employer are weighed against the employees' interest in speaking out. But in the case of "speech made by an employee in his or her professional capacity,"[82] the government's interests categorically trump the employees' interests: "Supervisors must ensure that their employees' official communications are accurate, demonstrate sound judgment, and promote the employer's mission."[83] For example, in Ceballos's case, if "[his] superiors thought his memo was inflammatory or misguided, they had the authority to take proper corrective action."[84] And they apparently must be empowered to do so without the prospect of judicial oversight. For the contrary rule "would commit state and federal courts to a new, permanent, and intrusive role, mandating judicial oversight of communications between and among government employees and their superiors in the course of official business."[85] Lest the reader assume that mere efficiency was at stake, the majority explained that such oversight would be "inconsistent with sound principles of federalism and separation of powers."[86]

The result was to give employees greater protection when they go public with their concerns than when they confine themselves to the internal channels prescribed by the employer. The majority sought to dispel the apparent anomaly, and the perverse incentive this seems to create for the employee. As for the practical problem, the government employer can avoid it if it chooses: "Giving employees an internal forum for their speech will discourage them from concluding that the safest avenue of expression is to state their

---

[81] Id (emphasis added).

[82] Id.

[83] Id.

[84] Id at 1960–61.

[85] Id at 1961.

[86] Id.

views in public."[87] But if an anomaly remained, it was inherent in "the theoretical underpinnings of our decisions,"[88] which again are grounded in preserving the baseline expressive freedoms of ordinary citizens: "Employees who make public statements outside the course of performing their official duties retain some possibility of First Amendment protection because that is *the kind of activity engaged in by citizens who do not work for the government*."[89] And speaking on matters of public concern in the course of performing one's job is not the kind of activity engaged in by private sector employees? Of course it is, as hundreds of private sector whistle-blower and public policy cases attest.[90] But we are getting ahead of ourselves.

Two major issues were left for the future. First, because the parties agreed that Ceballos's memo was written "pursuant to his employment duties," the majority declined "to articulate a comprehensive framework for defining the scope of an employee's duties in cases where there is room for serious debate."[91] In response, however, to the concern that employers would respond to the decision by writing very broad job descriptions, the majority did note that "the listing of a given task in an employee's written job description is neither necessary nor sufficient to demonstrate that conducting the task is within the scope of the employee's professional duties for First Amendment purposes."[92] Second, responding to the dissent as well as numerous *amici*, the majority reserved for the future the question of whether "expression related to academic scholarship or classroom instruction implicates additional constitutional interests" in academic freedom that call for a different rule.[93]

In closing, the majority acknowledged that "[e]xposing governmental inefficiency and misconduct is a matter of considerable significance," and that "public employers should, 'as a matter of good judgment,' be 'receptive to constructive criticism offered by their

---

[87] Id.

[88] Id.

[89] Id (emphasis added).

[90] See, for example, *White v General Motors Corp.*, 908 F2d 669 (10th Cir 1990); *Garibaldi v Lucky Food Stores, Inc.*, 726 F2d 1367 (9th Cir 1984); *Wieder v Skala*, 609 NE2d 105 (NY 1992); *Hayes v Eateries, Inc.*, 905 P2d 778 (Okla 1995); *Ellis v City of Seattle*, 13 P3d 1065 (Wash 2001). See generally Marion G. Crain, Pauline T. Kim, and Michael Selmi, *Work Law: Cases and Materials* 178–219 (2005).

[91] *Garcetti*, 126 S Ct at 1961.

[92] Id at 1962.

[93] Id.

employees.'"[94] Moreover, those "dictates of sound judgment are reinforced" by whistle-blower protection laws, labor laws, and professional codes of conduct, and other laws that afford recourse to employees who expose wrongdoing.[95]

> We reject, however, the notion that the First Amendment shields from discipline the expressions employees make pursuant to their professional duties. Our precedents do not support the existence of a constitutional cause of action behind every statement a public employee makes in the course of doing his or her job.[96]

There were three opinions from the four dissenting Justices. All four dissenters took as their point of departure that, as Justice Stevens put it, "public employees are still citizens while they are in the office,"[97] and that the categorical exclusion of speech-that-is-the-job was unwarranted. At the same time, all four acknowledged that the case of speech-that-is-the-job raised distinct concerns that called for some tweaking of the *Pickering-Connick* formula. Justice Souter, for himself and Justices Stevens and Ginsburg, would afford protection in that case only if the employee "speaks on a matter of unusual importance"—for example, "official dishonesty, deliberately unconstitutional action, other serious wrongdoing, or threats to health and safety"—and "satisfies high standards of responsibility in the way he does it."[98] Justice Breyer would narrow the scope of protection even further to cases in which the employee was both professionally and constitutionally obligated to speak.[99] Even after raising the hurdle for protection, however, all of the dissenters would have protected Ceballos in the case at hand.

All nine Justices were thus in agreement on at least two key points: First, some of the speech left unprotected by *Garcetti* is valuable to public debate. Second, protecting that speech under the ordinary *Pickering-Connick* balancing test intrudes too deeply into the ability of government managers to direct and evaluate the employees through whom they pursue their mission. The Court divided not over the value of the speech but over whether the individual had

[94] Id, quoting *Connick*, 461 US at 149.

[95] Id.

[96] Id.

[97] Id at 1963 (Stevens dissenting).

[98] Id at 1967 (Souter dissenting).

[99] Id at 1974 (Breyer dissenting).

the right sort of interest in the speech in question to trigger constitutional protections at all, and to justify any intrusion into managerial prerogatives in dealing with that speech. For the majority,
the answer was no; it was therefore content to rely on responsible
government employers and wise legislatures to protect and encourage that speech for its instrumental value. For the dissenters,
the answer was yes, leading them to seek some way of protecting
some of that speech without unduly constraining conscientious
managers.

IV. Charting the Overlapping Domains of Employment and Citizenship

With *Garcetti* and *City of San Diego*, the Supreme Court has
marked out three segments of the spectrum of potential speech-
related disputes between public employees and employers, with the
domain of citizenship and personal liberty extending from one end
of the spectrum, the domain of employment from the other, and a
large overlap in the middle. Clearly an employee does not cease to
be a citizen or to enjoy First Amendment rights upon entering the
workplace, or when speaking about workplace issues, nor even necessarily in the conjunction of those two circumstances. Several of
the Court's decisions—*Givhan*, *Connick*, and *Waters*—affirm the
First Amendment's application to some "internal whistle-blowing"
that both takes place at work among co-workers and supervisors
and is about policies or practices within the employing agency itself.
Indeed, in the entire run of Supreme Court cases decided under
Pickering-Connick, in which the speech was either at work or related
to the work, the employee occupied both roles simultaneously: The
plaintiff was acting both as a citizen (thereby entitled to free speech
rights) and in some sense as an employee (thereby entitled to a less
fulsome version of those rights).

But while the domains of citizenship and employment overlap,
they are clearly not coextensive. *NTEU* and *City of San Diego* together appear to establish an outer boundary to the government's
power as employer over its employees—a boundary beyond which
the individual is a citizen *simpliciter*, and enjoys First Amendment
protections whether or not she is speaking on matters of public
concern.[100] *City of San Diego* locates that boundary further away

---

[100] To be sure, the Court is a bit coy about what protections apply to *NTEU*'s category

from the workplace than one might have expected; still, the existence of the boundary is important for citizens who are employed by the government. The oldest and most deeply rooted rationale for injecting the First Amendment into the public sector workplace is the need to shield citizens who happen to be employed by the government from the additional repressive powers that the government could exercise in its capacity as employer. The further the government reaches outside the workplace, the more it appears to be leveraging its power as employer into a repressive regulatory role. *NTEU*, as read in *City of San Diego*, essentially pulls out the first of *Pickering*'s justificatory threads—the preservation of citizens' basic freedoms from the added coercive power the government can wield as employer—and weaves an extra-protective cloak out of it for speech that takes place outside the workplace and is unrelated to work.[101]

The question is what happens as we move along the spectrum toward speech that is related to the work, and eventually to speech-that-is-the-work: Clearly the government's interests as employer become stronger. But does the employee's interest as citizen also weaken, and even run out? *Garcetti* holds that it does. *Garcetti* establishes a boundary to the domain of citizenship and of individual freedom, past which the individual is an employee *simpliciter*. When the employee is acting pursuant to her job duties, she doffs her hat as citizen altogether and loses even the intermediate protections of *Pickering-Connick*. Of course, *Connick* itself establishes such a domain—a "free-fire zone," if you will—by holding that speech that is work related but not on matters of public concern, such as speech on purely personal job-related grievances, is entirely unprotected by the First Amendment. The Court in *Garcetti* expanded that "free-fire zone" to include even speech on matters of public concern

---

of speech that is "unrelated to the employment." *City of San Diego*, 543 US at 80. The Court says that regulating such speech requires a "governmental justification 'far stronger than mere speculation.'" Id, quoting *NTEU*, 513 US at 465, 475 (1995). One should hope so. The Court also makes it clear that this speech is more protected than *Pickering-Connick* speech. But it does not say that "full-strength" First Amendment protections apply. So while I refer to the "super-protections" of *NTEU*, I cannot say exactly what those protections are.

[101] As noted above, one may also think of this end of the spectrum in terms of the basic rationale articulated in *Waters* for allowing the government greater power as employer to regulate the speech of its employees: Only when speech is related to the citizen's government employment and has a potential impact on the mission of the employing agency is there any basis for diluting the First Amendment restrictions on the government's power to regulate speech. *Waters v Churchill*, 511 US at 674–75.

where it is part of the employee's job performance. Can that boundary be justified?

Let us be clear: There is no particular virtue or logic to symmetry here. Nothing in the boundedness of the government's power as employer over citizen employees militates for the boundedness of individuals' role or rights as citizens. On the contrary, the very solicitude for freedom of expression that is manifest in *NTEU* weighs against enlarging the government's "free-fire zone" to include all speech-that-is-the-job. The needs of the government employer, while they shape and limit the public employee's speech rights, do not have the same constitutional significance and do not demand the same solicitude as those speech rights.[102] So if the public employees' rights and role "as citizen" run out at some point in the employment relationship, it must be for reasons other than doctrinal symmetry.

A. AN ILLUSORY BASELINE: THE "LIBERTIES THE EMPLOYEE MIGHT HAVE ENJOYED AS A PRIVATE CITIZEN"

To be sure, the further courts are asked to reach *inside* the employment relationship, the more the employee becomes subject to the heightened interests of the government in controlling the speech of the employees through whom it seeks to serve the public. But *Garcetti* purports to rest not primarily on the weight of those managerial interests but rather on the quality of the employee's interest in speech: "Restricting speech that owes its existence to a public employee's professional responsibilities does not infringe any liberties the employee might have enjoyed as a private citizen."[103] This formulation is part of a recurring motif in the *Garcetti* majority opinion: the effort to anchor the free speech rights of public employees to the "liberties the employee might have enjoyed as a private citizen." To this same end, the majority constructed a new "goal of treating public employees like 'any member of the general public,'"[104] and put considerable weight on whether

---

[102] Invocation of "sound principles of federalism and the separation of powers" in support of minimizing judicial intervention, see *Garcetti*, 126 S Ct at 1961, does not alter this conclusion. Those principles could be invoked in support of nearly any refusal to enforce individual rights against the government; they function as little more than make-weight for the denial of the rights claim.

[103] Id at 1960.

[104] Id at 1959, quoting *Pickering v Board of Education*, 591 US 563, 573 (1968).

Ceballos's speech was or wasn't "the kind of activity engaged in by citizens who do not work for the government."[105] According to *Garcetti*, the intrinsic liberty interests of the employee—her interest in speaking "as a citizen"—begin and end with the "liberties the employee might have enjoyed as a private citizen."

This recurring motif seems to gesture toward an ambitious doctrinal undertaking: replacing a collection of individual and instrumental interests behind the protection of public employees' speech with a conceptually coherent baseline of "liberties the employee might have enjoyed as a private citizen." The First Amendment is to be called upon only to prevent the government from using its power as employer to diminish the employee's background liberties, not to expand those liberties beyond what the individual would have enjoyed absent government employment. "Our responsibility is to ensure that citizens are not deprived of fundamental rights by virtue of working for the government."[106] The use of this baseline effectively elevates one rationale for protecting speech—the fear that the government is "leverag[ing] the employment relationship to restrict, incidentally or intentionally, the liberties employees enjoy in their capacities as private citizens"[107]—to preeminence. And that is what is missing in *Garcetti*, according to the majority: The public employer is not "leveraging" the employment relationship when it is merely dictating how the job is to be done. And if the government is not leveraging its power but merely exercising its normal and necessary power as employer, then it does not infringe any intrinsic liberty interest of the employee-citizen.

Tethering public employee speech rights to the "liberties the employee might have enjoyed as a private citizen" seems to submerge the instrumental value of those rights, and the special role of public employees in enriching and informing civic discourse and maintaining governmental accountability. But the majority suggested that this latter goal required no special safeguards: "Refusing to recognize First Amendment claims based on government employees' work product does not prevent them from participating in public debate," nor from seeking "constitutional protection

---

[105] Id at 1961.
[106] Id at 1958, quoting *Connick*, 461 US at 147.
[107] Id.

for their contributions to the civic discourse."[108] According to the majority, both the individual and the public interests at stake are sufficiently protected as long as public employees are no less free than ordinary citizens to contribute to public debate.

The aim for parity with the rights of ordinary citizens pointed in the right direction (though not far enough) in *City of San Diego*: The speech of public employees that is "unrelated to the employment"—that is neither at work nor about the work—should be basically as free from government restrictions as the same speech by any other citizen. So far, so good. But at least for speech that is work related—that is, for nearly the entire run of public employee speech cases from *Pickering* to *Garcetti*—this simple idea quickly collapses into incoherence. The problem is that there are two sharply contrasting ways to conceptualize "the goal of treating public employees like 'any member of the general public'": We could seek parity with either the rights of ordinary citizens as against the government or with the rights of ordinary citizens against their own employers—their rights "as citizens" or their rights at work. Neither offers a viable approach to public employee speech rights under the First Amendment.

On the other hand, we might treat public employees like "any member of the general public" by giving them the free speech rights that ordinary citizens have as against adverse government action. That approach would generate much stronger and broader First Amendment rights than now exist. The problem lies not with the speech that is off-duty and "unrelated to the employment," for which *NTEU* indeed prescribes more or less full-strength free speech protections. But for speech that is related to work, we would presumably be seeking to mimic the First Amendment treatment of adverse government action against an ordinary citizen for something she said at her private sector workplace or about her private employer or as part of her job. Nearly all such speech would be protected against government action (whether or not it was of public concern). If that were our reference point, the plaintiffs in *Connick* and in *Garcetti* itself would have prevailed, because the First Amendment obviously would protect private sector employees in their position from being punished by the state because of their speech. It is thus perfectly clear that this is not what the

---

[108] Id at 1960.

majority meant to propose by its reference to the rights of ordinary citizens.

So perhaps the majority meant to treat public employees like "any member of the general public" by giving them the same free speech rights against their (public) employer as ordinary private sector employees have against their (private) employer. A hint that this is what the majority had in mind lies in its observation that "[g]overnment employers, like private employers, need a significant degree of control over their employees' words and actions."[109] The problem is that most private employers can exercise almost unlimited "control over their employees' words and actions" if they choose to, for ordinary private sector employees—those who are terminable at will, as most are—enjoy very little freedom of speech as against their employer. They have no federal constitutional speech rights and only a sprinkling of nonconstitutional speech rights, most of which vary from state to state.[110]

So if the majority means to remind us that a private sector employee could typically be fired for speech-that-is-the-job of which his employer disapproved, we should remember that most private sector employees could also have been fired for the speech at issue in *Pickering, Mt. Healthy, Rankin,* and even *NTEU*. To anchor the free speech rights of public employees to those of private sector employees vis-à-vis their employers would require wholesale reversal of the Court's public employee speech jurisprudence. Incidentally but ironically, that might include *Connick*: a private sector Myers could *not* lawfully have been fired for her questionnaire about workplace grievances, for the single broadest charter of free speech rights in the private sector workplace, the National Labor Relations Act, protects "concerted activity for mutual aid or protection" of employees; and that would include Myers's questionnaire.[111] In the main, however, to give public employers the power to censor and punish employee speech that private employers have as to at-will employees would take us back to the heyday of the "rights-privileges" distinction and virtually

---

[109] Id at 1958.

[110] See generally Cynthia Estlund, *What Do Workers Want? Employee Interests, Public Interests, and Freedom of Expression under the National Labor Relations Act*, 140 U Pa L Rev 921, 927–33 (1992).

[111] See National Labor Relations Act § 7, 29 USC § 157 (2000). On the ironic reversal of priorities under the First Amendment and the NLRA, see Estlund, 140 U Pa L Rev (cited in note 110).

wipe out public employee speech rights. That also cannot be what the majority meant to suggest.

We might come a bit closer to the mark—closer to the contours of existing public employee speech doctrine, that is—if we gave public employers the power to restrict their employees' speech that private employers have in a "for cause" setting. That seems an odd analogy to choose, as it is the exceptional private employee who enjoys that protection. But it does line up rather nicely with pre-*Garcetti* case law: A "for cause" standard would give employers virtually no power to control speech that is off-duty and unrelated to the job (like *NTEU*); greater but still restricted power to control speech that is at work or otherwise "related to the employment" (like *Pickering-Connick*); and even greater *but still restricted* power to control speech-that-is-the-job. Therein lies the rub: The discharge of a for-cause employee, even where it is based on speech-that-is-the-job, must be justified. That is precisely what *Garcetti* refuses to require. So that cannot be what the majority had in mind in referring to the "liberties the employee might have enjoyed as a private citizen"—though perhaps that is what it should have had in mind. And perhaps, as I will suggest later, this analogy provides a way out of the conundrum presented by these cases.

In any event, the goal of preserving the "liberties the employee might have enjoyed as a private citizen" can mean neither the liberties of ordinary private citizens vis-à-vis the government nor, by analogy, the liberties of ordinary private citizens vis-à-vis their private employer. But what else can it mean? It does not help to ask whether the speech in question is "the kind of activity engaged in by citizens who do not work for the government."[112] Citizens who do not work for the government not only write letters to the editor, speak at public meetings, and converse with their co-workers about politics, as the *Garcetti* majority assumed; they also speak out about organizational misconduct and expose threats to the public welfare, health, and safety, sometimes pursuant to their job duties. Do they do the latter while on the public payroll? Of course not; but that begs the question. Do they do so in their capacity as citizens? That, again, is the very question on which we are seeking traction; it does not answer itself. Do they enjoy the rights and liberties of citizens when they do so? That depends again on

---

[112] *Garcetti*, 126 S Ct at 1961.

whether we mean their rights as against their employer (in which case they might not, but then neither do they have the right to speak at a public meeting free from reprisals) or their rights as against government interference (in which case they almost certainly do, but that seems beside the point).

When we scratch the surface of the majority's recurring references to the "liberties the employee might have enjoyed as a private citizen," they appear to be less an aid to analysis than a rhetorical trope. The incoherence of that trope is manifest in one sentence from *Garcetti*: In acknowledging that some speech that takes place at work is protected, the majority says: "Many citizens do much of their talking inside their respective workplaces, and it would not serve the goal of treating public employees like 'any member of the general public,' to hold that all speech within the office is automatically exposed to restriction."[113] But of course, under employment at will, most citizens *can* be freely fired for most of the talking that they do inside their respective workplaces. So in one sense it *would* "serve the goal of treating public employees like 'any member of the general public'" to allow them to be fired for speech at the workplace; but at the same time it would *not* serve that goal to allow the *government* to restrict their workplace speech.

Perhaps I have overestimated the majority's ambitions; these references may be meant not to orient our general approach to public employee speech but only our approach to the *Garcetti* problem: With regard to speech that is part of one's job, the private citizen typically has no claim of liberty vis-à-vis her employer; therefore, Ceballos has none either.[114] This tells us only that, for this case, the majority chooses to empower the public employer by adopting the analogy of private sector employment at will. It tells us precisely nothing about *why* the majority chooses that analogy in this case but not in others.

---

[113] Id at 1959, quoting *Pickering*, 591 US at 573.

[114] Of course, the private sector employee might enjoy a common law or statutory right to speak up as a whistle-blower, even as to speech that is part of his job. On that score, too, the *Garcetti* majority's ruling does follow this analogy by noting that some on-the-job speech might have similar nonconstitutional protections. Id at 1962.

B. THE MEANING OF WORK TO CITIZENS AND THE MEANING OF
   CITIZENSHIP TO PUBLIC EMPLOYEES

So we are back to the drawing board: Does it make sense to put public employee speech-that-is-the-job outside the scope of the employee's role "as citizen"? The *Garcetti* majority does not really question the instrumental value of Ceballos' speech, and of much speech-that-is-the-job, to public discourse and to the political accountability of the government agency, or to critical engagement and discourse within the agency. The question is whether the individual has the right sort of interest of her own—"as a citizen"—in freedom of expression. The majority disparages the employee's interest in the freedom of speech-that-is-the-job as an interest in "personal gratification" and "job satisfaction."[115] But one could equally describe an employee's interest in speaking outside the workplace on topics unrelated to the work as an interest in "personal gratification." The question in either case is whether the speech is within the employee's liberties "as a citizen"; the majority's rhetorical swipe, like its more elaborate trope of the "liberties the employee might have enjoyed as a private citizen,"[116] begs that question.

Those who choose to become public employees may do so out of a variety of motives, but those motives commonly include a commitment to public service.[117] And public employers recruit employees on precisely this basis, as Justice Souter observed in his dissent: "Not to put too fine a point on it, the Human Resources Division of the L.A. County District Attorney's Office, Ceballos's employer, is telling anyone who will listen that its work 'provides the personal satisfaction and fulfillment that comes with knowing you are contributing essential services to the citizens of Los Angeles County.'"[118] Becoming a public servant effectively

---

[115] Id at 1960.

[116] Id.

[117] See *Garcetti*, 126 S Ct at 1966 (Souter dissenting); *Ceballos v Garcetti*, 361 F3d 1168, 1175 n 5 (9th Cir 2004).

[118] *Garcetti*, 126 S Ct at 1966 n 4 (Souter dissenting), citing Career Opportunities, http://da.co.la.ca.us/hr/default.htm. Justice Souter underscored the point in a lengthy footnote:

The United States expresses the same interest in identifying the individual ideals of a citizen with its employees' obligations to the Government. See Brief as *Amicus Curiae* 25 (stating that public employees are motivated to perform their duties "to serve the public"). Right now, for example, the U.S. Food and Drug Administration is appealing to physicians, scientists, and statisticians to work in the Center for

extends one's civic identity into the work that one does. Of course, it is not only through public sector work that one might work for the greater good. But it is a defining feature and a major draw of many government jobs that they afford the satisfaction of serving the public. The work these employees do for the public through their job may be a truer (and certainly a more frequent) expression of their character and self-conception as citizens than their rare letters to the editor or statements at public meetings.

The public employee who speaks out against perceived misconduct in the course of serving the public is a citizen *par excellence*. To say that the employee who speaks up is merely doing her job fails to reckon with the pressures that keep most employees silent in the face of misconduct—pressures that may now include the fear of discharge.[119] It is one thing to say that an employee's job requires her to speak up when she observes misconduct; it is quite another to compel an employee to observe the misconduct, to label it as such, and to step forward instead of looking the other way. Indeed, to say that the employee who speaks up against misconduct, *and is then fired for doing so,* was merely doing her job is not merely paradoxical but absurd. (Of course the employee might simply have been doing her job badly; but *Garcetti* makes that difference constitutionally irrelevant.) And the absurdity points to

---

Drug Evaluation and Research, with the message that they "can give back to [their] community, state, and country by making a difference in the lives of Americans everywhere." Career Opportunities at CDER: You Can Make a Difference, http://www.fda.gov/cder/career/default.htm. Indeed, the Congress of the United States, by concurrent resolution, has previously expressly endorsed respect for a citizen's obligations as the prime responsibility of Government employees: "Any person in Government Service should: . . . [p]ut loyalty to the highest moral principles and to country above loyalty to persons, party, or Government department," and shall "[e]xpose corruption wherever discovered," Code of Ethics for Government Service, H. Con. Res. 175, 85th Cong., 2d Sess., 72 Stat. B12. Display of this Code in Government buildings was once required by law, 94 Stat. 855; this obligation has been repealed, Office of Government Ethics Authorization Act of 1996, Pub. L. 104–179, §4, 110 Stat. 1566.

Id.

[119] It is no wonder that most employees who observe wrongdoing at work remain silent, for many of those who do blow the whistle on their employers report abuse by supervisors, ostracism by co-workers, and attacks on their competence, as well as discharge or other adverse employment actions, with consequences ranging from depression, severe anxiety, forced relocations, marital stress, and other health consequences. See Clyde H. Farnsworth, *Survey of Whistle Blowers Finds Retaliation but Few Regrets,* NY Times A22 (Feb 22, 1987); Marcia P. Miceli and Janet P. Near, *Blowing the Whistle: The Organization and Legal Implications for Companies and Employees* 79–80 (Lexington, 1992); Alan F. Westin, *Conclusion: What Can and Should Be Done to Protect Whistle Blowers in Industry,* in Alan F. Westin et al, eds, *Whistle-Blowing: Loyalty and Dissent in the Corporation* 132–33 (McGraw-Hill, 1981).

the fact that internal employee whistle-blowing and dissent often emerge from a deeply personal sense of civic and moral obligation, not just the dutiful performance of the job one is paid for.

The point may find support in the *Garcetti* scenario itself (or an imagined version of it). Suppose, for example, that Ceballos was one of a few Latino district attorneys in Los Angeles County; that the L.A. police were widely believed among the Latino minority to be biased against Latinos; and that Ceballos believed that the police affidavit in question reflected that bias. In that scenario, it is clear that Ceballos's statement of that belief would be as much an act of civic and moral responsibility as any letter to the editor. Far more than most letters to the editor, Ceballos risked defying his superiors, and perhaps his co-workers, as well as police department colleagues. The fact that he was also professionally obligated to speak up once having reached the conclusion that he did should not negate the civic character of the expression.

Under the Court's decision in *Garcetti*, all of these matters—the truth and reasoned nature of the speech, the employee's motives for speaking, the pressures that operate on the employee—are irrelevant. That is because, according to the Court, speech uttered by the employee as part of the job is not deemed to be his speech at all but that of the government; the government itself must speak through the employee and must have the right to control that speech.[120] The argument does have a potent logic where the government hires an employee to propagate a particular message or communicate specified information. An employee who is hired as public spokesperson for an agency and who proceeds to use her briefings to criticize the agency, or one who is hired to inform callers of emergency plans and instead rails against FEMA, should not be able to call upon the First Amendment to

---

[120] As the majority puts it:

> Restricting speech that owes its existence to a public employee's professional responsibilities does not infringe any liberties the employee might have enjoyed as a private citizen. It simply reflects the exercise of employer control over what the employer itself has commissioned or created. *Cf. Rosenberger v. Rector and Visitors of Univ. of Va.*, 515 US 819, 833 (1995) ("[W]hen the government appropriates public funds to promote a particular policy of its own it is entitled to say what it wishes.").

Garcetti, 126 S Ct at 1960. Judge O'Scannlain put the point more pungently: "[W]hen public employees speak in the course of carrying out their routine, required employment obligations, . . . their speech is, in actuality, the State's." *Ceballos v Garcetti*, 361 F3d 1168, 1189 (9th Cir 2004) (O'Scannlain, CJ, specially concurring).

contest resulting disciplinary action. Employees in such cases—even where their errant speech was undoubtedly on matters of public concern—arguably should not even be able to haul the government into court to defend disciplinary actions. *Garcetti*'s categorical rule insures that result. But of course *Garcetti*'s rule goes much further.

Garcetti's argument that the government "has commissioned," and essentially owns, the speech by which employees perform their jobs runs into difficulty when the job requires the exercise and expression of judgment and discretion by the employee—and especially when it requires the exercise of professional judgment as in Ceballos's case. In the case of an attorney or other professional, the employment relationship has built into it *both* some limitations on the speech-that-is-the-job *and* the requirement that the employee exercise professional judgment and discretion. But it is obviously not only members of the traditional learned professions who are expected, even required, to exercise and to express their judgment as part of their job. Nonprofessional employees may be hired as internal auditors or ombudsmen. Other employees may be encouraged as part of their job to offer suggestions or articulate concerns about the agency's operations. Many employees may find that part of their job is to speak up, disclose information, express critical judgments. They inevitably bring their civic and moral selves to that job.

So it seems deeply problematic to place the speech that fulfills those job duties beyond the reach of constitutional protection even when it is on matters of public concern and advances the public's interest in both information about and critical engagement within government agencies. But what kind of problem is it? If the problem is that employees are being encouraged or required to speak up as part of their job and then are punished for doing so, then it sounds as much like a breach of contract—the defeat of reasonable expectations grounded in the employment relationship—as an infringement of freedom of expression. Before pursuing this line of thought, let us examine the final and perhaps most potent argument for the narrow view adopted in *Garcetti*: securing the floodgates against the torrent of litigation, and the attendant burdens on government management, that would supposedly ensue if the broad view were adopted.

C. THE COST OF PROTECTING SPEECH-THAT-IS-THE-JOB: TOO MUCH
   LITIGATION, TOO MUCH INTRUSION INTO MANAGERIAL
   DISCRETION

The entire Court agreed on the instrumental value of much of
the speech at issue in *Garcetti*. The Court split over the nature of
the public employee's interest in speech-that-is-the-job. But underlying that split is a sharp division over the cost of protecting
that speech. Judge O'Scannlain put the matter in characteristically
strong terms: Under the Ninth Circuit approach, "what federal
or state employment-based decision can possibly evade intrusive
federal constitutional review?"[121] The Supreme Court majority in
Garcetti upped the ante: Protecting this speech would require "permanent judicial intervention in the conduct of governmental operations to a degree inconsistent with sound principles of federalism and the separation of powers."[122] But what this comes down
to is the familiar two-headed bogeyman that haunts the law of
wrongful discharge in both public and private employment: Opening the floodgates of litigation and accordingly constricting managerial discretion.

The "floodgates" argument has been trotted out often enough
to warrant a skeptical reception. Still, it is neither implausible nor
irrelevant. Many public employees perform their jobs primarily
through speech, and much of that speech presumably bears on
matters of public concern (to the extent it bears on what the agency
does for the public). Moreover, employees are probably penalized
more often for speech that is part of their job performance than
for "extracurricular" speech, whether it takes place at work or
outside of work. If all that is true, then under the Ninth Circuit
rule reversed in *Garcetti* a great many adverse personnel actions
based on how the employee performed the job would give rise to
a colorable First Amendment claim: they would cross the *Connick*
threshold and would then be subject to the balancing test. Government employers might win many of those cases at the balancing
stage, but the factual disputes and judgment calls that are necessary
within the balancing test will often require costly and protracted

---

[121] *Ceballos*, 361 F3d at 1190 (O'Scannlain specially concurring).
[122] *Garcetti*, 126 S Ct at 1961.

litigation (or sizable settlements under the threat of such litigation).[123]

Whether the resulting burdens of litigation and constraints on managerial discretion justify *Garcetti*'s categorical exclusion of claims based on speech-that-is-the-job depends largely on the importance of the speech that would thereby be left unprotected— how important for the employee citizen as well as for the public. But it should depend as well on whether there are other less burdensome ways to protect that speech than by applying the standard *Pickering-Connick* template. Let us consider an alternative approach.

V. A Due Process Solution to a First Amendment Problem

A version of the *Garcetti* problem arises in the private sector as well as in the public sector: An employee is fired for "blowing the whistle" on misconduct within the firm. If the misconduct implicates serious public policy concerns, most states now recognize a tort action for wrongful discharge in violation of public policy (and many afford statutory protection in some cases).[124] But those employees who blow the whistle to higher-ups inside the firm as part of their jobs have had mixed success under that doctrine.[125] The unfairness in firing an employee for doing what she was required to do seems to call for some remedy—some easing of the harsh mandate of employment at will. But courts have hes-

---

[123] Justice Souter in dissent contends that the "floodgates" argument is overstated in light of experience:

> First Amendment protection [for speech-that-is-the-job] has been available in the Ninth Circuit for over 17 years, and neither there nor in other Circuits that accept claims like this one has there been a debilitating flood of litigation. There has indeed been some: as represented by Ceballos's lawyer at oral argument, each year over the last five years, approximately 70 cases in the different Courts of Appeals and approximately 100 in the various District Courts.

126 S Ct at 1968 (citing Transcript of Oral Argument 58–59). But it is hard to know what that means in terms of lawsuits filed and settlements reached under the shadow of litigation.

[124] For a brief overview of state whistle-blower protections, see Elletta S. Callahan and Terry M. Dworkin, *The State of State Whistleblower Protection*, 38 Am Bus L J 99 (2000).

[125] According to one recent review of the common law cases, while many courts will protect "internal whistle-blowers," "[t]he general rule maintains that the whistleblowing employee must complain to outside government officials or law enforcement personnel in order to trigger the public policy exception." Frank J. Cavico, *Private Sector Whistleblowing and the Employment-at-Will Doctrine: A Comparative Legal, Ethical, and Pragmatic Analysis*, 45 S Tex L Rev 543, 601 (2004). See also Frank J. Cavico, *Employment at Will and Public Policy*, 25 Akron L Rev 497, 522 (1992).

itated. Internal whistle-blowing that is required by the employer may be seen as benefiting the employer and not the public. Moreover, internal whistle-blowing is presumably far more common that external whistle-blowing; protecting it might therefore produce both much more litigation and a greater intrusion into managerial prerogatives than protecting external whistle-blowing.

Some courts and commentators have addressed the problem by recasting it in contractual terms: Where an employee is hired to perform certain job duties, such as monitoring product safety or legal compliance, the implied covenant of good faith and fair dealing gives rise to an implied promise not to fire the employee (who may otherwise be terminable at will) based on the conscientious performance of those job duties.[126] The contractual solution extends common law protection to some internal whistle-blowers; but it is more closely tied to the employee's reasonable expectations and the employer's definition of the job, and it generates less fearsome liabilities than the tort remedy.

The *Garcetti* problem closely parallels the private sector problem of internal whistle-blowing; and a parallel solution to the problem may lie not squarely within free speech doctrine but in the quasi-contractual protections of due process. The Due Process Clause affords constitutional protection of employees' reasonable expectations regarding their job security. Employees whose jobs require the exercise and expression of judgment and discretion on matters of public concern should be deemed to enjoy a reasonable expectation that they will not be penalized for expressing that judgment and discretion in a responsible manner. That reasonable expectation should be implied into the employment contract as a matter of First Amendment policy, and should be protected against deprivation without due process of law: an administrative hearing on whether the employee was indeed subject to reprisals for speech on matters of public concern that was part of the conscientious performance of the job.

As compared to the judicial remedy rejected in *Garcetti*, the due process approach to "speech-that-is-the job" would lower the tem-

---

[126] See, e.g., *Wieder v Skala*, 609 NE2d 105 (NY 1992) (recognizing such a claim in the limited context of attorneys employed by law firms). Under the current draft of the new Restatement of Employment Law, it is a breach of the implied covenant of good faith and fair dealing to terminate employment "in order to . . . retaliate against the employee for performing the employee's obligations under the employment contract." *Draft Restatement (Third) of Employment Law* § 3.06.

perature and the stakes in these disputes; it would afford reasonable protection to employees' freedom of speech in this context while defusing both the impact of the law on employer discretion and the threat of proliferating litigation—concerns that were clearly operating in *Garcetti*. Before exploring further the virtues of the due process approach to the *Garcetti* problem, however, let us consider whether there is a plausible doctrinal path to that result within due process jurisprudence.

Public employees who have a "property interest" in continued employment cannot be deprived of that interest without "due process of law."[127] One has a "property interest" in employment if there are substantive constraints on the government's discretion to terminate employment. The constraints on employer discretion may be found in a statute or regulations, a written contract, an employee handbook or statement of employer policy, or other "mutually explicit understandings" about continued employment.[128] The typical public employee due process claim rests on an express assurance that the employee can only be fired "for good cause" or for some specified set of reasons such as misconduct and unsatisfactory performance. A for-cause employee who claims that he was fired without adequate cause has the right to pretermination notice of reasons and an informal opportunity to respond, and a full posttermination hearing before an impartial decision maker at which the employee may contest the decision.[129] If the employee prevails at the hearing, she is entitled to something approximating make-whole relief, such as back pay and reinstatement;[130] if she

---

[127] See *Board of Regents v Roth*, 408 US 564 (1972); *Perry v Sinderman*, 408 US 593 (1972). The typical dispute arises out of termination of employment, and that is my model here. But an employee may also have a property interest, and therefore due process rights, in freedom from disciplinary action, demotion, or the like as well.

[128] *Perry*, 408 US at 601.

[129] See *Cleveland Board of Education v Loudermill*, 470 US 532 (1985).

[130] It would, of course, hardly protect a property interest in continued employment to hold a hearing at which no cause is found for termination, but then to neither restore the job nor compensate for its loss. *Loudermill* thus assumes that a decision in the employee's favor at the requisite pre- or posttermination hearing will result in retention or restoration of employment. Id at 544–45. See also *Baird v Board of Educ.*, 389 F3d 685, 692–93 (7th Cir 2004) (property interest in employment entails right to pursue reinstatement remedy); *Archuleta v Colorado Dep't of Institutions*, 936 F2d 483, 491 (10th Cir 1991) (due process serves to "protect[] the plaintiff against arbitrary state action by restoring to her the property that was taken," e.g., by reinstatement). That some such remedy must be available to the employee who has a property interest in her job and who prevails at a due process hearing is implicit in the logic of due process, the purpose of which is to protect against "mistaken or unjustified deprivation" of protected liberty or property interests, *Carey v*

does not prevail, she may be entitled to some form of judicial review (though not a de novo trial).[131]

For the for-cause employee, then, the *Garcetti* problem already has a due process solution: If the employee is found to have been fired for doing his job properly, and for speaking up as the job required, he will prevail in the "good cause" hearing, and gain reinstatement and back pay. The employee's interest, as well as the public's interest in the employee's freedom to speak, is protected indirectly through job security and due process.[132] The *Garcetti* problem remains, however, for public employees who are terminable at will—as to whom there are no substantive constraints on the reasons for discharge. Those employees have no property interest in continued employment and therefore no right to due process in case of termination.[133]

But what about the due process rights of employees whose expectations regarding job security fall in between "for cause" and employment at will? A government employer might generally reserve the right to discharge at will and without cause, and yet rule out certain reasons for discharge. One might contend that any substantive limitation on the employer's discretion—even a single impermissible reason for discharge—should give rise to a limited property interest and a right to a hearing for the employee who claims to have been fired for the excluded reason. So, for example, if a public employer promises employees they will not be fired on the basis of their family status, and then allegedly does just that, the fired employee might be deemed to have a sufficient property

---

Piphus, 435 US 247, 259–60 (1978), and in the standard remedy for a due process violation under Section 1983: If the employee shows that a due process hearing, had it been held, would have found no cause for dismissal, the normal remedy is at least back pay and reinstatement (or a compensatory substitute). Id at 255.

[131] There is considerable uncertainty whether due process in this context requires access to judicial review of the merits of an administrative just cause determination. See Richard H. Fallon, Jr., *Some Confusions About Due Process, Judicial Review, and Constitutional Remedies*, 93 Colum L Rev 309, 335 & n 148 (1993). In *Loudermill*, the Supreme Court's one square consideration of what process is due in connection with the discharge of an employee with a property interest in continued employment, the Court required only a very informal pretermination "hearing" in that case, in part because the state's posttermination process included judicial review. 470 US at 545–46.

[132] As it often is. See Cynthia Estlund, *Free Speech and Due Process in the Workplace*, 71 Ind L J 101 (1995).

[133] Note, however, that if the government, in the course of termination, makes public charges that stigmatize the employee and damage his prospects for future employment, that implicates a "liberty interest" that triggers the right to a hearing to clear his name (but not to recover his job). See text accompanying notes 140–41.

interest in continued employment to entitle him to due process: a hearing on whether he was fired on the basis of family status, and a remedy if he was.

That reasoning suggests the makings of a due process solution to the *Garcetti* problem: When the government employer directs or encourages employees, as part of their job, to exercise and express their judgment or to disclose wrongdoing on matters of public concern, it implicitly promises them that they will not be subject to reprisals for doing so in a conscientious manner (even if they may otherwise be terminable at will). Or rather, we should imply such a promise as a First Amendment gloss on the contract—in the service of First Amendment values and the acknowledged public interest in the employee's speaking up. That implied contractual limitation on employer discretion should give rise to a limited property interest in employment and a right under the Due Process Clause to an impartial hearing if the employee claims to have been fired in breach of the implied assurance—that is, for speaking on matters of public concern as part of the conscientious performance of job duties assigned by the employer. A fair hearing does not of course mean a judicial hearing or a federal lawsuit. If the state provides a reasonable opportunity for a fair adversarial hearing on the relevant dispute before an impartial decision maker—through civil service laws or contractual grievance procedures or a whistle-blower protection law, for example—then the employee has gotten all that the Constitution guarantees her.

One difficulty is that the cases do not directly support the notion that a property interest arises solely from the prohibition of particular reasons for discharge. While the case law on this issue is sketchy, it suggests that a property interest in employment arises only if the substantive limitations on discharge are roughly equivalent to a "for cause" requirement.[134] A property interest might

---

[134] Clearly the paradigm case involves a "for cause" requirement. See *Logan v Zimmerman Brush Co.*, 455 US 422, 430 (1982) ("The hallmark of property, the Court has emphasized, is an individual entitlement grounded in state law, which cannot be removed except 'for cause'"). See also *Loudermill v Cleveland Board of Education*, 470 US 532, 538–39 (1985) (finding property interest based on statute providing for continued employment "during good behavior and efficient service," and prohibiting dismissal "except . . . for . . . misfeasance, malfeasance, or nonfeasance in office."). But I have found only one case, *Garrow v Gramm*, 856 F2d 203 (DC Cir 1988), explicitly rejecting the claim that a property interest in employment can be based solely on the prohibition of certain substantive grounds for discharge. The court in that case explained:

It is possible, of course, to imagine a statute that would create a property interest

be based on a statute or contract that excludes enough reasons for discharge so that it effectively requires a good reason for discharge, but probably not if it excludes only one or a few reasons for discharge.[135] This should probably come as no surprise. If the law were as hypothesized—if one or more legally prohibited reasons for discharge gave rise to a property interest and a right to due process—then all public employees would have due process rights; for even at-will employees are protected against discharge for some reasons, such as race or sex discrimination, or, for that matter, their off-duty speech on matters of public concern.[136] That is obviously not the law.

Nor is there a clear path around this obstacle by way of the Due Process Clause's protection of "liberty." To be sure, it would make perfect sense to say that a public employee who claims she was fired on the basis of protected speech in violation of the First Amendment has a "liberty interest" at stake and the right to a due process hearing on that claim.[137] It would be an altogether defensible reading of the Due Process Clause, and it would be a practical "prophylactic against [discharge] decisions improperly motivated by exercise of protected rights."[138] Unfortunately, the Court rejected that claim in *Board of Regents v Roth*.[139] The only circumstance in which public employees are clearly entitled to a due process hearing on the basis of a liberty interest—that is, absent

---

in continued employment without imposing an explicit "for cause" termination requirement. Such a statute might set forth so comprehensive a list of prohibited reasons for termination that an employee would reasonably have as great an expectation of continued employment as one who knows he cannot be fired except for cause.

Id at 206–07.

[135] Id.

[136] Of course the law might avoid that result by providing that, if the very statute or doctrine on which the employee relies for the substantive limit on employer discretion itself provides a fair process for challenging a termination in violation of that limit, no due process claim arises.

[137] It would make sense not only as a matter of logic but as a matter of constitutional policy. The at-will employee who suspects she may have been fired on the basis of protected speech has a potential First Amendment claim; but absent any right to notice of the reasons for her discharge or an opportunity to respond, she is greatly handicapped in the recognition and assertion of that claim. See generally Estlund, 71 Ind L J 101 (cited in note 132).

[138] This was the reasoning of the Court of Appeals in *Roth v Board of Regents*, 446 F2d 806, 810 (7th Cir 1971); it was rejected by the Supreme Court. *Roth*, 408 US 564, 575 n 14 (1972).

[139] 408 US at 575 n 14.

a property interest in continued employment—is when the government's stated reason for adverse action imposes a stigma on the employee and impairs his standing in the community or his future employment prospects.[140] In that "stigma-plus" case the employee is entitled to a "name clearing hearing."[141]

So under existing due process law, an employer's promise—express or implied—that an employee will not be fired for speaking on matters of public concern in the conscientious performance of her job appears to give rise to neither a property interest nor a liberty interest so as to trigger due process requirements. But perhaps it should. An employee's interest in not being fired for speaking on matters of public concern as part of her job combines elements of both "property," in that it is based on reasonable (albeit limited) expectations of continued employment, and of "liberty," in that it implicates her freedom of expression on the job. Even if it falls short of a full-fledged First Amendment right—mainly, it seems, because of the burden the resulting litigation would impose on government managers—it is a substantial interest for which due process provides the right sort of protection.

The reasoning behind this hybrid property-liberty interest may seem unsatisfyingly ad hoc. But it is at least as consonant with the functions of due process as the reasoning behind the "liberty interest" that is implicated when one is fired from public employment for reasons that are stigmatizing. It is hard to see why the public employee's interest in reputation, where it is coupled with job loss, is more of a protected "liberty interest" than the public employee's freedom to speak on matters of public concern as part of her job duties, where it is coupled with job loss. Indeed, the interests at stake in the two contexts are interestingly parallel: Both claims couple a tangible injury such as loss of a job (but without a property interest in the job) with an intangible injury that raises constitutional concerns but does not rise to the level of a free-standing constitutional right.[142] Neither injury alone triggers due process rights; together they do (or should).

---

[140] See *Roth*, 408 US at 573; *Wieman v Updegraff*, 344 US 183, 191 (1952).

[141] It is called "stigma-plus" because the injury to reputation alone is insufficient without some additional tangible loss such as termination of employment. See *Owen v City of Independence*, 445 US 622, 633 n 13 (1980).

[142] In the "stigma-plus" context, the intangible injury is the government's infliction of a "badge of infamy." Alone that injury does not rise to the level of a constitutional "liberty"

At bottom, the rationale for recognizing a liberty interest in the "stigma-plus" context is that due process, in the form of a "name clearing hearing," offers a sensible form of redress for a serious wrong that implicates constitutional concerns and would otherwise go unremedied. That is the case here, too: Being fired for speaking conscientiously pursuant to one's job duties on matters of public concern is as serious an injury, and it is at least as sensibly redressed by the ordinary workings of due process. To be sure, the Court has cautioned against pouring any and all substantial individual interests into the "liberty" vessel.[143] But nothing in the Court's due process jurisprudence closes the door to all newly recognized liberty interests in the public employment context or otherwise. Indeed, the Court has said (albeit not in so many words since the 1970s): "'Liberty' and 'property' are broad and majestic terms. They are among the '[g]reat [constitutional] concepts . . . purposely left to gather meaning from experience.'"[144] The experience reflected in *Garcetti* has brought to light a new problem for which due process offers an apt solution. So with due regard for the heavy burden of persuasion that a novel claim such as this must meet, let us consider how, and how well, due process can solve the First Amendment problem presented in *Garcetti*.

To begin with, we should situate this proposal within the venerable tradition of crafting procedural solutions to First Amendment problems.[145] Some of those procedural solutions are prophylactic in nature; they are designed to protect against the accidental suppression of speech that is in fact protected. This First Amendment due process tradition was reviewed by the plurality in *Waters v Churchill*,[146] which itself adopted a procedural solution to a problem that may arise in an ordinary public employee speech case: The employer fires an employee for saying X (which would be unprotected), but the employee claims she actually said Y (which would be protected). Under *Waters*, the re-

---

interest; coupled with job loss or debarment from other job opportunities, it does. See *Paul v Davis*, 424 US 693, 710 (1976).

[143] Id at 698–99.

[144] *Roth*, 408 US at 571, quoting *National Mutual Insurance Co. v Tidewater Transfer Co.*, 337 US 582, 646 (1949) (Frankfurter dissenting).

[145] See generally Henry P. Monaghan, *First Amendment "Due Process,"* 83 Harv L Rev 518 (1970) (reviewing the development and advocating the expansion of procedural protections of First Amendment rights).

[146] 511 US 661, 669–71 (1994).

viewing court is to look to "the facts as the employer *reasonably* found them to be," that is, based upon an investigation that was reasonable under the circumstances.[147] *Waters* thus extended to the at-will employee a smidgen of the "prophylactic" due process that the Court rejected in *Roth*: Before firing an employee for what might have been protected speech, the employer must do enough of an investigation to be reasonably certain that the speech was not protected.

It is not only on prophylactic grounds that the Court has relied on procedures to protect speech. In *Bush v Lucas*,[148] the Court had to decide whether federal employees who claim a violation of First Amendment rights have a constitutional cause of action analogous to that which state and local employees have under Section 1983.[149] The plaintiff, who claimed he had been demoted on the basis of protected speech, was covered by federal civil service laws: he could not be fired or demoted without cause, and had the right to "elaborate, comprehensive . . . procedures—administrative and judicial—by which improper action may be redressed."[150] The Court assumed that plaintiff's First Amendment rights had been violated and that the Congressional scheme provided a less fulsome remedy for this violation than would a federal lawsuit; monetary relief was not fully compensatory, and no punitive damages were available.[151] But the Court declined to imply a new right of action for a constitutional violation that was "fully cognizable" within the civil service system and subject to "meaningful remedies."[152] *Bush v Lucas* was deeply colored by the Court's reluctance to imply new rights of action against the federal government, particularly when Congress had constructed "an elaborate remedial system . . . step

---

[147] Id at 677–78. The plurality chose a middle ground between Justice Stevens's more speech-protective approach (what matters is what the employee actually said as found by the reviewing court), see id at 694–99 (Stevens dissenting), and Justice Scalia's less speech-protective approach (what matters is what the employer believed was said), see id at 686–94 (Scalia concurring).

[148] 462 US 367 (1983).

[149] The question was whether to create a *"Bivens* action," after *Bivens v Six Unknown Federal Narcotics Agents*, 403 US 388 (1971), parallel to the Section 1983 action recognized in *Pickering* and its sequelae.

[150] *Bush*, 462 US at 385.

[151] Id at 372–73.

[152] Id at 386. The Court reserved judgment on whether a *Bivens* remedy would be available for a First Amendment violation that could not be remedied under the civil service laws. Id at 391.

by step, with careful attention to conflicting policy consider-ations."[153] But the important point in the present context is the Court's conclusion that the administrative procedures and rem-edies available under civil service laws may afford sufficient redress even for speech that is clearly protected.

The procedural solution proffered here is neither a prophylactic in the face of factual uncertainty about whether the First Amend-ment is implicated, as in *Waters*, nor a substitute remedy for a recognized First Amendment violation, as in *Bush v Lucas*. It serves instead as a supplement to the First Amendment, a practical way to fill a gap in protection that *Garcetti* deemed necessary in light of the cost of providing that protection. The speech in *Garcetti* is important enough to protect through a due process hearing even though it is too costly to protect through a full-blown First Amendment lawsuit.

Due process provides an elegant solution to the *Garcetti* prob-lem. As compared to federal litigation, a due process hearing is less costly and disruptive, and generates more modest remedies; accordingly, the shadow cast by the prospect of adjudication would be less burdensome. The due process approach reduces not only the cost and burden of adjudication but also the bite that the Constitution takes out of managerial discretion. For the central issue in the hearing would be whether the employee was fired for speaking conscientiously in the performance of the job as the em-ployer defined it (reasonably and in good faith). The proposed scheme would leave the employer largely free to define the job and to evaluate job performance, but would constrain its ability to penalize the employee for doing that job, at least when she does so in the form of speech on matters of public concern.

A serious objection to this scheme lies precisely in the em-ployer's ability to define the job, and thus potentially to manipulate the scope of employees' freedom of expression about matters of public concern. The manipulation might take a variety of forms. The employer might deny at the threshold that the speech at issue was within the employee's job duties. But of course the effect of that denial would be to leave the employee free to sue the employer

---

[153] The question, said the Court, was "whether an elaborate remedial system that has been constructed step by step, with careful attention to policy considerations, should be augmented by the creation of a new judicial remedy for the constitutional violation at issue." Id at 388. In that context, the Court found "special factors counseling hesitation" in implying an additional judicial remedy. Id at 378–79 (citing *Bivens*, 403 US at 396).

in court under *Pickering-Connick*. So the employer might instead claim strategically that the speech at issue *was* part of the employee's job performance, thus channeling her dispute into an administrative rather than a judicial hearing. That is the sort of strategic pleading that the dissenters predicted *Garcetti* would produce; but the incentive to do so would be much reduced if it would land the government not in *Garcetti*'s "free-fire" zone but in an administrative hearing.[154]

The bigger risk to employees arises within the administrative hearing process itself: Having conceded that the speech was uttered in the course of performing the job, the employer may still seek to define *satisfactory* job performance so as to narrowly circumscribe the employee's freedom to disclose or discuss matters of public concern. So, in *Garcetti*, for example, the district attorney might concede that Ceballos's memo was written in the course of his job as prosecutor (thus steering the case into administrative channels), but might contend in the hearing that it violated procedures for reviewing and approving prosecutors' statements, or a rule against "controversial" statements or "criticism of superiors." Nearly any case of speech-that-is-the-job may offer the employer this opportunity to define for itself the scope of the employee's freedom to speak.[155]

The problem arises out of one of the claimed virtues of the hybrid due process regime: It aims to give greater weight to employer discretion in prescribing and evaluating employees' job performance than *Pickering-Connick* gives in the ordinary free speech case. But wholesale deference to the employer's definition of the job, and of the speech required by the job, might swallow up the protections that this hybrid regime aims to afford employee speech. At worst it would collapse into the *Garcetti* rule that employee speech-that-is-the-job is altogether unprotected because it is in effect the speech of the government employer itself. To avoid this result it is crucial to keep in mind the constitutional under-

---

[154] Moreover, the government's claim that an employee's speech was uttered as part of her job performance would tend to foreclose certain arguments the employer might otherwise wish to make about the supposed disruptiveness of the speech.

[155] Indeed, a similar problem confronts any "just cause" scheme; the employer has considerable latitude to define what counts as "just cause," and thus might undercut the employee's job security. The difference here is that, first, employers might be especially tempted to proscribe critical or controversial speech; and, second, "just cause" has a long history of judicial and arbitral precedent against which to judge the employer's claims.

pinnings of the employee's right to a hearing. The First Amendment policies at stake, including the value of critical engagement and tolerance of dissent within government agencies, should stiffen courts' resolve (on judicial review) and constrain employers' ability to define away the freedom to speak on matters of public concern. That may sound vague and unmanageable, but it is no more so than the First Amendment constraints on the nature of the legitimate managerial concerns that can be weighed against employee free speech interests in the balancing phase of a *Pickering-Connick* lawsuit. In either case, some government interests (or job requirements), such as avoiding criticism, are too far at odds with the basic commitments of democracy and free expression to pass muster.

In some of these cases, as in *Garcetti*, the First Amendment constraints will line up rather neatly with, or at least be informed by, the ethics and obligations of the employee's profession, which ought to be implied into the job requirements of professional jobs. On the other hand, some jobs, such as public spokesperson for an agency, may entail rather rigid managerial control over the content of the employee's speech. And there are some high-level managers whose public pronouncements will inevitably be thoroughly identified with the agency. There are some jobs, in other words, in which the speech of the employee *is* effectively that of the government employer; in some cases, this may justify withholding the mixed free-speech-due-process protections suggested here. But in most cases, considerations such as these—the risk that an individual's statements may be attributed to the agency—can be folded into the issue before the due process decision maker: Did the employee suffer adverse action because of speech on matters of public concern that was uttered in the conscientious performance of her job as the employer legitimately defined it?

A practical puzzle remains: How to encourage rather than discourage the institutionalization of internal criticism and disclosure. There are two sides to this puzzle: How to encourage employers to create institutional mechanisms for internal criticism and disclosures, and how to encourage employees to use those mechanisms. It is not so easy to do both, for employers might be more inclined to create internal channels for dissent if that would secure immunity from liability; yet employees may be more willing to speak, internally or externally, if they enjoy legal protection in doing so.[156]

These issues were tossed back and forth, more like grenades than like sustained argumentation, between the majority and dissents in *Garcetti*. The dissenters in *Garcetti* criticized the majority's rule of no protection for speech-that-is-the-job for its tendency to encourage employees to take complaints and concerns to the public rather than to their employer.[157] The majority responded that employers could avoid this result by creating "internal policies and procedures that are receptive to employee criticism."[158] But of course employees who chose to use those internal procedures pursuant to their job duties would be unprotected under *Garcetti* against reprisals. The dissenters also predicted that employers would respond to the new *Garcetti* rule by rewriting job descriptions to include as much potential dissenting speech as possible.[159] Of course, this might be seen as a constructive, even hoped-for, response: incorporating criticism and dissent into the job itself. But the effect under *Garcetti*, and the presumed purpose, would be to insulate the agency from litigation, and deprive the employee of any constitutional protection, under *Pickering-Connick*. As such, the majority responded, somewhat defensively, that judges would be able to see through such a subterfuge.[160]

The due process approach might clear a path through the minefield of conflicting incentives by reducing the weight of liability to something that both employers and employees could live with. Under the due process approach, employers who actually did incorporate internal criticism and disclosure into employees' job duties would be free from the threat of direct First Amendment litigation, but would be accountable in a constitutionally prescribed administrative hearing, if they punished employees for that

---

[156] The problem of encouraging employers to create, and employees to use, internal complaint mechanisms was addressed in the sexual harassment context in *Burlington Industries, Inc. v Ellerth*, 524 US 742 (1998), and *Faragher v City of Boca Raton*, 524 US 775 (1998). The *Faragher/Ellerth* approach—an affirmative defense against some discriminatory harassment liability where the employer did but the employer did not act reasonably to redress alleged harassment internally—bears scrutiny in the whistle-blowing context as well. But I do not explore it further here.

[157] *Garcetti*, 126 S Ct at 1963 (Stevens dissenting).

[158] Id at 1961.

[159] Id at 1961–62 n 2 (Souter dissenting).

[160] Id at 1965.

criticism. Employers who failed to institutionalize criticism might find that it breaks out anyway in the form of public or extracurricular on-the-job dissent; and in that case efforts to squelch it would trigger not an administrative hearing but a First Amendment lawsuit. For their part, employees who chose to speak up pursuant to their job duties and to do so through prescribed procedures would lose out on the prospect of a direct First Amendment lawsuit; but they would get the benefit of a faster and cheaper due process hearing at which they could contest any adverse actions based on their speech.

VI. Taking the Due Process Solution Beyond Garcetti?

The due process solution to the *Garcetti* problem has much to recommend it. So much, in fact, that we should consider whether it is a solution to the larger problem of public employee free speech rights. The difficult task of reconciling the competing demands of citizenship and work—of individual liberty and organizational efficacy—has preoccupied the Court not only in the *Garcetti* context but across the full gamut of *Pickering-Connick* cases. Was a federal lawsuit really the best way of vindicating McPherson's right to talk politics with her co-worker? Or Pickering's right to sound off on school board priorities? How many McPhersons and Pickerings are actually able to exercise their right to file a federal lawsuit against their employers? And at what cost both to them and to their employers? Might the legitimate interests of government employers and of employees in these cases perhaps be better served by a less costly, less time-consuming, and more accessible administrative hearing process—one that meets the demands of due process, including judicial review and the prospect of make-whole relief? We might accomplish that by reconceiving the right at stake in the ordinary public employee free speech contest as a liberty interest sufficient to trigger the protections of due process, rather than as a freestanding First Amendment right. Only when the employer failed to afford due process to the employee who claimed that her free speech rights were infringed would the employee have a constitutional cause of action.

The due process solution is addressed to the problem of reconciling the roles of citizenship and employment where they overlap; it should not apply where the government is simply using its power as employer to reach beyond the employment nexus into the individual's life as citizen—that is where the employee is penalized for speech that is "unrelated to the employment" under *NTEU*. Where the government leverages its authority as employer to intrude into the employee's civic and private life, a federal lawsuit remains the appropriate forum for vindicating the employee's free speech interests. But for the main run of public employee free speech contests involving speech that is either at work or otherwise related to the work, an administrative process may provide adequate (or even better, because faster and cheaper) recourse and remedies.

The Court in *Bush v Lucas* reached a similar result by an alternate route in the very particular context of the federal civil service. The Court declined to create an implied constitutional remedy under *Bivens* in light of Congress's express provision of an adequate statutory remedy for civil service employees: "Just cause" protections, backed by an extensive administrative hearing process and meaningful remedies (mainly reinstatement, back pay, and lost benefits), were deemed to provide adequate protection for the First Amendment rights of federal civil service employees.[161] The question on the table is whether that compromise should be extended to other public employees by way of the due process solution described above.

The Court confronted an intriguingly parallel question in private sector employment, and again affirmed the adequacy of the non-judicial forum: In *Gilmer v Interstate/Johnson Lane Corp.*,[162] the Court held that an employee's agreement to arbitrate rather than litigate future employment claims was enforceable; the less elaborate, less costly, and speedier arbitral forum was deemed to be an adequate substitute for federal litigation even in the context of federal antidiscrimination claims. *Gilmer* provoked a flood of critical commentary, legal controversies, and empirical studies.[163] But propo-

---

[161] *Bush* did not decide "whether the Constitution itself requires a judicially-fashioned damages remedy in the absence of any other remedy to vindicate the underlying right, unless there is an express textual command to the contrary." *Bush*, 462 US at 378, n 14. The Court did not need to reach that question because "existing civil service remedies for a demotion in retaliation for protected speech are clearly constitutionally adequate." The implication, however, is that Congress could expressly foreclose the *Bivens* remedy without providing a constitutionally adequate statutory remedy. Id.

[162] 500 US 20 (1992).

[163] For a useful summary of the legal and empirical controversies after *Gilmer*, see Richard A. Bales, *A Normative Consideration of Employment Arbitration at Gilmer's Quinceañera*, 81 Tulane L Rev 331 (2006).

nents of mandatory arbitration have largely won over the courts with their contention that arbitration, where it meets basic requirements of "due process," represents a fair quid pro quo for employees: it trades off some of the formality and procedural safeguards of litigation for a process that is cheaper, faster, and more likely to afford the employee "some kind of hearing" before an impartial decision maker than is the civil litigation process.[164]

The legal issues in *Bush* and in *Gilmer* were obviously entirely distinct. Still, the two cases reflect parallel policy judgments. In both settings, important employee rights in which the public has a major stake were deemed to be adequately safeguarded by a nonjudicial process that is less elaborate but purportedly more accessible and efficient than that afforded by federal litigation. In both settings, too, a major concern is whether the interest of the public that is at stake in these controversies is adequately protected in the lower-profile nonjudicial process. That concern is especially acute, and has never been adequately addressed by the Court, in the context of private arbitration; in *Bush* and in the due process solution suggested here, the substitute forum would still be public in nature. But the public interest in public employees' freedom to speak on matters of public concern is arguably more at the heart of the right itself here than is the public interest in individuals' freedom from invidious discrimination (which was deemed adequately protected through private arbitration of individual claims).

So the idea of converting most public employee speech rights— those in which the speech is not "unrelated to the employment" under *NTEU* and *City of San Diego*—from freestanding First Amendment rights into "liberty interests" protected by due process requires more systematic consideration than I attempt to give it here.[165] But such consideration seems well warranted. And it should include the question whether, once having reduced the burden of employee free speech claims on managerial discretion and judicial dockets, we might reconsider *Connick*'s categorical denial of protection to speech that

---

[164] The arbitral forum must also make available the same remedies that would be available in court. That makes the quid pro quo of arbitration different from the quid pro quo entailed by substituting an administrative process and "meaningful" but less extensive remedies, as in *Bush*.

[165] Another matter that would require careful consideration is whether extending the due process regime to the general run of public employee free speech claims would actually undermine some of the advantages claimed for the "due process solution" to the *Garcetti* problem.

is not of sufficient public concern. Recall the Court's statement of its holding in *Connick*, which *Garcetti* extended:

> We hold only that when a public employee speaks not as a citizen upon matters of public concern, but instead as an employee . . . , absent the most unusual circumstances, a federal court is not the appropriate forum in which to review the wisdom of a personnel decision taken by a public agency allegedly in reaction to the employee's behavior.[166]

But perhaps an administrative hearing *is* the appropriate forum in which to review such a decision.

Even those who are deeply committed to employees' freedom of expression at the workplace and about their work and their employers—and I count myself as one—have to question whether the theoretical availability of a federal cause of action, and the extremely remote prospect of a judicial trial, can protect that freedom of expression. Very, very few public employees who believe that their free speech rights have been infringed by their employers will ever sue, much less get "some kind of hearing" in court, on their claim. To be sure, federal civil litigation may cast a heavy enough shadow over public employers' litigation posture and personnel decisions to induce them to respect employees' speech rights or to settle claims generously without a trial. It is not only the employees who file and prosecute lawsuits who benefit from the law's protections. But it is not at all clear that the more certain and speedier prospect of an administrative hearing will cast a less effective shadow. Employees' readier and quicker access to a less elaborate nonjudicial hearing process may make up for its less fearsome quality and produce a comparable deterrent effect (as well as a more satisfactory dispute-resolution procedure from the perspective of aggrieved individuals). That is the sort of question that needs to be answered before pressing ahead with the wholesale transformation of First Amendment claims into "liberty interests" protected through due process. It is a question on which the ongoing debate and especially the empirical research on employment arbitration may useful.

CONCLUSION

　　The overlapping domains of citizenship and employment

---

[166] *Connick*, 461 US 138, 147 (1983) (emphasis added).

that the public employee occupies in the vast majority of free speech controversies, from *City of San Diego* at the outer edge of the workplace nexus to *Garcetti* at its innermost core, have generated a steady flow of difficult legal issues, not only in the Supreme Court but obviously throughout the federal courts, for nearly forty years. In one way or another all of those issues stem from the effort to recalibrate the First Amendment's constraints on the sovereign's power over the citizens to a set of constraints on personnel management in the public workplace. That effort has been invaluable in expanding the liberty of public employees to participate in public life inside and outside of their workplaces, in enriching public debate about government's performance and mission, and in opening up government agencies to greater internal debate and criticism. But there is no denying that federal litigation is a blunt instrument that can be wielded by relatively few employees, and at a cost to both plaintiffs and defendants that often seems out of all proportion to the task of correcting an illegally motivated adverse personnel action.

The entanglement of roles and the clashing commitments of employment and citizenship are most vexing in the *Garcetti* context; indeed, more vexing than the Court's categorical rejection of the First Amendment claims in that case admits. At least in the *Garcetti* context, a more sensible solution is available under the Due Process Clause through the recognition of a hybrid property-liberty interest in not being penalized for speaking on matters of public concern as part of the conscientious performance of one's job. The prospect of extending that solution to the wider field of public employee speech disputes that are "related to the employment" is tantalizing; but it calls for further thought and further study.

Central goals of the law of public employee speech are to liberate and encourage employees to speak up honestly and conscientiously on matters of public concern, on and off the job, and to induce employers to respect the interests of employees and the public in communicating on those public matters. As means to those ends, what is wanted is not more constitutional lawsuits, nor even necessarily more fulsome constitutional rights, but more speech-friendly institutional arrangements. While the venerable traditions of the First Amendment have illuminated the path ahead, the eminently flexible tools of due process may be better suited to the construction of those institutional arrangements.

LILLIAN R. BEVIER

FULL OF SURPRISES—AND MORE TO
COME: RANDALL v SORRELL, THE
FIRST AMENDMENT, AND CAMPAIGN
FINANCE REGULATION

On March 27, 2002, President Bush signed the Bipartisan Campaign Reform Act of 2002[1] (BCRA). BCRA was a sweeping campaign finance regulation measure among whose major provisions were restrictions on political party soft money and independent corporate and union issue advertising during election campaigns. The act was immediately challenged on constitutional grounds, and complex litigation ensued in which eleven separate lawsuits were consolidated and assigned to a three-judge District Court. On December 10, 2003, the lawsuit culminated in a "stunning triumph for campaign finance reform"[2] when in *McConnell v FEC*[3] a 5–4 majority of the Supreme Court sustained the act's major provisions.[4]

Lillian R. BeVier is David and Mary Harrison Distinguished Professor, University of Virginia Law School.

AUTHOR'S NOTE: Thanks to Lisa Perrygo and Stephen Reis, University of Virginia Law School Class of 2008, for valuable research help.

[1] 116 Stat 81 (2002).

[2] Richard Briffault, *McConnell v. FEC and the Transformation of Campaign Finance Law*, 3 Election L J 147 (2004).

[3] 540 US 93 (2003).

[4] For a concise summary of the *McConnell* litigation and of the Court's principal holdings, see Briffault, 3 Election L J at 150–61 (cited in note 2).

The majority in *McConnell* purported to leave *Buckley v Valeo*,[5] the Court's seminal campaign finance case, intact. The extent to which it actually did so is open to question.[6] One aspect of *Buckley* that *McConnell* apparently did not dismantle, however, was the analytical framework that distinguished between expenditure and contribution limitations in terms of both the First Amendment burdens that such limits impose and the state interests that justify them. According to *Buckley*, individual expenditure limits impose more of a burden on First Amendment rights than contribution limits do. In addition, contribution limits may be justified by the government interest in preventing corruption or its appearance. Individual expenditure limits can be justified neither by the state's interest in preventing corruption, by an interest in equalizing resources, nor by an interest in preventing wasteful or excessive spending on campaigns for federal office. Though the Court in *Buckley* did not "say in so many words that different standards might govern expenditure and contribution limits,"[7] it did imply that contribution limits would be subjected to somewhat less strict First Amendment scrutiny than limits on individual expenditures. This inclination to engage in somewhat less strict scrutiny of contribution than expenditure limitations morphed, via such cases as *Nixon v Shrink Missouri Government PAC (Shrink)*,[8] into what in *McConnell* became a posture of explicit and unskeptical deference to legislative judgment about the need for them.[9]

The *Buckley* Court rejected limits on independent expenditures by individuals, but it did not have before it a challenge to the

---

[5] 424 US 1 (1976) (per curiam).

[6] For an elaboration of the ways in which *McConnell* rejected *Buckley*'s underlying premises, see Lillian R. BeVier, *McConnell v. FEC: Not Senator Buckley's First Amendment*, 3 Election L J 127 (2004).

[7] *Nixon v Shrink Missouri Government PAC*, 528 US 377, 387 (2000).

[8] Id.

[9] Evidence for the claim in text abounds in the *McConnell* majority opinion. See, for example, *McConnell*, 540 US at 137 (recognizing Congress's "particular expertise" about the impact of particular campaign finance practices); id at 154 ("not unwarranted for Congress to conclude"); id at 158 ("we respect Congress' decision to proceed in incremental steps"); id (referring to Congress's "vastly superior knowledge" about the interactions between political party committees and federal officeholders); id at 165 (according "substantial deference to the predictive judgments of Congress"); id at 167 (deferring to "Congress' judgment" concerning state party soft money); id at 185 ("we will not upset Congress' eminently reasonable prediction"); id at 188 ("Congress is fully entitled to consider the real-world differences between political parties and interest groups"); and id at 207 (deferring to Congressional line drawing concerning the scope of the regulation of electioneering communication).

corporate or union expenditure prohibitions, which in fact had been in place since the Tillman Act of 1907[10] and the Federal Corrupt Practices Act of 1925.[11] Thus, in sustaining the prohibitions that BCRA imposed on independent expenditures by corporations and labor unions for "electioneering communications"—broadcast ads that mention candidates for federal office by name within specified times before primaries or general elections[12]—*McConnell* was not constrained by *Buckley*'s holding that limits on independent *individual* expenditures could not be proscribed. Instead of the *Buckley* prohibition on expenditure limits to constrain it, the *McConnell* Court drew support for deference to limits on independent corporate expenditures from some of its recent cases—such as *Austin v Michigan Chamber of Commerce*[13] and *FEC v Beaumont*[14]—in which it had sustained such limits based on the premise that it is appropriate to have "respect for the legislative judgment that the special characteristics of the corporate structure require particularly careful regulation."[15]

Though *McConnell* left the *Buckley* framework formally intact, it rejected the fundamental premises upon which the *Buckley* per curiam had rested. I have previously summarized *Buckley*'s fundamental premises as follows:

> *Buckley* is an affirmation of free political speech, an expression of skepticism about legislative trustworthiness in regulating political campaign speech, and a concomitant rejection of all but the narrowest rationales for its regulation. Its animating premises are that speech about issues and candidates during election campaigns is of the utmost constitutional value; that limitations on contributions to and expenditures on such speech are the func-

---

[10] 34 Stat 864 (1907).

[11] 43 Stat 1070 (1925). The Court has never acknowledged the fact that, on account of the ease of its evasion and its emasculation by courts, the Tillman Act had not in fact put an end to corporate political spending. See generally John R. Bolton, *Constitutional Limitations on Restricting Corporate and Union Political Speech*, 22 Ariz L Rev 373, 374–402 (1980) (summarizing history of efforts to regulate corporate and labor union political activity before the FECA).

[12] BCRA defines "electioneering communication" as "any broadcast, cable, or satellite communication" that "refers to a clearly identified candidate for Federal office" made within 60 days before a general . . . election . . . or 30 days before a primary." 2 USCA § 434(f)(3)(A)(i) (West Supp 2003).

[13] 110 S Ct 1391 (1990).

[14] 123 S Ct 2200 (2003).

[15] *McConnell*, 124 S Ct at 695 (internal quotations omitted).

tional equivalent of regulations of speech itself; that limitations of both must be subjected to careful scrutiny, though somewhat less scrutiny might be warranted for contribution limitations because they affect only "speech by proxy"; that the only interest sufficiently compelling to sustain limitations on either contributions or expenditures is the interest in preventing the appearance or actuality of corruption—with corruption narrowly conceived as "large contributions . . . given to secure a political *quid pro quo* from current and potential officeholders."[16]

By contrast, the Court in *McConnell* viewed things quite differently, as Richard Briffault noted:

> Instead of treating campaign finance restrictions as a threat to freedoms of speech and association and therefore a challenge to constitutional values, the Court gave great weight to the interests in fair, informed democratic decision-making it found to be advanced by contribution limitations, disclosure requirements, and restrictions on corporate and union treasury funds. . . . The *McConnell* majority clearly viewed many of BCRA's restrictions and requirements not as burdens on speech but as desirable efforts to promote democracy.[17]

McConnell hardly put an end to controversy about campaign finance practices and how they should be regulated. Nor did BCRA put an end to or slow the flow of money to political campaigns. Indeed, during the 2004 presidential campaigns, so-called 527 organizations (named after the section of the Internal Revenue Code pursuant to which they were organized)[18] spent millions of unregulated dollars on the election campaigns of both candidates.[19] Sen-

---

[16] BeVier, 3 Election L J at 128 (cited in note 6) (internal citations omitted).

[17] Briffault, 3 Election L J at 148–49 (cited in note 2). Professor Briffault describes the Court as having *"explained"* that "contribution limits, like other measures aimed at protecting the integrity of the process, tangibly benefit public participation in political debate." Id at 249 (emphasis supplied). It is fair, however, to wonder whether, rather than "explaining" that contribution limits benefit public participation, it would have been more accurate to have described the Court as having "asserted" that they do. This is because there exists in fact little empirical evidence that contribution limits have any such beneficial effect. See, for example, David M. Primo and Jeffrey Milyo, *Campaign Finance Laws and Political Efficacy: Evidence from the States*, 5 Election L J 23, 25 (2006) (Court in *McConnell* did not "offer any evidence that legal reforms influence public opinion about the integrity of the democratic process, perhaps because the link is taken to be self-evident.").

[18] 26 USCA § 527 (establishing the requirements for "political organizations" to avoid paying income taxes).

[19] Center for Responsive Politics, online at http://.crp.org.

ators McCain and Feingold fulminated about this activity,[20] and bills were introduced to regulate this new challenge to the success of their regulatory enterprise.[21] Bloggers also became politically active and a force to be reckoned with, and regulation of their activity was called for too. The FEC, however, came to their rescue by writing regulations that exempted most of them from BCRA's regulatory net.[22]

This essay focuses on a different but no less important post-*McConnell* development in the law regarding the First Amendment constraints on campaign finance restrictions. In *Randall v Sorrell*,[23] the Supreme Court addressed the constitutionality of an ambitious set of campaign finance regulations that the state of Vermont enacted. On the merits, the *Randall* result was perhaps not unexpected, but the Court's several opinions cannot be said to have clarified the law. Moreover, the opinions suggest that the future of *McConnell*'s reframing of the Court's approach to campaign finance regulation is a very uncertain thing indeed.

In 1997, when BCRA was still but a gleam in the eyes of Senators McCain and Feingold, the Vermont legislature enacted the very stringent campaign finance law that became known as Act 64[24] and took effect immediately after the 1998 elections. Among Act 64's provisions were mandatory expenditure limits on the amount candidates for state office could spend on their campaigns during two-year election cycles as well as limits on individual and party contributions to state candidates. Soon after Act 64 became law, a group of individuals challenged it on First Amendment grounds. The United States District Court for the District of Vermont invalidated the spending limits and the limits on contributions to political parties, but sustained the other contribution limits.[25] Both sides appealed. In a lengthy opinion, a divided panel of the Second Circuit

---

[20] Senator Russ Feingold, "On the Issues: Campaign Finance Reform—The Future of Reform," online at http://feingold.senate.gov/issues_future_reform.html (stating that "one of the most significant failures of the FEC in recent years was its decision not to address the explosion of so-called 527 groups in the 2004 presidential election).

[21] S 271 (109th): 527 Reform Act of 2005; HR 513 (109th): 527 Reform Act of 2006; HR 4948 (109th): Ethics Reform Act of 2006; HR 4975 (109th): 527 Reform Act of 2006; HR 4988 (109th): House Ethics Reform Act of 2006; S 1053 (109th): 527 Reform Act of 2005; S 2511 (109th): 527 Reform Act of 2006.

[22] 11 CFR §§ 100, 110, and 114 (2006).

[23] 126 S Ct 2479 (2006).

[24] Pub Act No 64, codified at Vt Stat Ann, Tit 17, § 2801 et seq (2002).

[25] *Randall v Sorrell*, 118 F Supp 2d 470 (2000).

upheld all of Act 64's contribution limits.[26] The Second Circuit was persuaded that *Buckley* had left the door open to a state to enact expenditure limits in pursuit of its interests in preventing corruption or its appearance and in limiting the amount of time state officials must spend raising campaign funds *if* the state could demonstrate that its interests in doing so were compelling and that they were threatened by unlimited expenditures. And, upon exhaustively recounting the evidence that the state had introduced to make this demonstration, the Second Circuit pronounced itself satisfied that, if the state could prove that Act 64's expenditure limits were narrowly tailored, the expenditure limits could be sustained. Accordingly, it remanded the case to the district court for findings on the narrow tailoring issue.

In *Randall*, the Supreme Court by a vote of 6–3 reversed the Second Circuit and invalidated both Act 64's expenditure limitations and its contribution limitations on First Amendment grounds. The result in *Randall* is important and interesting for at least two reasons. First, *Randall* was the first time a direct challenge had been mounted to *Buckley*'s holding regarding limitations on individual expenditures. In rejecting the challenge, the Court explicitly reaffirmed *Buckley*. Second, the Court had never before invalidated contribution limitations on the ground that they were too low. That they did so in a 6–3 decision so close on the heels of *McConnell* was not to have been expected.

I. The Opinions in Randall

A. JUSTICE BREYER

Justice Breyer announced the Court's judgment, but only Chief Justice Roberts joined his opinion in its entirety.[27] Invoking the principle of stare decisis—"the rule of law demands that adhering to our prior case law be the norm"[28]—Justice Breyer insisted that

---

[26] *Randall v Sorrell*, 382 F3d 91 (2004).

[27] Justice Alito concurred in the judgment, but declined to join the parts of Justice Breyer's opinion that addressed and rejected respondents' argument that, at least with respect to Vermont's expenditure limitations, *Buckley* should reconsider and overrule *Buckley*. Justice Alito thought that the request to "'revisit *Buckley*,'" 126 S Ct at 2500, had been "an afterthought almost," id, and that the respondents had failed adequately to discuss either the doctrine of stare decisis in general or the circumstances in which it would be "appropriate to reconsider a prior constitutional decision." Id.

[28] Id at 2489.

the result he reached was consistent with, indeed that it was compelled by, *Buckley*. That "well-established precedent," he wrote,
made it clear that the expenditure limitations were unconstitutional. Moreover, though its command was not quite so easily
discerned in this regard, *Buckley*'s rationale also required the Court
to strike down the contribution limitations.

With respect to the expenditure limitations, Justice Breyer not
only cited *Buckley* but quoted from it extensively, most notably
perhaps endorsing the *Buckley* Court's observation that expenditure restrictions "'reduc[e] the quantity of expression by restricting
the number of issues discussed, the depth of their exploration, and
the size of the audience reached.'"[29] And, paying virtually no heed
to the evidentiary record, nor to the substantial amounts of testimony on which the Second Circuit had relied, he gave short
shrift to the state's asserted interest in "protect[ing] candidates
from spending too much time raising money rather than devoting
that time to campaigning among ordinary voters."[30] Respondents
claimed that the *Buckley* Court had not fully considered this state
interest. No doubt this was the reason respondents thought it
worth while attempting to build record support for it. Their efforts
were wasted on Justice Breyer. To him, the "connection between
high campaign expenditures and increased fundraising demands"[31]
was "perfectly obvious."[32] And he insisted that it had been apparent
to—and adequately considered by—the *Buckley* Court.

Justice Breyer found it more difficult to square his conclusion
on Vermont's contribution limits with *Buckley* and with its progeny,
since the Court had never before overturned contribution limits
on the ground that they were too low. Still, Justice Breyer noted,
the Court had "recognized . . . that contribution limits might
sometimes work more harm"[33] than good. And he went on to note
a concern he had previously expressed in his concurring opinion
in *Shrink* (an opinion to which he had conspicuously *not* referred
in his discussion of the expenditure limitations[34]), that "too low a
limit [might] magnify the 'reputation-related or media-related ad-

[29] Id at 2488 (citing *Buckley*, 424 US at 19).
[30] Id at 2490.
[31] Id.
[32] Id.
[33] Id at 2491–92.
[34] See text accompanying notes 8–9.

vantages of incumbency and thereby insulat[e] legislators from
effective electoral challenge.'"³⁵ Thus, claiming to be "[f]ollowing
. . . *Buckley*,"³⁶ and despite acknowledging that the Court "ordinarily"³⁷ and appropriately defers to legislative judgment about
the amount of contributions that should be permitted, Justice
Breyer discerned a mandate to "exercise independent judicial judgment"³⁸ with respect to Vermont's limits. Danger signs that the
limits were unconstitutionally low abounded: they applied per
election cycle; they applied both to contributions from individuals
and to contributions from political parties; they were below the
limits the Court upheld in *Buckley* as well as below the lowest limit
the Court had previously upheld; indeed, they were the lowest in
the country. These danger signs impelled Justice Breyer independently to examine the record. When he did so, he determined that
the limits were insufficiently closely drawn to achieve the state's
interests.

Without making explicit the constitutional criteria that guided
his judgment, Justice Breyer identified five factors that led him to
his conclusion. First, the contribution limits would restrict the
amount of money available to challengers. Second, the limits on
party contributions would hamper parties' effort to target their
efforts to competitive races. Third, the low contribution limits
were exacerbated by Act 64's inclusive treatment of volunteer services. Fourth, the contribution limits were not adjusted for inflation. And fifth, the record contained no "special justification"³⁹
for such low and restrictive limits. The penultimate paragraph of
this section of his opinion summarizes Justice Breyer's conclusion
that Act 64's contribution limitations "go . . . too far."⁴⁰ They

> threaten . . . to inhibit effective advocacy by those who seek
> election, particularly challengers; . . . they mute the voice of
> political parties; they hamper participation in campaigns
> through volunteer activities; and they are not indexed for in-
> flation.⁴¹

³⁵ Id at 2492.
³⁶ Id.
³⁷ Id.
³⁸ Id.
³⁹ Id at 2499.
⁴⁰ Id at 2500.
⁴¹ Id at 2499.

Justice Breyer's description of the five factors is quite detailed, but his opinion leaves many things uncertain. It does not, for example, specify the relative weight that should be given to the factors; whether any of the five factors might be dispositive; whether all would need to be present in the same degree; whether other factors might also be relevant; or, more concretely, how high the contribution limits would have to be in order to change the result in a future case.

B. JUSTICE KENNEDY

Justice Kennedy's concurrence appears to have been motivated by his previously expressed and persistent doubts that the "universe of campaign finance regulation"[42] that the Court has created is either coherent or consistent with a proper reading of the First Amendment. This Court-made universe requires the Court to "explain why $200 is too restrictive a limit while $1,500 is not,"[43] he pointed out, but the Justices have neither their own experience nor any well-established body of law from which to seek guidance for making such distinctions. Though unwilling to join in Justice Breyer's opinion, which implied that making such determinations is well within the Court's ken, Justice Kennedy endorsed the plurality's judgment because it comported with "the legal universe we have ratified and helped create."[44]

C. JUSTICE THOMAS

Joined by Justice Scalia, Justice Thomas concurred in the judgment but disagreed with the plurality's rationale. He once again insisted that *Buckley* was wrongly decided in the first place[45] because it "provides insufficient protection to political speech."[46] He added that *Buckley* had been applied in an incoherent and unprincipled fashion, and that stare decisis accordingly posed no barrier to overruling it.

Justice Thomas only briefly reiterated his fundamental disagree-

---

[42] Id at 2501.

[43] Id.

[44] Id.

[45] Justice Thomas previously announced his conclusion to this effect in several cases. He cites to them in his *Randall* dissent. See id at 2502.

[46] Id.

ment with *Buckley*. His view has consistently been that contribution limits do not, as *Buckley* and its progeny have held, infringe First Amendment rights any less severely than do expenditure limits. Both kinds of limits, he argued, should be subjected to strict scrutiny, which both would fail.

Justice Thomas's principal thrust, however, was not directed at *Buckley* itself but rather at what he regarded as the plurality opinion's demonstration that "*Buckley*'s limited scrutiny of contribution limits is 'insusceptible of principled application. . . .'"[47] Justice Thomas argued that neither step of Justice Breyer's two-step inquiry—the determination that "danger signs" exist, followed by the exercise of independent judicial judgment evaluating the restrictions' tailoring—"can be reduced to a workable inquiry."[48] The plurality opinion left uncertain just how the Court is to determine whether limits are dangerously low, and it compounded this error by engaging in what Justice Thomas characterized as an "odd review" that combined "unrelated factors"[49] to reach its conclusion that Act 64's restrictions are insufficiently narrowly drawn. Parsing these factors left Justice Thomas unconvinced either that they were relevant or that they succeeded in distinguishing Vermont's limits from those the Court has sustained in other cases. What Justice Thomas's opinion amounts to, in the end, is an effort to demonstrate that the plurality opinion does not comport with rule of law values because "its discussion offers nothing resembling a rule at all."[50] "*Buckley*," he complained,

> as the plurality has applied it, gives us license to simply strike down any limits that just *seem* to be too stringent, and to uphold the rest. The First Amendment does not grant us this authority. *Buckley* provides no consistent protection to the core of the First Amendment, and must be overruled.[51]

D. JUSTICE STEVENS

Justice Stevens's dissent joined Justice Souter's in concluding

---

[47] Id at 2503 (citation omitted).
[48] Id.
[49] Id at 2504.
[50] Id at 2506.
[51] Id.

that Act 64 was constitutional in its entirety. But, coming at the matter from different premises entirely from those that guided the Justices who joined the judgment, and assuming a more vehement posture than Justice Souter on the matter of expenditure limits, Justice Stevens argued that *Buckley*'s holding in this regard should be overruled. He cited a number of factors that provided him with the requisite justification for revisiting *Buckley*'s holding.

First, Justice Stevens argued that *Buckley* itself "upset a long-established practice."[52] Second, the Court's post-*Buckley* reiteration of the distinction between contribution and expenditure limits occurred "primarily in cases affirming the validity of contribution limits or their functional equivalents,"[53] and thus the Court had not in fact addressed the stare decisis implications of *Buckley*'s expenditure limits holding. In addition, when the *McConnell* Court (in the opinion by Justices Stevens and O'Connor) invoked stare decisis to justify sustaining the contribution limits there at issue, it also adverted to the *"'respect that the Legislative and Judicial Branches owe to one another.'"*[54] The *Buckley* Court did not show respect to the legislative branch when it refused to defer to the legislature's judgment regarding the necessity for expenditure limitations.

At this point, Justice Stevens's dissent turned for support to Justice White, invoking that Justice's refusal to abandon his opposition to *Buckley* regarding expenditure limitations: "As Justice White recognized, it is quite wrong to equate money and speech."[55] A candidate, Justice Stevens went on to assert, "can exercise due care to ensure that her message reaches all voters,"[56] and as confirmation he offered several examples of effective political speech that did not require significant expenditure by the candidate.

Turning to the government interests that support expenditure limitations, Justice Stevens was persuaded that such limitations were justified by the interest in preventing corruption as well as the interest in "'protect[ing] equal access to the political arena,

---

[52] Id at 2507

[53] Id.

[54] Id (emphasis in original) (citation omitted).

[55] Id at 2508, citing Justice White's opinion concurring in part and dissenting in part in *Buckley*, 424 US at 263.

[56] Id at 2509.

[and] free[ing] candidates and their staffs from the interminable burden of fundraising.'"[57] Justice Stevens was troubled by the amount of time that fundraising requires from officeholders, because he was convinced that it "leaves them too busy to handle their public responsibilities effectively."[58] And he did not find in the record evidence to convince him that the interests offered in support of expenditure limitations were pretexts for protecting incumbents.

The "final point"[59] that Justice Stevens made to support his conclusion was an assertion that the Framers would have been on his side. Despite acknowledging that "[s]peculation about how the Framers would have legislated if they had foreseen [modern campaign practices] cannot provide us with definitive answers,"[60] he nevertheless claimed that "they would have been appalled by the impact of modern fundraising practices on the ability of elected officials to perform their public responsibilities."[61]

E. JUSTICE SOUTER

Justice Souter's view was that the Court of Appeals was right to remand to the district court for further inquiry regarding Act 64's expenditure limitations and right to conclude that the contribution limits satisfy the Court's prior cases. On the expenditure limits issue, Justice Souter read *Buckley* differently from the plurality: he read it not to have squarely or sufficiently addressed what he referred to as the "time-protection" interest,[62] and thus to require fact-finding on the question whether there is a need to "slow the fundraising treadmill."[63] Justice Souter was convinced that the record was incomplete, and the Court was therefore wrong

---

[57] Id (citing his dissenting opinion in *Colorado Republican Federal Campaign Comm. v Federal Election Comm'n*, 518 US 604, 649–50 (1996)). The legitimacy of the interest in equalizing resources was unambiguously rejected in *Buckley*, 424 US 48–49. Though that aspect of the *Buckley* opinion was not explicitly invoked by the plurality in *Randall*, it was implicitly affirmed when in the context of announcing its refusal to overrule *Buckley* on this point the plurality adverted to the "other governmental interests" that were advanced—and rejected—in that case. 126 S Ct at 2488.

[58] Id at 2509.

[59] Id at 2510.

[60] Id.

[61] Id.

[62] Id at 2511.

[63] Id at 2512.

to have foreclosed "the ability of a State to remedy the impact of the money chase on the democratic process."[64]

The contribution limits, in Justice Souter's view, though low, did not represent "remarkable departures" from either those the Court had previously upheld or those that other states had adopted and that had achieved judicial sanction. He stressed that his point, in adverting to prior cases that upheld legislative judgments, was "that the consistency in *legislative* judgment tells us that Vermont is not an eccentric party of one, and that this is a case for the judicial deference that our own precedents say we owe here."[65] In addition, he remained unpersuaded that the plurality's suspicion that the low contribution limits were incumbent-protective was warranted by reality.

Finally, Justice Souter addressed a number of the details about the contribution limits that had bothered the plurality. Counting a volunteer's expenses against that person's contribution limits, as Act 64 did, might indeed be a "colossal nuisance."[66] That reality would not necessarily imply that the act would limit volunteer activity. The failure to index the contribution limits to inflation, Justice Souter said, might render the limits problematic in the future, but did not affect their present validity. That the parties were subjected to the same contribution limits as individuals, along with other restrictions on party activity, might justify a wholesale reexamination of the situation of political parties, but standing alone the provision did not suffice to condemn the act. Last, reaching Act 64's presumption of coordinated expenditures on the part of political parties, which the plurality had had no occasion to reach, Justice Souter found the presumption insignificant. The presumption is so easily rebuttable, he insisted, that its burden could not be described as onerous.

II. WHAT'S NEXT AFTER RANDALL?

In what follows, I will make two principal points. First, I will argue that perhaps the most remarkable aspect of *Randall* is not its result but Justice Breyer's opinion. Second, I will suggest that *Randall* makes plain that the Court is profoundly divided about

---

[64] Id.

[65] Id at 2513.

[66] Id at 2515.

how to approach campaign finance regulations and that, where the divisions have to do with matters of principle—such as whether First Amendment values are genuinely implicated when legislatures enact campaign finance restrictions—there appears to be little room for or inclination to compromise. Thus, an answer to the question of what the future holds for campaign finance regulations must await a case in which the voices of Chief Justice Roberts and Justice Alito can be more clearly heard, their views more clearly articulated, than they were in *Randall*. *Wisconsin Right to Life v FEC*[67] may prove to be such a case.

A. JUSTICE BREYER'S SURPRISE

Randall, of course, was the first campaign finance case to be decided on the merits after *McConnell*, in which the majority opinion regarding the principal portions of BCRA could be read to have "reframed the way the Court addresses the constitutionality of campaign finance regulation,"[68] and to have "thoroughly repudiated *Buckley*'s First Amendment premises."[69] Because the expenditure limitations of Act 64 represented, and were apparently designed as, a direct challenge to *Buckley*, reform advocates no doubt felt that they were doctrinally as well poised for victory in the Supreme Court as they had been since before the Supreme Court in *Buckley* reversed the decision of the D.C. Circuit. Still, because the *McConnell* Court had been closely divided and the dissenting opinions unyielding and sharply critical, *McConnell* was rightly regarded as a precarious victory.[70] Had Justice Alito not replaced Justice O'Connor, one of the authors of the principal majority opinion in *McConnell*,[71] the *Randall* result might well have been a surprise. But because of this personnel change on the Court, it was not. What was surprising—what, indeed, could hardly have been anticipated—was that Justice Breyer would have voted with

---

[67] 2006 WL 3746669 (DDC), cert granted, 2007 WL 123974 (US).

[68] Briffault, 3 Election L J at 148 (cited in note 2).

[69] BeVier, 3 Election L J at 127 (cited in note 6).

[70] See Briffault, 3 Election L J at 149 (cited in note 2) ("*McConnell* is as precarious a victory for reform as it is sweeping. Both the specific holding and the Court's basic approach to campaign finance restriction could be dramatically transformed if and when the membership of the Court changes.").

[71] Chief Justice Roberts replaced Chief Justice Rehnquist, who dissented from the principal majority opinion in *McConnell*. It was not expected that views of the late Chief Justice and his successor would differ greatly on the issue of campaign finance regulation.

the new majority. Even more surprising is that he would have written the opinion that he wrote, and that his was the opinion that the new members of the Court joined on the merits.

Justice Breyer joined the majority in *McConnell*, voting to uphold the BCRA's most significant provisions restricting soft money contributions and prohibiting corporate and union expenditures on "electioneering communications." An important aspect of that majority opinion was explicit adoption of an exceptionally lenient standard of review of and deference to the legislative judgments that BCRA embodied regarding the need for regulation of campaign finance practices. The *McConnell* majority opinion that Justice Breyer joined said that Congress—that is, the legislative branch— has "particular expertise"[72] when it comes to predicting the likely effects of campaign finance practices. Congress must be given "sufficient room to anticipate and respond to concerns about circumvention of regulations designed to protect the integrity of the electoral process."[73] A lenient standard of review "shows proper deference to Congress' ability to weigh competing constitutional interests in an area in which it enjoys particular expertise."[74]

In addition to joining the majority in *McConnell* in its enthusiastic and uncritical deference to legislative judgment, Justice Breyer in his concurrence in *Shrink* had insisted that, when it came to campaign finance regulations, "constitutionally protected interests lie on both sides of the legal equation"[75] and thus a "presumption against constitutionality is out of place."[76] In addition, he said, the *Buckley* language that explicitly rejected "the concept that government may restrict the speech of some elements of our society in order to enhance the relative voice of others"[77] "cannot be taken literally."[78]

Thus, it could not easily have been foreseen that Justice Breyer would conclude in *Randall* that both Act 64's expenditure limitations and its contribution limitations were unconstitutional. And the opinion in which he explained his conclusions contained more

---

[72] *McConnell*, 540 US at 137.

[73] Id.

[74] Id at 136–37.

[75] 538 US at 400.

[76] Id at 401.

[77] *Buckley*, 424 US at 48–49.

[78] 538 US at 402.

surprises still. If the *McConnell* majority did indeed reframe the Court's approach to the constitutionality of campaign finance regulations, Justice Breyer's *Randall* opinion looks like something of an effort to *re*-reframe it. It certainly endorses aspects of *Buckley* that, in light of *McConnell*, his *Shrink* concurrence, and his off-Court writing, might well have been thought inconsistent with his views.

Particularly surprising was Justice Breyer's resolute summoning of and reliance upon the virtues of stare decisis and, more importantly, his conclusion that *Buckley*'s command that expenditure limitations are "'constitutionally invalid'"[79] was an unyielding one. Justice Breyer's commitment to precedent as a rule of decision is at best a sometime thing.[80] In invoking it with respect to the expenditure limitations in *Randall*, he may have discerned advantages in addition to and quite other than those inherent in vindicating the values of certainty and stability to which he appealed. It permitted him to put the possibility that he would reexamine *Buckley* off the table and, by then characterizing Act 64's expenditure limits as "not substantially different from those at issue in *Buckley*,"[81] to insist that the *Buckley* Court was sufficiently aware of the time-protection rationale that "fuller consideration" of it would not "have changed [the] result."[82] Thus he was able to avoid having to join issue with his *Shrink* concurrence, which seemed most definitely to have pointed in an opposite direction. For example, in *Shrink* Justice Breyer suggested that *Buckley* might be "reinterpret(ed) to make less absolute the contribution/expenditure line, particularly in respect to independently wealthy candidates, whose expenditures might be considered contributions to their own campaigns"[83] and in practically the same breath made explicit his view that *only* if *Buckley* could be read "to give the

---

[79] 126 S Ct at 2488.

[80] See Stephen Breyer, *Active Liberty: Interpreting Our Democratic Constitution* 116 (Vintage, 2005) (emphasizing the importance of judges in constitutional cases taking account of "real-world consequences" and differentiating that approach from that of judges who would place nearly exclusive interpretive weight on "language, history, tradition, or precedent."). In his writing, Justice Breyer concedes that "a court focused on consequences may decide a case in a way that radically changes the law. But this is not always a bad thing." Id at 119.

[81] 126 S Ct at 2490.

[82] Id.

[83] *Shrink*, 528 US at 405 (2000) (Breyer concurring).

political branches sufficient leeway to enact comprehensive solutions to the problems posed by campaign finance"[84] would he be
willing to be bound by the precedent it supposedly set.

In this context, it is perhaps worth noting that the principal
justification offered by the state for Act 64's expenditure limits in
Randall, and the only one that Justice Breyer's opinion took any
pains to address,[85] was the "time-protection" rationale. Perhaps,
therefore, his opinion stands only for the proposition that expenditure limitations cannot be defended *as means to reduce the amount
of time candidates devote to fundraising*. To limit the reach of his
opinion in this way would be helpful to reform advocates in the
future. No doubt on account of a deliberate strategy that seems
not only to have infused the tenor of the legislative debates in
Vermont but dictated the arguments that the state would offer,
the defense of the expenditure limitations in *Randall* rested exclusively on variations of the "unequal access is a signal of corruption"
themes that the majority in *McConnell* had emphasized along with
the time-protection rationale. In other words, Vermont did not
claim to enact nor did it defend Act 64's expenditure limitations
in reliance on the more fundamental ground that such limits serve
a legitimate interest in equalizing the resources available to political candidates. The *Buckley* Court, in what was surely the most
controversial and contested aspect of its decision, had squarely
rejected the First Amendment legitimacy of such an interest. In
his *Shrink* concurrence, in the context of elaborating his view that
Shrink was a case where "constitutionally protected interests lie
on both sides of the legal equation,"[86] Justice Breyer had insisted
that the words it used in doing so "cannot be taken literally."[87] In
addition to the First Amendment interest in protecting the rights
of candidates and their supporters, he implied that the interest on
the regulation side was a *First Amendment* interest in "democra-

---

[84] Id.

[85] Justice Breyer brushed away the state's argument that the expenditure limitations were
necessary as means to deter corruption. The state had not shown, he said, "any dramatic
increase in corruption or its appearance in Vermont [since *Buckley*]; nor have they shown
that expenditure limits are the only way to attack that problem." *Randall*, 126 S Ct at
2489–90.

[86] *Shrink*, 528 US at 400 (Breyer concurring).

[87] Id at 401.

tiz[ing] the influence that money itself may bring to bear upon the electoral process."[88]

Since Vermont did not invoke equalization in defense of Act 64, it did not clearly invite Justice Breyer to bring this aspect of his *Shrink* concurrence to bear on his analysis of the expenditure limitation at issue in *Randall*. Still, it remains a puzzle of his *Randall* opinion that Justice Breyer failed to quote this aspect of his *Shrink* concurrence. Nor did he specifically address the question whether, in refusing to overrule *Buckley*, he meant to endorse *Buckley* as it was originally understood—that is, as pretermitting pursuit of political equality as a legitimate First Amendment interest—or only as his *Shrink* opinion would have reinterpreted it, namely, to permit legislation justified by a *First Amendment* interest in "limiting the political rights of some so as to make effective the political rights of the entire electorate."[89]

The second unanticipated aspect of Justice Breyer's opinion in *Randall* is that, rather than deferring to the legislature's judgment regarding the level at which the contribution limits had been set— as the Court had been increasingly explicit about doing since *Buckley*[90]—it engaged in the "careful, precise, and independent judicial review"[91] the promise of which had been honored only in the breach in every previous case. It engaged in this review despite reiterating the judgment that the Court is not able to "determine with any degree of exactitude the precise restriction necessary to carry out the statute's legitimate objectives."[92] But there is "some lower bound [at which point] the constitutional risk to the democratic electoral process becomes too great,"[93] and when those "outer limits" are reached, the Court has no alternative but "to exercise . . . independent judicial judgment"[94] to the end of "assessing the proportionality of the restrictions."[95]

---

[88] Id.

[89] Id at 402 (citation omitted).

[90] For a summary of the Court's progression toward increasingly deferential review of legislative judgments regarding the contribution limitations as corruption-prevention devices, see BeVier, 3 Election L J at 129–36 (cited in note 6).

[91] *Shrink*, 528 US at 400.

[92] *Randall*, 126 S Ct at 2492.

[93] Id.

[94] Id.

[95] Id.

It was hardly to have been anticipated that Justice Breyer would be moved to depart from his posture of deference with regard to the contribution limits. Once having done so, however, it was practically a foregone conclusion that he would find that Act 64's limits could not survive scrutiny. Still, answers to two important questions do not emerge from his opinion. Apart from adverting to the fact that they are "substantially lower than both the limits we have previously upheld and comparable limits in other states,"[96] Justice Breyer did not specify why he thought Act 64's limits were so low as to constitute "danger signs" that challengers might be prevented "from mounting effective campaigns."[97] Both Justice Thomas from one side and Justice Souter from the other offered powerful reasons to question both Justice Breyer's apparent premises and his conclusion on this point. And, though his recitation of the five factors that led him to conclude that the danger signs meant real trouble contains a myriad of details, his conclusion is undertheorized, good for the resolution of the case at hand but suggesting little about the resolution of the next one.[98]

B. AN UNCERTAIN FUTURE FOR CAMPAIGN FINANCE REGULATION

The range of *Randall* opinions makes plain that *McConnell* cannot be regarded as a permanent resolution of the issue of the First Amendment's constraints on campaign finance regulations. The decision also makes plain that the *McConnell* majority's "refram[ing] of] the way the Court addresses the constitutionality of campaign finance regulation"[99] was indeed a precarious victory for reformers.

The members of the present Court remain as deeply divided as, if not more divided than, their *McConnell* opinions revealed them to be,[100] and the two newest members of the Court have yet to weigh in. The opinions reveal that unbridgeable chasms persist

---

[96] Id at 2494.

[97] Id at 2492.

[98] See Cass R. Sunstein, *One Case at a Time: Judicial Minimalism on the Supreme Court* 9, 58 (Harvard, 1999) (highlighting Justice Breyer's tendency to be "minimalist" and focus "only on what is necessary to resolve particular disputes," rather than developing "broad rules" to resolve future cases).

[99] Briffault, 3 Election L J at 148 (cited in note 2).

[100] They may be more divided than the *McConnell* opinions revealed them to be because Justice Stevens in *Randall* suggested that he had gotten off the First Amendment boat almost entirely. In his *McConnell* majority opinion, he at least paid lip service to the notion that First Amendment review of campaign finance regulations was called for.

about how to answer the most fundamental questions. That contribution and expenditure limitations might represent a genuine threat not just to the individual rights of candidates and citizens but to political freedom more generally is nowhere acknowledged by those who embrace reform. On the other hand, those who are suspicious of regulation cannot bring themselves to concede that unlimited giving to and spending on political campaigns might seriously threaten the integrity of the democratic process.

The Justices continue to talk past each other, just as the academic commentators do.[101] As I understand them, the positions the Justices have staked out are as follows. Of the six-member majority that agreed on the result in *Randall*, only two Justices—Scalia and Thomas—seem squarely to occupy what I will call the freedom side of the chasm that separates the Justices from one another with regard to the First Amendment and campaign finance regulation. In their view, distinguishing between contribution and expenditure limitations is wrong not because expenditure limitations should sometimes be sustained (which is the view of the three dissenters, as well—perhaps[102]—of Justice Breyer). Rather it is wrong because, in dictating a more lenient standard of review for contribution than expenditure limitations, it provides insufficient protection to free political speech. The Court should subject both contribution and expenditure limitations to the most rigorous review. Though persuaded that *Buckley*'s contribution/ expenditure distinction is indefensible, Justices Scalia and Thomas continue to embrace the parts of the *Buckley* per curiam that the *McConnell* majority seems clearly, if implicitly, to have rejected.[103] Justices Scalia and Thomas think *Buckley* was right to affirm that "contribution and expenditure limitations operate in an area of the most fundamental First Amendment activities;"[104] that it was right to equate the regulation of political giving and spending not with the regulation of conduct but with the regulation of speech; and that it was right to reject the challengers' arguments that

---

[101] Contrast Spencer Overton, *Judicial Modesty and the Lessons of McConnell v. FEC*, 3 Election L J 305 (2004) (arguing *McConnell* properly defers to Congressional expertise in the area of campaign finance), with Bradley A. Smith, *McConnell v. Federal Election Commission: Ideology Trumps Reality, Pragmatism*, 3 Election L J 345 (2004) (arguing campaign finance laws interfere with First Amendment rights).

[102] See notes 68–98 and accompanying text.

[103] See BeVier, 3 Election L J at 128–40 (cited in note 6).

[104] *Buckley*, 424 US at 14.

campaign finance restriction should be subjected to the more lenient scrutiny of regulations of conduct that *O'Brien* dictates.[105] For Justices Scalia and Thomas, the operative premise with respect to legislative judgments regarding the necessity for campaign finance regulation is one of deep distrust, not unquestioning deference.

Justice Kennedy is closest to Justices Scalia and Thomas on the continuum of views on the Court about the First Amendment and campaign finance regulation. He is inclined, as they are, to view campaign finance regulations as abridging important speech interests, and to subject them to more rather than less stringent review. However, rather than their apparent intractability about the imperative nature of strict scrutiny of *all* contribution and expenditure limitations, he has suggested that the Court would do well to scrap the entire *Buckley* apparatus of judicial decisions so that legislatures could start at square one and try some new experiments.[106] But instead of time after time insisting that *Buckley* should be overruled, he has attempted—as he did in *Randall*—to conform his judgments to its dictates and to "the universe of campaign finance regulation" created in its wake.

Because Justice Breyer's *Randall* opinion so unexpectedly attempted to straddle the two sides of the First Amendment chasm, and because the principles on which it rested are opaque, the most one can say with confidence about the side he will find himself on is that it will depend on the facts of the regulatory provisions at issue, on the interests put forward to justify them, and on his own assessment of whether the regulatory provisions enhance or diminish democratic self-government. In overturning Act 64's expenditure limitations on the authority of *Buckley*, Justice Breyer did affirm that there is First Amendment value in "unlimited political expression."[107] He rejected neither *Buckley*'s proposition that First Amendment interests are implicated by both expenditure and contribution limitations (thus agreeing in principle with Justices Scalia, Thomas, and Kennedy) nor the proposition that, with re-

---

[105] *United States v O'Brien*, 391 US 367 (1968) (holding that, "when 'speech' and 'nonspeech' elements are combined in the same course of conduct, a sufficiently important governmental interest in regulating the nonspeech element can justify incidental limitations on First Amendment freedoms.").

[106] *Shrink*, 528 US at 409–10.

[107] *Randall*, 126 S Ct at 2488.

spect to contribution limitations, deference to legislative judgments about the necessity and amount of the restrictions should be the norm (thus endorsing the *McConnell* majority's position).

Justices Souter, Ginsburg, and Stevens occupy the deference-to-legislators side of First Amendment chasm. These three Justices are in agreement with—indeed, they were in large part the engineers of—the post-*Buckley* trend toward the ever more deferential review of contribution limitations that culminated in the majority opinion in *McConnell*. Thus, far from regarding these developments with the dismay that they occasion for Justices Scalia, Thomas, and Kennedy, they regard them as benign, wholly appropriate, and completely faithful to the First Amendment. In place of a premise of distrust of legislative regulation of political giving and spending, they operate from the premise that legislatures enjoy a significant institutional advantage with respect to campaign finance. Legislators, after all, are "seasoned campaigners,"[108] to whom judges should defer on account of their "'greater institutional expertise . . . in the field of election regulation.'"[109]

With his *Randall* dissent, Justice Stevens laid claim to sole occupancy of the farthest reaches of the deference side of the First Amendment chasm. It seemed clear to him that *Buckley* was "quite wrong to equate money and speech."[110] In other words, he has not been persuaded that it abridges individual citizens' and candidates' freedom of speech to limit their freedom to decide how much money to spend on speech during election campaigns. Accordingly he would abandon serious First Amendment scrutiny of both contribution and expenditure limitations and review them with the minimal deference the Court currently accords to time, place, and manner regulations.[111]

Thus the continuum of views on the Court about the First Amendment and campaign finance regulation. One view is that

---

[108] Id at 2509 (Stevens dissenting).

[109] Id at 2513 (Souter dissenting) (quoting *Shrink*, 528 US at 402 (Breyer concurring)).

[110] *Randall*, 126 S Ct at 2508 (Stevens dissenting).

[111] See Kathleen Sullivan and Gerald Gunther, *First Amendment Law* 279–80 (Foundation, 2d ed 2003) (noting that "scrutiny on recent time, place and manner cases has most commonly been quite deferential on the substantiality of the state's interests, as well as the relationship of the means chosen to the implementation of those interests. The Court's implementation of the requirement that a regulation be 'narrowly drawn to further a substantial government interest'—a requirement common to both symbolic expression claims and time, place, and manner restrictions—does not involve strict scrutiny, or serious inquiry into availability of 'less restrictive means' to implement the government interest.").

the First Amendment demands strict scrutiny of and the adoption of a premise of distrust toward contribution and expenditure limits. A second view is that there are First Amendment interests on both the freedom and the regulation side of contribution and expenditure limits. A third view is that, though there are First Amendment interests on the freedom side, they are minimal and easily trumped by the combination of important government interests favoring restrictions and the comparative institutional advantage reflected in—and the corollary premise of judicial deference to—legislative judgments regarding their necessity. Justice Stevens appears now to embrace a fourth view, namely, that when the only activities being regulated are the giving and spending of money, there are *no* First Amendment interests of any significance on the freedom side of the equation. "Money," he declares, "is property; it is not speech."[112]

Thus, it seems, debate on these issues has reached an impasse. Notwithstanding Justice Breyer's attempt to straddle it in *Randall*, the chasm that separates the Justices from one another appears unbridgeable. After all that has been written on the issue already, one who thinks that basic freedoms are not at stake when campaign finance regulations are enacted is not likely to become persuaded that they are. On the other hand, one who embraces the intuition that legislative judgments tend to be hostages to incumbent self-interest is unlikely to think that legislators are trustworthy rule-makers when it comes to deciding how much their challengers may spend in future elections. Those who believe that, because legislators know best how the electoral system works, they can be trusted to regulate it so as to protect challengers are unlikely to think that precisely because of their comparative advantage at understanding how the system works legislators are the system's *least* trustworthy guardians. And one who believes that the integrity of the very democratic process that the First Amendment protects is put at risk by excessive and unregulated spending on political campaigns and that the rights of the entire electorate cannot be secured without limiting the rights of some within it is likely to

---

[112] Justice Stevens first announced his view that "[m]oney is property; it is not speech" in *Shrink*, 528 US at 398. He elaborated: "The First Amendment doesn't provide same measure of protection to the use of money . . . as it provides to the use of ideas. . . . The right to use one's own money to hire gladiators, or to fund 'speech by proxy,' certainly merits significant constitutional protection. These property rights, however, are not entitled to the same protection as the right to say what one pleases." Id.

find the threat to political freedom too abstract and in any case too trivial in a state as active as ours to stand in the way of campaign finance reform efforts.

There would seem to be little if anything that could be said and little if any evidence that could be marshaled, by either side, which would stand much chance of persuading those on the other to reconsider their positions. Thus, Chief Justice Roberts and Justice Alito seem to hold the key to the First Amendment future of campaign finance regulation. *Wisconsin Right to Life v FEC* (hereafter *WRTL*),[113] which the Court will decide during the October 2006 term, may prove to be the case in which they are forced to tip their respective hands. It is likely to reveal whether the two new Justices tilt toward the Scalia/Thomas/Kennedy view or the Stevens/Souter/Ginsburg view. It may even reveal them to be straddlers, following Justice Breyer's example. Should they tilt toward the Scalia/Thomas/Kennedy view, however, *McConnell*'s premise of deference to legislative judgment about the necessity for campaign finance restrictions may well give way to a new majority's premise of distrust. If one or the other of them is drawn to the Stevens/Souter/Ginsburg brand of deference, on the other hand, then *McConnell* looks secure for the near future.

WRTL is an as-applied challenge to § 203 of the BCRA,[114] which the Court sustained against facial challenge in *McConnell*. Section 203 forbids corporations and unions to use general treasury funds to pay for broadcast ads that mention federal candidates by name within thirty days of a primary or sixty days of a general election. Wisconsin Right to Life, a nonprofit advocacy corporation, wished to use general treasury funds to pay for broadcast ads during the relevant time period before the 2004 election. Because the ads that WRTL planned to run mentioned the name of Senator Feingold, who was going to be a candidate for reelection, they constituted "electioneering communications" within the meaning of § 203 and were thus prohibited. The ads contained no explicit reference to the coming election, however. Rather, they referred to the then-anticipated filibusters of judicial nominees. Their literal message urged citizens to contact Senators Kohl (who was not running for reelection) and Feingold (who was) and ask them to vote against

---

[113] 2006 WL 3746669 (DDC), cert granted, 2007 WL 123974 (US).

[114] Id at *1.

the filibusters. WRTL sought a preliminary injunction against the FEC's enforcement of § 203 as applied generally to all election-eering communications that constitute "grass roots lobbying" and specifically to the particular ads it wished to run. Concluding that "the reasoning of the *McConnell* Court [left] no room for the kind of 'as applied' challenge WRTL propounds before us,"[115] a three-judge district court initially denied WRTL's motion. The Su-preme Court disagreed, reading *McConnell* as having neither re-solved nor precluded an as-applied challenge and remanded the case.[116] On remand, District Judge Leon again wrote the opinion, granted WRTL's motion for summary judgment, and sustained its as-applied challenge to § 203. The court refused WRTL's re-quest that it carve out a general exception for "grass roots lob-bying" by corporations and unions. It held, however, that the par-ticular ads that WRTL had proposed to run in 2004 were genuine issue ads, that the government interests that justified regulating express advocacy did not justify regulation of genuine issue ads, and that the First Amendment required that the ads be exempt from § 203. In reaching its conclusion that the ads were genuine issue ads, the court refused to undertake a contextual analysis to determine WRTL's intent in running the ads and of the effect they were likely or were meant to have on the voting public. Instead, the court confined its analysis to the ads' literal content and limited its consideration to

> language within the four corners of the anti-filibuster ads that, at a minimum: (1) describes a legislative issue that is either currently the subject of legislative scrutiny or likely to be the subject of such scrutiny; (2) refers to the prior voting record or current position of the named candidate on the issue de-scribed; (3) exhorts the listener to do anything other than con-tact the candidate about the described issue; (4) promotes, at-tacks, supports or opposes the named candidate; and (5) refers to the upcoming election, candidacy, and/or political party of the candidate.[117]

Judge Roberts in dissent thought that in refusing to look at pur-pose and effect in judging the as-applied challenge, the court was

---

[115] *WRTL*, 2004 WL 3622736, *2 (DDC).

[116] *WRTL*, 126 S Ct 1016 (2006).

[117] *WRTL*, 2006 WL 3746669, *8 (DDC).

ignoring the implications of *McConnell*. In *McConnell*, said Judge Roberts, the Court looked "precisely to the purpose and effect of advertising in a facial challenge to the constitutionality of the electioneering communications provision."[118]

The Supreme Court granted review of the district court decision on January 19, 2007.[119] It set an expedited schedule for briefing and argument, indicating that its decision will be forthcoming in the October 2006 term. It is impossible to make a confident prediction about what that decision will be, and not merely because Chief Justice Roberts and Justice Alito have not yet tipped their hands. The Court in *WRTL* could either broaden the reach of § 203 or effectively eviscerate it. Which the Court will do—or whether it will pursue some third alternative—is anybody's guess.

WRTL's litigation posture—the way it has framed the issue before the Court—is one reason why prediction is difficult. WRTL is a nonprofit, nonstock ideological advocacy corporation, but it did not claim the organizational exemption from BCRA to which it might well have been entitled by *FEC v Massachusetts Citizens for Life*.[120] WRTL is after bigger game than simply an exemption for itself. It is seeking an exemption for "grass roots lobbying" in general—or "genuine issue ads" in particular—that would be available to *all* corporations and unions. Thus it has framed the issue as one having to do with First Amendment protection based on the *content of the speech*, not based on the *identity or characteristics of the speaker*. This presents a problem for one trying to predict how the Court will rule because of the way the opinions in *McConnell* were written. The majority opinion sustaining § 203 was surprisingly opaque on how to draw the line between "electioneering communications" on which expenditures by corporations and unions could be prohibited and political speech—"genuine issue ads"—on which they presumably could not be. Justice Stevens, somewhat grudgingly, acknowledged—or was willing to "assume[—]that the interests that justify the regulation of campaign speech might not apply to the regulation of genuine issue

---

[118] Id at 13 (Roberts dissenting).

[119] *WRTL*, 2007 WL 123974 (US).

[120] 107 S Ct 616 (1986) (creating an exemption from the prohibition on corporate spending for corporations that pursue ideological causes, are supported by ideologically motivated donors, and refuse contributions from business interests).

ads."[121] He was convinced, however, that, even though § 203 might prohibit some expenditures on genuine issue ads, it was not overbroad because "the vast majority" of prohibited ads were express advocacy or its functional equivalent.[122] Nor did the dissenters pay more attention than did the majority to the line-drawing problem that § 203 arguably poses. As Professor Briffault pointed out in his summary of the *McConnell* opinions, instead of concentrating on the differences between "electioneering communications" and genuine issue ads, the dissenting Justices focused on the constitutionality of "the underlying ban [on corporate and union expenditures] itself."[123] Nor is it obvious how the line should be drawn. If it is drawn the way the district court drew it, with attention only to ads' literal terms, corporations and unions will find it child's play to write ads whose literal terms mention incumbent candidates by name but which will be held to constitute issue advocacy. Drawing the line this way would go a long way to eviscerating § 203. On the other hand, if the line is drawn so that judges would have to determine from its context an ad's purpose and effect, then in practice very little would be gained by recognizing an as-applied exception to § 203 in principle.

The likely result in *WRTL* is also rendered uncertain by the position of the four dissenting Justices in *McConnell*. Each of them wanted to overrule *Austin v Michigan Chamber of Commerce*,[124] in which the Court first squarely held that the First Amendment permits legislatures to ban corporation and union independent expenditures on political advocacy on behalf of candidates. Three of those dissenting Justices are still on the Court. Justice O'Connor, who provided the necessary fifth vote to sustain § 203 in *McConnell*, has left. Thus, if Chief Justice Roberts and Justice Alito become persuaded, as Justices Scalia, Thomas, and Kennedy already are, that *Austin* was wrongly decided, then a five-Justice majority just might be assembled to overrule it. In that event, with regard to the ban on corporate and union spending at least, the line between electioneering communications and genuine issue advocacy would be beside the point. "Without *Austin*, § 203 would

---

[121] *McConnell*, 540 US at 206 n 88.

[122] Id.

[123] Briffault, 3 Election L J at 171 (cited in note 2).

[124] 494 US 652 (1990).

necessarily fail"[125] and there would be no need to decide either whether the First Amendment required an as-applied exception for genuine issue advocacy or, if so, how to know genuine issue advocacy when one sees it. Such an outcome is unlikely. None of the parties has seen fit to put the continuing validity of *Austin* in play. While the Court has not always confined itself to resolving the precise issues argued by the parties,[126] to hazard a guess—much less to predict—that they might not do so in *WRTL* would be foolhardy. The point is not that we ought to expect the Court to overrule *Austin*, even if the two new Justices tilt toward the Scalia/Thomas/Kennedy view of the First Amendment and campaign finance reform. Rather it is that, because their opinions in *McConnell* do not reveal even how Justices Scalia, Thomas, and Kennedy would draw the line that *WRTL* asks the Court to draw, we haven't the wherewithal to predict how they will draw it much less to predict what Chief Justice Roberts and Justice Alito will do.

One thing is clear. *WRTL* confronts the new Court with not one but two opportunities to reinvigorate First Amendment review of campaign finance regulation, and *Randall v Sorrell* suggests that *McConnell* was not necessarily the death blow that some had hoped and others feared.

---

[125] Briffault, 3 Election L J at 171 (cited in note 2).

[126] See, for example, *Dun & Bradstreet v Greenmoss Builders*, 472 US 749 (1985) (cert granted on the issue of whether the *New York Times* privilege extends to nonmedia defendants, whereas the Court decided that the privilege did not protect defendants being sued by private individuals suing for defamation about private matters).

JACOB E. GERSEN

OVERLAPPING AND UNDERLAPPING JURISDICTION IN ADMINISTRATIVE LAW

Perhaps the central question in administrative law is how decision-making authority should be allocated among political institutions. The nondelegation doctrine requires that Congress make certain policy choices by specifying an intelligible principle to guide agency discretion.[1] Nondelegation canons require that Congress speak with clarity when delegating especially important or broad discretionary authority to the executive.[2] Hard look review ensures that factual or scientific judgments are initially made by agencies, but with genuine judicial review of agency decision making.[3] The Administrative

Jacob E. Gersen is Assistant Professor of Law, The University of Chicago.

AUTHOR'S NOTE: My appreciation to Adam Cox, David Fontana, Anne Joseph O'Connell, David Strauss, Cass Sunstein, and Adrian Vermeule for extremely useful comments. Thanks to Helen Gilbert, Jessica Hertz, Stacey Nathan, Marc Tarlock, and Peter Wilson for excellent research assistance. Financial support was provided by the John M. Olin Foundation, the Lynde & Harry Bradley Foundation, and the Robert B. Roesing Faculty Fund.

[1] See *J. W. Hampton, Jr., & Co. v United States*, 276 US 394, 409 (1928). The vitality of the doctrine is hotly contested. Compare Eric A. Posner and Adrian Vermeule, *Interring the Nondelegation Doctrine*, 69 U Chi L Rev 1721 (2002), with Larry Alexander and Saikrishna Prakash, *Reports of the Nondelegation Doctrine's Death Are Greatly Exaggerated*, 70 U Chi L Rev 1297 (2003). For the Supreme Court's most recent pronouncement on the matter, see *Whitman v American Trucking Association*, 531 US 474 (2001).

[2] See Cass R. Sunstein, *Nondelegation Canons*, 67 U Chi L Rev 315, 321 (2000). Consider *FDA v Brown & Williamson Tobacco Corp.*, 529 US 120, 161 (2000); *MCI Telecom Corp. v AT&T Corp.*, 512 US 218, 234 (1994).

[3] See 5 USC § 706(2)(A) (2000); *Motor Vehicle Mfrs. Assn. v State Farm Mutual Auto Ins. Co.*, 463 US 29 (1983). See generally M. Elizabeth Magill, *Agency Choice of Policymaking*

Procedure Act's mandate for a rough separation of powers within agencies allocates decision-making authority to an administrative law judge and the collection of evidence to other officers or departments.[4] The *Chevron* doctrine allocates interpretive authority to agencies rather than courts.[5]

The particular allocation of authority that any of these doctrines entail might be readily contested, and many volumes have been filled with such debates.[6] For example, there is no shortage of work urging that courts should resolve questions of statutory interpretation de novo rather than deferentially,[7] or that the nondelegation doctrine should be more actively or less actively enforced.[8] These standard administrative law debates are now being replicated in other fields like foreign relations and national security.[9]

Most typically, these allocative disputes involve parceling out decision-making authority between courts and another political institution. For example, *Chevron* doctrine allocates interpretive authority between the judiciary and the executive. But increasingly, *Chevron* is being applied confusingly to interpretations of statutes that allocate interpretive authority either to multiple administrative

---

Form, 71 U Chi L Rev 1383, 1429–30 (2004); Sidney A. Shapiro and Richard E. Levy, *Judicial Incentives and Indeterminacy in Substantive Review of Administrative Decisions*, 44 Duke L J 1051, 1065 (1995). See also *Am. Paper Inst., Inc. v Am. Electric Power Service Corp.*, 461 US 402, 412 n 7 (1983).

[4] See 5 USC § 554(d) (2000).

[5] *Chevron USA, Inc. v Natural Resources Defense Council*, 467 US 837 (1984).

[6] For example, many commentators have urged that *Chevron* produces too much or too little deference. Compare Cynthia R. Farina, *Statutory Interpretation and the Balance of Power in the Administrative State*, 89 Colum L Rev 452 (1989) (too low); Jonathan T. Molot, *The Judicial Perspective in the Administrative State: Reconciling Modern Doctrines of Deference with the Judiciary's Structural Role*, 53 Stan L Rev 1 (2000) (too low); Cass R. Sunstein, *Law and Administration After Chevron*, 90 Colum L Rev 2071 (1990) (too low), with Thomas O. McGarity, *Some Thoughts on "Deossifying" the Rulemaking Process*, 41 Duke L J 1385 (1992) (too high); Richard J. Pierce, Jr., *Chevron and Its Aftermath: Judicial Review of Agency Interpretations of Statutory Provisions*, 41 Vand L Rev 301, 308–14 (1988) (too high); Peter L. Strauss, *One Hundred Fifty Cases per Year: Some Implications of the Supreme Court's Limited Resources for Judicial Review of Agency Action*, 87 Colum L Rev 1093 (1987) (too high).

[7] See, for example, Stephen G. Breyer, *Judicial Review of Questions of Law and Policy*, 38 Admin L Rev 363, 379 (1986).

[8] Consider Theodore J. Lowi, *The End of Liberalism: The Second Republic of the United States* (Norton, 2d ed 1979); Thomas O. Sargentich, *The Delegation Debate and Competing Ideals of the Administrative Process*, 36 Am U L Rev 419, 424 (1987); David Schoenbrod, *The Delegation Doctrine: Could the Court Give It Substance?* 83 Mich L Rev 1223, 1229 (1985). But see Posner and Vermeule, 69 U Chi L Rev at 1729 (cited in note 1).

[9] See, for example, Eric A. Posner and Cass R. Sunstein, *Chevronizing Foreign Law*, 116 Yale L J 1170 (2007); Derek Jinks and Neal Kumar Katyal, *Disregarding Foreign Relations Law*, 116 Yale L J 1230 (2007).

agencies or to a mix of federal and state institutions. These questions sound in the administrative law of preemption and shared jurisdiction statutes.

Such problems serve as the doctrinal backdrop for *Gonzales v Oregon*,[10] a case resolved in the 2006 Term of the Supreme Court. *Gonzales* involved a disputed interpretation of the Controlled Substances Act (CSA),[11] a statute that allocates decision-making authority to a number of federal and state entities. The Attorney General interpreted the CSA to preclude the prescription of drugs to facilitate assisted suicide for terminally ill patients, while an Oregon statute explicitly authorized such prescriptions.[12]

The underlying ethical and political questions in the case are obviously important and controversial. But *Gonzales* can also be used as a vehicle for revisiting and revising the conventional wisdom concerning agency interpretations of statutes that share jurisdiction between multiple political institutions.[13] Statutes of this sort create overlapping and underlapping jurisdictional schemes. This article examines the use by Congress and subsequent treatment by courts of overlapping and underlapping jurisdictional statutes in administrative law. Because overlapping and underlapping jurisdictional assignment can produce desirable incentives for administrative agencies, statutes of this sort are useful tools for managing principal-agent problems inherent in delegation. Unfortunately, courts often employ interpretive practices that undermine rather than support these regimes. *Gonzales* is a prime example.

I. DEATH, DIGNITY, AND DIVISION

A. BACKGROUND

In 1994, Oregon voters approved a ballot measure enacting the Oregon Death with Dignity Act (ODWDA).[14] The measure gives legal protection to state-licensed physicians who dispense or prescribe a lethal dose of drugs upon the request of a terminally ill patient if, and only if, the physicians comply with certain proce-

---

[10] 126 S Ct 904 (2006).

[11] 21 USCA § 801 et seq (2006).

[12] Oregon Death with Dignity Act, Or Rev Stat § 127.800 et seq (2003).

[13] On *Chevron* and preemption, see generally Nina A. Mendelson, *Chevron and Preemption*, 102 Mich L Rev 740 (2004).

[14] Or Rev Stat § 127.800 et seq (2003).

dural safeguards. To be eligible to request a prescription under the ODWDA, residents must receive a diagnosis from their attending physician that they have an incurable and irreversible disease that—within reasonable medical judgment—will cause death within six months.[15] Oregon physicians are then authorized to prescribe a lethal drug to facilitate the death of the terminally ill patient.

Prescribed drugs are regulated by the Controlled Substances Act (CSA), a voluminous statute that distributes authority to various federal and nonfederal agencies, including the Attorney General of the United States.[16] The CSA criminalizes the unauthorized distribution of substances classified in any of five schedules,[17] to which the Attorney General may add, remove, or reschedule substances after making specific findings. *Gonzales* involved Schedule II substances generally available to the public only pursuant to a written prescription issued by a physician.[18] A 1971 regulation promulgated by the Attorney General pursuant to CSA authority requires that every prescription for a controlled substance "be issued for a legitimate medical purpose by an individual practitioner acting in the usual course of his professional practice."[19] Violations of the CSA are investigated by the Drug Enforcement Agency (DEA) and carry significant criminal penalties. The specific drugs at issue in *Gonzales* are sometimes used in small doses for pain relief; but in large doses they are lethal. In 2004, thirty-seven patients ended their lives by ingesting a lethal dose of medication prescribed pursuant to the ODWDA.[20]

By the late 1990s, certain members of Congress were increasingly concerned about assisted suicide generally and the ODWDA specifically.[21] In 1997, a group of legislators invited the DEA to

---

[15] Or Rev Stat §§ 127.815, 127.800(12) (2003).

[16] 84 Stat 1242 (1970), codified as amended 21 USCA § 801 et seq (2006).

[17] 21 USCA §§ 841, 844 (2006).

[18] 21 USC § 829(a) (2000).

[19] 21 CFR § 1306.04(a) (2006).

[20] Or Dept of Human Servs, Seventh Annual Report on Oregon's Death with Dignity Act 20 (Mar 10, 2005).

[21] See Dan Eggen and Ceci Connolly, *Ashcroft Ruling Blocks Ore. Assisted-Suicide Law*, Wash Post A01 (Nov 7, 2001); Joe Rojas-Burke, *Showdown on Assisted Suicide Looms in Senate; Both Sides Know the Stakes Are High for the Right-to-Die Movement Across the Nation*, Oregonian A01 (Sept 19, 2000); *Meddling with Oregon's Law*, NY Times A14 (Oct 30, 1999).

prosecute or revoke the CSA registration of Oregon physicians who assisted suicide pursuant to the ODWDA.[22] Although the then head of the DEA responded favorably, Attorney General Janet Reno concluded that the DEA could not take the proposed action because the CSA does not authorize it to "displace the states as the primary regulators of the medical profession, or to override a state's determination as to what constitutes legitimate medical practice."[23] Legislation was introduced in Congress to delegate explicitly to the agency any requisite authority, but the bills did not garner enough support to pass.[24]

In 2001, John Ashcroft was appointed Attorney General. Oregon officials wrote to Attorney General Ashcroft in February 2001 to inquire whether the department was likely to change its position.[25] Initially, Ashcroft disclaimed any intention to alter the agency's view on the CSA and the ODWDA. However, drawing on analysis from an Office of Legal Counsel memorandum on the subject, Attorney General Ashcroft soon issued an Interpretive Rule stating that

> assisting suicide is not a "legitimate medical purpose" within the meaning of 21 C.F.R. 1306.04 (2001), and that prescribing, dispensing, or administering federally controlled substances to assist suicide violates the Controlled Substances Act . . . and that prescribing drugs for assisted suicide may render his registration . . . inconsistent with the public interest and therefore subject to possible suspension or revocation under 21 U.S.C. § 824(a)(4).[26]

The prior regulation, 21 CFR 1306.04 (issued in 1971), had interpreted the CSA to require that prescriptions be for a "legitimate medical purpose." The Ashcroft Interpretive Rule offered an in-

[22] Letter from Sen. Orrin Hatch and Rep. Henry Hyde to Thomas A. Constantine (July 25, 1997), reprinted in Hearings on S 2151 before the Senate Committee on the Judiciary, 105th Cong, 2d Sess 2–3 (1999).

[23] Letter from Attorney General Janet Reno to Sen. Orrin Hatch on Oregon's Death with Dignity Act (June 5, 1998), reprinted in Hearings on S 2151 before the Senate Committee on the Judiciary, 105th Cong, 2d Sess 5–6 (1999).

[24] See HR 4006, 105th Cong, 2d Sess, in 144 Cong Rec H 4240 (June 5, 1998); HR 2260, 106th Cong, 1st Sess, in 145 Cong Rec H 4614 (June 17, 1999).

[25] See Letter of Feb 2, 2001 in Brief for Patient-Respondents in Opposition, Appendix 55a, *Gonzales v Oregon*, 126 S Ct 904 (2006) (No 04-623).

[26] Dispensing of Controlled Substances to Assist Suicide, 66 Fed Reg 56607 (Nov 9, 2001).

terpretation of the preexisting regulation, concluding that prescribing drugs to facilitate the death of terminally ill patients is
not a "legitimate medical purpose." Because distribution of Schedule II drugs for nonauthorized purposes would constitute a violation of the CSA, the Ashcroft interpretation purported to make
conduct illegal that the ODWDA explicitly authorized. The Interpretive Rule was challenged in federal district court, resulting
in a permanent injunction against the Ashcroft directive.[27] The
Ninth Circuit held the Interpretive Rule invalid,[28] and the Supreme Court ultimately agreed.[29]

B. LEGAL QUESTIONS

Gonzales involved the intersection of a number of typically dis-
crete administrative law doctrines. First, what deference is due an
agency's interpretation of its own rule? Second, what deference
ought to be given to a statutory interpretation issued by a federal
agency that has the effect of displacing a state law? Third, should
deference be given to an agency's interpretation of a statute that
gives authority to multiple federal agencies? These are not new
questions, but it is rare to witness them arise simultaneously with
such stark results.

The government, and Justice Scalia in dissent, argued that the
case should have been resolved without legal fanfare. Courts generally defer to agencies on interpretations of statutes[30] and will
overturn an agency's interpretation of its own rules or regulations
only if "plainly erroneous."[31] Justice Scalia's dissent concluded that
the Interpretive Rule should have been easily upheld on either
ground. The majority opinion, per Justice Kennedy, took a rather
different tack, avoiding deference to the Interpretive Rule either
as an interpretation of the agency's own regulations or as an interpretation of a statute the agency administers.[32]

Much of Justice Kennedy's opinion relies on two ideas. First,
when a statute shares authority between agencies, deference should

---

[27] *Oregon v Ashcroft*, 192 F Supp 2d 1077, 1080 (D Or 2002).

[28] *Oregon v Ashcroft*, 368 F3d 1118, 1138 (9th Cir 2004).

[29] *Gonzales*, 126 S Ct at 925–26.

[30] *Chevron USA, Inc. v National Resources Defense Council*, 467 US 837 (1984).

[31] *Auer v Robbins*, 519 US 452 (1997); *Bowles v Seminole Rock & Sand Co.*, 325 US 410,
414 (1945).

[32] *Gonzales*, 126 S Ct 904, 914–17 (2006).

be given to the agency that has the relevant expertise—here not the Attorney General, but the Secretary of Health and Human Services.[33] Second, because the CSA shares authority between federal and state governments, no deference should be given to an interpretation that "displaces the States' general regulation of medical practice."[34] Both these presumptions undermined the Attorney General's claim to deference from the courts.[35] Properly understood, the Court's analysis contributes to an emerging doctrine known as *Chevron* Step Zero, which clarifies when judicial deference to agency views is appropriate. Neither of the employed presumptions is implausible, but nor is either inevitable. Given the increasing prominence of Step Zero in administrative law, and the frequency with which courts encounter shared jurisdiction statutes, clarifying this state of affairs is of some importance.

II. Overlapping and Underlapping Jurisdiction

Much of the analysis in *Gonzales* depends on how *Chevron* doctrine treats statutes that entail the ambiguously overlapping and underlapping jurisdiction of political institutions. Courts have long struggled with whether deference should be given to statutes administered by multiple federal agencies, and an administrative law variant of federalism principles specifies if and when courts should defer to agency decisions that preempt state law. Currently, *Chevron* doctrine instructs courts to defer to agency statutory interpretations when Congress has delegated law-interpreting authority. This determination, in turn, rests on a rational reconstruction of congressional intent about local judicial deference to agency interpretations. Therefore, to know whether Congress would want courts to defer to agency interpretations of shared jurisdiction statutes or to interpretations with preemptive effects, it is necessary to theorize about why Congress would rely on statutes that share authority in this way.

A. CONCEPTUAL BASICS

As one court recently noted, "we live in an age of overlapping

---

[33] Id at 914–17. See also 21 USCA §§ 811, 823(q) (2006).

[34] 126 S Ct at 923.

[35] Id.

and concurring regulatory jurisdiction."[36] The CSA is one prime example, but statutes that parcel out authority or jurisdiction to multiple agencies may be the norm, rather than an exception. Still, there are many variants of shared jurisdiction regimes, and all need not be treated identically by the law.

Suppose Congress is considering enacting a new statute to address policy space X, that there are only two governmental units, A and B, and that Congress wishes to allocate some authority to one entity and some authority to the other. Conceptually, Congress might allocate authority in any number of ways, but consider two dimensions of variation: *exclusivity* and *completeness*. With respect to exclusivity, Congress might grant authority to one agency alone or to both. With respect to completeness, Congress might delegate authority to act over the entire policy space or only a subset of the space. If both agencies receive concurrent authority to regulate in a field, there is jurisdictional overlap. When neither gets authority, there is jurisdictional underlap. Combining the dimensions of exclusivity and completeness yields four potential statutory schemes.

    1.   Congress could delegate *complete* and *exclusive* jurisdiction. Agency A is given the authority to regulate X_1, where X_1 is a subset of X ($X_1 \subset X$). Agency B is given authority to regulate X_2, where X_2 is a subset of X ($X_2 \subset X$). In the complete and exclusive regime, there is no policy authority held simultaneously by both agencies; that is, $X_1 \cap X_2 = \varnothing$. And the combination of the policy space regulated by both agencies is the entire policy space, $X_1 \cup X_2 = X$. If the space X is represented with a circle, a single line dissecting the circle marks the jurisdictional divisions, with A getting all authority on one side of the line and B all authority on the other.

    2.   Congress could delegate *incomplete* and *exclusive* jurisdiction. If the policy space X continues to represented by a circle, this statutory scheme excepts a subset of the policy space from the jurisdiction of either agency A or B. The remainder of the space is exclusively within either the jurisdiction of agency A or B. That is, the sets of authority delegated to agencies A and B remain disjoint, $X_1 \cap X_2 = \varnothing$. However, the union of A and

[36] *FTC v Ken Roberts Co.*, 276 F3d 583, 593 (DC Cir 2001), quoting *Thompson Medical Co. v FTC*, 791 F2d 189, 192 (DC Cir 1986). See also *FTC v Texaco, Inc.*, 555 F2d 862, 881 (DC Cir 1976). See generally *FTC v Cement Institute*, 333 US 683, 694–95 (1948).

B does not occupy all of the policy space; $X_1 \cup X_2 \subset X$. The important difference between regimes (1) and (2) is that some potential authority in the policy field that could have been given to an agency is not given to either agency. This is jurisdictional underlap.

3. Congress could delegate *complete* authority to agencies A and B, but with *nonexclusive* jurisdictional assignments. In this regime, all of the potential authority within space X is delegated, but some authority is given to both agencies. The authority might be perfectly overlapping, such that $X_1 = X_2 = X$. Or, more likely, each agency is given some exclusive jurisdiction, but some subset of authority is also jointly held by both agencies such that $X_1 \cap X_2 = X_3 \subset X$. That is, jurisdiction is partially overlapping.

4. Lastly, Congress might generate a *nonexclusive* shared jurisdiction scheme in which the grant of authority is *incomplete* (or nonexhaustive). At least some portion of each agency's authority is also shared with the other agency. What differentiates regime (4) from regime (3) is that there is also some subset of the policy space not clearly given to either agency, such that $X_1 \cup X_2 \subset X$. Regime (4) carves out a portion of potential authority that is not given to either government entity, although of course the scope and existence of this pocket will usually be ambiguous. Jurisdiction in this scheme is both overlapping and underlapping.

This description is not meant to be especially novel or controversial. The typology just describes generic ways to carve up authority among government units. The institutions to which authority is granted, A and B, might be two agencies like the Environmental Protection Agency (EPA) and the Occupational Safety and Health Administration (OSHA), or they might be two levels of government like the federal government and state governments. Institution A might be the National Labor Relations Board and Institution B an administrative law judge. If the typology cuts ice it is only because it gives conceptual clarity to the differences between statutory schemes which are often assumed to be the same, helping to theorize about why Congress would use each of these possible regimes.

B. REFINEMENTS

The levers of completeness and exclusivity are only two of many that Congress might adjust to vary agency authority. Congress might allocate overlapping jurisdiction, but give different policy tools to different agencies, perhaps giving rulemaking authority to one agency and enforcement authority to another, as Congress often does. Both agencies could act in the same policy area, but one could do so using rules and the other using adjudications.

Alternatively, holding the type of policy tools constant, both agencies might have overlapping authority, but one agency might be given dominant authority, either explicitly or implicitly. In the case of direct conflict between the two agencies on some legal question, one agency's decision might clearly control. For example, if one agency has rulemaking authority and another only enforcement authority, and the two agencies disagree on the meaning of a statutory term, the interpretation proffered by the agency with rulemaking authority might control or vice versa.[37] An agency with rulemaking authority might be given preference because the process of making rules better incorporates both democratic and informational expertise, but enforcement proceedings allow agencies to incorporate more particularized insights, so perhaps the opposite inference is just as plausible. That is, the mere fact of jurisdictional overlap leaves unresolved the important subsequent question of whether authority is equal or hierarchical.

In practice, jurisdictional boundaries between political institutions are also fuzzy or ambiguous. Outside the overlapping jurisdiction context, the ambiguous border problem animates an ongoing debate about whether *Chevron* deference should be given to agency determinations about the scope of the agency's own jurisdiction.[38] The outcome in many cases depends on whether agencies have jurisdiction and whether specific agency views warrant deference.[39] If defining jurisdictional borders is difficult generally, it promises to be even harder in shared jurisdiction regimes.

---

[37] See Part II.D.2.

[38] See, for example, Sunstein, 90 Colum L Rev at 2097 (cited in note 6).

[39] See, for example, *FDA v Brown & Williamson Tobacco Corp.*, 529 US 120 (2000); *Mississippi Power & Light Co. v Mississippi*, 487 US 357 (1988); *United States v Riverside Bayview Homes*, 474 US 121 (1985); *Massachusetts v EPA*, 415 F3d 50 (DC Cir 2005), rev'd and remanded, 127 S Ct 1438 (2007); *United Transportation Union v Surface Transportation Board*, 183 F3d 606 (7th Cir 1999); *Alaska v Babbitt*, 72 F3d 698 (9th Cir 1995).

If a statute clearly gives some jurisdiction to one agency to administer one portion of a statute, and clearly gives some jurisdiction to another agency to administer another portion of the statute, how should courts treat agency interpretations or assertions of authority with respect to a third portion of the statute, related to both other sections?

C. JUSTIFICATION

Overlapping and underlapping jurisdiction in a world with fuzzy borders is a practical mess for agencies, courts, and private parties. So why would Congress rely on shared jurisdiction schemes? Scholarship in political science and economics provides one answer. Delegation by Congress to other institutions creates agency problems. Overlapping and underlapping jurisdiction schemes can be understood as a partial response to these problems. More specifically, Congress might use overlapping or underlapping jurisdiction as a mechanism for encouraging the development and accurate revelation of information by agencies, or as a means of controlling agency conduct and substantive policy choices.

A central organizing principle of the delegation and oversight literature is that an enacting congressional coalition must balance the risk of legislative drift against the risk of bureaucratic drift. Congress could produce policy internally, but given limitations of time, resources, and the potentially lower costs of bureaucratic production, delegation to agencies will often prove a more desirable alternative. When Congress delegates, there is always a risk that the preferences of the enacting coalition in Congress will diverge from the views of the administrative agency.[40] That is, delegation involves agency problems.

The commentary is replete with suggestions about how and to what extent Congress can effectively control the bureaucracy, including the use of ex ante procedures,[41] ex post monitoring,[42] tem-

---

[40] See generally David Epstein and Sharon O'Halloran, *Delegating Powers: A Transaction Cost Politics Approach to Policy Making under Separate Powers* (Cambridge, 1999). See also Kenneth A. Shepsle, *Bureaucratic Drift, Coalitional Drift, and Time Consistency*, 8 J L Econ & Org 111 (1992).

[41] See Matthew D. McCubbins, Roger G. Noll, and Barry R. Weingast, *Structure and Process, Politics and Policy: Administrative Arrangements and the Political Control of Agencies*, 75 Va L Rev 431 (1989).

[42] See Matthew D. McCubbins and Thomas Schwartz, *Congressional Oversight Overlooked: Police Patrols versus Fire Alarms*, 28 Am J Pol Sci 165 (1984).

poral limitations,[43] budgetary appropriations,[44] and other forms of political influence.[45] This literature focuses on the use of ex ante and ex post mechanisms for generating or calibrating the incentives of agents to encourage them to act consistently with the interests of principals. Jurisdictional overlap and underlap should be understood as additional tools for structuring the incentives of administrative agencies. Congressional choice about how to structure delegated authority inevitably reflects the preferences of legislators and interest groups.[46] Just as procedural mechanisms like those set out in the Administrative Procedure Act (APA) can be used to control agency behavior, so too can overlapping and underlapping agency jurisdiction.

A statute that allocates authority to multiple government entities relies on *competing agents* as a mechanism for managing agency problems. Giving authority to multiple agencies and allowing them to compete against each other can bring policy closer to the preferences of Congress than would delegation to a single agent.[47] To illustrate, consider the problem of agency expertise.

A potential justification for the use of complete and exclusive jurisdiction (regime 1) is to facilitate the use of relevant agency expertise in the implementation of policy. If one agency has expertise in a field and a second agency in another, Congress should delegate to the most informed agency. The trouble with this view of expertise is that it is static and exogenous; but agency expertise is itself a function of many factors, including the degree of discretion given to the agency, the costliness of developing expertise, the degree of divergence between agency and congressional preferences, and other political influences like interest groups.[48]

[43] See Jacob E. Gersen, *Temporary Legislation*, 74 U Chi L Rev 247 (2007).

[44] See Michael M. Ting, *The "Power of the Purse" and Its Implications for Bureaucratic Policy-Making*, 106 Pub Choice 243 (2001).

[45] See, for example, Emerson H. Tiller, *Controlling Policy by Controlling Process: Judicial Influence on Regulatory Decision-Making*, 14 J L Econ & Org 114 (1998).

[46] See Terry M. Moe, *The Politics of Bureaucratic Structure*, in John E. Chubb and Paul E. Peterson, eds, *Can the Government Govern?* 267 (Brookings, 1989).

[47] See Anne Joseph O'Connell, *The Architecture of Smart Intelligence: Structuring and Overseeing Agencies in the Post-9/11 World*, 94 Cal L Rev 1655, 1704 (2006); Michael M. Ting, *A Strategic Theory of Bureacratic Redundancy*, 47 Am J Pol Sci 274, 287 (2003).

[48] See Matthew C. Stephenson, *Bureaucratic Decision Costs and Endogenous Agency Expertise*, J L Econ & Org (forthcoming 2007); Jonathan Bendor and Adam Meirowitz, *Spatial Models of Delegation*, 98 Am Pol Sci Rev 293 (2004); Philippe Aghion and Jean Tirole, *Formal and Real Authority in Organizations*, 105 J Pol Econ 1 (1997); Kathleen Bawn,

Agency expertise is neither static nor exogenous, but rather is a function of existing institutional arrangements. Like other mechanisms for mitigating principal-agent problems, the assignment of jurisdiction can be used to create incentives for agencies to invest in the development of expertise.

Consider regime 3, complete and overlapping jurisdiction. If agencies prefer to increase jurisdiction rather than decrease it, assigning overlapping jurisdiction at time 0 gives agencies an incentive to invest in information at time 1, so that their jurisdiction is not eliminated at time 2.[49] If Congress wants to take advantage of agency knowledge, but is concerned that agencies will shirk and fail to invest heavily enough in the development of expertise, manipulating jurisdiction can help manage that possibility. If one agency invests in developing expertise and the other does not, Congress can shift from regime 2 to regime 1, giving the agency that invested in expertise exclusive authority. The threat of jurisdictional loss is a sanction for the failure to produce desirable informational expertise.

What of jurisdictional underlap, as in regimes (2) or (4), where Congress has not clearly allocated authority over a subset of the policy space? Two agencies have jurisdiction over other parts of the statute, either exclusively (regime 2) or concurrently (regime 4). If ambiguous jurisdictional boundaries are the norm, underlapping jurisdiction can also produce desirable incentives. Suppose it is unclear whether either agency has jurisdiction at time 0. By investing in the development of relevant expertise and asserting jurisdiction at time 1, the agency demonstrates relevant expertise, and Congress (or a court) could redefine clear and potentially exclusive jurisdiction at time 2. If ex ante jurisdictional ambiguity is resolved in favor of an agency that develops expertise, ambiguous

Political Control versus Expertise: Congressional Choices about Administrative Procedures, 89 Am Pol Sci Rev 62 (1995); Steven Callander, *A Theory of Policy Expertise* (unpublished manuscript, 2006), online at http://harrisschool.uchicago.edu/Academic/workshops/pol_econ _papers/expertise5october2006.pdf; Sean Gailmard, *Discretion Rather than Rules: Choice of Instruments to Constrain Bureaucratic Policy-Making* (unpublished manuscript, August 2006), online at http://faculty.wcas.northwestern.edu/~spg763/menus.pdf. For earlier and more general analysis, see McCubbins, Noll, and Weingast, 75 Va L Rev 431 (cited in note 41); Mathew D. McCubbins, Roger G. Noll, and Barry R. Weingast, *Administrative Procedures as Instruments of Political Control*, 3 J L Econ & Org 243 (1987).

[49] Even this is not obvious. James Q. Wilson sought to explain why expansionist bureaucracies often shun new responsibilities. See *Bureaucracy: What Government Agencies Do and Why They Do It* (Basic Books, 1989). Agencies might lose a sense of mission, or jurisdictional expansion might introduce additional opportunities for failure.

underlap in time 0 can create a race to produce expertise and assert jurisdiction.

Understood in this way, both jurisdictional overlap and jurisdictional underlap use delegation to competing agents to control agency behavior. Jurisdictional overlap is like the stick; jurisdictional underlap the carrot. Both statutory schemes, however, can be sensibly understood as intentional mechanisms for mitigating agency problems inherent in delegation to other political institutions. Redundancy can also increase the reliability of bureaucratic performance, and using multiple agents may also provide for monitoring and reporting of agent behavior by competing agents themselves.[50]

This is not to say that jurisdictional overlap is a silver bullet for agency problems. Overlapping jurisdiction also creates a risk of shirking by both agencies when Congress observes only outcomes and not effort.[51] Moreover, redundancy in the assignment of bureaucratic tasks can also create duplicative monitoring and enforcement costs.[52] Overlapping jurisdiction, therefore, is not necessarily an ideal structure for delegation. But there is an implicit logic in the use of overlapping and underlapping jurisdictional schemes that can itself be traced to an elaborate theoretical literature in economics and political science.

If manipulating jurisdiction is an effective tool for constraining agencies, then several conclusions might follow. First, courts might adopt interpretive practices that support rather than undermine these statutory schemes. For example, a common view is that courts owe no *Chevron* deference to agency views of shared juris-

---

[50] For a discussion of related issues deriving from the appropriate allocation of function to government agencies, see David A. Weisbach and Jacob Nussim, *The Integration of Tax and Spending Programs*, 113 Yale L J 955 (2004).

[51] See Joseph O'Connell, 94 Cal L Rev at 1704 (cited in note 47); Ting, 47 Am J Pol Sci at 287 (cited in note 47); Charles Perrow, *Normal Accidents: Living with High-Risk Technologies* 332 (Princeton, 1999); Jean Tirole, *The Internal Organization of Government*, 46 Oxford Econ Papers 1 (1994). See also Jonathan B. Bendor, *Parallel Systems: Redundancy in Government* 244–45 (California, 1985); Dan S. Felsenthal and Eliezer Fuchs, *Experimental Evaluation of Five Designs of Redundant Organizational Systems*, 21 Admin Sci Q 474, 474 (1976); Rowan Miranda and Allan Lerner, *Bureaucracy, Organizational Redundancy, and the Privatization of Public Services*, 55 Pub Admin Rev 193, 193 (1995).

[52] See Andrew B. Whitford, *Adapting Agencies: Competition, Imitation, and Punishment in the Design of Bureaucratic Performance*, in George A. Krause and Kenneth J. Meier, eds, *Politics, Policy, and Organizations: Frontiers in the Scientific Study of Bureaucracy* 160 (Michigan, 2003); Gary J. Miller and Terry M. Moe, *Bureaucrats, Legislators, and the Size of Government*, 77 Am Pol Sci Rev 297, 310 (1983). But see William A. Niskanen, *Bureaucrats and Politicians*, 18 J L & Econ 617, 637 (1975) (competition decreases cost of monitoring).

diction statutes; Congress would not want courts to defer to the view of one agency when the statute is administered by many agencies. The competing agents framework suggests otherwise. Deference is a form of reward, which could encourage agencies to develop expertise and enter areas of ambiguous jurisdiction.

Second, the same framework has implications for deference and preemption, though the implications are less clear. When a statute allocates overlapping jurisdiction to state and federal entities, courts might endeavor to preserve concurrent jurisdiction, perhaps by refusing to defer to agency decisions to preempt state law. By the same token, in a case of jurisdictional underlap, where it is unclear whether either entity has jurisdiction, deference to pre-emptive decisions by the agency could be understood as a reward for moving into a field of ambiguous jurisdiction. The difficulty is that the state agency cannot do the same thing, and therefore the agents are competing on unequal footing. If a genuine conflict exists and the federal agency has clear authority, the state agency may not displace the federal agency's view. This asymmetry creates a wrinkle, but nonetheless it is a wrinkle that should be ironed out within the competing agents framework.

Lastly, courts have sometimes been hesitant to defer to agency views about their own jurisdiction, even setting aside the problem of overlap or underlap. The competing agents framework suggests this may be a mistake. Congress might well prefer that agencies be rewarded for developing expertise and asserting jurisdiction.

The competing agents framework is not inevitably correct, but it provides a way to structure the dispute in *Gonzales*. The CSA establishes a partially overlapping jurisdictional scheme· in which authority is shared between federal agencies and state government authorities. The Attorney General is authorized to add or remove drugs from CSA schedules.[53] For certain determinations, the Attorney General must consult with other governmental actors like the Secretary of Health and Human Services.[54] The Attorney General is authorized to issue rules,[55] and require registration,[56] but the precise contours of that authority and the appropriate infer-

---

[53] 21 USC § 811(a) (2000 & Supp 2004).

[54] See, for example, 21 USC § 811(d)(3)(C) (2000 & Supp 2004) (requiring the Attorney General and the Secretary of Health and Human Services to coordinate drug scheduling).

[55] 21 USC § 821 (2000 & Supp 2004).

[56] 21 USC §§ 822, 871 (2000).

ence to draw from those contours were fiercely disputed in the case. The CSA preserves state authority to regulate medical practice with a savings clause disclaiming an intent to occupy the field.[57] The outcome of the case turned on the extent of authority granted to the Attorney General, whether that authority was exclusive, overlapping, or underlapping, and, if overlapping, inferior or superior to the authority of other federal agencies and state authorities.

D. DOCTRINE

The core of the Court's analysis in *Gonzales* took place in the analytic framework of *Chevron* doctrine. The key question then is how the various statutory schemes fit into *Chevron* doctrine. The *Gonzales* majority hewed closely to the conventional wisdom, refusing to give deference to the Attorney General's interpretation of the statute. In part, this refusal was driven by the fact that the CSA is a shared jurisdiction statute that allocates authority not just between multiple federal agencies, but also federal and state authorities. The competing agents framework suggests this analysis was partially incomplete and partially incorrect. After a brief sketch of *Chevron* doctrine, this section focuses on the intersection of *Chevron* with overlapping jurisdiction statutes.

1. *Chevron basics. Chevron* established an analytic framework for judicial review of agency interpretations of statutes. At Step One of *Chevron*, judges ask whether the statute speaks to the "precise question at issue";[58] if so, then judges simply enforce its commands.[59] If the statute contains a gap—if, in other words, it is silent or ambiguous on the relevant question—then judges are to proceed to Step Two, at which they ask whether the agency interpretation of the statute is reasonable.[60]

---

[57] 21 USC § 903 (2000) ("No provision of this title shall be construed as indicating an intent on the part of the Congress to occupy the field in which that provision operates, including criminal penalties, to the exclusion of any State law on the same subject matter which would otherwise be within the authority of the State, unless there is a positive conflict between that provision of this title and that State law so that the two cannot consistently stand together.").

[58] *Chevron*, 467 US at 842.

[59] There are many subtle problems about Step One that I do not attempt to review here. For a comprehensive treatment, see Elizabeth Garrett, *Step One of Chevron v. Natural Resources Defense Council*, in John F. Duffy and Michael Herz, eds, *A Guide to Judicial and Political Review of Federal Agencies* (ABA, 2005).

[60] See *Chevron USA, Inc. v Natural Resources Defense Council*, 467 US 837, 845 (1984).

The decades after *Chevron* brought much wrangling over the scope, foundation, and application of the *Chevron* doctrine.[61] In an important series of cases, *Christensen v Harris County*,[62] *United States v Mead*,[63] and *Barnhart v Walton*,[64] the Supreme Court sought to clarify precisely when the *Chevron* deference framework applies and when it does not. The trilogy creates a third step of analysis in the *Chevron* framework, a sort of *Chevron* prequel, increasingly known as Step Zero.[65] The Step Zero doctrine requires that before proceeding to the *Chevron* two step, a court must first engage in a prior analytic inquiry to ascertain whether Congress would want courts to defer to agencies on this sort of interpretation of this sort of statute in this particular context. Step Zero is an increasingly important doctrine, and *Gonzales* is most naturally read as a Step Zero case.

Chevron's original justification was ambiguous. The *Chevron* majority cited several potential justifications for judicial deference to administrative agencies including comparative expertise and democratic accountability, in addition to an implicit congressional directive that courts ought to defer to agencies.[66] However, in *Mead* the Court followed existing commentary and suggested that *Chevron* rests on Congress's implicit delegation of law-interpreting authority to agencies.[67] In *Mead*, the Court held that a tariff classification ruling by the United States Customs Service was not entitled to *Chevron* deference.[68] The Court concluded that *Chevron* deference is appropriate "when it appears that Congress delegated authority to the agency generally to make rules carrying the force of law, and that the agency interpretation claiming deference was

---

[61] For an overview, see Cass R. Sunstein, *Chevron Step Zero*, 92 Va L Rev 187 (2006).

[62] 529 US 576 (2000).

[63] 533 US 218 (2001).

[64] 535 US 212 (2002).

[65] The term is originally from Thomas W. Merrill and Kristin E. Hickman, *Chevron's Domain*, 89 Geo L J 833, 872 (2001).

[66] *Chevron*, 467 US at 865.

[67] Mead, 533 US at 230 n 11, citing Merrill and Hickman, 89 Geo L J (cited in note 65). This rationale is a bit awkward given that the APA, which is the closest Congress has come to providing a general instruction on the allocation of law-interpreting authority, says that courts are to decide all relevant questions of law. See 5 USC § 706 (2000) ("To the extent necessary to decision and when presented, the reviewing court shall decide all relevant questions of law.").

[68] *Mead*, 533 US at 226.

promulgated in the exercise of that authority."[69] *Mead*'s language initially appeared to make Step Zero turn on procedural formality. The strongest cases for *Chevron* deference looked to be when an agency had been given rulemaking authority that the agency had actually used in promulgating the interpretation.[70] The weakest candidates for deference were the result of informal adjudication, a decision-making process that lacks any required procedural formality.[71] Unfortunately, the precise relationship between the delegation of force-of-law authority and procedural formality remained elusive. The Court clearly stated that a lack of procedural formality does not preclude *Chevron* deference.[72] And at least Justice Breyer thinks procedural formality is not a sufficient condition for *Chevron* deference either.[73]

How then are courts to determine whether Congress has (implicitly) delegated law-interpreting authority to an agency? Recent guidance has not been altogether clear. One answer was given by Justice Breyer in *Barnhart v Walton*.[74] In *Barnhart*, the Court upheld an interpretation of the term "impairment" in a Social Security Administration regulation. Although the interpretation had been issued in notice and comment rulemaking, Justice Breyer emphasized that deference could apply even though "the Agency previously reached its interpretation through means less formal than 'notice and comment' rulemaking."[75] Considering "the interstitial nature of the legal question, the related expertise of the

---

[69] Id at 226–27 (emphasis added).

[70] See *Shalala v Illinois Council on Long Term Care, Inc.*, 529 US 1, 20–21 (2000); *United States v Haggar Apparel Co.*, 526 US 380 (1999); *AT&T Corp. v Iowa Utilities Board*, 525 US 366 (1999); *Atlantic Mutual Insurance Co. v Commissioner*, 523 US 382 (1998); *Regions Hospital v Shalala*, 522 US 448 (1998); *United States v O'Hagan*, 521 US 642 (1997); *Smiley v Citibank (South Dakota), N.A.*, 517 US 735 (1996); *Babbitt v Sweet Home Chapter, Communities for Greater Ore.*, 515 US 687 (1995); *ICC v Transcon Lines*, 513 US 138 (1995); *PUD No. 1 of Jefferson City v Washington Department of Ecology*, 511 US 700 (1994); *Good Samaritan Hospital v Shalala*, 508 US 402 (1993); *American Hospital Association v NLRB*, 499 US 606 (1991); *Sullivan v Everhart*, 494 US 83 (1990); *Sullivan v Zebley*, 493 US 521 (1990); *Massachusetts v Morash*, 490 US 107 (1989); *K Mart Corp. v Cartier, Inc.*, 486 US 281 (1988); *Atkins v Rivera*, 477 US 154 (1986); *United States v Fulton*, 475 US 657 (1986); *Riverside Bayview Homes*, 474 US 121.

[71] See *Mead*, 533 US at 231.

[72] Id ("The fact that the tariff classification here was not a product of such formal process does not alone, therefore, bar the application of *Chevron*.").

[73] See *National Cable & Telecommunications Assn. v Brand X Internet Servs.*, 545 US 967, 1003–05 (2005) (Breyer, J, concurring).

[74] 535 US 212 (2002).

[75] Id at 221.

Agency, the importance of the question to administration of the statute, the complexity of that administration, and the careful consideration the Agency has given the question over a long period of time,"[76] *Chevron* deference was properly applied.[77] This view of *Chevron* echoes Justice Breyer's view of many years ago, arguing that judicial deference to agency interpretations of law should depend on a case-by-case consideration of the particular agency interpretation and the specific statutory scheme.[78]

Questions about *Chevron*'s scope had pre–Step Zero answers. But before the trilogy, they were answers without an analytic framework. A charitable reading of *Mead*, *Christensen*, and *Barnhart* is that they impose a structure on the decision of whether *Chevron* deference is appropriate.[79] To decide whether *Chevron* applies, judges should ask whether Congress is best taken to have delegated law-interpreting authority to the agency, that is, would Congress want courts to defer? The competing agents framework helps answer this question by offering a rational reconstruction of congressional intent about judicial deference and overlapping jurisdiction statutes. Any resolution of the Step Zero question ought at least to take account of this explanation; and if no better explanation is available, then the competing agents approach should prevail, on the ground that it is the best reconstruction of Congress's intentions.

2. *Chevron and shared jurisdiction*. When a statute is administered by multiple agencies, do agency views about statutory meaning receive deference in the *Chevron* framework? This question has long been disputed.[80] Today, it is best treated as a Step Zero inquiry, but before the court accepted the implicit congressional

---

[76] Id at 222.

[77] See Sunstein, 92 Va L Rev at 217 (cited in note 61) (discussing the passage and opinion).

[78] Breyer, 38 Admin L Rev at 379 (cited in note 7).

[79] Compare David J. Barron and Elena Kagan, *Chevron's Nondelegation Doctrine*, 2001 Supreme Court Review 201, 227, with Adrian Vermeule, *Mead in the Trenches*, 71 Geo Wash U L Rev 347 (2003); Lisa Schultz Bressman, *How Mead Has Muddled Judicial Review of Agency Action*, 58 Vand L Rev 1443, 1457 (2005).

[80] See Merrill and Hickman, 89 Geo L J at 851 (cited in note 65). See also *Sutton v United Airlines*, 527 US 471, 478–80 (1999); *Bragdon v Abbott*, 524 US 624, 642 (1998). As Merrill and Hickman point out, in the pre-*Chevron* case law, the fact that a statute was administered by multiple agencies was sometimes cited as a factor for giving reduced deference. See *New Haven Board of Education v Bell*, 456 US 512, 522 n 12 (1982); *General Electric Co. v Gilbert*, 429 US 125, 144–45 (1977).

directive theory of *Chevron*, some scholarship used democratic accountability and expertise to argue that deference to interpretation of shared jurisdiction statutes was inappropriate.[81] Although accountability and expertise are no longer sufficient to support *Chevron* deference, they remain relevant variables in the Step Zero inquiry if expertise or accountability would be reasons that Congress would prefer courts to defer to agencies.

In the shared jurisdiction context, however, neither expertise nor democratic accountability necessarily supports the no deference view. When several agencies share responsibility for administering a statute, all of them might have more expertise than the courts. And even outside the competing agents framework, two agencies with concurrent jurisdiction will generally be more responsive to democratic processes than any court is likely to be. Within the competing agents framework, multiple agencies with overlapping jurisdiction may well be both more expert and more accountable than a single agency with exclusive jurisdiction. Notwithstanding this view, agency expertise has regularly been used as a justification for not giving deference to agency views of shared jurisdiction statutes.

Consider agency interpretations of general statutes—statutes that bear on the business of multiple agencies like the Freedom of Information Act (FOIA) or National Environmental Policy Act (NEPA). "It is universally agreed that no single agency with enforcement power has been charged with administration of these statutes, and hence that *Chevron* does not apply."[82] Similarly, no deference is given to agency interpretations of the Administrative Procedure Act because "[t]he APA is not a statute that the Director is charged with administering."[83] Congress should not be taken to have implicitly delegated law-interpreting authority to any agency because no agency administers the statute.[84]

---

[81] See, for example, Daniel Lovejoy, Note, *The Ambiguous Basis for Chevron Deference: Multiple-Agency Statutes*, 88 Va L Rev 879 (2002).

[82] Merrill and Hickman, 89 Geo L J at 893 (cited in note 65).

[83] *Metropolitan Stevedore Co. v Rambo*, 521 US 121, 137 (1997) (internal citations omitted). The Court added that the "interpretation does not appear to be embodied in any regulation or similar binding policy pronouncement to which such deference would apply" and the "interpretation is couched in a logical non-sequitur." Id.

[84] The Supreme Court has never conclusively said that interpretations of statutes administered by multiple agencies do not qualify for *Chevron* deference, but *Metropolitan Stevedore Co.*, 521 US at 137, is probably the closest the Court has come. See also Merrill and Hickman, 89 Geo L J at 893 n 288 (cited in note 65).

To the extent that the APA, FOIA, and NEPA are statutes that apply to all agencies but are not truly "administered" by any agency, this view is perfectly reasonable. Accordingly, the lower courts generally do not defer to agency views in these settings, largely on expertise grounds.[85] To illustrate, consider *Professional Reactor Operator Society v NRC*.[86] The D.C. Circuit refused to give *Chevron* deference to the Nuclear Regulatory Commission's interpretation of the APA because the "Supreme Court has indicated . . . that reviewing courts do not owe the same deference to an agency's interpretation of statutes that, like the APA, are outside the agency's particular expertise and special charge to administer."[87]

However, not giving deference to an agency's view of a statute that it does not administer[88] implies little about whether deference is warranted for agency views of a statute that multiple agencies do administer. Unfortunately, the same basic analysis is often applied. For example, *Bowen v American Hospital Association*[89] involved a challenge to regulations promulgated by the Secretary of Health and Human Services. Section 504 of the Rehabilitation Act authorized "any head of an Executive Branch Agency . . . to promulgate regulations prohibiting discrimination against the handicapped."[90] Although the plurality overturned the regulations because they lacked a sufficient evidentiary basis, the plurality opinion also noted that where twenty-seven agencies had promulgated regulations forbidding discrimination on the basis of

---

[85] See, for example, *DuBois v United States Department of Agriculture*, 102 F3d 1273, 1285 n 15 (1st Cir 1996) (declining to apply *Chevron* to NEPA "because we [the court] are not reviewing an agency's interpretation of the statute that it was directed to enforce"). However, even here it is not clear shared jurisdiction is the appropriate framework for analysis. At least on the court's own terms, the correct parallel is whether the agency is one of several which enforces the statute. A somewhat stronger case is *Reporters Commn. for Freedom of the Press v United States Dept. of Justice*, 816 F2d 730, 734 (DC Cir 1987) ("[N]o one executive branch entity is entrusted with [FOIA's] primary interpretation"), revd on other grounds, 489 US 749 (1989).

[86] 939 F2d 1047 (DC Cir 1991).

[87] Id at 1051.

[88] See *Adams Fruit Co. v Barrett*, 494 US 638 (1990) (stating that *Chevron* deference to an agency interpretation of a statute the agency did not administer would be inappropriate); *Crandon v United States*, 494 US 152 (1990) (Scalia, J, concurring) (rejecting *Chevron* deference because the statute in question was not administered by any agency but by the courts).

[89] 476 US 610 (1986).

[90] Rehabilitation Act of 1973, Pub L No 93-113, 87 Stat 394, codified as amended at 29 USC § 794 (1986). See also *Bowen*, 476 US at 642.

handicap under section 504's authority, "[t]here is thus not the same basis for deference predicated on expertise as we found [in *Chevron*]."[91]

In *Sutton v United Air Lines, Inc.*,[92] the Court emphasized that no agency was given authority to issue regulations for the applicable provisions of the Americans with Disabilities Act (ADA), even though multiple agencies clearly had authority to administer other portions of the ADA.[93] The Court chose to treat one portion of the statute as "administered by no agency" notwithstanding that the statute itself was administered by multiple agencies. Even the dissent would have given deference to the agency only because the term at issue—"disability"—was used both in the portion of the statute the Equal Employment Opportunity Commission (EEOC) administers and in the more general portion of the statute not solely administered by the EEOC.[94] *Sutton* might be treated as a case of ambiguously underlapping jurisdiction. Given uncertainty about whether agencies with some responsibility for some portion of the statute have law-interpreting authority for some other portion of the statute, the Court elected to inhibit the assertion of law-interpreting authority by the EEOC. The competing agents framework suggests this is a mistake. Ambiguously underlapping jurisdiction may facilitate competition between two agencies. Enacting judicial obstacles only undermines these goals.

a) An exclusive jurisdiction canon. In many cases of concurrent jurisdiction, courts go to great length either to conclude that no agency was given law-interpreting authority (as above) or to conclude that *only one* agency was given law-interpreting authority. In so doing, the courts often rely on what appears to be a *presumption of exclusive jurisdiction*. In effect, this presumption imposes an additional cost on Congress to use overlapping jurisdiction effectively to discipline agency behavior. For example, *California v Kleppe*[95] involved the question of whether EPA and the Secretary of Interior had concurrent jurisdiction over air quality on off-shore oil rigs. The Ninth Circuit concluded that there was no overlapping jurisdiction because such authority would "impair or frustrate

---

[91] Id at 643 n 30.

[92] 527 US 471 (1999).

[93] Id at 479.

[94] Id at 514–15 (Breyer, J, dissenting).

[95] 604 F2d 1187 (9th Cir 1979).

the authority which [the statute] grants to the secretary."[96]

In *Martin v Occupational Safety & Health Review Commission*,[97] the Supreme Court was faced with a conflict between the Secretary of Labor and the Health Review Commission, both of whom have responsibility for implementing OSHA.[98] The Court rejected the Commission's interpretation, holding that the Secretary was the agency entitled to deference, not the Commission.[99] The Supreme Court appeared to rely on a presumption that Congress delegates law-interpreting or "force of law" authority to a single agency. This idea is even implicit in the way the Court phrased the issue presented: "[t]he question before us in this case is to which administrative actor—the Secretary or the Commission—did Congress delegate this 'interpretive' lawmaking power under the OSH Act."[100] Said the Court:

> Because historical familiarity and policymaking expertise account in the first instance for the presumption that Congress delegates interpretive lawmaking power to the agency rather than to the reviewing court, we presume here that Congress intended to invest interpretive power in the administrative actor in the best position to develop these attributes.[101]

ETSI Pipeline Project v Missouri[102] is similar. The case involved a dispute over whether the Flood Control Act of 1944[103] created overlapping or exclusive agency jurisdiction. The Flood Control Act granted authority to the Federal Power Commission, the Department of Agriculture, the Department of Interior, and the Secretary of War.[104] Both the Secretary of Interior and the Secretary of War asserted the authority to enter into contracts respecting

---

[96] Id at 1193–94. See also *Get Oil Out! Inc. v Exxon Corp.*, 586 F2d 726 (9th Cir 1978).

[97] 499 US 144 (1991).

[98] See generally Russell L. Weaver, *Deference to Regulatory Interpretations: Inter-Agency Conflicts*, 43 Ala L Rev 35 (1991); George Robert Johnson, *The Split Enforcement Model: Some Conclusions from the OSHA and MSHA Experiences*, 39 Admin L Rev 315 (1987).

[99] *Martin*, 499 US at 150.

[100] Id at 151.

[101] Id at 153.

[102] 484 US 495 (1988). See also Timothy K. Armstrong, *Chevron Deference and Agency Self-Interest*, 13 Cornell J L & Pub Policy 203, 246–47 (2004).

[103] Pub L No 78-534, 58 Stat 887, codified as amended at 33 USC § 701 et seq (2000).

[104] Id.

use of certain reservoirs.[105] Writing for a unanimous court,[106] Justice White concluded that the plain language of the statute granted exclusive authority to the Secretary of War, rather than the Secretary of Interior, who was claiming concurrent authority.

What might be inelegantly termed an *exclusive jurisdiction canon*[107] presumes that when Congress delegates power to the executive, it gives law-interpreting authority only to a single agency. Because *Mead* makes this inquiry the hurdle for *Chevron* deference, the presumption makes truly concurrent law-interpreting authority unlikely. It also reduces the effectiveness and increases the costs of using competing agents to control agency behavior. The presumption makes it more difficult for Congress to use regimes (3) or (4), and favors regimes (1) and (2).[108]

What explains the presumption of exclusive jurisdiction? Perhaps the presumption is a subset of democracy-reinforcing canons that sometimes manifest in the *Chevron* context.[109] Presuming that Congress does not give concurrent jurisdiction might facilitate greater democratic accountability because there is always one agency that has the authority to act with the force of law in a given policy domain. Citizens would know to whom to direct complaints and about whom to complain to Congress. Or the presumption might be taken to facilitate transparency. If the presumption merely requires that Congress speak clearly when delegating law-interpreting authority to multiple agencies, perhaps the clarity allows citizens to monitor Congress and reward or punish for the grant of concurrent jurisdiction accordingly.

These views are plausible, but ultimately not particularly persuasive. Private groups regularly monitor the actions of multiple agencies, and publication of agency actions in the Federal Register would seem to mitigate any ambiguity about which government agency is responsible for which policy. The complexity of statutory

---

[105] See *ETSI*, 484 US at 502–05. See 58 Stat at 890, 903–07.

[106] Justice Kennedy took no part in the consideration or decision.

[107] Weaver refers to a similar idea as "authority principles." See Weaver, 43 Ala L Rev at 38 (cited in note 98).

[108] This practice is not universal. Some courts grappling with potentially overlapping jurisdiction schemes have asserted that "when two regulatory systems are applicable to a certain subject matter, they are to be reconciled and, to the extent possible, both given effect," *Pennsylvania v ICC*, 561 F2d 278, 292 (DC Cir 1977), at least where they do not create "conflicting or incompatible obligations." *Ken Roberts Co.*, 276 F3d at 593.

[109] See Sunstein, 92 Va L Rev at 245 n 245 (cited in note 61).

schemes may undermine transparency, but that problem is hardly unique to overlapping jurisdictional schemes.

The cases themselves seem to ground the presumption in the idea of agency expertise.[110] As between two agencies, courts should presume that Congress delegated law-interpreting authority to the more expert agency rather than the less expert agency.[111] In *Gonzales* itself, one reason the majority did not defer to the Attorney General's interpretation was that the Attorney General lacked the relevant expertise. The majority concluded that the Secretary of Health and Human Services was given exclusive interpretive authority regarding health and medical practices.

When one agency has greater expertise than another agency, it is not ludicrous to suggest that courts should defer to the more expert one. But as noted above, this view of expertise is too static and exogenous. If concurrent jurisdictional schemes facilitate the development of agency expertise, then the exclusive jurisdiction presumption undermines the precise goal the presumption is supposed to serve.

b) Step Zero canons. Suppose the exclusive jurisdiction presumption were embraced. If the presumption is like a substantive canon, it raises an ongoing debate about when to apply substantive canons in the *Chevron* regime.[112] Take, for example, the canon of constitutional avoidance.[113] The canon might be applied at Step One of *Chevron*. If a statute allows for two interpretations, one of which raises a constitutional question, courts will generally adopt the interpretation that avoids the constitutional question. If only one plausible interpretation of the statute remains after applying the canon, then the statute is clear and unambiguous, and the case is resolved at Step One.[114] The constitutional avoidance idea could theoretically be invoked at Step Two as well, although courts rarely do so. Even if the text of the statute does not unambiguously preclude the interpretation (Step One), the interpretation is unreasonable because it is arguably unconstitutional. Historically, the

---

[110] See, for example, *Gonzales*, 126 S Ct at 937 (Scalia, J, dissenting).

[111] See *Martin*, 499 US at 153.

[112] See generally Sunstein, 67 U Chi L Rev 315 (cited in note 2).

[113] Id.

[114] See, for example, *Edward J. DeBartolo Corp. v Florida Gulf Coast Bldg. & Constr. Trades Council*, 485 US 568, 574–75 (1988); *Chamber of Commerce v FEC*, 69 F3d 600, 605 (DC Cir 1995).

major alternative was to treat certain substantive canons as *Chevron* trumps.[115] In the context of avoidance, courts should not defer at all to agencies when agencies advance interpretations that raise constitutional questions. Substantive canons displace *Chevron* entirely.

This was the pre-*Mead* thinking. However, *Mead* provides a structure for this analysis. Like other substantive canons, the presumption of exclusive jurisdiction is best conceived as part of a growing number of Step Zero canons. Consider the presumption that Congress does not delegate "major questions"[116] to agencies, and therefore no *Chevron* deference should be given on such matters.[117] As long as the goal of Step Zero is to ascertain whether Congress would want courts to defer to agencies on the particular interpretation of the particular statute, then the exclusive jurisdiction presumption fits most naturally at Step Zero. If Congress is presumed not to give law-interpreting authority to multiple agencies, applying the presumption at Step Zero should end the matter. No deference is warranted.

Although the presumption fits naturally at Step Zero, the competing agents framework suggests it is also wrong. The presumption undermines a potentially important set of mechanisms with which Congress creates desirable incentives for agencies. If the competing agents framework constrains the behavior of agencies, aligning outcomes more closely with the preferences of Congress, then the presumption of exclusive jurisdiction is democracy-undermining rather than democracy-reinforcing.

How ought these cases to be analyzed? A tentative suggestion is as follows.[118] First, courts should hesitate declining to defer to agency interpretations of either general statutes or statutory provisions that the agency does not clearly administer. Either of these scenarios might involve jurisdictional underlap and Congress might well prefer that ambitious agencies be rewarded for developing expertise and asserting an interpretation of a statutory term not clearly within their jurisdiction.

---

[115] See Mendelson, 102 Mich L Rev at 746–47 (cited in note 13); Sunstein, 90 Colum L Rev 2071 (cited in note 6).

[116] Sunstein, 92 Va L Rev at 243–44 (cited in note 61) (discussing the possibility of reading *MCI* and *Brown & Williamson* as Step Zero cases, but ultimately concluding they are best read as Step One cases).

[117] See *Walton*, 536 US 212; *Mead*, 533 US 218; *Christensen*, 529 US 576.

[118] Compare Merrill and Hickman, 89 Geo L J at 893–99 (cited in note 65).

For so-called joint-enforcement statutes that call on one agency
to promulgate regulations and another to enforce the statute via
adjudications, courts should give deference to both agencies, at
least absent an affirmative conflict between the two.[119] If overlapping jurisdiction helps incentivise agencies, then failing to give
reward expertise by giving deference frustrates Congressional
goals. Moreover, the touchstone of *Chevron* is whether Congress
has delegated the agency "the power to act with the force of law."[120]
Both rulemaking and formal adjudicatory powers confer such authority, and therefore the (not quite) necessary and (usually) sufficient condition for deference is met. The mere fact that Congress
has distributed lawmaking authority to several agencies does not
imply that Congress would not want courts to defer to agency
interpretations of statutory ambiguity,[121] and the competing agents
framework provides an affirmative reason why Congress would
want courts to do so.[122]

The competing agents theory of overlapping and underlapping
jurisdiction suggests that the exclusive jurisdiction idea is a mistake, and that more disputes about the meaning of concurrent
jurisdiction statutes should proceed past Step Zero. The proposal,
however, might generate at least two problems: the possibility of
inconsistent interpretations of a statute and a race to the courthouse steps.[123] Said one court, "[giving deference] would lay the
groundwork for a regulatory regime in which either the same
statute is interpreted differently by the several agencies or the one

---

[119] See id at 894. Consider the Occupational Safety and Health Act, the Mine Safety
and Health Act, and the Longshore and Harbor Workers' Compensation Act, discussed
therein.

[120] See Merrill and Hickman, 89 Geo L J at 895 (cited in note 65).

[121] See id at 893–99.

[122] This disagreement aside, it seems clear that the lower courts have trended away from
this preferred position. For example, in *Rapaport v Office of Thrift Supervision*, 59 F3d 212
(DC Cir 1995), the D.C. Circuit refused to give deference to a statutory interpretation
by the Office of Thrift Supervision because "that agency [OTS] shares responsibility for
the administration of the statute with at least three other agencies." Id at 216. As a matter
of circuit law, this is simply a mistake. The Court relied on *Wachtel v Office of Thrift
Supervision*, 982 F2d 581 (DC Cir 1993), where the court, in dicta, suggested deference
might not apply in such settings. Id at 585. *Wachtel*, in turn, relied on *Professional Reactor
Operator Society*, 939 F2d 1047. But the court simply referred to language of the Supreme
Court indicating that where an agency interprets a statute that it does not administer, no
deference is warranted. Id at 1052, citing *Chevron*, 467 US 837; *Adams Fruit Co.*, 494 US
638; and *Crandon*, 494 US 152 (Scalia, J, concurring).

[123] See *Rapaport*, 59 F3d at 216–17.

agency th✺t happens to reach the courthouse first is allowed to fix the meaning of the text for all."[124]

Even if superficially unseemly, there is nothing inherently troubling about a statutory term having different meanings in different policy spheres. *Chevron* is supposed to open up policy discretion for agencies that have significant expertise in the fields they regulate. When a single agency administers a statute that uses the same term in different parts of the statute, the term may be defined differently so long as there is a sufficient justification for doing so.[125] Similarly, a single agency is free to offer two different interpretations of a statutory term in two different time periods so long as adequate justification is given for the difference.[126] That two agencies regulating different fields would offer different interpretations is no more objectionable.[127] Alternatively, where one agency has rulemaking authority and another concomitant adjudication authority, courts could defer to either if no conflict exists or to the agency with rulemaking authority if a conflict does exist.[128]

The race to the courthouse steps may have been a genuine problem at one point. But the ideas embraced by *National Cable & Telecommunications Association v Brand X Internet Service*[129] suggest this is no longer a significant concern. In *Brand X*, the Court clarified the relationship between a prior judicial interpretation of a statute and an agency's subsequent and different interpretation of the same term.[130] The *Brand X* majority held that a "court's prior judicial construction of a statute trumps an agency construction otherwise entitled to *Chevron* deference only if the prior court decision holds that its construction follows from the unambiguous terms of the statute and thus leaves no room for agency discre-

---

[124] Id.

[125] See *Environmental Defense v Duke Energy Corp.*, 127 S Ct 1423 (2007); *K Mart*, 486 US at 293 n 4.

[126] See, for example, *Chevron*, 467 US 837.

[127] Unless of course the same parties are being regulated and the two interpretations are mutually inconsistent.

[128] See Merrill and Hickman, 89 Geo L J at 894–95 (cited in note 65).

[129] 545 US 967 (2005).

[130] For a proposal to address sequencing problems like this, see generally Kenneth A. Bamberger, *Provisional Precedent: Protecting Flexibility in Administrative Policymaking*, 77 NYU L Rev 1272 (2002).

tion."[131] Put differently, when a court rejects an agency position because the statute unambiguously requires the interpretation the court adopted, the agency may not later adopt a different position. When a court acknowledges statutory ambiguity, the agency maintains the flexibility to pick new interpretations in the future[132]— in effect picking an interpretation different from the one the prior court thought best.[133] When a court finds that a statute requires a given interpretation, the agency is bound; when a court finds merely that an agency position is permitted, the agency is not.

Brand X clarifies that first in time need not imply first in right with respect to statutory interpretation. One agency's interpretation upheld by the courts in one time period need only bind other agency interpretations if the interpretation is required by the statute (Step One) rather than merely permitted (Step Two). If the case is resolved at Step One, the same result would be required no matter which agency litigated the issue and with or without a deference regime. If not, both agencies would remain free to adopt alternative interpretations in the future, irrespective of which agency first breached the courthouse door. Like *Chevron* itself, *Brand X* is flexibility preserving, and deference to agency interpretations of overlapping jurisdiction statutes is perfectly in keeping with that impulse.[134]

3. *Chevron, federalism, and preemption.* Although much of the analysis thus far has focused on overlapping and underlapping jurisdiction schemes involving multiple federal agencies, variants of the same issues arise in the context of overlapping or underlapping jurisdiction between federal agencies and state authorities. The CSA allocates authority to multiple federal agencies and to state authorities, and therefore *Gonzales* implicates not only the courts' shared jurisdiction cases, but also the intersection of *Chevron* and preemption doctrine.[135]

---

[131] *Brand X*, 545 US at 982.

[132] Id at 983.

[133] See id at 1013–14 (Scalia, J, dissenting).

[134] See also Merrill and Hickman, 89 Geo L J at 894–95 (cited in note 65).

[135] For general treatments, see Mendelson, 102 Mich L Rev at 740 (cited in note 13); Peter J. Smith, *Pennhurst, Chevron, and the Spending Power*, 110 Yale L J 1187 (2001); Sunstein, 67 U Chi L Rev 315 (cited in note 2); Jack W. Campbell IV, *Regulatory Preemption in the Garcia/Chevron Era*, 59 U Pitt L Rev 805 (1998); Damien Marshall, Note, *The Application of Chevron Deference in Regulatory Preemption Cases*, 87 Geo L J 263 (1998); Howard P. Walthall, Jr., Comment, *Chevron v. Federalism: A Reassessment of Deference to*

a) Background. The history and desirability of preemption doctrine generally has been well canvassed elsewhere.[136] As to conflict preemption, federal requirements preempt state requirements either if compliance with both is impossible,[137] or if the state requirement "stands as an obstacle to the accomplishment and execution of the full purposes and objectives of Congress."[138] As to field preemption, a state requirement is preempted if the "scheme of federal regulation is so pervasive as to make reasonable the inference that Congress left no room for the States to supplement it."[139] The presumption against preemption articulated in *Rice v Santa Fe Elevator Corp.*[140] serves as strong to intermediate weight against preemption: Congress must speak with clarity to preempt state law,[141] but congressional intent determines preemptive effect.[142]

The intersection of administrative law with preemption analysis creates an added layer of complexity. As between a valid federal regulation implementing a statute and an actually conflicting state policy, the federal rule would preempt state law.[143] Where there is uncertainty about either the scope of the federal agency's authority,[144] the validity of the agency's statutory interpretation, the meaning of the agency regulation that could have preemptive effect, or whether the agency regulation creates a genuine conflict

---

Administrative Preemption, 28 Cumb L Rev 715 (1997); Paula A. Sinozich et al, *The Role of Preemption in Administrative Law*, 45 Admin L Rev 107 (1993); Richard J. Pierce, Jr., *Regulation, Deregulation, Federalism, and Administrative Law*, 46 U Pitt L Rev 607 (1985). The preemption literature is, of course, expansive. See, for example, Caleb Nelson, *Preemption*, 86 Va L Rev 225 (2000); Viet D. Dinh, *Reassessing the Law of Preemption*, 88 Geo L J 2085 (2000); Roderick M. Hills, Jr., *The Political Economy of Cooperative Federalism: Why State Autonomy Makes Sense and "Dual Sovereignty" Doesn't*, 96 Mich L Rev 813 (1998).

[136] Consider Nelson, 86 Va L Rev 225 (cited in note 135).

[137] See *Florida Lime & Avocado Growers, Inc. v Paul*, 373 US 132, 142–43 (1963).

[138] *Hines v Davidowitz*, 312 US 52, 67 (1941).

[139] *Medtronic, Inc. v Lohr*, 518 US 470, 508 (1996) (Breyer, J, concurring in part), quoting *Rice v Santa Fe Elevator Corp.*, 331 US 218, 230 (1947).

[140] 331 US 218 (1947).

[141] See id.

[142] See *Medtronic*, 518 US at 485.

[143] See, for example, *Geier v American Honda Motor Co.*, 529 US 861 (2000); *Norfolk Southern Railway v Shanklin*, 529 US 347 (2000); *United States v Locke*, 529 US 89 (2000); *Smiley*, 517 US 735; *Medtronic*, 518 US 470; *City of New York v FCC*, 486 US 57 (1988). See generally Richard Pierce, 1 *Administrative Law Treatise* § 3.5 (Aspen, 4th ed 2002).

[144] See Mendelson, 102 Mich L Rev at 738 (cited in note 13).

with state law,[145] courts must decide whether to defer to agency judgments.

The courts' analysis of *Chevron* and regulatory preemption has been somewhat uneven, and was at the center of *Watters v Wachovia Bank, N.A.*[146] The Supreme Court declined to resolve this question, however. Still, in the past several decades the Court has tended to uphold, if not defer to, agency views that bear on preemption questions. For example, in *Smiley v Citibank*,[147] a unanimous Court cited *Chevron* in upholding an agency interpretation of the statutory term "interest" that had the effect of preempting usury laws in most states.[148] However, in *Medtronic, Inc. v Lohr*,[149] the Supreme Court gave only "substantial weight" to an FDA determination that the Medical Devices Act preempted state common law claims,[150] while not technically deferring to the regulation.[151] In concurrence, Justice Breyer seemed to ground his agreement in concerns other than the mere fact of statutory ambiguity and implicit Congressional delegation that underlie *Chevron*.[152]

---

[145] When a federal agency acts within the scope of delegated power it can preempt state and local regulations. *City of New York*, 486 US at 64.

[146] 2007 WL 1119539 (US April 17, 2007). The relevant question in *Watters* was whether an interpretation of the Comptroller of the Currency of the National Bank Act that has the effect of preempting Michigan's laws is entitled to *Chevron* deference. The court did not resolve the issue, concluding "[t]his argument is beside the point, for under our interpretation of the statute, the level of deference owed to the regulation is an academic question." Id at *10.

[147] 517 US 735 (1996).

[148] In the lower courts, *Chevron* deference is sometimes applied, see, for example, *Center for Legal Advocacy v Hammons*, 323 F3d 1262 (9th Cir 2003) (applying *Chevron* framework, but rejecting agency view), and sometimes not, see, for example, *Massachusetts Association of HMOs v Ruthardt*, 194 F3d 176 (1st Cir 1999) (independent evaluation of statute's effect).

[149] 518 US 470.

[150] Id at 496. See also *Smiley*, 517 US at 739–41; *Lawrence County v Lead-Deadwood School District No. 40-1*, 469 US 256, 261–62 (1985) (substantially deferring to Interior Department finding of preemption of state law); *Hillsborough County v Automated Medical Labs, Inc.*, 471 US 707, 714 (1985) ("The FDA's statement is dispositive on the question of implicit intent to pre-empt unless either the agency's position is inconsistent with clearly expressed congressional intent.").

[151] See *Medtronic*, 518 US at 512 (O'Connor, J, dissenting in part) ("Apparently recognizing that *Chevron* deference is unwarranted here, the Court does not admit to deferring to these regulations, but merely permits them to 'inform' the Court's interpretation."). Justice O'Connor went on to note that it "is not certain that an agency regulation determining the preemptive effect of *any* federal statute is entitled to deference." Id (emphasis in original).

[152] Id at 506 (Breyer, J, concurring in part) ("To draw a similar inference [in favor of deference] here makes sense, and not simply because of the statutory ambiguity. The Food and Drug Administration (FDA) is fully responsible for administering the MDA. That

Elsewhere, the Court has treated agency views regarding pre-emption as entitled to some though not dispositive weight.[153] Nonetheless, if a federal agency has clear statutory authority to preempt state law via regulations, the federal rule is supreme so long as properly promulgated.[154] As a result, underlying disputes in litigation are largely about statutory authority and regulatory effects.[155]

The commentary is somewhat divided about whether deference is owed to agency views that bear on preemption.[156] The standard reasons for not giving *Chevron* deference are several. First, some scholars have taken the view that *Chevron* deference is inappropriate because of a mismatch in institutional competence and democratic structure.[157] If deference is given to agency judgments about preemption, questions bearing on "state interests" would be resolved by agencies rather than Congress. Because the representational structure of Congress is allegedly more attuned to state interests than are agencies controlled by the executive,[158] agencies should be prevented from making preemption determinations. The executive branch is sometimes said to be more likely to represent national interests, whereas Congress is more likely to rep-

---

responsibility means informed agency involvement and, therefore, special understanding of the likely impact of both state and federal requirements, as well as an understanding of whether (or the extent to which) state requirements may interfere with federal objectives. The FDA can translate these understandings into particularized pre-emptive intentions accompanying its various rules and regulations.") (internal citations omitted).

[153] Consider *Geier*, 529 US at 883 ("We place some weight upon DOT's interpretation of [the statute's] objectives and its conclusion, as set forth in the Government's brief, that a tort suit such as this one would stand as an obstacle to the accomplishment and execution of those objectives.") (internal quotation marks omitted).

[154] See id at 883; *United States v Shimer*, 367 US 374, 382 (1961). See also *City of New York*, 486 US at 64.

[155] See generally Paul A. McGreal, *Some Rice with Your Chevron? Presumption and Deference in Regulatory Preemption*, 45 Case W Res L Rev 863, 866 (1995).

[156] Compare Mendelson, 102 Mich L Rev 740 (cited in note 13) (no deference); Dinh, 88 Geo L J at 2087 (cited in note 135) (same); Campbell, 59 U Pitt L Rev at 832 (cited in note 135) (no deference); with Pierce, 1 *Administrative Law Treatise* § 3.5 (cited in note 143) (yes deference); Bradford R. Clark, *Separation of Powers as a Safeguard of Federalism*, 79 Tex L Rev 1321, 1425 (2001) (deference to agencies' finding of preemption threatens federalism); S. Candice Hoke, *Preemption Pathologies and Civic Republican Values*, 71 BU L Rev 685 (1991) (criticizing deference to agencies' findings of preemption as threat to meaningful local governance); Marshall, 87 Geo L J 263 (cited in note 135) (deference inappropriate because agencies lack political accountability).

[157] See, for example, Campbell, 59 U Pitt L Rev at 832 (cited in note 135).

[158] See id. See also Sunstein, 67 U Chi L Rev at 331 (cited in note 2).

resent state or regional interests.[159] The weakness in this view is that it both overstates the protections inherent in Congress and understates the ability of Congress to protect state sovereignty interests against invasion by agencies. Agency organic statutes are crafted by Congress, and to the extent that Congress wants to protect state interests, it can do so through the standard mix of ex ante and ex post constraints. Indeed, jurisdictional boundaries are one mechanism for doing so.

A second justification for the "no deference to agency views on preemption" position is grounded in expertise. Agencies might lack expertise with respect to the distribution of overall government authority, and "the intrinsic value of preserving core state regulatory authority."[160] But to the extent that federal jurisdiction is overlapping with state authorities, this expertise might easily develop over time. In the CSA context, there were repeated interactions between Oregon and federal authorities. It could be that Attorney General Reno's decision not to preempt Oregon law was too attuned to state interests, or that the later Ashcroft decision to preempt the state law was insufficiently respectful of those interests, but there is little in the case itself to suggest a uniform bias in favor of preemption and against the preservation of statute authority.

A third commonly cited reason for not giving deference to agency statutory interpretations that displace state law is that the agency is effectively interpreting the scope of its own jurisdiction. Some commentary argues that granting deference on preemption-related questions would increase the risk that agencies would inappropriately expand their own authority at the expense of the states.[161] Notwithstanding several opportunities to do so, the Supreme Court has not offered a definitive answer about whether there is a "scope of jurisdiction" exception to *Chevron*.[162]

Both before and after *Chevron*, some authority suggested courts

---

[159] See generally Herbert Wechsler, *The Political Safeguards of Federalism: The Role of the States in the Composition and Selection of the National Government*, 54 Colum L Rev 543 (1954).

[160] Mendelson, 102 Mich L Rev at 741–42 (cited in note 13). Mendelson also argues that giving deference to agency views on preemption might result in inadequately constrained decision-making processes. Id.

[161] See id at 740.

[162] See Merrill and Hickman, 89 Geo L J 833 at 844 n 54 (cited in note 65); Sunstein, 90 Colum L Rev at 2097 (cited in note 6).

owe no deference when an agency interprets its own jurisdiction.[163] Others, led by Justice Scalia, urged that interpretive questions about jurisdiction are no different from other interpretive questions; often it is impossible to distinguish jurisdictional questions from nonjurisdictional ones.[164] When the FDA concludes tobacco is a drug and the agency's organic statute grants the FDA jurisdiction to regulate drugs, is the initial determination jurisdictional or not? The lower courts are divided as well,[165] but in shared jurisdiction schemes, the no deference view tends to predominates.[166]

The counterpoint on deference to jurisdictional decisions was articulated some years ago by Justice Brennan: one reason deference is owed to agency interpretations is that Congress has "entrusted" the agency with administering the statute.[167] If *Chevron* rests on an implicit delegation of law-interpreting authority, perhaps it is awkward to infer that Congress intended agencies to define the scope of their own power, authority, or jurisdiction.[168] Any alternative view would be inconsistent with at least some strains of Anglo-American law.[169]

Still, if there were no risk of bias or self-interested agency behavior, Congress might prefer to entrust agencies with the task of determining the scope of their own jurisdiction.[170] And even if agencies might act in their narrow self-interest, there is a trade-

---

[163] See *Dole v United Steelworkers*, 494 US 26, 43 (1990) (White, J, dissenting); *Social Security Board v Nieretko*, 327 US 358, 369 (1946) ("An agency may not finally decide the limits of its statutory power.").

[164] See *Mississippi Power & Light Co.*, 487 US at 381–82 (1988) (Scalia, J, concurring).

[165] Compare *Air Courier v United States Postal Service*, 959 F2d 1223, 1225 (3d Cir 1992) (Becker, J, concurring) (deference to jurisdictional questions should be limited), with *Oklahoma National Gas Co. v FERC*, 28 F3d 1281, 1283–84 (DC Cir 1994) (deference to jurisdictional judgments appropriate).

[166] *Collins v NTSB*, 351 F3d 1246, 1252–53 (DC Cir 2003) (no deference to jurisdictional determination when statute is implemented by multiple agencies); *Rapaport*, 59 F3d at 216 (same); *Wachtel*, 982 F2d at 585 (same); *ACLU v FCC*, 823 F2d 1554, 1567 n 32 (DC Cir 1987) ("highly unlikely that a responsible Congress would implicitly delegate to an agency the power to define the scope of its own power.").

[167] *Mississippi Power & Light Co.*, 487 US at 386.

[168] See Merrill and Hickman, 89 Geo L J at 910 (cited in note 65); Sunstein, 90 Colum L Rev at 2099 (cited in note 6) ("Because congressional instructions are crucial here, courts should probably refuse to defer to agency decisions with respect to issues of jurisdiction— again, if we assume that the distinction between jurisdictional and nonjurisdictional questions is easily administrable.").

[169] See Sunstein, 90 Colum L Rev at 2097 (cited in note 6).

[170] See generally Armstrong, 13 Cornell J L & Pub Policy 203 (cited in note 102).

off between expertise and accountability on the one hand and the risk of self-interested action on the other. These problems are not unique to jurisdictional judgments.[171]

Ultimately, the no deference to jurisdictional judgments view rests on unproven background assumptions about the behavior of administrative agencies. The running theme (with few exceptions[172]) is agency overreaching. Agencies might maximize jurisdiction, but they may also maximize budgets or autonomy.[173] Agencies may overreach, but they often underreach as well, and there is no reason to be systematically more concerned with overreaching than underreaching.[174] More to the point, if agencies prefer more authority, then overlapping and underlapping jurisdictional schemes make use of this tendency, generating desirable incentives for agency behavior rather than resisting institutional inclinations.

b) Preemption at Step Zero. When state interests are not at issue, the competing agents framework suggests courts should defer to agency views of statutes more often than current doctrine does. However, when a statute uses overlapping or underlapping jurisdiction to allocate authority between federal and state actors, things are somewhat more complicated. Like the generic shared jurisdiction deference question, the agency preemption question is properly analyzed at Step Zero. Should Congress be taken to have implicitly delegated law-interpreting authority to an agency with respect to statutory interpretations implicating preemption? The answer to that question will depend on the structure of the specific statutory scheme, but again, the overlap-underlap framework emphasizes a set of relevant variables that is both important and often overlooked.

Deferring to the agency's view on preemption issues may un-

---

[171] See Sunstein, 90 Colum L Rev at 2100–2101 (cited in note 6). See also Quincy M. Crawford, Comment, *Chevron Deference to Agency Interpretations That Delimit the Scope of the Agency's Jurisdiction*, 61 U Chi L Rev 957, 969–70 (1994).

[172] See id at 2100 ("It should follow that agencies will not receive deference when they are denying their authority to deal with a large category of cases.").

[173] See, for example, William A. Niskanen, Jr., *Bureaucracy and Representative Government* 36–42 (Aldine, Atherton, 1971). See also Wilson, *Bureaucracy* at 118–19 (cited in note 49); Anthony Downs, *Inside Bureaucracy* 26 (Little, Brown, 1989).

[174] In practice, it may be exceedingly difficult to distinguish these two factors. For example, was the EPA's decision not to regulate greenhouse gases during the second Bush administration a function of politics, expertise, or both? See *Massachusetts v EPA*, 126 S Ct 1438 (2007). See also Daryl Levinson, *Empire-Building Government in Constitutional Law*, 118 Harv L Rev 915, 935 (2006).

dermine the use of the competing agents framework because the views of the state actor (one of the agents) are jettisoned. In essence, one of the two competing agents would be given authority to end unilaterally the regulatory competition that the statute establishes. If so, then the competing agents framework suggests an alternative reason for not deferring to agency views that have preemptive effects, without invoking the questionable argument that courts should not defer to agencies' determinations of their own jurisdiction or dubious assumptions about agency interests and the political process.

This conclusion is not especially strong, however, and it should yield in the face of contrary considerations. Another way of stating the point is that when a statute shares jurisdiction between federal agencies and state authorities, there is no potential for genuine jurisdictional underlap. Either the state has authority or the federal agency does. Giving deference to agency views would provide an additional incentive for federal agencies to develop expertise, enter the field, and assert jurisdiction. But because judicial deference to agency views would also short-circuit the regulatory competition, the argument against implicit Congressional delegation and therefore *Chevron* deference is weaker. This conclusion is admittedly tentative, but note that it is perfectly in keeping with the *Rice* presumption, even though it derives from a somewhat different intuition. The problem is not preserving state authority against federal intrusion, but supporting a set of mechanisms that Congress might use to generate incentives for other governmental units.

Another alternative would be to aggressively review agency determinations in favor of preemption, but to readily defer to agency views concluding no preemption.[175] This would be more supportive of competing agents regimes, but awkward in the implicit delegation framework. Would Congress delegate the authority to interpret decisions that reach outcome X, but not outcome Y? Perhaps, but there is little in existing doctrine to provide a rigorous conceptual foundation for this idea.

Lastly, note that "dual federalism,"[176] which relies on the notions of "mutually exclusive" spheres of state and federal authority to

---

[175] This regime has been proposed to address agency bias or overreaching as well. See Walthall, 28 Cumb L Rev at 754–58 (cited in note 135).

[176] Edward S. Corwin, *The Passing of Dual Federalism*, 36 Va L Rev 1 (1950).

support dual sovereigns,[177] can be understood as a variation on the theme of the exclusive jurisdiction canon. In federalism jurisprudence, the trend has been away from efforts to enforce mutually exclusive spheres of authority and toward concurrent jurisdiction,[178] a shift that is perfectly in keeping with the competing agents framework. This trend in federalism jurisprudence toward concurrent rather than exclusive jurisdictional schemes mirrors the proposed shift toward supporting concurrent jurisdiction for federal agencies.

III. GONZALES V OREGON

Gonzales v Oregon involved the interpretation of a statute that shared jurisdiction and authority horizontally between multiple federal agencies and vertically between federal agencies and state government authorities. The precise contours of any overlapping or underlapping jurisdiction were ambiguous. Accordingly, the Attorney General's authority to displace Oregon's statute was contested, as was the question whether the Attorney General should receive deference for his view.

The 1971 Rule required that every prescription for a controlled substance be issued for a legitimate medical purpose by an individual practitioner acting in the usual course of his professional practice.[179] The 1971 Rule was not challenged in *Gonzales*. Rather, at issue was the validity of the Attorney General's 2001 Interpretive Rule, which interpreted the 1971 Rule, concluding that using controlled substances to assist suicide is not a "legitimate medical practice"[180] as that term is used in the 1971 Rule, and that therefore the CSA prohibits dispensing or prescribing drugs for that purpose.[181]

It is not hard to imagine a world in which *Gonzales* is an easy

---

[177] See generally Martin H. Redish, *The Constitution as Political Structure* 26 (Oxford, 1995); Alpheus Thomas Mason, *The Role of the Court*, in Valerie A. Earle, ed, *Federalism: Infinite Variety in Theory and Practice* 8, 24–25 (F. E. Peacock, 1968). For an overview and discussion in the context of foreign affairs, see Ernest Young, *Dual Federalism, Concurrent Jurisdiction, and the Foreign Affairs Exception*, 69 Geo Wash L Rev 139, 143 (2001). See also Larry Kramer, *Understanding Federalism*, 47 Vand L Rev 1485 (1994).

[178] See Young, 69 Geo Wash L Rev at 143–45 (cited in note 177).

[179] 21 CFR § 1306.04(a), 36 Fed Reg 7799 (Apr 24, 1971), redesignated at 38 Fed Reg 26609 (Sept 24, 1973), and amended at 39 Fed Reg 37986 (Oct 25, 1974).

[180] 21 CFR § 1306.04.

[181] 66 Fed Reg 56607 (Nov 9, 2001).

case. Indeed, perhaps it is Justice Scalia's world. Justice Scalia contended that the case involved three sufficient reasons to uphold the Attorney General's interpretation.[182] As an interpretation of an agency's own regulation, the Interpretive Rule might have been given the high level of deference of *Auer v Robbins*.[183] Under *Auer*, an agency's interpretations of its own regulations are controlling unless "plainly erroneous or inconsistent with the regulation."[184]

The majority thought *Auer* deference inappropriate, because the Attorney General's Interpretive Rule did "little more than restate the terms of the statute itself."[185] This setting, the majority said, was unlike *Auer*, where the interpretation offered by the Secretary of Labor (of regulations exempting certain law enforcement officers from the Fair Labor Standards Act of 1938) gave specificity to a general statutory command. As the majority concluded, an agency may not receive *Auer* deference merely by restating the terms of the statute in a regulation and then subsequently purporting to interpret the regulation.[186] "[T]he language the Interpretive Rule addresses comes from Congress, not the Attorney General," the Court said, and "the near-equivalence of the statute and regulation belies the Government's argument for *Auer* deference."[187] Within the *Auer* framework, the Interpretive Rule would very likely have been upheld.

What of *Chevron* deference for the Interpretive Rule? To start with, the majority conceded that, once within the *Chevron* framework, Step One of *Chevron* would be satisfied: "All would agree, we should think, that the statutory phrase 'legitimate medical purpose' is a generality, susceptible to more precise definition and open to varying constructions, and thus ambiguous in the relevant sense."[188] The majority continued:

---

[182] *Gonzales v Oregon*, 126 S Ct 904, 926 (2006) (Scalia, J, dissenting). Justice Scalia concluded the Attorney General's interpretation should have been upheld either as a de novo interpretation, or the agency's interpretation of a statute reviewed deferentially in the *Chevron* framework, or the agency's interpretation of its own regulation reviewed even more deferentially in the *Auer* framework.

[183] Id at 927.

[184] *Auer v Robbins*, 519 US 452, 461 (1997). See also *Bowles v Seminole Rock & Sand Co.*, 325 US 410, 414 (1945).

[185] *Gonzales*, 126 S Ct at 915.

[186] Id at 916.

[187] Id at 915.

[188] Id at 916.

Chevron deference, however, is not accorded merely because the statute is ambiguous and an administrative official is involved. To begin with, the rule must be promulgated pursuant to authority Congress has delegated to the official.[189]

Enter Step Zero.

A. STEP ZERO AND SWITCHED PRESUMPTIONS

For many years, *Chevron* was taken to be a global presumption in favor of judicial deference to agencies. In the face of statutory silence or ambiguity, judges would defer to agencies on matters of statutory interpretation. In the aftermath of *Mead*, the direction of this presumption may be shifting. Courts apparently will not defer to agency interpretations of statutes absent some affirmative indication that Congress delegated law-interpreting authority.

In *Gonzales*, the Court first asserted that the Step Zero hurdle is cleared if "the statute gives an agency broad power to enforce all provisions of the statute."[190] However, where the specific delegation provision fails to grant such broad authority to the agency, more analysis is required. Importantly, in overlapping jurisdiction statutes, this generally sufficient condition for *Chevron* deference will almost never be met unless authority is completely overlapping. This reading of *Mead* amounts to a bias against concurrent regulatory authority in the *Chevron* framework. The majority concluded that the CSA delegates to the Attorney General only "limited powers, to be exercised in specific ways"[191] rather than the sufficient general authority. Because the CSA gives the Attorney General the authority to make rules and regulations to carry out "registration and control" and for the "efficient execution of his functions," the majority concluded that the Attorney General does not have general "force of law" authority to implement the entire

---

[189] Id, citing *United States v Mead Corp.*, 533 US 218, 226–27 (2001).

[190] *Gonzales*, 126 S Ct at 916 (emphasis added). See also *National Cable & Telecommunications Assn. v Brand X Internet Servs.*, 545 US 967, 980 (2004) (finding *Chevron* deference appropriate to an FCC regulation because Congress delegated authority to prescribe such rules and regulations as may be necessary in the public interest to carry out the provisions of the Act); *Household Credit Services, Inc. v Pfennig*, 541 US 232, 238 (2004) (deferring under *Chevron* doctrine to Federal Reserve board regulation because Congress delegated authority to make regulations as necessary or proper to effectuate the purposes of the statute).

[191] *Gonzales*, 126 S Ct at 917.

statute.[192] The Interpretive Rule could pass muster under Step Zero only if it was related to one of the two explicit delegation provisions, and the majority thought it inadequately tethered to either. In essence, the Court concluded that the statute does not create overlapping interpretive authority between the Attorney General and the Secretary on medical matters.[193] The Interpretive Rule was not issued via notice and comment rulemaking, as required for rules promulgated under the relevant section.[194] And, the majority concluded that the Interpretive Rule could not be "justified" under the registration portion of the statute because it failed to undertake the five-factor analysis required of such rules[195] and concerned more than just registration.[196]

---

[192] For example, section 821 gives the Attorney General authority "to promulgate rules and regulations and to charge reasonable fees relating to the *registration* and *control* of the manufacture, distribution, and dispensing of controlled substances and to listed chemicals." 21 USC § 821 (2006) (emphasis added). Section 871(b) gives the Attorney General authority "to promulgate and enforce any rules, regulations, and procedures which he may deem necessary and appropriate for the efficient execution of his functions under this subchapter." 21 USC § 871(b) (2006).

[193] With respect to the control provision, the Attorney General can make regulations for the "control" of drugs, but control is defined for purposes of the subchapter: "The term 'control' means to add a drug or other substance, or immediate precursor, to a schedule under part B of this subchapter, whether by transfer from another schedule or otherwise." See 21 USC § 802(5) (2006). To exercise this scheduling authority the Attorney General must follow a set of procedures that include requesting a scientific and medical evaluation from the Secretary of Health and Human Services. 21 USC § 811 (2006). Because the Interpretive Rule was not issued via notice and comment rulemaking, as required for rules promulgated under the relevant section, and because it did not follow the specified procedures of consultation, the majority thought the control provision clearly inadequate to support the rule. Section 821 is in subchapter C rather than subchapter B, which is guided by the statutory definition the majority cites. Subchapter C relates to registration of manufacturers, distributors, and dispensers of controlled substances. Subchapter B relates to scheduling. These are technical debates about the reach of statutory definitions, which need not be definitively resolved here.

[194] This is a readily contestable point. Interpretive rules are excepted from notice and comment requirements of the APA, and so long as an interpretive rule interprets a validly issued regulation, it would be perfectly valid (authorized). To say the least, the Court's reading of "control" is far from obvious, or as Justice Scalia urged "manifestly erroneous." *Gonzales*, 126 S Ct at 929.

[195] See 21 USC § 823(f) (2006):

(1) The recommendation of the appropriate State licensing board or professional disciplinary authority.
(2) The applicant's experience in dispensing, or conducting research with respect to controlled substances.
(3) The applicant's conviction record under Federal or State laws relating to the manufacture, distribution, or dispensing of controlled substances.
(4) Compliance with applicable State, Federal, or local laws relating to controlled substances.
(5) Such other conduct which may threaten the public health and safety.

[196] *Gonzales*, 126 S Ct at 918.

Because dispensing controlled substances without being registered to do so is a crime,[197] the majority concluded that the Interpretive Rule "purports to declare that using controlled substances for physician-assisted suicide is a crime, an authority that goes well beyond the Attorney General's statutory power to register or deregister."[198] This would be "extraordinary authority." This part of the opinion connotes a series of cases in which the Court declined to give deference to agencies on "major questions."[199] These cases were decided before *Mead*, and *Gonzales* indicates that the "major questions" exception fits neatly into the Step Zero analytic.

Each of these interpretive moves is an attempt to narrowly define the scope of the Attorney General's authority in the CSA.[200] By tracing law-interpreting authority to very specific statutory provisions, the majority effectively shrank the agency's jurisdiction and the potential law-interpreting authority associated therewith. The narrower the Attorney General's statutory jurisdiction gets, the less plausible the inference that Congress implicitly delegated law-interpreting authority that would warrant judicial deference.[201]

The Court made a number of arguments that clearly implicate the overlapping and underlapping jurisdiction analysis. First, the Court reasoned that it would not interpret ambiguous general authority broadly in the face of specific and prescribed grants of authority.[202] Given the alleged breadth of the authority claimed by the Attorney General, and the silence or ambiguity of the CSA, the statute was best read to preclude *Chevron* deference because Congress does not confer broad authority through an implicit

---

[197] 21 USC § 841 (2006).

[198] *Gonzales*, 126 S Ct at 918.

[199] Sunstein, 92 Va L Rev at 243–44 (cited in note 61).

[200] Prior to 1984, the Attorney General's registration authority was limited, allowing for deregistration only for a false application, felony conviction, or state denial of license; the Attorney General was required to register any physician authorized by the state. *Gonzales*, 126 S Ct at 917; Pub L No 91-513, 84 Stat 1253 (1970), codified at 21 USC § 301 et seq (1976). After the 1984 Amendments, the Attorney General could also deny or revoke registration if such registration is found to be "inconsistent with the public interest." 21 USC §§ 823(f), 824(a) (2006).

[201] Moreover, the 1971 Rule that the 2001 Interpretive Rule purported to interpret was issued prior to the 1984 Amendments, which the majority took as further evidence that the Attorney General lacked authority.

[202] See *Gonzales*, 126 S Ct at 918, citing *Federal Maritime Commission v Seatrain Lines, Inc.*, 411 US 726, 744 (1973). *Seatrain Lines* reasoned that ambiguous provisions would not be read to extend agency authority in light of specific grants.

delegation.[203] Justice Scalia disagreed. By giving the Attorney General sole and explicit charge for administering the registration and deregistration provisions, Congress "implicitly (but clearly) gave the Attorney General authority to interpret those criteria—*whether or not* there is any explicit delegation provision in the statute."[204] After all, *Chevron* itself was a case of implicit delegation.[205] The majority read the alleged statutory ambiguity to create exclusive jurisdictional assignments, while Justice Scalia would have interpreted the statute to create concurrent law-interpreting authority.[206] Given the mix of explicit and implicit delegated rulemaking authority, Scalia found the majority's conclusion that the statute gives exclusive federal authority over scientific and medical determinations to the Secretary of Health and Human Services "not remotely plausible."[207]

B. APPLYING THE EXCLUSIVE JURISDICTION PRESUMPTION

The majority also relied on the general statute and exclusive jurisdiction presumptions discussed above, and was unwilling to give deference to agency interpretations of terms used in multiple parts of the same statute.[208] The Attorney General's regulations interpreted the term "public interest," but as the Court said: "[i]t is not enough that the terms 'public interest,' 'public health and safety,' and 'Federal law' are used in the part of the statute over which the Attorney General has authority."[209] To further the inference that Congress would not want courts to defer to the Attorney General on such matters the court noted that:

---

[203] See *Gonzales*, 126 S Ct at 921–22.

[204] Id at 936 (Scalia, J, dissenting) (emphasis in original).

[205] *Chevron USA, Inc. v Natural Resources Defense Council*, 467 US 837, 844 (1984).

[206] Justice Scalia reasoned that because § 821 gives the Attorney General authority to promulgate rules and regulations relating to the registration and control of the manufacturing, distribution, and dispensing of controlled substances, the statute should be read to delegate interpretive authority to the Attorney General for all of Part C of the CSA, §§ 821–30. *Gonzales*, 126 S Ct at 936–37 (Scalia, J, dissenting).

[207] Id at 937.

[208] The Court relied on *Sutton v United Air Lines*, 527 US 471 (1999). Recall that in *Sutton*, the Court rejected an argument that EEOC could receive *Chevron* deference for its interpretation of "disability" because the ADA is administered by many agencies, despite the fact that the EEOC was given authority to implement a subchapter of the ADA. See 527 US at 514 (Breyer, J, dissenting).

[209] *Gonzales*, 126 S Ct at 919.

The Attorney General does not have the sole delegated authority under the CSA. He must instead share it with, and in some respects defer to, the Secretary, whose functions are likewise delineated and confined by the statute. The CSA allocates decisionmaking powers among statutory actors so that medical judgments, if they are to be decided at the federal level and for the limited objects of the statute, are placed in the hands of the Secretary.[210]

This passage might be read to support concurrent jurisdiction, but in practice it did not. Despite a statute that clearly shares authority between these two institutional actors, the majority concluded law-interpreting authority for *Chevron* purposes was only delegated to one agency—the Secretary. As such, the opinion appears to embrace the exclusive jurisdiction presumption as part of a Step Zero analysis. Again, this presumption makes a plausible, but ultimately unsatisfying, inference about congressional intent and its relation to expertise:

Because historical familiarity and policymaking expertise account in the first instance for the presumption that Congress delegates interpretive lawmaking power to the agency rather than to the reviewing court, we presume here that Congress intended to invest interpretive power in the administrative actor in the best position to develop these attributes.[211]

The majority reasoned that because the Interpretive Rule involved a quintessentially medical judgment, the CSA was best read (via the presumption) to preclude rather than grant the Attorney General the authority to act with the force of law in the promulgation of the Interpretive Rule. Therefore, no *Chevron* deference was warranted.

C. APPLYING THE MODIFIED STEP ZERO PREEMPTION PRESUMPTION

The majority also used a modified presumption against preemption to analyze Step Zero. When deciding whether to defer to the Attorney General's interpretation of the CSA, the majority explicitly disclaimed reliance on clear statement principles, but

---

[210] Id at 920.

[211] Id at 921, quoting *Martin v Occupational Safety and Health Review Commission*, 499 US 144, 153 (1991).

nonetheless invoked related presumptions to justify its inference against an implicit Congressional delegation:

> Just as the conventions of expression indicate that Congress is unlikely to alter a statute's obvious scope and division of authority through muffled hints, the background principles of our federal system also belie the notion that Congress would use such an obscure grant of authority to regulate areas traditionally supervised by the States' police power. It is unnecessary even to consider the application of clear statement requirements or presumptions against pre-emption to reach this commonsense conclusion.[212]

This is a dense and somewhat cryptic passage, but the key seems to be that courts will presume Congress has not delegated law-interpreting authority to issue rules that have the effect of displacing state policy, at least in "traditional" fields of state regulation.[213] The Court could have said that agency interpretations that create positive conflicts with state law are not entitled to *Chevron* deference.[214] The Court might also have applied its presumption against preemption,[215] or a clear statement rule,[216] to preserve the state law. But it did neither.[217] Read properly as Step Zero analysis, this passage indicates that *Chevron* deference will not generally be given to agency interpretations of statutes generating conflicts with state law, at least in fields traditionally of state or local concern like the regulation of the medical profession.

The majority reasoned that the CSA constitutes a comprehensive federal regime for regulating drug trafficking and drug use,[218] but that the CSA is concerned only secondarily with the regulation of the medical profession.[219] The statute's text and design manifest "no intent to regulate the practice of medicine generally," partic-

---

[212] *Gonzales*, 126 S Ct at 925 (internal citations omitted).

[213] Id.

[214] Justice Scalia argued in dissent that the Interpretive Rule does not purport to preempt state law even by conflict preemption because a federal law that precludes physician-assisted suicide would not create a positive conflict with a state law authorizing physician-assisted suicide unless the state law mandated physician-assisted suicide rather than merely authorizing it. Id at 934 (Scalia, J, dissenting).

[215] See *Rush Prudential, HMO, Inc. v Moran*, 536 US 355, 387 (2002).

[216] See *United States v Bass*, 404 US 336, 349 (1971).

[217] See *Gonzales*, 126 S Ct at 925.

[218] See generally *Gonzales v Raich*, 545 US 1, 13 (2006).

[219] See *Gonzales*, 126 S Ct at 922.

ularly given the structure and limitations of federalism.[220] Because the CSA presumes and expressly utilizes state regulation of the medical profession under the police powers,[221] and the statute contains an express preservation clause,[222] the statute should not be read lightly to preempt state regulation of the medical profession.[223]

As long as Congress has acted pursuant to a legitimate grant of constitutional power, the federal government can clearly set national standards that preempt state law even though regulation of health and safety is primarily and historically a matter of local concern.[224] The Interpretive Rule proffered an interpretation of the CSA that created an inconsistency between federal law and the ODWDA. On its face, the majority seems to use a modified Step Zero presumption against preemption. Congress will not be taken to delegate law-interpreting authority when a federal agency asserts authority in a way that butts up against traditional state concerns. The majority's emphasis on the statute's "silence on the practice of medicine generally"[225] suggests a rebuttable presumption, as does the emphasis on implicit rather than explicit authorization. However, the majority took the specific delegations of rulemaking authority in the CSA to be insufficient to rebut this modified presumption. The CSA might or might not provide authority for the Attorney General to preempt the ODWDA—a matter of clear disagreement in the case—but the modified Step Zero presumption against preemption implies that courts will more often resolve these questions de novo than within the *Chevron* deference framework.

---

[220] Id at 923.

[221] See, for example, 21 USC § 823(f) (2006) (making compliance with the laws of the state in which the potential registrant practices necessary to dispense controlled substances). See also 21 USC § 802(21) (2006).

[222] See 21 USC § 903 (2006).

[223] See *Gonzales*, 126 S Ct at 923. The majority continued: "In the face of the CSA's silence on the practice of medicine generally and its recognition of state regulation of the medical profession it is difficult to defend the Attorney General's declaration that the statute impliedly criminalizes physician-assisted suicide. This difficulty is compounded by the CSA's consistent delegation of medical judgments to the Secretary and its otherwise careful allocation of powers for enforcing the limited objects of the CSA." Id at 924. This passage conflates de novo interpretation of the CSA with the scope of the Attorney General's jurisdiction, which in turn contributes to the Step Zero analysis.

[224] See id at 923. See also *Hillsborough County v Automated Medical Laboratories, Inc.*, 471 US 707, 717 (1985).

[225] *Gonzales*, 126 S Ct at 924.

D. SUMMARY

In the overlapping and underlapping jurisdiction framework, the Attorney General's Interpretive Rule is an assertion of ambiguous jurisdiction. By not clarifying the precise boundaries of the Attorney General's authority, Congress could be taken to have provided for the possibility that the Attorney General would develop expertise and assert jurisdiction. The majority's inference of exclusive rather than concurrent law-interpreting authority in the CSA undermines the use of jurisdiction to generate incentives for agencies. If the competing agents framework constitutes a reasonable reconstruction of congressional intent, then the trend in the courts toward an inference of exclusive law-interpreting authority is inconsistent with the foundation of Step Zero. The majority's focus on expertise—tailoring deference to relevant knowledge—is laudable. But the Court's view of expertise is too static. Expertise develops over time. When the Court uses the exclusive delegation canon to presume that Congress wants only a single agency to receive deference for relevant interpretations, it adopts a short-term resolution to what is a long-term challenge and enacts obstacles to the formation of better regulatory policy.

Unlike the exclusive jurisdiction presumption, which I have argued undermines the competing agents framework, the Step Zero modified preemption presumption can be understood as competing agents-supporting, although imperfectly so. The majority's reluctance to defer to an agency view that would have the effect of displacing state judgments could support the use of creative statutory design in domains like the CSA. The preservation of concurrent jurisdiction helps avoid premature termination of the checks on behavior that competing agents can produce.

The overlap-underlap framework will clearly not always resolve Step Zero inquiries. However, by offering a theory of why Congress would use statutes with overlapping and underlapping jurisdiction, the competing agents framework more closely aligns the Step Zero inquiry with actual congressional dynamics. If a rational reconstruction of congressional intent is to be the cornerstone of Step Zero, courts will increasingly need elaborate theoretical frameworks to analyze whether Congress is best taken to request deferential or de novo review of agency decisions.

IV. CONCLUSION

Gonzales v Oregon is a rich case for administrative lawyers. Beyond the nuanced moral and policy debates that physician-assisted suicide raises, the statutory and regulatory framework is remarkably complex. Ultimately, what drove the Court's analysis was the relationship between statutes that share jurisdiction among various federal and state authorities and the *Chevron* deference framework. As such, the case constitutes part of an important emerging Step Zero doctrine that sorts administrative judgments into those that qualify for judicial deference and those that do not.

The Court seemed to adopt two interpretive presumptions that reduce the likelihood of deference for interpretations of shared jurisdiction statutes. The first presumes that Congress gives law-interpreting authority to a single government entity. If real, the presumption makes the use of overlapping and underlapping jurisdictional schemes more costly and less effective. The second presumes that Congress does not implicitly grant law-interpreting authority to agencies with respect to interpretations that would impinge on state interests. This modified preemption presumption of Step Zero is a close cousin to the *Rice* presumption against preemption, but the Court apparently conceives of them as different tools.

Gonzales also illustrates fault lines in the *Chevron* doctrine itself. *Chevron* asks whether agencies or judges should make interpretive decisions. This was an important first-generation *Chevron* problem: courts versus agencies, when, where, and why? Increasingly, however, courts are being called on to allocate authority within the executive branch and between state and federal governments. *Chevron* may be the right lens through which to view such disputes, but these second-generation questions require more nuanced analysis of politics and policy. The competing agents framework suggests greater attention to the justification for, and dynamics of, overlapping and underlapping jurisdiction schemes in administrative law.

ANN WOOLHANDLER

INTERSTATE SOVEREIGN IMMUNITY

In *Nevada v Hall*, the Supreme Court held that the Constitution does not prevent a state from opening its courts to suits against other states. The Court therefore affirmed a California damages judgment against Nevada arising from an automobile accident in California.[1] More recently, in *Franchise Tax Board v Hyatt*, the Court unanimously allowed a Nevada resident's case in a Nevada court to proceed against California for an allegedly abusive tax investigation.[2] In a footnote, the Court declined to reconsider the question of the defendant state's constitutional immunity, noting that the defendant had not pressed that issue.[3]

Hall and *Hyatt* may give the impression that allowing state court suits against sister states involves only a grudge match between California and Nevada.[4] But *Hyatt* was one of dozens of suits that individuals have pursued against states in the courts of other states

---

Ann Woolhandler is William Minor Lile Professor and Class of 1948 Research Professor, University of Virginia Law School.

AUTHOR'S NOTE: My thanks to Michael Collins, Richard Fallon, Toby Heytens, John Jeffries, Dan Meltzer, Caleb Nelson, and George Rutherglen for comments on earlier drafts, and to Dan Espensen and Julie Podlesni for research assistance.

[1] 440 US 410 (1979).

[2] 538 US 488 (2003).

[3] Id at 497.

[4] See *The Supreme Court, 1978 Term, Constitutional Law, Sovereign Immunity, State Tort Liability in Another State's Courts*, 93 Harv L Rev 189, 198 (1979) (suggesting that suits against states in another state's courts would remain a rarity, requiring no rigid formula for choice of law); Tom A. Jerman, Note, *Nevada v. Hall: Sovereign Immunity, Federalism and Compromising Relations Between Sister States*, 1980 Utah L Rev 395, 406 (predicting there would be few cases against states in other states' courts).

following *Nevada v Hall*. And while a suit over a car wreck that occurred in the forum state may seem unexceptionable, the state courts have entertained other cases involving claims for injuries caused by escaped detainees,[5] by a state university's threatened withdrawal of a Ph.D.,[6] by coaches' demands on a college athlete,[7] and by a state university financial officer's allegedly reneging on an investment contract.[8] The Supreme Court's allowing a suit arising from a tax investigation in *Hyatt*, moreover, suggests that the Court is disinclined to impose limits on suits against states in sister states' courts, other than the minor restraints of minimum contacts for personal jurisdiction and nonarbitrariness for choice of law.

The initial commentary on *Hall* was mixed, with some scholars voicing approval[9] and others noting its discordance with the Supreme Court's Eleventh Amendment jurisprudence.[10] This discor-

---

[5] See *Peterson v Texas*, 635 P2d 241 (Colo App 1981) (allowing suit for damages to a car caused by escapees from a Texas youth rehabilitation program).

[6] *Faulkner v University of Tennessee*, 627 S2d 362 (Ala 1992), cert denied, 510 US 1101 (1994).

[7] *Oregon v Superior Court of Los Angeles County*, 29 Cal Rptr 2d 909 (Cal Ct App 1994) (treating dismissively claims of comity where it was alleged that the University of Oregon had promised a California athlete adequate medical treatment and where the athlete subsequently suffered a stroke while playing for the University of Oregon in California).

[8] *Ehrlich-Bober & Co. v University of Houston*, 404 NE2d 726 (NY 1980).

[9] See, for example, John M. Rogers, *Applying the International Law of Sovereign Immunity to the States of the Union*, 1981 Duke L J 449, 467 (approving the result in *Hall*, but arguing that sister-state immunity should be governed by international sovereign immunity standards); David L. Shapiro, *Wrong Turns: The Eleventh Amendment and the Pennhurst Case*, 98 Harv L Rev 61, 79–80 (1984) (discussing with approval the *Hall* Court's observation that the "question whether one sovereign entity is immune from suit in the courts of another has long been recognized as a question for the forum to resolve according to its law" (footnote omitted)); compare Chris Martiniak, *Hall v. Nevada, 440 U.S. 410 (1979): State Court Jurisdiction over Sister States v. American State Sovereign Immunity*, 63 Cal L Rev 1144, 1166 (1975) (discussing the case before the Supreme Court decision, and favoring a federal law to govern suits against states); Comment, *The Abolition of Sister State Immunity: Nevada v. Hall and Territorial Sovereignty*, 60 BU L Rev 601, 619, 622–23 (1980) (viewing the decision favorably and arguing that the Supreme Court's appellate review would protect states from unfairness); *Recent Developments: Constitutional Law—State Sovereign Immunity—Nevada v. Hall*, 56 Wash L Rev 289, 304 (1981) (concluding that that jurisdiction should "be limited to that which is necessary to preserve the sovereignty of the forum state without creating an undue infringement upon that of the defendant state"); *The Supreme Court, 1978 Term*, 93 Harv L Rev at 194–95 (cited in note 4) (approving the result in *Hall*, but suggesting that some limits might be necessary to prevent interference with self-government).

[10] See, for example, Glenn H. Reynolds, *Penumbral Reasoning on the Right*, 140 U Pa L Rev 1333, 1343 (1992) (quoting with approval then-Justice Rehnquist, who criticized the decision as contrary to the "logic of the Framers' careful allocation of responsibility among the state and federal judiciaries"); Gary Simson, *The Role of History in Constitutional Interpretation: A Case Study*, 70 Cornell L Rev 253, 267 (1985) (faulting the *Hall* opinion for its inattention to the history); Margaret G. Stewart, *The State as an Unwilling Defendant:*

dance became more pronounced after the Supreme Court held in *Alden v Maine*[11] that Congress cannot use its powers under the Commerce Clause to subject a state to suit on a federal question claim in the state's own courts.[12]

This article explores in greater depth why *Hall* and *Hyatt* were incorrectly decided, as a matter of the constitutional framers' intent, structure, and text, as well as historical practice, and practical results. Part I visits the founding era to show that state immunity in the courts of other states was foundational to all sides of the debate on whether Article III effected a waiver of state immunity. Part II

Reflections on Nevada v. Hall, 59 Neb L Rev 246, 278 (1980) (concluding that *Hall* runs against the grain of American federalism); Comment, *The Eleventh Amendment, Sovereign Immunity and Full Faith and Credit: No Constitutional Refuge for a State as Defendant*, 42 U Pitt L Rev 57, 84–85 (1980) (criticizing the decision).

[11] 527 US 706, 739 (1999) (distinguishing *Hall* on the ground that the Court should be warier of unstated limitations on state power than federal power).

[12] See Richard H. Fallon, Jr., Daniel J. Meltzer, and David L. Shapiro, *Hart and Wechsler's The Federal Courts and the Federal System* 1060 (Foundation, 5th ed 2003) (questioning whether *Hall* was still good law after *Alden*); Daniel J. Meltzer, *State Sovereign Immunity: Five Authors in Search of a Theory*, 75 Notre Dame L Rev 1011, 1037–38 n 110, 1048 n 153 (2000) (noting *Alden*'s tension with *Hall* and also noting the anomalous possibility of suits against states in sister states' courts on federal questions under *Hall*); David L. Shapiro, *The 1999 Trilogy: What Is Good Federalism?* 31 Rutgers L J 753, 754–60 (2000) (in writing disapprovingly of *Alden*, asking, "If the notion of state sovereign immunity really did matter in our federal system, would we permit a state itself to be sued not only by the federal government and by another state in a federal court *and* to be sued in another state on a private state law claim"? (footnotes omitted)); Carlos Manuel Vázquez, *Sovereign Immunity, Due Process, and the Alden Trilogy*, 109 Yale L J 1927, 1936 (2000) (suggesting that because *Alden* did not overrule *Hall*, states might be made liable on federal causes of action in the courts of sister states, although questioning this suggestion given that *Alden* indicated that Congress could not subject states to damages liability in any forum); see also Thomas H. Lee, *Making Sense of the Eleventh Amendment: International Law and State Sovereignty*, 96 Nw U L Rev 1027, 1092, 1096 (2002) (arguing that the international law interpretation of state immunity indicates that states should not be suable in the courts of other states, but that states should be able to espouse the state-law-based claims of their citizens in suits against other states in the federal courts, and that states should be entitled to immunity in the courts of other states to the same extent as in the federal courts); Alfred Hill, *In Defense of Our Law of Sovereign Immunity*, 42 BC L Rev 485, 582–84 (2001) (arguing that the original understanding was that states could not be sued in state or federal courts without consent, although arguing that on its facts *Nevada v Hall* was not necessarily wrong, but that the California court should have to apply the law that the Supreme Court would in a suit between the states for redress); Vicki C. Jackson, *Seductions of Coherence, State Sovereign Immunity, and the Denationalization of Federal Law*, 31 Rutgers L J 691, 731 (2000) (discussing *Hall* as consistent with [the now overruled] *Hilton v South Carolina Rys Comm'n*, 502 US 197 (1991), in allowing states to be sued outside of the federal courts); J. Brian King, *The State Political Process Theory of the 11th Amendment*, 19 Rev Litig 355, 358, 396 (2000) (noting *Hall*'s conflict with *Alden*, and arguing that sovereign immunity is inherent to a state and should only be waived pursuant to the state's democratic process); James E. Pfander, *Rethinking the Supreme Court's Original Jurisdiction in State-Party Cases*, 82 Cal L Rev 555, 587, 655, 658 (1994) (arguing that states could not be sued in courts of other states, but that states should be amenable to federal claims in the Supreme Court's original jurisdiction).

argues that the Eleventh Amendment was built on the same premise that states could not be sued in sister states. Part III shows that both federal and state courts proceeded on assumptions of interstate sovereign immunity for 180 years—until *Hall*. Part IV discusses post-*Hall* decisions in the state courts, and why recognition of a constitutional immunity for states would produce better results.

I. Unamended Article III and Assumptions of State Nonsuability in Sister-State Courts

Article III extended the federal judicial power to "Controversies . . . between a State and Citizens of another State."[13] It also provided for Supreme Court original jurisdiction in cases "in which a State shall be Party." In *Chisholm v Georgia*, in which a South Carolina citizen sued Georgia in the Supreme Court for payment for goods, the majority of Justices held that the Constitution abrogated state immunity.[14] This in turn led to the Eleventh Amendment's provision that the "Judicial power of the United States shall not be construed to extend" to suits commenced against a state by "Citizens of another state."[15]

Article III's state/citizen diversity provisions and the Eleventh Amendment explicitly address only federal court jurisdiction, thus making possible *Hall's* decision that state immunity in the courts of other states is largely unaffected by the Constitution.[16] Justice Stevens's opinion in *Hall* asserts that the "the question whether one State might be subject to suit in the courts of another State was apparently not a matter of concern when the new Constitution was being drafted and ratified."[17] This statement may be true in the limited sense that the framers would not have thought such suits possible, and therefore were not worried that they would occur. If, however, Stevens's statement means that the founders had nothing on their minds with regard to state jurisdiction over sister states,

---

[13] US Const, Art III, § 2, cl 1.

[14] 2 US (2 Dall) 419 (1793).

[15] The arguments made herein are also generally similar for state/alien diversity, but for simplicity this article will only refer to state/citizen diversity.

[16] 440 US at 421 (reasoning that Article III and the Eleventh Amendment as well as debates about them were focused on the federal judicial power).

[17] Id at 418–19.

it is incorrect.[18] Rather, the impossibility of unconsented *in personam* suits against states in the courts of other states was a foundation on which all sides of the framing era debates built their argument as to whether Article III's state/citizen diversity provisions effected a waiver of state immunity.

Those at the Philadelphia convention engaged in little discussion of the state/citizen diversity provision. The Committee of Detail proposed it under the convention's directive to provide for jurisdiction over questions involving the national peace or harmony.[19] Whether it was meant to encompass only state-as-plaintiff or also state-as-defendant suits, the committee's committing state/citizen cases to the Supreme Court's original jurisdiction suggests the sensitivity of such jurisdiction and a wish to guarantee a federal forum even if lower federal courts went uncreated.

During ratification and through the Court's *Chisholm* decision, debate arose over whether Article III and the state/citizen diversity provision (1) preserved state immunities,[20] or (2) effected a waiver of sovereign immunity. Both positions are still reflected in the modern debate about the scope of sovereign immunity.[21] The first bol-

---

[18] See King, 19 Rev Litig at 392 (cited in note 12) ("It is not true that the states were not concerned about suit in other state courts at the time of ratification; the issue was just not before them at that time."); Simson, 70 Cornell L Rev at 267 (cited in note 10) (observing "the absence of any mention of state courts in the eleventh amendment does not strongly imply an intent to exclude state courts from the amendment's coverage").

[19] See Max Farrand, ed, 2 *The Records of the Federal Convention of 1787* 46 (July 18) (Yale, 1911) (recording the agreement without opposition by the Committee of the Whole to James Madison's proposal "that the jurisdiction shall extend to all cases arising under the Natl. laws: And to such other questions as may involve the Natl. peace & harmony"), discussed in William A. Fletcher, *A Historical Interpretation of the Eleventh Amendment: A Narrow Construction of an Affirmative Grant of Jurisdiction Rather than a Prohibition Against Jurisdiction*, 35 Stan L Rev 1033, 1045–46 (1983) (noting this general direction to the Committee of Detail); see also Federalist 80 (Hamilton) in Philip B. Kurland and Ralph Lerner, eds, 4 *The Founders' Constitution* 240, 241 (Chicago, 1987) ("The power of determining causes between two STATES, between one state and the citizens of another, and between the citizens of different states, is perhaps not less essential to the peace of the union than that which has been just examined" (cases in which foreigners are parties)).

[20] One may further subdivide this view, at least for purposes of the modern debate, into a belief that the original Article III did not abrogate existing state immunities and a view that the original Article III implicitly incorporated a firm state immunity. See notes 21–22.

[21] For a description of the immunity and diversity views, see Peter W. Low and John C. Jeffries, Jr., *Federal Courts and the Law of Federal-State Relations* 931–33, 938–40 (Foundation, 5th ed 2004); see also Fletcher, 35 Stan L Rev at 1060–61, 1130 (cited in note 19) (arguing that the Eleventh Amendment's failure to mention suits by in-state citizens suggests that the drafters did not intend to reach federal question cases, and that the amendment "left both admiralty and federal question jurisdiction to operate according to their own terms, authorizing federal courts to entertain private citizens' suits against the states whenever based on valid substantive federal law"). There is a vast volume of schol-

sters the "immunity" view that state immunity was implicit in the Constitution and that the Eleventh Amendment restored and more fully constitutionalized this original understanding.[22] The second lends support to the "diversity" theory—that the Eleventh Amendment does not imply sovereign immunity in federal question cases, particularly for actions provided by congressional statutes and perhaps for implied constitutional claims as well.[23] But during the de-

---

arship on state sovereign immunity which includes other approaches as well as variations on the two principal approaches that this article will discuss. One major view, which might also be seen as a variation on the diversity view, is the congressional abrogation or separation of powers approach. See Low and Jeffries, *Federal Courts* at 940–41 (describing this view). This approach sees the Eleventh Amendment as signaling that the federal courts acting without congressional authorization cannot make states liable, but allows for Congress to make states liable. This view shares with the diversity view that federal question cases may be excepted from sovereign immunity, although it requires congressional action which the diversity theory would not necessarily require. See, for example, John E. Nowak, *The Scope of Congressional Power to Create Causes of Action Against State Governments and the History of the Eleventh and Fourteenth Amendments*, 75 Colum L Rev 1413, 1425 (1975) (arguing that the drafters of Article III's state/citizen diversity provision "meant *Congress* to have the power to grant jurisdiction in suits by a citizen of one state against another state"); id at 1440–41 (arguing that the Eleventh Amendment was primarily addressed to suits by Tories against states and that no evidence exists that the states similarly feared congressionally authorized suits). Most of the arguments here that address the diversity view would likely be applicable to the congressional abrogation view.

This article, however, does not attempt to address the consistency of *Hall* and *Hyatt* to all the variant views of state sovereign immunity. Some approaches may be consistent with those cases. See, for example, Lawrence C. Marshall, *Fighting the Words of the Eleventh Amendment*, 102 Harv L Rev 1342, 1371 (1989) (arguing for the plausibility of a plain meaning approach to the Eleventh Amendment); Martha A. Field, *The Eleventh Amendment and Other Sovereign Immunity Doctrines: Part One*, 126 U Pa L Rev 515, 544–45 (1977) (seeing the Eleventh Amendment as only restoring a common law but not a constitutional immunity, even as to cases within its literal terms, thus leaving Congress and to an extent the courts with leeway to adjust to changing notions of the doctrine).

[22] See *Hans v Louisiana*, 134 US 1, 10 (1890); *Alden v Maine*, 527 US 706, 722–25 (1999); Charles Warren, 1 *The Supreme Court in United States History* 91, 96 (Little, Brown, 1922) (arguing that it was only because of assurances that states could not be sued that the Constitution was ratified, and that *Chisholm* "fell upon the country with a profound shock"). It is helpful but not necessary to the immunity position to see state immunity as hardwired into the original Article III. One could take a less definitive view of the original Article III, but see the Eleventh Amendment as effectively reading back such a hardwired immunity into Article III.

[23] See, for example, John V. Orth, *The Judicial Power of the United States: The Eleventh Amendment in American History* 28–29 (Oxford, 1987) (arguing that given the lack of clear evidence on intent, the "safest course" was to accept the "plain meaning" of the state/citizen provision as making states suable); Akhil Reed Amar, *Of Sovereignty and Federalism*, 96 Yale L J 1425, 1468–74 (1987) (arguing that the original Article III state/citizen diversity clause should be read as providing for symmetrical jurisdiction of state v. citizen and citizen v. state cases, although faulting the Court for failing to follow Georgia law of immunity in a case presenting no issue of federal law); see also id at 1475 (arguing that the Eleventh Amendment meant that state/citizen diversity would no longer prove an independent basis for jurisdiction, but "the existence of such an alignment would not *oust* jurisdiction that was independently grounded—for example, in federal question or admiralty cases); John J. Gibbons, *The Eleventh Amendment and State Sovereign Immunity: A*

bates on the ratification of the Constitution and thereafter, the opposing positions as to whether Article III waived state immunity shared the underlying premise that the states could not be subjected to unconsented *in personam* suits in the courts of other states.

A. ARGUMENTS THAT ARTICLE III PRESERVED STATE IMMUNITIES

Caleb Nelson has illuminated how it was possible to read Article III as preserving state immunity, despite its providing for state/citizen diversity. Under both common-law immunity of sovereigns in their own courts, as well as law-of-nations immunity of sovereigns in other sovereigns' courts, states were not subject to compulsory process in suits by individuals; rather, the defendant state's consent was required. Both types of immunity were in the nature of a lack of amenability to personal jurisdiction or compulsory process.[24] A case required a plaintiff, a defendant, and a judge, and without a defendant that could be properly served and brought under the court's authority, there was no case. Given the pervasiveness of this view, Nelson concludes that those drafting and ratifying the Constitution might sensibly have entertained the view that Article III—despite its wording—made no inroad on state immunity in suits at the instance of individuals.

Nelson provides repeated references in the ratification debates

---

Reinterpretation, 83 Colum L Rev 1889, 1913 (1983) (arguing that the best evidence from the ratifying conventions was that the original Article III allowed states to be sued in the federal courts, particularly as to treaty violations); id at 1937 (arguing that the Eleventh Amendment did not affect federal question jurisdiction).

To hold a diversity or related position that allows for federal question suits against states one need not necessarily see the original Article III as affirmatively abrogating state immunity. See, for example, Fletcher, 35 Stan L Rev at 1054, 1077 (cited in note 19) (concluding that the state/citizen diversity provision would have had a more prominent place in the ratification debates had it been widely thought to abrogate state immunity by its own force, and also that neither the immunity nor potential liability of the states to private suits under federal law was clearly established under the Constitution). For example, one could see the original Article III as leaving common-law immunities intact, with the possibility of either judicial or congressional abrogation. See, for example, Vicki C. Jackson, *The Supreme Court, the Eleventh Amendment, and State Sovereign Immunity*, 98 Yale L J 1, 6–7, 44 (1988) (arguing that sovereign immunity is inapplicable to federal questions, but that the common law of sovereign immunity acts as an abstention doctrine that allocates federal question cases against states to state courts, with the possibility of Supreme Court direct review).

[24] Caleb Nelson, *Sovereign Immunity as a Doctrine of Personal Jurisdiction*, 115 Harv L Rev 1559, 1574 (2002). While deriving from these various immunities, the immunity was not necessarily on all fours with either. See, for example, *Chisholm v Georgia*, 2 US (2 Dall) 419, 449 (1793) (Iredell dissenting) (arguing that the law of nations was not directly applicable to the issue).

to states' not being subject to compulsory process in any court.[25] In responding to Antifederalist arguments that Article III effected a waiver of suits against states at the instance of individuals, for example, John Marshall stated, "It is not rational to suppose, that the sovereign power shall be dragged before a Court."[26] James Madison argued, "It is not in the power of individuals to call any state into court,"[27] and Hamilton said, "It is inherent in the nature of sovereignty not to be amenable to the suit of an individual *without its consent.*"[28] The Massachusetts Federalists in the ratifying convention thought compulsory process against a state laughable.[29]

To what courts were the framers referring when arguing the impossibility of suits against states in a court (and by extension the impossibility of suing them in the new federal courts without their consent)? It seems reasonable to conclude that the references encompassed both suits in the states' own courts as well as in sister states' courts. As commentators have noted, sovereign immunity drew on notions both of home-state and foreign-state immunity,[30] the latter involving suits in the courts of other sovereigns. And as James Pfander has pointed out, the framers were familiar with the 1781 case of *Nathan v Virginia*[31] in which the Pennsylvania court declined, on the basis of international concepts of immunity of one sovereign in the courts of another, to allow an attachment of Virginia property.[32] The proposed federal courts, moreover, would

---

[25] Nelson, 115 Harv L Rev at 1587 (cited in note 24).

[26] Debates of the Virginia Convention (June 20, 1788), in John P. Kaminski and Gaspare J. Saladino, eds, 10 *Documentary History of the Ratification of the Constitution* 1433 (Madison 1993), discussed in Nelson, 115 Harv L Rev at 1593 & n 160 (cited in note 24).

[27] Jonathan Elliott, ed, 3 *The Debates in the Several State Convention on the Adoption of the Federal Constitution* 533 (James Madison) (Lipincott, 2d ed 1836) ("*Elliot's Debates*"); see also *Hall*, 440 US at 436 & n 3 (Rehnquist dissenting) (quoting this and other sources).

[28] Federalist 81 (Hamilton), in 4 *The Founders' Constitution* at 242, 244 (cited in note 19).

[29] See Nelson, 115 Harv L Rev at 1593 (citing sources) (cited in note 24).

[30] See Pfander, 82 Cal L Rev at 559 (cited in note 12) (referring to the source of immunity as both the common-law immunities of states in their own courts, and also law-of-nations immunity in the courts of other sovereigns); see also Lee, 96 Nw U L Rev at 1028, 1040 (cited in note 12) (drawing on international law immunities to explain state immunities); Peter J. Smith, *States as Nations: Dignity in Cross-Doctrinal Perspective*, 89 Va L Rev 1, 73, 97–99 (2003) (discussing law-of-nations immunity but arguing that the analogy suggests allowing congressional abrogation, just as *Nevada v Hall* allows for sister-state abrogation).

[31] 1 Dall 77 n (Pa CP 1781).

[32] Pfander, 82 Cal L Rev at 587 (cited in note 12) (arguing that *Nathan* should be seen as a decisive rejection of state suability in the courts of other states); Nelson, 115 Harv L Rev at 1578–79 (cited in note 24) (discussing *Nathan* as support for the proposition

be more analogous to the courts of other states or sovereigns than to a state's own courts. Thus the framers' references to the impossibility of suits against a state in any court most plausibly included suits in the courts of another state.

B. ARGUMENTS THAT ARTICLE III WAIVED STATE IMMUNITIES

Alternative to the view that Article III's state/citizen diversity provision preserved state immunities was the view that, despite the disclaimers of some Federalists, the provision effected a waiver of state immunity in the federal courts. There were two major subdivisions of persons who so argued: Antifederalists who thought the waiver was another reason not to ratify the Constitution, and Federalists who thought the waiver desirable.

As one might expect, the Antifederalist arguments were premised on the states' not previously being suable in any court absent consent. Thus the Federal Farmer stated, "How far it may be proper so to humble a state, as to oblige it to answer to an individual in a court of law, is worthy of consideration: the states are now subject to no such actions."[33] The Federal Farmer—in the course of expressing the fear that the federal courts would swallow up state jurisdiction—again manifested the belief that, under the Articles of Confederation, states could not be sued:

> By Art. 3. Sect. 2. the powers of the federal judiciary are extended (among other things) to all cases between a state and citizens of another state—between citizens of different states—between a state or the citizens thereof, and foreign state, citizens, or subjects. Actions in all these cases, *except against a state government*, are now brought and finally determined in the law courts of the states respectively.[34]

Brutus similarly argued that the new Constitution improperly subjected states to "answer in courts of law at the suit of an individual,"

---

that states were not seen as answerable to suits by individuals). But see Fletcher, 35 Stan L Rev at 1075–76 (cited in note 19) (suggesting that it was critical to the result in *Nathan* that the Pennsylvania executive branch did not favor suability).

[33] Federal Farmer No. 3 (Oct 10, 1787), in 4 *The Founders' Constitution* 227 (cited in note 19); see also Federal Farmer No. 18 (Jan 25, 1788), in id at 233 (arguing that no action against a state government by any citizen or foreign citizen ought to be allowed).

[34] Federal Farmer No. 3 (Oct 10, 1787), in 4 *The Founders' Constitution*, at 227 (cited in note 19) (emphasis added).

noting, "the states now are subject to no such actions."[35]

Similarly, Federalists who thought the Constitution effected a desirable waiver of state immunity built their arguments on the foundation that states could not be sued in the courts of other states. Professor Pfander, in support of his argument that states should be subject to suit in federal question cases as part of the Supreme Court's original jurisdiction, shows that waiver Federalists argued that state/citizen diversity jurisdiction was necessary due to the impossibility of calling states to account in the courts of other states.[36] Edmund Pendleton, addressing the Virginia convention, explained the provision for federal jurisdiction over controversies in which the state was a party: "The impossibility of calling a sovereign state before the jurisdiction of another sovereign state, shows the propriety and necessity of vesting this tribunal with the decision of controversies to which a state shall be a party."[37]

Edumund Randolph, who had participated in the framing of Article III, also saw the Supreme Court's original jurisdiction as addressing the inability of states to be sued in the courts of other states. In his 1790 Report on the Judiciary he stated that:

> [A]s far as a particular state can be a party defendant, a sister state cannot be her judges. Were the states of America unconfederated, they would be as free from mutual controul as other disjoined nations. Nor does the federal compact narrow this exemption, but confirms it, by establishing a common arbiter in the federal judiciary, whose constitutional authority may administer redress.[38]

Randolph, as the attorney for Chisholm in his suit against Georgia in the Supreme Court, would later argue that under the Confed-

---

[35] Brutus No. 13 (March 20, 1788), in 4 *The Founders' Constitution* 237, 238 (cited in note 19).

[36] Pfander, 82 Cal L Rev at 635–37 (cited in note 12).

[37] 3 *Elliot's Debates* at 549 (cited in note 27) (remarks of Edmund Pendleton), discussed in Pfander, 82 Cal L Rev at 635 (cited in note 12). But see *Chisholm v Georgia*, 2 US (2 Dall) at 474 (Jay) (stating that before the Constitution, "Each State was obliged to acquiesce in the measure of justice which another State might yield to her, or to her citizens").

[38] 1790 Report to Congress by Attorney General Edmund Randolph, reprinted in Maeva Marcus, ed, 4 *The Documentary History of the Supreme Court, 1789–1800* 130 (Columbia, 1992) ("*DHSC*"), discussed in Pfander, 82 Cal L Rev at 637 (cited in note 12).

eration, "the States retained their exemption from the forensic jurisdiction of each other."[39]

C. ISSUES OF STATE SUABILITY WOULD BE RESOLVED IN THE FEDERAL COURTS.

Thus both sides of the debate as to whether Article III effected a waiver of sovereign immunity and both Federalists and Anti-federalists saw the lack of state suability in the courts of sister states as the beginning point of their arguments. It is likely that all would have agreed on a further point: to the extent states were subject at all to involuntary *in personam* suits at the instance of a noncitizen of that state, such jurisdiction would be in the federal courts.[40] This would follow from the assumption that the states had no such preexisting jurisdiction. It was a common view of the founding generation, moreover, independent of their view of whether Article III effected a waiver of immunity, that federal jurisdictional concurrency extended only to cases that had been in the aboriginal jurisdiction of the state courts.[41] Thus, waiver Federalist Randolph saw the jurisdiction over unconsented suits

---

[39] *Chisholm*, 2 US (2 Dall) at 423. Justice Iredell in *Chisholm* argued that because the 1789 Judiciary Act had made the Supreme Court's jurisdiction over state/citizen suits concurrent, the Court could only exercise such jurisdiction as the state courts exercised at the time the act was passed, and that no actions against the states were then maintainable. Id at 436–37.

[40] See *Chisholm*, 2 US (2 Dall) at 448 (Iredell dissenting) ("A State is altogether exempt from the jurisdiction of the Courts of the *United States*, or from any other exterior authority, unless in the special instances where the general Government has power derived from the Constitution itself"); William A. Fletcher, *The Diversity Explanation of the Eleventh Amendment: A Reply to Critics*, 56 U Chi L Rev 1261, 1296 (1989) ("The source for the Court's holding that Georgia's sovereign immunity was abrogated [in *Chisholm*] was not the common law, but rather the only federal law with bearing on the case—the state-citizen diversity clause."); Rogers, 1981 Duke L J at 470 (cited in note 9) (arguing that Article III should be read as giving states a federal forum in which to have their issues of immunity determined, in accordance with immunity law derived from international sovereign immunity law).

[41] Michael G. Collins, *The Federal Courts, the First Congress, and the Non-Settlement of 1789*, 91 Va L Rev 1515, 1541 & n 94 (2005) (discussing manifestations of this belief); compare *Rhode Island v Massachusetts*, 37 US (12 Pet) 657, 724 (1838) (in taking jurisdiction of an interstate boundary dispute, reasoning "it is evident, that there remained no power in the contending states to settle a boundary controverted between themselves, as states competent to act by their own authority on the subject matter, or in any department of the government, if it was not in this"); Federalist 82 (Hamilton) (May 28, 1788), in 4 *The Founders' Constitution* 245, 246 (cited in note 19) (indicating that there would be concurrent jurisdiction where the states had preexisting authority); John Marshall, Virginia Ratifying Convention (June 20, 1788), in 4 *The Founders' Constitution* 247 (cited in note 19) (noting that states would not lose jurisdiction of cases that they now decide).

against states as exclusive, based on his premise that the state courts had no preexisting jurisdiction over such suits.[42]

This did not mean that state/citizen diversity as a whole was exclusive, nor did the 1789 Judiciary Act make it so.[43] Rather, all acknowledged that state/citizen diversity encompassed suits where states were plaintiffs and suits in which states consented to jurisdiction—all of which could be within the states' preexisting jurisdiction and thus would be presumptively concurrent.[44] In addition, true *in rem* actions in sister-state courts may have been a possibility, as reflected in the Pennsylvania Attorney General's argument against the attachment in the 1781 Pennsylvania case *Nathan v Virginia* that the attachment there sought was merely to secure the presence of the defendant and was not truly *in rem*.[45]

Thus, similar to cases involving foreign ministers that were also in the Supreme Court's original jurisdiction and believed to affect

---

[42] See text accompanying note 38–39. Even using a presumption of state jurisdictional concurrency as to all matters within the federal courts' jurisdiction, state jurisdiction over unconsented *in personam* suits against other states would be derivative of the grant of power to the federal courts, and could generally be expected to follow federal court decisions. And to the extent state concurrent jurisdiction over such cases was derivative of federal jurisdiction, the Eleventh Amendment divested it.

[43] Act of Sept 24, 1789, ch 20, § 13, 1 Stat 73, 80–81 (providing for Supreme Court jurisdiction in "all controversies of a civil nature, where a state is a party, except between a state and its citizens," and also providing that this jurisdiction was exclusive except in suits "between a state and citizens of other states, or aliens"). In addition, the lower federal courts have generally been allowed when congressionally authorized to hear cases within the Supreme Court's original jurisdiction, see Fallon et al, *The Federal Courts* at 271 (cited in note 12). The 1789 Judiciary Act did not give the lower federal courts jurisdiction over state/citizen diversity cases, but did give the circuit courts jurisdiction, concurrent with state courts, where an "alien is a party." Act of Sept 24, 1789, ch 20, § 11, 1 Stat 73, 78. The reference, however, was likely to citizen/alien diversity. See Dennis J. Mahoney, *A Historical Note on Hodgson v. Bowerbank*, 49 U Chi L Rev 725, 732–33 (1982) (discussing assumptions that the provision referred to cases in which a domestic citizen was a party).

[44] Compare *Delafield v Illinois*, 2 Hill 159, 1841 NY LEXIS 201 (1841) (in action brought by Illinois to enjoin the defendant from selling certain Illinois bonds, rejecting the defendant's argument that the Supreme Court had exclusive jurisdiction).

[45] *Nathan v Virginia*, 1 Dall 77 n (Pa C P 1781) ("That though the goods of a sovereign, as well as of an individual, might be liable for freight, or duties, or subject to forfeiture; yet in those cases, there was a lien on the goods, they were answerable, and the process was *in rem*; in this case, it was *in personam*; and the goods were attached merely to compel the party's appearance to answer the plaintiff's demand."), discussed in Nelson, 115 Harv L Rev at 1579 (cited in note 24); see also *Chisholm v Georgia*, 2 US (2 Dall) 419, 425 (1793) (argument for Chisholm by Edmund Randolph) (discussing authority for summoning a prince where he was proprietor of lands in the dominion of another); *Schooner Exchange v M'Faddon*, 11 US (7 Cranch) 116, 145–46 (1812) (discussing arguments that the property of a foreign sovereign is not distinguishable from that of a private party, and without indicating an opinion, noting there is a distinction between private property held by someone who happens to be a prince, and a military ship).

the peace and harmony of the nation, the extent of immunity in state/citizen diversity would be determined largely in federal and not states courts. Assuming a narrow immunity (e.g., had a *Chisholm* regime prevailed), the Court might nevertheless have disallowed suits on state bonds,[46] or perhaps eventually have disallowed full respondeat superior liability against the sovereign—as in modern Section 1983 litigation against local governments. Had the Court decided for a robust immunity in *Chisholm*, issues of consent and the allowability of *in rem* jurisdiction might have arisen in the Court's original jurisdiction as well as in state courts.[47]

The Court might have treated such immunity decisions under unamended Article III as general law; alternatively, the Court might have treated the immunities as matters of federal constitutional or federal common law.[48] Even if the Court initially discussed state immunity as a matter of general law, however, it likely would have eventually treated the law of state immunity as a form of either federal constitutional[49] or subconstitutional law.[50]

---

[46] See *Chisholm*, 2 US (2 Dall) at 479 (Jay) (indicating that states' suability might not extend to all demands, such as on state bills of credit issued before the Constitution was promulgated); id at 425 (argument of Edmund Randolph for Chisholm) (arguing that the states' suability for some actions would not mean suability for all).

[47] To the extent immunities might be seen as matters of federal constitutional or common law, a denial of such immunity would be reviewable under Section 25 of the First Judiciary Act and later provisions for review. The Supreme Court might have occasion to review such determinations when issues of judgment recognition arose. See text accompanying notes 62–72.

[48] The Court would not necessarily have specified federal common law as distinct from general law. There would be little need to specify so long as state court decisions did not deviate substantially from those of the federal courts.

[49] Many areas that were once somewhat vaguely sourced between general constitutional and common law and federal constitutional law are now seen as constitutional. See Michael G. Collins, *Before Lochner—Diversity Jurisdiction and the Development of General Constitutional Law*, 74 Tulane L Rev 1263 (2000). For example, the common-law remedies available against individual officers that together with governmental immunities define the law of governmental accountability is an area where the general law and constitutional law interacted to form modern constitutional baselines for remedies. See Ann Woolhandler, *The Common Law Origins of Constitutionally Compelled Remedies*, 107 Yale L J 77, 130–31 (1997) (discussing the move from a general law concept of reasonableness in rate regulation to a constitutional one).

[50] The Court has long handled many other issues of interstate relations according to rules of federal common law. See, for example, *Hinderlider v La Plata River Cherry Creek Ditch Co.*, 304 US 92, 110 (1938) (stating that the law of neither state could be conclusive in an interstate water dispute); *Rhode Island v Massachusetts*, 37 US (12 Pet) at 724 (indicating that there was no authority in the states to decide an interstate boundary dispute); Caleb Nelson, *The Persistence of General Law*, 106 Colum L Rev 503, 508–09 (2006) (noting that commentators "have agreed that the Constitution implicitly strips the states of lawmaking power" over interstate issues such as boundary and water disputes, and that such matters post-*Erie* are considered to be federal common law). An attempt by one state's

Obviously, had the states remained unconfederated, no such federalization would have occurred. Rather, recognition of foreign sovereign immunity would have started as a matter of general law within the various states. Eventually, the courts, legislatures, and executives of these independent sovereigns might have claimed the previously unclaimed power to make other sovereigns liable to unconsented *in personam* suits. But the states did unite under the Constitution, and Article III meant that future development of interstate immunity law would occur in the Supreme Court and was no longer left primarily to state decision makers.

Quite apart from the Supreme Court's original jurisdiction over state/citizen diversity, the provision for ordinary diversity jurisdiction in the Constitution and judiciary acts provided an avenue for federal court resolution of disputes when a citizen of one state complained of a wrong inflicted by an officer of another state. In determining the extent of individual officer immunity and liability, the federal courts could effectively determine the extent of state immunity and accountability. The founders were familiar with suits against officers for their trespassory harms as an accommodation of the rule of law and sovereign immunity. Thus, in arguing for the Eleventh Amendment, "A True Federalist" stated:

> When an injury is done to the person, or to the property of an individual citizen of another state, he clearly has a remedy against the immediate aggressor. . . . Suppose the Legislature of Massachusetts should pass an act or resolve, directing the sheriff of a county, or any other officer, or man, to seize, or take the property of a citizen of New Hampshire or Connecticut; and the officer or man directed should obey: the man who should be thus injured would bring his action into the Circuit Court of the United States, against the officer, or acting person, for the trespass.[51]

The Constitution thus seemed to assure the role of the federal courts as the primary arbiters of state immunity in suits by out-of-staters, whether or not one saw the provision of state/citizen di-

---

courts, at the instance of one of its citizens, to limit the immunity of another state involves a clash of sovereignties similar to an attempt by one state's courts to determine the water rights of another state. In both cases, one might conclude that the allocation of power to the federal courts and the structure of the union imply a lack of state lawmaking power.

[51] *A True Federalist*, Independent Chronicle, Mar 2 and 6, 1797, reprinted in Maeva Marcus, ed, 5 *The Documentary History of the Supreme Court, 1789–1800* 629, 630 (Columbia, 1994) ("*DHSC*").

versity as effecting a broad waiver of state suability. Article III was enacted against a background assumption that the states could not entertain suits against one another. The allocation of jurisdiction over state/citizen suits to the Supreme Court indicated that involuntary *in personam* jurisdiction over the states—if allowed at all— would be exercised in the federal courts. And this allocation of authority made sense in a system attempting to reduce interstate tensions.

II. The Eleventh Amendment and its Effect on Prior Assumptions of State Nonsuability in Courts of Sister States

A. framers' assumptions

The Court in *Chisholm v Georgia* famously held that an individual could sue an unconsenting state under the state/citizen diversity for a state or general law assumpsit claim.[52] The commentary both for and against proposals to overturn *Chisholm* discussed the issue interchangeably as the "suability" of states *vel non* and their suability in federal court,[53] reflecting the starting point that states could not be subject to compulsory process in state courts. For example, the Connecticut legislature sought an

---

[52] 2 US (2 Dall) 419 (1793).

[53] See, for example, Proceedings of the South Carolina Senate (Dec 17, 1793), in 5 *DHSC* 610, 610–11 (cited in note 51) (stating that "it is the decided sense of the Legislature . . . that the power of compelling a State to appear, and answer to the plea of an individual, is utterly subversive of the separate dignity and reserved independence of the respective States" and instructing their Congressmen to seek amendments to remove any article of the Constitution "which can be construed to imply, or justify a decision that a state is compellable to answer in any suit, by an individual, or individuals in any Court of the United States."); John Hancock's Address to the Massachusetts General Court (Sept 18, 1793), in 5 *DHSC* at 416 ("I cannot conceive that the People of this Commonwealth, when they, by their Representatives in Convention, adopted the Constitution of a General Government, expected that each State should be held liable to answer on *compulsory civil process*, to every individual resident in another State or in a foreign kingdom."); Independent Chronicle, Sept 16, 1793, in 5 *DHSC* 415 ("THE great and interesting question of the 'SUABILITY' of the State, is to come before the Legislature of Massachusetts on Wednesday next"); Letter from Fisher Ames to Alexander Hamilton (Aug 31, 1793), in 5 *DHSC* 415 ("It is supposed, the Legislature will vote their cens[ure] of the suableness of a state & request congress to propose an amendment"); Letter from James Hillhouse to Samuel Huntington (Mar 5, 1794), in 5 *DHSC* 619, 623 (reporting that the House had concurred with the resolution of the Senate to amend the Constitution "so far as respects the suability of States"); Letter from Philip John Schuyler to Rufus King (Jan 31, 1794), in 5 *DHSC* at 623 ("The [New York] senate has sent a resolution to the assembly on the subject of the Suability of a state"); Zephaniah Swift to David Daggett (Mar 5, 1794), in 5 *DHSC* 624 ("A Resolve to amend the Constitution in respect of the Suability of States has passed the Senate and House of Representatives").

amendment "so that in future no State can on any Construction of the Constitution be held liable . . . to make answer in any Court, on the suit, of any Individual or Individuals whatsoever."[54]

As noted above, there are two polar views of how to interpret the Eleventh Amendment's provision that "[t]he Judicial power of the United States shall not be construed to extend to any suit in law or equity, commenced or prosecuted against one of the United States by Citizens of another State."[55] Both are primarily concerned with the extent of state suability in the federal courts, but neither is readily compatible with an understanding that the states were suable in the courts of sister states.

The major premise of the "diversity" view—that the Eleventh Amendment only rejected state liability on common-law or state-law claims but not federal claims—fits ill with an assumption that states might be liable as involuntary defendants in courts of sister states on those very claims as to which the Amendment reinstated their immunity in the presumably more impartial federal courts.[56] In addition, to the extent that the diversity theory presupposes a waiver of immunity in the original Constitution that was only partly withdrawn by the Eleventh Amendment, the Framers' waiver arguments (as noted above) assumed there was no jurisdiction in state courts over unconsented actions against a sister state.

The supposition that an individual could sue a state in the courts of another state is similarly incompatible with an "immunity" view of the Eleventh Amendment. To hold an immunity view but not to include immunity to suits in sister-state courts results in odd logic: Immunity of states from unconsented suits was sufficiently entrenched that Article III's provisions for state/citizen diversity should not be read as abrogating such immunity; the Eleventh Amendment restored and further constitutionalized this understanding, even beyond the wording of the amendment. But even if

---

[54] Resolution of the Connecticut General Assembly (Oct 29, 1793), in 5 *DHSC* 609 (cited in note 51), discussed in Nelson, 115 Harv L Rev at 1600 & n 203 (cited in note 24).

[55] The Amendment continues, "or by Citizens or Subjects of any Foreign State."

[56] Compare Fletcher, 35 Stan L Rev at 1035, 1071 (cited in note 19) (while arguing that the reaction to *Chisholm* was merely a way of preserving a state's immunity under its own law, even when sued in federal court, also recognizing that general law governed many such actions, such that the immunity might extend beyond that provided by the laws of the defendant state).

the principle of nonsuability of states in courts of other states is a premise for reading a broad immunity into Article III and the Eleventh Amendment, state courts nevertheless may subject sister states to unconsented *in personam* suits.

B. CONSTITUTIONAL VERSUS GENERAL LAW

It might be argued that whatever the apparent historical anomaly of allowing suits against states in the courts of other states, there is no textual support in the Eleventh Amendment or elsewhere in the Constitution for forbidding suits against states in sister states' courts. After all, the Constitution constituted and limited federal, not state, courts.[57] And accordingly, the diversity and immunity views are directed to the scope of federal and not state jurisdiction. Interstate immunities, the argument would continue, were merely matters of general law that cannot be located in the Constitution.

The constitutional location of sovereign immunity, however, may be found by reading Article III together with the Eleventh Amendment (although historical background is also required). As discussed above, Article III's provision for state/citizen diversity and the original jurisdiction of the Supreme Court in state-as-party cases meant that any aboriginal power in the state courts to hold each other involuntarily liable to individuals' suits had been ceded to the federal courts, and would be decided (most likely in the Supreme Court) as a matter of what would be effectively federal law, not state law. The Eleventh Amendment specified and constitutionalized what this federal law would be for state/citizen suits (at least those arising under state law): states could not be made involuntary defendants.

This textual reading is supported not only by historical understandings, but also by constitutional structure. As then-Justice Rehnquist noted in his *Hall* dissent, the Eleventh Amendment's framers necessarily thought they had put an end to states "as unconsenting defendants in foreign jurisdictions, for, . . . they would

---

[57] See *The Supreme Court: 1978 Term*, 93 Harv L Rev 1 at 192–93 (cited in note 4) (arguing that neither the debate over Article III nor the adoption of the Eleventh Amendment is conclusive as to the result in *Hall* "since they both dealt only with the limits of *federal* judicial power); compare David L. Shapiro, 31 Rutgers L J at 753 (cited in note 12) (arguing that history did not compel the result in *Alden v Maine*, 527 US 706 (1999)); *The Supreme Court—Leading Cases*, 113 Harv L Rev 200, 207 (1999) (faulting the Court's *Alden* opinion for reading "historical truths into evidentiary gaps").

have otherwise perversely foreclosed the neutral federal forums only to be left to defend suits in the courts of other States."[58]

The alternative argument, noted above, is that the Eleventh Amendment has nothing to say about immunity in state courts. The immunity of states in sister states' courts was merely a matter of state or general law[59] that the states over time were free to change so as to make sister states liable. Indeed, this is *Hall*'s view.[60] But a textual constitutional problem arises when one considers enforcement. If one state's courts may, without offense to the Constitution, make another state liable to individuals' suits, then it would presumably follow that the defendant state must recognize this supposedly constitutionally valid judgment as a matter of constitutional full faith and credit. The Eleventh Amendment, however, would seem to pose a direct textual barrier to the federal courts' requiring enforcement of the judgment under the full faith

---

[58] See 440 US at 437 (Rehnquist dissenting); id at 431 (Blackmun dissenting) (arguing that framers would have been more concerned with states' being called before the courts of sister states than before federal courts); see also Reynolds, 140 U Pa L Rev at 1341–42 (cited in note 10) (praising Rehnquist's dissent for his appropriate use of penumbral reasoning).

[59] Even if one believes that the Eleventh Amendment has nothing to say about immunity in state courts and that members of the founding generation expected general law to govern this issue, one need not conclude that individual states must therefore be able to change the governing principles. To be sure, many principles that might once have been associated with the general law are now classified purely as matters of state law. Where interstate relations are concerned, however, some other such principles are now classified as matters of federal common law, and are not subject to change by the legislative power of any individual state. See, for example, *Hinderlider*, 304 US at 110 (prescribing federal common-law rule for an interstate water dispute); Hill, 42 BC L Rev at 582–84 (cited in note 12) (arguing that the state courts should have to follow the same law that the Supreme Court would follow in a suit between two states). For a federal common-law argument to work, however, one might have to assume that the Supreme Court, on direct review of state court judgments as well as of actions to enforce state court judgments, is not limited by the literal terms of the Eleventh Amendment. But see text accompanying notes 64–73. Such a federal common law might take its content from Eleventh Amendment jurisprudence (in which case there would be little difference from a constitutional immunity) or from other sources, such as foreign sovereign immunity law.

[60] See *Hall*, 440 US at 416–18 (analogizing sister-state immunity to foreign sovereign immunity and thus treating it as a matter of comity). But see Jerman, 1980 Utah L Rev at 409 (cited in note 4) (noting that the analogy of states to foreign nations was inapt because of the possible requirement that the defendant state recognize the forum state's judgment under the Full Faith and Credit Clause); Rogers, 1981 Duke L J at 465 (cited in note 9) (noting that California courts were different from the courts of another country in that its decisions were appealable to the United States Supreme Court). The argument for state power to hold another state liable might be that the states retained such powers (although unrecognized and long dormant) despite the original federal grant of state/citizen diversity, or, alternatively, that such powers reverted to them when the Eleventh Amendment took away federal jurisdiction.

and credit provisions, thus indicating that the state-court judgment is constitutionally invalid.[61]

Suppose, for example, that a state court were to take jurisdiction of an individual's suit against another state on a state-law-based claim. Further assume that the defendant state defaults, and the forum state's courts enter a judgment. The judgment creditor/plaintiff brings an enforcement suit in the defendant state. The defendant state's courts deny enforcement.[62] If the plaintiff then sought Supreme Court review to force recognition on the resisting defendant state, the enforcement suit would seem to fall squarely within the prohibition of the Eleventh Amendment: "The Judicial power of the United States shall not be construed to extend to any suit in law or equity, commenced or prosecuted against one of the United States by citizens of another State."[63] Nor is there anything surprising in this result, for a constitutional prohibition on federal court assistance in enforcement manifests the unexceptionable notion that the Constitution, at least post–Eleventh Amendment, did not give the federal

---

[61] Compare Martiniak, 63 Cal L Rev at 1163, 1166 (cited in note 9) (noting a possible Eleventh Amendment problem with federal assistance in enforcing judgments against states, but recommending some federal enforceability under full faith and credit provisions). It might be possible to argue that a judgment might be entered that would be valid within the forum but not necessarily entitled to recognition elsewhere. Such a de facto judgment would have done little good in an era when states presumably held few assets outside their borders. What is more, a judgment that is not entitled to recognition based on federal constitutional grounds is generally considered subject to collateral attack even in the forum state. See, for example, *Pennoyer v Neff*, 95 US 714, 732 (1877) (indicating that a judgment not entitled to recognition due to lack of personal jurisdiction would not be good in the rendering state).

[62] Compare *In re Thompson's Estate*, 97 SW2d 93, 97–98 (Mo 1936) (refusing to hold up an estate's final settlement for an action where service allegedly had been made on an agent of administrators of a Missouri estate in Louisiana, based on the lack of official authority of the administrator out of state); Note, *Nevada v. Hall: The Death Knell of Interstate Sovereign Immunity*, 9 Cap U L Rev 113, 125 (1979) (noting possible problems of enforcement of judgments against states).

[63] Because it was the defendant state that sought Supreme Court review in *Hall* and *Hyatt*, the literal Eleventh Amendment problem was not so squarely presented. The Supreme Court's review was by consent of the states that had requested it, and the Court could properly take jurisdiction to deny state liability, although it ended up taking jurisdiction to affirm it. Consider what would have happened had the *Hall* plaintiff lost in the California courts, based on a holding that the federal Constitution forbad a suit against a sister state. It would seem that a violation of the Eleventh Amendment would occur were the Supreme Court to take jurisdiction of the case in order to hold that the state could be liable, the case being one "commenced or prosecuted against one of the United States by Citizens of another State." US Const, Amend XI; see also Marshall, 102 Harv L Rev at 1360 (cited in note 21) (stating that "even if it was expected that the Supreme Court would review state court decisions in suits against states, it was not at all clear that it would reverse state court decisions which dismissed complaints on the grounds of state sovereign immunity").

courts power to make one state liable at the instance of a citizen of another state on a state law claim.

It might be objected that the Eleventh Amendment is inapplicable to the Supreme Court's direct review of state court judgments.[64] As I have argued elsewhere, the Supreme Court's cases should not be read so broadly, in a way that is inconsistent with the Eleventh Amendment.[65] For the most part, when the Court has held states involuntarily liable for monetary remedies as defendants on direct review[66]—such as in compelling tax refund remedies—the state has otherwise consented to make itself liable for monetary remedies for the particular type of suit, and has substituted itself for an individual officer defendant against whom such a remedy might be constitutionally compelled.[67] Thus the Court has generally stayed within the strictures of its federal constitutional sovereign immunity jurisprudence in exercising its appellate jurisdiction, despite occasionally flirting with a forum-allocation version of sovereign immunity.[68]

True, even enforcing a judgment when the state as defendant consented to the initial suit might be said to violate the literal terms of the Eleventh Amendment. But consented suits were always deemed to be an area where immunity did not reach, and where the Court has not literally enforced the Eleventh Amendment.[69] Caleb Nelson

---

[64] *McKesson Corp. v Division of Alcoholic Beverages and Tobacco*, 496 US 15, 31 (1990) (in reversing a state's denial of tax refund remedies, stating that "the Eleventh Amendment does not constrain the appellate jurisdiction of the Supreme Court over cases arising from state courts."); see also Rogers, 1981 Duke L J at 470 (cited in note 9) (arguing that the Supreme Court has authority to review the scope of state suability in the courts of other states under the state/citizen diversity provision of Article III).

[65] Woolhandler, 107 Yale L J at 152–53 (cited in note 49).

[66] Cases such as *Cohens v Virginia*, 19 US (6 Wheat) 264 (1821), may be explained both by a notion of consent as well as by the case not being initiated against a state. Id at 406–12.

[67] See Carlos Manuel Vázquez, *What Is Eleventh Amendment Immunity?* 106 Yale L J 1683, 1771 (1997) (taking this view); Woolhandler, 107 Yale L J at 152–53 (cited in note 49) (same).

[68] Compare *Hilton v South Carolina Public Rys Comm'n*, 502 US 197 (1991) (allowing a FELA suit against a state to proceed in state court) with *Alden v Maine*, 527 US 706 (1999) (holding that Congress lacked power under the Commerce Clause to subject unconsenting states to private suits for damages in state courts).

[69] Very few stick to a totally literal view of the Eleventh Amendment. The diversity view allows for suits the defendant consented to if otherwise within the court's jurisdiction. (In addition, the diversity view sees the language of the amendment as a limitation only on Article III's state/citizen diversity provisions, and thus reads the words of the Eleventh Amendment as not extending to federal causes of action by a citizen of one state against another state.) The immunity view argues for sovereign immunity broader than the literal

has explained this anomaly by showing that the doctrine of sovereign immunity was in the nature of an immunity from personal jurisdiction.[70] And once a state consented or was properly deemed to have consented according to constitutional immunity law, then the consent cannot necessarily be withdrawn.[71] By contrast, using the appellate jurisdiction to force unconsented damages suits on the states on state law claims is not only contrary to the letter of the Eleventh Amendment, but also allows for liability for the very state-law-based claims that the Eleventh Amendment was aimed at foreclosing—even under a diversity view.[72]

One holding a diversity view might perhaps argue that, because sovereign immunity is inapplicable to federal question cases, there would be no sovereign immunity bar to the Court's taking a case on direct review to require that a state as a matter of federal full faith and credit recognize a sister-state judgment against itself. The diversity view, however, in treating sovereign immunity as not barring federal question cases against states, is primarily referring to cases where federal law actually is an essential element of the initial claim for relief and not to any case that may involve a federal issue. For example, a defendant state's raising an immunity defense to a citizen of another state's state-law claim against it does not automatically mean that the state loses on the defense because the case now arises under *federal* law. An action to enforce a state-law judg-

---

words of the Eleventh Amendment, but generally would allow for consented suits, even if violative of the amendment's literal language (e.g., if the state wanted to substitute itself for an individual defendant in a federal question case brought by an out-of-stater). Compare *Clark v Bernard*, 108 US 436, 447 (1883) (holding that the Eleventh Amendment was a personal privilege that could be waived by the state). The Court's allowance of legislation under Section 5 of the Fourteenth Amendment that violates the express terms of the Eleventh Amendment is based on the Fourteenth Amendment's being later in time and its alteration of state/federal relations. See, for example, *Fitzpatrick v Bitzer*, 427 US 445, 455 (1976).

[70] Nelson, 115 Harv L Rev at 1565 (cited at note 24).

[71] Compare *Reich v Collins*, 513 US 106, 113–14 (1994) (holding that the state could not hold out a postdeprivation remedy, then take the position after the taxpayer had paid that only predeprivation remedies were available); *McKesson Corp. v Florida Division of Alcoholic Beverages and Tobacco*, 496 US 18, 50 (1990) (holding that where a state requires taxpayers to pay and seek a refund, rather than allowing injunctions, the state must provide an opportunity to obtain later relief).

[72] In addition this article argues that the diversity view is consistent with state courts' having no power to entertain an unconsented *in personam* suit against a sister state, and that the Supreme Court on direct review of a state court could not exercise its jurisdiction to hold a state liable to such a suit without violating the Eleventh Amendment. See text accompanying notes 64–73. And an initially invalid judgment against a sister state in state court would not become valid because it was now presented as an enforcement action with federal full faith and credit issues rather than as an original action.

ment thus is not necessarily the type of claim for relief under federal law that the diversity theory would treat as escaping the Eleventh Amendment.

One might, however, argue that an enforcement action implicitly embodies as part of the complaint a federal claim under the Full Faith and Credit Clause. But the incarnation of the suit as an enforcement action should not obliterate the fact that the action is one to enforce a state/citizen, state-law-based claim. Certainly there is nothing central to the diversity view that would require such a bootstrap of what remains essentially a state/citizen suit.[73]

To see why full faith and credit requirements do not change the underlying nature of the claim as a state/citizen suit arising under state law, imagine that Congress purported to require defendant states to recognize the law and judgments of other states making defendant states liable at the instance of individuals. Such a federal statute would amount to a choice-of-law provision, and the applicability of a federal statute specifying which state's law to apply surely would not change the action from a state/citizen diversity suit arising under state law into one arising under federal law (in the sense presumably used by the diversity theorists for designating cases in which immunity can be abrogated). To the contrary, the Eleventh Amendment (even if read in accordance with the diversity theory) would still bar the lower federal courts from hearing the case, because the case would still amount to a state/citizen diversity case under state law. And were the Supreme Court to take jurisdiction of an enforcement action brought in the defendant state's courts to force recognition on a resisting state, the Supreme Court too would be acting contrary to the Eleventh Amendment.

C. STRUCTURAL LIMITATIONS ON CONGRESSIONAL POWER TO
   ENFORCE FULL FAITH AND CREDIT

To suppose that an unconsenting state might be forced by the federal courts to recognize a judgment by a citizen of another state also leads to anomalous results with regard to Congress's power to enforce the full faith and credit provisions of the Constitution. Those holding the immunity view generally assume that sovereign immunity imposes limitations on congressional power to make

---

[73] See Fletcher, 35 Stan L Rev at 1096 (cited at note 19) (arguing against states' having an obligation to hear cases that the Eleventh Amendment bars from the federal courts).

states liable on both constitutional as well as common-law claims in federal or state courts.[74] Under the current state of immunity law, for example, Congress presumably cannot make states liable on their bonded indebtedness under any of its enumerated powers. Rather, Congress is empowered to make states liable primarily when properly legislating under Section 5 of the Fourteenth Amendment.[75] Taking this prohibition as a given, could Congress nevertheless legislate under the Full Faith and Credit Clause that states must recognize judgments on their bonded indebtedness that individuals obtain in sister states? If the answer is yes, then constitutional limitations on Congress's legislative power deriving from state sovereign immunity seem illusory.[76] On the other hand, if the Eleventh Amendment limits congressional legislative power under the Full Faith and Credit Clause, then by extension the Court should be under a similar limitation forbidding its enforcing a judgment arising from an unconsented suit against a state obtained in another state's courts.

One might, however, combine with a diversity theory a broad view of Congress's enumerated powers, such that Congress in exercising its Article I regulatory powers could federalize common-law actions and obliterate state immunities. Thus, the argument would go, Congress in indirectly forcing liability on the states via full faith and credit legislation would not be exceeding what it could do directly under its Commerce Clause powers.

But Congress's greater power to federalize many common-law claims would not necessarily include the lesser power to force recognition of judgments in actions that had not actually been federalized. Federalization of state law claims, after all, may entail Congress's providing rules of decision,[77] regulating private parties in

---

[74] See *Alden v Maine*, 527 US 706 (1999) (holding that limitations on congressional power applied as to making states liable in state as well as federal court).

[75] Section 2 of the Thirteenth and Fifteenth Amendments would also be exceptions. In addition, there is an exception for bankruptcy legislation. See *Central Virginia Community College v Katz*, 126 S Ct 990, 996, 1000, 1005 (2006) (relying on the supposed plan of the Constitution and the *in rem* nature of bankruptcy proceedings).

[76] Compare Vázquez, 109 Yale L J at 1936–37 (cited in note 12) (arguing that *Alden* seems to undermine an implication from *Hall* that Congress might make states liable in the courts of sister states).

[77] Compare *Verlinden BV v Central Bank of Nigeria*, 461 US 480, 491 & n 17 (1983) (avoiding an issue of whether Congress might provide protective jurisdiction to foreign sovereigns by holding that whether a statutory exception to immunity existed was a federal issue in all claims under the Foreign Sovereign Immunities Act of 1976, Pub L No 94–583, 90 Stat 2891–98, codified at 28 USC §§ 1330, 1602–11).

parallel circumstances,[78] and allowing for original federal court jurisdiction.[79] It seems doubtful that Congress's Article I powers allow
it merely to abrogate state immunity simpliciter, as would be the case
were Congress to mandate recognition of any action against a state
by an out-of-stater. A diversity theory must distinguish claims
brought by individuals against a state that are actually based on federal
law for which Congress may abrogate immunity from those only
potentially based on federal law for which the Eleventh Amendment
continues to provide immunity. Otherwise the diversity theory of
immunity concedes no immunity even in a diversity setting.[80]

Thus far this article has attempted to show that as a matter of
constitutional history, jurisdictional structure, and text, it makes
little sense to allow states to entertain involuntary *in personam* suits
against sister states. These arguments, moreover, are consistent with
both of the modern polar views on sovereign immunity. The article
will now address post–Eleventh Amendment historical practice in
the federal and state courts regarding state suability. (Discussion of
jurisdictional structure and of the variant views of the Eleventh
Amendment will occasionally resurface.)

III. Historical Practice in the Courts

A. ACTIONS IN FEDERAL COURTS

The Supreme Court for the next 180 years following the Eleventh Amendment continued to manifest framing-era assumptions

---

[78] Compare *Reno v Condon*, 528 US 141, 151 (2000) (not addressing the argument that
Congress may only regulate states by laws that apply to individuals as well as states, because
the statute at issue would meet any general applicability requirement).

[79] See Michael G. Collins, *Article III Cases, State Court Duties, and the Madisonian Compromise*, 1995 Wis L Rev 39 (showing that many thought that the states would have option
not to entertain many federal claims).

[80] Under a diversity view, one might argue that Congress's Article IV full faith and
credit powers provide a basis for congressional legislation to require defendant states to
recognize other states' laws and judgments subjecting a defendant state to liability. But as
discussed in text accompanying note 73, Congress's specification of which state's law
applied would not change the action from a state/citizen diversity suit arising under state
law into a federal question case arising under federal law (in the sense that would allow
abrogation of immunity under the diversity view). Thus the case would remain one that
the federal courts could not assist in enforcing under the Eleventh Amendment, even if
the amendment is considered to be only a limit on Article III's state/citizen diversity
provision and not on federal question cases. Compare Fletcher, 56 U Chi L Rev at 1297
(cited in note 40) ("The Eleventh Amendment, in overruling *Chisholm*, repealed the grant
of jurisdiction that had required the state to submit to suit under the common law, and
thus prevented the federal government from finding that a state had given up its sovereign
immunity in suits brought under non-federal law").

that the states were immune from unconsented suits in both the federal courts and the courts of other states. In *Beers v Arkansas*, for example, Chief Justice Taney stated that, "It is an established principle of jurisprudence in all civilized nations that the sovereign cannot be sued in its own courts, or in any other, without its consent and permission."[81] And in *Hans v Louisiana*, the Court quoted with approval language from an earlier case, "that neither a State nor the United States can be sued as defendant in any court in this country without their consent, except in the limited class of cases in which a State may be made a party in the Supreme Court of United States by virtue of the original jurisdiction conferred on this Court by the Constitution."[82] The states manifested similar assumptions as the federal courts, as discussed more fully in Section IIIB.

Rather than suits against unconsenting states themselves, many suits involving a citizen of one state and an official of another proceeded by way of suits against the officer as an individual under the citizen/citizen diversity. As noted above, the framers seemed to have contemplated such suits as a way to test the legality of the actions of state officers, and regular diversity remained the avenue of choice for challenges by out-of-staters to the legality of state action, even for many years after the 1875 advent of federal question jurisdiction.[83]

Diversity suits against state officers were brought as general law or state law tort claims, under which an officer lost his immunity if his acts were unauthorized under state law or if state law authorized the action but was unconstitutional. As is well known, officers could generally be liable for both damages and injunctive relief for unjustified trespassory harms and threats thereof, but were not generally liable for contractual liabilities they had un-

---

[81] 61 US (20 How) 527, 529 (1857); *Hans v Louisiana*, 134 US 1, 17 (1890) (quoting this language); see also *Hall*, 440 US at 437–38 (Rehnquist dissenting) (quoting this and other similar statements by the Court).

[82] 134 US at 17, quoting *Cunningham v Macon & Brunswick RR*, 109 US 446, 451 (1883); see also Philip L. Martin, *The New Interpretation of Sovereign Immunity for the States*, 16 Cal W L Rev 39, 45 (1980) (noting that the Court's last pronouncement on state suability in the courts of other states before *Hall* was its statement in *Western Union v Pennsylvania*, 368 US 71, 80 (1961): "It is plain that Pennsylvania courts, with no power to bring other States before them, cannot give such hearings.").

[83] Woolhandler, 107 Yale L J at 85–101 (cited in note 49) (discussing diversity as a method of raising federal questions).

dertaken as the disclosed agent of the state.[84] The availability and unavailability of actions against individual officers limned the federal constitutional law of sovereign immunity.[85]

Most such diversity cases involved suits by an out-of-stater against an officer for acts the officer took in the officer's home state, and were brought in the federal courts of the officer's home state.[86] Individual liability worked equally well, at least in theory, when an officer acted tortiously outside of his home state. If the out-of-state officer committed an unjustified tort according to the law of the forum state, a defense that he was acting under the authority of his home state would generally be insufficient.[87]

Several cases reached the Supreme Court in which officers kidnapped a suspect from a sister state or foreign country rather than using normal rendition procedures. The Court repeatedly refused to release the complaining prisoner, but noted that civil damages as well as criminal prosecution under the law of the place from which the offender was kidnapped could be available.[88] For example, in *Mahon v Justice*, the Court assumed that West Virginia could criminally prosecute a Kentucky official who, having been sent to receive a fugitive, had instead kidnapped him.[89] In *Pettibone v Nichols*, also involving an interstate kidnapping, the Court quoted with approval language from an English case, "if the act complained of were done against the law of the foreign country, that country might have

---

[84] See David Engdahl, *Immunity and Accountability for Positive Government Wrongs*, 44 U Colo L Rev 1 (1972) (analyzing the differences in individual liability for tort and contract).

[85] See, for example, *Reagan v Farmers' Loan & Trust Co.*, 154 US 362, 390 (1894) (in diversity case, allowing suit against individual officers to enjoin enforcement of unreasonably low rates).

[86] See generally Woolhandler, 107 Yale L J at 85–108 (cited in note 49).

[87] Compare *United States Fidelity and Guaranty Co. v Hill*, 162 SE 604, 604 (NC 1932) (allowing suit against a North Carolina sheriff in North Carolina by a Maryland surety that had paid out on a South Carolina judgment on the sheriff's bond, after the sheriff had kidnapped a South Carolina suspect); id (noting that the bonding company had removed the initial action to federal court in South Carolina).

[88] See, for example, *Ker v Illinois*, 119 US 436, 444 (1886) (refusing to grant relief to a convicted defendant kidnapped from Peru by the officer sent to receive him, but noting the possibility of a trespass and false imprisonment action against the kidnapper); *Sosa v Alvarez-Machain*, 542 US 692, 697, 737 n 28 (2004) (while refusing to allow an Alien Tort Statute [8 USC § 1350 (2000)] claim for kidnapping a suspect from Mexico, noting that "Sosa might well have been liable under Mexican law").

[89] 127 US 700, 706 (1888). It seems improbable, however, that Kentucky would have agreed to extradition. See *Kentucky v Dennison*, 65 US (24 How) 66, 110 (1860) (refusing to force the governor of Ohio to extradite a person accused of assisting the escape of a slave from Kentucky), overruled by *Puerto Rico v Branstad*, 483 US 219 (1987) (holding that states could not refuse to honor other states' extradition requests).

vindicated its own law. If it gave her [the prisoner] a right of action she may sue upon it."[90] Analogously, individuals could sue federal officials in state courts for damages for their individual torts (although in such cases authorization under federal law—as distinguished from the law of another state—would generally provide a complete defense).[91]

True, it might be difficult for a plaintiff to get jurisdiction over an out-of-state official without following him to his home state. Of course it is only since the last century that we have come to think that a plaintiff has a strong entitlement to sue an out-of-stater *in personam* in the plaintiff's home state. But whether the official were sued in his own state or had been served within the plaintiff's state, diversity jurisdiction would often be available, assuming a sufficient amount in controversy, at the instance of the party suing or sued outside his home state.[92] This jurisdiction would keep issues of out-of-state officer suability and immunity largely under the federal courts' control, and help to prevent biased determinations of either liability or immunity that might occur in state court. Attempts at suing the state itself would largely have to be in the defendant state's own courts on its own terms, absent a viable consent theory for an out-of-state suit. Thus the ability to sue the individual officer together with the diversity jurisdiction provided a continuing Article III avenue for federal control of suits between an official and citizens of a different state, even after the Eleventh Amendment foreclosed the state/citizen diversity route.

---

[90] 203 US 192, 215 (1906) (quoting *Ex parte Scott*, 9 B & C 446 (17 ECL 204) (1829)); see also id (refusing to distinguish *Mahon* on the argued ground that in *Mahon* the acts had not been authorized by the officials' home state); id (citing state authorities); compare *Cook v Hart*, 146 US 183, 192–93 (1892) (discussing a party's attempt to distinguish prior cases in which the illegality of arrest did not lead to the prisoner's release on the ground that "they were cases of tort, for which the injured party could sue the tortfeasors").

[91] See, for example, *Bivens v Six Unknown Federal Narcotics Agents*, 403 US 388, 391 n 4 (1971) (alluding to the Department of Justice's policy to remove all suits in state courts for trespass or false imprisonment against federal officers); Michael G. Collins, *The Unhappy History of Federal Question Removal*, 71 Iowa L Rev 717, 767 (1986) (discussing suits against federal officers in state courts, and progressively greater removability to federal courts).

[92] Compare *United States Fidelity and Guaranty Co. v Hill*, 162 SE 604, 605 (NC 1932) (referring to removal of a suit commenced in a South Carolina court against the Maryland bonding company for a North Carolina sheriff whose deputies kidnapped a person from South Carolina).

B. ACTIONS IN STATE COURTS

The state courts manifested the same working assumption as the federal courts that constitutional and general law immunity principles prevented states from being made involuntary parties in suits in other states. For example, in disallowing a quasi *in rem* action against Georgia-owned property in an attempt to collect on state bonds, the Tennessee Supreme Court stated that it could not allow the suit "without overturning, or disregarding principles long established, and so well-grounded in reason and the philosophy of the law, as to be impregnable to attack."[93] The South Dakota Supreme Court discussed the reaction to *Chisholm* in denying jurisdiction over a worker's compensation claim arising from the defendant North Dakota's mining activities in South Dakota.[94] And a New York state court rebuffed an attempt to attach Illinois funds in New York for payment on defaulted Illinois bond coupons, citing *Osborn* as support for why naming the state treasurer could not be used to sue the state in this case.[95]

Also, similar to the federal courts, the state courts indicated that individual state officers might be the proper defendants when they committed wrongs outside of their home state—at least so long as personal jurisdiction were obtained.[96] And of course an ag-

---

[93] *Tappan v Western & Atlantic Railroad Co.*, 71 Tenn (3 Lea) 106, 113, 1879 LEXIS 43, *10 (1879).

[94] See *Paulus v South Dakota*, 227 NW 52, 54–55 (ND 1929) (also discussing arguments of Hamilton, Madison, and Marshall that states were not suable under the original Article III, and reasoning from the immunity that states enjoyed in federal courts); *Dalrymple's Estate*, 31 Pa CC 77, 1905 WL 3920, *10 (Pa Orph 1905) (in holding that Pennsylvania was not bound by a Wisconsin court's determination that the decedent was domiciled in Wisconsin, noting "the record does not show notice or service on the commonwealth . . . nor indeed, could the commonwealth of Pennsylvania be made a party without its continuing assent. Hans v. Louisiana, 24 Fed Rep. 55" [24 F 55 (CC La 1885), aff'd, 134 US 1 (1890)]); compare *Grain Growers' Grain Co. v Michigan*, 204 NW 838, 838 (ND 1925) (in suit against the state for breach of a contract for the sale of twine, dismissing the case as unappealable, but noting that *Paulus v South Dakota*, 201 NW 867 (ND 1924), had been overlooked by the parties and "it is difficult to see why the rule announced in that case is not applicable under the facts here").

[95] *Stockwell v Bates*, 10 Abb Pr (ns) 381 (NY Sup Ct 1871).

[96] See *Florida State Hospital for the Insane v Durham Iron Co.*, 21 SE2d 216, 218, 219 (Ga 1942) (adverting to the possibility of suits against individuals, although also noting that attachments might be possible where a state owned property in another state for commercial purposes, but only as to matters related to the conduct of such business); compare *Winfield v Mapes*, 4 Denio 571, 1847 NY LEXIS 178 (NY S Ct 1847) (holding the named overseers of the poor of a Pennsylvania county liable for a penalty in an action commenced by New York superintendents of the poor under a New York statute that forbade bringing a pauper from outside the state into a county or town with the intent to make the county or town chargeable for the pauper's expenses); see also id at **3

grieved party might also sue in the officer's home state.[97]

The few suits in the state courts that were brought against states or state-owned entities, moreover, were based on consent, property ownership, or commercial activity, often in combination; such allowance of suits was in line with extant federal-court exceptions to state and federal governmental immunities. Perhaps the largest group of cases holding a state could be made a less-than-voluntary party were those arising from Georgia's ownership, with the approval of the Tennessee legislature, of a railroad in Tennessee.[98] The Tennessee Supreme Court allowed suits relating to the rail-

---

(reasoning that the defendants' acting in conformity with Pennsylvania law made no difference); *United States Fidelity and Guaranty Co.*, 162 SE at 604 (bonding company's suit against a North Carolina sheriff after the bonding company had been sued in South Carolina for the sheriff's kidnapping someone in South Carolina).

[97] The cases herein are primarily against local officials or local government entities. See *Board of Directors of Darke County Infirmary v Overman*, 60 NE 1017, 1017–19 (Ind 1901) (holding that Ohio officials lacked standing to mandate that an Indiana sheriff receive an insane person who had been improperly removed to Ohio by the sheriff's predecessor, although indicating that an action in Indiana against the county to recover expenses might be allowed); *Warren County, Mississippi v Hester*, 54 So2d 12, 16 (La 1951) (in a suit in Louisiana by a Mississippi county against a Madison Parish, La., tax assessor for taxes on a toll bridge paid under protest, holding that Louisiana public property exemption covered only that of Louisiana and its subdivisions); *Wilson v Helmbold*, 13 Ohio NP (ns) 222 (Ohio Com Pl 1912) (declining to take jurisdiction over a case in which a former night jail guard alleged that the mayor of a Kentucky town sued as an individual had assaulted and imprisoned the plaintiff, all occurring in Kentucky); *Brower v Watson*, 244 SW 362, 367 (Tenn 1922) (reasoning that one state will not take jurisdiction of a matter which concerns the internal police regulations of another state, such that the Tennessee courts would not entertain jurisdiction of an action by a Mississippian against an official of that state on his official bond, for a cause of action arising there); *Pickering v Fisk*, 6 Vt 102 (1834) (refusing to entertain an action by the treasurer of New Hampshire against a New Hampshire county sheriff and his sureties for failing to collect and return an execution); *Indiana v John*, 5 Ohio (S Hammond) 217 (1831) (reaching a similar result as to an Indiana bond that was held to be penal). But compare *Flower v Allen*, 5 Cow 654, 666 (NY 1825) (entertaining on the merits an action against overseers of the poor of a Vermont town sued apparently individually for medical services to a pauper rendered in Vermont by New York doctors); id (Senator Spencer, dissenting in part) (questioning "whether the courts of one State will entertain suits for the official misconduct of officers of another State.").

[98] See *Georgia v City of Chattanooga*, 264 US 472, 478 (1924). Georgia began building the Western and Atlantic Railroad in 1837 with public funds and did not separately incorporate it. Id at 478. The Georgia courts allowed suits for railroad business, by naming the railroad superintendent. See *Western & Atlantic RR v Carlton*, 28 Ga 180, 182 (1859) (allowing claims for damage to hogs). From December 27, 1870, onward, the railroad was operated by several long-term lessees. See *Georgia v City of Chattanooga*, 264 US at 478 (noting that the Nashville, Chattanooga & St. Louis Railway's lease would expire in 1969); *Georgia v Southern Ry Co.*, 255 F 369, 375–76 (ND Ga 1918) (discussing various leases). Plaintiffs apparently brought suits arising after 1870, including actions under the Federal Employers' Liability Act, 53 Stat 1404 (1939), 45 USC §§ 51–60 (2000) ("FELA"), against the lessees. See, for example, *Western & Atlantic RR v Hughes*, 278 US 496 (1929) (holding that there was sufficient evidence to go to the jury in a FELA case). Actions involving disposition of lands owned by Georgia, however, necessarily included the state as a party.

road's business[99] and the railroad's commercial property within Tennessee.[100] For example, the railroad's real estate was subjected to eminent domain proceedings, including by a Tennessee city— a result the Supreme Court would approve.[101]

These railroad cases were consistent with commercial exceptions to state immunity that the federal courts themselves recognized. In *Bank of the United State v Planters' Bank of Georgia*, the Supreme Court allowed a federal court suit against a banking corporation partly owned by the state, stating, "It is, we think, a sound principle, that when a government becomes a partner in any trading company, it divests itself, so far as concerns the transactions of that company, of its sovereign character, and takes that

---

[99] See, for example, *Hutchinson v Western & Atlantic RR Co.*, 53 Tenn (6 Heisk) 634 (1871) (holding that even though Georgia was the sole shareholder of the railroad, and the operation of steamers on the Tennessee River was not authorized by the charter granted to Georgia by Tennessee, the railroad could be liable to the widow of a mate who died from injuries when two of its steamers collided); *Western & Atlantic RR Co. v Taylor*, 53 Tenn 408 (1871) (allowing suit on change bills issued by the Georgia-owned railroad); see also id at 416 (stating with respect to the argument that the bills were prohibited bills of credit that the state's making the bills receivable for taxes was not pledging the faith of the state for payment).

[100] See, for example, *East Tenn, Va & Ga Ry Co. v Nashville, Chattanooga & St. Louis Ry Co.*, 51 SW 202, 203 (Tenn Ch App 1897) (although refusing to sell the allegedly jointly owned railroad property, rejecting Georgia's demurrer, and noting that the suit was brought for the administration of property in Tennessee for purposes of which the right to enter Tennessee had been granted); id (also noting that the Tennessee statute had given Georgia the right previously granted to the Nashville & Chattanooga Railroad, and the latter act included a right to sue and be sued).

[101] *Georgia v City of Chattanooga*, 264 US at 479 (refusing to grant Georgia's request for injunction against the city's condemnation of part of its railroad yard). Georgia conceded that the state of Tennessee could condemn the land, but contested the city's right to do so. Id at 479. The Court reasoned that, "Having acquired land in another State for the purpose of using it in a private capacity, Georgia can claim no sovereign immunity or privilege in respect of its expropriation." Id at 479–80; compare *Burbank v Fay*, 65 NY (20 Sickles) 57, 62 (1875) (rejecting a challenge to the state of New York's closing a basin that had once been owned by Massachusetts but that had been conveyed to private parties, noting that the State had assumed merely the possession of a private proprietor).
Comparably, at times the Supreme Court indicated that states might condemn land owned by the United States, if not reserved and used for public purposes. See *United States v Chicago*, 48 US (7 How) 185, 194–95 (1849) (although not allowing the city's condemnation of Fort Dearborn, which the United States held "by an original cession . . . and afterwards appropriated for specific public object," stating, "It is not questioned that land within a State purchased by the United States as a mere proprietor, and not reserved or appropriated for any special purpose, may be liable to condemnation for streets or highways, like the land of other proprietors, under the rights of eminent domain"); see also *United States v Railroad Bridge Co.*, 27 F Cases 686, 689–91, 694 (CC ND Ill 1855) (over objections of the United States, and despite the land's technically falling outside of a statute authorizing roads across certain federal lands, refusing to enjoin use of federal land that was no longer used for public purposes for a bridge authorized by the state).

of private citizen."[102] The Court extended this reasoning to a bank completely owned by a state,[103] as well as to other commercial ventures in which states held ownership interests including railroads.[104] These suits were compatible with sovereign immunity based on a notion that states were not acting as states when engaged in certain commercial activities.[105]

Indeed, state liability arising from owning railroads was the preeminent Supreme-Court-approved toehold for state damages liability under Commerce-Clause-based legislation[106] prior to *Union Gas's*[107] opening wider prospects of state suability under the Commerce Clause, and *Seminole Tribe's*[108] closing them. And the Ten-

---

[102] 22 US (9 Wheat) 904, 907 (1827).

[103] *Bank of Kentucky v Wister*, 27 US (2 Pet) 318, 323 (1829) (quoting *Planters' Bank*); compare *Curran v Arkansas*, 56 US (15 How) 304, 308–09 (1853) (holding on direct review that funds of an insolvent bank owned by the state, of whose remaining assets the state had taken possession, remained a fund for creditors). But see id at 309 (also noting that the state supreme court in this suit had held the state liable to suit, and "as this is purely a question of local law, depending on the constitution and statutes of the State" the Court would follow that decision in holding that the state had consented to suit).

[104] See, for example, *Louisville, Cincinnati & Charleston RR Co. v Letson*, 43 US (2 How) 497, 550–51 (1844) (rejecting objection to jurisdiction based on state's being a member of the corporate railroad defendant); see also *Georgia v City of Chattanooga*, 264 US at 482 (in approving of Chattanooga's condemnation of Georgia railroad property, citing *Planters' Bank* to support the proposition that Georgia had divested itself of its sovereign character when it engaged in the railroad business in Tennessee).

[105] Thus in a case such as *Wister*, where jurisdiction was apparently based on diversity, the suit would not necessarily be one "against one of the United States" in violation of the Eleventh Amendment. The lack of textual conflict was facilitated by not naming the state as a formal party defendant. See 27 US at 318, 323.

[106] See *Hilton v South Carolina Rys Comm'n*, 502 US at 202–03 (holding that the FELA creates a cause of action against state-owned railroads enforceable in state courts); *Parden v Terminal Ry of the Alabama State Docks Dept.*, 377 US 184, 192 (1964) (rejecting a sovereign immunity defense to FELA liability for a state-run railroad, reasoning, *inter alia*, that Alabama had consented to suit by beginning to operate a railroad twenty years after the FELA's promulgation); id at 193 (citing lower court cases rejecting sovereign immunity defenses to the FELA); both overruled by *Alden*, 527 US at 712, 737–38 (holding that an action under the Fair Labor Standards Act of 1938, 29 USC §§ 201–09 (2000), that could not be brought in federal court against the state also could not be brought in state court). See also *Texas State RR*, 34 ICC Val Rep 276, 277 (1930) (rejecting the state's challenge to the authority of agency's authority, citing Georgia Supreme Court cases involving the Western & Atlantic Railroad); compare *United States v California*, 297 US 175, 180, 183–84 (1936) (unanimously holding that United States could sue the state for a $100 fine under the Federal Safety Appliance Act in connection with the state's operation of a belt railroad, the reserved power of the states being subordinate to congressional power to regulate interstate commerce).

[107] *Pennsylvania v Union Gas Co.*, 491 US 1 (1989) (holding that congressional commerce legislation could abrogate state immunity).

[108] *Seminole Tribe of Florida v Florida*, 517 US 44 (1996) (holding that congressional commerce legislation could not abrogate state immunity).

nessee Supreme Court relied on *Planters' Bank* to support suits against the Georgia railroad.[109]

In addition to the railroad cases, there were a handful of other cases against states, most of which similarly had analogues in federal cases recognizing exceptions to sovereign immunity.[110] A Maryland decision allowed taxation of part of a bridge that was in Maryland and of which Virginia owned part of the capital stock, a result that was supported, as counsel argued, by *Planters' Bank*.[111] There were occasional additional suggestions, particularly in cases allowing taxation of municipal property in another state, that state property in another state might similarly be taxed.[112] These sug-

---

[109] See, for example, *Western & Atlantic RR v Taylor*, 53 Tenn at 414–15 (relying on *Planters' Bank* in holding that the Georgia-owned railroad could be sued on change bills it had issued); compare *Taggart v Holcomb*, 116 P 251, 253–54 (Kan 1911) (citing *Planters' Bank* and other federal cases in support of allowing a tax on Kansas City, Missouri's waterworks in Kansas, which the Kansas court here deemed to be held for proprietary purposes), review denied, 226 US 599 (1912); *City of Cincinnati v Reeves*, 167 SW2d 709, 714 (Ky 1942) (citing *Georgia v City of Chattanooga*, 264 US 472, to support taxation of income that the city received from leasing its railroad properties in Kentucky).

[110] A case that seems contrary to the federal cases was *Susquehanna Canal Co. v Pennsylvania*, 72 Pa 72, Pa LEXIS 205, *7–9 (1872) (affirming a decision allowing Pennsylvania to collect a tax on a Pennsylvania canal company's debt payments to its creditor, the State of Maryland, which was to be taken as a deduction from the amount due to the creditor, and reasoning more generally that a forum state could tax property of another state within the latter's boundaries). The court below whose opinion the Pennsylvania Supreme Court affirmed had reasoned from commercial activity cases such as *Planters' Bank*. The result, however, seems inconsistent with *United States v Railroad Co.*, 84 US (17 Wall) 322, 332–33 (1872), which did not allow the federal government to tax money due from a railroad to Baltimore, based on intergovernmental tax immunities. The Court treated the tax as one on the creditor and not the corporation. Id at 326–27.

[111] *O'Neal v the Virginia and Maryland Bridge Co. at Shepherds Town*, 18 Md 1, 1861 Md LEXIS 62, *30–31 (1861) (argument of counsel, citing *Planters' Bank* to allow taxation of a bridge to the extent it was in Maryland); compare *Hoagland v Streeper*, 145 NE2d 625, 631–32 (Ill 1957) (holding that there was jurisdiction in an Illinois court to enjoin a Missouri city that owned a bridge partly in Illinois from conveying the bridge to the state of Missouri, although indicating that Missouri could not be made a formal party); id at 629–30 (relying on an *in rem* theory and on *Cunningham v Macon and Brunswick RR Co.*, 109 US 446, 450 (1883), and also noting that the ownership of roads and bridges in another state is considered a private function), discussed in Martiniak, 63 Cal L Rev at 1148 n 21 (cited in note 9).

[112] See Martiniak, 63 Cal L Rev at 1148 (cited in note 9). This taxation sometimes extended to property that if owned by an in-state municipality would have been considered to he held for a public purpose. See id at 1148 n 20 (noting the accepted rule that a municipality "forfeits all claim to sovereignty with respect to property it has acquired or non-governmental activities it performs in another state."); *Minnesota v City of Hudson*, 42 NW2d 546, 548 (Minn 1950) (allowing the state to impose a personal property tax on a portion of a Wisconsin city's toll bridge that was in the state of Minnesota, reasoning that the "sovereign character of the state owning property in another state ceases at the state line, with the consequence that its ownership of property in the foreign state is in its corporate capacity without any sovereign or public attributes"); id at 549 (collecting cases allowing taxation of municipal property owned in another state); see also *Taxation of a*

gestions, however, loosely paralleled the Supreme Court's allowing federal taxation of South Carolina's liquor dispensaries as commercial, despite intergovernmental tax immunities.[113] And state courts sometimes voiced a belief that *in rem* actions might be allowed against state property,[114] as did the federal courts.[115]

The state cases actually making states involuntary parties were not numerous and for the most part did not deviate materially from

---

Bridge Owned by Kentucky Located in West Virginia, 37 W Va Op Atty Gen 125, 1937 LEXIS (1937) (rendering an opinion that West Virginia could tax the portion of a Kentucky-owned bridge that was in West Virginia).

[113] Compare *South Carolina v United States*, 199 US 437, 463 (1905) (allowing the tax on liquor dispensary) with *Collector v Day*, 78 US (11 Wall) 113 (1870) (holding that the federal government could not tax the salary of a state judge). See also *South Carolina v United States*, 199 US at 458 (reasoning that the framers would not have anticipated that the state would attempt to monopolize a business previously carried on by individuals); id at 461 (also adverting to the well-known distinctions between the public and private business of municipal corporations); compare *City Council of Augusta, Georgia v Timmerman*, 233 F 216 (4th Cir 1916) (approving South Carolina county officials' taxation of a Georgia city's abutments for a dam on the South Carolina side of a river). But see *South Carolina v United States*, 199 US at 464–67 (White, joined by Peckham and McKenna, dissenting) (discussing cases that suggested a contrary result, and particularly *United States v Railroad Co.*, 84 US (17 Wall) 322 (1872), which did not allow the federal government to tax money due from a railroad to the city of Baltimore).

[114] The eminent domain cases discussed in note 101 and accompanying text seem to have been the principal instances where an *in rem*-type action proceeded against a state. In addition, a New York judge in an 1845 case, although sustaining a demurrer by agents of the state of Indiana because no specific relief was asked of them, opined that the court would be able to take jurisdiction over the state if it had a lien on the stock whose ownership was to be determined in the proceeding. The court indicated that "there is nothing in that constitution to deprive the court of chancery of this state of all the jurisdiction on the subject which it possessed before that constitution was adopted." This might sound like a broad claim to aboriginal state court jurisdiction, had the opinion not continued: "true this court has not the power, absolutely, to compel a sovereign state to perform a decree, which may be made against such state. And if the state of Indiana should be made a party defendant in this suit, it would not be with any expectation of compelling it to transfer to the complainant the stock standing in its name . . . [b]ut it would be to enable the state to appear and protect its right . . . ." *Garr v Bright*, 1 Barb Ch 157, 5 NY Ch Ann 337 (NY Ch 1845).

[115] Before the decision in *Ex parte New York*, 256 US 490 (1921), it was thought that states might be subject to jurisdiction *in rem* in admiralty. See Fletcher, 35 Stan L Rev at 1080 (cited in note 19). Fletcher notes Justice Story's statement that in *in rem* actions "the jurisdiction of the court is founded upon the possession of the thing; and if the state should interpose a claim for the property, it does not act merely in the character of a defendant, but as an actor." Joseph Story, 3 *Commentaries on the Constitution of the United States* 561 (Hillard, Gray, 1833); see also Charles H. Weston, *Actions Against the Property of Sovereigns*, 32 Harv L Rev 266, 268–71 (1919) (noting that *The Davis*, 77 US (10 Wall) 15 (1870), allowed for libeling of cotton owned by the United States for salvage, but that the case might be limited to salvage claims, and that the dominant position at the time of the article was that foreign-government-owned ships even used for trade should not be subject to private attachment); compare *Central Virginia Community College v Katz*, 126 S Ct 990, 996, 1000, 1005 (2006) (relying on the *in rem* nature of bankruptcy proceedings to allow congressional abrogation of state sovereign immunity).

circumstances in which the states might be liable in federal courts.[116] And just as the state courts looked to Supreme Court precedent such as *Hans* for the general principle of immunity, they looked to the Supreme Court's decision in *Planters' Bank* for a commercial/consent exception to that immunity.[117]

C. WAS THE ABSENCE OF SUITS AGAINST STATES MERELY A MATTER OF PERSONAL JURISDICTION?

Reinforcing the impossibility of suing a state in a sister state were rules of personal jurisdiction.[118] A litigant could not effect service on the state *in personam* by suing a responsible official outside of the home state. Thus it was virtually impossible to make a claim to good personal service on a state in the courts of another state.[119]

Illustrating the impossibility of getting effective service were cases involving administrators of estates, who were treated as officials of the courts that appointed them. In *Vaughn v Northup*, for example, the Court held that a Kentucky administrator was not subject to suit in the District of Columbia upon his personal service there at the instance of Virginia claimants to the estate he administered.[120] This was true even though the administrator had traveled to the district to claim money due to the decedent from the federal government, pursuant to a congressional statute placing him on the footing of a domestic administrator with regard to

---

[116] There would naturally be some differences. For example, because a state is not a citizen for purposes of diversity jurisdiction over suits between citizens of different states, and there is no statutory grant of lower-court jurisdiction for cases between a citizen of one state against another state, a federal court would not have jurisdiction over a claim by an out-of-stater directly against the state on a state law cause of action, even with consent. The Supreme Court, however, would not be barred from enforcing such an action. See text accompanying notes 69–72.

[117] To the extent one embraces such a commercial exception, one might think that expansive modern doctrines of what counts as "commerce" (for purposes of Congress's powers under Article I) should produce a concomitant expansion in the exception to state sovereign immunity. But there is no real logical connection between these two things. To the extent that courts recognized a commercial exception to sovereign immunity in cases such as *Planters' Bank*, the distinction was not so much commerce vs. noncommerce as it was state vs. nonstate. Under current doctrine, a state may easily engage in activities that are at once commerce and sovereign (such as employing police).

[118] Nelson, 115 Harv L Rev at 1628 & n 298 (cited in note 24) (discussing the difficulties state courts would have had acquiring personal jurisdiction over another state).

[119] Compare *Chisholm*, 2 US (2 Dall) at 419 (noting that this federal action had been commenced by service on the governor and attorney general in the district of Georgia).

[120] 40 US (15 Pet) 1 (1841).

collection against the United States.[121] Justice Story for the Court stated, "both upon principle and authority," that the administrator was not "liable to be sued here, in his official character, for assets lawfully received by him." He reasoned that "every grant of administration is strictly confined in its authority and operation to the limits of the territory of the government which grants it, and does not, de jure, extend to other countries."[122]

On the one hand, this impossibility of obtaining personal jurisdiction for an *in personam* suit is supportive of state immunity in the courts of other states. On the other hand, one might argue that the growth of long-arm jurisdiction means states are now suable. After all, the argument would go, the inability to effect personal service on the state outside of the state was also once true for private corporations sued outside of their states of incorporation. One could not obtain proper service on a corporation by serving even a chief officer out of state just as one could not obtain service on a state by serving a state officer out of state.[123] Thus one might argue that just as corporations became increas-

---

[121] Id at 7.

[122] Id; see also *In re Thompson's Estate*, 97 SW2d 93 (Mo 1936) (reaching a similar result where plaintiffs brought a libel by serving an agent of the administrators in a different state, and discussing authorities); Joseph Story, *Conflict of Laws* § 513 (Little, Brown, 5th ed 1857) ("It has hence become a general doctrine of the common law, recognized both in England and America, that no suit can be brought or maintained by any executor or administrator, or against any executor or administrator, in his official capacity, in the courts of any other country, except that from which he derives his authority to act in virtue of the probate and letters of administration there granted to him"); *Restatement (First) of the Law of Conflicts of Law* § 512 (stating the general rule that claims against an administrator cannot be maintained outside the state of administration, and discussing some exceptions). Federal bankruptcy trustees, the Court held, could sue in districts other than that of their appointment and in state courts. See *Lathrop v Drake*, 91 US 516 (1875) (holding that bankruptcy trustees could sue in other districts); *Claflin v Houseman*, 93 US 130, 143 (1876) (holding that bankruptcy trustees could sue in state courts).

[123] Compare *Bank of Augusta v Earle*, 38 US (13 Pet) 519, 589–90 (1839) (in allowing a Georgia corporation to sue in the Alabama federal court due to the presumption that a state would accord comity to corporations of other states, stating that "a corporation can have no legal existence out of the boundaries of the sovereignty by which it is created"); discussed in Charles A. Wright and Arthur A. Miller, 4 *Federal Practice and Procedure* § 1066 (West, 2002) (stating that under *Earle*, a corporation had no existence outside of its state of incorporation and could only be sued there; also indicating that *Earle* was seen as creating a barrier to serving a corporation through an officer outside of the state of incorporation, citing *McQueen v Middleton Mfg. Co.*, NY Sup Ct 1819, 16 Johns R 5, 7); Gerard Carl Henderson, *The Position of the Foreign Corporation in American Constitutional Law: A Contribution to the History and Theory of Juristic Persons in Anglo-American Law* 77 (Harvard, 1918) (indicating that until toward the mid-nineteenth century, the widely prevalent view was that attachment was the only process available against corporations incorporated in other states).

ingly subject to personal jurisdiction, so too should sister states.

States' immunity from suit, however, while in a sense a matter of personal jurisdiction and enforced through its mechanisms, was never treated as an identical issue. Whereas attachment alone worked to secure jurisdiction over individuals or corporations, suits against states required not merely attachment[124] but also a commercial/consent or other recognized exception to sovereign immunity. Thus, the Tennessee Supreme Court, which allowed suits against Georgia relating to its railroad business in Tennessee, rebuffed an attempt to collect on Georgia bonds by attaching railroad property.[125] As noted by a Georgia court, a state's ownership of property in another state did not subject the state to "promiscuous suits"[126] as it might for a corporation or individual defendant. And in *Stockwell v Bates*, when a holder of unpaid Illinois bond coupons attached Illinois funds on deposit in New York, the court vacated the attachment, stating that "no judgment can be had, so as to attach money of the State, and thereby coerce its appearance."[127] Similarly when states sued as plaintiffs in other states, unrelated setoffs were not allowed.[128]

---

[124] See, for example, *Grain Growers' Grain Co. v Michigan*, 204 NW 838, 838–39 (ND 1925) (indicating that a contract action commenced by garnishment (substituted service of summons) should be dismissed); *Nathan v Virginia*, 1 Dall 77 n (Pa CP 1781) (preconstitutional case, refusing to allow an attachment of Virginia-owned goods as a means to obtain jurisdiction where the attachment was only to secure the presence of the defendant state).

[125] *Tappan v Western & Atlantic RR Co.*, 71 Tenn 106 (1879) (in a suit commenced by attachment of eight acres of property that the state of Georgia owned in Chattanooga as part of its operation of a railroad that was partly in Tennessee, dismissing amended bill on bonds issued by the state of Georgia); compare *Paulus v South Dakota*, 201 NW 867, 869–70 (ND 1924) (dismissing a suit against South Dakota for worker's compensation benefits, and rejecting an argument that the state by raising a question of the regularity of the attachment proceedings, waived its sovereignty and submitted to the jurisdiction of the district court).

[126] *Florida State Hospital for the Insane v Durham Iron Co.*, 21 SE2d 216, 220 (Ga 1942) (dismissing levy against land owned by Florida, because even if it were assumed that the state operated the property as a commercial rather than sovereign enterprise, the plaintiff had not shown that the suit originated out of the operation of the farm); id at 219 (in noting that there was authority for the proposition that when a state acquired property in another state, it divests itself of sovereignty, observing that this latter rule applies only as to commercial business).

[127] 10 Abb Pr (ns) 381 (NY Sup Ct 1871).

[128] *Moore v Tate*, 11 SW 935, 937 (Tenn 1889) (holding that a defendant in Alabama's suit on commercial paper could not use as a setoff an independent claim on the bonds of the state). The Tennessee court noted that it would not allow such a setoff against Tennessee, and that all states as far as it knew extended the same privileges as the forum state enjoyed. Id at 937. The court noted that otherwise "bonded indebtedness of a state, issued in its sovereign and political capacity, predicated entirely upon the faith and credit of the

In the period from *International Shoe*'s adoption of the minimum contacts approach to personal jurisdiction in 1945 until *Nevada v Hall* in 1979, moreover, suits against states remained rarities,[129] indicating that the states saw the immunity of sister states as not merely a matter of personal jurisdiction. Rather, the assumption, as some post-*Hall* state court decisions noted, was that sister states could not be sued as a matter of constitutional immunity transcending restraints on personal jurisdiction.[130] Thus, although the difficulties of obtaining personal jurisdiction over states for the first century and a half of the republic reinforced the notion that states were immune from *in personam* suits in the courts of other states, the nonsuability of states was not sourced solely in restraints on personal jurisdiction.

IV. POST-HALL DEVELOPMENTS

A. DISRUPTION OF THE FOUNDING-ERA STRUCTURE

The founding generation put into place a jurisdictional structure that assumed that the courts of one state would generally be inappropriate forums for suits brought by one of their residents against another state. Under unamended Article III, such suits, if allowed at all, would generally fall within the Supreme Court's original jurisdiction. Once the Eleventh Amendment foreclosed this option, regular citizen/citizen diversity remained available for residents of one state suing officers of another, and out-of-state plaintiffs frequently invoked this jurisdiction against in-state officers. In addition, states could allow suits in their own courts against themselves on their own terms.

Nevada v Hall's holding that states enjoy no constitutional im-

---

state . . . might be made the subject of suit by such indirection. So too every taxpayer might discharge his obligation to the government." Id. But see *Massachusetts v Davis*, 160 SW2d 543 (Tex App 1942) (allowing a (related) wrongful garnishment counterclaim to a Massachusetts tax suit on a judgment for taxes), aff'd in part, rev'd in part, 168 SW2d 216 (Tex 1942) (affirming Massachusetts's recovery and reversing the grant of recovery on the taxpayer's counterclaim); id at 221 (stating it was unnecessary to consider whether a state can be held liable for damages in a sister state for wrongful garnishment).

[129] See *Hall*, 440 US at 414 (noting that the question of whether a state can be sued in courts of another state had never been answered by the Court).

[130] See, for example, *Ehrlich-Bober v University of Houston*, 404 NE2d 726, 729 (NY 1980) (noting "that it was long thought that a State could not be sued by the citizens of a sister state except in its own courts"); *Recent Developments*, 56 Wash L Rev at 304 (cited in note 9) (noting that prior to *Hall* it was "widely assumed that a state could not be sued without its consent in the courts of another state").

munity in the courts of other states upset this rational jurisdictional structure. Under *Hall*, out-of-staters will frequently forgo suing only individual officers as to whom a federal diversity forum would often be available,[131] or suing defendant states in the defendant states' courts, in favor of suing defendant states in the plaintiffs' home-state courts.[132] The current diversity and removal statutes, moreover, would not seem to allow for the defendant state's removal of such suits to federal court.[133] With both a constitutionally based immunity and a federal forum foreclosed, restraints on suits against states in other states' courts now largely depend on the forum state's decisions as to choice of law and comity. The only federal constraints are minimum contacts,[134] and nonarbitrariness in choice of law under the Due Process and Full Faith and Credit Clauses, both of which are quite limited.

When the Court thus forswears federal authority in an area by giving only minimal constitutional scrutiny, one may appropriately ask whether the institutions to which decisional power has defaulted are superior to the federal courts. The intent of the framers

---

[131] The plaintiff may be able to join local defendants to defeat removal under current requirements of complete diversity.

[132] See *Hall*, 440 US at 442 (Rehnquist dissenting) (noting that, "Despite the historical justification of federal courts as neutral forums, now suits against unconsenting States by citizens of different States can *only* be brought in the courts of other States.").

[133] See 28 USC §§ 1332(a)–(c), 1441(a)–(d) (2000); *Hall*, 440 US at 442 (Rehnquist dissenting) (noting the impossibility of state removal under the diversity jurisdiction); *Hawsey v Louisiana Dept. of Social Services*, 934 SW2d 723, 725 (Tex App 1996) (noting that although the case had been removed by federal officer defendants, the claims against the Louisiana department had been remanded to the Texas state court); Comment, *Constitutional Law—Neither the Eleventh Amendment Nor Any Other Provision of the United States Constitution Supports One State's Claim of Sovereign Immunity in the Courts of Another State, Nevada v. Hall*, 10 Cumb L Rev 579, 590–91 (1979) (while generally commending the result in *Hall*, noting problem that removal was not possible); Mitchell N. Berman, Note, *Removal and the Eleventh Amendment: The Case for District Court Remand Discretion to Avoid a Bifurcated Suit*, 92 Mich L Rev 683, 695–96 (1993) (concluding that a case in which a private party and a state are defendants is not removable in diversity, independent of Eleventh Amendment problems).
Removal might be possible where defendants are sued on a mixture of federal and state law claims. If the state enjoys no immunity in state court on the state-law claims, then its removal may be deemed a waiver of the sovereign immunity defense. Compare *Lapides v Board of Regents of University System of Georgia*, 535 US 613, 619 (2002) (holding that the state waived federal-court immunity to state law claims by removing a federal question suit that included state law claims as to which it had waived its immunity in state court); Fallon et al, *The Federal Courts* at 1037–38 (cited in note 12) (discussing problems with the waiver-by-removal decisions).

[134] The state is not necessarily a person protected by the Fifth and Fourteenth Amendments' Due Process Clauses, but courts generally treat minimum contacts analysis as applicable to them. See note 143.

of Article III and the Eleventh Amendment, the text of the Amendment, the federal structure and jurisdictional history as discussed above, all suggest that state courts are not the preferred forums for suits against sister states. There is little reason, moreover, to think that state courts are more trustworthy to entertain suits against sister states now than they were in the founding era. A defendant state would be unlikely to leave the union or invade the forum state due to the latter's exercise of jurisdiction, but that does not suggest that the forum would be any fairer. Rather, incentives to take a multilateral or reciprocal approach that might benefit all states are weak in a fifty-state union where there are few clear punishments for noncooperation.[135]

What is more, by the time the Court decided *Hall*, a lack of reciprocity had manifested itself in the very area of law to which the Court had now relegated interstate sovereign immunity: conflicts of law. The states have generally employed an interest analysis that begins with a presumption that a state's primary interest is to protect its own citizens at the expense of out-of-state interests.[136]

There have been many suggestions that the Court should federalize conflicts law generally,[137] and some suggestions that the

---

[135] See, for example, Erin A. O'Hara and Larry E. Ribstein, *From Politics to Efficiency in Choice of Law*, 67 U Chi L Rev 1151, 1177 (2000) (noting the practical problems of states' achieving reciprocity in conflicts of law, particularly given competing considerations of favoring local plaintiffs and attracting litigants); compare Michael W. McConnell, *A Choice-of-Law Approach to Products-Liability Reform*, in Walter Olson, ed, *New Directions in Liability Law* 90, 92–93 (Academy of Political Science, 1988) (referring to the rich literature in the field of taxation and rate regulation showing that policies are favored by the states where the costs will be borne by other states).

[136] See William H. Allen and Erin A. O'Hara, *Second Generation Law and Economics of Conflict of Laws: Baxter's Comparative Impairment and Beyond*, 51 Stan L Rev 1011, 1023 (1999) (criticizing interest analysis and citing recent empirical works confirming that interest analysis leads to more frequent application of forum law than other regimes); Lea Brilmayer, *Interest Analysis and the Myth of Legislative Intent*, 78 Mich L Rev 392, 408 (1980) (criticizing parochialism of interest analysis); Douglas Laycock, *Equal Citizens of Equal and Territorial States: The Constitutional Foundations of Choice of Law*, 92 Colum L Rev 249, 274–75 (1992) (stating that Brainerd Currie's approach of preference for local citizens remained embedded in interest analysis, and that Currie's whole scheme takes the view that the interests of outsiders do not count); McConnell, *A Choice-of-Law Approach to Products-Liability Reform* at 93 (cited in note 135) (criticizing interest analysis for loading the dice in favor of the plaintiff, favoring larger recovery, and its beginning assumptions that states are interested only in obtaining benefits for their own residents); Gene R. Shreve, *Choice of Law and the Forgiving Constitution*, 71 Ind L J 271, 271 (1996) (criticizing the parochialism of interest analysis).

[137] See Fallon et al, *The Federal Courts* at 636–40 (cited in note 12) (noting the first edition's statements that allowing state choice of law rules to govern in diversity reintroduces the problem *Erie* sought to address of having different law apply to the same

Court should federalize the conflicts rules of state suability.[138] The Court, however, declined to follow the latter suggestions in *Hyatt*.[139] The Court's common law in this small area of state suability might suggest that the whole area of conflicts of law would be appropriate for a federal common law—which the Court seems disinclined to undertake. By involving the Court in elaborating the conditions of state liability, moreover, a federalized conflicts regime for suits against states would highlight the anomaly of the Court's recog-

---

primary conduct); Henry Hart, *The Relations Between State and Federal Law*, 54 Colum L Rev 489, 513–15 (1954) (indicating that between citizens of different states, issues of choice of law "are essentially federal, in the sense that they involve, by hypothesis, more than one state. To the solution of no other type of controversy is the diversity jurisdiction better adapted."); compare Michael Gottesman, *Draining the Dismal Swamp: The Case for Federal Choice of Law Statutes*, 80 Geo L J 1, 16 (1991) (proposing that Congress legislate choice of law rules "wherever a subject is a frequent source of litigation with multistate implications, and the costs of indeterminacy and/or non-neutrality have grown unacceptable"); Donald T. Trautman, *The Relation Between American Choice of Law and Federal Common Law*, 41 L & Contemp Prob 105, 126 (Spring 1977) (arguing that federal common law should develop only in response to identified federal needs not adequately served by state law, and often should merely provide an outer boundary).

[138] See Hill, 42 BC L Rev at 583 (cited in note 12) (arguing that California might have sued Nevada in the Supreme Court in *Hall*, and that the law that should be applied in a lower court considering the case should be that which the Supreme Court would have applied); *The Supreme Court, 1978 Term*, 93 Harv L Rev at 196 (cited in note 4) (recommending greater policing of choice of law to prevent unfairness to state defendants). One might imagine a regime, for example, in which states would generally be sued in their own courts, as virtually all states would like to be.

While generally requiring that a state be sued in its home forum, a federalized conflicts of law regime in some cases, such as those involving auto accidents, might provide that the substantive law and damages ceilings of the state where the accident occurred apply. See Richard Posner, *Economic Analysis of Law* 602–03 (Aspen, 6th ed 2003) (arguing for place of injury rule for choice of law in torts, as reflecting states' comparative regulatory advantage); Allen and O'Hara, 51 Stan L Rev at 1043–44 (cited in note 136) (arguing for a place of injury rule in torts to promote predictability of the law governing primary behavior). The auto accident, however, provides no paradigm when the breach of duty largely occurs in the officer's home state but the injury is elsewhere. In such cases the law of the officer's home state might generally apply. Compare Gottesmann, 80 Geo L J at 11–13 (cited in note 137) (suggesting specific rules for a federalized choice of law regime). But see Laycock, 92 Colum L Rev at 311–14 (cited in note 136) (arguing that the forum should not be able to give a preference to forum law, nor employ a public policy exception).

[139] 538 US at 495 (noting that the court had tried balancing state interests for conflicts of law decisions under the Full Faith and Credit Clause, but that it had proved unsatisfactory); see also Scott Fruehwald, *The Rehnquist Court and Horizontal Federalism: An Evaluation and a Proposal for Moderate Constitutional Constraints on Horizontal Federalism*, 81 Denver U L Rev 289, 305–08 (2003) (discussing the Court's refusal to federalize the question of which state's law should apply as a matter of full faith and credit, and more generally discussing the Rehnquist Court's lesser concern for horizontal than vertical federalism); id at 314 (concluding that the result in *Hyatt* was correct, because Nevada had at least as strong an interest as California in applying its law).

nizing immunity in federal but not state courts, and run headlong into the Eleventh Amendment.[140]

B. RESULTS IN THE STATES

Results in the states post-*Hall*, while mixed, indicate that states cannot uniformly expect fair treatment, much less recognition of immunity, as defendants in the courts of other states.[141] These results indicate that the framers were correct to design a jurisdictional system providing federal court jurisdiction for controversies between citizens of one state and officers of another.

After *Nevada v Hall* foreclosed a federal constitutional immunity,[142] defendant states typically argue that the sister-state forum should apply the defendant state's own immunity law as a matter of choice of law or comity. The defendant state might assert that the forum state should respect (*a*) the defendant state's limitations of suit to its own courts,[143] (*b*) the defendant state's notice, administrative exhaustion, and time limitations provisions, or (*c*) the defendant state's absolute bar to liability in some cases, or its damages ceilings in others.

One may roughly sketch three approaches to these requests for the defendants' rules to apply. The first and most comity-respect-

---

[140] See text accompanying notes 62–63.

[141] Compare Kermit Roosevelt III, *The Myth of Choice of Law: Rethinking Conflicts*, 97 Mich L Rev 2448, 2535–37 (1999) (stating that sister states and their domiciliaries are likely candidates for discrimination because they lack electoral voice, and arguing that the Full Faith and Credit and Privileges and Immunities Clauses protect against such discrimination in conflicts of laws).

[142] Conflicts scholars sometimes cite *Hall* and *Hyatt* as supporting a public policy limitation to one state's full faith and credit obligations to apply the policies of another state. See, for example, Richard S. Myers, *The Public Policy Doctrine and Interjurisdictional Recognition of Civil Unions and Domestic Partnerships*, 3 Ave Maria L Rev 531, 534–35 (2005) (discussing *Hyatt* as strongly supporting such a public policy exception); Lynn D. Wardle, *Non-Recognition of Same-Sex Marriage Judgments Under DOMA and the Constitution*, 38 Creighton L Rev 365, 382–83 (2005) (citing *Hall* for a public policy exception).

[143] An argument that there is no personal jurisdiction will have a similar effect. See, for example, *Hoskinson v California*, 812 P2d 1068, 1070–72 (Ariz Ct App 1990) (in a case in which California provided no liability and Arizona would have allowed it, finding a lack of personal jurisdiction where a California parole official was alleged to have negligently failed to revoke parole, leading to murder in Arizona; id at 1071 n 3 (overruling a prior similar case (*Chavez v Indiana for Logansport State Hosp.*, 596 P2d 698 (Ariz 1979)) as to the personal jurisdiction issue); *Underwood v University of Kentucky*, 390 So2d 433, 435 (Fla App 1980) (dismissing a defamation suit against a state university press that was held not to be doing business in the state).

ing would honor the defendant states' requests as (a),[144] (b),[145] or (c).[146] Following this comity-respecting approach will generally lead to dismissal, with refiling in the home state a possibility in many cases.[147] For example, in *K.D.F. v Rex*, the Texas Supreme Court dismissed a suit against the Kansas Employees Retirement System arising out of a business deal involving oil and gas property in Texas, recognizing that both Texas and Kansas had similar interests in enforcing their forum restriction provisions requiring

---

[144] See, for example, *Levert v University of Illinois*, 857 So2d 611 (La App 2003) (holding that plaintiffs should sue in Illinois over not getting tickets they had ordered through the Illinois ticket office even if no class action were available in Illinois, particularly given that Illinois recognized sister-state immunity); *King v Northern Indiana Commuter Transportation Dist.*, 785 NE2d 35 (Ill App 2003) (declining to exercise jurisdiction where an Illinois plaintiff alleged injuries resulting from being put off of an Indiana-run train in Illinois); *Simmons v Montana*, 670 P2d 1372 (Mont 1983) (refusing both on personal jurisdiction and comity grounds to take jurisdiction over Oregon in a malpractice case arising from Oregon's performance of certain medical tests under agreement with Montana, where the case could be filed in Oregon); *Hawsey v Louisiana Dept. of Social Services*, 934 SW2d 723 (Tex App 1995) (where Texan sued Louisiana child support agency over arrest and publication of his child support arrears, dismissing for possible refiling in Louisiana).

[145] *Crair v Brookdale Hospital Medical Center*, 728 NE2d 974 (NY 2000) (dismissing two state universities from a suit alleging defective human growth hormone, where New York had similar but not identical requirements of filing notice of claims); compare *Mejia-Cabral v Eagleton School*, 10 Mass L Rptr 453, 1999 Mass Super LEXIS 353, *3 (Mass Super 1999) (dismissing a third-party complaint against the state by a school sued for allowing the escape of a detained juvenile, so as to allow the use of Connecticut's claim procedures that required authorization from the Claims Commissioner or the legislature); id at *3 (noting that Massachusetts does not allow itself to be sued for negligence in selection of a treatment facility for a juvenile offender); *Williams v Washington*, 885 P2d 845 (Wash Ct App 1994) (applying Oregon's shorter limitations period to a suit against it by an Oregon resident as to accident on the Washington side of the bridge, and noting there was no point in sending the case to Oregon to have it there dismissed).

[146] See, for example, *Schoeberlein v Purdue University*, 544 NE2d 283 (Ill 1989) (dismissing suit that failed to comply with the governmental limitations period of the forum and defendant state, and also indicating that the defendant state's lower liability limits could apply); *Reed v University of North Dakota*, 543 NW2d 106 (Minn Ct App 1996) (dismissing student athlete's suit based on North Dakota sovereign immunity law at the time the events occurred in North Dakota, although Minnesota had waived sovereign immunity).

[147] Accepting arguments under (a) generally also entails acceptance of (b) and (c), and will lead to dismissal, with the possibility of refiling depending on the defendant state's laws as to (b) and (c). If a state raises an issue under (b), its acceptance often leads to dismissal, sometimes with a possibility of refiling in the home state upon compliance. Accepting arguments under (c) only, uncombined with arguments under (a) and (b), may lead to either dismissal if there is an absolute bar to suit, or to the case proceeding in the forum but using some parts of the defendant state's laws, such as a damages limitation. The latter result has occurred in suits against local governmental entities. See, for example, *Lemons v Cloer*, 206 SW3d 60, 2006 Tenn App LEXIS 285 (Tenn App 2006) (in suit involving Georgia plaintiffs' suit against a Georgia school district and its driver for accident in Tennessee, holding that Georgia's $300,000 damages cap would apply, although Tennessee had no cap).

suits against the state to be in its own courts.[148] And in *Newberry v Georgia Department of Industry and Trade*, where there were multiple additional defendants to a claim based on the plaintiff's tripping over electrical wires at a trade show, the South Carolina Supreme Court was willing to recognize Georgia's claim to absolute immunity under Georgia law, although that immunity was greater than South Carolina would accord itself.[149]

A second approach involves ignoring defendant-state forum limitation provisions,[150] notice and time limits,[151] and liability and damages limitations,[152] and applying the forum's law of state suability. Application of the forum's own law may lead to dismissal,[153] or to the case proceeding on the merits. For example, in *Struebin*

---

[148] 878 SW2d 589 (Tex 1994).

[149] 336 SE2d 464 (SC 1985). But see *Melton v Crowder*, 452 SE2d 834 (SC 1995) (taking jurisdiction of a car accident case against North Carolina based on finding that although North Carolina required actions against agencies to be brought before its industrial commission, it was not absolute in this, having once allowed a third-party complaint in the regular courts).

[150] See, for example, *Ehrlich-Bober & Co. v University of Houston*, 404 NE2d 726 (NY 1980) (in suit alleging a breach of contract over investment transactions, where the defendants acted by phone from Texas, refusing to honor Texas provisions for suit against the state in particular courts). But see *Crair v Brookdale Hospital Medical Center*, 728 NE2d 974 (NY 2000) (dismissing state universities from suit arising from alleged defective human growth hormone on the ground that it was not against New York policy to apply state notice of claim provisions when New York had similar although not identical provisions).

[151] See, for example, *McDonnell v Illinois*, 748 A2d 1105, 1106 (NJ 2000) (in allowing an age discrimination suit against Illinois by an employee stationed in a New Jersey revenue office, noting that the plaintiff could have sued in Illinois courts but had failed to comply with the 180-day requirement for bringing claims), cert denied, 531 US 818 (2000); compare *Radley v Transit Authority of Omaha*, 486 NW2d 299 (Iowa 1992) (not requiring compliance with Nebraska notice requirements for suit against a city transit authority when Iowa lacked similar requirements).

[152] See, for example, *Perrino v Yeager*, 1991 Conn Super LEXIS 2211 (in an auto accident case, stating that it would be repugnant to state policy to apply Texas's $250,000/$500,000 limits where Connecticut had none); *Kent County v Shepherd*, 713 A2d 290 (Del 1998) (rejecting Maryland's $50,000 limit on liability for auto accident in Delaware); compare *Reynolds v Lancaster County Prison*, 739 A2d 413 (NJ Super Ct App Div 1999) (in case against a local government entity of Pennsylvania, holding that application of the Pennsylvania $500,000 limit would be against New Jersey public policy).

[153] See, for example, *Solomon v Supreme Court of Florida*, 816 A2d 788 (DC 2002) (in defamation claim against, *inter alia*, the state bar for suspension of attorney while the bar was meeting in the District of Columbia, recognizing the absolute immunity for the bar where the disciplinary agents of the District of Columbia bar would receive absolute immunity); *Clement v Indiana*, 524 NE2d 36 (Ind Ct App 1988) (according immunity to Kentucky entities and state and local officials where both states had immunity and operated under the Uniform Act of Fresh Pursuit); compare *Hansen v Scott*, 687 NW2d 247 (ND 2004) (according immunity to Texas Department of Corrections officials sued individually in connection with a murder in North Dakota by a Texas parolee where North Dakota officials would be immune under similar circumstances).

v Illinois, the Iowa court took jurisdiction over a suit against Illinois alleging that it had negligently maintained part of a bridge that was in Iowa, and refused to apply Illinois's $100,000 liability limit.[154]

A forum's applying to a defendant state the same rules as it would apply to the forum state may sound reasonable even if it leads to taking jurisdiction and defendant-state liability. But while the forum purports to apply its own law as to suits against governmental entities, it implicitly ignores a part of forum law that coincides with the defendant state's law (and as to which there is arguably no true conflict): a preference or requirement that governmental entities be sued in their home forums. And as to other issues, state courts' assertions that they would allow actions to go forward against their own states in the same circumstances have sometimes been rather questionable.[155] For example, in *Hyatt*, the United States Supreme Court lauded the Nevada court's supposedly sensitive application of conflicts law in holding that California would be immune, as would Nevada, for negligence but not intentional torts. The Nevada court, however, without citation treated the suit for a bad faith tax investigation as unaffected by the administrative exhaustion requirements for tax cases in both states.[156]

---

[154] 322 NW2d 84 (Iowa 1982).

[155] Compare *Laconis v Burlington County Bridge Comm'n*, 583 A2d 1218 (Pa Super Ct 1990) (where accident occurred due to accumulation of water on a Pennsylvania road (PennDot Road), holding the New Jersey county bridge commission liable where the commission operated the interstate bridge that led up to the road and had previously tried to correct the problems of water accumulation on PennDot Road); id at 1223 (also disallowing an appeal of the district court's disallowing the commission to join Pennsylvania as a defendant due to the commission's failure to take an interlocutory appeal). But see *Flamer v New Jersey Transit Bus Operations*, 607 A2d 260 (Pa Super Ct 1992) (distinguishing *Laconis* and dismissing a suit by Pennsylvania residents injured on a New Jersey bus in New Jersey without prejudice to refiling in New Jersey, and noting that both states had damages limits).

[156] The Nevada Supreme Court treated the case as separate from the California administrative case, such that administrative exhaustion requirements could be ignored. *Franchise Tax Board of California v Eighth Judicial District Court of Nevada*, 2002 Nev LEXIS 57, at *8; compare *Malecon Tobacco v Department of Taxation*, 59 P3d 474, 475–77 (Nev 2002) (requiring exhaustion of administrative remedies in a tax case, and noting exceptions for facial constitutional challenges and futility); *County of Washoe v Golden Road Motor Inn*, 777 P2d 358, 359–60 (Nev 1989) (holding that the lower court lacked subject matter jurisdiction over claims of incorrect assessment as to some tax years due to lack of exhaustion, and affirming the assessments as to other years by a standard that the taxpayer must show clear and convincing evidence that the valuation was "unjust and inequitable"); id at 360 (indicating that the taxpayer could only meet this burden if "the state board applied a fundamentally wrong principle or refused to exercise its best judgment, or that

Similarly, in *Mianeck v Second Judicial District Court*,[157] the Nevada Supreme Court allowed a suit against the Wisconsin Department of Corrections for not warning the people with whom a parolee went to live that the parolee had been convicted of child molestation. The Nevada Court decided that the case involved operational rather than discretionary acts such that there would be no immunity were Nevada the defendant.[158] A few years later, by contrast, the same court decided that failure of a Nevada county sheriff's department to respond to a report that a person (who eventually died of exposure) was lying along a roadside in need of assistance was discretionary rather than operational.[159]

Under the third approach, the forum court does not even purport to accord the defendant state the same rules that it would apply to its home state.[160] For example, in *Faulkner v University of Tennessee*, the plaintiff complained that academic officials at the main University of Tennessee campus threatened to withdraw a doctorate he received after participating in a program for NASA employees in Alabama.[161] The university officials offered the plaintiff a hearing upon notifying him of their concerns about his degree, and exhaustion of administrative remedies was required by

---

the assessment was so excessive as to create an implication of fraud and bad faith" (citation omitted)).

[157] 658 P2d 422, 424 (Nev 1983).

[158] Id at 424.

[159] See *Parker v Mineral County*, 729 P2d 491 (Nev 1986). Given disparate Nevada holdings as to the operational versus discretionary distinction, one cannot definitely conclude that the decision against Wisconsin resulted from prejudice, but the party-based grants of federal jurisdiction were intended to obviate both subtle as well as blatant discrimination in state courts. Compare *Maturi v Las Vegas Metropolitan Police Dept.*, 871 P2d 932, 933–34 (Nev 1994) (holding that handcuffing a suspect who alleged he told officers of his back injuries and pain was discretionary rather than operational and therefore immune) with *Nevada v Silva*, 478 P2d 591, 593–94 (Nev 1970) (although suggesting it was a close case, at a time when damages were limited to $25,000, holding that state could be liable for honor prisoner's raping someone, in that the manner in which the camp was supervised was primarily operational).

[160] Compare Laycock, 92 Colum L Rev at 288–305 (cited in note 136) (arguing that equality of states should be a foundational principle of conflicts rules).

[161] 627 So2d 362 (Ala 1992), cert denied, 510 US 1101 (1994). His professors had approved his dissertation, but academic officials at the Tennessee campus later notified him that they had concluded his dissertation lacked original work. 627 So2d at 364; compare *Head v Platte County, Missouri*, 749 P2d 6, 10 (Kan 1988) (in suit against a county and officials for giving information leading to the arrest of the wrong person, indicating that the court would not apply another state's immunity laws, and stating, "We believe that when considering comity, Kansas courts should give primary regard to the rights of its own citizens and persons who are within the protection of this state.").

both Tennessee and Alabama law.[162] The Alabama court never-theless allowed the plaintiff to pursue an Alabama state court action without exhaustion, noting that "[t]he defendant cites no authority for the proposition that Alabama's exhaustion of remedies doctrine would extend to a remedy provided by a foreign agency."[163] The Court also declined to accord any other possible immunities that Alabama courts would have accorded to Alabama, reasoning that Tennessee was neither sovereign nor politically accountable in Alabama, and that Alabama's primary interest was in redress for its own citizens.[164] Similarly in *Peterson v Texas*, the Colorado appellate court refused to grant Texas, when sued for property damages caused by escapees from a youth rehabilitation program, the same immunity it would have given Colorado.[165]

The results in decisions that take the second approach (following the forum's law as to governmental defendants) and third approach (following the forum's law as to private defendants), although defensible under modern conflicts law, do not dispel concerns that a defendant state may suffer hometown justice when another state retains jurisdiction of a case against the defendant state. The first approach discussed above (giving respect to the defendant state's law) generally results in the case proceeding if at all in the defendant state's own courts. Resurrecting a constitutionally based immunity would effectively compel a result similar to the first approach: states could be sued only in their own courts and on their own terms.[166] Plaintiffs could sue individual officers

---

[162] *Faulkner*, 627 So2d at 365; see also id at 366 (Houston dissenting) (arguing that if the failure to exhaust would bar the action in Tennessee, it should bar the action in Alabama).

[163] Id at 365.

[164] Id at 366; compare *Schoeberlein v Purdue University*, 544 NE2d 283, 289 (Ill 1989) (Calvo dissenting) (arguing that Illinois's only harm from failing to recognize Indiana immunity was that other states might fail to recognize Illinois's immunity law).

[165] 635 P2d 241 (Col App 1981); see also *Veroczi v Big Y Foods*, 1997 Conn Super LEXIS 2795, *3 (although the Connecticut Claims Commissioner would have to waive sovereign immunity on particular claims if they were against Connecticut, holding that Florida enjoyed no such immunity in Connecticut).

[166] In the conflicts of law area, scholars have argued for a federal law of conflicts in order to reach a multilateral approach that states cannot reach themselves. See William Baxter, *Choice of Law and the Federal System*, 16 Stan L Rev 1, 1–22 (1963) (arguing for rules based on hypothetical bargains that the states would make in the conflicts context); Allen and O'Hara, 51 Stan L Rev 1011 (cited in note 136) (discussing Baxter's recommendations, including that federal courts should develop choice of law under the Full Faith and Credit Clause and use diversity to foster comparative impairment analysis); Trautman, 41 L & Contemp Prob at 106–08 (cited in note 137) (describing with approval

in appropriate cases,[167] in which case diversity would frequently be an option for the party suing or sued outside his home state. Recognition of sister-state immunity, which relegates plaintiffs who wish to sue a state to the defendant state's courts, might seem to compromise the deterrence and compensation goals of the potential forum state with more liberal liability and damages rules. This may be true, but no more than federal deterrence and compensation goals are compromised by plaintiffs' inability to sue the state itself under Section 1983 and Commerce Clause legislation. In both cases, the clash between one sovereign's regulatory power and another's immunity may be resolved by the ability to sue the

cases in which multistate policies reflecting the needs of the community of jurisdictions involved outweigh domestic law concerns, and arguing that federal common law should operate as a floor or ceiling to implement such multistate policies).

The Court has manifested a preference that officials be sued in their home states. See *LeRoy v Great Western United Corp.*, 443 US 173, 180, 184–85 (1979) (holding that Idaho officials should be sued there, by interpreting then-existing 28 USC § 1391 (b) provision for venue "where the claim arose" as giving the plaintiff discretion to choose between districts only when they were of approximately equal plausibility and not where there was one obvious locus); compare *Pennzoil v Texaco*, 481 US 1, 6–7 (1987) (in case dismissed on abstention grounds, noting that the plaintiffs had filed the suit in the New York federal courts rather than in the Texas [state] courts); *Butterworth v Hill*, 114 US 128 (1885) (holding that the provision of the venue statute that required suits where persons resided or could be found meant that a suit against the Commissioner of Patents had to be in the District of Columbia, and his acceptance of service of a suit in the federal court in Vermont did not waive the venue objection); *Costlow v Weeks*, 790 F2d 1486 (9th Cir 1986) (affirming dismissal for improper venue of a civil rights action brought in Washington federal court against Alaska officials where the events giving rise to the action had occurred primarily in Alaska). But see *Stroman Realty v Antt*, 20 F Supp 2d 1050, 1052–53 (SD Tex 1998) (despite pending Florida enforcement proceedings, taking jurisdiction in Texas over Florida officials who were trying to force the Texas-resident plaintiff who participated in the secondary market for time share condominiums in Florida to comply with Florida's licensing requirements for real estate brokers); *Roussel v Boren*, 1978 US Dist LEXIS 14515 (ED La) (taking jurisdiction over a suit to enjoin Oklahoma officials from enforcing their anti-takeover provisions as to a Louisiana business attempting to take over an Oklahoma insurance company). The Supreme Court's decision in *LeRoy* indicated that *Roussel* was incorrect under then-applicable venue provisions, compare *LeRoy*, 443 US at 185 (indicating the claim arose where the contested law and regulation emanated from) with *Roussel*, 1978 US Dist LEXIS 14515 at *38–39 (indicating the claim arose where the regulatory impact was felt). The *LeRoy* Court, however, declined to rule on the personal jurisdiction issue, 443 US at 180–81; compare Charles A. Wright, Arthur R. Miller, and Edward H. Cooper, 15 *Federal Practice and Procedure* § 3806 (West, 1986) (questioning result in *LeRoy* in light of amendments providing for venue in "a judicial district in which a substantial part of the events . . . giving rise to the claim occurred").

[167] Indeed, some might argue that suit against the officer is a mere formal change, because the state will likely defend and indemnify him in many cases (depending on state law). See, e.g., Vázquez, 109 Yale L J at 1950 (cited in note 12) (stating that de jure officer liability is likely to mean de facto state liability). While this may often be true, the state will at least have the advantage of not being the named deep-pocket defendant before a jury. To the extent indemnification is limited to the sums that a defendant actually pays out on a judgment, the state may be able to limit its exposure.

individual officer for his tortious violations.[168] What is more, recognition of sister-state immunity provides reciprocal benefits to
all states by directing suits against them to their own courts—a
result states might reach if they were to bargain, and indeed, as
argued here, reflects the constitutional bargain.

Conclusion

No one seriously argues that the framers approved of individuals' making states involuntary defendants in the courts of
other states; at most they argue for founding-era inadvertence.
But Article III's provision for state/citizen diversity as well as the
Eleventh Amendment's withdrawal of such jurisdiction for state-
as-defendant suits were both premised explicitly and implicitly on
the states' not being suable in the courts of sister states. The
founding era left in place a structurally coherent scheme whereby
an out-of-state plaintiff could sue a defendant state in its own
courts according to the defendant state's consent, or the plaintiff
could sue the officer. In the latter case, federal diversity jurisdiction
would often be an available option, and out-of-staters frequently
did sue officers in the federal courts of the officer's home state.
Restoring state sovereign immunity in the courts of other states
would reinstate this sensible jurisdictional allocation.

---

[168] Officer immunities may bar suits in some cases, but this is also true as to federal
constitutional suits under Section 1983.

JONATHAN F. MITCHELL

APPRENDI'S DOMAIN

Recent Supreme Court decisions have extended the Sixth Amendment right of jury trial to some, but not all, disputed factual questions at sentencing. *Apprendi v New Jersey*,[1] for example, held that the jury right attaches to any sentencing factor (other than recidivism) that increases the maximum allowable punishment for a crime. That means that if the law normally provides a ten-year maximum sentence for a firearms offense, but a "sentencing factor" raises that ceiling to thirty years in cases where the defendant used the firearm to commit murder, a jury must resolve that sentencing enhancement. At the same time, the Court has refused to extend the jury right to "mitigating" sentencing factors.[2] So if the law provides a thirty-year maximum sentence for the aforementioned firearms offense, which drops to ten years if the defendant shows that he did *not* use the firearm to commit murder, the jury need not resolve that factual issue. And the Court has similarly refused to extend the jury right to facts that mandate minimum sentences without increasing the maximum allowable punishment.[3]

Jonathan F. Mitchell is Visiting Assistant Professor, University of Chicago Law School.

AUTHOR'S NOTE: Thanks to Stephanos Bibas, Josh Bowers, Richard Epstein, Toby Heytens, Orin Kerr, Alison LaCroix, Jessica Lowe, Tom Miles, Trevor Morrison, Adam Mortara, Eric Posner, Nicholas Quinn Rosenkranz, Jacqueline Ross, David Strauss, and Cass Sunstein for helpful comments on earlier drafts, and to Nathan Cardon for outstanding research assistance. I wrote portions of this article while I was a visiting researcher at Georgetown University Law Center, and I am grateful to Associate Dean Lawrence Gostin and the Law Center for accommodating me during that time. Errors are mine alone.

[1] 530 US 466 (2000).

[2] Id at 490 n 16.

[3] See *Harris v United States*, 536 US 545 (2002).

These court decisions fail to provide a coherent or sensible rule for distributing power between judge and jury. This is because the Supreme Court has inexplicably decided that all facts subject to the Sixth Amendment jury requirement must also be proved beyond a reasonable doubt, and charged in indictments in federal prosecutions, as if they were "elements" of substantive crimes. Because previous cases had limited the Court's proof-beyond-a-reasonable-doubt requirement to the "elements" of substantive offenses, this has produced a jurisprudence in which the jury right, like the reasonable-doubt rule, attaches only to "elements" of crimes or their "functional equivalents." So when *Apprendi* extended the jury right to sentencing facts that increase a defendant's maximum allowable punishment, the Court simultaneously held that such facts were "functional equivalent[s] of [ ] element[s],"[4] which prosecutors must prove beyond a reasonable doubt. And when the Court refused to extend the jury right to other sentencing facts, it based those decisions on its view that such facts are not "elements" of crimes subject to the Court's proof-beyond-a-reasonable-doubt requirement.[5]

This tie-in arrangement between the jury right and the proof-beyond-a-reasonable-doubt requirement is mistaken. The right of jury trial should extend well beyond the "elements" of crimes (and their "functional equivalents") and should encompass all disputed questions of fact that purport to aggravate *or mitigate* a defendant's guilt or punishment. But the courts should not necessarily require that these jury facts be charged by prosecutors or proved beyond a reasonable doubt as if they were "elements" of substantive crimes. Indeed, *Apprendi*'s historical claim that sentencing enhancements were treated as "elements" of offenses whenever they increased a defendant's maximum punishment is demonstrably mistaken. And the platitudes from Joel Prentiss Bishop's nineteenth-century treatises,[6] which the pro-*Apprendi* Justices repeatedly invoke to support

---

[4] *Apprendi*, 530 US at 494 n 19; see also id at 483 n 10 ("Put simply, facts that expose a defendant to a punishment greater than that otherwise legally prescribed were by definition 'elements' of a separate legal offense.").

[5] See *Harris*, 536 US at 549 (plurality opinion) (holding that sentencing factors that establish mandatory minimums "are not elements, and are *thus not subject to the Constitution's . . . jury . . . requirements*") (emphasis added); *McMillan v Pennsylvania*, 477 US 79, 93 (1986) (refusing to extend the right of jury trial to a "sentencing consideration" because it is "not an element of any offense").

[6] See, e.g., Joel Prentiss Bishop, 1 *Criminal Procedure* § 81 at 51 (Little, Brown, 2d ed

this assertion,[7] are patently false and did not accurately describe the law in actual court decisions of that era.[8] Nineteenth-century courts repeatedly held that first-degree murder did not need to be charged in indictments as an "element" of a substantive crime, even though it increased a defendant's maximum allowable punishment from life imprisonment to death, and even though it was decided by juries. These court decisions instead regarded first- and second-degree murder as mere grades of punishment within the unitary offense of murder, and enforced a jury right that extended well beyond the facts that prosecutors were required to charge and prove as components of a substantive crime. The Court should therefore reaffirm and expand *Apprendi*'s Sixth Amendment holding, and overrule its reasonable-doubt holding and its corresponding implication that all "jury facts" must be treated as "elements" of substantive crimes.

I

The federal Constitution granted judges significant powers, including life tenure and salary protection, but did so with the understanding that a strong jury right would limit judicial power. To that end, the Sixth Amendment provides that "[i]n all criminal prosecutions, the accused shall enjoy the right to a speedy and public trial, by an impartial jury of the state and district wherein the crime shall have been committed."[9] But once the Supreme Court in *Apprendi* resolved to extend this jury right to certain factual disputes at sentencing, it became hard to justify a regime that limits the jury right to a subset of those factual issues. Numerous sources from before, during, and after the nation's founding indicate that the scope of the jury right hinged on the distinction between questions of fact and questions of law, not on whether a fact might "aggravate" or "mitigate" a defendant's guilt or punishment, or on whether it qualifies as an "element" of a crime.

One must first understand how the Constitution's text and early

---

1872) (cited hereafter as "Bishop") (stating that nineteenth-century indictments were required to include "every fact which is legally essential to the punishment").

[7] See *Apprendi*, 530 US at 489 n 15 (citing 1 Bishop at § 81 at 51) (cited in note 6); id at 510 (Thomas, J, concurring), quoting 1 Bishop at § 81 at 51 (cited in note 6); see also *Blakely v Washington*, 542 US 296, 301–02 (2004), quoting 1 Bishop at § 87 at 55 (cited in note 6).

[8] See Section V.

[9] See US Const, Amend VI. See also US Const, Art III, § 2 ("The trial of all crimes, except in cases of impeachment, shall be by jury").

American practice regarded the criminal jury as a structural mechanism designed to limit the power of individual judges and preserve
popular participation in the judiciary.[10] Article III of the Constitution provided that "[t]he trial of all crimes, except in cases of
impeachment, *shall be by jury*," and this was originally understood
as providing a nonwaivable jury in federal criminal trials.[11] Many
state constitutions were likewise understood to provide a nonwaivable jury in felony criminal cases,[12] which defendants could avoid
only by pleading guilty and waiving their entire right to trial.[13] In
refusing to permit criminal defendants to consent to bench trials,
courts noted that such trials would confer power on judges beyond
that which the law allowed,[14] sometimes even describing the jury's

---

[10] See Akhil Reed Amar, *The Bill of Rights as a Constitution*, 100 Yale L J 1131, 1182–99
(1991); Vikram David Amar, *Jury Service as Political Participation Akin to Voting*, 80 Cornell
L Rev 203, 218 (1995); Herbert J. Storing, *What the Anti-Federalists Were For* 19 (Chicago,
1981) (describing the jury as a means to preserve "the role of the people in the *administration* of government"). See also John Adams, 2 *The Works of John Adams* 253 (Little,
Brown, 1850) (Charles F. Adams, ed) (diary entry, Feb 12, 1771) ("[T]he common people
[ ] should have as complete a control" over the judiciary as over the legislature); Letter
from Thomas Jefferson to L'Abbé Arnoux (July 19, 1789), reprinted in Thomas Jefferson,
15 *The Papers of Thomas Jefferson* 282, 283 (Princeton, 1958) (Julian Boyd, ed) ("Were I
called upon to decide whether the people had best be omitted in the Legislative or Judiciary
department, I would say it is better to leave them out of the Legislative."); Letters From
The Federal Farmer (XV), in Herbert J. Storing, ed, 2 *The Complete Anti-Federalist* 320
(Chicago, 1981) (writing that the jury "secure[s] to the people at large, their just and
rightful controul in the judicial department"); Letters From The Federal Farmer (IV), in
id at 249 ("It is essential in every free country, that common people should have a part
and share of influence, in the judicial as well as in the legislative department."); Alexis de
Tocqueville, 1 *Democracy in America* 293–94 (Vintage, 1945) ("The institution of the jury
. . . places the real direction of society in the hands of the governed, . . . and not in that
of the government. . . . The jury system as it is understood in America appears to me to
be as direct and as extreme a consequence of the sovereignty of the people as universal
suffrage.").

[11] See *Thompson v Utah*, 170 US 343, 353–54 (1898).

[12] See, e.g., *Harris v People*, 21 NE 563, 565 (Ill 1889); *Cancemi v People*, 18 NY 128,
138 (1858); *Hill v People*, 16 Mich 351, 355–59 (1868); *State v Lockwood*, 43 Wis 403, 405
(1877); *State v Ellis*, 60 P 136, 137–38 (Wash 1900); *State v Mansfield*, 41 Mo 470, 479
(1867); *Michaelson v Beemer*, 101 NW 1007, 1008 (Neb 1904).

[13] Cf. John H. Langbein, *On the Myth of Written Constitutions: The Disappearance of
Criminal Jury Trial*, 15 Harv J L & Pub Pol 119, 121 (1992) (noting that criminal defendants could waive the right to jury trial by pleading guilty).

[14] See, e.g., *Harris v People*, 21 NE 563, 564 (Ill 1889) ("But while a defendant may
waive his right to a jury trial [by pleading guilty], he can not by such waiver confer
jurisdiction to try him upon a tribunal which has no such jurisdiction by law. . . . For
the trial of felonies the judge alone is not the court. The judicial functions brought into
exercise in such trials are parceled out between him and the jury, and so long as there is
no law authorizing it, the functions to be exercised by the jury might just as well be
transferred, by agreement of the parties, to the clerk or sheriff as to the judge."); *Cancemi
v People*, 18 NY 128, 138 (1858) (holding the right of jury trial nonwaivable on the ground
that "the trial must be by the tribunal and in the mode which the constitution and laws

role in jurisdictional terms.[15] Nonwaivability was a paradigmatic example of how the criminal jury was understood to limit the power of individual judges.[16]

The idea of a nonwaivable criminal jury eventually fell out of fashion.[17] But this trend did not repudiate, nor is it inconsistent with, the idea that the criminal jury plays an important structural role in limiting judicial power and preserving popular control in the judiciary. Rather, it is best seen as an allowance that a defendant's right *not* to be tried by a jury (perhaps rooted in due process, or a broader autonomy principle) may trump the structural dimension of the jury guarantee. Indeed, the Supreme Court has made clear that the jury right, even at the state level, continues to serve systemic values beyond protecting individual defendants. In *Taylor v Louisiana*,[18] for example, the Court held that excluding women from juries violated a *male* defendant's Sixth Amendment right of jury trial. It allowed the defendant to challenge his conviction if his jury had not been drawn from "a fair cross section of the community,"[19] even if the juror exclusions skewed the jury pool in favor of the defendant's race, sex, or social class, and without regard to whether

---

provide."); *State v Mansfield*, 41 Mo 470, 478 (1867) ("His right to be tried by a jury of twelve men is not a mere privilege; it is a positive requirement of the law. . . . [H]e has no power to consent to the creation of a new tribunal unknown to the law to try his offence.").

[15] See, e.g., *Morgan v People*, 26 NE 651 (Ill 1891) ("Consent of the defendant . . . can not confer jurisdiction upon the judge, or dispense with a finding of the fact of guilt before a jury."); *Neales v State*, 10 Mo 498, 500 (1847) ("It is exclusively the province of a jury to try the issue of not guilty, and the consent of the defendant for the court to try the same [ ] cannot confer such power on the court."); *Craig v State*, 30 NE 1120, 1122 (Ohio 1892) ("[T]he court of common pleas had no authority to try the case without [a jury]. It was a mode of trial unknown to the law. The legislature had not clothed the court with that form of jurisdiction, and no act or consent of the accused could create or confer a jurisdiction not established by law."); see also Charles Hughes, *Hughes' Criminal Law* § 2979, at 776 (Bowen-Merrill, 1901) ("A jury cannot be waived in a felony case—even by agreement or consent of the defendant. It is jurisdictional, and consent can never confer jurisdiction."); Stewart Rapalje, *A Treatise on Criminal Procedure* § 151, at 227 (Bancroft-Whitney, 1889) ("A trial without jury is a trial without jurisdiction.").

[16] See John Proffatt, *A Treatise on Trial by Jury* § 113, at 157 (S. Whitney, 1877) ("[T]he constitutional provisions do not concede the right to waive the jury in criminal cases; for it is deemed, in such cases there are more than personal interests involved, that the rights and interests of the public are also concerned.").

[17] See, e.g., *Patton v United States*, 281 US 276, 298–99 (1930) (allowing criminal bench trials in Article III courts); Susan C. Towne, *The Historical Origins of Bench Trial for Serious Crime*, 26 Am J Legal Hist 123, 145 (1982).

[18] 419 US 522 (1975).

[19] Id at 527.

such exclusions were harmless.[20] In so holding the Court relied on the jury's role as an instrument of popular sovereignty; excluding groups from jury duty was "at war with our basic concepts of a democratic society and representative government."[21]

Only until very recently, it was widely understood that criminal juries served these structural functions by preventing trial judges from resolving disputed questions of fact. William Blackstone declared that "[t]he principles and axioms of law . . . should be deposited in the breasts of the judges. . . . But in settling and adjusting a question of fact . . . a competent number of sensible and upright jurymen . . . will be found the best investigators of truth and the surest guardians of public justice."[22] And Lord Coke wrote that "ad quaestionem facti non respondent judices [judges do not answer a question of fact] . . . ad quaestionem juris non respondent juratores [jurors do not answer a question of law]."[23] Section nine of the Judiciary Act of 1789 also embraced this view of the criminal jury's role. After establishing exclusive jurisdiction in the federal district courts over certain crimes and offenses, the Act provided that "*the trial in issues of fact,* in the district courts, in all causes except civil causes of admiralty and maritime jurisdiction, *shall be by jury.*"[24] And while opinion at the time of the Founding was divided as to whether the criminal jury should also decide questions of law,[25]

---

[20] Id at 538–39 (Rehnquist, J, dissenting) (protesting that the Court had reversed a conviction "without a suggestion, much less a showing, that the appellant has been unfairly treated or prejudiced in any way by the manner in which his jury was selected.").

[21] Id at 527 (quoting *Smith v Texas*, 311 US 128, 130 (1940)). See also *Blakely v Washington*, 542 US 296, 305–06 (2004) (describing the jury right as "no mere procedural formality, but a fundamental reservation of power in our constitutional structure. Just as suffrage ensures the people's ultimate control in the legislative and executive branches, jury trial is meant to ensure their control in the judiciary"); *Georgia v McCollum*, 505 US 42 (1992) (holding that criminal defendants may not use preemptory challenges in a racially discriminatory manner, even if a defendant would benefit from doing so).

[22] See William Blackstone, 3 *Commentaries on the Laws of England* *380 (Chicago, 1979).

[23] See, e.g., Edward Coke, 1 *Commentary on Littleton* § 155b (J. & W. T. Clarke, 19th ed 1832); see also Edward Wynne, 3 *Eunomus: or Dialogues Concerning the Law and Constitution of England* 217 § 53 (B. White, 2d ed 1785); *R. v Poole*, 95 Eng Rep 15, 18 (KB 1734); Welsh S. White, *Fact-Finding and the Death Penalty: The Scope of a Capital Defendant's Right to Jury Trial*, 65 Notre Dame L Rev 1, 4 (1989).

[24] Judiciary Act of 1789 § 9, 1 Stat 73, 77 (1789) (emphases added).

[25] Compare Federal Farmer (XV), Storing, 7 *The Complete Anti-Federalist* at 319–20 (cited in note 10) (arguing that criminal juries should have the right to "decide both as to law and fact, whenever blended together in the issue put to them"); with Thomas Jefferson, Letter to the L'Abbé Arnoux (July 19, 1789) (cited in note 10) (arguing that juries "are not qualified to judge questions of law"). See also Mark Howe, *Juries as Judges of Criminal Law*, 52 Harv L Rev 582 (1939).

no one ever suggested that trial judges should displace the jury's role in resolving factual disputes. Many state criminal codes expressly provided that juries were to resolve disputed questions of fact,[26] and early state-court decisions similarly described the criminal jury's role as extending beyond the elements of crimes to include all disputed questions of fact, leaving judges to decide questions of law.[27]

The Supreme Court of the United States continued to endorse this view of the criminal jury throughout the early twentieth century. Even when it rejected the "nonwaivable" jury in *Patton v United States*,[28] the Court emphasized that the jury's constitutional role presumptively extends to all issues of fact.[29] And several modern court decisions recognized that criminal juries should resolve disputed questions of fact, even when such facts do not qualify as "elements" of crimes.[30] Most significantly, a 1961 opinion by Judge Henry Friendly extended the Sixth Amendment jury right beyond "elements" to sentencing factors that mitigate a defendant's sentence. In that case, *United States v Kramer*,[31] the relevant statute

---

[26] See, e.g., Iowa Code § 4439 (1873); Dig Stat Ark, ch 52 § 149 (1848); Mo Rev Stat, ch 138, art 6, § 1 (1845); 7 Tex Crim Proc, art 676 (1879); Stat Okla (Terr), ch 68, art 10, § 4 (1893); Cal Stat 255 § 398 (1851); Gen Laws Kan, ch 32, § 215 (1862); Or Rev Stat 264, at ch 37, § 2 (1855).

[27] See *Commonwealth v Porter*, 51 Mass 263, 276 (1845) (opinion of Shaw, CJ); *Commonwealth v Anthes*, 71 Mass 185, 198 (1855) (opinion of Shaw, CJ); *Duffy v People*, 26 NY 588, 595 (1863); *Harris v People*, 21 NE 563, 563 (Ill 1889); *Commonwealth v Garth*, 30 Va 761, 762 (1827); *Townsend v State*, 2 Blackf 151, 157–58 (Ind 1828); *People v Barthleman*, 52 P 112, 114 (Cal 1898); *State v Hudspeth*, 51 SW 483, 487 (Mo 1899); *State v Dickinson*, 55 P 539, 541 (Mont 1898); *State v Magers*, 57 P 197, 201 (Or 1899); *State v Lightfoot*, 78 NW 41, 44 (Iowa 1899); *People v Cignarle*, 17 NE 135, 140 (NY 1888). See also *State v Spayde*, 80 NW 1058, 1059 (Iowa 1899); *McCullough v State*, 34 SW 753, 754 (Tex Ct Crim App 1896).

[28] 281 US 276 (1930).

[29] Id at 312 ("Trial by jury is the normal and, with occasional exceptions, the preferable mode of disposing of issues of fact in criminal cases above the grade of petty offense."). See also *Dimick v Shiedt*, 293 US 474, 485–86 (1934); *Quercia v United States*, 289 US 466, 469 (1933).

[30] See, e.g., *Ake v Oklahoma*, 470 US 68, 81 (1985) (stating that juries are to be "primary factfinders" on the issue of a criminal defendant's psychiatric condition); *Sherman v United States*, 356 US 369, 377 (1958) (noting the unanimous view of the federal courts of appeals that entrapment defenses fall within the jury's purview); *United States v Southwell*, 432 F3d 1050 (9th Cir 2006) (holding that a criminal defendant has a constitutional right to a unanimous jury verdict on the affirmative defense of insanity). See also *United States v Jackalow*, 66 US 484, 487 (1861) (holding that the jury should determine whether a criminal offense was committed out of the jurisdiction of a state, because it was "not a simple question of law").

[31] 289 F2d 909 (2d Cir 1961).

provided that anyone convicted of theft of United States property "[s]hall be fined not more than $10,000 or imprisoned not more than ten years, or both; *but if the value of such property does not exceed the sum of $100*, he shall be fined not more than $1,000 or imprisoned not more than one year, or both."[32] The court recognized that the value of the property was not an "element of the crime," but rather was a "fact going only to the degree of punishment."[33] Nevertheless, Judge Friendly's opinion held that the district court should instruct the jury to determine not only whether Kramer was guilty of "the offense charged," but also whether the property had a value of in excess of $100.[34] The Court simply took for granted the proposition that "the Sixth Amendment entitles a defendant to have that fact determined by the jury rather than by the sentencing judge."[35]

Given the jury's structural role in limiting judicial power, and the authorities from the eighteenth through the twentieth centuries holding that juries served this function by keeping judges from deciding questions of fact, the most natural response for the *Apprendi* Court was to extend the Sixth Amendment jury right to *any* disputed factual question that aggravates or mitigates a defendant's guilt or punishment. But the Supreme Court did not adopt this approach, because it had unwittingly tied the jury right to its proof-beyond-a-reasonable-doubt requirement, which attaches only to "elements" of crimes. Section II discusses the Court's reasonable-doubt jurisprudence and explains why the Court's "elements" test, which defines the scope of the reasonable-doubt rule, should not similarly define the scope of the Sixth Amendment jury guarantee.

II

A

Long before *Apprendi*, the Supreme Court held that the Due Process Clause requires prosecutors to prove certain facts beyond a reasonable doubt in criminal prosecutions.[36] But the Court did not extend this requirement to every question of fact that affects

---

[32] Id at 920 n 8 (emphasis added) (quoting 18 USC § 641 (1994) (modified 1994)).

[33] 289 F2d at 921.

[34] Id.

[35] Id.

[36] See, e.g., *In re Winship*, 397 US 358, 364 (1970).

a defendant's guilt or punishment. *Martin v Ohio*,[37] for example, upheld a state's requirement that criminal defendants prove self-defense, an "affirmative defense" that absolves defendants of guilt. *Patterson v New York*[38] approved a statute that required murder defendants to prove that they killed while acting "under the influence of extreme emotional disturbance for which there was a reasonable explanation or excuse."[39] This "mitigating circumstance," if proved, would reduce the crime from murder to first-degree manslaughter.[40] And *McMillan v Pennsylvania*[41] refused to extend the Court's proof-beyond-a-reasonable-doubt requirement to "sentencing considerations" that were not components of a substantive crime.

All these decisions limited the constitutional reasonable-doubt rule to facts characterized as "elements."[42] "Elements" are facts that the prosecution must establish in every case to secure a conviction for a criminal "offense."[43] Facts on which a criminal defendant must offer evidence, by contrast, did not qualify as "elements." An "affirmative defense," for example, is an issue on which a defendant bears the burden of production; the prosecutor need not offer any proof unless the accused produces enough evidence to put the fact in issue.[44] "Mitigating circumstances" are facts on which a criminal defendant rather than the government carries the burden of persuasion.[45] And facts that affect only a defendant's sentence, rather than his guilt or innocence of an offense, also did not qualify as "elements" of a substantive crime.

Because legislatures define the substantive criminal law, this

---

[37] 480 US 229 (1987).

[38] 432 US 197 (1977).

[39] Id at 206, 218–19 (quoting NY Penal Law § 125.25(1)(a) (McKinney 2006)).

[40] NY Penal Law § 125.20(2) (McKinney 2006).

[41] 477 US 79 (1986).

[42] See *Martin*, 480 US at 233–34; *Patterson*, 432 US at 210; *McMillan*, 477 US at 85–86.

[43] See, e.g., *Richardson v United States*, 526 US 813, 817 (1999). See also *Black's Law Dictionary* 559 (West, 8th ed 2004) (defining "element" as "[a] constituent part of a claim that must be proved for the claim to succeed").

[44] See Model Penal Code § 1.12(2) (ALI 1962). Once the accused satisfies his burden of production, then the burden of *persuasion* might rest with either the prosecution or the defense. See id at § 1.12(4).

[45] See, e.g., 18 USC § 3593(c) (2000 & Supp 2002) (providing that capital defendants must establish mitigating factors by a preponderance of the information); *United States v Washman*, 128 F3d 1305, 1307 (9th Cir 1997) ("The defendant has the burden of proof with respect to any sentence reduction based upon a mitigating factor.").

proof-beyond-a-reasonable-doubt requirement amounted to little more than a default rule that legislatures could avoid by characterizing facts as affirmative defenses, mitigating circumstances, or sentencing considerations. If a jurisdiction wanted to amend its statutory-rape laws so that guilt or punishment would depend on the perpetrator's knowledge of the victim's age, it could make such knowledge an "element" of the crime, which would trigger the Court's reasonable-doubt rule. But it could instead opt to establish the defendant's *lack* of knowledge as an "affirmative defense" or a "mitigating circumstance" that would not implicate the Court's proof-beyond-a-reasonable-doubt requirement.[46] Or it might enact a "sentencing factor" that requires higher minimum penalties in cases where the defendant knew the victim was underage. That would likewise avoid the Court's reasonable-doubt rule.

The Supreme Court recognized that legislatures might go to extremes in structuring their criminal codes to evade the proof-beyond-a-reasonable-doubt requirement,[47] and emphasized that "there are obviously constitutional limits beyond which the States may not go" in this regard.[48] The Court insisted that every crime contain at least one "element" subject to the reasonable-doubt standard,[49] though it did not further specify these "obvious[] constitutional limits" on legislative attempts to avoid the Court's reasonable-doubt rule. The Court did, however, acknowledge the obvious: That the "applicability of the reasonable-doubt standard" has "always been dependent on how a State defines the offense that is charged in any given case."[50]

B

Several commentators have criticized this formalism in the

---

[46] See, e.g., 18 USC § 2243(a), (c) (2000 & Supp 2006) (criminalizing consensual sexual acts with minors under the age of sixteen and at least four years younger than the defendant, yet providing that in such prosecutions, "it is a defense, which the defendant must establish by a preponderance of the evidence, that the defendant reasonably believed that the other person had attained the age of 16 years").

[47] See *Patterson*, 432 US at 210–11 & n 12.

[48] See id at 210.

[49] See id (stating that a legislature cannot "declare an individual guilty or presumptively guilty of a crime," and cannot "create a presumption of all of the facts essential to guilt") (quoting *McFarland v American Sugar Rfg. Co.*, 241 US 79, 86 (1916), and *Tot v United States*, 319 US 463, 469 (1943)).

[50] See 432 US at 211 n 12.

Court's reasonable-doubt jurisprudence, and have urged the Court to expand the reasonable-doubt rule beyond "elements" to include affirmative defenses or mitigating circumstances.[51] But this was not a realistic option for the Supreme Court. First, there was no source of authority for the Court to impose such an expansive reasonable-doubt rule as a constitutional requirement. The Constitution's text does not mention standards of proof in criminal cases, so the Court instead relied on tradition to justify its reasonable-doubt rule as a constitutional due-process requirement.[52] Yet the traditional scope of proof beyond a reasonable doubt was limited. Both English and American law long required criminal defendants to bear some burden of proof on "affirmative defenses" such as insanity and self-defense.[53] Prohibiting this time-honored burden-shifting in the name of a rule found in tradition would be an opportunistic and unprincipled use of tradition as a source of legal authority. This is not, however, a reason to similarly limit the right of jury trial, which has a different historical pedigree. There is no long-standing tradition suggesting that certain categories of facts should be excluded from the jury's factfinding role. Indeed, to the extent that history informs the meaning of the criminal jury guarantee, it suggests that juries should simply resolve "questions of fact," regardless of the standard of proof.[54]

Second, an expansive reasonable-doubt rule could defeat one of the Court's stated purposes for imposing proof beyond a reasonable doubt as a constitutional requirement. When the Court inferred this standard-of-proof requirement from the Due Process Clause, it explained that such a rule was necessary to "command the respect and confidence of the community in applications of

---

[51] See generally Barbara D. Underwood, *The Thumb on the Scales of Justice: Burdens of Persuasion in Criminal Cases*, 86 Yale L J 1299 (1977); Donald A. Dripps, *The Constitutional Status of the Reasonable Doubt Rule*, 75 Cal L Rev 1665 (1987); Scott E. Sundby, *The Reasonable Doubt Rule and the Meaning of Innocence*, 40 Hastings L J 457 (1989).

[52] See, e.g., *Winship*, 397 US at 361–62 (observing that the proof-beyond-a-reasonable-doubt standard "dates at least from our early years as a Nation" and noting the "virtually unanimous adherence to the reasonable-doubt standard in common-law jurisdictions"). But see Anthony A. Morano, *A Reexamination of the Development of the Reasonable Doubt Rule*, 55 BU L Rev 507, 519–24 (1975) (claiming that states did not regularly employ the reasonable-doubt rule until the 1820s, and that many other states did not instruct juries in reasonable-doubt terms until 1850 or later).

[53] See, e.g., Blackstone, 4 *Commentaries* *201 (cited in note 22) (stating that at common law the criminal defendant bore the burden of proving "all [ ] circumstances of justification, excuse or alleviation").

[54] See Section I.

the criminal law."[55] But if the Supreme Court required prosecutors to disprove all affirmative defenses or mitigating facts beyond a reasonable doubt, many jurisdictions would repeal or constrict the scope of existing defenses and be reluctant to recognize new ones. The upshot would be more crude and overinclusive definitions of crimes that do not sufficiently account for mitigating circumstances,[56] forcing less culpable defendants to rely on more capricious and less transparent devices such as prosecutorial discretion or jury nullification. Such an outcome could actually sap public respect for the criminal justice system, contrary to the goals that led the Court to constitutionalize the reasonable-doubt rule in the first place.

But again, these concerns should not necessarily lead to corresponding limits on the scope of the Sixth Amendment jury right. It is doubtful that extending the jury right to affirmative defenses or mitigating facts would tilt the substantive criminal law in a manner that provokes legislative correction. Expanding the jury's factfinding role at the expense of judges would not be likely to increase the odds of acquittal in the way that heightening the government's burden of proof would; indeed, empirical data show that acquittal rates are actually lower in jury trials than in bench trials.[57] But even if the political branches were to respond by removing certain facts from the jury's domain by broadening the scope of criminal liability, such a response would not undermine the purposes of the jury guarantee by, for example, allowing judges to resolve disputed issues of fact. Finally, even if an expansive jury role will hurt some criminal defendants in the long run by provoking legislative responses that broaden substantive crimes or toughen sentences, such considerations should be as irrelevant as they were in *Taylor*, where the Court's decision might have worked to the long-term detriment of criminal defendants, yet the Court

---

[55] *Winship*, 397 US at 364.

[56] See *Patterson*, 432 US at 207–09, 214 n 15.

[57] See, e.g., James P. Levine, *Jury Toughness: The Impact of Conservatism on Criminal Jury Verdicts*, 29 Crime & Delinquency 71, 78, 85–87 (1983) (analyzing nearly 125,000 jury trials and over 50,000 bench trials in federal and state jurisdictions throughout the United States and concluding that juries were more likely to convict than judges); Andrew D. Leipold, *Why Are Federal Judges So Acquittal Prone?* 83 Wash U L Q 151, 152 (2005) (noting that from 1989 to 2002, the average conviction rate in federal court was 84 percent for jury trials, but 55 percent for bench trials).

elided these concerns in its efforts to vindicate popular participation in the judicial branches of government.

Third, when the Constitution allows governments to abolish
affirmative defenses or mitigating circumstances, it is hard to justify a constitutional barrier to regimes that merely ease the government's burden of proof on such facts.[58] But this sort of reasoning, which holds that a legislature's "greater power" to abolish
a defense logically entails the "lesser power" to define the standards of proof, cannot justify similar limits on the right of jury
trial. Because the jury right is a structural right designed to promote popular sovereignty and limit judicial power over factfinding,
there is nothing illogical about insisting that juries determine affirmative defenses or mitigating circumstances while acknowledging a legislature's "greater power" to repeal any such defenses or
mitigating facts. In either case, the principle of popular sovereignty
will be preserved, either by the jury's factfindings, or by the decision of elected officials that an issue should not be relevant in
determining guilt or punishment. On top of that, the Sixth
Amendment's text provides a right of jury trial "in all criminal
prosecutions," no matter how a legislature chooses to define its
substantive criminal law. That a legislature *might* remove facts
from the jury by making the substantive criminal law more harsh
does not render the Sixth Amendment jury right inapplicable when
it provides affirmative defenses and mitigating facts in criminal
prosecutions as a matter of grace. The reasonable-doubt rule, by
contrast, lacks these structural dimensions, and there is no textual
hook in the Constitution that suggests its scope, so it is far more
sensible for the Court to regard it as a default rule, applicable
only to facts characterized as "elements," which avoids the illogical
consequences from a more expansive rule.

Each of these considerations compelled the Court to limit the
reasonable-doubt rule to the "elements" of criminal offenses, but
none of them justifies similar limits on the constitutional jury
guarantee. Yet the Supreme Court's cases have simply assumed
that the jury right, like the reasonable-doubt rule, should attach
only to "elements" of offenses or their "functional equivalents."

---

[58] See *Patterson*, 432 US at 207–08. See also Ronald Jay Allen, *Mullaney v. Wilbur, the
Supreme Court, and the Substantive Criminal Law—an Examination of the Limits of Legitimate
Intervention*, 55 Tex L Rev 269, 284–85 (1977); John Calvin Jeffries, Jr. and Paul B. Stephan
III, *Defenses, Presumptions, and Burden of Proof in the Criminal Law*, 88 Yale L J 1325, 1345
(1979).

Section III explains the origins of this misguided idea and shows how it became the foundation of the Court's *Apprendi* jurisprudence. The culprits are two 1986 Supreme Court decisions: *Cabana v Bullock*[59] and *McMillan v Pennsylvania*.[60]

III

A

In 1986, the Supreme Court issued two decisions that used the concept of "elements" to define the scope of the Sixth Amendment right to "trial [ ] by an impartial jury." The first of these cases, *Cabana v Bullock*, held that the Sixth Amendment did *not* require juries to make "*Enmund* findings" in death-penalty trials.[61] These findings had been required by an earlier Court decision that limited capital punishment to persons who killed, attempted to kill, or intended to kill.[62] The respondents in *Cabana* argued that such *Enmund* findings were "constitutionally equivalent to elements of an offense,"[63] and the Court rejected this contention. But its opinion went further, suggesting that the respondents' Sixth Amendment claim failed *because* the *Enmund* findings were not "elements" of the substantive crime of murder. Wrote the Court:

> A defendant charged with a serious crime has the right to have a jury determine his guilt or innocence. . . . [O]ur ruling in *Enmund* does not concern the guilt or innocence of the defendant—*it establishes no new elements of the crime of murder that must be found by the jury*.[64]

This left an unfortunate implication that the Sixth Amendment jury right extends only to "elements." Yet the Court did not in any way explain why the concept of "elements" should determine the scope of a jury's constitutional factfinding responsibilities.

---

[59] 474 US 376 (1986).

[60] 477 US 79 (1986).

[61] See 474 US 376. The Supreme Court's later decision in *Ring v Arizona*, 536 US 584 (2002), casts doubt on *Cabana*'s continued validity. See notes 109–10 and accompanying text.

[62] See *Enmund v Florida*, 458 US 752, 801 (1982).

[63] Brief for Respondent, *Cabana v Bullock*, No 84-1236, *22 (filed Sept 9, 1985) (available on Lexis at 1984 US Briefs 1236).

[64] *Cabana*, 474 US at 385 (emphasis added).

McMillan v Pennsylvania[65] established a more explicit link between the jury right and the "elements" of crimes subject to the
Court's reasonable-doubt rule. There the Court upheld a state law
that imposed a five-year mandatory minimum sentence in cases
where a judge found, by a preponderance of the evidence, that
the defendant "visibly possessed a firearm" when committing his
crime.[66] The statute insisted that this was not an element of an
offense, but a sentencing factor to be considered only after a defendant's conviction for a predicate crime.[67] Yet the petitioners
maintained that the "visible possession of a firearm" finding was
akin to an element and should therefore be subject to the Court's
reasonable-doubt rule.

The Court rejected this contention, concluding that the "visible
possession of a firearm" should not be treated as an element and
need not be proved beyond a reasonable doubt.[68] It emphasized
that a legislature's definitions of crimes are "usually dispositive,"[69]
and accepted Pennsylvania's characterization of this fact as a "sentencing factor" affecting only the level of punishment for a crime.[70]
The Court mentioned two situations in which legislative designations of "sentencing factors" might present more serious constitutional concerns: First, the Court warned against sentencing
factors that serve as "a tail which wags the dog of a substantive
offense."[71] The Court did not elaborate on the meaning of that
phrase, nor did it provide examples. Second, the Court wrote that
the petitioners' reasonable-doubt claim "would have at least more
superficial appeal" if the "visible possession" finding increased the
maximum allowable punishment for a crime, rather than increasing
only the *minimum* punishment.[72] The Court's overall analysis,
however, recognized considerable legislative control over standards of proof, consistent with prior decisions establishing the
reasonable-doubt requirement as a default rule that legislatures

---

[65] 477 US 79 (1986).

[66] See id at 81 n 1 (quoting 42 Pa Cons Stat § 9712(a) (1982)).

[67] See id at 81 n 1 (quoting 42 Pa Cons Stat § 9712(b) (1995)) ("Provisions of this
section shall not be an element of the crime").

[68] Id at 88.

[69] Id at 85.

[70] Id at 85–86.

[71] Id at 88. See also id at 89–90.

[72] Id at 88.

may avoid by characterizing facts as something other than "elements."

The petitioners in *McMillan* also argued that the Sixth Amendment required a jury to decide whether they "visibly possessed a firearm." But they did *not* base this claim on their earlier argument that this fact was akin to an "element." Instead, the petitioners maintained that the Sixth Amendment jury right should attach to *any* factual determinations concerning the alleged criminal conduct, regardless of whether such facts qualified as "elements" or whether they increased or decreased a defendant's sentence.[73] They conceded that "historical facts" such as a defendant's criminal history need not be submitted to juries because such facts do not pertain to underlying criminal conduct.[74] Indeed, the D.C. Circuit's decision in *Jordan v United States District Court for the District of Columbia*[75] had previously endorsed this distinction between facts relating to "the manner in which a crime was committed" and "historical" facts such as recidivism, requiring juries to determine the former but allowing judges to decide the latter.[76] The petitioners' brief cited that case along with numerous legal authorities supporting the view that juries should resolve disputed questions of fact relating to underlying criminal conduct.[77]

But the *McMillan* Court held, without any analysis, that the right of jury trial extends only to "elements" of crimes, and not to "sentencing factors." Noting its earlier conclusion that the "visual possession of a firearm" finding was not an element, the Court wrote that the petitioners' Sixth Amendment claim "merit[ed] little discussion," and tossed it aside in a perfunctory sentence: "Having concluded that Pennsylvania may properly treat visible possession as a sentencing consideration and not an element of any offense, we need only note that there is no Sixth Amendment right to jury sentencing, even where the sentence turns on specific findings of

---

[73] See, e.g., Brief for Petitioners, *McMillan v Pennsylvania*, No 85-215, *33–38 (filed Dec 2, 1985) (available on Westlaw at 1985 WL 670131).

[74] See id at *33 n 38.

[75] 233 F2d 362 (DC Cir 1956).

[76] Id at 367.

[77] See, e.g., Brief for Petitioners at *35 (cited in note 73) (citing Edward Wynne, 3 *Eunomus, or Dialogues Concerning the Law and Constitution of England* § 53, at 205–07 (1768)); id at *35 n 40 (quoting John Hawles, *The Englishman's Right: A dialogue between a Barrister at Law, and a Juryman* 8 (R. Janeway, 1680)).

fact."[78] This was a woefully inadequate response to the petitioners' argument.

First, the petitioners never asserted anything resembling a "right to jury sentencing." They advanced a more limited and nuanced claim: That the Sixth Amendment required juries to determine all "critical facts" relating to the alleged criminal conduct, as opposed to "historical facts" such as a defendant's character and background. To be sure, some of these "critical facts" may affect the ultimate sentencing decision. In *McMillan*, for example, the "visible possession of a firearm" finding would lead to a minimum five-year prison sentence. But requiring a jury to decide such "critical facts" is a far cry from requiring the jury to choose the ultimate sentence. Indeed, the petitioners' brief expressly disclaimed any constitutional right to jury sentencing, and carefully explained why their argument did not imply such a right.[79] Their argument no more implicated a "right to jury sentencing" than the Supreme Court's holding in *Ring v Arizona*[80] that juries must find statutory aggravating factors in death penalty cases.[81]

Second, the *McMillan* Court gave no reasons for limiting the jury right to the "elements" subject to the Court's reasonable-doubt rule. Its opinion parroted the slapdash analysis in the respondents' brief, which asserted (without reasons or citations) that the Sixth Amendment jury right extends only to "elements" of crimes,[82] and raised the straw man of a right to jury sentencing in response to the petitioners' Sixth Amendment argument.[83] But neither the Court nor the respondents attempted to explain why the "elements" test should define the jury's constitutional fact-finding role. This silence was especially puzzling given that the Second Circuit's *Kramer* opinion, authored by Judge Friendly, had already extended the Sixth Amendment jury right beyond the "el-

---

[78] *McMillan*, 477 US at 93 (citing *Spaziano v Florida*, 468 US 447, 459 (1984)).

[79] See, e.g., Brief for Petitioners at *38 (cited in note 73).

[80] 536 US 584 (2002).

[81] See id at 597 n 4 ("*Ring's* claim is tightly delineated: He contends only that the Sixth Amendment required jury findings on the aggravating circumstances asserted against him. . . . [H]e [does not] argue that the Sixth Amendment required the jury to make the ultimate determination whether to impose the death penalty.") (emphasis added).

[82] See Brief for Respondent, *McMillan v Pennsylvania*, No 85-215, *12–13 (filed Oct 1985) (available on Westlaw at 1985 WL 670135).

[83] See id at *13 ("[T]he relevant inquiry is whether the sixth amendment requires a sentencing jury. It is clear that the sixth amendment carries no such requirement. There is no sixth amendment right to jury sentencing") (citing *Spaziano*, 468 US at 460).

ements" of criminal offenses to "sentencing facts" that affected only a defendant's punishment.[84]

In every case subsequent to *McMillan*, the Justices and the Court's practitioners have labored under its unsupported premise that the jury right is coextensive with the reasonable-doubt rule, attaching only to "elements" of crimes. Several post-*McMillan* decisions, for example, refused to extend the right of jury trial to aggravating factors that render a defendant eligible for capital punishment on the ground that such facts are not "elements" of crimes.[85] And in *Sullivan v Louisiana*,[86] the Court made the connection even more explicit, writing, "It is self-evident, we think, that the Fifth Amendment requirement of proof beyond a reasonable doubt and the Sixth Amendment requirement of a jury verdict are interrelated."[87] *Sullivan* went on to hold that a constitutionally deficient reasonable-doubt instruction violated the defendant's *Sixth Amendment right of jury trial*, because "the jury verdict required by the Sixth Amendment *is a jury verdict of guilty beyond a reasonable doubt*."[88] It did not account for the possibility that the Sixth Amendment might require jury findings on factual issues outside the scope of the reasonable-doubt rule.[89]

Perhaps the most dramatic post-*McMillan* opinion linking the scope of the jury right with the reasonable-doubt rule and the concept of "elements" was Justice Scalia's dissent in *Monge v California*.[90] *Monge* held that a court's refusal to find a sentencing enhancement is not an "acquittal" of an "offense" for purposes of the Double Jeopardy Clause. Justice Scalia's dissent, however, ar-

---

[84] See *United States v Kramer*, 289 F2d 909, 920–21 (2d Cir 1961). See also notes 31–35 and accompanying text.

[85] See, e.g., *Clemons v Mississippi*, 494 US 738, 745–46 (1990); *Hildwin v Florida*, 490 US 638, 639–41 (1989); *Walton v Arizona*, 497 US 639, 647–49 (1990). The Court overruled these cases in *Ring v Arizona*, 536 US 584, 609 (2002) (holding that statutory aggravating factors in death-penalty cases are the "functional equivalent" of "elements," and must therefore be found by a jury) (quoting *Apprendi*, 530 US at 494 n 19).

[86] 508 US 275 (1993).

[87] Id at 278.

[88] Id (emphasis added).

[89] See also *United States v Gaudin*, 515 US 506, 510 (1995) ("[The Fifth and Sixth Amendments] require criminal convictions to rest upon a jury determination that the defendant is guilty of every element of the crime with which he is charged, beyond a reasonable doubt."); id at 511 ("The Constitution gives a criminal defendant the right to demand that a jury find him guilty of all the elements of the crime with which he is charged.").

[90] 524 US 721 (1998).

gued that sentencing enhancements that increase a defendant's maximum allowable sentence are akin to "elements" of a separate, aggravated "crime," and that refusals to find such enhancements represent "functiona[l] acquit[als]" of such crimes.[91] Then he went even further, claiming that the concept of "elements" defined the scope of the Sixth Amendment right of jury trial as well as the Double Jeopardy Clause and the reasonable-doubt rule:

> "The fundamental distinction between facts that are elements of a criminal offense and facts that go only to the sentence provides the foundation for our entire double jeopardy jurisprudence. . . . *The same distinction also delimits the boundaries of other important constitutional rights, like the Sixth Amendment right to trial by jury and the right to proof beyond a reasonable doubt.*"[92]

Justice Scalia's *Monge* dissent presaged the Court's *Apprendi* jurisprudence in two ways. First, it expressly linked the right of jury trial with the reasonable-doubt rule, and limited both to "elements" of "crimes." Second, it sought to give meaningful content to the jury right and other constitutional provisions by setting forth an expansive view of "elements" that does not depend on labels used in criminal codes, and turns instead on whether a fact increases the range of punishment to which a defendant is exposed. Subsection B describes how the Court's *Apprendi* jurisprudence endorsed and expanded on the approach that Justice Scalia urged in *Monge*.

B

Apprendi v New Jersey perpetuated the Supreme Court's link between the jury right and the reasonable-doubt rule. The petitioner had pleaded guilty to a firearms offense that normally carried a maximum penalty of ten years' imprisonment.[93] But the trial court imposed a twelve-year sentence because of New Jersey's hate-crimes law, which increased the maximum allowable sentence to twenty years' imprisonment if a trial judge finds, by a preponderance of the evidence, that the defendant acted with a "purpose

---

[91] See id at 741 (Scalia, J, dissenting).

[92] Id at 738 (Scalia, J, dissenting) (emphasis added).

[93] See NJ Stat Ann § 2C:43-6(a)(2) (West 2006).

to intimidate" an individual because of race.[94] The petitioner protested that this regime violated his right of jury trial and the Court's proof-beyond-a-reasonable-doubt rule.

Once again, the Court proceeded as if the jury right and the reasonable-doubt rule were identical in scope. The Court described its proof-beyond-a-reasonable-doubt requirement as "the companion right" to the right of jury trial,[95] with each extending to the "elements" of crimes: "*Taken together*, these rights indisputably entitle a criminal defendant to 'a jury determination that [he] is guilty *of every element of the crime with which he is charged*, beyond a reasonable doubt.'"[96]

Unlike prior decisions, however, the *Apprendi* Court refused to limit these protections to facts designated as "elements" in criminal codes, an approach that would allow legislatures to circumvent the jury right by redesignating "elements" as "sentencing factors."[97] Instead, the Court decided that the concept of "elements" should depend on *effects* at sentencing rather than labels used in statutes. It claimed that historical practice showed that "facts that expose a defendant to a punishment greater than that otherwise legally prescribed were by definition 'elements' of a separate legal offense."[98] From this observation the Court held that any fact, other than the fact of a prior conviction,[99] that increases the penalty for a crime beyond the "maximum authorized statutory

---

[94] See NJ Stat Ann § 2C:44-3(e) (West 2001) (repealed by 2001 NJ Sess Law Serv 443 (West)).

[95] *Apprendi*, 530 US at 478.

[96] Id at 477 (emphases added) (citations omitted). See also id at 484 (describing the extent of "*Winship*'s due process *and associated jury protections*") (emphasis added); id at 483–84 ("[P]ractice must at least adhere to the basic principles undergirding the requirements of trying to a jury all facts necessary to constitute a statutory offense, and proving those facts beyond reasonable doubt.").

[97] See id at 494 (noting that "[l]abels do not afford an acceptable answer") (citation omitted); see also *Ring*, 536 US at 605 ("[T]he characterization of a fact or circumstance as an 'element' or a 'sentencing factor' is not determinative of the question 'who decides,' judge or jury.").

[98] *Apprendi*, 530 US at 483 n 10. The Court also cited with approval the portions of Justice Thomas's concurrence that argued that courts historically treated such sentencing enhancements as elements of separate, aggravated crimes. Id (citing *Apprendi*, 530 US at 501–04 (Thomas, J, concurring)).

[99] The Court excluded recidivist sentencing enhancements because of its decision in *Almendarez-Torres v United States*, 523 US 224, 226–27 (1998) (holding that 8 USC § 1326(b)(2) (2000), which enhances penalties for recidivist criminals, was not an "element" of a crime and need not be charged in an indictment, even if it increases the maximum punishment that could otherwise be imposed).

sentence" is the *"functional equivalent of* an element of a greater offense,"[100] and must be submitted to a jury and proved beyond a reasonable doubt.[101] The Court distinguished *McMillan*, where the sentencing enhancement increased only the minimum punishment, and did not raise the statutory maximum.[102]

Justice Thomas's concurrence argued for an even broader view of "elements."[103] He agreed that courts should look beyond a legislature's designations, but he thought that "elements" should include any fact established by law as a basis for *imposing or increasing* punishment, even if such facts do not raise the "statutory maximum" punishment.[104] He urged the Court to overrule *McMillan*, because facts establishing mandatory minimums increase a defendant's punishment and should therefore be deemed "elements." But he acknowledged that "fact[s] that mitigat[e] punishment" are not "elements" subject to the constitutional jury or standard-of-proof requirements.[105]

Post-*Apprendi* decisions continued to link the scope of the jury right with the reasonable-doubt rule and the concept of "elements." In *Harris v United States*,[106] the Court reaffirmed *McMillan's* holding that sentencing facts that impose mandatory minimums, without increasing a defendant's maximum allowable punishment, are not "elements" for constitutional purposes, and need not be charged by prosecutors, submitted to juries, or proved beyond a reasonable doubt. The plurality opinion, like *McMillan*, assumed that the jury's constitutional factfinding responsibilities extended only to "elements" of crimes, and did not consider the possibility that they might extend beyond that; the plurality wrote that facts that "are not elements *are thus not subject to the Constitution's . . . jury . . . requirements*."[107] Justice Breyer concurred in the judgment but reiterated his continued disagreement with *Ap-*

---

[100] *Apprendi*, 530 US at 494 n 19 (emphasis added).

[101] Id at 490. See also id at 494 n 19 ("[W]hen the term 'sentence enhancement' is used to describe an increase beyond the maximum authorized statutory sentence, . . . it fits squarely within the usual definition of an 'element' of the offense.").

[102] See id at 487 n 13.

[103] See id at 499–523 (Thomas, J, concurring).

[104] Id at 501 (Thomas, J, concurring).

[105] See id at 500, 501 (Thomas, J, concurring).

[106] 536 US 545 (2002).

[107] Id at 549 (plurality opinion) (emphasis added).

prendi's holding; he claimed that he could not "easily distinguish *Apprendi v New Jersey* from this case."[108] But whatever tension may exist between *Apprendi* and the *Harris* plurality opinion, they have this much in common: Each opinion links the jury right with the reasonable-doubt rule and limits both to the "elements" of crimes or their "functional equivalents."

Three more decisions reaffirmed and clarified the scope of *Apprendi*. *Ring v Arizona*[109] held that aggravating factors that render a defendant eligible for capital punishment are "functional equivalent[s]" of "element[s]," which must be found by a jury beyond a reasonable doubt.[110] *Blakely v Washington*[111] clarified that *Apprendi* applies to any fact that increases the maximum sentence that could be imposed based *solely* on facts found by a jury or admitted by the defendant.[112] Finally, *United States v Booker*[113] found the Federal Sentencing Guidelines unconstitutional to the extent that they allowed judicial factfinding to increase a defendant's maximum allowable penalty. To remedy this constitutional defect, the Court decided to invalidate the statutory provisions that made the Guidelines mandatory.[114] As advisory Guidelines, judicial factfinding would no longer alter "statutory maximum" sentences and would not implicate the *Apprendi* rule. Throughout its opinion, however, the Court reaffirmed and recited *Apprendi*'s formulation that linked the scope of the jury right with the reasonable-doubt rule.[115]

Figure 1 illustrates the Court's current approach to the constitutional jury and standard-of-proof requirements in felony prosecutions. This approach leaves the bottom-left and top-right boxes as null sets.[116] But tying the jury right with the reasonable-doubt

---

[108] Id at 569 (Breyer, J, concurring in the judgment).

[109] 536 US 584 (2002).

[110] Id at 609 (quoting *Apprendi*, 530 US at 494 n 19). This overruled earlier decisions holding that the Sixth Amendment did not require jury findings on such aggravating factors. See note 85.

[111] 542 US 296 (2004).

[112] See id at 303–04 ("In other words, the relevant 'statutory maximum' is not the maximum sentence a judge may impose after finding additional facts, but the maximum he may impose *without* any additional findings.").

[113] 543 US 220 (2005).

[114] Id at 244–68.

[115] See, e.g., id at 230–31, 244.

[116] Because the Supreme Court has held that juries are not required for "petty" offenses, see, e.g., *Blanton v City of North Las Vegas*, 489 US 538 (1989), there may be situations in certain nonfelony prosecutions where the Court's jurisprudence would require proof be-

| Standard of Proof: | Factfinder: | |
	Right to Jury Determination	No Right to Jury
Proof Beyond Reasonable Doubt Required	Elements *"Apprendi* facts" (or "Functional Equivalents" of Elements)	
Less than Proof Beyond Reasonable Doubt Allowed		All Other Sentencing Factors

FIG. 1

rule has created two serious problems in the Court's *Apprendi* jurisprudence. Section IV shows that the Court has failed to provide "intelligible content" to the right of jury trial because it has trapped the jury right within the reasonable-doubt rule's formalism. Because the Court cannot extend the reasonable-doubt rule to affirmative defenses and "mitigating" circumstances, its *Apprendi* jurisprudence excludes "mitigating" sentencing facts from the jury's domain, producing an overly formalistic jury right that is easily evaded by legislatures. Worse, there is no sound basis on which to distinguish "aggravating" from "mitigating" sentencing facts for purposes of the Sixth Amendment jury right. Deciding that a so-called "mitigating" fact has *not* been proved will increase a defendant's sentence from that which would otherwise be imposed, no less than finding that an "aggravating" fact *has* been proved. Section V shows that *Apprendi*'s all-too-limited efforts to expand the jury right have led courts to adopt overbroad and historically indefensible understandings of "elements" and "crimes."

IV

A

Although the Supreme Court claims that *Apprendi* gives "intelligible content to the right of jury trial,"[117] its failure to extend

---

yond a reasonable doubt without requiring a jury determination. But as for felony prosecutions, the Court treats the jury right and the reasonable-doubt rule as coterminous.

[117] *Blakely*, 542 US at 305.

the jury right to facts that *mitigate* punishment allows legislatures and sentencing commissions to continue to shift factfinding power from juries to judges, either by converting "elements" of crimes into affirmative defenses, or by transforming aggravating sentencing facts into mitigators that describe the absence of aggravating conduct.[118] This loophole is a result of the Court's unwillingness to extend the reasonable-doubt rule to such facts, and its unwarranted assumption that the jury right can extend no further.

To see this, suppose a legislature or sentencing commission provided a penalty range of ten to twenty years for a firearms offense, which drops to five to ten years if the defendant proves, by a preponderance of the evidence, that he did *not* act "with a purpose to intimidate an individual or group of individuals because of race." Neither *Apprendi*'s holding nor the more expansive rule urged in Justice Thomas's concurrence would have anything to say about this, even though the judge decides whether the defendant will be exposed to a sentence beyond ten years' imprisonment.[119] The courts would intervene only if they regarded the "purpose to intimidate" issue as a "tail which wags the dog of a substantive offense."[120]

The *Apprendi* Court was unfazed by this scenario. It predicted that the political branches would acquiesce, and would not try to recast sentencing enhancements as "mitigating facts" that describe the absence of aggravating conduct. Such action "seems remote," the Court explained, because "structural democratic constraints" would discourage legislatures or sentencing commissions from evading the jury right in this fashion.[121] For this reason, the Court felt that it was not necessary to extend the jury right to mitigating sentencing facts.

---

[118] See *Apprendi*, 530 US at 540–43 (O'Connor, J, dissenting); *Blakely*, 542 US at 339 (Breyer, J, dissenting); *Jones v United States*, 526 US 227, 267 (1999) (Kennedy, J, dissenting); Frank O. Bowman III, *Beyond Band-Aids: A Proposal for Reconfiguring Federal Sentencing After Booker*, 2005 U Chi Legal F 149, 197 (noting that the conversion of aggravating factors into mitigators "was for some time following *Blakely* the favored option of important decisionmakers in the Justice Department and among some key congressional staff"); Stephanos Bibas, *Originalism and Formalism in Criminal Procedure: The Triumph of Justice Scalia, the Unlikely Friend of Criminal Defendants?* 94 Geo L J 183, 198 (2005) (concluding that *Apprendi* "will not suffice to prevent erosion of" the jury right because it is "remarkably easy to evade").

[119] See *Apprendi*, 530 US at 490 n 16; id at 501 (Thomas, J, concurring).

[120] *McMillan*, 477 US at 88.

[121] *Apprendi*, 530 US at 490 n 16.

The Court's reliance on "structural democratic constraints" as a means to protect the jury's factfinding responsibilities from legislative evasion is not convincing. Any such decision to rely on political safeguards over judicial enforcement of a constitutional norm should be justified by institutional considerations. There must be concrete reasons to believe either that courts are ill-equipped to fully enforce a constitutional principle, or that the political branches will respect a constitutional norm without the courts' help. The Court's reluctance to enforce a strong "nondelegation doctrine," for example, can be defended by institutional difficulties in fashioning a principled judicial doctrine that distinguishes between permissible and impermissible delegations.[122] And court decisions that rely on "political safeguards" to protect norms of constitutional federalism provide specific institutional reasons to be sanguine about Congress's willingness to respect state prerogatives.[123] This sort of institutional analysis is necessary to prevent the concept of "political safeguards" from becoming a convenient cubbyhole into which judges can relegate disfavored constitutional provisions for underenforcement.

Yet the *Apprendi* opinion did not note any institutional problems that might arise if courts were to extend the jury right to mitigating sentencing facts. Although Justice Breyer's dissent asserted that such a regime would be impracticable, on the ground that there are "far too many potentially relevant sentencing factors to permit submission of all (or even many) of them to a jury,"[124] this seems an overstatement. Such regimes are already the norm for capital sentencing; the Federal Death Penalty Act (and many state laws) require jurors to make findings on every relevant mitigating and aggravating factor during the sentencing phase.[125] And the number

---

[122] See, e.g., *Mistretta v United States*, 488 US 361, 415 (1989) (Scalia, J, dissenting) ("[W]hile the doctrine of unconstitutional delegation is unquestionably a fundamental element of our constitutional system, it is not an element readily enforceable by the courts. . . . [W]e have almost never felt qualified to second-guess Congress regarding the permissible degree of policy judgment that can be left to those executing or applying the law."); see also Cass R. Sunstein, *Is the Clean Air Act Unconstitutional?* 98 Mich L Rev 303, 311 (1999) (describing the nondelegation doctrine as a "genuine, but judicially underenforced, constitutional norm").

[123] See, e.g., *Garcia v San Antonio Metropolitan Transit Authority*, 469 US 528, 551 (1985); see generally Herbert Wechsler, *The Political Safeguards of Federalism*, 54 Colum L Rev 543 (1954); Larry D. Kramer, *Putting the Politics Back into the Political Safeguards of Federalism*, 100 Colum L Rev 215 (2000).

[124] *Apprendi*, 530 US at 557 (Breyer, J, dissenting).

[125] See, e.g., 18 USC § 3593(d) (2000).

of mitigating facts in such capital cases is potentially infinite; federal law requires jurors to consider "*any* mitigating factor" beyond the eight enumerated factors in the death-penalty statute.[126] California's Penal Code similarly requires jurors to consider "[a]ny other circumstance which extenuates the gravity of the crime,"[127] which, in one capital case, allowed jury consideration of a dance choreography prize that the defendant received while in prison.[128] The widespread use of such regimes makes it difficult to see any institutional problems with requiring juries to find mitigating sentencing facts along with sentencing enhancements that raise the maximum punishment.

More importantly, the *Apprendi* opinion offered no reasons to believe that political processes will preserve a meaningful factfinding role for the jury, absent a requirement that juries find all disputed sentencing factors, including mitigators. Jury factfinding in criminal sentencing has little political currency. During recent House Judiciary Committee hearings on responses to *Booker*, none of the four witnesses proposed a system in which the jury would play any factfinding role at sentencing.[129] Nor is this surprising. Even William Blackstone, who praised the criminal jury as "the grand bulwark" of English liberties,[130] recognized that jury factfinding produces "inconveniences,"[131] and strong political constituencies naturally coalesce behind more convenient principles such as equality and even-handedness in the criminal justice system. Tough-on-crime politicians want sentencing uniformity and predictability as a means to promote deterrence. And politicians that sympathize with the criminal defense bar, or with criminal suspects, are equally unlikely to advocate a system that produces disparities in criminal punishment. On top of this, the future criminal defendants who might benefit from jury factfinding are unknown, and cannot lobby for an expansive jury right. For all these

---

[126] See 18 USC § 3593(c) (2000 & Supp 2002) (emphasis added). See also 18 USC § 3593(d) (2000).

[127] Cal Penal Code § 190.3(k) (West 2006).

[128] See *Boyde v California*, 494 US 370, 382 n 5 (1990).

[129] See *United States v. Booker: One Year Later—Chaos or Status Quo?* Hearing before the Subcommittee on Crime, Terrorism, and Homeland Security, 109th Cong, 2d Sess (2006); see also Douglas A. Berman, *Tweaking Booker: Advisory Guidelines in the Federal System*, 43 Houston L Rev 341, 371–72 (2006).

[130] Blackstone, 4 *Commentaries* at *342 (cited in note 22).

[131] Id at *343–44.

reasons, the right of jury trial seems an especially poor candidate for reliance on political safeguards or for treatment as an "underenforced constitutional norm."[132]

Apprendi therefore amounts to little more than an option for legislatures or sentencing commissions to choose between jury fact-finding (by creating sentencing facts that purport to "aggravate" a defendant's maximum allowable sentence) or judge fact-finding (by creating "mitigating" sentencing facts that describe the absence of aggravating conduct). Although the reasonable-doubt rule is similarly structured as a default rule that legislatures may evade, in that situation the court could not justify an expansive rule that attaches to "affirmative defenses," or "mitigating circumstances," so an easily evaded standard-of-proof requirement was the lesser of two evils. But the Court's valid reasons for limiting the reasonable-doubt requirement as a default rule do not carry over to the jury right,[133] and it is hard to see how treating the jury right as a default rule is consistent with the Supreme Court's stated goal of giving "intelligible content" to the right of jury trial.

B

Apprendi's conception of the jury right suffers from a more serious problem: There is no coherent basis to distinguish "facts in aggravation of punishment" from "facts in mitigation"[134] for purposes of the right of jury trial. Consider again the hypothetical discussed in subsection A, where conviction for a firearms offense triggers a penalty range of ten to twenty years, which drops to five to ten years if the defendant proves, by a preponderance of the evidence, that he did *not* act "with a purpose to intimidate an individual or group of individuals because of race." This regime is functionally identical to what the Supreme Court nixed in *Apprendi*; in both cases the defendant's maximum sentence will be increased ten years if a judge concludes that it is more likely than not that he acted with a biased purpose to intimidate. The only difference is that the defense (rather than the prosecution) bears the burden of proof on the "purpose to intimidate" issue. But

---

[132] See Lawrence Gene Sager, *Fair Measure: The Legal Status of Underenforced Constitutional Norms*, 91 Harv L Rev 1212 (1978).

[133] See Section II.B.

[134] See *Apprendi*, 530 US at 490 n 16.

legislative choices that allocate burdens of proof should not affect constitutional requirements regarding the identity of the fact-finder; the Court's contrary view is another unfortunate result of its decision to link the jury right with its standard-of-proof requirements.

Neither *Apprendi* nor subsequent cases made a serious effort to explain how "aggravating" and "mitigating" facts can be distinguished for Sixth Amendment purposes, given that a failure to find a "mitigating" fact enhances a defendant's maximum sentence just as surely as an "aggravator." All that *Apprendi* had to say was that judicial determinations of "mitigating" facts "neither expos[e] the defendant to a deprivation of liberty greater than that authorized by the [jury's] verdict," nor "impos[e] upon the defendant a greater stigma than that accompanying the jury verdict alone."[135] But this analysis is circular; the extent of punishment and stigma "authorized" by the jury's verdict itself depends on whether the defendant can establish the relevant "mitigating facts."

Justice Thomas's concurrence defended this distinction between "aggravating" and "mitigating" sentencing facts by arguing that the jury right should extend only to facts that are "a basis for imposing or increasing punishment."[136] This, however, is a non sequitur. When a "mitigating" circumstance decreases a defendant's maximum allowable sentence, the absence of that circumstance is a "basis for imposing" any punishment exceeding the mitigated penalty range. Recall *Patterson v New York*, where New York provided an affirmative defense for those who killed "under the influence of extreme emotional disturbance."[137] That the defendant had *not* acted under the influence of "extreme emotional disturbance" was the "basis" for sentencing him to life imprisonment, rather than a reduced penalty. Even though the defendant bore the burden of proof on this issue, the factual determination was as much a "basis" for his punishment as the fact that he caused the death of another human being. Each fact was necessary to expose him to life imprisonment.

The Court's *Apprendi* jurisprudence fails to recognize that sentencing facts are "aggravating" or "mitigating" only in relation to

---

[135] Id.

[136] See id at 501 (Thomas, J, concurring).

[137] NY Penal Law § 125.25(1)(a).

some baseline from which departures are measured.[138] Just as the failure to confer a property-tax exemption can "penalize" a constitutional right,[139] so too the refusal to find a "mitigating" fact can "increase" a defendant's otherwise applicable maximum sentence. To see this, consider once again our earlier hypothetical, where conviction for a firearms offense triggers ten to twenty years' imprisonment, unless the defendant proves, by a preponderance of the evidence, that he did *not* act with a "purpose to intimidate an individual or group of individuals because of race," which drops the penalty to five to ten years. One might view this sentencing fact as "lowering" the maximum sentence from twenty to ten years in cases where the defendant satisfies his burden of proof. This perspective uses the twenty-year maximum sentence as its benchmark, the highest possible penalty the judge could impose. Yet one might instead view a defendant's failure to satisfy his burden of proof as triggering a "penalty" that raises his maximum punishment from ten to twenty years. This view uses the lower of the two sentencing ranges as the baseline for measurement.

Blakely v Washington[140] purported to adopt a baseline when it defined the "statutory maximum" as the highest sentence a judge may impose "solely on the basis of the facts reflected in the jury verdict or admitted by the defendant."[141] The Court explained: "[T]he relevant 'statutory maximum' is not the maximum sentence a judge may impose after finding additional facts, but the maximum he may impose *without* any additional findings."[142] It is not immediately clear what this means; modern sentencing regimes almost always require *some* assessment of factual evidence before a "maximum sentence" can be ascertained. Consider again our aforementioned hypothetical sentencing regime; the judge must make some decision regarding whether the defendant satisfied his burden of proof on the "purpose to intimidate" mitigator before *any* "maximum sentence" can be ascertained. If he decides that the

---

[138] Cf. Cass R. Sunstein, *Lochner's Legacy*, 87 Colum L Rev 873 (1987).

[139] See *Speiser v Randall*, 357 US 513 (1958).

[140] 542 US 296 (2004).

[141] See id at 303 (emphasis omitted).

[142] See id at 303–04. See also *Cunningham v California*, 127 S Ct 856, 869 (2007) (holding that "the jury's verdict alone" must authorize a sentence to comport with the Sixth Amendment).

defendant proved that he did not act with a biased "purpose to intimidate," the maximum punishment is ten years. Otherwise the judge would decide that the defendant failed to carry his burden of proof on this issue, which triggers a twenty-year maximum. *There is no* "statutory maximum" that can be ascertained without *some* decision regarding a party's ability to carry his burden on the existence of sentencing facts.

The *Blakely* Court seems to be suggesting that its "statutory maximum" baseline is the highest sentence a court may impose, if all sentencing facts are resolved adversely to the party bearing the burden of proof. On this view, when a party fails to satisfy its burden of proof with regard to a sentencing fact, there is no "finding" that alters the baseline punishment. That means that when criminal defendants bear the burden of proof with regard to a sentencing fact, it is a "mitigating fact" that need not be submitted to the jury. By contrast, when prosecutors bear the burden of proof with regard to a sentencing fact, it is an "aggravating fact" and belongs to the jury if it increases the baseline maximum punishment.

But the Court has provided no reasons why the scope of the jury right should depend on the party that bears the burden of proof, and none is apparent. A determination that a "mitigating" sentencing fact has not been established exposes the defendant to punishment beyond that which he would otherwise receive; the effect is no different from finding an aggravating fact that increases the maximum punishment beyond what could otherwise be imposed. The only difference is that the defendant has been assigned the burden of proof in the former case. The Constitution may allow legislatures or sentencing commissions to choose how to allocate burdens of proof given the limited scope of the reasonable-doubt rule,[143] but why should this affect what the Constitution requires regarding the identity of the factfinder, especially when there is no difference in the effect of the factfinder's decision? Allowing the right to a jury determination to depend on legislative decisions to allocate the burdens and standards of proof seems arbitrary.

Not only is this baseline arbitrary, it is almost entirely within the control of the political branches. When constitutional rights

---

[143] See Section II.

are at stake, the Supreme Court rarely allows its analysis to proceed from baselines over which the political branches have near-plenary control. That much is clear from the many decisions in the Court's "unconstitutional conditions" genre.[144] It is hard to see why the Sixth Amendment jury right should be different in this regard, nor has the court suggested a reason why. While the Court allows the scope of its constitutional reasonable-doubt requirement to depend on decisions of the political branches, those limits are necessary to prevent the Court from overstepping its authority by expanding the reasonable-doubt requirement beyond its traditional scope, and to avoid creating incentives for crude and over-inclusive criminal laws that would defeat the Court's stated purposes for the reasonable-doubt rule.[145] None of these reasons carries over to the jury right.

Finally, some sentencing statutes do not specify which party bears the burden of proof, making it difficult to determine whether a sentencing fact increases or decreases the "statutory maximum" under *Blakely*. Consider a few provisions of the federal drug statutes, which establish a range of penalties that depend on drug type and quantity.[146] For persons convicted of distributing marijuana, 21 USC § 841(b)(1)(C) provides a maximum sentence of twenty years, plus fine. But then 21 USC § 841(b)(1)(D) provides that persons distributing less than fifty kilograms of marijuana may be punished with a sentence of no more than five years' imprisonment (plus fine). And 21 USC § 841(b)(4) goes even further, saying that those who distributed only "a small amount of marijuana for no remuneration" may not be imprisoned for more than one year. Yet nowhere does the statute specify whether the prosecution or the defense must prove whether the amount of marijuana falls within the ranges provided in sections 841(b)(1)(D) or 841(b)(4).[147] Hence, the statute does not indicate whether the "statutory maximum" under *Blakely* should be the twenty years' imprisonment plus fine provided in section 841(b)(1)(C), the five years' impris-

---

[144] See, e.g., *FCC v League of Women Voters*, 468 US 364, 399–401 (1984); *Sherbert v Verner*, 374 US 398, 405–06 (1963); *Arkansas Writers' Project v Ragland*, 481 US 221, 229 (1987).

[145] See Section II.B.

[146] See 21 USC § 841(b)(1)–(4) (2000 & Supp 2002).

[147] See *United States v Brough*, 243 F3d 1078, 1079 (7th Cir 2001) ("[T]he statute [§ 841] does not say who makes the findings or which party bears what burden of persuasion.").

onment plus fine provided in section 841(b)(1)(D), or the one year in prison plus fine allowed by section 841(b)(4). Judges are left with little guidance in choosing from among these options.[148]

In some respects, *Apprendi*'s attempt to distinguish "aggravating" and "mitigating" facts contains echoes of the "right/privilege" distinction that used to hold sway in constitutional law.[149] The Justices might think that facts that purport to increase a defendant's maximum allowable punishment implicate his "right" to be free from confinement, whereas facts that decrease the maximum punishment confer a "privilege" and therefore do not implicate the Sixth Amendment jury right. Justice Scalia's *Apprendi* concurrence contained shades of this reasoning, claiming that it was "not unfair to tell a prospective felon that if he commits his contemplated crime he is exposing himself to a jail sentence of 30 years—and that if, upon conviction, he gets anything less than that he may thank the mercy of a tenderhearted judge."[150]

The problem with this view is that mitigating facts that lower a defendant's maximum allowable sentence do not confer "privileges" or "mercy" when they represent *legal entitlements* to be free from certain levels of punishment. A judge who wrongfully withholds this entitlement does not fail to dispense mercy, but deprives the defendant of a legal claim to freedom. That such deprivation is accomplished by the failure to find a mitigating fact, as opposed to the finding of a sentencing enhancement, should make no difference for purposes of the jury right. The Supreme Court has recognized as much in its procedural due process cases, which have abandoned "right/privilege" analysis and protect all "entitlements" created by law.[151] Similar reasoning should extend the jury right to "mitigating" sentencing facts, no less than aggravating

---

[148] Cf. *United States v Outen*, 286 F3d 622, 637–39 (2d Cir 2002) (holding that the "default" penalty for marijuana possession is the five-year term in 21 USC § 841(b)(1)(D) rather than the one-year term in 21 USC § 841(b)(4)); *United States v Campbell*, 317 F3d 597, 603 (6th Cir 2003) (same).

[149] See, e.g., *Barsky v Board of Regents*, 347 US 442, 451 (1954) (upholding the suspension of a physician's license on the ground that the license was "a privilege granted by the State under its substantially plenary power to fix the terms of admission"); William W. Van Alstyne, *The Demise of the Right-Privilege Distinction in Constitutional Law*, 81 Harv L Rev 1439 (1967).

[150] *Apprendi*, 530 US at 498 (Scalia, J, concurring). See also *Harris*, 536 US at 565 (plurality opinion) (stating that conviction "authorize[s]" the government "to impose any sentence below the maximum").

[151] See, e.g., *Board of Regents v Roth*, 408 US 564 (1972).

ones. But the Court cannot adopt this approach under its current jurisprudence because it is unwilling to countenance a corresponding expansion in the proof-beyond-a-reasonable-doubt requirement and the concept of "elements."

V

A

Section IV showed that the Supreme Court has failed to give "intelligible content" to the jury's constitutional factfinding role because of its unjustifiable decision to link the jury right with the reasonable-doubt rule. Yet the problems caused by this linkage are even more far reaching. Under the Supreme Court's precedents, whenever courts expand the jury right, they must bring along the reasonable-doubt rule and, with it, the "elements" label. As a result, *Apprendi*'s well-meaning efforts to strengthen the jury's factfinding role have produced a regime in which prosecutors must prove certain sentencing enhancements beyond a reasonable doubt, and allege such facts in indictments in federal prosecutions, as if they were "elements" of a substantive crime.[152] In the Supreme Court's words, a nonrecidivist fact that increases a defendant's maximum allowable sentence must be treated as "the functional equivalent of an element of a greater offense."[153]

The *Apprendi* Court and Justice Thomas's concurring opinion defended this outcome by claiming that sentencing enhancements had always been regarded as "elements" of substantive crimes whenever they increased a defendant's maximum allowable punishment.[154] They each relied on Joel Prentiss Bishop's assertion

---

[152] See, e.g., *United States v Cotton*, 535 US 625, 632 (2002). See also, e.g., *United States v Fields*, 242 F3d 393, 395–96 (DC Cir 2001) (holding that drug quantity under 21 USC § 841(b) "is an element of the offense" if it results in a sentence that exceeds the statutory maximum, and that "the Government must state the drug type and quantity in the indictment"); *United States v Promise*, 255 F3d 150, 152 (4th Cir 2001) (holding that drug quantities under § 841(b) "must be treated as elements of aggravated drug trafficking offenses [and] charged in the indictment."); *United States v Doggett*, 230 F3d 160, 164–65 (5th Cir 2000) (holding that drug quantity under § 841(b) is an "element" of a crime, which "must be stated in the indictment"); *United States v Rebmann*, 226 F3d 521, 524–25 (6th Cir 2000) (describing drug quantity under § 841(b) as "elements of the offense"); *United States v Rogers*, 228 F3d 1318, 1327 (11th Cir 2000) (holding that drug quantity under § 841(b) "must be charged in the indictment"). But see *United States v Bjorkman*, 270 F3d 482, 489–90 (7th Cir 2001) (denying that *Apprendi* facts constitute "elements" of substantive crimes).

[153] *Apprendi*, 530 US at 494 n 19.

[154] See id at 483 n 10.

that nineteenth-century indictments were required to include "every fact which is legally essential to the punishment."[155] But this statement from Bishop's Criminal Procedure treatise is flatly wrong; numerous nineteenth-century cases held that first-degree murder findings were not required to be charged in indictments as "elements" of a greater crime, even though they increased the maximum allowable sentence from life imprisonment to death, and even though they were to be determined by juries. These cases demonstrate that the Court's expansive concept of "elements" is historically indefensible, and that juries' factfinding prerogatives have often extended beyond the "elements" of substantive crimes required to be alleged in indictments and proved beyond a reasonable doubt.

B

Justice Scalia's *Monge* dissent first propounded the idea that sentencing enhancements should be deemed "elements" of substantive crimes whenever they expose a defendant to a new range of punishment.[156] Two years later, the *Apprendi* Court endorsed this view, claiming that, as a historical matter, "facts that expose a defendant to a punishment greater than that otherwise legally prescribed were by definition 'elements' of a separate legal offense."[157] To support this historical assertion, the Court cited nineteenth-century treatises.[158] One of these was the second edition of Bishop's Criminal Procedure treatise, which claimed that "every fact which is legally essential to the punishment" must be charged in an indictment and be treated as an ingredient of a substantive

---

[155] See id at 489 n 15 (quoting 1 Bishop § 81 at 151 (cited in note 6)); id at 510 (Thomas, J, concurring) (same).

[156] See 524 US at 737–38 (Scalia, J, dissenting). See also notes 90–92 and accompanying text.

[157] *Apprendi*, 530 US at 483 n 10. See also *Cunningham v California*, 127 S Ct 856, 864 (2007) ("*Apprendi* said that any fact extending the defendant's sentence beyond the maximum authorized by the jury's verdict would have been considered an element of an aggravated crime . . . by those who framed the Bill of Rights.") (quoting *Harris v United States*, 536 US 545, 557 (2002) (plurality opinion)).

[158] See id at 480 (citing John Archbold, *Pleading and Evidence in Criminal Cases* 51 (H. Sweet, 15th ed 1862) (John Jervis, ed)); id at 489 n 15 (relying on 1 Bishop at § 81 at 51 (cited in note 6)). See also *Blakely*, 542 US at 301–02 (quoting Bishop in support of its claim that the jury must determine "all facts 'which the law makes essential to the punishment'") (quoting 1 Bishop at § 87 (cited in note 6)).

crime.[159] Bishop was among the preeminent nineteenth-century treatise writers on American law, and had been described by the *Central Law Journal* in 1885 as "the foremost law writer of the age."[160] Justice Thomas's *Apprendi* concurrence also relied on Bishop's treatise as evidence of "the traditional understanding. . . . regarding the elements of a crime,"[161] along with a handful of nineteenth-century state-court decisions.[162] The Supreme Court later endorsed all of these sources as "relevant authorities" supporting *Apprendi*'s expansive theory of elements.[163] None of these opinions, however, considered actual nineteenth-century court decisions involving sentencing categories in first-degree murder statutes. If they had, they would have realized that state courts almost uniformly rejected Bishop's view of the indictment, as well as the proposition that sentencing enhancements must be treated as elements of substantive criminal offenses whenever they increase a defendant's maximum allowable punishment.

Although *Apprendi* claimed that distinctions between "elements" and "sentencing factors" were unknown "during the years surrounding our nation's founding,"[164] the states have in fact employed "sentencing factors" since the early days of the nation's history. And numerous state-court decisions recognized that these facts were not "elements" of substantive crimes and did not need to be charged by prosecutors, even when they increased the maximum allowable punishment.[165] In 1794, only three years after ratification of the Bill of Rights, Pennsylvania enacted a statute that divided the crime of murder into two degrees: Murder in the first degree was limited to murders "perpetrated by means of poi-

---

[159] See *Apprendi*, 530 US at 489 n 15, quoting 1 Bishop at § 81 (cited in note 6).

[160] Stephen A. Siegel, *Joel Bishop's Orthodoxy*, 13 Law and Hist Rev 215, 215 (1995) (quoting Note, *Mr. Bishop as Law Writer*, 21 Cent L J 81, 81 (1885)). A note in the *American Law Review* heaped similar praise on Bishop. See Note, *A Deserved Tribute*, 18 Am L Rev 853, 853–54 (1884).

[161] *Apprendi*, 530 US at 510–12 (Thomas, J, concurring) (citing Bishop (cited in note 6) and Joel Prentiss Bishop, *New Criminal Procedure or New Commentaries on the Law of Pleading and Evidence and the Practice in Criminal Cases* (Flood, 4th ed 1895)).

[162] See id at 502–09, 512–18 (Thomas, J, concurring) (citing relevant state-law cases).

[163] See *Blakely*, 542 US at 302.

[164] *Apprendi*, 530 US at 478.

[165] See, e.g., *Hanon v State*, 63 Md 123, 126 (1885) ("The mere affixing by statute of a penalty different from that at common law, or adjusting it to specified circumstances of aggravation or mitigation, where the crime or misdemeanor is in its nature susceptible of such variations, without losing its essential character, *is not the creation of a distinct offence*.") (emphasis added).

son, or lying in wait, or by any other kind of wilful, deliberate and premeditated killing, or which shall be committed in the perpetration or attempt to perpetrate any arson, rape, robbery, or burglary."[166] All other kinds of murders were second degree. Many other states adopted similar schemes. But only murder in the first degree was punishable by death, so a first-degree finding was the nineteenth-century analogue to a statutory "aggravating factor" in modern death-penalty statutes. Each would be a quintessential "*Apprendi* fact" under the Supreme Court's current jurisprudence, and would be regarded as the "functional equivalent of an element of a greater offense."[167]

But nineteenth-century courts did not regard a first-degree murder finding as an "element" of an aggravated crime, even though such findings increased the maximum allowable sentence from life imprisonment to death, and even though the law required jury determinations as to the degree of murder in cases that went to trial. *White v Commonwealth*[168] was the first published decision construing Pennsylvania's first-degree murder statute, and all the justices of the state supreme court agreed that the first-degree murder statute did not divide murder into separate offenses. The majority opinion held that indictments need not charge the degree of murder because "first-degree" murder was merely a sentencing category within a unitary offense rather than an element of a separate, aggravated crime:

> "All that [the statute] does, is to define the different kinds of murder, which shall be ranked in different classes, and be subject to different punishments. *It has not been the practice since the passing of this law, to alter the form of indictments for murder in any respect; and it plainly appears by the act itself, that it was not supposed any alteration would be made.* It seems taken for granted, that it would not always appear on the face of the indictment of what degree the murder was."[169]

The dissenting opinion agreed that Pennsylvania's first-degree

---

[166] See 4 Journal of the Senate 242–46 (Pa 1794). See also Gen Laws Pa, ch 124 § 2 (Johnson 1849).

[167] See *Ring v Arizona*, 536 US at 609 (quoting *Apprendi*, 530 US at 494 n 19).

[168] 6 Binn 179 (Pa 1813).

[169] See id at 183 (opinion of Tilghman, CJ) (emphasis added).

murder statute "creates no new offence as to willful and deliberate murder. . . . Different degrees of guilt exist under the general crime of murder."[170] Even though the Pennsylvania statute conferred a right to a jury determination as to the first-degree murder finding,[171] no one on the court regarded this jury fact as part of a substantive criminal offense, even as it increased the maximum allowable punishment from life imprisonment to death.

After *White*, the Pennsylvania Supreme Court continued to hold that prosecutors need not charge the degree of murder in indictments.[172] Other jurisdictions that divided murder into degrees likewise held that murder indictments need not mention the degree of the crime. These included the highest courts of Alabama,[173] Arkansas,[174] California,[175] Colorado,[176] Idaho,[177] Maine,[178] Maryland,[179] Massachusetts,[180] Michigan,[181] Minnesota,[182] the territory of Montana,[183] Nevada,[184] New Jersey,[185] New Hampshire,[186] New

---

[170] Id at 188 (Yeates, J, concurring in part and dissenting in part).

[171] See Gen Laws Pa, ch 124, § 2 (Johnson 1849).

[172] See, e.g., *Commonwealth v Gable*, 7 Serg & Rawle 423, 427 (Pa 1821) (opinion of Tilghman, CJ); id at 429 (Gibson, J, dissenting); *Commonwealth v Flanagan*, 7 Watts & Serg 415, 418 (Pa 1844); *O'Mara v Commonwealth*, 75 Pa 424, 429–30 (Pa 1874) (quoting *White*, 6 Binn at 182–83 (opinion of Tilghman, CJ)).

[173] See, e.g., *Noles v State*, 24 Ala 672, 693 (1854).

[174] See, e.g., *McAdams v State*, 25 Ark 405, 416 (1869). But see *Cannon v State*, 31 SW 150, 153 (Ark 1895) (suggesting that first-degree murder should be alleged in indictments).

[175] See, e.g., *People v Murray*, 10 Cal 309, 310 (1858).

[176] See, e.g., *Garvey v People*, 6 Colo 559, 563 (1883).

[177] See, e.g., *State v Ellington*, 43 P 60, 61 (Idaho 1895).

[178] See, e.g., *State v Verrill*, 54 Me 408, 415–16 (1867).

[179] See, e.g., *Ford v State*, 12 Md 514, 529–30 (1859).

[180] See, e.g., *Green v Commonwealth*, 94 Mass 155, 170–71 (1866).

[181] See, e.g., *People v Doe*, 1 Mich 451, 457–58 (1850).

[182] See, e.g., *State v Lessing*, 16 Minn 75, 78 (1870).

[183] See, e.g., *Territory v Stears*, 2 Mont 324, 327–28 (1875).

[184] See, e.g., *State v Millain*, 3 Nev 409, 442 (1867).

[185] See, e.g., *Titus v State*, 7 A 621, 623 (NJ 1886) (stating that New Jersey's first-degree murder statute "did not create any new crime, but 'merely made a distinction, with a view to a difference in the punishment, between the most heinous and the less aggravated grades of the crime of murder.' . . . [I]t [is] not necessary to set out in the count that the alleged killing was 'willful, deliberate, and premeditated,' [and] it cannot be necessary to show that the killing was in the commission of a rape, which is another of the categories of the same section.") (quoting *Graves v State*, 45 NJL 347, 358 (NJ 1883)).

[186] See, e.g., *State v Williams*, 23 NH 321, 324 (1851).

York,[187] Tennessee,[188] Texas,[189] Virginia,[190] West Virginia,[191] and Wisconsin.[192] While each of these courts held that murder indictments need not specify the degree of the crime, courts would not hold indictments invalid when they did so.[193] The California Supreme Court, for example, held that courts should simply disregard attempts in indictments to designate a degree of murder.[194] And it allowed such indictments to sustain convictions for *any* degree of murder, even if higher than the degree specified in the indictment.[195] In so holding the court stressed that prosecutors and grand juries should not be allowed to designate sentencing categories at the charging stage; rather, such decisions should be made at the time of the defendant's conviction for a crime by the relevant factfinder, either a jury (in cases where the defendant opts for a trial) or trial judge (in cases where the defendant waives his right of trial by pleading guilty).[196] The court seemed intent on preventing these sentencing categories from becoming a regime of "charge-offense" sentencing, and would not allow indictments to control sentencing decisions.[197] All these decisions are directly contrary to the views of Bishop, who wrote that, according to

[187] See, e.g., *Cox v People*, 80 NY 500, 514 (1880).

[188] See, e.g., *Mitchell v State*, 16 Tenn 514, 527 (1835); id at 530–34 (Catron, CJ, concurring); see also *Hines v State*, 27 Tenn 597, 598 (1848).

[189] See, e.g., *Gehrke v State*, 13 Tex 568, 573–74 (1855).

[190] See, e.g., *Commonwealth v Miller*, 3 Va 310, 311 (1812).

[191] See, e.g., *State v Schnelle*, 24 W Va 767, 779 (1884).

[192] See, e.g., *Hogan v State*, 30 Wis 428, 439–42 (1872).

[193] See, e.g., *People v Dolan*, 9 Cal 576, 583 (1858).

[194] See *People v King*, 27 Cal 507, 512 (1865). See also *People v White*, 22 Wend 167, 175–76 (NY 1839); *Stears*, 2 Mont at 328; *Kirby v State*, 15 Tenn 259, 264 (1834).

[195] See, e.g., *People v Nichol*, 34 Cal 211, 217 (1867). See also *Stears*, 2 Mont at 327.

[196] See, e.g., *King*, 27 Cal at 512 ("The trial jury, and not the grand jury, determine the degree of the crime, and the former should not be embarrassed by the opinion of the latter."); *Nichol*, 34 Cal at 217 (noting that the duty to fix the degree of crime is "expressly cast upon the trial jury, and the designation of the degree by the Grand Jury is, therefore, as idle as a recommendation to the mercy of the Court appended to a verdict of guilty of murder in the first degree.").

[197] See also *Ellington*, 43 P at 61 ("How are the jury to find the degree? From the descriptive allegations in the indictment, or from the evidence on the trial? . . . [T]he answer is unavoidable, as it is conclusive, that the degree of the crime is *solely for the trial jury*, and it is not requisite or essential that the words defining the degrees of murder should be set forth in the indictment to constitute a good indictment for murder in the first degree under our statutes.") (emphasis added); *Stears*, 2 Mont at 327–28; *State v Thompson*, 12 Nev 140, 147–48 (1877); *State v Rover*, 10 Nev 388, 391 (1875); *Mitchell*, 16 Tenn at 533 (Catron, CJ, concurring).

"those principles of natural reason and justice which are inherent in the case, . . . the indictment for murder, where the statute divides it into two degrees, should, if murder of the first degree is meant to be proved against the prisoner, contain those allegations which show the offence to be in this degree."[198]

Several of these state-court decisions considered and rejected the claim in Bishop's treatise that indictments "must contain an allegation of every fact which is legally essential to the punishment to be inflicted."[199] *State v Millain*[200] expressly disapproved Bishop's views while rejecting a claim that first- and second-degree murder were separate offenses, requiring distinct indictments.[201] The court noted that "Mr. Bishop has laboured with zeal and ingenuity to show the distinct nature of the two offenses,"[202] but nevertheless concluded that "it was not the intention of the legislature, in making the distinction in the two classes of murder, to require a distinct indictment for each."[203] Indeed, the court noted the "almost [ ] uniform practice" in other States allowing a generic murder indictment to sustain convictions for first-degree murder.[204] In denying the petition for rehearing, the court emphasized that it had "read with great care and attention the arguments of Mr. Bishop as to the necessity of an indictment for murder drawing the distinction between murder of the first and second degree."[205] But this did not persuade the court to change its previous decision upholding the indictment.[206]

Hogan v State[207] also rejected Bishop's views in a case where a murder indictment omitted the degree. The dissenting opinion invoked Bishop's treatise and argued that the indictment was

---

[198] 2 Bishop at § 586 at 308 (cited in note 6).

[199] 1 Bishop at § 81 at 51 (cited in note 6). See also id at § 540 ("[T]he indictment must . . . contain an averment of every particular thing which enters into the punishment"); *Apprendi*, 530 US at 510 (Thomas, J, concurring) (citing these provisions in Bishop's treatise).

[200] 3 Nev 409 (1867).

[201] See id at 439–40.

[202] Id.

[203] Id at 442.

[204] Id.

[205] Id at 479.

[206] Id.

[207] 30 Wis 428 (1872).

bad,[208] but the majority opinion rejected this view, even while recognizing that an indictment "must fully set out the crime charged."[209] The majority noted the long-standing view in Wisconsin that murder indictments need not specify a degree to sustain a conviction for murder, even in the first degree. And it wrote that "[t]he acquiescence of a bar so able and learned as the bar of Wisconsin, and for so long a period, . . . and this without a word of dissent from the bench, brings such rule almost within the operation of the maxim, '*stare decisis*.'"[210] The court also observed that the state legislature had expressly approved the use of common-law form indictments in prosecutions for first-degree murder, and the court refused to hold the statute unconstitutional. It therefore felt "constrained to hold that such express averment in unnecessary, and that an indictment in the common law form is sufficient."[211]

Finally, in *State v Verrill*,[212] the defendant had been convicted and sentenced for first-degree murder based on an indictment that did not allege the degree, even though the state constitution had been construed to require "that *all the elements of*, or facts necessary to, the crime charged, shall be fully and clearly set out" in an indictment.[213] On appeal, the defendant cited Bishop's treatise[214] to support his claim that his indictment should have alleged first-degree murder. But the court rejected the defendant's claim. Even though the first-degree murder finding increased the maximum punishment, it did not need to be charged in the indictment because it was not an element of a crime. The court explained: "*There is still but one crime denominated murder*, as at the common law, although by the provisions of the statute there are two degrees of that crime, liable to different punishments."[215]

---

[208] See id at 443 (Dixon, CJ, concurring in part and dissenting in part).

[209] Id at 439 (majority).

[210] Id at 441.

[211] Id at 440.

[212] 54 Me 408 (1867).

[213] Id at 414 (emphasis added).

[214] See id at 410 (citing Joel Prentiss Bishop, 2 *Criminal Procedure* §§ 562–97 at 317–53 (Little, Brown, 1st ed 1866)).

[215] Id at 415 (emphasis added). Other decisions rejected Bishop's claim that indictments should allege every fact essential to guilt. See, e.g., *Ellington*, 43 P at 61–62; *Territory v Bannigan*, 46 NW 597, 599 (Dakota 1877) (noting that "a long array of authorities" stands against Bishop's assertion that indictments for first-degree murder "should" allege the degree).

All these jurisdictions made clear that they did not regard first- and second-degree murder as separate offenses. Instead, they viewed the degrees of murder as nothing more than sentencing categories within a unitary offense, even though a first-degree murder finding boosted the maximum punishment from imprisonment to death.[216]

A few jurisdictions did require murder indictments to allege the degree of the crime.[217] The Iowa Supreme Court, for example, held in *Fouts v State*[218] that a common-law indictment for murder, which did not specify the degree of crime, could not support conviction and punishment for first-degree murder. But the court recognized that its approach was in the minority, noting that common-law murder indictments were "perhaps good in nearly every other state in the Union."[219] And subsequent Iowa Supreme Court decisions again noted that *Fouts* was opposed to the views expressed in court decisions from other jurisdictions.[220] The Missouri Supreme Court likewise acknowledged that other states had adopted a "different practice," refusing to require indictments to allege first-degree murder, even under "statutes using somewhat similar phrases in declaring what shall be murder in the first degree, and what in the second degree."[221]

So while a few jurisdictions adopted Bishop's view that indictments must charge every fact that increases a defendant's punishment, the first-degree murder cases show that most jurisdictions rejected it, and did not necessarily regard sentencing enhancements as "elements" of separate, aggravated crimes that must be

---

[216] See also *Commonwealth v Gardner*, 77 Mass 438, 444 (1858); *People v Haun*, 44 Cal 96, 98 (1872); *Thompson*, 12 Nev at 146; *Simpson v State*, 19 SW 99, 102 (Ark 1892); *State v Tatro*, 50 Vt 483, 493 (1878) (quoting Francis Wharton, *A Treatise on the Criminal Law of the United* States § 1103 at 500 (Kay, 4th ed 1857)); *Mitchell*, 16 Tenn at 526.

[217] See, e.g., *Finn v State*, 5 Ind 400, 403 (1854); *Fouts v State*, 4 Greene 500, 503–04 (Iowa 1854); *State v McCormick*, 27 Iowa 402, 411–12 (1869) (citing Joel Prentiss Bishop, 2 *Commentaries on the Law of Criminal Procedure, or Pleading, Evidence, and Practice in Criminal Cases* § 584 at 333 (Little, Brown, 1st ed 1866) to support *Fouts*'s holding, and reiterating that "the degree [of murder] must be alleged"); *State v Jones*, 20 Mo 58, 60–61 (1854); *State v Brown*, 21 Kan 38, 49–50 (1878).

[218] 4 Greene 500 (Iowa 1854).

[219] Id at 503.

[220] See *State v Johnson*, 8 Iowa 525, 529 (1859) (discussing *Fouts*); *McCormick*, 27 Iowa at 408 ("We are aware that the cases are not uniform respecting the question whether, to constitute a good indictment for murder in the first degree, it is necessary to allege that the killing was willful, deliberate and premeditated.").

[221] See *Jones*, 20 Mo at 61.

charged in indictments, even when they raise the maximum punishment. The Supreme Court has not acknowledged or discussed these nineteenth-century first-degree murder cases, yet it relies on Bishop's views to support revisionist understandings of "elements" and "crimes." The first-degree murder cases demonstrate, however, that these statements from Bishop's treatise were aspirational rather than an accurate description of nineteenth-century American practice (much less evidence of what the U.S. Constitution requires). Bishop himself recognized that the law of first-degree murder could not be reconciled with his claim that indictments must charge "every fact which is legally essential to the punishment" as an element of a crime.[222] Indeed, he bemoaned the holdings of those cases, writing that "to a lamentable extent have our courts, not consulting the teachings of our books of the law, or resorting to accurate reasonings, done, upon the subject of the indictment [in first-degree murder cases], the very highest champion blundering."[223] The Supreme Court might prefer Bishop's aspirations to the actual practice of nineteenth-century state courts as a matter of policy, but that by itself is not a legitimate basis on which to impose a constitutional rule regarding the meaning of "elements" or the requirements of the Fifth Amendment's Indictment Clause.[224]

Although Justice Thomas's *Apprendi* concurrence supplemented his reliance on Bishop's treatise with a handful of nineteenth-century state-court decisions that spoke favorably of Bishop's views, many of those same courts interpreted their first-degree murder statutes in a manner irreconcilable with Bishop's views of the indictment and Justice Thomas's understanding of "elements."[225] At most, Justice Thomas's historical evidence shows that

---

[222] See, e.g., 3 Joel Prentiss Bishop, *New Criminal Procedure* §§ 500, 561–89 (Flood, 2d ed 1913).

[223] See, e.g., id at § 500 at 277.

[224] See Stephanos Bibas, *Judicial Fact-Finding and Sentence Enhancements in a World of Guilty Pleas*, 110 Yale L J 1097, 1132 (2001) (noting that Bishop's "speculation about 'natural reason' and 'abstract justice' is no basis for discerning the original meaning of the Fifth and Sixth Amendments"); cf. John Hart Ely, *Foreward: On Discovering Fundamental Values*, 92 Harv L Rev 5, 16–22 (1978).

[225] Compare *Apprendi*, 530 US at 511–12 (Thomas, J, concurring) (citing, among others, state-court decisions from Texas, Maryland, and Maine that spoke approvingly of Bishop's views) with *Gehrke*, 13 Tex at 573–74 (holding that an indictment charging murder in its common-law definition is sufficient to sustain conviction and punishment for murder in the first degree); *Ford*, 12 Md at 549 (holding that there was "no defect in the indictment" that charged the defendant with common-law murder without specifying the degree). See

some sentencing enhancements were charged in indictments in *some* situations. But there was no obligation, constitutional or otherwise, to treat *every* fact that increases the maximum allowable punishment as an element of a substantive crime.

As further proof that the states did not regard sentencing enhancements as "elements" of substantive crimes, some states *would not permit* a criminal defendant to plead guilty to a specific degree of murder. They allowed him to plead guilty only to the unitary offense, and the trial judge would fix the degree and sentence, given that the defendant's guilty plea waived his right to a jury.[226] This was an early example of "real-offense" sentencing based on the defendant's actual conduct, rather than charging decisions or plea bargains.[227] And this continued well into the twentieth century. The California Supreme Court, for example, held that trial courts must fix the degree of burglary whenever the defendant pleaded guilty to a generic burglary indictment.[228] These state-court decisions regarded "degrees" of crimes as real-offense sentencing categories rather than "elements" of substantive offenses that could be the subject of plea bargaining. The federal courts have no historical basis for mandating that sentencing enhance-

---

also *Verrill*, 54 Me at 415–16 (rejecting the defendant's argument that "the indictment does not set out a murder in the first degree, therefore insufficient to sustain the verdict").

[226] See, e.g., *Weighorst v State*, 7 Md 442 (1855) ("[T]he act does not authorize the accused to plead guilty of murder in the second degree. If he confesses at all he must plead to the indictment for murder, and it is then made the duty of the court, by examination of witnesses, to determine the degree of the crime, and to give sentence accordingly."); *Dick v State*, 3 Ohio St 89, 93 (1853) ("The prisoner is not allowed to determine the degree of the crime, by a confession with reference to the form and manner of the charge against him; but the degree must be found by the court, from the evidence, without regard to the form of the confession, or the mode in which the crime is charged in the indictment."); *Wells v State*, 104 SW2d 451, 452 (Ark 1937) (jury must find degree of murder even when defendant pleads guilty to an indictment charging first-degree murder); *Martin v State*, 38 SW 194, 196 (Tex Crim 1896) ("[A defendant] may plead guilty to murder, but the degree must be found by a jury."); *Wicks v Commonwealth*, 4 Va 387, 392–93 (1824) ("But the Law goes on to say, 'but if such person be convicted by confession, the Court shall proceed, by examination of witnesses, to determine the degree of the crime, and to give sentence accordingly.' Now, if the Indictment must charge the offence to be murder in the first degree or second degree, and if the accused confesses he is guilty of the crime charged upon him by the Indictment, what further enquiry upon that subject can be had?"). But see *State v Kring*, 74 Mo 612, 620 (1881) (noting that defendant entered a plea of guilty to murder in the second degree); *State v Shanley*, 18 SE 734, 736 (W Va 1893) (noting that a defendant "may plead guilty of murder in the first degree").

[227] See, e.g., Stephen Breyer, *The Federal Sentencing Guidelines and the Key Compromises Upon Which They Rest*, 17 Hofstra L Rev 1, 8–12 (1988) (explaining the differences between "charge-offense" and "real-offense" sentencing).

[228] See *People v Jefferson*, 52 Cal 452, 454–55 (1877) (citing Cal Penal Code § 1192 (1872)); see also *People v Stratton*, 24 P2d 174, 176 (Cal App 1933).

ments be treated as elements of separate, aggravated criminal offenses that prosecutors must charge and prove beyond a reasonable doubt.

But the nineteenth-century law of first-degree murder fully supports *Apprendi*'s decision to expand the jury right to sentencing factors. Every jurisdiction that divided murder into degrees required juries to fix the degree of the crime, even though they did not treat this jury fact as an "element" of a substantive criminal offense. The only exception was when the defendant waived his right to trial by pleading guilty.[229] But at the time, guilty pleas waived all rights that otherwise would apply at trial;[230] even jurisdictions that regarded the criminal jury as "nonwaivable" recognized that guilty pleas obviated any factfinding role for the jury.[231] In cases that did go to trial, many state courts jealously guarded the jury's prerogative to fix the degree of murder, holding that a jury verdict of "guilty" that did not specify the degree of murder was a nullity, and could not support *any* punishment, even for the lowest possible degree.[232] They would not permit trial

---

[229] See *Hallinger v Davis*, 146 US 314 (1892). A few states, however, still required juries to determine the degree of murder even if the defendant pleaded guilty. See, e.g., Dig Laws Ala 412–13, at §§ 1–2 (Slade 1843).

[230] See, e.g., *People v Popescue*, 177 NE 739, 744 (Ill 1931); *State v Kaufman*, 2 NW 275, 276 (Iowa 1879); *People v Noll*, 20 Cal 164, 165 (1862).

[231] See, e.g., S. Chesterfield Oppenheim, *Waiver of Trial by Jury in Criminal Cases*, 25 Mich L Rev 695, 715 (1927).

[232] See, e.g., *State v Reddick*, 7 Kan 143, 154–55 (1871) (noting "[a] long train of decisions . . . [that] have held such a defect fatal" and holding that a murder verdict that fails to specify the degree "is not sufficient to base a judgment upon"); *Williams v State*, 60 Md 402, 403 (1883) ("A general verdict of 'guilty' on an indictment for murder, is a *bad verdict*, and on such a verdict no judgement can be pronounced."); *Tully v People*, 6 Mich 273, 273 (1859) ("[It] is imperative that the jury in their verdict . . . shall determine the degree of crime. The judgment must be reversed."); *Robertson v State*, 42 Ala 509, 510 (1868) ("The verdict, in this case, fails to ascertain the degree of murder in which the defendant was guilty, and the court erred in passing sentence upon the verdict."); *People v Marquis*, 15 Cal 38, 38 (1860) ("[T]he jury shall designate in their verdict the degree of the offense. This they have not done, and the Court . . . cannot assume that they designed, from a general finding, to fix the grade of the crime. . . . For this error, the judgment must be reversed, and the case remanded for a new trial."); *State v Rover*, 10 Nev 388, 391 (1875) ("[A] verdict which fails to designate the degree of murder of which the jury find the defendant guilty, is so fatally defective that no judgment or sentence can be legally pronounced thereon."); *State v Redman*, 17 Iowa 329, 331 (1864) ("[A] verdict in such a case is fatally defective, unless the jury find specifically the degree of murder."); *Stears*, 2 Mont at 331 ("[T]he verdict in the case of murder must express the degree of the crime, or no judgment can be entered thereon."). See also *McGee v State*, 8 Mo 495, 496 (1844); *Hogan*, 30 Wis at 435–36; *People v Campbell*, 40 Cal 129, 138–40 (1870); *Kearney v People*, 17 P 782, 782 (Colo 1888); *People v Shafer*, 1 Utah 260, 264 (1875); *Buster v State*, 42 Tex 315, 319–20 (1874); *Allen v State*, 26 Ark 333, 333–34 (1870); *M'Pherson v State*, 17 Tenn 279, 279 (1836); *Cobia v State*, 16 Ala 781, 783 (1849); *Hall v State*, 12 So 449, 452 (Fla 1893).

judges to fix the degree of crime when the jury verdict failed to do so; to hold otherwise would allow judges to overstep limits on their power imposed by the constitutional jury guarantees.[233]

All these jurisdictions insisted that juries should determine the degree of murder, not because it was an "element" of a criminal "offense" (it wasn't), but because they thought juries should resolve disputed questions of fact that affect a defendant's sentence. The Texas Court of Criminal Appeals, for example, held that juries should decide "every grade of crime"[234] suggested by the evidence, and based its conclusion on the ground that degrees of crime presented "question[s] of fact upon which the jury alone may speak."[235] It rejected any suggestion that trial courts could decide questions of fact for the jury: "A doctrine more subversive of our law, more alarming in its tendency, and more fatal to that bulwark of Anglo-Saxon liberty, the jury system, could not be suggested *than that this court could settle questions of fact for the jury*."[236] Similar views were expressed in other state-court decisions.[237] These first-degree murder regimes clearly understood the jury's factfinding responsibilities as extending well beyond the "elements" of criminal offenses or their "functional equivalents."

Of course, none of these nineteenth-century legal authorities purported to interpret the meaning of the Sixth Amendment's jury guarantee. These all involved state court decisions and laws enacted before the Sixth Amendment even applied to the states. Yet

---

But see *Simpson*, 19 SW at 102 (allowing prisoner to be sentenced for second-degree murder when jury's verdict failed to specify the degree).

[233] See, e.g., *State v Montgomery*, 11 SW 1012, 1013 (Mo 1889) ("[N]o one else but the jurors can perform the duty thus enjoined."); *Kirby*, 15 Tenn at 263 ("[T]he court has no power to proceed to judgment unless the degree of the crime be ascertained by the verdict of the jury."); *Cobia*, 16 Ala at 783 ("[T]he degree [must] be ascertained by the verdict of the jury, and if this be not done, the court has no power to render judgment at all. The judge without the intervention of the jury cannot ascertain the degree of guilt").

[234] *Jones v State*, 26 SW 1082, 1086 (Tex Crim 1894).

[235] Id (quoting *Halliburton v State*, 22 SW 48 (Tex Crim 1893)).

[236] Id (emphasis added).

[237] See, e.g., *People v Constantino*, 47 NE 37, 41 (NY 1897) (holding that juries must resolve the degree of murder because it "was plainly a question of fact."); *Craft v State*, 3 Kan 450, 485 (1866) (stating that juries must fix the degree of murder as "the exclusive judges of all questions of fact" and "[i]n that behalf their power is exclusive and supreme."); *People v Kennedy*, 54 NE 51, 53 (NY 1899) (describing degrees of homicide as presenting "a question of fact for the jury" while recognizing that "the jury is the ultimate tribunal" for resolving "questions of fact arising upon conflicting evidence"); *State v Welch*, 15 SE 419, 422 (W Va 1892) ("The question whether the act was murder in the first or second degree was one of fact for the jury exclusively.").

even before incorporation, every state constitution has always guaranteed the right of jury trial in criminal cases,[238] and in many such provisions the wording is identical to the Sixth Amendment.[239] And while there was very little case law interpreting the Sixth Amendment in the eighteenth and nineteenth centuries, the unanimous view among the states that juries should fix the degree of murder in cases that went to trial, even though this fact was not charged in indictments as an "element" of a substantive crime, is at least persuasive evidence of what the right of jury trial meant in the early years of our nation's history.[240] And it further shows that there is nothing anomalous or unprecedented about extending the jury right beyond the facts that prosecutors must charge and prove as components of a substantive offense.

VI

The problems discussed in the two preceding sections are a direct result of the Court's decision to link the jury right with the reasonable-doubt rule and the concept of "elements." This section will sketch and defend a much broader view of the jury right, one that is not tied to the Court's standard-of-proof requirements, but that is based on the traditional understanding of the jury as a separation-of-powers mechanism within the judiciary that limits the power of judges over factfinding.

On this view, the jury right should, at a minimum, extend to *all* disputed questions of fact that determine a defendant's guilt or punishment, regardless of standards of proof. This approach would limit the sentencing judge's powers to resolving questions of law, or applying law or exercising discretion in accordance with undisputed facts or facts found by a jury. Although commentators have shown that this distinction between factual and legal ques-

---

[238] See *Duncan v Louisiana*, 391 US 145, 153 (1968).

[239] See, e.g., SD Const, Art VI, § 7 ("In all criminal prosecutions the accused shall have the right . . . to a speedy public trial by an impartial jury of the county or district in which the offense is alleged to have been committed.").

[240] Cf. generally Eric A. Posner and Cass R. Sunstein, *The Law of Other States*, 59 Stan L Rev 131 (2006) (relying on the Condorcet Jury Theorem to claim that when a large majority of states make a certain decision based on a certain shared belief, and the states are well motivated, there is good reason to believe that the decision is correct, provided that certain conditions are met).

tions is not always clear,[241] and difficult cases will arise at the margins, the Constitution's text assumes the soundness of this distinction. In defining the civil jury's role, the Seventh Amendment provides that "*no fact tried by a jury*, shall be otherwise re-examined in any Court of the United States, than according to the rules of the common law,"[242] which not only recognizes the distinction between factual and legal questions but also reinforces the principle that resolving disputed questions of fact is central to a jury's constitutional task. The Supreme Court continues to use this distinction to define the roles of judge and jury in civil litigation,[243] and it has shown to be workable, even as the Court must occasionally step in to resolve hard cases.[244] In the criminal context, any distinction between "questions of fact" and "questions of law" will necessarily be one of degree. A relatively easy case would involve sentencing categories that depend on whether a defendant "visibly possessed a firearm" during his crime, as this would involve a particularized inquiry into what happened. Still, this might present "questions of law" for the court if the parties disagree over the meaning of "visibly possessed." In such situations the judge could instruct the jury on the meaning of those words, leaving the jury to apply the court's interpretation of the law to the facts of the case. Or the court might require the jury to return specialized findings limited to factual questions about past conduct. Recidivist sentencing enhancements will also involve questions of fact for the jury: the existence of prior felony convictions. Although, again, questions of law for the court may arise if the parties disagree over the legal definitions of "felony" or "misdemeanor."

Expanding the jury right along these lines would raise important questions for quasi-discretionary sentencing regimes that depend on judicial factfinding, such as the post-*Booker* Federal Sentencing

---

[241] See generally, e.g., James Bradley Thayer, *"Law and Fact" in Jury Trials*, 4 Harv L Rev 147 (1890); Nathan Isaacs, *The Law and the Facts*, 22 Colum L Rev 1, 11–12 (1922) ("[W]hether a particular question is to be treated as a question of law or a question of fact is not in itself a question of fact, but a highly artificial question of law.").

[242] US Const, Amend VII (emphasis added).

[243] See, e.g., *Colgrove v Battin*, 413 US 149, 157 (1973) ("[T]he purpose of the jury trial in . . . civil cases [is] to assure a fair and equitable resolution of factual issues."); *Gasoline Prods. Co. v Champlin Ref. Co.*, 283 US 494, 498 (1931) ("All of vital significance in trial by jury is that issues of fact be submitted for determination . . . by the jury. . .").

[244] See generally, e.g., *Markman v Westview Instruments, Inc.*, 517 US 370 (1996).

Guidelines. After finding the pre-*Booker* Guidelines unconstitutional, the *Booker* Court held that sentencing courts must calculate and consider the Federal Guidelines range, but may impose sentences outside that range in light of other concerns.[245] Appellate courts must review these sentences for "reasonableness."[246] Under this regime, judicial factfinding will influence the ultimate sentence imposed, but, unlike the sentencing regimes considered in *McMillan*, *Apprendi*, *Harris*, and *Blakely*, it will not fix concrete minimum and maximum sentences.

The *Booker* remedy was a product of the Court's cramped interpretation of the Sixth Amendment jury right, limited to facts subject to the Court's reasonable-doubt rule. From that perspective, the Court needed only to amend the Guidelines so that no finding of fact increased a defendant's maximum allowable sentence, and the constitutional objections melted away. But once one jettisons the Court's link between the jury right and the reasonable-doubt rule and focuses on the jury's role as a structural constitutional guarantee, then the real constitutional problem lies with the Guidelines' failure to maintain a proper division of power between judge and jury. They allow judges to intrude on the jury's factfinding responsibilities by resolving disputed questions of fact that determine a defendant's range of punishment. *Booker*'s "remedy" does little to allay these constitutional concerns. It continues to allow judges to decide factual issues that alter a defendant's range of punishment, but softens the impact of such findings by allowing judges to consider other factors in the process.[247] Given the importance of the jury's role as factfinder to constitutional structure, one should look askance at any scheme that allows judges rather than juries to resolve disputed questions of fact that must be considered when deciding what sentence to impose, especially in light of empirical evidence suggesting that "voluntary guidelines" affect judges' sentencing practices like mandatory guidelines.[248] The need, recognized by Blackstone, to protect the jury

---

[245] See 543 US at 245–46, 261.

[246] Id at 261.

[247] See, e.g., Michael W. McConnell, *The Booker Mess*, 83 Denver L Rev 665, 677–78 (2006) (noting that the *Booker* remedy does little to address the Sixth Amendment concerns under the pre-*Booker* Guidelines system).

[248] See, e.g., John F. Pfaff, *The Continued Vitality of Structured Sentencing Following Blakely: The Effectiveness of Voluntary Guidelines* 48, 54 UCLA L Rev 235, 283 (2006) (noting that judges often comply with "voluntary guidelines" because "(1) they provide useful infor-

guarantee "from all secret machinations which may sap and undermine it,"[249] should lead the Court to extend the jury right to disputed questions of fact even under advisory sentencing guidelines. This would also include factual findings in capital sentencing regimes that rely on "guided discretion."

Finally, one must consider the constitutionality of fully discretionary sentencing regimes. Discretionary sentencing has a long pedigree; both at common law and throughout our nation's history, judges have been given discretion to choose levels of fines, whipping, or imprisonment up to a prescribed statutory maximum.[250] And the Supreme Court has held that the Sixth Amendment imposes no barrier to fully discretionary sentencing, even though a judge might exercise his discretion in accordance with his own perception of the facts, without asking a jury to resolve any disputed factual issues that he might deem relevant.[251] On the other hand, a so-called "hanging judge" might systematically impose tough sentences without considering or resolving factual questions in the process. These discretionary regimes *allow* judges to base a defendant's sentence on factual determinations that were not submitted to a jury, but do not *require* them to do so. Still, the idea that an individual judge can act as a sentencing commission unto himself is troubling if the jury right is meant to limit judicial power over factfinding.

There are two possible approaches in considering the Sixth Amendment's implications for discretionary sentencing. One is to require sentencing judges to ask juries for special findings whenever there are genuine disputes between the parties as to issues of fact that the judge might deem relevant to his ultimate sentencing decision. This would be similar to a capital sentencing regime that gives the judge discretion whether to sentence a defendant to life imprisonment or death, but requires the jury to resolve relevant factual disputes and provide a nonbinding sentencing recommen-

---

mation; (2) legislatures can threaten to replace them with more mandatory systems; and (3) judges can be held accountable for noncompliance (outside of appellate reversal)").

[249] Blackstone, 4 *Commentaries* at *343 (cited in note 22).

[250] See, e.g., An Act for the Punishment of certain Crimes against the United States §§ 25, 26 , 1 Stat 112, 117, 118 (1790) (setting forth penalties of imprisonment "not exceeding" a certain number of years, and authorizing fines "at the discretion of the court"); John Baker, *An Introduction to English Legal History* 584 (Butterworths, 3d ed 1990).

[251] See, e.g., *Booker*, 543 US at 233 ("[W]hen a trial judge exercises his discretion to select a specific sentence within a defined range, the defendant has no right to a jury determination of the facts that the judge deems relevant.").

dation to the judge.[252] Of course, such a rule will be difficult for appellate courts to enforce, as discretionary sentencing regimes allow trial judges to conceal their true motives and reasons for imposing a particular sentence. This may explain why even the most pro-*Apprendi* Justices have never been willing to impose such limitations on purely discretionary sentencing regimes, content to leave the jury right as an "underenforced constitutional norm" in this context. But declaring a rule that requires sentencing judges to submit factual disputes to juries would help preserve the jury's structural role without taking the more radical step of imposing a constitutional ban on discretionary sentencing regimes.

Another possibility is to draw a constitutional distinction between the binary factfinding required by sentencing guidelines and the probabilistic weighing of evidence allowed by a fully discretionary sentencing regime.[253] Sentencing guidelines require the sentencer to treat a fact as established, or not, depending on whether a burden of proof is met. Fully discretionary sentencing imposes no such requirement. It allows the decision maker to adjust sentences based on mere probabilities and to calibrate the effect on a sentence in light of such probabilities. A sentencer might take into account a 10 percent likelihood that a defendant carried a gun during the crime, along with an 80 percent likelihood that his difficult upbringing affected his moral culpability. In doing this, a judge isn't forced to resolve questions of fact in a binary way; he's allowed to weigh different probabilities and use those to adjust his sentence. This at least provides a possible means by which to distinguish the "sentencing factors" that must be found by juries from the fully discretionary sentencing regimes that have always been thought constitutional.

In all events, defining the jury right in accordance with "questions of fact" would truly give "intelligible content" to that right by closing the door on most attempts to avoid the jury through legislative draftsmanship. And this approach has a substantial pedigree in historical sources and early state-court decisions that emphasize the jury's structural role in preventing judges from resolving factual questions. The Supreme Court, however, cannot extend the jury right in this manner unless it stops linking the

---

[252] See, e.g., 11 Del Code Ann § 4209 (2006).

[253] I thank Nicholas Quinn Rosenkranz for suggesting this concept of "probabilistic factfinding."

jury right with the reasonable-doubt rule. Under the current case law, any expansion of "jury facts" leads to a concomitant expansion in facts subject to the reasonable-doubt standard, and the Justices will not (and should not) hold that all facts legally relevant to guilt or punishment must be proved beyond a reasonable doubt.[254] Such a holding would overrule *Patterson v New York* and prohibit states from requiring criminal defendants to bear the burden of proof on affirmative defenses such as self-defense or insanity. Even Justice Thomas, who has embraced the most expansive theory of "elements," was unwilling to go that far.[255] But if the Court severs its link between these constitutional protections, it could extend the jury right to *all* defenses and sentencing facts, without requiring prosecutors to charge and prove such facts beyond a reasonable doubt.

At the same time, the Supreme Court should limit the reasonable-doubt rule and the concept of "elements" to something akin to their pre-*Apprendi* scope. This would include facts labeled as "elements" in criminal codes, along with facts that the Supreme Court might deem a "tail which wags the dog of a substantive offense,"[256] but not every sentencing fact that increases the ceiling on a defendant's punishment. The historical evidence described in Section V is merely the latest in a long string of criticisms leveled at court decisions that require prosecutors to charge and prove sentencing enhancements beyond a reasonable doubt, as if they were "elements" of a substantive crime. Professor Stephanos Bibas, for example, has criticized *Apprendi* for increasing prosecutorial power, giving them more "crimes" to charge and strengthening their hand in plea-bargaining negotiations.[257] Justice Breyer has argued that *Apprendi* could harm criminal defendants by forcing them to contest prejudicial sentencing facts during the guilt phase of trial rather than a bifurcated sentencing proceeding,[258] and he has further complained that *Apprendi* will lead to cruder

---

[254] See Section II.B.

[255] See, e.g., *Apprendi*, 530 US at 501 (Thomas, J, concurring); *Harris*, 536 US at 575 (Thomas, J, dissenting).

[256] *McMillan*, 477 US at 88.

[257] Bibas, 110 Yale L J at 1168–70 (cited in note 224); see also *Blakely*, 542 US at 331 (Breyer, J, dissenting).

[258] See, e.g., *Blakely*, 542 US at 335 (Breyer, J, dissenting) ("How can a Constitution that guarantees due process put these defendants, as a matter of course, in the position of arguing, 'I did not sell drugs, and if I did, I did not sell more than 500 grams' . . . ?").

	Factfinder:	
Standard of Proof:	**Right to Jury Determination**	**No Right to Jury**
Proof Beyond Reasonable Doubt Required	Elements	
Less than Proof Beyond Reasonable Doubt Allowed	Affirmative Defenses All Sentencing Factors	

FIG. 2

punishments by requiring sentences to be based on facts charged by prosecutors rather than real-offense conduct.[259]

But these problems arise only because some courts regard *Apprendi*'s "jury facts" as components of substantive crimes that prosecutors must charge and prove beyond a reasonable doubt. If *Apprendi* had simply required juries to decide *all* disputed questions of fact at sentencing, without any expansion of the reasonable-doubt rule and the concept of "elements," it could have protected the jury's factfinding role without relying on false historical claims regarding the meaning of "elements," and without giving rise to the pragmatic concerns noted by Professor Bibas and Justice Breyer. Indeed, the nineteenth-century first-degree murder cases demonstrate that jurisdictions *can* require juries to determine sentencing factors without adding new charging weapons to the prosecutor's arsenal, and that jury factfinding can coexist with "real-offense" sentencing and bifurcated sentencing proceedings.[260] None of the concerns noted by Professor Bibas and Justice Breyer should undermine *Apprendi*'s Sixth Amendment holding, once we jettison the Court's link between the jury right and the "elements" of crimes subject to the Court's reasonable-doubt rule.

Figure 2 illustrates this alternative approach, which expands the jury right to all questions of fact, but limits the reasonable-doubt rule to its pre-*Apprendi* scope. Compare the above proposal to the Court's current approach, shown in figure 3.

One challenge for this proposed approach is the prospect that

---

[259] See *Apprendi*, 530 US at 555–56 (Breyer, J, dissenting).

[260] See Section V.B.

	Factfinder:	
Standard of Proof:	**Right to Jury Determination**	**No Right to Jury**
Proof Beyond Reasonable Doubt Required	Elements "*Apprendi* facts" (or "Functional Equivalents" of Elements)	
Less than Proof Beyond Reasonable Doubt Allowed		All Other Sentencing Factors

FIG. 3

legislatures might evade the reasonable-doubt rule (and the Fifth Amendment's Indictment Clause) by relabeling "elements" of crimes as "sentencing factors." Of course, this problem is already present in the current *Apprendi* regime, which allows legislatures to avoid the reasonable-doubt rule by establishing "mitigating" sentencing factors or "affirmative defenses," or facts that establish mandatory minimum punishments. And one might think that *Winship*'s proof-beyond-a-reasonable-doubt requirement is best left as a default rule, given the historical and practical barriers to a more expansive regime.[261] But for those who are not content to leave *Winship* as a mere default rule, this possibility of legislative evasion must be taken seriously.

Fortunately, rejecting *Apprendi*'s reasonable-doubt holding will not necessarily leave the concept of "elements" completely at the mercy of the political branches. Even before *Apprendi*, the Supreme Court indicated that it would look past statutory labels if it deemed a fact to be a "tail which wags the dog of a substantive offense."[262] While the *Blakely* Court ridiculed this standard as hopelessly subjective,[263] nothing prevents the Court from adopting a more determinative constitutional standard for "elements" that stops short of *Apprendi*'s historically indefensible view that includes every sentencing fact that increases the ceiling on a defendant's

---

[261] See Section II.B.
[262] See *McMillan*, 477 US at 88.
[263] See *Blakely*, 542 US at 302 n 6, 307–08.

punishment.[264] Exploring all the possibilities in this regard would require another article, but one should not conclude that the doctrinal benefits from avoiding *Apprendi*'s expansive concept of "elements" will come at the cost of eviscerating proof beyond a reasonable doubt as a constitutional requirement.

VII

Although the Supreme Court uses the concept of "elements" to define boundaries for the reasonable-doubt rule, that should not define the scope of a criminal defendant's right of jury trial. The Supreme Court went off track in *McMillan v Pennsylvania*,[265] when it collapsed the jury trial and standard-of-proof claims into a unitary inquiry, holding that the jury right extends only to "elements" of criminal offenses subject to the Court's reasonable-doubt rule. This has infected the Court's *Apprendi* jurisprudence, which proceeds as if the right of jury trial and the reasonable-doubt rule are coextensive.

Because the Supreme Court has linked the jury right with the proof-beyond-a-reasonable-doubt standard, it is unable to extend the jury right in a manner that meaningfully protects the jury's constitutional factfinding role, because it cannot countenance a corresponding expansion in the reasonable-doubt rule and the concept of "elements." At the same time, when the Court *has* extended the jury right to certain sentencing enhancements, the accompanying expansion in the reasonable-doubt rule has produced a revisionist concept of "elements" that cannot be justified on historical or pragmatic grounds. In sum, the *Apprendi* jurisprudence has given us the worst of both worlds: a circumscribed jury role that is easily evaded, and an overbroad theory of "elements" that lacks historical support, gives new powers to prosecutors that were not conferred by legislatures, and brings needless pragmatic and doctrinal complications to court decisions that broaden the right of jury trial. All of this stems from the Court's assumption that the jury right goes hand-in-hand with the reasonable-doubt rule and the concept of "elements," a premise that originalists and pragmatists alike should reject.

The Court should therefore sever its link between the jury right

---

[264] Cf. *Patterson*, 432 US at 216–32 (Powell, J, dissenting).

[265] 477 US 79 (1986).

and the reasonable-doubt rule, expanding the former while constricting the latter. Juries should resolve any disputed question of fact that purports to aggravate *or mitigate* a defendant's range of punishment. But sentencing factors should not be regarded as "functional equivalents of elements" that prosecutors must charge and prove beyond a reasonable doubt whenever they increase a defendant's maximum allowable punishment. This approach would protect the jury's constitutional factfinding prerogatives while avoiding the historical and doctrinal problems arising from an overbroad understanding of "elements." And such a framework should satisfy most of *Apprendi*'s defenders and critics. *Apprendi*'s supporters should approve a regime that actually provides "intelligible content" for the jury right, unlike the Court's current jurisprudence. And once "jury facts" are decoupled from the "elements" of crimes that must be proved beyond a reasonable doubt and charged in indictments in federal prosecutions, court decisions that expand the jury right will no longer increase prosecutorial power, limit the use of "real-offense" sentencing, or force prejudicial sentencing facts into the guilt phase of trial.

JOHN HARRISON

STATE SOVEREIGN IMMUNITY AND CONGRESS'S ENFORCEMENT POWERS

Amid the current Justices' sharp disagreements on sovereign immunity there is one important point of agreement. According to the cases, the Constitution imposes significant limits on Congress's power to create private causes of action against nonconsenting states.[1] On this point four of the Justices strongly dissent.[2] The cases, however, recognize an exception with respect to one particular congressional power. Relying on *Fitzpatrick v Bitzer*, the Court holds that Congress may provide for private causes of action against nonconsenting states when it exercises its enforcement powers under Section 5 of the Fourteenth Amendment.[3] On this point there is

John Harrison is the D. Lurton Massee, Jr., Professor of Law, University of Virginia.

AUTHOR'S NOTE: Thanks to Caleb Nelson and Michael Collins for helpful comments and Josh Bartz for excellent research assistance.

[1] The leading case is *Seminole Tribe of Florida v Florida*, 517 US 44 (1996). The doctrine and its justification are most fully explained in *Alden v Maine*, 527 US 706 (1999), which held that Congress may subject states to regulation under the Fair Labor Standards Act with its authority under the Commerce Clause, but may not create private causes of action against the states.

[2] Justices Stevens, Souter, Ginsburg, and Breyer continue to reject the doctrine of *Seminole Tribe*. See, e.g., *Alden*, 427 US at 760 (Souter, J, joined by Stevens, Ginsburg, and Breyer, JJ, dissenting).

[3] *Fitzpatrick v Bitzer*, 527 US 445 (1976). As formulated by the Court the *Fitzpatrick* exception involves only Section 5 of the Fourteenth Amendment, not the enforcement clauses of the Thirteenth and Fifteenth Amendments (Section 2 in each case). It is hard to imagine, however, that the Court would treat the Thirteenth and Fifteenth Amendments differently from the Fourteenth. Nor, as appears below, is there any reason to believe that the people who framed the Reconstruction amendments thought that the enforcement powers differed from one another in this respect. The Court has not addressed Congress's

no dissent. Indeed, the late Chief Justice, author of the primary case limiting Congress's power, *Seminole Tribe*, was also the author of *Fitzpatrick*.

Fitzpatrick is quite brief. It resolved the question of congressional power under Section 5 in very short compass, with virtually no inquiry into the original understanding.[4] Subsequent cases have not expanded on its analysis, and have not even asked whether it makes sense in light of more recent doctrinal developments.[5]

This article examines the correctness of *Fitzpatrick*. It asks questions at three levels of abstraction. Part I investigates the understandings of the people who participated in framing the Reconstruction amendments, using the debates on the Fourteenth and Fifteenth Amendments and on the enforcement legislation that Congress adopted from 1866 to 1871. It concludes that they probably did not believe that the amendments gave Congress power to create private causes of action against states. Part II deals with the purpose of the Fourteenth Amendment as deduced from the circumstances surrounding its enactment. The amendment was proposed in part to make clear that Congress could adopt the Civil Rights Act of 1866. Part II considers and rejects the argument that, whatever the subjective views of the framers, in order to accomplish its goal of sustaining the act, the Fourteenth Amendment had to give Congress power to override sovereign immunity. Part III asks whether the structural reasoning underlying *Fitzpatrick* is sound given the assumptions of *Seminole Tribe* and *Alden*, and maintains that it is not. Part IV brings the threads together, briefly concluding that if *Seminole Tribe* and *Alden* are correct then *Fitzpatrick* is not.

I. The Expectations of the Framers

This section seeks to uncover the Reconstruction framers' expectations concerning Congress's power under the enforcement

power under the other amendments that have enforcement clauses, such as the Nineteenth, nor will I.

[4] *Fitzpatrick* resolves its principal issue in a few pages, 427 US at 453–56, mainly addressing *Ex parte Virginia*, 100 US 339 (1880), which upheld criminal punishment of a state judge who violated the ban on race discrimination in jury selection contained in the Civil Rights Act of 1875. The Court did not rely on any evidence from the framing of the Fourteenth Amendment other than the amendment's text.

[5] Only one commentator has inquired into the question of the original understanding in any depth. John E. Nowak, *The Scope of Congressional Power to Create Causes of Action Against State Governments and the History of the Eleventh and Fourteenth Amendments*, 75 Colum L Rev 1413 (1975). My conclusions differ from Professor Nowak's.

clauses to create causes of action for private people against non-consenting states. The Thirteenth Amendment was proposed in 1865 by the 38th Congress, the Fourteenth Amendment in 1866 by the 39th, and the Fifteenth Amendment in 1869 by the 40th. The 39th Congress adopted the Civil Rights Act of 1866, which when adopted was justified mainly on the Enforcement Clause of the Thirteenth Amendment; Section 1 of the Fourteenth Amendment was designed in part to provide a firmer constitutional foundation for the 1866 act, as doubts had been expressed as to whether the Thirteenth Amendment genuinely could support the legislation. The 41st Congress adopted the Voting Rights Act of 1870, which enforced the Fourteenth and Fifteenth Amendments, as did the Ku Klux Act of 1871, adopted by the 42d Congress. Because so many of the people who proposed the amendments also supported the implementing civil rights acts, some of the best available evidence of their understanding of the new constitutional provisions comes from their contemporaneous statutes implementing those provisions.

All of that work took place against the background of well-established principles governing remedies for unlawful government action, including unconstitutional statutes. Also part of the background, although somewhat less thoroughly fleshed out, was judicial doctrine protecting the states from federal control. This part begins with a review of the mid-nineteenth-century law on those topics, and then turns to Congress during Reconstruction.

A. DOCTRINES OF STATE SOVEREIGNTY IN THE NINETEENTH CENTURY

1. *Public law remedies in a system based on governmental immunity from suit.* In order to understand what the framers and ratifiers of the Reconstruction amendments thought about remedies under the enforcement clauses, it is necessary to know about the remedies against government with which they were familiar. As of the mid-nineteenth century those remedies included a number of ways of getting government decisions into court and obtaining redress, including damages, but they did not include lawsuits by private individuals against nonconsenting states.

Most basic of all the pieces of the public law remedial system was (as it still is) the principle that invalid government acts are legal nullities, and in particular that unconstitutional laws and government decisions are legal nullities.[6] Nullity of unlawful official acts could be relied on by private people in a variety of litigation contexts. Perhaps the most basic was the context in which the government was not the defendant but the plaintiff, or prosecutor. In criminal proceedings or other government enforcement actions, defendants could argue that they were being prosecuted under a law that was unconstitutional, or under a state law that was inconsistent with a valid federal statute.[7] Challenges to the validity of state laws also could be raised in litigation between private parties.[8]

Affirmative relief against the government itself, or rather something close to it, was mainly available through that staple of nineteenth-century public law litigation, the suit against a government officer. Officer suits could be used to challenge the validity of a legal authority on which an official acted, or the lawfulness of the official's own decision. Damages were routinely available, albeit from the officer personally and not the public treasury. An individual who suffered harm at the hands of an official to an interest protected by the private law would follow a well-established structure to seek redress. The individual would sue the officer, usually in tort, alleging the injury. The officer would plead justification pursuant to official authority, for example a statute authorizing action that otherwise would be wrongful. The individual in turn would argue that the officer had exceeded his authority or that the legal authority was itself invalid, for instance because of a constitutional defect.[9]

---

[6] "The sanction of nullity is pervasive in the whole theory of American public law." Henry M. Hart, Jr., and Albert M. Sacks, *The Legal Process: Basic Problems in the Making and Application of Law* 154 (William N. Eskridge, Jr., and Philip P. Frickey, eds, 1994). See *Marbury v Madison*, 1 Cranch 137 (1803) (statutes contrary to the Constitution are legal nullities).

[7] See, e.g., *Cohens v Virginia*, 6 Wheat 264 (1821) (invalidity of state criminal statute raised as a defense).

[8] See, e.g., *Fletcher v Peck*, 6 Cranch 87 (1810) (Georgia legislative action held invalid under Contracts Clause in action between private parties).

[9] An example of an officer suit for trespass damages is *M'Connell v Hampton*, 12 Johns 234 (NY Sup Ct 1815), arising out of the War of 1812. M'Connell was arrested by the U.S. military and sued the commanding officer, Hampton, for assault and false imprisonment. Hampton pled his authority under federal law, but the trial court found that the arrest was unlawful and the jury imposed heavy damages of $9,000. The New York Court of Appeals, finding the damages clearly excessive, remanded for a new trial. Id at 234–35. A similar case was *Smith v Shaw*, 12 Johns 257 (NY Sup Ct 1815). Shaw was arrested on suspicion of being a spy and sued the custodial officer for trespass and false imprisonment, winning damages.

If an officer was threatening to do something that would be a tort if done by a private person without official privilege, the validity of the officer's authority could be challenged in advance through an injunctive proceeding, provided the usual requirements for an injunction were met.[10] To compel the performance of an official duty, however, the remedy was generally not injunctive, but rather a common law writ designed specifically for officers, mandamus.[11] Mandamus, like all the other remedies discussed so far, in form ran against the officer personally, and indeed under traditional rules of pleading it was brought on behalf of the government, on the relation of the real plaintiff in interest, against the officer.[12] Mandamus of course had limits, the most important of which confined it to compelling clearly marked, nondiscretionary duties, like the delivery of a commission. Officers were also subject to personal sanctions for unlawful conduct, including civil penalties and criminal prosecution.[13] Finally, sovereign immunity could be waived.[14]

All the clever lawyering with officer suits resulted from a premise of the system: states and the United States could not be sued without their consent. As Justice Story said in his *Commentaries on the Constitution*, "It is a known maxim, justified by the general sense and practice of mankind, and recognized in the law of nations, that it is inherent in the nature of sovereignty not to be amenable to the suit of any private person, without its own con-

---

[10] In *Osborn v Bank of the United States*, 9 Wheat 738 (1824), the bank sought and obtained from the lower federal court an injunction against Osborn, the state auditor for Ohio, directing him not to carry out his stated intention to seize property of the bank in order to collect an Ohio tax.

[11] See, e.g., James L. High, *A Treatise on Extraordinary Remedies, Embracing Mandamus, Quo Warranto, and Prohibition* 4 (1874) (mandamus is directed to officers, inferior courts, and public corporations to compel them to perform an official duty).

[12] Id at 302–03. An example of the pleading convention at work is the classic Taney Court case of *Kendall v United States ex rel Stokes*, 12 Pet 524 (1838) (Circuit Court for the District of Columbia may issue mandamus to federal officials in the district). Kendall was the Postmaster General, Stokes a post office contractor with a dispute under the contract.

[13] For example, the Fugitive Slave Act of 1850 provided criminal punishment and civil liability for U.S. marshals who failed to perform their duties under the act. Act of Sept 18, 1850, ch lx, § 5, 9 Stat 462.

[14] The antebellum constitutions of Delaware and Pennsylvania empowered their legislatures to authorize suits against those states on terms chosen by the legislatures. Del Const of 1831, Art I, § 9; Pa Const of 1838, Art IX, § 11. Congress waived federal sovereign immunity in contract, and provided that the Court of Claims would adjudicate such actions, in 1863. Act of Mar 3, 1863, ch 92, 12 Stat 765.

sent. This exemption is an attribute of sovereignty, belonging to every State in the Union: and was designedly retained by the national government."[15] Story went on to explain the system of officer suits for torts and, sometimes, waiver of sovereignty immunity for contract claims.[16]

Sovereign immunity was a familiar principle in federal and state court. In *Beers v Arkansas*[17] the Supreme Court of the United States stated the point broadly: "It is an established principle of jurisprudence in all civilized nations that the sovereign cannot be sued in its own courts, or in any other, without its consent and permission." It was taken for granted that the sovereign could not be sued, so the questions that actually came up mainly involved the boundary between impermissible suits against the government and permissible suits against officers and other agents. The Supreme Court of Pennsylvania found that the city of Pittsburgh was on the immune side of the line, explaining that "it is the prerogative of a sovereign to be exempt from coercion by action" and that the city was within that principle.[18] Sovereign immunity might produce results contrary to natural justice, the court explained, but it was the law.[19] In similar fashion, in a tort suit against the superintendent of a railroad owned by the state of Georgia, the Supreme Court of Georgia held for the defendant: "the general rule where the State is the party doing the injury, is, that there is no judicial remedy of any sort. The State cannot be sued."[20] The issue that is so contested today, whether Congress could create a cause of action for a private person against a nonconsenting state, seems not to have arisen in the nineteenth century.

The system just described applied to states and the United States. Matters were somewhat more complicated and more uncertain with respect to local governments. Some of the complexity and uncertainty arose from the fact that different kinds of local governments, which today would be treated as belonging to a

---

[15] Joseph Story, 3 *Commentaries on the Constitution of the United States* 538, § 1669 (1833) (footnotes omitted).

[16] Id at 539–40, §§ 1670–71.

[17] 20 How 527, 529 (1858).

[18] *O'Connor v Pittsburgh*, 18 Pa St R 187, 189 (1851) (tort action for damage to property resulting from lowering the grade of a street).

[19] Id.

[20] *Walker v Spullock*, 23 Ga 436, 438 (1857).

single legal category, were then often regarded as quite distinct. Counties were usually treated as subdivisions of states, partaking of the legal status of the state; they were distinguished from municipal corporations properly speaking, which were incorporated in much the same manner as a private corporation.[21] Municipal corporations, separately incorporated entities that perform government functions such as towns and cities, were often seen as intermediate between states and private corporations; Cooley said that for purposes of tort the sovereign immunity of municipal corporations depended on the function being performed.[22]

Another source of complexity and uncertainty arose from the difference between the two great branches of nineteenth-century private law, tort and contract. By the time of the Civil War it was reasonably well established that local governments generally were subject to lawsuits on their contracts, and in particular on their debts.[23] With respect to torts, however, the situation was less clear, but localities do seem sometimes to have had part of the states' sovereign immunity.[24]

2. *State immunity from federal control.* With respect to intergovernmental immunity the mid-nineteenth-century law was clear in one direction: as *M'Culloch v Maryland*[25] illustrated, the federal government was not subject to state control when it acted within its sphere. Matters were less clear in the other direction, when the United States acted on the states as such. One such interaction was generally, but not universally, accepted: the Supreme Court of the United States had appellate jurisdiction over the state courts

[21] John F. Dillon, 1 *Commentaries on the Law of Municipal Corporations* 44 (4th ed 1890) (counties are political divisions of states and deal with matters of state, not municipal, concern).

[22] Thomas M. Cooley, *A Treatise on the Law of Torts* *619–22 (2d ed 1880) (discussing tort liability and immunity of municipal corporations).

[23] By the 1860s cases involving bonds issued by local governments were a staple of the Supreme Court's docket, mainly coming through the diversity jurisdiction; Fairman treated the matter at length in his Holmes Devise volumes. Charles Fairman, 6 *History of the Supreme Court of the United States: Reconstruction and Reunion, 1864–88, Part One* 918–1116 (1971).

[24] 2 Dillon (cited in note 21) at 1156: "We find it impossible to state, by way of definition, any rule sufficiently exact to be of much practical value which will *precisely embrace the torts for which a civil action* will, in the absence of a statute declaring the liability, lie against a municipal corporation."

[25] 4 Wheat 316 (1819) (states may not tax federally created corporations).

as to cases within the Article III jurisdiction.[26] Beyond appellate jurisdiction and a few other specialized contexts, such as presidential command of the militia when called to federal service, federal power to control state officers and the instrumentalities of state government was widely denied.[27] It is likely everyone but a few extreme supporters of federal authority believed that there were important limits on the national government's ability to command the states as such.

When state intergovernmental immunity came up during debates on the Reconstruction amendments and civil rights acts, the most significant case was probably *Prigg v Pennsylvania*,[28] which dealt with state and federal authority concerning fugitive slaves. Prigg was convicted in Pennsylvania court for recapturing an escaped slave without using the procedures set out in a Pennsylvania statute. The Court, through Justice Story, found that the Pennsylvania statute was preempted by the federal Fugitive Slave Act of 1793. The Fugitive Slave Clause of Article IV of the Constitution provides that persons held to service or labor in one state who escape to another are to be delivered up to the person to whom the labor is due.[29] It does not explicitly provide for any federal power to implement it, but the Court found such a power implicit. Justice Story reasoned that the Constitution, by creating the right of recaption, imposed a duty to respect the right. The duty is found in the federal Constitution, not a state constitution, and does not mention the states. Thus the power to enforce the duty must vest with the national government.[30] As part of that argument the Court embraced a principle of state autonomy: the Constitution "does not point out any state functionaries, or any state action to carry its provisions into effect. The states cannot, therefore, be compelled to enforce them."[31]

Opponents of slavery relied on *Prigg*, as Justice Story may have intended, for the proposition that state officials were to have noth-

---

[26] *Martin v Hunter's Lessee*, 1 Wheat 304 (1816) (Supreme Court of the United States has appellate jurisdiction over state courts with respect to cases within the federal judicial power under Article III).

[27] When state militia are called into federal service, the President is their commander-in-chief. US Const, Art II, § 2, para 1.

[28] 16 Pet 539 (1842).

[29] US Const, Art IV, § 2, para 3.

[30] 16 Pet at 615–16.

[31] Id.

ing to do with returning runaway slaves.[32] Because the infrastructure of the federal government was in those days quite limited, confining the enforcement of the clause to federal officers and courts was a substantial restriction on slaveholders' ability to recapture. *Prigg*'s defense of the states from federal duties became popular with opponents of slavery, and it is not surprising that it was cited during the Reconstruction debates by both Republicans, who had long endorsed it for that reason, and Democrats, who favored states' rights generally.

A similar Taney Court case that restricted federal power and provided a practical victory for antislavery forces was *Kentucky v Dennison*,[33] which involved the return of a fugitive from justice. Article IV provides that such fugitives are to be returned to the state from which they fled on demand of the executive authority of that state. Under the same 1793 statute at issue in *Prigg*, Congress had made it the duty of the Governor of the receiving state to return the fugitive. Willis Lago was indicted in Kentucky for helping a slave escape and flee to Ohio. Kentucky demanded that Ohio Governor William Dennison deliver Lago. Dennison refused and Kentucky sued in the original jurisdiction of the Supreme Court, seeking mandamus against Dennison.

The Court, through Chief Justice Taney, indicated that Governor Dennison's refusal was unjustified but refused to grant relief. Although the federal statute purported to impose a duty on the Governor, that was only a moral duty, not one that could be enforced in federal court.[34] "And we think it clear, that the Federal Government, under the Constitution, has no power to impose on a state officer, as such, any duty whatever, and compel him to perform it; for if it possessed this power, it might overload the officer with duties which would fill up all his time, and disable him from performing his obligations to the State."[35] Congress

---

[32] Story himself characterized *Prigg*'s doctrine of federal exclusivity as a victory for freedom. R. Kent Newmyer, *Supreme Court Justice Joseph Story: Statesman of the Old Republic* 372 (1985). In response to *Prigg*, several northern legislatures explicitly forbade state officers to assist in the recovery of fugitive slaves, which is just what Story said he had in mind. Id at 373. Paul Finkelman argues that in fact Story sacrificed the interests of slaves, and of intellectual honesty, in order to strengthen national power. Paul Finkelman, *Story Telling on the Supreme Court: Prigg v Pennsylvania and Justice Joseph Story's Judicial Nationalism*, 1994 Supreme Court Review 247.

[33] 24 How 66 (1861), overruled in part, *Puerto Rico v Branstad*, 483 US 219 (1987).

[34] 24 How at 107.

[35] Id at 107–08.

could authorize state officers and institutions to perform certain functions, and had authorized state courts to entertain federal actions, but it could not compel state cooperation.[36]

After the Reconstruction amendments were adopted, but while Congress was still implementing them with enforcement legislation, the Court decided another state immunity case that reflected a strong principle of state autonomy and that made its way into the congressional debates. *Collector v Day*[37] held that a state judge did not have to pay the income tax Congress imposed during the Civil War. Echoing John Marshall, the Court explained that the power to tax is the power to destroy, and Congress has no power to destroy the states or their officers.[38] In dissent, Justice Bradley drew another theme from *M'Culloch*, arguing that it was one thing for the common government of all to tax state officers just as it taxed its own officers, and another thing for one state to tax federal officers and instrumentalities, which were the agents not just of that state but of all the others; Bradley thus rejected complete symmetry between state and federal immunity.[39]

As far as the Supreme Court was concerned, even during Reconstruction states still had substantial protections from federal power. In describing the judicial doctrine I do not mean to imply that all Republicans would have agreed; Bradley, who dissented in *Day*, was a Grant appointee. But the Court's opinion in that case was joined by six Republican appointees, including the first Republican Chief Justice, whose relatively brief tenure may best be remembered for a statement that summarized moderate Republican thinking about the federal union: "Not only, therefore, can there by no loss of separate and independent autonomy to the States, through their union under the Constitution, but it may not unreasonably be said that the preservation of the States, and the maintenance of their governments, are as much within the design and care of the Constitution as the preservation of the

---

[36] Id at 108–09.

[37] 11 Wall 113 (1871).

[38] Justice Nelson quoted the famous passage about the power to tax being the power to destroy, 11 Wall at 123, and then explained that state immunity from federal interference was symmetrical with federal immunity from state interference: "the States within the limits of their powers not granted, or, in the language of the tenth amendment, 'reserved,' are as independent of the general government as that government within its sphere is independent of the States," id at 124.

[39] Id at 128–29 (Bradley, J, dissenting).

Union and the maintenance of the National government. The Constitution, in all its provisions, looks to an indestructible Union, composed of indestructible States."[40]

B. THE CIVIL RIGHTS ACT OF 1866 AND THE FOURTEENTH AMENDMENT

At the center of this inquiry is the First Session of the 39th Congress, which opened in December 1865 and sat into the summer of 1866. That session adopted the Civil Rights Act of 1866 and proposed the Fourteenth Amendment.[41] The 1866 act is doubly important here, because it is closely connected to the enforcement clauses of both the Thirteenth and Fourteenth Amendments. Section 1 of the act forbade the states from discriminating on the basis of race, color, or previous condition of servitude with respect to a list of legal entitlements, entitlements then referred to as civil rights.[42] It was directed against the Black Codes, statutes adopted by postwar southern state legislatures that discriminated against the freed slaves with respect to their basic rights of property, contract, and access to the courts.[43] Section 2 of the act made it a federal crime for anyone acting under state law to violate Section 1.[44] It was explicitly directed against state officers and thereby implicated congressional power to act against the states.

Proponents of the 1866 act relied mainly on the Thirteenth Amendment as the source of Congress's power to adopt it. They argued that race discrimination was a badge or incident of slavery, and that freedom entailed equality with other citizens with respect to civil rights. Congress could legislate on the subject because of its power under Section 2 of the Thirteenth Amendment to enforce the substantive provisions of Section 1.[45] The debate on the

---

[40] *Texas v White*, 7 Wall 700, 725 (1869) (Chase, CJ).

[41] The Civil Rights Act of 1866 is Act of Apr 9, 1866, ch xxxi, 14 Stat 27.

[42] Id, § 1, 14 Stat 27. Today the phrase "civil rights" often refers to antidiscrimination norms. It did not in 1866. Rather, civil rights were the basic legal advantages that citizens enjoyed, primarily rights of property, contract, and protection through the legal system. The Civil Rights Act of 1866 was so called, not because it was an antidiscrimination rule, but because it was an antidiscrimination rule about civil rights.

[43] See Fairman at 110–15 (cited in note 23) (summarizing Black Codes).

[44] Act of Apr 9, 1866, ch xxxi, § 2, 14 Stat 27.

[45] Senator Lyman Trumbull of Illinois, Chairman of the Senate Judiciary Committee, was the principal drafter of the 1866 act and its manager in the Senate. Discussing the Black Codes, Trumbull said that "any statute which is not equal to all, and which deprives

act was thus in large part a debate about the extent of congressional power under the very first Reconstruction Enforcement Clause.

While the Republicans who controlled the 39th Congress were able to pass the Civil Rights Act over President Johnson's veto, there were lingering doubts about its validity; the act forbade race discrimination against people who had never been slaves as well as against former slaves, and it operated in both former slave states and states that had never had slavery, so its connection to the Thirteenth Amendment was doubtful.[46] Moreover, like any statute, the 1866 act could be repealed, and some Republicans feared that it would be as soon as the Democrats regained control of Congress.[47] Thus one purpose of the Fourteenth Amendment was to put the substantive rule of the Civil Rights Act into the Constitution and to ensure that Congress had power to adopt the act, including the parts of it that would not follow from a self-executing constitutional antidiscrimination rule. Section 5 of the Fourteenth Amendment was therefore designed in part to support the enforcement provisions of the 1866 act, including in particular the criminal penalties imposed on state officers by Section 2 of the statute.

Proponents of the Civil Rights Act did not say that Section 2 of that legislation represented, or that Section 2 of the Thirteenth Amendment authorized, a significant federal intrusion into state autonomy. Rather, they presented the criminal penalty in Section 2 of the act as an ordinary application of individual accountability for officers and of federal supremacy. Senator Trumbull explained that it involved nothing new. Section 2 did not punish the law or the community, but the individual person who violated federal

---

any citizen of civil rights which are secured to other citizens, is an unjust encroachment upon his liberty; and is, in fact, a badge of servitude which, by the Constitution, is prohibited." Cong Globe, 39th Cong, 1st Sess 474 (1866). Trumbull went on to argue that Section 2 of the Thirteenth Amendment "vests Congress with the discretion of selecting that 'appropriate legislation' which it is believed will best accomplish the end and prevent slavery," id at 475, and that the penalty in Section 2 of the 1866 act, along with the act's other enforcement provisions, were "the machinery to carry [the Constitution] into effect," id.

[46] See William E. Nelson, *The Fourteenth Amendment: From Political Principle to Judicial Doctrine* 104 (1988) (Section 1 of Fourteenth Amendment designed in part to obviate constitutional problems with Civil Rights Act of 1866).

[47] Cong Globe, 39th Cong, 1st Sess 2896 (1866) (Senator Howard explains that Section 1 of Fourteenth Amendment is designed to put antidiscrimination rule of Civil Rights Act into Constitution).

law.[48] Trumbull also denied that the act would punish a judge who in good faith refused to follow it on constitutional grounds. He maintained that criminal intent would be absent in such a situation.[49] As for state judges who knowingly refused to follow valid federal law, they should be punished. Indeed, Trumbull explained, Congress had provided for similar punishment of state officials ever since it enacted the Crimes Act of 1790, which imposed criminal penalties on officers who served process on foreign diplomats contrary to the law of nations.[50] Trumbull scoffed at the suggestion that state law could authorize an officer to violate federal law. That would place state officials above the law. The southern secession legislatures had conspired against the United States; surely state law could not have protected them from prosecution.[51] Provided that Section 1 of the act was itself constitutional, Section 2 rested on ordinary federal supremacy. Trumbull did not invoke any special feature of the Thirteenth Amendment that would authorize otherwise impermissible federal intrusion into state autonomy.

One leading Democratic legal thinker in the Senate, Reverdy Johnson of Maryland, seems to have agreed with Senator Trumbull about congressional enforcement power. Johnson opposed the Civil Rights Act, arguing that it struck at the legislative and judicial power of the states and raised the feared specter of consolidated federal power.[52] He did not, however, deny that Congress could punish state officers when it acted within its enumerated powers. Johnson distinguished Section 2 of the Civil Rights Act from the 1790 Crimes Act on which Trumbull relied on the grounds that Congress had an enumerated power to enforce the law of nations.[53] Johnson apparently believed that when Congress acted within its granted authority it could impose individual criminal punishment on state officers. The problem for him seems to have been that the whole act, starting with the substantive rule of Section 1, went

[48] Id at 1758.

[49] Id.

[50] Id. The ban on serving process on foreign diplomats is in Act of Apr 30, 1790, ch ix, § 26, 1 Stat 118, which made it a crime for a government officer to execute a writ on a protected diplomat.

[51] Cong Globe, 39th Cong, 1st Sess 1758 (1866).

[52] Id at 1775–78.

[53] Id at 1778.

beyond Congress's enumerated authority and thereby invaded the legislative domain of the states.[54]

In the House, too, supporters of the act said that the Section 2 criminal penalty involved no innovation and no serious intrusion into state autonomy. Representative James Wilson, chairman of the House Judiciary Committee, believed that the bill enforced both Section 1 of the Thirteenth Amendment and the Privileges and Immunities Clause of Article IV.[55] Representative Samuel Shellabarger of Ohio, a leading Republican legal theorist in the House, similarly regarded Section 2 of the act as unproblematic.[56] It simply punished a violation of an act of Congress.[57]

Debate in Congress in 1866 focused on issues that mattered in 1866, not issues that matter now. Thus the debate on the Fourteenth Amendment was concerned mainly with Section 2, which changed the basis of apportionment for the House and the Electoral College, and Section 3, which imposed political disabilities on many former Confederates. Section 1, which has become the principal font of substantive constitutional doctrine, received much less attention, and Section 5, with which this article is concerned, received hardly any. When Thaddeus Stevens introduced the amendment in the House on behalf of the Joint Committee

---

[54] Not only Reverdy Johnson found himself in agreement with Trumbull on the constitutional point. Senator Garrett Davis of Kentucky, as heated and voluble an opponent as the Civil Rights Act had, when pressed was forced to agree with respect to federal power to punish state officers. During a lengthy speech in support of President Johnson's veto, Davis too responded to Trumbull's argument based on earlier statutes such as the 1790 Crimes Act. His answer was the same as Reverdy Johnson's. The difference, Davis said, was that those earlier federal laws were directed against unconstitutional state laws, and officers who were instruments of wrong and oppression under them. Id at App 185.

[55] Id at 1115–18; id at App 157. With respect to Article IV, Representative Wilson departed from judicial orthodoxy, which then as now held that the clause forbade discrimination by states with respect to civil rights against Americans from out of state. See, e.g., *Paul v Virginia*, 8 Wall 168 (1869) (Privileges and Immunities Clause of Article IV forbids discrimination against citizens of other states). It is not clear whether Wilson believed that Article IV forbade discrimination with respect to privileges and immunities or was a substantive guarantee of basic rights to all citizens. The important point here is that Article IV was part of the original Constitution, so in enforcing it Congress could not rely on any new authority granted by the Thirteenth Amendment. Wilson seems to have thought that the Thirteenth Amendment supported the Civil Rights Act only insofar as the act applied to freed slaves.

[56] "Now, sir, I have no difficulty in regard to the constitutionality of the second section of this bill, provided we have the power to enact the first section." Cong Globe, 39th Cong, 1st Sess 1293 (1866).

[57] Id at 1294.

on Reconstruction, his initial speech did not even mention the enforcement provision.[58]

Senator Jacob Howard of Michigan, who introduced the amendment in the Senate on behalf of the joint committee, did discuss Section 5 and did say something that bears on this inquiry. Howard explained that constitutional restrictions on the states did not, by themselves, imply congressional power to enforce them. If Congress was to have such power with respect to the Fourteenth Amendment, and in particular the restrictions of Section 1, it had to be granted explicitly.[59] Howard thus presented Section 5 as extending Congress's substantive authority, adding to the list in Article I, Section 8. He did not say that it granted a power different from others in its ability to reach into state sovereignty. And his example of a proper exercise of the Section 5 grant was minimal: "It enables Congress, in case the States shall enact laws in conflict with the principles of the amendment, to correct that legislation by a formal congressional enactment."[60] From Howard's description one might have concluded that Section 5 was there just in case Section 1 turned out not to be self-executing in the fashion of most other constitutional restrictions on the states.

Representative John Bingham of Ohio, member of the Joint Committee on Reconstruction and principal drafter of the second sentence of Section 1 of the Fourteenth Amendment, indicated that the point of a provision like Section 5 was to ensure that Congress had power to adopt provisions like Section 2 of the Civil Rights Act. While the act was pending before Congress, Bingham, on behalf of the Joint Committee on Reconstruction, introduced in the House a precursor to Section 1 of the Fourteenth Amendment.[61] The proposed amendment was in form a grant of power to Congress, authorizing it to pass all laws necessary and proper to protect the privileges and immunities of citizens and to secure

---

[58] Id at 2459. Others mentioned Section 5 only to say that it did not need to be discussed. Representative Boyer, who opposed the amendment, said that it was not necessary to remark on Section 5, id at 2467, while Representative Miller, who supported it, explained that Section 5 was too plain to admit of argument, id at 2511.

[59] Id at 2765. As discussed below, Howard's premise, while held by many, was also often rejected: there was substantial controversy concerning congressional authority to enforce prohibitions in the absence of any enumerated power for that purpose.

[60] Id at 2768.

[61] Id at 1033.

to all persons equal protection of life, liberty, and property.[62] Bingham maintained that the states were already required to respect
privileges and immunities by Article IV of the Constitution, and
to give equal protection to life, liberty, and property by the Due
Process Clause of the Fifth Amendment.[63] The problem, he explained, was that this obligation was enforced only by the state
officers' oath to support the Constitution, which had proven inadequate. Congress needed power to punish "by penal enactment"
state officers who violated their oaths.[64] Bingham was one of those
who said that limitations on the states, without more, did not entail
congressional power to enforce those limitations.[65] He said that
Congress needed power to enforce an obligation that federal law
already imposed on state officers, not that it needed a wholly new
kind of authority over state governments as such.

In the Fourteenth Amendment itself Bingham's earlier proposal
was broken into two pieces, the substantive part going into Section
1 and the power in Congress going into Section 5. The significance
of that change remains a matter of interest.[66] It did not change
Bingham's explanation of the need for enforcement power. Speaking in favor of the Fourteenth Amendment itself, Bingham said
that Section 1 repaired the want of power in the whole people to
protect privileges and immunities and ensure equal protection.[67]
Although he clearly contemplated that it would enable Congress
to punish officers individually, he did not indicate that it would
authorize legislation regulating the states themselves.

Opponents of the Fourteenth Amendment spent little time with
Section 5. When they did address it their concern seems to have
been that it was a new font of federal power in areas previously

---

[62] Id at 1034.

[63] Id.

[64] Id at 1090. "The question, is simply, whether you will give by this amendment to the
people of the United States the power, by legislative enactment, to punish officials of
States for violation of the oaths enjoined upon them by their Constitution?" Id.

[65] Id at 1093 (distinguishing between bills of rights and grants of power). Although he
was in favor of enforcing state officers' obligations through criminal statutes, Bingham
objected to Section 2 of the Civil Rights Act because it made errors of judgment by state
officers a crime. Id at 1291.

[66] In *City of Boerne v Flores*, 521 US 507 (1997), the Court relied on the change from
Bingham's proposal to the Fourteenth Amendment's combination of Sections 1 and 5 for
its conclusion that the "Fourteenth Amendment's history confirms the remedial, rather
than substantive, nature of the Enforcement Clause," id at 520.

[67] Cong Globe, 39th Cong, 1st Sess 2542 (1866).

governed by the states, not that it would enable Congress to regulate the states as such. Senator Hendricks pointed to the experience with Section 2 of the Thirteenth Amendment, which had
been represented by its sponsors as a minor clause but had become
a source of national control over the rights of citizens.[68] Representative Harding of Kentucky made essentially the same point,
saying that Section 5 would transfer to Congress all power over
the rights of citizens.[69]

If Section 5 of the Fourteenth Amendment was supposed to
differ from other federal powers with respect to Congress's power
to regulate the states as such, no one on either side mentioned it.
And no one breathed a word about sovereign immunity from suit.
Its leading advocates provided examples of its application, nullity
and actions against officers but not states, that were familiar in a
system that assumed that states could not be sued as such.

C. THE FIFTEENTH AMENDMENT AND ITS ENFORCEMENT CLAUSE

While the Enforcement Clause of the Fourteenth Amendment
received little attention in Congress, the Enforcement Clause of
the Fifteenth received hardly any, especially from its supporters.
There were plenty of other issues. The amendment itself was
highly controversial. Not only was black suffrage a matter of bitter
dispute, north and south, but also the amendment was brought
before a lame-duck session of Congress that convened in December 1868, shortly after General Grant had been elected President
on a Republican platform according to which suffrage in the loyal
states was a matter for them to decide.[70] Opponents said that the
Republicans were engaged in a breach of faith, having promised
that northern states would resolve the suffrage question for themselves only to break their pledge within weeks.[71]

Moreover, the precise content that the amendment should have
was the subject of much debate. One question was whether it

---

[68] Id at 2940.

[69] Id at 3147.

[70] The 1868 Republican platform said that while equal suffrage for loyal men in the
South was clearly necessary, the question of suffrage in the loyal states, which meant the
North, was up to the people of those states. Donald Bruce Johnson and Kirk H. Porter,
eds, *National Party Platforms, 1840–1972* 39 (5th ed 1975).

[71] William Gillette, *The Right to Vote: Politics and the Passage of the Fifteenth Amendment*
56 (1965) (Democrats denounce Republican change of position and breach of faith).

should protect only the right to vote or also the right to hold office.[72] That issue was especially salient because the majority of the reconstructed legislature in Georgia had expelled its black members on the grounds that they had been enfranchised but not entitled to hold office.[73] Another issue was whether the amendment should be limited to race or should also extend to other grounds of discrimination, such as religion, place of birth (as, for example, in a foreign country), or education.[74] All this had to be thrashed out in a short session that had to end, when the terms of its members ended, on March 4, 1869.

During these somewhat chaotic proceedings, supporters of the amendment said virtually nothing about the Enforcement Clause. They hardly even mentioned the Civil Rights Act of 1866, which at that point was the only example of enforcement legislation. Opponents gave Section 2 of the amendment a little more attention, but not much. Senator Willard Saulsbury, Democrat of Delaware, said that it would put elections themselves under congressional control, with federal canvassers and judges of election.[75] No one on either side discussed remedies, including whether remedies would run against individuals or states as such. Sovereign immunity from suit was not touched on. Only with the Voting Rights Act of 1870, adopted the following year by the first session of the 41st Congress, did anyone focus seriously on questions of enforcement and remedies under the Fifteenth Amendment.

D. THE VOTING RIGHTS ACT OF 1870

Soon after the Secretary of State announced that the Fifteenth Amendment had been ratified, Republicans in Congress began work on a statute to enforce it.[76] In nineteenth-century America there was always an election coming up, so this legislation was hurried through.

Republicans seem to have been especially concerned that re-

---

[72] See id 70 (whether to include right to hold office comes before House-Senate conference committee).

[73] Earl M. Maltz, *Civil Rights, the Constitution, and Congress, 1863–1869* 143–44 (1990) (action of Georgia legislature refusing to seat black members).

[74] Gillette (cited in note 71) at 59 (Senate rejected proposal to ban discrimination on the basis of race, color, nativity, property, education, or religious belief).

[75] Cong Globe, 40th Cong, 3d Sess App 163 (1869).

[76] The Voting Rights Act of 1870 is Act of May 31, 1870, ch cxiv, 16 Stat 140.

calcitrant states and localities would evade the Fifteenth Amendment through racially discriminatory administration of the procedural rules about voting, especially voter registration requirements. Registration at that point was required in some states but by no means all.[77] In the states that had it, the registrars could refuse to put black voters on the rolls even though the law allowed them to register and vote. Anticipating that it would be hard to detect such low-level discrimination, the Republicans proposed to remedy it through enforcement legislation. The act as adopted imposed substantial penalties on state officials who refused to allow a voter to register, or otherwise to qualify to vote, on the basis of race, color, or previous condition of servitude.[78] It also provided that if a voter offered to perform any act required to qualify to vote, such as registration, and was wrongfully refused, the offer would itself count as the act required.[79] Thus a qualified voter who sought to register and was turned away on account of race would be allowed to vote on election day, despite not having qualified under applicable state law.

Voters were not the only beneficiaries of the act. Candidates for specified offices who claimed to have been defeated because of the unlawful exclusion of qualified voters were given a remedy to recover the office to which they were entitled.[80] The scenario contemplated by the act's sponsors was a Republican candidate who was defeated because black voters were excluded. In a move presaging the next major civil rights statute, to be enacted the following year, the Voting Rights Act also sought to deal with private violence against voters.[81]

In its remedial apparatus the 1870 act used the standard tools of nineteenth-century public law. Foremost among those tools was nullity, which was generally believed to follow automatically from the Fifteenth Amendment, but which was reinforced by Section

---

[77] Most states did not require registration before the 1870s, but some did, beginning with Massachusetts in 1801. Alexander Keyssar, *The Right to Vote: The Contested History of Democracy in the United States* 151–52 (2000).

[78] Act of May 31, 1870, ch cxiv, § 2, 16 Stat 140.

[79] Id, § 3, 10 Stat 140–41.

[80] Id, § 23, 16 Stat 146.

[81] Id, §§ 4–6, 16 Stat 141. Not all of the act enforced the Fifteenth Amendment. Congress also exercised its power over the manner of conducting elections to the House of Representatives, putting into the bill several provisions designed to prevent fraud at the polls. Id, §§ 19–22, 16 Stat 144–46.

1 of the act just for good measure.[82] Officers were subject to civil liability and criminal punishment.[83] Officer suits against allegedly unlawfully elected incumbents were also part of the package.[84]

The act did not, however, create any causes of action against the states, nor did anyone raise the possibility that it should. This is noteworthy because at the time the right to vote, when conferred on an individual by the laws of suffrage, was generally considered a property right protected by the common law. If one private individual used violence to prevent another from voting, the law of tort would give a remedy for the injury to the victim's right to the franchise.[85] More important for our purposes is that this interprivate rule was, in standard fashion, extended to officers to create a public law remedy. Wrongful interference by an official with the right to vote could, depending on the circumstances, give rise to an action for damages on the part of the voter.[86] In providing for civil recovery of a stated sum, the Voting Rights Act was specifying liquidated damages for deprivation of the franchise.

Today it would be natural to say that the main source of disenfranchisement of legally qualified voters contrary to the Fifteenth Amendment would be state laws that violated it, and that the natural remedy would be an action for damages against the state involved when any racially discriminatory laws on voting were carried out. Yet while the Voting Rights Act reinforced the nullification of such laws by the Fifteenth Amendment, it did not provide for damages against the states if such laws were executed despite their nullity. It did provide for damages against officers in such situations, consistent with the principle of individual official liability, but not state liability, for torts.[87]

---

[82] Id, § 1, 16 Stat 140 (no race discrimination with respect to the right to vote, any state law to the contrary notwithstanding).

[83] Sections 2 and 3 of the act provided that injured voters could recover a $500 forfeiture from officials who violated them and also made offending officers liable to fine and imprisonment. Id, §§ 2–3, 16 Stat 140–41.

[84] Id at § 23, 16 Stat 146.

[85] Thomas M. Cooley, *A Treatise on the Law of Torts* *298 (2d ed 1880) (actual force used to prevent voting constitutes aggravated trespass, threat of force gives rise to cause of action if reasonable individual would have been deterred from voting).

[86] Id at 297–98. Senator Edmunds pointed out that an officer committed an actionable wrong by interfering with the right to vote. Cong Globe, 41st Cong, 2d Sess 3563 (1870).

[87] A damages remedy against states probably would have been especially tempting for the Republicans for partisan reasons. The states that were most likely to retain and carry out discriminatory laws were those that were least Republican; because blacks strongly

While no one suggested a remedy against the states as such, there was some discussion of the nature of Congress's enforcement power under Section 2 of the Fifteenth Amendment. Only a little of it came from Republicans, who were in a hurry to adopt the legislation. One of the few Republicans who discussed the enforcement power in any depth was Senator John Pool, of North Carolina. Pool explained that enforcement must be against individuals, not the states themselves, because a state could not be punished for a crime.[88] Drawing a distinction between punishing officers as individuals and as officers, he emphasized that only the former was permissible and pointed to Section 2 of the Civil Rights Act of 1866 as an example.[89] Pool then pulled what may have been the rabbit out of his hat, arguing that if it was permissible to punish officers as individuals, it should be possible to punish purely private people who interfered with the right to vote; thus Congress could punish Ku Klux Klansmen who went in disguise on the highway to intimidate voters.[90]

One moderate Republican, Senator Joseph Fowler of Tennessee, took a quite narrow view of the enforcement power.[91] He believed that Section 2 of the Fifteenth Amendment did not extend Section 1, and that the only remedy available under either was nullity.[92]

favored the Republican party, the temptation to disenfranchise them was strongest for states controlled by the Democrats.

[88] Cong Globe, 41st Cong, 2d Sess 3611 (1870).

[89] Id.

[90] Id at 3611–12.

[91] Fowler's views are worth attention because of his position on the political spectrum. Born and raised in Ohio, he moved first to Kentucky and then Tennessee, where he lived for several years before being driven out when Tennessee seceded. Fowler returned to his adopted state in 1862 as part of former Senator Andrew Johnson's military government. He was elected to the Senate in 1865 by the Republican legislature established under presidential reconstruction, but was not seated until 1866, after Tennessee ratified the Fourteenth Amendment. In his policy views Fowler was a moderate Republican. A lifelong opponent of slavery, he opposed secession but remained committed to strong states' rights under the Constitution. Fowler supported Tennessee's 1865 abolition of slavery and enfranchisement of the freed slaves, and voted for the Reconstruction acts that imposed race-blind suffrage on the other former Confederate states. But he opposed making suffrage a matter for the federal Constitution and voted against the Fifteenth Amendment. Fowler voted to acquit Johnson in the impeachment trial, supported Grant in 1868, and switched to Greeley in 1872. Allen Johnson and Dumas Malone, eds, 6 *Dictionary of American Biography* 564 (1931). Fowler was thus a member of two crucial constituencies for the Republican party: antislavery Unionists who believed strongly in states' rights, and Unionists from the upper South. As his votes for military reconstruction but against Johnson's conviction indicate, he was sometimes on the decisive margin of the Republican coalition.

[92] Cong Globe, 41st Cong, 2d Sess App 421 (1870). Fowler allowed that the drafters of Section 2 may have wanted it to go farther than nullity, but denied that it did so. Id.

Criminal punishment of state officers, he asserted, would destroy local self-government.[93]

Other Republicans, many not so moderate as Fowler, were also concerned lest Congress go too far. Lyman Trumbull was not happy with the remedy for defeated candidates; the Fifteenth Amendment was about the right to vote, not to hold office.[94] Senator Oliver Morton of Indiana was disturbed with phrasing suggesting that the act could reach denial of the vote for reasons other than race.[95] Morton, like Trumbull, was also doubtful as to the remedy for defeated candidates, again because the Fifteenth Amendment was about voting, not office.[96]

Democrats, as would be expected, took a narrow view of congressional power. As far as they were concerned the main remedy under the Fifteenth Amendment was the nullity of inconsistent state laws. Perhaps Congress could also reach state officers in their personal capacity, but that was doubtful. Senator Allen Thurman of Ohio, a former justice of Ohio's Supreme Court, argued that the Fifteenth Amendment was a prohibition on the states and that its proper remedy was therefore nullity.[97] Thurman flirted with implicitly endorsing Section 2 of the Civil Rights Act of 1866, admitting that Congress might be able to punish state officers who executed invalid laws, but drew the line at punishing wholly private interference with the right to vote; that was a matter for the states.[98]

As Thurman's remarks indicate, the Democrats may have reconciled themselves to punishment of officers who carried out invalid laws. Of like mind to Thurman was Senator Charles Casserly, Democrat of California. Nullity and perhaps suits against officers were the remedies, nothing more.[99] Senator Garrett Davis of Ken-

---

[93] Id at 421–22.

[94] Id at 3570.

[95] Id at 3571.

[96] Id at 3681.

[97] Id at 3661.

[98] Id at 3661–62.

[99] Id at App 472–73. Asked by Republican Matthew Carpenter of Wisconsin whether Congress could deal with Ku Klux under the Fourteenth Amendment, Casserly replied that the two amendments were the same in their remedies. "Both refer expressly to States. Both in terms operate on States as such. Both deal with the acts of a State; with the constitution or law of a State; and if you will, for the sake of the argument, with an officer of the State acting under color of a State law or constitution against the prohibition of either amendment." Id at 473. Congress had no power to punish wholly private acts. Id.

tucky, who implicitly conceded as much in the debate on the 1866 act, came closer to doing so explicitly in 1870, saying that limitations on states apply to individuals only when they are state officers.[100] His point was that punishing wholly private acts was beyond congressional power. Whether that was true dominated debate on the next major piece of civil rights legislation.

E. THE KU KLUX ACT OF 1871

In the Ku Klux Act, also called the Civil Rights Act of 1871, Congress made aggressive use of its powers under the enforcement clauses after extensive debate as to the extent of those powers.[101] As its common name indicates, the statute was aimed at violence by the Ku Klux Klan and similar terrorist organizations in the South. Section 1 of the act, the ancestor of the statute now generally known as 42 USC 1983, created a private cause of action for violations of constitutional rights by persons acting under color of state law.[102] Subsequent sections covered conduct by persons not acting under color of state law and who were thus wholly private.[103] Section 1, a civil remedy against state actors modeled on Section 2 of the 1866 act, was not very controversial. The provisions that dealt with wholly private individuals were highly controversial because the claims of congressional power on which they rested threatened to subvert the principle of enumerated federal power.

The statute itself used the standard tools of public law remedies and therefore avoided authorizing lawsuits against the states themselves. It was directed wholly against individuals, not against governmental entities as such.

The debates offer much useful information, although nothing absolutely conclusive. Congress never explicitly discussed the possibility of private remedies against nonconsenting states, although it came tantalizingly close to doing so when considering such a remedy against municipal corporations. I will first consider the

---

In what may have been a less guarded moment during the same debate, Senator Casserly said without hedging that Section 2 of the Fifteenth Amendment enabled Congress to deal with officers acting under color of state law. Id at 3671.

[100] Id at 3666. Davis's views on the 1866 act are discussed above.

[101] Act of Apr 20, 1871, ch xxii, 17 Stat 13.

[102] Id, § 1, 17 Stat 13.

[103] Id, §§ 2, 6, 17 Stat 13–15.

bearing on state sovereign immunity of the general issues of federalism that arose during the framing of the Ku Klux Act, and then turn specifically to Senator Sherman's proposal to impose monetary liability on municipalities.

While liability of state officers was a central feature of the act throughout its development in Congress, no one proposed liability for the states themselves. This may have reflected constitutional scruples, but it may also have reflected the priorities of the Republicans who controlled Congress. By 1871 all the ex-Confederate states had gone through some form of reconstruction, and although not all of them were under Republican control, the state governments themselves were not the primary problem. The primary problem was the Klan, private individuals engaged in criminal acts.[104] Public officials were a secondary issue; they might be conniving with or intimidated by the Ku Klux Klan, but were not themselves engaging in much murder, battery, and arson.

A number of speakers did indicate that Congress could not reach the states themselves, and while significant, those statements must be discounted somewhat, at least when made by Republicans. For example, Senator Oliver Morton of Indiana, a Republican supporter of the legislation, observed at one point that a state could not be indicted or punished as such, and that Congress had to act on individuals.[105] States were forbidden to coin money, he noted, but that prohibition was to be enforced by making it a crime to coin money under state authority.[106] While that certainly indicates that Morton believed in significant state immunity from suit, it may have been something of a rationalization. Republicans who wanted to deal with private violence faced the problem that Section 1 of the Fourteenth Amendment addresses the states, not private people. One way to defend the seemingly more expansive step of legislating as to individuals is to say that because of the federal structure, legislation as to individuals is the only remedial mechanism available.[107]

---

[104] See Eric Foner, *Reconstruction, America's Unfinished Revolution, 1863–1877* 425–44 (1988) (describing Klan activities).

[105] Cong Globe, 42d Cong, 1st Sess App 251 (1871).

[106] Id at App 251.

[107] To be sure, this argument may actually reach only far enough to justify Section 1 of the Ku Klux Act and Section 2 of the 1866 act, both of which gave remedies against individuals acting under color of state law and were directed primarily against public

Morton was not alone in seeking to justify remedies against individuals on the grounds that there could be no remedy directly against the states. John Bingham explained that penal laws against the enforcement of unconstitutional state statutes were proper because "the United States punishes men, not States, for a violation of its law."[108] According to Representative Mercur, a Republican from Pennsylvania, when states denied equal protection it was proper for Congress to provide that protection itself because the state could not be compelled to do so. The Equal Protection Clause, he said, "cannot be enforced by a bill in equity to compel specific performance of it; but if a State denies this equal protection, the United States Government must step in and give that protection which the state authorities neglect or refuse to give."[109] Republican Representative David Lowe of Kansas believed that the enforcement of the Fourteenth Amendment must go beyond the nullification of unconstitutional state legislation, but that the next step was action against individuals, not affirmative relief against states as such. Federal courts could not, he said, give a mandamus to require a state to perform its duty under the Equal Protection Clause. "There is no legal machinery for that purpose. There can be none."[110] Congress had to act directly.[111] Democrats

---

officials with respect to their official acts.

At least one Republican, Senator Daniel Pratt of Indiana, even said that government officers could not be punished as individuals, saying that jurors, sheriffs, and constables who failed to perform their duty to provide equal protection were beyond the reach of Congress. "We cannot touch any State official for malfeasance, or misfeasance, or nonfeasance." Id at 506. If Pratt was correct, Section 2 of the 1866 act was invalid.

[108] Id at App 86.

[109] Id at App 182.

[110] Id at 376.

[111] In similar fashion, Senator George Edmunds justified action against individuals on the grounds that actions against states as such were beyond Congress's power. Using as an example Article I, Section 10's prohibition on state treaty making, he asked what could be done if Vermont entered into its own extradition treaty with Britain. The United States, he said, "can institute no process against that State to set aside the treaty," so the only alternatives were war or federal action directly on individuals. Id at 692. Edmunds relied on *Prigg* for the proposition that Congress could do something, albeit not act on states directly, to enforce state duties. Id.

Senator Frederick Frelinghuysen, Republican of New Jersey, also said that action against individuals was proper because direct action against a state was unavailable. The United States, he said, "cannot deal with the States or with their officials to compel proper legislation and its enforcement; it can only deal with the officers who violate the privileges and immunities of citizens of the United States." Id at 501. In both affirming and denying Congress's power to reach officers, Frelinghuysen probably had in mind a distinction between an action to compel protection, which he thought could not be created, and a damages action against an officer who invaded constitutional rights, which he thought could be.

THE SUPREME COURT REVIEW

who opposed the Ku Klux Act did not say that the states were the proper target as opposed to private individuals who were not even government officers. Instead they took an even more limited view of congressional enforcement power under Section 5. Some said that remedies under the Fourteenth Amendment were limited to invalidity of unconstitutional official actions and that Congress could go no farther. Thus Representative McHenry, Democrat of Kentucky, said that Section 1 of the amendment was directed to the states and enforced through nullification of state acts; Congress therefore could not reach private individuals under Section 5 of the amendment.[112] He did not say that the limitation to states implied that Congress could make them suable by private people.

For different reasons, Democrats and Republicans generally agreed, at least in their official positions, that direct enforcement of the Constitution against states as such was at best highly problematic and probably impermissible. No one said that Congress had the power to create such a remedy.

Congress did come close to debating its power to impose monetary liability on states as such when it considered an amendment to the Ku Klux Act originally proposed by Senator Sherman. Sherman's amendment would have imposed tort liability on municipal corporations when outrages were committed within their jurisdictions and the victims could not collect from the actual perpetrators.[113] His argument was that wealthy and politically powerful southerners could put a stop to Klan violence if they wanted to, and that because they were the primary taxpayers for municipalities the prospect of municipal liability would give them a strong incentive to act.[114] The Senate adopted the proposal but the House conferees objected to it on constitutional grounds and it was not adopted by Congress.[115] Instead, the statute imposed similar liability on private individuals, not municipal corporations,

---

[112] Id at 429.

[113] The history of Sherman's proposal is discussed at length in *Monell v New York City Dep't of Social Services*, 436 US 658, 665–83 (1978). As the Court explains, a first version of Senator Sherman's proposal was adopted by the Senate without debate; that version imposed liability on individuals, not local governments. Id at 666. The version that imposed liability on municipalities, and that was debated at length as discussed presently, came from the first of two conference committees on the Ku Klux Act. Id at 666–67.

[114] Cong Globe, 42d Cong, 1st Sess 761 (1871) ("people of property" in South must be made liable if they fail to raise the hue and cry when lawless violence takes place).

[115] 436 US at 668.

who had the power to prevent Klan violence but failed to do so.[116]

One supporter of the Sherman amendment made an argument that could lead one to believe that he thought Congress had power to override sovereign immunity. Senator Edmunds of Vermont, an important Republican legislative leader on legal issues, explained that the proposal was constitutional because Section 1 of the Fourteenth Amendment imposed duties of protection on the states, and states act through municipalities.[117] Standing alone, that statement certainly indicates that the liability could just as easily have been imposed on the states.

Yet Edmunds was among those who said that Congress could not act on the states as such.[118] One possibility is that he was simply being inconsistent, taking whatever position favored his goals at the moment. Edmunds was a sophisticated lawyer, though, and Democrats were hardly bashful about calling Republicans liars, so he had reason to maintain consistency. And Edmunds's seemingly contradictory positions can be reconciled if the inference from municipalities to states is rejected. He may have believed that municipal corporations were the perfect targets for liability because they shared the states' obligation to provide the equal protection of the law, and on that score were like states and unlike private people, but did not share the states' immunity from lawsuits, and were in that respect like private people and not like states.

If that is what Edmunds was thinking, his reasoning was internally consistent and consistent with that of other supporters of the Sherman amendment, who justified municipal liability on the grounds that municipal liability to suit was well established. Representative Shellabarger of Ohio relied on the fact that lawsuits against municipal corporations in contract were well accepted, and reasoned that liability in tort should be no different.[119] The rules of contractual liability for states were quite different from those for municipalities, however, and Shellabarger's argument would not have worked for states.[120] Had he meant to rely on the stronger

---

[116] Id at 668–69.

[117] Cong Globe, 42d Cong, 1st Sess 756 (1871).

[118] Id at 692.

[119] Id at 752.

[120] As discussed above, under general principles of sovereign immunity, states were not liable on their contracts unless they consented to suit.

claim that states too were subject to suit under Section 5, he probably would have embraced it.

Senator Sherman himself relied on the liability of municipal corporations to suit, not on a deduction from the potential liability of states themselves. Ridiculing the provision with which the second conference committee replaced his proposal, he argued that if a railroad could be sued, so could a county, because both were corporations made by the states.[121] Counties were sued all the time, he complained, and the House should not have rejected his plan in favor of a form of private liability that he deemed worthless.[122]

A few participants used logic similar to Edmunds's, and may have believed states could be sued, but probably did not. Senator Frederick Frelinghuysen, Republican of New Jersey, who opposed Sherman's proposal, said that Congress operates on individuals and states, not parts of states.[123] Thus it could not make municipal corporations liable for keeping the peace. From the statement that Congress operates on states one might conclude that Frelinghuysen believed in state liability, but as noted above he too thought that there were significant limits on Congress's power to provide for affirmative relief against states themselves.[124] Another participant who may possibly have believed in state suability was Representative Charles Willard, a Republican from Vermont who opposed the measure. Willard said that Sherman's provision "would be liable to very much less objection, both in regard to its justice and its constitutionality, if it provided" for suits directly against states.[125] Willard, however, did not say whether the much lesser constitutional objection would still have been fatal, and may not have wanted to commit himself. As an opponent, he did not have to; to say that if this could be done at all it would have to be done against the states and not their components is not to say that it could be done.

Democratic opponents of the Sherman amendment were of course hostile to liability for municipalities. Some of them argued that municipal suability did indeed imply state suability and made this a reductio ad absurdum argument against Sherman's proposal.

---

[121] Id at 820.

[122] Id at 821.

[123] Id at 776–77.

[124] Id at 501.

[125] Id at 791.

One who took this line was the other senator from Ohio, Democrat Allen Thurman. Thurman said that if Senator Sherman's theory was correct, Congress could create an action against a state "with more semblance of constitutional law" than against a county.[126] How much semblance that would be came out presently, when Thurman observed that on Sherman's reasoning a state could be made liable for damages, its capitol sold to satisfy a judgment, and the state paralyzed.[127] In discussing liability for the states themselves as opposed to municipalities, Thurman was presenting a parade of horribles, not a more modest alternative.

Representative Michael C. Kerr of Indiana, a leading Democrat and later Speaker of the House when the Democrats regained control, had a similar response to the municipal liability proposal. He said that if Congress could do this it could invade the treasuries and control the ministerial officers of the states, destroying local self-government.[128] Municipal liability for contract was quite different as far as Kerr was concerned, in part because municipalities were sued under the state's own law of contract.[129]

The group whose views may matter most for these purposes, and whose views mattered most for the fate of Sherman's proposal, were the Republicans in the House who opposed it on constitutional grounds and led to its defeat. Their argument was that Congress had no power to assign responsibilities to state instrumentalities, including municipal corporations. Whether municipalities should have law enforcement functions and be accountable for them was up to the states, not Congress. Thus, for example, Representative Austin Blair, Republican of Michigan, argued that Congress had no power to set the functions and obligations of state instrumentalities.[130] Blair cited the recently decided *Collector v Day* in support of state immunity and responded to Shellabarger's argument about contractual liability by distinguishing the enforcement of an obligation a municipality had entered into itself from the creation of a new obligation.[131] Only the states, not Congress, could assign duties to state-created public bodies. John Bing-

---

[126] Id at 772.

[127] Id.

[128] Id at 788–89.

[129] Id at 789.

[130] Id at 795.

[131] Id.

ham agreed, arguing that while it was true that some states had a form of municipal liability much like what Senator Sherman had proposed, such liability had to come from the state involved.[132] Representative John Farnsworth, Republican of Illinois, echoed the doctrine of *Prigg*, according to which Congress could not impose duties on state officials.[133]

The Republican-controlled House made its constitutional objections stick in the second conference committee. As Republican Luke Poland of Vermont, a conferee on the part of the House, explained, he and his House colleagues had told their Senate counterparts that the House had taken a stand on the state immunity issue. "Congress [they told the Senators] had no constitutional power to impose any obligation upon county or town organizations, the mere instrumentality for the administration of State law."[134] In response the conference committee proposed a substitute that would impose liability on individuals who had the duty to prevent Klan violence and failed to do so rather than on government entities.[135]

How would those who endorsed the House view have responded to a proposal to create a private action against the states themselves? Most likely Democrats would have been horrified, as Thurman and Kerr indicated. As for Republicans, their views are harder to deduce. It is certainly coherent to believe both that Sherman's proposal was unconstitutional and that Congress may make states themselves liable. The gravamen of the constitutional objection to municipal liability was that it usurped the states' power to determine the functions and duties of their various instrumentalities. Imposing liability on a state treasury would not do that. It would not violate the rule of *Prigg*, at least as narrowly conceived.

It nevertheless is likely that most of those who agreed with the House would also have found state liability for damages unconstitutional. Those who relied on *Collector v Day* thought that case relevant even though it involved a state judge, not a municipal officer, and a tax, not the imposition of a substantive duty. If they viewed a tax as an impermissible imposition on state autonomy, despite Congress's broad taxing power, they likely would have

---

[132] Id at 798.

[133] Id at 799.

[134] Id at 804.

[135] Id.

viewed a money damages remedy in the same light. At the level of constitutional structure the underlying federalism policy supporting the immunity of state officers from federal regulation was very hard to square with congressionally created damages remedies against the states. The Court in *Dennison*, for example, explained that Congress could not impose duties on state officers because those duties might take them away from performing important state functions.[136] Immunity doctrine was about the power to set priorities and allocate resources; that power had to remain with the states, not Congress. One of the main objectives of imposing monetary liability, then and now, is to affect behavior and thereby the allocation of resources; Senator Sherman justified his proposal specifically in terms of its deterrent effect. If Congress can impose monetary liability on the states, it has a powerful tool to determine the priority of the many functions that state governments must perform. If Congress could not, under Section 5, choose the state officers who were to provide the protection of the laws, it likely also could not decisively shape those officers' incentives by imposing liability on the state.

F. UNDERSTANDINGS IN THE RECONSTRUCTION CONGRESS

The foregoing evidence warrants several conclusions about the consciously held views of senators and representatives who participated in proposing and implementing the Reconstruction amendments. Some of those conclusions can be firmer than others. One that is quite firm, and of considerable interest, is that there was no general understanding, even among Republicans, that Congress could create damages actions for individuals against states.

This appears most clearly from the debates on the Ku Klux Act. Had the participants in that debate taken it to be the accepted Republican view that Congress could override state sovereign immunity, the arguments would have been very different. For one thing, Republicans would not have been able to get away with justifying regulation of private people on the grounds that states could not be regulated. Democrats would have pointed to the well-

---

[136] See 24 How at 107–08 (if Congress could impose duties on state officers it could overload them with responsibilities and take them away from their functions under state law). The Court relied on the same reasoning in *Alden*, explaining that immunity from private lawsuits preserves the states' ability to establish their own priorities concerning the use of public resources. 527 US at 750–51.

known Republican position that Congress could create damages remedies against states and would have demanded to know why their hypocritical opponents refused to do so. And the discussion of Senator Sherman's proposal would not have proceeded as it did. Instead, that discussion would have begun with the premise that liability of the kind Sherman proposed could be imposed on the states themselves, and would have moved from there. Opponents would have had to explain why choosing municipalities for liability was unconstitutional even though making the state liable was not. Such an explanation would have been available to them, but had state liability to lawsuits been generally accepted they would have had to articulate that explanation, which in fact they did not do. In 1871 there was no consensus that Congress's Section 5 power could be used to override state sovereign immunity.

Debates on the Fourteenth and Fifteenth Amendments themselves confirm that such a Republican consensus did not exist when they were being drafted, any more than it existed a few years later at the time of the Ku Klux Act. Neither proponents nor opponents of either amendment discussed the possibility that either enforcement clause could be used to make states liable to individuals for damages. If that power had been understood to be part of the proposal, either Republicans would have defended it or Democrats would have denounced it in so many words, along with their other complaints about the annihilation of state autonomy and the reduction of the people under a consolidated despotism. Moreover, if Republicans were taking the position that the Enforcement Clause of the Thirteenth Amendment could be used to authorize private lawsuits against states, they likely would have cited that strong federal power in support of Section 2 of the Civil Rights Act of 1866, rather than justifying it as an ordinary example of federal supremacy.

Another conclusion that can be accepted with high confidence is that the sponsors of the amendments did not represent the enforcement clauses as an innovation with respect to federal power over the states. As just noted, supporters of the Civil Rights Act did not say that its Section 2 rested on any novel power over the states; they said that it was nothing out of the ordinary. They were not claiming any such power under Section 2 of the Thirteenth Amendment, and not suggesting that an amendment adopted to secure the Civil Rights Act would need to give any such power. Then in the debates on the Fourteenth Amendment itself its advocates explained Section 5 as filling a complete absence of enumerated power with respect to restrictions on the states, not as granting Congress a kind of special authority that it lacked under the grants in Article I, Section 8. Those who thought Section 5 of the Fourteenth Amendment unnecessary mainly believed that it was redundant of the Necessary and Proper Clause, the most generic of grants to Congress.

While Democrats complained that the enforcement powers would upset federalism, they mainly or exclusively were concerned about the principle of enumerated powers, not structural protections of intergovernmental immunity. Representative Aaron Harding of Kentucky, one of the few participants to mention Section 5 of the Fourteenth Amendment, said that it would give Congress power over citizens' rights.[137] Democrats treated those provisions as new and unjustified equivalents of the Commerce Clause.

Next comes the central question: What were the views of senators and representatives, especially Republicans, as to whether the enforcement clauses could be used to create causes of action for private parties against nonconsenting states? Here the answer must be given with less confidence, but most probably a substantial and decisive bloc of Republicans, indeed, probably a majority of them, believed that it could not be done.

As explained above, the background legal context was one in which private lawsuits against nonconsenting states were unknown, and instead a system of officer suits provided affirmative relief for government wrongs. State intergovernmental immunity was found in the Supreme Court's doctrine. Acting against that background, the Reconstruction Congresses enacted a series of enforcement statutes that used remedies against officers and not against states. In the Voting Rights Act and the Ku Klux Act they also operated directly on private people, despite the state action problem with doing so. And when the Senate proposed a measure that was as close as anyone came to state liability, the House voted it down. Congress legislated in this fashion, avoiding the creation of lawsuits against states, even though many of the problems it was addressing, especially the Black Codes and disenfranchise-

---

[137] Cong Globe, 39th Cong, 1st Sess 3147 (1866).

ment, had their source in state statutes. The implication from these actions is strong that the supporters of the enforcement legislation did not believe that option available to them.[138]

Actions speak loudly, but words often speak more clearly. Supporters of the Fourteenth Amendment said that Section 5 was needed to remedy a lack of power but not that it would create an authority more intrusive with respect to the states than Congress had elsewhere. John Bingham spoke of the need for a power to punish officers, and no one said that the amendment would enable Congress to act on states as such. After both amendments were adopted, when it was too late to arouse fear in marginal voters, many Republicans said that the enforcement powers did not authorize Congress to create remedies against states as such. In 1871 Republicans in the House rejected the Sherman amendment on stated grounds highly protective of states, and probably implying rejection of causes of action against states, while no supporter of the amendment clearly rested it on a power to create such causes of action. As for Democrats, their minimalist view of the enforcement powers and their strong attachment to state autonomy imply that they would have rejected causes of action against states, and in 1871 two leading Democrats argued on the assumption that such remedies were impermissible.

Moreover, the main acknowledged weak point in the existing remedial system was not particularly relevant. That weak point

---

[138] Nowak maintains that the debates on the Fourteenth Amendment "make it clear that both the drafters and the opponents of the fourteenth amendment assumed that the federal courts would be given an inherent power to enjoin the activities of state government which were in violation of the amendment." Nowak (cited in note 5) at 1455. He identifies no drafter, supporter, or opponent who said that, nor have I found one. Instead, he relies on the following inference: "There seemed to exist throughout the debates an assumption upon the part of all of the proponents of the fourteenth amendment that its mere existence would somehow force the state to bring their laws into conformity with its principles. If the amendment was widely viewed as self-executing, it follows that the federal courts must have been endowed with the power to issue injunctions to order compliance." Id (footnote omitted). The premise contained in the first quoted sentence is largely correct, but the conclusion in the second sentence is unsound. Proponents assumed that the Fourteenth Amendment would be self-executing insofar as it nullified inconsistent state law, and that it would take its place along with other federal constitutional limitations on the states that were enforced through the system of remedies described in this article. There is no indication that they thought it would be enforced in an as-yet-to-be-determined way. The remedies with which they were familiar did not include injunctive actions against states but nevertheless gave practical effect to the principle that unconstitutional state laws are void. It would be many years before the Supreme Court approved a remedy along the lines Professor Nowak describes, and even then it did so only through officer suits. See, e.g., *Ex parte Young*, 209 US 123 (1908).

involved government contracts and especially government debt. Officers were responsible for their own torts but not for the contracts of their disclosed principal, the sovereign, so an officer could not be sued for damages if a government failed to perform its contract and in particular defaulted on its bonds. Story identified government contracts as the area in which legislative waiver of sovereign immunity was most needed.[139] Some of the most clever ways around sovereign immunity were designed to ensure that governments would in some fashion be responsible for their debts.[140] Thus if in 1866 a sophisticated lawyer had been asked to identify the field in which a power to override state sovereign immunity would do the most good, the answer almost certainly would have involved government bonds. Although many such lawyers sat in Congress, and were no doubt well aware of the problem, they had no reason to associate it with slavery, race discrimination, or violence against freed slaves and Republicans. Indeed, Section 4 of the Fourteenth Amendment actually forbade the payment of some kinds of state indebtedness.

Most likely, then, a majority of the participants in the framing and early enforcement of the Reconstruction amendments believed that state immunity from lawsuits was both a general principle of public law and an aspect of state intergovernmental immunity from national power. They regarded the new enforcement powers as not differing in kind from Congress's existing powers, which they believed to be implicitly limited by state autonomy. Being familiar with a system of constitutional remedies that provided individuals with extensive protection without subjecting states as such to lawsuits, they saw no need for a fundamental change to it. The area in which that system was subject to the most criticism, state debt, was not before them. When they came to enforce the amendments, they avoided any attempt to override state immunity from lawsuit, using instead the familiar tools of nullity and remedies against officers. In framing the amendments they did not want to give

---

[139] 3 Story (cited in note 15) at 539–40, § 1671 (because agents are not responsible for their principals' contracts, those with contract claims against the United States must look to Congress for a remedy).

[140] One leading example of the legal subtleties employed because of sovereign immunity was found in the Virginia Funding Act of 1871. Reginald C. McGrane, *Foreign Bondholders and American State Debt* 367–68 (1935). The Virginia mechanism, which sought to reassure bond purchasers by enabling them to litigate their claims in a defensive posture, rather than as plaintiffs against a nonconsenting state, was vindicated by the Supreme Court in the *Virginia Coupon* Cases. See *Poindexter v Greenhow*, 114 US 270 (1885).

Congress a power to subject nonconsenting states to private law-suits, and in enforcing them they did not try to use such a power.

Probably some Republicans thought, or would have thought if they had thought about it, that Congress could create causes of action against nonconsenting states. They were likely in a minority in their own party and an even smaller minority in Congress.

II. Section 5 and the Imperative of the Civil Rights Act of 1866

Section 5 was included in the Fourteenth Amendment in large part to make sure that Congress had power to adopt the Civil Rights Act of 1866, the constitutionality of which was disputed. One controversial aspect of the 1866 act was Section 2, which imposed criminal liability on state officers for the performance of their duty under state law. Doing so was a substantial interference with state autonomy. In order to achieve its goal, the Fourteenth Amendment had to be strong enough to authorize that level of interference. If criminalizing state officers' official acts required a novel form of federal power that was highly intrusive into the operations of state governments, then there is a strong argument that Section 5 differed from other federal powers in this respect, and was uniquely capable of overriding state sovereign immunity. Proponents of the Fourteenth Amendment like Senator Trumbull denied that they were proposing any such novel power, but it is conceivable that they were pulling a Trojan Horse, supporting a measure that had far-reaching implications that they did not want to announce or that they did not even fully appreciate themselves.[141]

If it took a substantial expansion of federal power over the states in order to validate Section 2 of the Civil Rights Act, then there is good reason to think that Section 5 represented such an expansion. But even under the law of intergovernmental immunity as it stood in 1866, Senator Trumbull was very likely right in arguing that the criminal penalty in the Civil Rights Act was not

---

[141] The possibility that the meaning of an enactment might diverge from what its sponsors said or believed about it was not lost on members of Congress. Early in the Senate's consideration of the Civil Rights Act, Senator Trumbull had assured his colleagues that it would not reach suffrage. Senator Saulsbury, Democrat of Delaware and an opponent of the act, was not reassured. "The question is not what the Senator means, but what is the legitimate meaning and import of the terms employed in the bill." Cong Globe, 39th Cong, 1st Sess 477 (1866).

an impermissible intrusion into state autonomy, and that such
penalties could be imposed in order to implement any otherwise
valid exercise of federal power. His main premise was as sound
then as it is now: under the Supremacy Clause, valid federal law
trumps state law, so a state may not authorize its officers to violate
federal law. A state that sought to solve a fiscal crisis by counter-
feiting federal securities could not immunize its officers from personal prosecution when they sold fake United States paper. To be
sure, a prosecution would interfere with the implementation of
state policy, but the whole nineteenth-century system of public
law remedies, which centered on the personal responsibility of
officers, had that effect. It was nevertheless thought to be consistent with state sovereignty, and in particular with state sovereign
immunity from lawsuit, precisely because the direct effect was on
the officers personally, with only an indirect effect on the state
involved.

If there was a constitutional problem with Section 2 under standard intergovernmental immunity principles, it would have to have
been more subtle than ordinary trumping of state law by federal
law, and indeed than some interference with state officers. Two
possible difficulties are worth considering. One arises from the
fact that Section 2 acted on state officers as such, albeit by imposing a penalty that they would bear personally, rather than just
including them within a norm that applied more generally. In
American federalism, questions naturally arise any time Congress
regulates the official acts of state officers, and *Dennison* long stood
for the proposition that "the Federal Government, under the Constitution, has no power to impose on a State officer, as such, any
duty whatever, and compel him to perform it."[142] Section 2, however, did not impose a new duty. It attached a criminal penalty to
the violation of the duty created by the oath demanded by Article
VI, and Article VI singles out "the Judges in every State" as bound
to respect the supremacy of federal law "any Thing in the Constitution or Laws of any State to the contrary notwithstanding."[143]
If the Civil Rights Act was itself constitutional, state officers, including judges, had a duty created by the Constitution and owed
to the United States to treat the statute as binding despite any

---

[142] *Kentucky v Dennison*, 24 How 66, 107 (1861).
[143] US Const, Art VI, para 2.

contrary state law. That duty was indeed deeply disruptive of state sovereignty. It came, not from Congress, but from Article VI, which is the principal locus of the Constitution's fundamental modification of state sovereignty. For Congress to enforce it was a far smaller interference with state autonomy than for the Constitution to create it in the first place.[144]

Second, the act's critics were especially outraged by what they characterized as an interference with the good-faith exercise by state decision makers of their official responsibilities.[145] A state judge who believed the Civil Rights Act unconstitutional and refused to follow it could be prosecuted for a conscientious action. If prosecuted, of course, the judge could raise as a defense the unconstitutionality of Section 1 of the act, so a conviction would

---

[144] Section 2 of the 1866 act was consistent with the holding and reasoning of *Dennison*, which concluded that Congress could not, and therefore should be understand not to have sought to, impose a judicially enforceable duty on a governor. The Rendition Clause of Article IV, which was at issue in *Dennison*, differs from Article VI in a crucial respect: it imposes a duty on the rendering state, not on any officer. A fleeing fugitive "shall on Demand of the executive Authority of the State from which he fled, be delivered up, to be removed to the state having Jurisdiction of the Crime." US Const, Art IV, § 2, para 2. In identifying the executive of the rendering state as the authority to perform the rendition, see Act of Feb 12, 1793, ch vii, § 1, 1 Stat 302, Congress was imposing a duty on a specific officer that did not come directly from the Constitution. This distinction may seem minor, but it is quite important under Chief Justice Taney's rationale for the outcome. He was concerned that if Congress had such a power it could impose duties on an officer that would interfere with his state functions and would be "incompatible with the rank and dignity to which he was elevated by the State." 24 How at 107–08. Both of those undesirable effects would result from a congressional power to impose a duty on an officer chosen by Congress, such as the Governor. They would not result from congressional enforcement of an obligation already derived from the Constitution itself.

[145] Senator Edgar Cowan of Pennsylvania, a conservative Republican, was troubled by the application of Section 2 to state judges and suggested to Senator Trumbull that the proper remedy for honest judicial error was through the appellate process, not criminal prosecution. He doubted whether judges could be held responsible for honest errors of law. Cong Globe, 39th Cong, 1st Sess 475–76 (1866). The next day Cowan said that Section 2 was shocking as applied to judges and again said that the proper response was through writ of error. Id at 500. In the House, Representative George Miller of Pennsylvania, another Republican, moved unsuccessfully to exempt state judges from Section 2 and instead expand the appellate jurisdiction of the federal courts. Id at 1156. Representative Henry Raymond, a conservative Republican from New York, complained that Section 2 of the act would invade the rights of the states and the state courts. Id at 1267.

Democrats were also generally shocked by Section 2 of the act. Senator Garrett Davis of Kentucky called it "monstrous and absurd" to punish state officers for carrying out their oaths. Id at 1415. Senator Willard Saulsbury, Democrat of Delaware and an ardent friend of states' rights, said that the people would resist the enforcement of Section 2 by force. Id at 1809.

The objection to prosecution of state judges for good-faith error had both a constitutional and a policy aspect, and probably some members of Congress who thought Section 2 valid also thought it unwise. Indeed, as noted, Lyman Trumbull himself thought that it would not apply to honest judicial error, which would lack criminal intent.

be possible only if the courts determined that the judge had in fact acted improperly. That is not to say that the prospect of prosecution would not interfere at all with the judge's decision; some state judges who were convinced that Section 1 was invalid might nevertheless enforce it for fear of being convicted on what they would regard as an erroneous ground.

While this reduction of judicial independence gave pause to some Republicans and many Democrats, it was not so severe as it may seem and not sufficiently severe to count as an unprecedented invasion of state sovereignty, even by the more demanding standards of 1866. Judges are generally not immune from criminal prosecution for crimes relating to their office, most notably bribery.[146] A judge who had accepted a gift, believing it to have been lawful, albeit legally doubtful, might then bend over backwards to avoid any seeming favoritism to the giver. The judge's official actions thus could be influenced by the possibility of a prosecution that might not in fact be well founded. Yet the possibility that a judge could act in that fashion, as indeed some judge almost certainly has at some point, does not fatally undermine judicial independence. Moreover, as noted before, in the nineteenth century personal tort responsibility by nonjudicial officers was a central public law remedy. The prospect of such liability under valid federal law was not thought to invade the sovereignty of the state for whom the officer worked, even though it affected official decisions.

However strong the objections to Section 2 may have been on policy grounds, they were weak on constitutional grounds. A reasonable, legally sophisticated observer in 1866 thus would not have concluded that in order to validate the Civil Rights Act, Section 5 of the Fourteenth Amendment had to give power to invade state sovereignty of a kind that Congress did not possess under other constitutional grants. Trumbull was right when he minimized the impact of Section 2 on state sovereignty.

If the criminal penalty for state officers did not require a novel congressional power as of 1866, it is reasonable to ask whether Section 5 of the Fourteenth Amendment was needed at all. Putting aside the enforcement of Sections 2, 3, and 4 of the amendment, with respect to Section 1, the enforcement power did perform an

---

[146] Bribery is identified as grounds for impeachment by Article II, Section 4 of the Constitution, and Congress has provided for criminal punishment of judges who accept bribes ever since the Crimes Act of 1790, Act of Apr 30, 1790, ch ix, § 21, 1 Stat 117.

important function even if it was not actually necessary. It resolved, with respect to the Fourteenth Amendment, the long-simmering debate over Congress's power to enforce constitutional limitations on the states.

That debate had gone on for decades by 1866 and was reviewed several times in the First Session of the 39th Congress. Representative James Wilson believed that the Necessary and Proper Clause, as interpreted in *M'Culloch*, gave Congress power to enforce limitations on the states.[147] More plausibly as a matter of case law, Wilson also relied on *Prigg v Pennsylvania* for the proposition that when the Constitution recognized individual rights, in *Prigg* the slaveholder's right of recaption, it implicitly gave Congress the power to enforce those rights.[148] Representative Wilson invoked *Prigg* in response to John Bingham, who took the other side of the venerable debate, according to which a constitutional restriction by itself did not bring along any congressional power.

As discussed above, Representative Bingham said that a congressional enforcement power was needed because without one Congress could do nothing when state officers violated federal rules that applied to them.[149] Senator Howard made the same point when he introduced the Fourteenth Amendment in the Senate: restrictions on the states are not powers for Congress, so Section 5 was needed to enable Congress to secure the rights set out in Section 1.[150] By providing such a power, Section 5, and the other enforcement clauses, disposed of a serious objection, one founded in a conceptual and textual distinction between limitations on the states and powers of the national government. The enforcement clauses thus perform an important function even if they do not authorize Congress to upset the existing federal balance, which their supporters never claimed they did.

III. Structure and Purpose

Although *Fitzpatrick* preceded *Seminole Tribe* and *Alden*, it now operates as an exception to the latter cases' general principle.

---

[147] Cong Globe, 39th Cong, 1st Sess 1118 (1866).

[148] Id at 1294.

[149] Id at 1090.

[150] Id at 2765–66.

That principle is structural; it is an inference from the overall constitutional scheme, not the product of any explicit provision.[151] The post-*Fitzpatrick* Court's reasoning begins with the premise that the separate political and legal existence of the states, their sovereignty, is a basic feature of the Constitution, even though American states are not fully sovereign entities.[152] Immunity from lawsuits by private plaintiffs, the Court says, is an integral aspect of sovereignty.[153] Because it is so basic, there is a strong presumption that sovereign immunity remains intact, and in particular that grants of power to Congress do not imply power to override it.[154]

Applying this approach, the Court has concluded that none of the Article I powers it has so far encountered meets the standard, but that Section 5 of the Fourteenth Amendment does. Why the latter is true is not so clear from *Fitzpatrick* and the passages in later cases endorsing it, which are quite brief in their treatment of the issue. One thing the Court has pointed to is the fact that the enforcement clauses attach to substantive limitations that refer specifically to the states.[155] That specificity must somehow be the key to the exception.

It cannot be the key, however, that the substantive limitations and thus the enforcement clauses apply to the states. Whatever the Justices who joined *Fitzpatrick* may have thought, the Court

---

[151] *Alden* involved Congress's power to create causes of action against states that would be heard in state courts, and so did not involve the Eleventh Amendment, but the broader principle of state sovereign immunity. "This separate and distinct structural principle is not directly related to the scope of the judicial power established by Article III, but inheres in the system of federalism established by the Constitution." 527 US at 730.

[152] The Court in *Alden* explained that state sovereignty consists of both reserved powers in areas not covered by grants to the national government and of the principle that the national government operates directly on private people, not through and by controlling the states. 527 US at 714–15. "The States thus retain 'a residuary and inviolable sovereignty.' The Federalist No. 39, at 245. They are not relegated to the role of mere provinces or political corporations, but retain the dignity, though not the full authority, of sovereignty." Id at 715.

[153] "The generation that designed and adopted our federal system considered immunity from private suits central to sovereign dignity." Id at 715.

[154] "In exercising its Article I powers Congress may subject the States to private suits in their own courts only if there is 'compelling evidence' that the States were required to surrender this power to Congress pursuant to the constitutional design." Id at 730–31 (quoting *Blatchford v Native Village of Noatak*, 501 US 775, 781 (1991)).

[155] "By imposing explicit limits on the powers of the States and granting Congress the power to enforce them, the Amendment 'fundamentally altered the balance of state and federal power struck by the Constitution.'" 527 US at 756 (quoting *Seminole Tribe*, 517 US at 59).

has since decided that substantive application to the states does not distinguish the enforcement powers from, for example, the commerce power. Rather, the Court in *Alden* was at pains to explain that the Fair Labor Standards Act bound Maine.[156] Thus the enforcement powers are not distinct in that they may be used to legislate in a fashion that binds the states.

If application to the states is not the distinguishing feature of the enforcement powers, that feature must be their reference specifically to the states, which are not named in the ordinary Article I powers. Yet this just means that the enforcement clauses are more limited than most congressional authorities, which also apply, and indeed primarily apply, to private people. It may seem strange to think that a more limited power is for that very reason more intense.

Despite the seeming paradox, there is a reasonable argument along these lines. Whenever the question is whether some grant to Congress includes authority to override state sovereign immunity, the answer must come from comparing the cost of impairment with the value of allowing it. With respect to most congressional authority, the value is relatively small, because the marginal importance of a remedy against the states is comparatively small. Congress's regulation of interstate commerce will not be much disrupted if the Fair Labor Standards Act has an exception for private lawsuits against the states. According to the premise of *Alden*, however, subjecting a state to a private lawsuit imposes a heavy cost on sovereignty itself.[157]

The comparison may be different with the enforcement powers, however, because they apply only or primarily to the states. Any limitation on Congress's power over the states is thus no small margin, the argument would go, but a substantial compromise of the whole point of the provision. In that context, one may think, the balance tips the other way, so that a limited restriction on state sovereignty is justified in order to avoid gutting another part of the Constitution.

If one accepts the rest of the Court's sovereign immunity doc-

---

[156] "The constitutional privilege of a State to assert its sovereign immunity in its own courts does not confer upon the State a concomitant right to disregard the Constitution or valid federal law." 527 US at 754–55.

[157] Id at 748–53 (describing substantial disruption to state sovereignty that would result from congressional power to abrogate state sovereign immunity).

trine, that reasoning is not persuasive. Two factors need to be considered in deciding whether a reasonable constitution maker who embraced both state sovereignty and enforcement of the Reconstruction amendments would think that the former must yield for the latter to be truly meaningful. One is the importance of sovereign immunity to the Constitution's overall design, the second the importance of a power to override sovereign immunity for adequate enforcement of the Reconstruction amendments.

State sovereignty, whatever its precise content, is the foundational structural principle. "Without the States in union there could be no such political body as the United States."[158] *Seminole Tribe* and *Alden* assert that immunity from suit is in turn a basic aspect of sovereignty. If that is true, then a congressional power to override state immunity is a substantial change, and a significant cost to a basic commitment.

Second, sovereign immunity from private lawsuits is in fact a relatively small qualification of the overall system of public law remedies through which constitutional limitations are enforced. Even if states cannot be subjected to private suits for money damages without their consent, violations of the Constitution will hardly go unredressed. Rather, the other remedies that have been developed, in large part on the assumption that lawsuits directly against the government will not be available, protect individuals from unconstitutional decisions. As the earlier review of public law remedies in the nineteenth century shows, waivers of sovereign immunity are not needed in order to have an extensive system of relief from wrongful, and unconstitutional, government action. That system is to be sure not complete, because sometimes the only really effective remedy is an action against the government as such for damages, but it is very broad.

The argument for *Fitzpatrick* rests specifically on the character of the Reconstruction amendments: they limit the states and empower Congress. A closer look at their shared content, however, shows that their common substantive theme makes them especially susceptible to effective enforcement through the classic constitutional remedy, nullity alone. Nullity operates by excising offending parts of the legal system while leaving the rest in place. Thus the Contracts Clause nullifies state laws that impair the

---

[158] *Lane County v Oregon*, 7 Wall 71, 76 (1869).

obligation of contracts, so that contracting parties have the rights and obligations that they would have had absent the unconstitutional legislation. The Contracts Clause need not and does not create the obligation of contracts, which comes from the law of contract.[159] Underlying the Contracts Clause is the assumption that the states will in general have a reasonable law of contract that will in unusual circumstances be disrupted by unwise debtor-relief legislation. The Contracts Clause nullifies the latter, leaving the former in place. In a remarkably economical move, it provides constitutional protection to contract rights without actually creating a constitutional law of contract.

All three Reconstruction amendments share a common basic principle: equality, or nondiscrimination, of one kind or another. Each of the amendments operates by raising a hitherto disadvantaged group to the legal status of a previously more advantaged reference group. First came the elimination of the most extreme form of discrimination of all, that between slaves and free people. Slaves lack basic legal advantages that free people have. Most basic of all is the right to bodily integrity and liberty, which slaves lack: their masters may physically confine them and compel them to work and thus may take actions with respect to their slaves that would be torts if done to free people.[160] A slave who is made free obtains all the legal rights of freedom. Eliminating slavery puts an end to a profound discriminatory divide.

As was forced home on Republicans in 1865 and 1866, however, emancipation by itself leaves intact forms of discrimination other than that between slaves and free people. American slavery was tightly bound with race, and the end of the legal discriminations associated with slavery was not the end of legal discrimination on the basis of race. The earlier elimination of slavery in the North had not eliminated race discrimination there.[161] In the self-recon-

---

[159] In *Ogden v Saunders*, 12 Wheat 213 (1827), the Court held that prospective limitations on contract rights were consistent with the Contracts Clause because there is no impairment if the obligation of contract never arose between the parties in the first place, and whether a contractual obligation arises depends on the nonconstitutional law of contract, not the Constitution itself.

[160] One standard way for a purported slave to test in court whether he was in fact free was to bring an action for battery against his master. See, e.g., *Scott v Sanford*, 19 How 393 (1857) (action for battery to try freedom).

[161] Before the Civil War northern blacks were subject to discrimination "in virtually every phase of existence." Leon F. Litwack, *North of Slavery: The Negro in the Free States, 1790–1860* 64 (1961). For example, five free states—Indiana, Illinois, Iowa, Ohio, and

structed South one of the first steps of the restored state governments was to enact the Black Codes, laws that substantially cur-
tailed the civil rights of the freed people. Discrimination against
blacks replaced discrimination against slaves, or continued even
though discrimination against slaves had ended. In response the
Republicans enacted the Civil Rights Act of 1866 and the Fourteenth Amendment, which were designed to end race discrimination with respect to the basic rights of citizenship. In similar
fashion the Fifteenth Amendment ended race discrimination with
respect to another major legal advantage, the right to vote.

When the Reconstruction amendments raised members of previously disadvantaged groups to a state of parity with members of
previously more advantaged groups, they did so with respect not
only to rights but also remedies. A former slave received not only
the right to personal liberty and bodily security enjoyed by a free
person, but also the remedies protecting that right. Personal liberty is vindicated by the most celebrated public law remedy of all,
the writ of habeas corpus, by which unlawful detention can be
challenged. In the Habeas Corpus Act of 1867, Congress made
sure that freed slaves would be able to bring habeas actions in
federal as well as state court if they were restrained of liberty
contrary to the Thirteenth Amendment.[162]

Remedies figured explicitly in the Civil Rights Act of 1866,
which provided that all citizens were to have the benefit of all
proceedings for the protection of person and property that were
enjoyed by white citizens, the previously more advantaged reference group.[163] Section 1 of the Fourteenth Amendment picked
up the antidiscrimination rule of the statute.

The principle of nondiscrimination also applied to remedies
against government and government officials. An officer suit was
a proceeding for the protection of legal rights and hence covered

---

California—prohibited testimony by blacks in cases in which a white person was a party.
Id at 93.

[162] The 1867 act gave the federal courts jurisdiction to grant writs of habeas corpus "in
all cases where any person may be restrained of his or her liberty in violation of the
Constitution, or of any treaty or law of the United States." Act of Feb 5, 1867, ch xxviii,
14 Stat 385. Its principal purpose was to provide a federal remedy for freed slaves. Lewis
Mayers, *The Habeas Corpus Act of 1867: The Supreme Court as Legal Historian* 33 U Chi L
Rev 31, 33–43 (1965).

[163] The act prohibited race discrimination with respect to the rights "to make and enforce
contracts, to sue, be parties, and give evidence," and secured "full and equal benefit of all
laws and proceedings for the security of person and property" that protected white citizens.
Act of Apr 9, 1866, ch xxxi, § 1, 14 Stat 27.

by the Civil Rights Act and the Fourteenth Amendment. When
the new system of nondiscrimination was in place, therefore, previously disadvantaged people received the benefit of a remedial
system that people who enjoyed important legal advantages had
devised for themselves and presumably believed to be reasonable.
If enfranchised white citizens thought that they needed waivers
of sovereign immunity, they would have them. If they did not have
waivers of sovereign immunity, that was because they thought
waiving sovereign immunity to be unnecessary given the relief
otherwise available. The genius of antidiscrimination is that it
works so well with the sanction of nullity: if there is a generally
sound legal system that excludes some people, the easy solution
is to extend it to those people and otherwise leave it unchanged.

For that reason the rationale for giving Congress power to override state sovereign immunity, rather than being especially strong
with respect to the Reconstruction amendments, is especially weak
with respect to them. Most of the necessary work, including with
respect to remedies against the government, is done by the nondiscrimination norm itself, operating through nullity. That norm
will bring with it a whole system of remedies already in place. And
if Congress finds it necessary to add additional relief, officer suits
and similar mechanisms provide a substantial set of options. Preserving the sovereignty of the states, which according to *Alden*
and *Seminole Tribe* entails immunity from lawsuit, requires only a
quite modest limitation on remedial authority: Congress cannot
act to give disadvantaged individuals one particular remedy when
it is not available to more advantaged individuals.

If sovereign immunity is really central to the constitutional
structure, that is not much of a price to pay for it. The rationale
of the Reconstruction amendments does not demand that they
alter the structure in that fashion. The amendments can easily
accommodate states that retain their sovereign immunity from
lawsuit. In that respect they differ from the other context in which
the Court has found an implicit limitation on state immunity, that
of lawsuits by other states of the Union and the United States.[164]

In that latter context state sovereignty itself has been fundamentally changed, so it is no surprise that immunity from lawsuits
changes with it. States of the Union resemble fully sovereign en-

---

[164] See *Alden*, 527 US at 755–56 (Constitution contemplates suits by other states and
the United States).

tities in many ways. But American states differ from fully sovereign entities in one basic feature: they are permanently associated with other, similar entities, and through that association constitute a greater political body. A paradigmatic sovereign is wholly independent, knowing no legal superior; indeed, not being subjected to any other power is often part of the definition of sovereignty.[165] States of the Union do not have that characteristic, and in particular do not have that characteristic with respect to one another and with respect to the national government. Their obligations as members of the Union trump state law and may not be renounced unilaterally.

Association with other states and with the United States thus effects an essential transformation of the very political and legal character of members of the Union. Transforming immunity from suit along with it does not imply that sovereignty was also compromised when the Constitution was amended to impose additional limitations on states already subject to some limitations and to make clear that there is a power to enforce those limitations. The people who created the Union called it a *novus ordo seclorum*, a new order for the ages; they remade the concept of sovereignty. Important as they are, amendments to their scheme operate within it, not by remaking it.

IV. THE CORRECTNESS OF FITZPATRICK

If the *Seminole Tribe* doctrine is correct, *Fitzpatrick* is inconsistent with the text, structure, and history of the Constitution.[166] As a textual matter, one power of Congress is like another, at least as long as none of them explicitly deals with state sovereign immunity. The structural argument that would distinguish the Reconstruction enforcement powers from Congress's other powers is not sound. *Fitzpatrick*'s reading of Section 5 is probably

---

[165] H. L. A. Hart, refining John Austin's concept of sovereignty, explained that "the same negative characterization of the Queen in Parliament, as *not* habitually obeying the orders of others, roughly defines the notion of *independence* which we use in speaking of the separate legal systems of different countries." H. L. A. Hart, *The Concept of Law* 25 (2d ed 1994). "If, following Austin, we call such a supreme and independent person or body of persons the sovereign, the laws of any country will be the general orders backed by threats which are issued either by the sovereign or subordinates in obedience to the sovereign." Id.

[166] This conclusion leaves open the question whether *Fitzpatrick* should be retained for reasons of stare decisis.

inconsistent with the dominant expectations of the Fourteenth Amendment's supporters and is not required by the amendment's association with the Civil Rights Act of 1866. *Fitzpatrick* is the part that does not fit.

For those who believe that *Seminole Tribe* is incorrect, the question of *Fitzpatrick* is more difficult, and more interesting. It depends on the answer to a recurring problem that has no standard solution. Legal enactments, including constitutional amendments, often rest on presuppositions about the legal system that they change. They usually take those presuppositions for granted, rather than enacting them. At a later time, it may come to seem that the early assumptions about the still earlier law were incorrect. The question then arises whether the enactment should be interpreted to have included its presuppositions, even though it does not do so explicitly and even though the assumptions have been rejected.

If *Seminole Tribe* is wrong, then as an original matter the Constitution did not provide for sovereign immunity, except through the specific text of the Eleventh Amendment. The evidence presented in this article, however, provides good reason to conclude that by the time the Reconstruction amendments were adopted, it was widely believed that the Constitution did provide for sovereign immunity, and did so with a principle broader than the text of the Eleventh Amendment. If that presupposition is read into the enforcement powers of the Reconstruction amendments, then rather than being uniquely able to override state sovereign immunity, those powers are uniquely unable to do so. Whether to read the amendments as including their drafters' assumptions is of course a hard question. Doing so encounters many objections, but it has the virtue of consistency with the concrete expectations of the drafters about what they were going to accomplish. Depending on how these issues are resolved, it is possible that both *Seminole Tribe* and *Fitzpatrick* are incorrect, and the Court has it exactly backwards.

KEITH E. WHITTINGTON

PRESIDENTS, SENATES, AND FAILED SUPREME COURT NOMINATIONS

After a decade of stability on the U.S. Supreme Court, in which new vacancies and appointments were eagerly anticipated but long deferred, three nominees for the Supreme Court were sent by the president to the Senate in the space of four months in 2005. Only two of those nominees reached the Court, with the troubled nomination of Harriet Miers being withdrawn before the Senate Judiciary Committee even began its formal deliberations. The appointments process did not play out as many expected.

The shadow of the failed 1987 nomination of Robert Bork has loomed over the judicial appointments process, and the recent vacancies were widely expected to produce a large-scale confirmation battle, with the prospect of nominees being defeated as Bork was. At the outset of Ronald Reagan's second term of office, Laurence Tribe foreshadowed that battle by calling on senators to take a judicial nominee's substantive views into account when deciding on confirmation and to resist presidential efforts to shift the Court in a more conservative direction.[1] Two decades later, at the outset of George W. Bush's second term of office, Cass Sunstein offered similar advice to Democratic senators, looking to the earlier defeat

Keith E. Whittington is William Nelson Cromwell Professor of Politics, Princeton University.

AUTHOR'S NOTE: I thank Mitch Berman, H. W. Perry, Rick Pildes, Scot Powe, David Yalof, and the editors for their helpful comments and Kimberley Pearce for research assistance.

[1] Laurence H. Tribe, *God Save This Honorable Court* (Random House, 1985).

of Bork as a normative model.[2] The increased polarization of American politics raises the prospect of greater conflict over judicial nominations and presumably the greater likelihood of their defeat.[3] Scholars and interest groups have urged, with some apparent success, the Democratic caucus in the Senate to adopt an explicitly ideological test for voting for judicial nominees with a goal of defeating otherwise qualified nominees.[4] Others have held up the nineteenth-century confirmation process, with its greater rate of failed nominations and less apparent deference to presidential selections, as a normative model for the future.[5]

But 2005 did not recreate 1987. The confirmation process for both John Roberts and Samuel Alito was tamer than many expected or hoped. It was the nomination of the apparently more liberal nominee, Harriet Miers, that failed, defeated in large part by conservatives in the president's own party. At the same time, both Roberts and Alito received far more negative votes on the floor of the Senate than would once have been expected given the absence of serious questions about their personal characters or qualifications.[6]

It is time that we paid more attention to failed Supreme Court nominations. A focus on how controversial a nomination might be can obscure the fact that even controversial nominees are generally successful in passing through the Senate and getting to the Court. We ultimately want to account not for controversy but for success or failure in the confirmation process. No doubt presidents and nominees care most about success or failure. Justices have no less power on the Court for having won confirmation by a slim margin rather than by acclamation. They can serve just as long; their opin-

---

[2] Cass R. Sunstein, *Radicals in Robes* 13–20, 31 (Basic, 2005).

[3] See, e.g., Jeffrey A. Segal, Charles M. Cameron, and Albert D. Cover, *A Spatial Model of Roll Call Voting: Senators, Constituents, Presidents, and Interest Groups in Supreme Court Confirmations*, 36 Am J Pol Sci 96 (1992); Charles R. Shipan and Megan L. Shannon, *Delaying Justice(s): A Duration Analysis of Supreme Court Confirmations*, 47 Am J Pol Sci 654 (2003); Lee Epstein and Jeffrey A. Segal, *Advice and Consent* 102–19 (Cambridge, 2005).

[4] Neal A. Lewis, *Democrats Readying for a Judicial Fight*, NY Times (May 1, 2001), A19; Edward Walsh, *Panel Debates Senate's Role on Court Choices*, Wash Post (June 27, 2001), A23.

[5] See, e.g., Jeffrey K. Tulis, *Constitutional Abdication: The Senate, the President, and Appointments to the Supreme Court*, 47 Case W Res L Rev 1331 (1997).

[6] With 42 votes cast against him, Alito's confirmation vote is comparable to that of Clarence Thomas or William Rehnquist, whose confirmations involved serious ethical controversies as well as ideological disagreement.

ions and their votes count for just as much. The game, in the modern Senate in the absence of a filibuster, is to get to fifty-plus-one. The rest is symbolism.

The history of failed Supreme Court nominations can help clarify basic aspects of the politics of judicial appointments. Recent commentary would have led us to expect that the more ideologically extreme Roberts and Alito would have the greatest difficulty being confirmed, not the apparently more moderate Miers. The historical record, by contrast, would have suggested that, given a Republican majority in the Senate, it was Miers, rather than Roberts or Alito, who had the most to fear in the confirmation process. Within the context of unified government and absent scandal, Supreme Court nominees with solid credentials and judicial philosophies that place them within the mainstream *of their own* political parties—nominees like Roberts and Alito—should be expected to succeed. Getting to fifty-plus-one in the Senate means securing the base. Within unified government, it is nominees who are distrusted by the party faithful who fail.

The most salient feature of the Bork nomination was not that he was conservative—the point emphasized by commentators then and now—but that the Senate at the time of the nomination was controlled by the opposition party. Divided government has always been risky for Supreme Court nominees.

The modern era in this regard is unusual in one respect, however, and in this the Bork nomination is indicative of something distinctly new. It is in the modern era, with the defeat of Clement Haynsworth Jr. and G. Harrold Carswell under President Richard Nixon and Bork under President Reagan, that such nominees have failed outside of a presidential election year.[7] The particular perspective on separation of powers provided by failed Supreme Court nominations certainly reinforces the importance of the interaction of the constitutional scheme with the rise of political parties, but the re-

---

[7] The feature of the modern era also suggests the need to modify the presidentialist perspective of Balkin and Levinson's partisan entrenchment thesis. To their admonition that "if you don't like what the Court is doing now, you (or your parents) shouldn't have voted for Ronald Reagan," the name of the appropriate senator should be added. Jack M. Balkin and Sanford Levinson, *Understanding the Constitutional Revolution*, 87 Va L Rev 1045, 1076 (2001). Control of Congress matters as well to partisan entrenchment. See also Howard Gillman, *How Political Parties Can Use the Courts to Advance Their Agendas: Federal Courts in the United States, 1875–1891*, 96 Am Pol Sci Rev 511 (2002).

lationship between these two fundamental features of the American political system has not been stable over time.[8]

The record of failed Supreme Court nominations also provides a different perspective on the historical pedigree of normative arguments for a more aggressive senatorial role in the appointments process. Although scholars such as Laurence Tribe are right that substantive judicial philosophy has sometimes been taken as relevant to Senate deliberations on Supreme Court nominees, until the modern era such factors were only determinative when the opposition party held the majority of the Senate *and* the defeat of the nomination meant that a new president would fill the vacancy. Before the modern era, the opposition party did not stand as an obstacle to presidents placing their picks on the Court until the president became a lame duck. Partisan warfare over Supreme Court nominees had once been confined to the last months of a presidential term of office. It no longer is. Others, such as Jeffrey Tulis, have argued that the modern Senate has "abdicated" its historic constitutional role of contesting presidential nominations to the Supreme Court, suggesting that the failed Bork nomination was once the norm.[9] The Miers episode is far more resonant of the nineteenth-century experience, however, than is that of Bork. More generally, however, the assertiveness of the nineteenth-century Senate, though real, is not one that we would likely want to recreate or one that we could revive even if we wanted to do so.

To understand why some nominations have failed when so many others succeed and how the politics of Supreme Court appointments has changed over time, this article examines the record of failed nominations. The first section briefly establishes some basics about the confirmation process and the record of failure. The second section will extract some of the important factors that have caused failed Supreme Court nominations over the course of American history and that help to explain why the nineteenth century was so distinctive. The partisan control of the Senate and the White House and the electoral calendar have played important roles in determining the success or failure of Supreme Court nominations, but those relationships have not been stable over time. Notably, where unified government once posed the most danger to the president's

[8] Cf. Daryl J. Levinson and Richard H. Pildes, *Separation of Parties, Not Powers*, 119 Harv L Rev (2006).

[9] See Tulis, 47 Case W Res L Rev (cited in note 5).

selection of Supreme Court nominees, divided government is now the primary source of risk for presidential nominees. The concluding section will note a few lessons for the future.

I. The Confirmation Process and Those Who Were Called but Did Not Serve

The founders created the possibility of failed Supreme Court nominations with the design of the appointments process. Article II of the Constitution specifies that the president "shall nominate, and by and with the Advice and Consent of the Senate, shall appoint . . . Judges of the supreme Court."[10] The involvement of these two independent institutional actors, the president and the Senate, in a two-stage appointments process creates the possibility of deadlock. A majority of the Senate may refuse, perhaps repeatedly, to confirm the president's selections to fill vacancies in the judiciary.[11]

As with much else in the Constitution, the appointments process is the result of a compromise in the Philadelphia convention. James Madison's "Virginia Plan" implied that the president would have the sole power to execute laws and appoint officers.[12] Conceptually, the power of appointment seemed executive in nature and more closely associated with the administration of laws than the making of them.[13] As a practical matter, the experience since the American Revolution seemed to suggest that the appointment power was best placed in a single set of hands. After independence, many states had reacted against the colonial experience, in which the royal governor could use the appointment power to consolidate English control over the colonial governments, by restricting the appointment pow-

---

[10] US Const, Art II, § 2.

[11] The text of the Constitution does not specify what will constitute adequate evidence of "advice and consent of the Senate" in the case of appointments, but the implication and practice has been that a majority vote is adequate for confirmation. The textual silence, however, leaves room for argument about the propriety of filibusters and other procedural devices that effectively prevent a vote on a nominee or require a higher threshold than a simple majority to confirm an appointment. See Michael J. Gerhardt, *The Constitutionality of the Filibuster*, 21 Const Comm 445 (2004).

[12] The Virginia Plan called for the "executive rights vested in Congress by the Confederation" to be transferred to a "National Executive," but did not specify what those were. It also indicated that the judiciary would consist of "tribunals to be chosen by the National Legislature," which might imply the legislative selection of individual judges. James Madison, *Journal of the Federal Convention* 62 (ed E. H. Scott, Albert, Scott, 1893). Madison later indicated that he thought the appointment power was included in the executive power. Id at 87.

[13] Id at 87.

ers of the executives in the state governments.[14] The Confederation
government did not even have a chief executive or distinct executive
branch, so any administrative appointments were made by Congress.[15] The result often seemed to be irresponsibility and discord.
Once it became apparent in the debates of the federal convention
that some would oppose presidential appointment of judges on the
grounds that it seemed too monarchical and others would oppose
legislative appointment of judges on the grounds that it bred in-
trigue, factionalism, and incompetence, Madison and others groped
for a compromise.[16] As Gouverneur Morris concluded, the scheme
finally adopted in Article II sought to balance the "responsibility"
of presidential nomination with the "security" of Senate confirmation.[17]

Although the requirement of Senate confirmation places a check
on the presidency, the Senate and the president are not equal players
in the appointments process. The president has intrinsic advantages
over the Senate, at least in the case of high-profile positions like
the members of the Supreme Court. As Alexander Hamilton noted
in his commentary on the presidency in *The Federalist Papers*, the
only consequence of the rejection of an individual nominee is that
the president gets to choose again.[18] The Senate only possesses a
negative; it does not have the formal authority to dictate a particular
selection. Presidential persistence might well pay off. To the extent
that leaving a given position vacant is an unattractive option to the
Senate, whether because the position is seen as too important to
leave unfilled (as is likely the case with Supreme Court Justices),
because delay in confirmations would only invite a series of unilateral recess appointments of "acting" officials, or because the office
in question provides particular benefits to senators or their constituents, the president can limit the Senate's choice set within a
fairly narrow range.[19] A presidential reputation for determination

[14] Marc W. Kruman, *Between Authority and Liberty* 111–23 (North Carolina, 1997).

[15] Articles of Confederation, Art IX.

[16] James Madison, *Journal of the Federal Convention* at 108–9 (cited in note 12).

[17] Id at 681.

[18] Federalist 66 (Alexander Hamilton) in Clinton Rossiter, ed, *The Federalist Papers* 403 (New American Library, 1961).

[19] There may be some positions that for reason of ideology a president might be content to leave vacant, thus placing pressure on senators sympathetic to the mission of the office in question to accept a nominee rather than have the position crippled by a long-term vacancy. On the other hand, senators may be willing to accept long-term vacancies in

in regard to appointments can force senators to adjust their expectations for an appointment in the president's favor. With the prerogative of nomination and the proper reputation in the capital, presidents can lead senators to calculate whether an otherwise objectionable nominee is nonetheless "the best that we are going to get from this administration."[20]

Presidents have other advantages within the appointments process as well. As the founders expected, decisions are easier to make within the unitary and hierarchical executive than a collective body such as the Senate. Once a nomination is made, senators opposed to the nomination must bear the organizational costs of mobilizing a majority of their colleagues against the nomination and sustaining that majority when confronted with a new nominee. The president has an agenda-setting advantage in considering a possible nomination.[21] In considering whether to make a potentially controversial appointment, the president can often choose whether, when, and for which office to engage in such fights. In his choice of nominee, the president can also choose how to frame the issues of the confirmation, potentially defusing opposition by such stratagems as doubling up on a nomination (as President Ronald Reagan did with the joined appointments of William Rehnquist and Antonin Scalia) or appealing to racial or ethnic loyalties (as President George H. W. Bush did with Clarence Thomas) or choosing polished professionals rather than ideological firebrands (as President George W. Bush did with John Roberts and Samuel Alito). Relatedly, presidents enjoy a potential information advantage in making a nomination, having already sought to exclude potential nominees who would be relatively vulnerable to Senate opposition and to select nominees who can be expected to perform their duties in ways that will be satisfying to the president (of course, the informational advantage

---

some positions, such as district or circuit court judges, thereby giving them greater leverage in the game of confirmation chicken with the president.

[20] To apply the point that presidential scholar Richard Neustadt made more generally in his study of presidential leadership within the world of negotiation and compromise in Washington, D.C., the president's reputation in bargaining is crucial in establishing how much political capital he might be willing to expend in a confirmation fight. If the president has a reputation for determination, and thus is seen as willing to absorb the costs of an extended confirmation battle, then senators might well settle quickly. If the president instead has a reputation for avoiding such fights (perhaps in the interest of preserving other priorities), then senators have an incentive to resist a presidential nomination in the expectation that a more attractive nominee will soon be forthcoming. See Richard E. Neustadt, *Presidential Power and the Modern Presidents* (1991).

[21] See Michael J. Gerhardt, *The Federal Appointments Process* 43 (Duke, 2003).

is only relative and contingent, as numerous administrations have discovered). Finally, the mere fact of presidential nomination creates a presumption in favor of the nominee. The burden falls on opposition senators to find suitable public reasons to justify rejecting a nominee.[22]

Such presidential advantages have made themselves felt in practice. The vast majority of presidential nominations—for any office— are successful.[23] Senate confirmation is the default outcome within the appointments process. Obstruction and delay within the Senate is far more of an obstacle to presidential nominations than is the prospect of outright defeat.[24] Only about 1 percent of all Cabinet-level nominations have been defeated on the floor of the Senate.[25] The record is comparable for sub-Cabinet-level appointments.[26] The Senate rarely says no to the president on his choices for filling the executive branch, but it may take its time in saying yes.

The president has not been quite as successful in filling vacancies in the judicial branch, but the presidential record is still formidable. Over the course of the nation's history, there have been 148 nominations to the Supreme Court.[27] Just under a fifth of these presidential selections have failed to be confirmed by the Senate. The Senate has created more difficulty for the president in filling the third branch of government than in filling the subordinate offices of the executive, but the odds remain very much in the president's favor.

This article focuses on the politics of failed Supreme Court nominations. "Failure" is used here in its most basic sense: the failure to win Senate confirmation for a nomination. Most obviously, this focus lays aside the problem of appointment "mistakes," or Justices who do not perform as the appointing president would have expected or preferred. The lost opportunity to shape the Court or push it in a desired direction is, from one perspective, an instance

---

[22] See id at 44. That burden may not exist in low-profile posts, where practices such as the "blue slip" allow individual senators to obstruct a nomination with little or no explanation.

[23] See id at xx–xxi.

[24] Nolan McCarty and Rose Razaghian, *Advice and Consent: Senate Responses to Executive Branch Nominations 1885–1996*, 43 Am J Pol Sci 1122 (1999).

[25] See Gerhardt, *The Federal Appointments Process* at xx (cited at note 21).

[26] See id at xxi.

[27] See list ast http://www.senate.gov/pagelayout/reference/nominations/Nominations.htm. My count excludes those nominations on which "no action" was taken.

of nomination "failure."[28] Presidents (and historians) may regard their appointments as failures if they do not serve long or well on the bench, for example. A survey of academics evaluated eight Justices as "failures," presumably for such reasons.[29] More notoriously, presidents may regard their appointments as failures if they do not adhere to the substantive commitments of the administration. Thus, President Dwight Eisenhower is frequently said to have thought in hindsight that the appointments of Earl Warren and William Brennan to the Court were mistakes.[30] "Failures" of this sort are beyond the range of this article.

A somewhat less obvious problem is the difficulty in pinning down the number of presidential selections that failed to reach the bench. Relatively easy to lay aside are potential nominees who decline the presidential invitation before the nomination is transmitted to the Senate. Somewhat trickier is the exclusion of nominations that are made known to the public but abandoned before they are officially made to the Senate. Such episodes may range from indecisiveness on the part of presidents and judicial candidates, "trial balloons" leaked to the press, and nominations that derail before they even get started. Excluding this group from consideration leaves out the ill-starred announcement by President Ronald Reagan that Judge Douglas Ginsburg would be his next Supreme Court nominee in 1987, but it has the advantage of drawing a bright line between the public consideration of potential judicial candidates and official nominations subject to Senate deliberation.[31] A final line that is drawn here is the exclusion of official nominations that are subsequently withdrawn and renewed. Thus, the initial nomination of John Roberts to the position of Associate Justice to replace Sandra

---

[28] See Michael Ebeid, *Influencing the Supreme Court: Democratic Accountability and the Presidential Threat to Judicial Independence* (Ph.D. diss, Yale University, 1999); Stefanie A. Lindquist, David A. Yalof, and John A. Clark, *The Impact of Presidential Appointments to the U.S. Supreme Court: Cohesive and Divisive Voting with Presidential Blocs*, 53 Pol Res Q 795 (2000).

[29] See Henry J. Abraham, *Justices, Presidents, and Senators* 370 (Chatham House, 1999).

[30] On Eisenhower's views of Warren and Brennan, see Stephen J. Wermiel, *The Nomination of Justice Brennan: Eisenhower's Mistake? A Look at the Historical Record*, 11 Const Comm 515 (1994); Michael A. Kahn, *Shattering the Myth about President Eisenhower's Supreme Court Appointments*, 22 Pres St Q 47 (1992).

[31] See "Supreme Court Nominations" on the website of the U.S. Senate (http://www.senate.gov/pagelayout/reference/nominations/Nominations.htm#official). On Douglas Ginsburg, see Ronald Reagan, *Remarks Announcing the Nomination of Douglas H. Ginsburg to be an Associate Justice of the United States Supreme Court, October 29, 1987*, in Public Papers of the Presidents of the United States: Ronald Reagan, 1987 (1988).

Day O'Connor is excluded rather than counted as a failure because the nomination was withdrawn in favor of his successful appointment to be Chief Justice upon the death of William Rehnquist, as are nominations such as Eisenhower's initial submission of John Marshall Harlan II's name to the Senate just before the expiration of the Eighty-Third Congress. Such "nominations not confirmed" are more a matter of bookkeeping than failure within the politics of Supreme Court appointments.[32]

This article focuses on those nominations to fill vacancies on the Supreme Court that were clearly rejected by the Senate, whether through direct action or deliberate inaction. By these criteria, there have been twenty-seven failed Supreme Court nominations, twenty-seven instances of a nomination being submitted to the Senate and subsequently permanently withdrawn by the president, voted down by the Senate, or voted to be permanently postponed by the Senate (see App. A). These failed Supreme Court nominations have involved sixteen presidents, ranging from George Washington to George W. Bush, and twenty-five candidates (two individuals had the misfortune of being rejected twice by the Senate). In total, 18 percent of the presidential nominations to fill vacancies on the Supreme Court have failed.

Failed Supreme Court nominations have been a common but not regular feature of American political history. The remainder of this article is concerned with what accounts for these failures and what lessons we might learn from them.

II. ACCOUNTING FOR FAILED SUPREME COURT NOMINATIONS

What accounts for failed Supreme Court nominations? Any reasonable answer must make sense of one particularly striking feature of figure 1: the nineteenth century was different. One contribution of this article is in indicating exactly how the nineteenth century was different, and how those differences relate to the success and failures of the Supreme Court nominations since the turn of the twentieth century. This article argues that failed Supreme Court nominations can be accounted for by three primary, and partly related, factors: divided government, the timing of vacancies relative

---

[32] For a list that includes such nominations, see Henry B. Hogue, "Supreme Court Nominations Not Confirmed, 1789–2004," Congressional Research Service Report for Congress (March 25, 2005) (available at http://www.fas.org/sgp/crs/misc/RL31171.pdf).

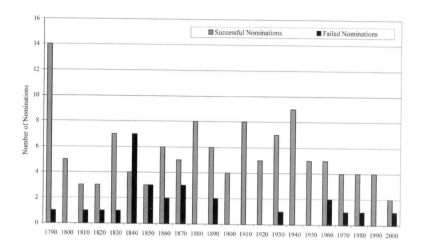

FIG. 1.—Supreme Court nominations by decade. The appointments made in 1789, the first year of the federal government under the U.S. Constitution, are included in the decade of the 1790s. The series ends with the appointment of Samuel Alito in 2006.

to the electoral calendar, and the personal characteristics of the nominees themselves. As it happens, all three factors are also relevant to explaining the transformation in the politics of Supreme Court appointments associated with the close of the nineteenth century. This section begins with a first cut at nominally divided government, with the White House and the Senate under different party control, across American history. It then introduces the electoral calendar and the significance of the proximity of a presidential election for the success of Supreme Court nominations. It then takes a second cut at divided government and examining more closely some apparent anomalies from the previous discussion. It concludes with a closer look at the surprising cases of failed nominations during unified government.

A. DIVIDED GOVERNMENT—A FIRST CUT

The American presidential system, with its independent election of the legislature and the chief executive, creates the possibility of divided government. The bicameral structure of Congress also allows for the possibility of divided party control of the two chambers of the legislature, but for appointment politics what matters is the control of the White House and the Senate and that is the

TABLE 1
SUPREME COURT NOMINATIONS BY PARTY CONTROL, 1789–2006

	Divided Government	Unified Government
Number confirmed	18	103
Number not confirmed	8	19
Failure rate (%)	31	16

focus here. Divided government has not been the norm in American history. For the White House and the Senate to be controlled by two different parties has only been common in the late nineteenth and late twentieth centuries, and was a fairly rare circumstance for most of the rest of American history.[33] Given this backdrop, it is not surprising that most nominations are made during periods of unified government. Over 80 percent of nominations have occurred when the president and the Senate are of the same party.

Divided government is a very difficult environment for Supreme Court nominations. Even though only 18 percent of all nominations occur during periods of divided government, a third of all the failed nominations occurred during these periods. As table 1 indicates, the failure rate for Supreme Court nominations during divided government is twice as high as the failure rate during unified government. Notably, even a slim Senate majority in the president's favor has been sufficient to make the difference. Despite the potential availability of the filibuster in the Senate, and thus arguably an expanded "gridlock interval" within which the minority party can obstruct the actions of the majority party, narrow majorities are not much different than large Senate majorities in approving presidential nominations to the Supreme Court.[34]

That failed Supreme Court nominations would be more likely during periods of divided government is not exactly surprising.[35]

[33] Joel H. Silbey, *Divided Government in Historical Perspective, 1789–1996*, in Peter F. Galderisi, ed, *Divided Government* (Rowman & Littlefield, 1996); Gary W. Cox and Samuel Kernell, eds, *The Politics of Divided Government* 3 (Westview, 1991).

[34] The failure rate for appointments made when the president's party controls a majority of less than 55 percent of the Senate is just 11 percent. There is no evidence of filibuster activity on Supreme Court nominations before 1968. On the expanded gridlock interval in the Senate theoretically created by the supermajority cloture rule, see Keith Krehbiel, *Pivotal Politics* 35–38, 64–73 (Chicago, 1998).

[35] See also John Anthony Maltese, *The Selling of Supreme Court Nominees* 5–8 (Johns Hopkins, 1995).

In general, we would expect more political conflict and disagreement during periods of divided government than during periods of unified government, and it is often thought that divided government would produce greater gridlock in the operation of the government and make cooperation between the president and Congress more difficult across a variety of government activities. Even so, there is some disagreement about how much gridlock divided government actually produces, and it might be thought that presidents would anticipate any possible obstacle that opposite-party Senate majorities might create and make the needed adjustment in their appointment strategies.[36] At least for the confirmation of Supreme Court Justices, however, divided government does appear to create real difficulties for presidents.

The folk wisdom about the obstructions created by divided government in the legislative arena is not often extended to the realm of Supreme Court appointments, which are sometimes portrayed as normatively and descriptively "above politics." The confirmation record of Supreme Court nominations indicates that the normal expectation about the significance of divided government should be extended to our thinking about Supreme Court appointments. Across American history, the appointment of Supreme Court Justices has not been separated from the normal dynamics of partisan politics. Presidents fare much better in getting their preferred nominees on the Court when their own party controls the Senate. If failed Supreme Court nominations are not the rule during divided government, they are at least commonplace.

Looking at the track record of Supreme Court nominations during unified and divided government across all of American history ignores the tendency, visible in figure 1, for Supreme Court nominations to have had greater trouble in the years prior to 1900.

---

[36] See generally David R. Mayhew, *Divided We Govern* (Yale, 1991) (finding no effect on legislative output from divided government); Krehbiel, *Pivotal Politics* at 51–75 (cited in note 34) (arguing that legislative process encourages formation of large lawmaking majorities); Charles M. Cameron, *Veto Bargaining* 83–150 (Cambridge, 2000) (arguing that lawmakers will anticipate presidential vetoes and incorporate presidential preferences into legislation); David W. Brady and Craig Volden, *Revolving Gridlock* 13–32 (Westview, 1997) (arguing for importance of legislative institutions in creating gridlock). See also Bryon J. Moraski and Charles R. Shipan, *The Politics of Supreme Court Nominations: A Theory of Institutional Constraints and Choices*, 43 Am J Pol Sci 1069 (1999) (arguing that presidents adjust to the Senate in their appointment strategy); Glen S. Krutz, Richard Fleisher, and Jon R. Bond, *From Abe Fortas to Zoe Baird: Why Some Presidential Nominations Fail in the Senate*, 92 Am Pol Sci Rev 871 (1998) (finding that divided government did not increase chance of failure of presidential nominations).

TABLE 2
SUPREME COURT NOMINATIONS BY PARTY CONTROL BEFORE AND AFTER 1900

	Before 1900		After 1900	
	Divided Government	Unified Government	Divided Government	Unified Government
Number confirmed	6	58	12	45
Number not confirmed	5	16	3	3
Failure rate (%)	46	22	20	6

Divided government was not significantly more common before the twentieth century; rather, the significance of divided and unified government for Supreme Court confirmations changed in the twentieth century. As table 2 indicates, the president's prospects over the past century improved under both divided and unified government relative to the earlier period. There have been fewer Supreme Court nominations in the years since 1900 than in those before it (an average of one nomination every 1.3 years before and one nomination every 1.8 years after, a difference that is only partly attributable to the higher failure rate of pre-1900 nominations), but presidents have been more successful in winning confirmation for their nominations whether or not their party controls the Senate (though they still do better when their party controls than when it does not).

Before 1900, presidents nominating Supreme Court Justices during periods of divided government would seem to have no better chance of success in the Senate than in a coin flip. Although the odds of failure during divided government have remained high since 1900, it is striking (at least in comparison to our first century's experience) that presidents could, in the twentieth century, normally expect their nominees to be confirmed even when the Senate was in the hands of the opposition.

B. THE ELECTORAL CALENDAR, LAME DUCKS, AND FAILED
   NOMINATIONS

To begin to understand the divergence between the experience of the nineteenth century and that of the twentieth century, another factor needs to be added to the partisan control of the government: the electoral calendar. The U.S. government works, of course, to the rhythm of a fixed electoral cycle. Presidents face election every four years, and although individual senators face election every six years, the Senate is affected by an election every two years. Supreme Court vacancies are not directly tied to this calendar but instead intersect it more or less at random depending on the vagaries of deaths and resignations. The timing of these vacancies, however, matters greatly to how successful the nominations to fill those vacancies will be.

The American electoral calendar is fixed, but it has not been entirely stable across two hundred years of history. The Constitution of 1787 specified that Congress would assemble on the first Monday of December, unless otherwise directed by law.[37] Until the early twentieth century, the result was that the new Congress first met and the new president was inaugurated on March 4.[38] The Twentieth Amendment to the Constitution altered that schedule, specifying that Congress would meet January 3 and the new president would be inaugurated on January 20, beginning with Franklin Roosevelt in 1937.[39] The consequence of the Amendment was to significantly reduce the lame-duck period between when a new Congress and president were elected and when they assumed their offices.[40]

Both the extended lame-duck period and strategic calculations associated with the electoral calendar had significant implications for Supreme Court appointment politics in the nineteenth century. Lame-duck presidents have made fourteen nominations to the Supreme Court. The last of those lame-duck appointments occurred in 1893. Lame-duck nominations were a common feature of nineteenth-century appointment politics, accounting for 16 percent of all the nominations made before 1900, but there have been no lame-duck nominations in over a century. Lame-duck nominations also had a high rate of failure. Half of those nominations failed.

Lame-duck nominations were not doomed to failure. They interacted in predictable ways with partisan interests. As table 3 indicates,

---

[37] US Const, Art I, § 4.

[38] See Michael Angelo Mussman, *Changing the Date for Congressional Sessions and Inauguration Day*, 18 Am Pol Sci Rev 108 (1924).

[39] US Const, Amend XX.

[40] "Lame duck" is here used in the narrow sense of officeholders whose successors have already been elected. "Late term" is used to refer to officeholders whose successors will be elected within six months. The meaning and significance of the Twentieth Amendment are explored in Bruce Ackerman, *The Case against Lameduck Impeachment* (Seven Stories, 1999).

TABLE 3
LAME-DUCK NOMINATIONS AND PARTY CONTROL

	Divided Government	Unified Government
Number confirmed	0	7
Number not confirmed	3	4

nominations by outgoing presidents were doomed to failure when the Senate was controlled by the opposition party. Unsurprisingly, an opposition-controlled Senate always preferred to wait for their own party's president-elect to assume office and fill the vacancy on the Court rather than confirm a lame-duck nomination. The most startling thing about this scenario is that presidents even made the attempt.[41] Nonetheless, apparently working on the belief that they possessed a duty and responsibility to act to fill any vacancy that arose during their term of office and on the hope that a qualified nominee could rise above party feelings, both National Republican John Quincy Adams and Whig Millard Fillmore sent Supreme Court nominations to Democratic-controlled Senates in the waning days of their administrations only to see them unceremoniously tabled.[42] The vacancies were quickly filled by Democratic presidents and Senates immediately after the inaugural.

By contrast, the same-party Senate was generally eager to confirm the lame-duck nominations of outgoing presidents.[43] In the months after the election of 1800, the Federalist Senate not only approved a new Judiciary Act expanding and strengthening the federal courts but it also twice voted to confirm John Adams's selections for Chief Justice before the hated Thomas Jefferson could occupy the White House.[44] A Democratic Senate quickly endorsed Martin Van Buren's choice of Peter Daniel to fill a vacancy two days before the Whigs

---

[41] In each case, the president *and* his party were being replaced at the inaugural. If John Quincy Adams and Millard Fillmore had been able to look forward to their partisan successors filling the vacancy, then they might have been more content to stay their hands.

[42] Nonetheless, the supporters of John Adams's nominee, John Crittenden, complained of the "infernal precedent" being set by "impeding the action of the whole Government" on "party ground" during the lame-duck period. See David J. Danelski, *Ideology as a Ground for the Rejection of the Bork Nomination*, 84 Nw U L Rev 900, 907 (1990).

[43] The surprising exceptions of the four unified-government rejections of lame-duck nominations are discussed in text at notes 56–63.

[44] Adams's first choice, John Jay, declined to serve. On the final days of the Federalist government, see Bruce Ackerman, *The Failure of the Founding Fathers* 111–245 (Harvard, 2005); Richard E. Ellis, *The Jeffersonian Crisis* (Oxford, 1971); Stanley Elkins and Eric McKitrick, *The Age of Federalism* 691–750 (Oxford, 1993).

TABLE 4
TIMING AND SUCCESS OF SUPREME COURT NOMINATIONS

Time until Presidential Election	After Election (Lame Duck)	Within Six Months (Late Term)	Within Twelve Months	More than Twelve Months
Number confirmed	7	2	21	91
Number not confirmed	7	3	3	14
Failure rate (%)	50	· 60	13	13

were slated to take over both the presidency and the Senate. More idiosyncratic, and uncharitable, was the congressional action to create two new seats on the Supreme Court on the eve of Andrew Jackson's departure from the capital.[45] Despite the fact that Jackson's own vice president, Martin Van Buren, was to be his successor, Jackson sent the names of his selections for those two seats to the Senate on his last day in office.

The last lame-duck nomination was also the most difficult. When a vacancy opened on the Court after the election of 1892, the defeated Republican President Benjamin Harrison hoped to immediately fill it, denying the seat to his successor, Democrat Grover Cleveland, and what would be only the second Democratic Senate since the Civil War. The Republican leadership in the narrowly divided Senate, however, sent word that the Democratic minority was prepared to obstruct any confirmation through the end of the session. Harrison outmaneuvered the opposition, however, by nominating a former Democratic senator, Howell Jackson, who had been appointed as federal circuit court judge during the first Cleveland administration.[46] The Democratic senators could hardly hold up Jackson's nomination. Although the outgoing Republicans were unable to entrench one of their own on the high court, they were at least able to choose which Democrat would receive the appointment.

Late-term nominations are only a step removed from lame-duck nominations, and they too have difficulty being confirmed. As table 4 indicates, when presidential elections are impending, failed Supreme Court nominations are more likely. Moreover, of the four-

---

[45] 5 Stat 176 (1837).

[46] Richard D. Friedman, *The Transformation in Senate Response to Supreme Court Nominations: From Reconstruction to the Taft Administration and Beyond*, 5 Cardozo L Rev 1, 40 (1983).

teen failed nominations that have been lame-duck or late-term efforts, only one occurred after 1900. Late-term and lame-duck
nominations account for all but two of the failed Supreme Court
nominations prior to the Civil War and for over 60 percent of the
failed nominations prior to 1900. With the election in sight, and
with it the possibility of a new president, opponents of the incumbent president have an incentive to obstruct any nomination in the
Senate and gamble that the next president will nominate a more
desirable candidate for the vacancy on the Supreme Court. The
lateness of the hour creates both the desire and the means to prevent
a vacancy from being filled, countering the advantage that normally
falls to a determined president.

One of the six failed nominations since 1900 occurred in these
circumstances, when President Lyndon Johnson was unable to secure confirmation of Associate Justice Abe Fortas to replace Chief
Justice Earl Warren. This was an instance of a strategic retirement
gone awry. Politically debilitated by the Vietnam War, Lyndon
Johnson had already announced that he would not stand for reelection in 1968. Once Robert Kennedy was killed during the Democratic primaries that summer, Warren became convinced that the
Democrats would not be able to defeat the expected Republican
presidential nominee, Richard Nixon, who was not only a long-
time political rival of Warren's from their days in California but
who was also mounting a "law-and-order" campaign that was as
critical of the Warren Court as it was of the Johnson administration.
Fearful that he would not be able to outlast a Nixon presidency,
the seventy-seven-year-old Warren submitted his resignation, effective with the confirmation of a successor, to Johnson with the
understanding that Fortas would be his replacement. Despite a large
Democratic majority in the Senate, the Fortas nomination ran into
immediate difficulty. Conservative Democrats in the Senate pillo-
ried Fortas at his confirmation hearings and the Republican candidate Nixon and the media questioned the propriety of the coordinated resignation-nomination on the eve of the election.
Johnson was forced to withdraw the nomination rather than force
a certain defeat in a recorded vote, and President Richard Nixon
accepted Warren's resignation upon assuming office in 1969.[47]

Lame-duck and late-term nominations in unfavorable political

---

[47] Lucas A. Powe, Jr., *The Warren Court and American Politics* 468–75 (Harvard, 2000).

circumstances bedeviled the nineteenth century but were practically unknown in the twentieth century.[48] They account for much of the differential failure rates between the two periods. Of course, the timing of vacancies on the Court largely determines the timing of nominations. Why so many vacancies of this sort in the nineteenth century and so few afterward? Luck cannot be ruled out entirely. Chief Justice William Rehnquist could have died on an election eve during a period of divided government rather than in an odd-numbered year during a period of unified government. But presidents since the nineteenth century have not just been unusually lucky.

An unanticipated side effect of changes in the structure of the government has systematically reduced the incidence of such vacancies. First, prior to the Twentieth Amendment the lame-duck period was much longer, creating more time during which vacancies might occur and making it more difficult to simply wait for the next president to fill any vacancies that might arise. The adoption of the Twentieth Amendment has reduced the odds of lame-duck vacancies and resultant high-risk, lame-duck nominations. Second, Congress took legislative steps in the twentieth century to encourage Justices, and federal judges generally, to retire rather than die in office by creating more generous pensions and terms of retirement.[49] These efforts have been more far-reaching in their consequences for the lower courts than for the Supreme Court, but even so the Justices are more willing to walk away from the job now than they once were.[50] Chief Justice Rehnquist's mode of departure was once the standard. Now Justice Sandra Day O'Connor's is not uncommon.

The failed lame-duck and late-term nominations were almost uniformly predictable given the political situations at the time that the vacancies arose. Absent the strategic miscalculation of the sort

---

[48] Midterm elections have posed no special difficulties for the confirmation of Supreme Court nominees. It is the prospect of change in the nominating institution, not the confirming institution, that appears to matter.

[49] David N. Atkinson, *Leaving the Bench* (Kansas, 1999); Artemus Ward, *Deciding to Leave* 136–43 (SUNY, 2003).

[50] Peverill Squire, *Politics and Personal Factors in Retirement from the United States Supreme Court*, 10 Pol Beh 180, 181 (1988); Christopher J.W. Zorn and Steven R. Van Winkle, *A Competing Risks Model of Supreme Court Vacancies, 1789–1992*, 22 Pol Beh 145, 154–56 (2000). See also James F. Spriggs II and Paul J. Wahlbeck, *Calling It Quits: Strategic Retirements on the Federal Courts of Appeals, 1893–1991*, 48 Pol Res Q 573, 588–91 (1995); Albert Yoon, *As You Like It: Senior Federal Judges and the Political Economy of Judicial Tenure*, 2 J Emp L St 495 (2005).

TABLE 5
CAUSES OF VACANCIES RESULTING IN LAME-DUCK AND LATE-TERM NOMINATIONS

	Death	Resignation	New Seat	Unsuccessful Prior Nomination
Pre-1830	1	1	0	1
1831–1900	6	0	2	6
Post-1900	0	2	0	0

that caught up Warren, Johnson, and Fortas, few Justices would have chosen to step down from the bench given those conditions and thereby create the circumstances for an extended confirmation battle over a successor. The Justices can choose the time of their retirement, but they cannot choose the time of their death. Modern Justices looking at a divided government have generally chosen to retire a safe distance from future elections so as to minimize the likelihood that their seats would become entangled in election-year politics. As table 5 indicates, there have been only two late-term (and no lame-duck) nominations since 1900. The strategic miscalculation of the Warren retirement has already been noted. The other was the result of Charles Evan Hughes leaving the Supreme Court in order to claim the 1916 Republican presidential nomination. In those circumstances, Republican senators could hardly object to President Woodrow Wilson filling the vacant seat prior to the election. The GOP was simply willing to trade the Supreme Court seat for the apparent strength of a Hughes candidacy, which almost succeeded in unseating Wilson from the presidency. The number of late-term and lame-duck nominations in the period between 1830 and 1900 is also multiplied by the stubborn determination of two presidents, John Tyler and Millard Fillmore, to refuse to accept "no" for an answer from the Senate. Rather than facing political reality and accepting that the late-term vacancy would be filled by the next president, as Lyndon Johnson did after the Fortas nomination imploded, Tyler and Fillmore persisted in trying to find a nominee that the Senate would accept despite the political season.[51] Tyler's persistence was in fact partly rewarded when the Senate finally confirmed the lame-duck nomination of Samuel Nelson just days before James Polk's presidential inaugural.

---

[51] The one lame-duck nomination resulting from an unsuccessful prior nomination before 1830 was not the result of a Senate rejection but rather the result of John Jay declining to accept the post of Chief Justice to which he had been nominated and confirmed.

TABLE 6
SUPREME COURT NOMINATIONS BY TIMING AND PARTY CONTROL

	Divided Government		Unified Government	
	Late-Term	Not Late-Term	Late-Term	Not Late-Term
Pre-1900:				
Number confirmed	0	6	8	50
Number not confirmed	4	1	5	11
Post-1900:				
Number confirmed	0	12	1	44
Number not confirmed	0	3	1	2

C. "DIVIDED GOVERNMENT": A SECOND CUT

It is now appropriate to unpack the concept of party government to explain some of the apparent anomalies in the tables above. As table 1 indicates, divided government has been risky but not fatal for nominees, but table 2 also pointed out the fact that divided government was far more risky for nominees in the nineteenth century than it has been since. Why have nominations fared as well as they have under conditions of divided government? At the same time, table 3 included its own surprise in that not all lame-duck nominations during unified government have been success-ful. Taking into account the electoral calendar and looking more closely at the workings of divided and unified government will help explain these apparent anomalies.

Table 6 focuses our attention on how partisanship and timing intersect to facilitate or hamper the confirmation of Supreme Court nominees, and how that relationship has changed over time. As table 2 indicates, divided government presented extreme dif-ficulties for nominations in the nineteenth century but has been much less of an obstacle since 1900. Table 6 indicates the reason for this. In the nineteenth century, presidents near the end of their terms made several attempts to place Justices on the Supreme Court even though the Senate was in opposition hands, and none of those attempts was successful. Since the nineteenth century, no president at the end of his term has attempted to appoint a Su-preme Court Justice without also having same-party control of the Senate.[52] It is the combination of divided government and

---

[52] Eisenhower, for example, gave William Brennan a recess appointment, waiting until after his own reelection before putting Brennan's name before the Senate. Had Adlai Stevenson won the presidential election in 1956, Brennan would likely never have been converted into a formal nomination.

late-term appointments that has historically been fatal to Supreme Court nominations. In such circumstances, the Senate could reasonably expect to wait the president out.

Through most of American history, divided government was not an obstacle to Supreme Court nominations when the vacancies did not occur near a presidential election. Before 1969, there was only a single exception: Andrew Jackson's January 1835 nomination of Roger Taney to be Associate Justice. On the final day of the Twenty-Third Congress, the lame-duck but Whig-controlled Senate narrowly defeated the Taney nomination. The gesture was purely symbolic. The Whigs had lost control of the Senate in the midterm election of 1834. President Jackson had two more years in office and a friendly Senate on the way. There was little doubt that the president would soon be able to fill the seat. As it happened, John Marshall died before the Twenty-Fourth Congress assembled, so that when Taney was successfully renominated for the Court his appointment was to fill the role of Chief Justice rather than Associate Justice. It is difficult now to appreciate the depth of loathing the Whigs felt for Roger Taney at the time of his original nomination, and as a consequence just how exceptional his defeat on the Senate floor was. Taney had been Jackson's loyal lieutenant, serving first as his attorney general and helping to draft the veto messages that so inflamed partisan passions before the presidential elections of 1832.[53] It was these vetoes that first fed the formation of the Whig Party as an organized opposition to "King Andy" and the emerging Democratic Party.

Far more serious for Taney, however, were the events of 1833 and his involvement in the president's final moves against the Bank of the United States. Having vetoed the rechartering of the Bank in the summer of 1832 and been resoundingly reelected in the fall, Jackson announced his resolve in 1833 to remove the federal government's deposits from the Bank, crippling it. When his Treasury Secretary refused to go along with the plan, Jackson fired him and replaced him with Taney, who had already indicated his belief in the legality and sound policy of the removal plan. As acting Secretary of the Treasury, Taney immediately issued the necessary instructions, setting in motion what would become the

---

[53] Carl Brent Swisher, *Roger B. Taney* 190–97 (Macmillan, 1935); Charles Warren, 2 *The Supreme Court in United States History* 254–365 (Little, Brown, 1922).

financial panic of 1837.[54] The Whigs, apoplectic at what they took to be Jackson's most extreme abuse of executive power yet but unable to launch an impeachment without the cooperation of the Democratic House of Representatives, were reduced to passing an unprecedented resolution of censure in the Senate in March of 1834.[55] The Senate could, and did, refuse to confirm Taney as Treasury Secretary that summer. It was the first time the Senate had ever rejected a Cabinet nomination. The outgoing Whigs undoubtedly enjoyed the opportunity to take another swing at Taney when Jackson nominated him to the Supreme Court just a few months later. It is hard to imagine a comparable appointment in the modern era. Politically, it would have been like Gerald Ford nominating Richard Nixon to the Supreme Court instead of John Paul Stevens in 1975, or Bill Clinton resigning from the presidency after his 1998 impeachment and Al Gore immediately nominating him for a vacancy on the Court. Even so, Taney fell just three votes short of being confirmed to the Supreme Court just six months after the same Senate had rejected his confirmation as Treasury Secretary by a ten-vote margin.

By comparison, the rejection by Democratic Senates of the midterm Supreme Court nominations of Republican presidents looks like a historically new level of activism in the exercise of the confirmation power. When he nominated Judge Clement Haynsworth Jr. in the fall of 1969, Richard Nixon had not yet reached the first anniversary of his inauguration as president. He was no lame duck, and the Democratic majority in the Senate could not expect to hold the position open for a president of their own party. The same situation prevailed when Nixon nominated G. Harrold Carswell after Haynsworth was defeated and when Ronald Reagan nominated Robert Bork in the summer of 1987. With the exception of the Taney nomination in 1835, presidents had not encountered significant Senate resistance to their Supreme Court nominations within divided government as such. The threat of ideologically based defeat of Court nominations, without an overhanging election, is a modern phenomenon.

As surprising, from a modern perspective, as the traditional deference of the Senate to presidential nominations during divided

---

[54] Robert V. Remini, *Andrew Jackson and the Bank War* (Norton, 1967).

[55] 10 Reg Deb 58 (1833); 13 Reg Deb 433–44 (1837).

government is the lack of deference to presidential nominations during unified government. Particularly striking are the five failed late-term nominations during unified government before 1900 shown in column 3 of table 6 (the one such failure since 1900 was Abe Fortas). The expectation would be that partisans would leap at the chance to entrench one of their own on the Supreme Court rather than leaving a vacancy for their successors to fill, burning the midnight oil if necessary as John Adams did with his appointments. The fate of the 1968 Fortas nomination is an indication that "unified government" can be a messy category. The importance of the "conservative coalition" of Republicans and Southern Democrats in Congress, a coalition that helped defeat Fortas, might call into question the easy classification of divided and unified government in the postwar period.[56]

If the conservative coalition complicates the concept of unified government in 1968, the partisan alignments during the five pre-1900 late-term defeats blow it apart. The last of the five came in February 1861, with President James Buchanan's nomination of Jeremiah Black to fill the vacancy left by the death of Justice Peter Daniel several months earlier. By 1861, the lame-duck Buchanan's Democratic majority in the Senate had evaporated as Southern senators resigned to join their home states in secession. At the time of Black's nomination, the Republicans held a one-seat advantage in the Senate, and Black was voted down in a straight party-line vote.[57]

The other four were nominations by President John Tyler, who presided over a government that was only nominally unified under a common party label. Tyler had been a prominent, if idiosyncratic, Virginia politician. Serving in the U.S. Senate during the Jackson administration, Tyler found himself no longer willing to support the president during the deposit removal crisis. Considering the strong support for Jackson in the Virginia legislature, however, Tyler felt honor-bound to resign from the Senate and allow the legislature to select a representative more in tune with their own commitments.[58] Constitutional scruples over executive power had made him a Whig in the Jacksonian era, but like others in the

---

[56] See Paul Frymer, *Ideological Consensus within Divided Party Government*, 109 Pol Sci Q 287 (1994).

[57] 11 *Journal of the Executive Proceedings of the United States Senate* 278 (1861).

[58] Warren, *Supreme Court in United States History* at 2:288 (cited in note 53).

South he was a "states' rights" Whig, or, as he later told the press, he was a "Jeffersonian Republican" who had never departed from the "principles of the old Republican Party."[59] He was recruited onto the bottom of the Whig presidential ticket in 1840 in order to help lure Southern conservatives like himself to cross party lines, and the Whigs did capture both the White House and Congress in that election.[60] President William Henry Harrison's death weeks after his inaugural put the self-conscious Jeffersonian constitutionalist into the Oval Office just as Congress under the leadership of Henry Clay and former president John Quincy Adams hoped to embark on an activist, nationalist program that depended on the constitutional sensibilities of John Marshall.

The relationship between the president and the congressional Whigs quickly deteriorated, with Tyler and Clay plotting against each other and with Adams, barely able to admit that Tyler even was the president, authoring reports in the House of Representatives calling for his impeachment.[61] Unable to reach a compromise, Tyler effectively gutted the Whigs' legislative program with his vetoes and was struggling to find supporters among Democrats and other Southern independents.[62]

By the time a vacancy opened up on the Court in the final year of his presidency, Tyler had essentially been written out of the party and could expect to receive no deference from the Senate majority. After the Senate rejected his first choice for the seat and another death on the Court created a second vacancy, the leading Whig paper declared that "better the bench be vacant for a year" than filled by a Tyler appointee.[63] Not one to be intimidated and with months still to go before his term of office would be over, Tyler was determined to try again. At one point the president was camped out in a Senate anteroom scribbling names on slips of paper to be passed on to the chamber floor as the Senate shot down one nomination after another, for the Supreme Court and for other offices.[64] One senator later recalled that "[n]ominations

---

[59] Quoted in Oliver Perry Chitwood, *John Tyler* 191 (D. Appleton-Century, 1939).

[60] Robert Seager II, *And Tyler Too* 132–35 (McGraw-Hill, 1963).

[61] John Quincy Adams, *The Diary of John Quincy Adams* 522 (Longmans, Green, 1929) ("styles himself president"); Seager, *And Tyler Too* at 167 (cited in note 60).

[62] Robert J. Morgan, *A Whig Embattled* 38–55, 157–71 (Nebraska, 1954).

[63] *The U.S. Judiciary*, National Intelligencer (April 27, 1844), 2.

[64] Thomas H. Benton, 2 *Thirty Years' View* 630 (D. Appleton, 1865).

and rejections flew backwards and forwards as in a game of shuttle-cock—the same nomination, in several instances, being three times rejected . . . within the same hour."[65] After the Democrat James Polk surprised the capital by beating Henry Clay in the presidential election of 1844, the Senate finally relented and accepted one of Tyler's Supreme Court nominations: New York chief justice Samuel Nelson. In the course of winning this one victory, Tyler racked up six failed Supreme Court nominations, including one "late term" and three "lame-duck" nominations.

Amazingly, the Tyler presidency was not unique in the nineteenth century. Andrew Johnson, the third vice president to ascend to the Oval Office upon the death of the president (Tyler was the first), was cut from similar cloth. Johnson was a nationalist protégé of Andrew Jackson's from Old Hickory's home state of Tennessee. Johnson was serving in the U.S. Senate when Tennessee seceded, and he was one of the few who chose to stay in Washington rather than follow his state into the Confederacy. His loyalty was later rewarded when Abraham Lincoln appointed him to be the military governor when Tennessee was recaptured for the Union. A minority president in 1860 and mired in a long internecine war, Lincoln needed to broaden his base in 1864 and help frame the war as a national effort rather than a partisan one. Like Tyler before him, Johnson was added to the "Union Party" ticket as a man whose constitutional scruples had led him to break from his party and his region.[66] And as with Tyler, the party managers got more than they had bargained for when that independent-minded token of ticket balancing assumed the presidency in 1865.

By the time Johnson sought to fill a vacancy on the Court in April 1866, he too was effectively a president without a party. Over the two prior months, the president had vetoed the key pieces of congressional Reconstruction and publicly denounced Republican congressional leaders as no better than the secessionists.[67] The Republicans responded by organizing a veto-proof majority in Congress and renouncing the president. By the fall, Johnson would be campaigning against congressional Republicans in the midterm elections of 1866 and trying to organize his own party under the

---

[65] Id at 2:629.

[66] Eric Foner, *Reconstruction* 44–45 (Harper & Row, 1989).

[67] Id at 240–49.

Union label.[68] Before then, however, the Senate simply ignored his nomination of Henry Stanbery (the reputed author of one of the veto messages) for the Supreme Court. Instead, the House and Senate began deliberations on a judicial reform bill that would eliminate not only the seat for which Stanbery had been nominated but the next seat that might become vacant as well, reducing the Court from ten Justices (where the Republicans had set it in 1863, when Lincoln still held the appointing power) to eight (it was brought back up to nine after the inauguration of Ulysses Grant).[69] Stanbery instead accepted an appointment to be Johnson's attorney general, and later served on the president's defense team at his impeachment. The rejection of Johnson's Supreme Court nominee, like those of Tyler's and Buchanan's, occurred during unified government only in a nominal sense.

Far from being a golden age of Senate activism and responsibility, the nineteenth century was an age of presidential misfortune. Much of the nineteenth-century Senate's record of bold rejections of Supreme Court nominations was solely the product of lame-duck presidents and divided government. In such circumstances, the modern Senate would undoubtedly be equally "bold." It is not the Senate that has changed; it is the circumstances of nomination.

At the same time, the modern Senate is bolder than its predecessors, and has broken from nearly two centuries of precedent in rejecting the midterm nominations of opposite-party presidents. The modern Senate is far more obstructionist during divided government than it was over the course of its history. It once took the nomination of a Roger Taney to trigger a nomination failure in an opposite-party, midterm Senate. It no longer does. Whatever else may be said of them, Clement Haynsworth and Robert Bork were no Roger Taney.

D. SUPREME COURT NOMINEES AND ORDINARY POLITICS DURING UNIFIED GOVERNMENT

The combination of the electoral calendar and divided government largely accounts for seventeen of the twenty-seven failed

---

[68] Keith E. Whittington, *Constitutional Construction* 114–15 (Harvard, 1999).

[69] Warren, *Supreme Court in United States History* at 3:144–45 (cited in note 53); Friedman, 5 Cardozo L Rev at 22–24 (cited in note 46).

Supreme Court nominations. The remaining ten failed nominations occurred during genuinely unified governments that were not hampered by the electoral clock. Nearly all of these occurred before 1900—three before 1860, five more before 1900, and two since 1900. Although these nominations were made in what would seemingly be the most favorable circumstances, they were also made in circumstances in which the president's fellow partisans in the Senate had the luxury of sending the president back to the well, confident that a like-minded Justice would eventually be confirmed. In such circumstances, senators in the president's own party can afford to indulge secondary considerations about individual nominees. Particularly in the nineteenth century, the range of those secondary considerations was rather broad.

John Rutledge was the first Supreme Court nominee to be rejected by the Senate. His nomination by George Washington in 1795 was seemingly unobjectionable. Rutledge had already served on the Court as one of Washington's first picks in 1789, before resigning in order in 1791 to accept the job of chief justice in his home state of South Carolina. When John Jay stepped down from the position of Chief Justice, having been elected governor of New York while he was serving on a diplomatic mission in England, Washington returned Rutledge to the Court with a recess appointment in the summer of 1795. When his name officially came before the Senate in December, there had been nine Supreme Court confirmations, all by voice vote and without controversy. By then, however, Rutledge had become a controversial figure. The treaty that Jay had negotiated in England secured the peace and improved America's trading position, but it was widely perceived as to have conceded too much to England and to have done nothing about the emotional issue of the seizure of American ships and impressment of American sailors by the English navy. Sometimes violent demonstrations against the treaty erupted on the streets, the Washington administration was subject to caustic criticism in the press, and the House of Representatives nearly blocked the implementation of the treaty after the more accommodating Senate had ratified it.[70] While still in South Carolina, Rutledge had delivered an angry speech denouncing the treaty. Reports of the speech reached the nation's capital before Rutledge himself

---

[70] Elkins and McKitrick, *Age of Federalism* at 416–22 (cited in note 44).

did.[71] With the 1796 elections on the horizon and a bitter partisan split emerging over American foreign policy, support for the Jay Treaty was a litmus test issue for the Federalists. Rutledge was sent packing, with the same senators voting for his confirmation as had voted against the ratification of the treaty.[72]

In the spring of 1811, James Madison's nomination of Alexander Wolcott was turned down by the Senate. The death of William Cushing created a vacancy on the Court that would necessarily be challenging for Madison to fill. The expectation that the Justices would be drawn from the geographic circuit for which they would be responsible meant that the nominee would have to be drawn from New England. Although the Republicans had made headway in New England, it was still a Federalist section and an area of Republican weakness. It was as if George Bush were to limit himself to choosing a Supreme Court nominee from New Hampshire. There are Republicans to be found there, but the pickings are slim and they are not very representative of the party as a whole. The timing was not propitious either. The Jeffersonian embargo, unsuccessfully designed to keep the United States out of a war with Britain, hit the shipping and commercial interests of New England especially hard, and the scandal over the Yazoo land claims was still ongoing and tainted many of the region's best lawyers in the eyes of the Republicans.[73] Supporting this federal power over shipping was the critical issue for any Jeffersonian appointee from the region, but insistence on this principle further limited the field of possible candidates. Madison's top choices declined the job. Wolcott, a long-time custom-house collector, was undistinguished, but industrious, loyal, and free of scandal. Wolcott's energy in collecting the import duties and enforcing the embargo had left him deeply unpopular in his home region, and he was largely unknown in the rest of the country.[74] When

---

[71] Id at 526–27.

[72] The bloc of ten senators was the same except that Georgia's James Jackson voted against the treaty (but was absent during the Rutledge vote) and South Carolina's Jacob Read voted for Rutledge (but was absent for the treaty vote). *Journal of the Executive Proceedings* at 1:196 (cited in note 57). In lobbying against Rutledge, Alexander Hamilton argued that the judge was "deranged." See Danelski, *Ideology and the Rejection of Bork* at 903 (cited in note 42).

[73] Warren, *Supreme Court in United States History* at 1:407 (cited in note 53).

[74] Id at 1:410–13; Morgan D. Dowd, *Justice Joseph Story and the Politics of Appointment*, 9 Am J Legal Hist 265, 275–76 (1965).

the New Englanders vigorously objected, the Republicans could not move themselves to rally to the cause, and the Senate sent him back to Connecticut.[75]

The third such failure before secession was James Polk's nomination of George Woodward at the end of 1845. Polk seemed little interested in the vacancy on the Court, which had carried over from the preceding Tyler administration. He had offered the position to his secretary of state, James Buchanan, but Buchanan eventually declined.[76] In choosing Woodward, a lower court state judge in Pennsylvania with no broad reputation, Polk followed the advice of his vice president, George Dallas, rather than his secretary of state. In choosing between the two Pennsylvania Democratic leaders in offering this political plum, however, the president's nomination of Woodward was seen as a slap at Buchanan.[77] Worse, it soon emerged that Woodward was a nativist, which was hardly a plus within what was generally the pro-immigrant party.[78] Enough Democrats defected to sink the nomination.

The five postbellum failures were each the result of political infighting. The era marked the highpoint of patronage politics, and presidents and senators engaged in several pitched battles across these decades over who would control the appointment power. Patronage was the lifeblood of party organizations, and appointments of all sorts were highly clientelistic. The struggle was most routinely over such lucrative posts as custom-house official and postmaster, but Supreme Court Justices and department secretaries were not immune from either the constant calculation of political power or the claims of prerogative of individual senators.[79]

President Grant lost three Supreme Court nominations in intraparty struggles. Grant came to the presidency on the strength of his celebrity as a victorious general, and the management of his fractious and demanding coalition proved not to be his strong suit. When Congress created a new seat on the Court in 1869,

---

[75] The position eventually went to Joseph Story, who had little reputation beyond being a smart and ambitious young lawyer and consequently had little political baggage.

[76] Abraham, *Justices, Presidents, and Senators* at 80 (cited in note 29).

[77] Warren, *Supreme Court in United States History* at 2:420–21 (cited in note 53).

[78] Id at 2:421.

[79] See generally Wilfred E. Binkley, *President and Congress* 187–204 (Vintage, 3rd ed 1962); Sean Dennis Cashman, *America in the Gilded Age* 151–52 (Nebraska, 3rd ed 1993); Ari Hoogenboom, *Outlawing the Spoils* (Illinois, 1961).

Grant offered his trusted attorney general for the position. Ebenezer Hoar was a respected legal professional and reformer, and his nomination won plaudits from civil service reformers in the press. The nomination received the opposite reaction from the senators, who had already been repeatedly affronted by the attorney general on judicial appointments and civil service reform during his short tenure in the Justice Department.[80] Though it was immediately apparent that Hoar would not be confirmed, he was left to wait for nearly two months before he was finally voted down. At the beginning of his second term, Grant again turned to his attorney general, this time George H. Williams, to fill the position of Chief Justice. Williams had very different problems than Hoar, however. He had been a frontier lawyer in Oregon, and he was widely regarded as out of his depth in the role of attorney general, let alone of Chief Justice. Although the senators initially seemed willing to go along with the nomination, growing criticism from the press and the professional bar in the east convinced the nominee and the president to abandon the effort.[81] Within days, Grant submitted the name of his friend, Caleb Cushing, for the center seat. Cushing had impeccable credentials and unquestioned legal skills, but at seventy-four he was well above the normal age for a Supreme Court nominee and was widely seen as unprincipled and a political opportunist. It was an open question as to whether that would have been enough to stop his confirmation, but he became politically untouchable after the surprising revelation of an 1861 letter of recommendation for an acquaintance seeking a political job from Jefferson Davis, then the president of the Confederacy.[82] Such letters were the common currency of public life in the nineteenth century, but publicity was not kind to this particular example of the professional courtesies of politicians. His nomination was hastily withdrawn.

Grover Cleveland, who had managed to place two Justices on the Court without incident when the Senate was in Republican hands, lost his first two nominations with the Senate in Democratic hands. By 1893, presidents had largely won the constitutional

---

[80] Warren, *Supreme Court in United States History* at 3:223–29 (cited in note 53); John S. Goff, *The Rejection of United States Supreme Court Appointments*, 5 Am J Legal Hist 357, 364–65 (1961).

[81] Warren, *Supreme Court in United States History* at 2:275–78 (cited in note 53).

[82] Id at 3:280–81; Goff, 5 Am J Legal Hist at 365–66 (cited in note 80).

struggle with the Senate over appointments and the civil service system was officially in place. Nonetheless, the Democratic senator from New York, David B. Hill, managed to outmaneuver the president when Cleveland sought to replace the deceased Justice Samuel Blatchford with another New Yorker. Cleveland and Hill, both former governors, were old rivals from New York state politics. Cleveland was a reformer, who had soon moved to the national stage. Hill was a machine politician, and as a U.S. senator he was a key player in New York politics.[83] Cleveland had hoped to ignore Hill's recommendations in order to make his own selections from the state. His first pick, William Hornblower, was a leader of the New York bar, but he had also recently exposed the electoral fraud of one of Hill's allies and implicated Hill in the process. In a short-handed holiday-season session of the Senate, Hill was able to rally a majority to his appeal for senatorial courtesy. Defiant, Cleveland immediately sent Wheeler Peckham's name forward. Peckham was a prominent corporate attorney, but he had also been involved in antimachine investigations and was even more offensive to Hill. The Senate again backed Hill.[84] In order to fill the position, Cleveland turned outside of New York entirely and turned senatorial courtesy in his favor, successfully nominating Senate majority leader Edward White of Louisiana to the Court. With the next vacancy, more than a year later, Cleveland gave in and nominated Hill's choice of Rufus Peckham, Wheeler's brother and someone who had stayed out of machine politics.

The two such failed nominations since 1900 reflect presidential missteps both familiar and distinct from the politics of the nineteenth century. Judge John Parker's nomination by Herbert Hoover in 1930 ran aground on the emerging shoals of interest-group politics. When Hoover selected the respected Republican circuit-court judge from North Carolina, the AFL and the NAACP launched an aggressive campaign to block his confirmation. The AFL regarded his decisions on the circuit court to be hostile to unions, and the NAACP argued that he was hostile to black interests, publicizing a statement from an earlier North Carolina gubernatorial campaign in which Parker endorsed black disen-

---

[83] Herbert Bass, *"I Am a Democrat"* (Syracuse, 1961).

[84] Allan Nevins, *Grover Cleveland* 568–72 (Dodd, Mead, 1948); Friedman, 5 Cardozo L Rev at 52–54 (cited in note 46); Carl A. Pierce, *A Vacancy on the Supreme Court: The Politics of Judicial Appointment, 1893–94*, 39 Tenn L Rev 555 (1972).

franchisement. The combination was enough to swing some Progressive Republicans against Parker and defeat the nomination by two votes.[85] Both the involvement of organized interest groups and the focus on substantive issues related to the work of the Court distinguished Parker's failed nomination from others. With a handful of centrist senators holding the balance of power, the public campaign was able to weaken party loyalty enough to defeat the nomination even during a period of unified government, forcing Hoover to pull his coalition back together with the nomination of Owen Roberts. George W. Bush's recent nomination of Harriet Miers never reached the floor of the Senate, as her name was withdrawn when it became apparent that there was little enthusiasm among Republican senators for the little-known nominee who was close only to the president. With conservative interest groups at best conflicted about a nominee with weak credentials and no track record, support seemed to erode rather than grow as she made the rounds to visit individual senators.[86] Like U.S. Grant and George Williams in 1874, Bush and Miers decided not to test the loyalty of the Republican senators.

III. Lessons

Some have argued that the nineteenth century was a kind of golden age of Senate scrutiny of Supreme Court nominees. Just as Congress as a whole in this period seemed to take its responsibility for deliberating on the scope of its own constitutional powers and for evaluating the constitutionality of legislative proposals seriously, so the elevated rejection rate of Supreme Court nominees may suggest a Senate more engaged with the task of offering its advice and consent to the appointment of judges.[87] In sharp contrast to a modern "politics of deference" in which the Senate may have abdicated its role in the appointments process, the earlier Senate, it is said, exercised greater independence and

---

[85] See Richard L. Watson, *The Defeat of Judge Parker: A Study in Pressure Groups and Politics*, 50 Miss Valley Hist Rev 213 (1963); Richard Davis, *Electing Justice* 26–28 (Oxford, 2005); Maltese, *Selling of Supreme Court Nominees* at 49–51 (cited in note 35).

[86] Robin Toner, David D. Kirkpatrick, and Anne E. Kornblut, *Steady Erosion in Support Undercut Nomination*, NY Times (Oct 28, 2005), A16.

[87] See Donald G. Morgan, *Congress and the Constitution* (Harvard, 1966) (arguing that there has been a decline in responsibility in Congress for constitutional deliberation since the late nineteenth century).

was more activist in performing its constitutional function.[88]

There is little question that failed Supreme Court nominations were more common in the nineteenth century. Of the twenty-seven presidential nominations to the Supreme Court that have met with failure over the course of American history, twenty-one of them came before 1900, 78 percent of the total. A full quarter of all the Supreme Court nominations made in the nineteenth century failed to get through the Senate. By contrast, only 10 percent of the nominations made since 1900 have failed.

But this failure rate for Supreme Court nominations was not the only distinguishing feature of the nineteenth-century Senate. The period before the twentieth century was different in other ways as well that would not seem to make it an obvious model for contemporary confirmation politics. It is hard to judge the relative quality of deliberation in that period. Until the early twentieth century, it was routine for the Senate to conduct most of its discussion of appointments in executive session, closed to the public and reporters. It was only when the election of senators was thrown open to regular citizens, rather than state legislatures, that the Senate suddenly discovered the need to conduct its business in public. The first public hearing on a nomination and the first public appearance at a hearing of a judicial nominee did not occur until the twentieth century.[89] But neither did the nominee go to the Senate in private. Senators could seek out information about the nominee, but they could not expect to question the nominee himself.

Even presidents, in this age before easy long-distance communication and travel, could not expect always to meet the prospective nominee. Presidents also did not always do the advance spade work to ensure that a nominee would be broadly acceptable to the Senate, or even would be willing to accept the nomination. This gave rise to the rather peculiar phenomenon of the Supreme Court nominee who won confirmation but declined to serve. George Washington twice sent nominations to the Senate and received its assent to Supreme Court appointments only to be later informed that the individuals did not want the job. Four other presidents had the same difficulty with nominees (the last in 1882).

Divided government (in effect, if not always in name) has ac-

---

[88] See Tulis, 47 Case W Res L Rev (cited in note 5). See also Mariah Zeisberg, *The Constitution of Conflict* (Ph.D. diss, Princeton University, 2005).

[89] Gerhardt, *The Federal Appointments Process* at 67 (cited in note 21).

counted for most failed Supreme Court nominations over the course of American history. At times, the partisan division has been nearly pathological, with Senates resolving to block essentially any nominee that a president might put forward (as with party apostates John Tyler and Andrew Johnson) or spitefully delaying the confirmation of particularly hated nominees (as with Roger Taney).[90] More often, divided government has operated to block nominees when it is expected that an intervening election will soon resolve the disagreement. Divided government has meant that lame-duck and late-term presidents could not expect to fill any vacancies that might arise in the remaining months of their term of office. When a change of administration is not imminent, divided government has historically not been an obstacle to presidents placing their choice of Justice on the Court. Whether out of strategic calculation, a broader sense of deference, or simple approval of the individuals the presidents have chosen, Senate majorities have generally not tried to exercise a veto over the Supreme Court nominations of opposite-party presidents.

Divided government in recent decades has been different. The defeat of Haynsworth, Carswell, and Bork in the Nixon and Reagan administrations were the first, and thus far only, instances in which the party controlling the Senate rejected the nominee of the opposite party controlling the White House without an election in sight. Within the context of "normal" divided government, the modern Senate has been, by historical standards, extraordinarily activist in evaluating Supreme Court nominees. Consequently, this has also been the first era in which Supreme Court nominations failed for primarily ideological reasons, because the party that controlled the Senate was hostile to the jurisprudential goals of the president and was willing therefore to veto presidential choices for the Supreme Court. Somewhat surprisingly, divided government had historically worked to free presidents, at least until late in their terms, to choose as they would from the ranks of their own partisans. The modern Senate has instead shrunk the range of presidential discretion during divided government, attempting to cut off the farther ideological wing of the president's coalition from the available pool of Supreme Court nominees. During the Nixon administration, that meant pull-

---

[90] See also Silbey, *Divided Government in Historical Perspective* at 14–17 (cited in note 33) (characterizing early episodes of divided government as ones of "disarray" and "vicious acrimony").

ing back from the "Southern strategy" and largely abandoning the search for "strict constructionists." During the Reagan, Bush, and Clinton administrations, that meant looking for more centrist nominees or stratagems for shielding nominees from normal senatorial scrutiny.

Senate confirmation activism in the nineteenth century came in the context of unified rather than divided government and was largely disconnected from jurisprudential concerns. Presidents were frequently blocked from appointing their first choice to the Supreme Court when their own party controlled the Senate. With the Senate safely in friendly hands, party discipline could be relaxed and senators did not need to rally around their president's nominee. Instead, the Senate in such circumstances frequently applied litmus tests of its own, and those litmus tests were usually political rather than jurisprudential. Nominees could not embarrass the party on touchy electoral issues, like the Jay Treaty or nativism, and they could not offend the parochial interests of powerful individual senators. The Senate has sometimes acted as a kind of quality control under such circumstances, forcing presidents to withdraw nominees who come under attack from the outside as unqualified, but they have hardly been diligent or systematic in performing that function.

It is this sort of activism that has declined since the nineteenth century, with only a tiny fraction of nominees failing to be confirmed by same-party presidents since the days of Grover Cleveland. Since the collapse of what Woodrow Wilson dubbed "congressional government" at the end of the Gilded Age, senators have largely deferred to presidents of their own party when it comes to the selection of Supreme Court Justices.[91] Supreme Court appointments within unified government have become a presidential prerogative, requiring little consultation or consideration of senatorial interests. It requires a dramatic misstep (Miers) or a faltering party (Parker and Fortas) to lose a nominee to a same-party Senate. This shift in power within the political parties from the Senate to the president has been accompanied by an increased public focus of jurisprudential credentials and commitments and the near eclipse of confirmation debate over issues about the nominee that cannot be packaged as relevant to the evaluation of "judicial character."

After the Senate confirmation of John Roberts and Samuel Alito,

---

[91] Woodrow Wilson, *Congressional Government* (Houghton, Mifflin, 1885).

some wondered whether the Democratic strategy for resisting President Bush's Supreme Court nominations had failed.[92] For the Democrats to have been able to defeat the president's nominations, without the help of a major gaffe from the nominees themselves, from their position in the minority would have been truly exceptional. The willingness of a large number of Democratic senators to cast votes against Roberts and Alito despite the fact that their confirmations were assured marks an escalation in the intensity of the ideological conflict surrounding Supreme Court appointments. There is now apparently more to be gained politically from being seen futilely taking a stand against the opponent's nominee than with showing support for a new Supreme Court Justice, for politically tarring the Supreme Court rather than rallying behind it.

The lesson of the Bork nomination, and the broader experience of recent decades, is that the opposition party can and will reject Supreme Court nominees when they control the Senate. The opposition party has never defeated a president's Supreme Court nominee from a minority position. The roots of failure for Supreme Court nominations are to be found in the Senate's majority. It would have been truly unprecedented for the Senate to have failed to confirm Roberts or Alito given the circumstances of their nominations and the characteristics of the nominees. It would no longer be surprising, however, if these same nominations would have failed had they been made during a period of Democratic control of the Senate. The question then becomes how determined a president is to press his natural advantages in the appointments process and how narrowly he defines victory. The modern, more aggressive Senate has heightened the stakes for Supreme Court nominations during periods of divided government. Presidents who primarily want to avoid confirmation battles with the Senate will have to cede ground to the other party in choosing a nominee. Presidents who value placing their own choice on the Court will have to be prepared for an extended fight, and the possibility of making multiple nominations for a vacancy.

---

[92] See John Crea, *After Alito, Liberal Groups Look to Reload*, Legal Times (Feb 27, 2006), 18; Lois Romano and Juliet Eilperin, *Republicans Were Masters in the Race to Paint Alito, Democrats' Portrayal Failed to Sway the Public*, Wash Post (Feb 2, 2006), A1; Seth Stern, *A Risky Strategy for Judging Judges*, CQ Weekly Report (Jan 23, 2006), 218.

Appendix A

Failed Supreme Court Nominations, 1789–2006

Nominee	President	Date of Nomination	Divided Government	Senate Action
John Rutledge	G. Washington	Dec. 10, 1795	No	Rejected
Alexander Wolcott	J. Madison	Feb. 4, 1811	No	Rejected
John Crittenden	J. Q. Adams	Dec. 18, 1828	Yes	Postponed
Roger Taney	A. Jackson	Jan. 15, 1835	Yes	Postponed
John Spencer	J. Tyler	Jan. 9, 1844	No*	Rejected
Reuben Walworth	J. Tyler	March 13, 1844	No*	Tabled
Edward King	J. Tyler	June 5, 1844	No*	Tabled
Reuben Walworth	J. Tyler	Dec. 10, 1844	No*	Tabled
Edward King	J. Tyler	Dec. 10, 1844	No*	Tabled
John Read	J. Tyler	Feb. 8, 1845	No*	No Action
George Woodward	J. Polk	Dec. 23, 1845	No	Rejected
Edward Bradford	M. Fillmore	Aug. 21, 1852	Yes	Tabled
George Badger	M. Fillmore	Jan. 10, 1853	Yes	Postponed
William Micou	M. Fillmore	Feb. 24, 1853	Yes	No Action
Jeremiah Black	J. Buchanan	Feb. 6, 1861	No*	No Action
Henry Stanbery	A. Johnson	April 16, 1866	No*	No Action
Ebenezer Hoar	U.S. Grant	Dec. 15, 1869	No	Rejected
George Williams	U.S. Grant	Dec. 2, 1873	No	Withdrawn
Caleb Cushing	U.S. Grant	Jan. 9, 1874	No	Withdrawn
William Hornblower	G. Cleveland	Dec. 6, 1893	No	Rejected
Wheeler Peckham	G. Cleveland	Jan. 22, 1894	No	Rejected
John Parker	H. Hoover	March 21, 1930	No	Rejected
Abe Fortas	L. Johnson	June 26, 1968	No	Withdrawn
Clement Haynsworth	R. Nixon	Aug. 18, 1969	Yes	Rejected
G. Harrold Carswell	R. Nixon	Jan. 19, 1970	Yes	Rejected
Robert Bork	R. Reagan	July 7, 1987	Yes	Rejected
Harriet Miers	G. W. Bush	Oct. 7, 2005	No	Withdrawn

Sources.—U.S. Congress, Senate, *Journal of the Executive Proceedings of the Senate of the United States of America*, various editions; Party Division in the Senate, 1789–Present (http://www.senate.gov/pagelayout/history/one_item_and_teasers/partydiv.htm).

* White House and Senate only nominally under same-party control.